I0819647

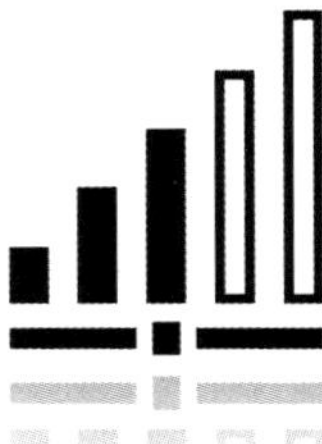

ON RECORD 1981 G. BROWN

CONTENTS

ON RECORD ENTRIES ARE NOT ORDERED ALPHABETICALLY, BUT ORGANIZED INTUITIVELY— A MIXTURE OF SEGUES BY MUSICAL GENRE OR STYLE.

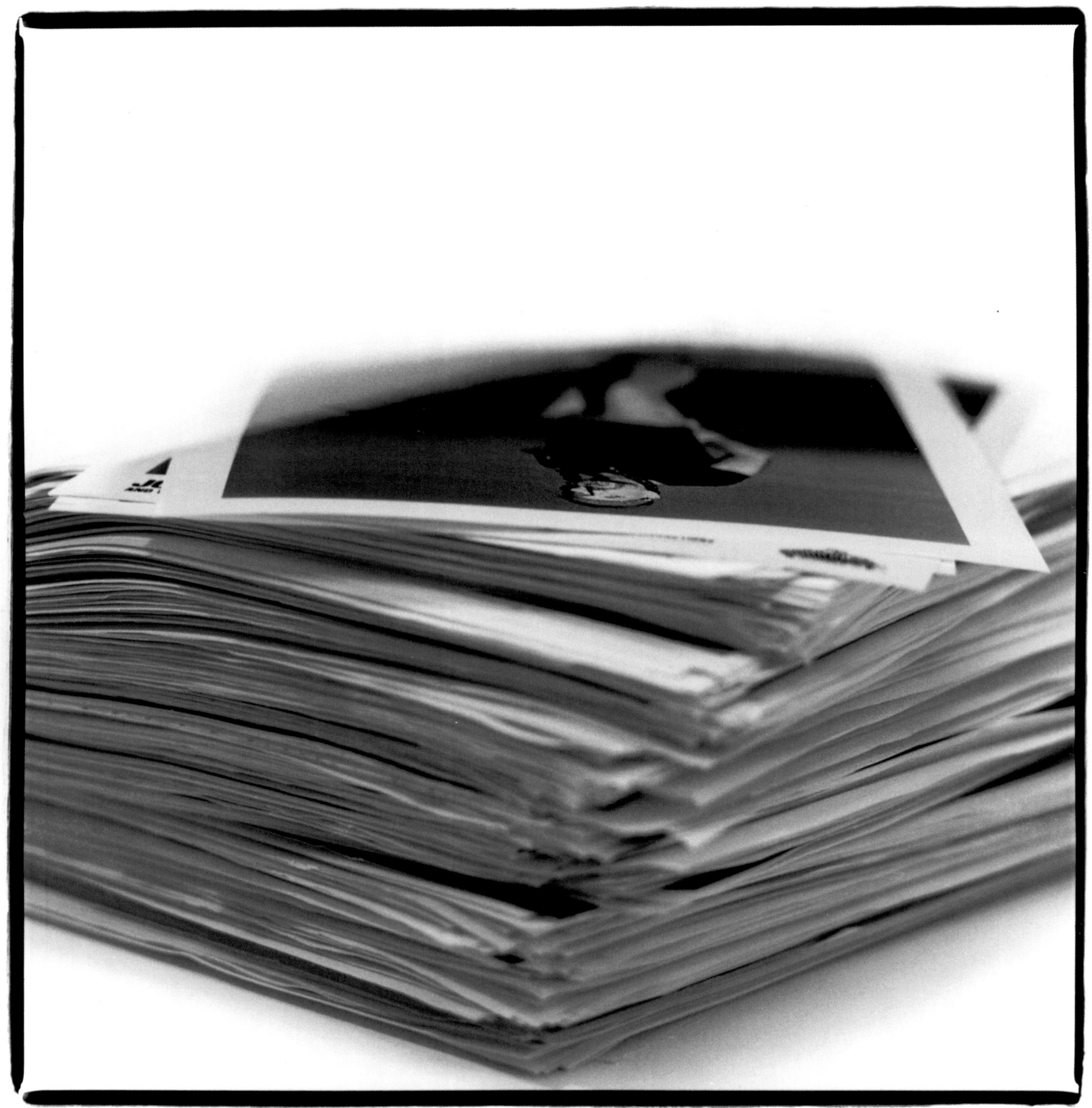

PHOTOGRAPH BY STEPHEN COLLECTOR

ON RECORD VOL. 4 1981

WRITING ABOUT popular music for a major daily newspaper in the Seventies presented some unique challenges. I contracted with *The Denver Post*, where conservative editors and execs had yet to gain an appreciation for my beat. Sex and drugs and rock 'n' roll? It was essentially verboten to mention two out of the three.

The big bugaboo was overnight concert reviews. I was charged with filing my pieces by 10 p.m.—a deadline that meant I'd miss the last portion of any arena or theater production (late-starting club shows were out of the question). I perceived the dictum as a lack of respect—sportswriters were allowed to file later, as they'd never be expected to report on a ballgame after the seventh inning or third quarter.

Change was finally effected with the help of the Grateful Dead. Improvisation set the band apart from any other headlining act at the time—the members performed different songs from show to show and played each song differently from show to show. They didn't put on pat, prepared gigs with peaks and valleys in place. Sometimes the music wouldn't catch fire until the end of a marathon second set.

In 1981, with the band slated to play at McNichols Sports Arena in Denver, I stated my case that my deadline had to be extended, or—and this was considered a radical idea—allow me to watch the entire show and write a more considered review the next day ("But then it isn't news!").

The *Post* acquiesced. In the ensuing years, no longer encumbered by time restraints, I got to cover the Dead extensively—talking with reluctant messiah Jerry Garcia, detailing Mickey Hart's various pursuits in musical anthropology and discovering Bob Weir's wayward Colorado prep-school roots. Best of all, during his 18-month tenure as a member, Bruce Hornsby allowed me to sit right on the stage behind his piano bench—a once-in-a-lifetime vantage point to witness the sort of musical telepathy the group facilitated.

My pal David Gans, who has written definitively about the Grateful Dead through the decades, stewarded me through the nuances. I assumed a group of scrawny Deadheads we encountered in the parking lot were trolling for tempeh, figuring they were partial to the newly fashionable alternative food. Turned out they were looking for tickets to the show in Tempe, Arizona.

My amended deadlines were a footnote to the musical events of 1981. MTV went on the air for the first time, offering cable subscribers around-the-clock music videos introduced by veejays. Simon & Garfunkel performed a free reunion concert in New York City's Central Park, attended by over a half-million fans. Reggae figurehead Bob Marley was lost to cancer, while Ozzy Osbourne bit the head off a dove at a CBS Records gathering in Los Angeles.

The Human League's "Don't You Want Me" and Soft Cell's "Tainted Love" made the first stirrings of synth-pop writ large, and Phil Collins' "In the Air Tonight" popularized the gated reverb drum sound that became ubiquitous. The success of the "Stars on 45" concept led to a short-lived medley craze.

I received all their records for review, waded through their press kits and attended their concerts. I was and am a very lucky boy. Please allow me to share. — **G. Brown**

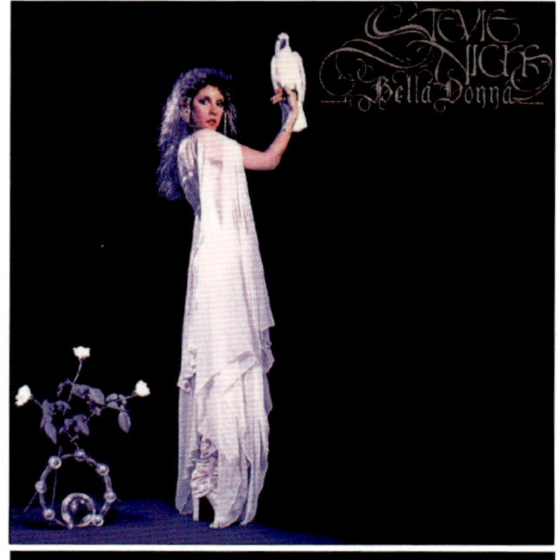

Billboard 200: *Bella Donna* (No. 1)
Billboard Hot 100: "Stop Draggin' My Heart Around" (#3); "Leather and Lace" (#6); "Edge of Seventeen" (#11); "After the Glitter Fades" (#32)

Bella Donna, Stevie Nicks' solo debut album, was one of the year's most hotly anticipated recordings.

ACCLAIMED FOR her throaty croon and mystical look, Stevie Nicks had sold millions of records as a key member of Fleetwood Mac. Favorites like "Rhiannon" and "Dreams" (the band's only No.1 hit) made her a focal point and only fueled anticipation for the start of her solo career. Nicks had amassed a large stockpile of material that she had been unable to record and release with Fleetwood Mac because each album had to accommodate the band's three songwriters.

"I write three of four songs every month or two," Nicks said. "And since I never get more than that many on a Fleetwood Mac album, the backlog grows."

While remaining a member of Fleetwood Mac, Nicks released *Bella Donna*, which topped the charts and yielded a number of hits. She'd originally written the country-tinged "After the Glitter Fades," a tale of heartache in Hollywood, back in 1972. "Leather and Lace," originally demoed in 1975, was cut with Don Henley.

"Waylon Jennings asked me to write a song for him and Jessi Colter," Nicks explained. "After I wrote 'Leather and Lace,' they broke up. Waylon wanted to cut it by himself and I said, 'No! You can't do that—I spent too long working on getting the psychology of the two characters right. It's got to be a duet, sung by the right man and the right woman.' So Waylon didn't do it, and I wouldn't do it until Don and I sang it."

There was one outside song—Tom Petty and his Heartbreakers joined Nicks for the performance of his seething "Stop Draggin' My Heart Around." Petty's wife Jane came up with the title for "Edge of Seventeen," Nicks' most recent composition.

"The album, in a sense, was my finding out if I could still make something on my own," Nicks said. "You start to doubt yourself after seven years of Fleetwood Mac—my life was completely, undeniably wrapped around the band."

Bella Donna was the product of her active spirit. "I can't just sit down and 'write a song'—mine are more like running commentaries on my life. I'll probably have 15 or 20 songs on a given theme—life with Fleetwood Mac, audiences, being on the road—by the time I'm 60. At this rate, I may never catch up." ■

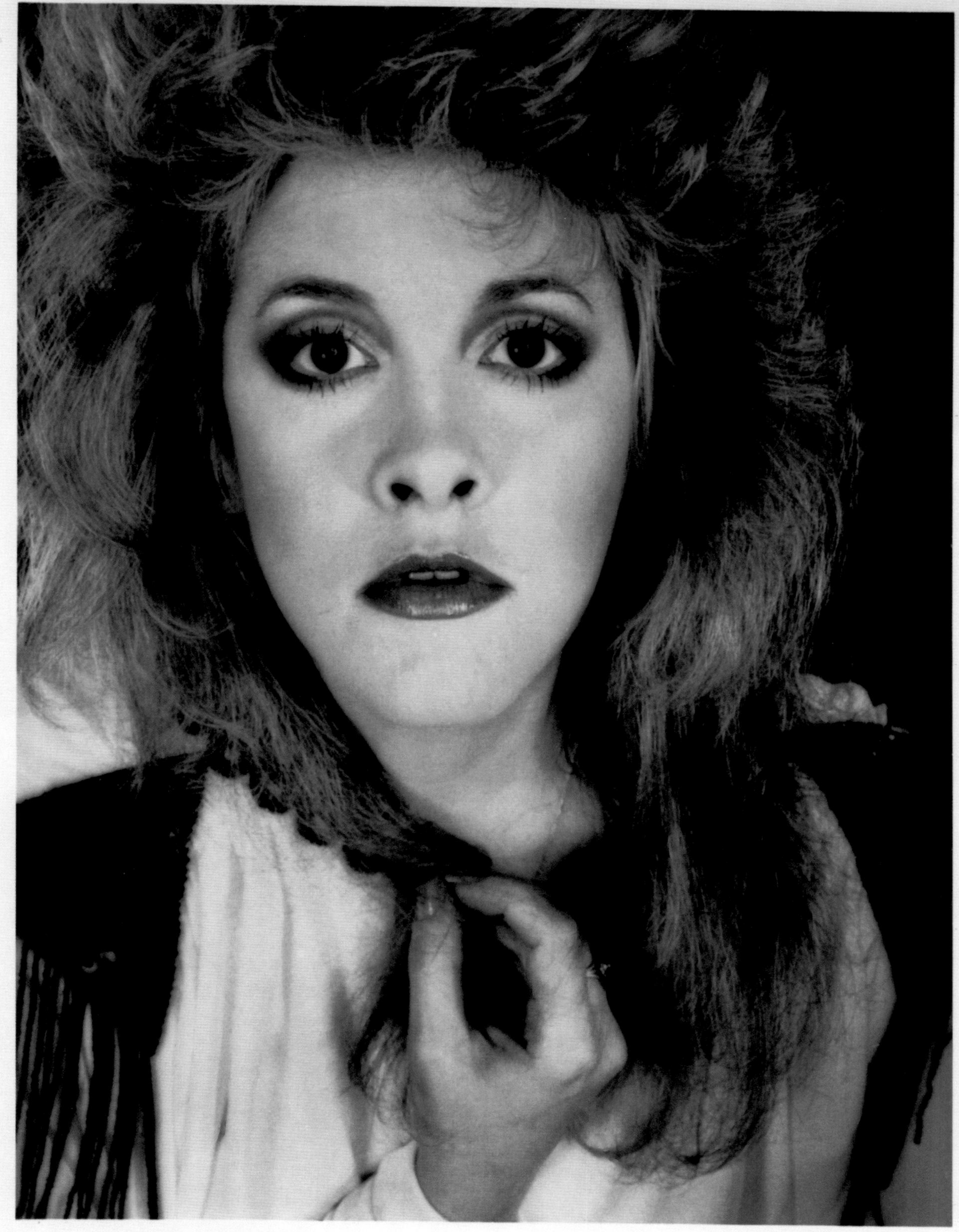

STEVIE NICKS

TITLE: Modern
SUBJECT: Records
EST. 1980

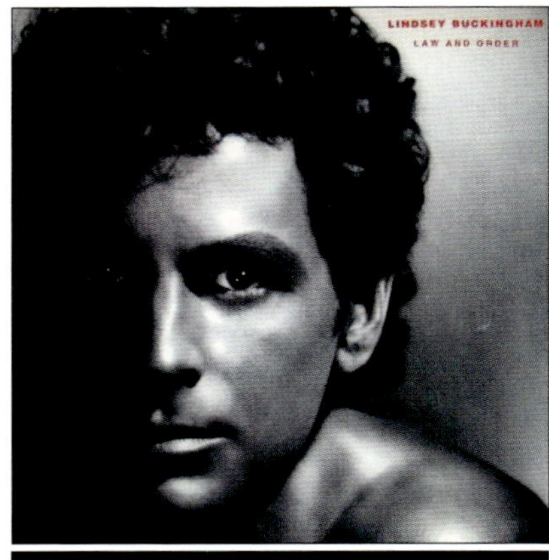

Billboard 200: *Law and Order* (No. 1)
Billboard Hot 100: "Trouble" (#9)

Lindsey Buckingham's inventiveness was still in evidence on *Law and Order* and his first solo hit, "Trouble."

FLEETWOOD MAC'S 1979 studio album, *Tusk*, was an ambitious work, and its quirky charm could be attributed directly to Lindsey Buckingham. The eccentric guitarist's daring arrangements and intricately layered production offset his already-familiar talents as a singer and instrumentalist. Despite generally favorable reaction in the rock marketplace, *Tusk* put Buckingham on the spot.

"It hurt my feelings a little bit," he noted in retrospect. "All of a sudden the band was turning to me saying, 'It's your fault we didn't sell *x* number of albums.' But that was the risk we took in doing something experimental in the first place."

Buckingham released *Law and Order*, a solo album that was more compact but captured the same antic verve that had marked *Tusk*. Buckingham played virtually all of the instruments, but the record still exuded moments of spontaneity and tension that were usually absent in such overdubbing exercises. One of the more accessible tracks, "Trouble," featured drumming by Fleetwood Mac's Mick Fleetwood and became a Top 10 single for Buckingham.

"I had tried playing the drums on it, but it wasn't happening," Buckingham noted. "Mick came in one night and we stayed until four in the morning doing takes. But there wasn't one we felt was solid enough from start to finish. So we decided to cut a short tape loop of Mick's drum track, only four seconds over and over again. The irony was that the original reason for having Mick play on the song was to approach the track completely live, as opposed to my usual technique. Ultimately, we achieved just the opposite."

"Bwana" conjured up images of a "jungle cartoonland" thanks to Buckingham's manic vocal, while "Love from Here, Love from There" found him breaking down the roles of a Dixieland jazz band (cornet, clarinet, trombone) and emulating them on guitars. "I'll Tell You Now" and "That's How We Do It in L.A." were edgy stylistic forays.

"I'm just enamored of the idea of retaining a certain freshness and individuality," he explained. "So much of what you hear on the radio sounds the same. Take Quarterflash, which sounds like Pat Benatar and early Fleetwood Mac—it's got all the elements that are acceptable to the largest amount of people, and therefore it's doing well. That's not a healthy thing, I don't think."

Law and Order gave Buckingham the chance to express his musical vision to his own satisfaction.

"I did get a little spoiled, engineering and being as creative as I wanted," Buckingham admitted. "In Fleetwood Mac's situation, you have to scale down your involvement. It's just the politics of five people. Sometimes when we're all in there it's a little crazy, like Circus Maximus." ■

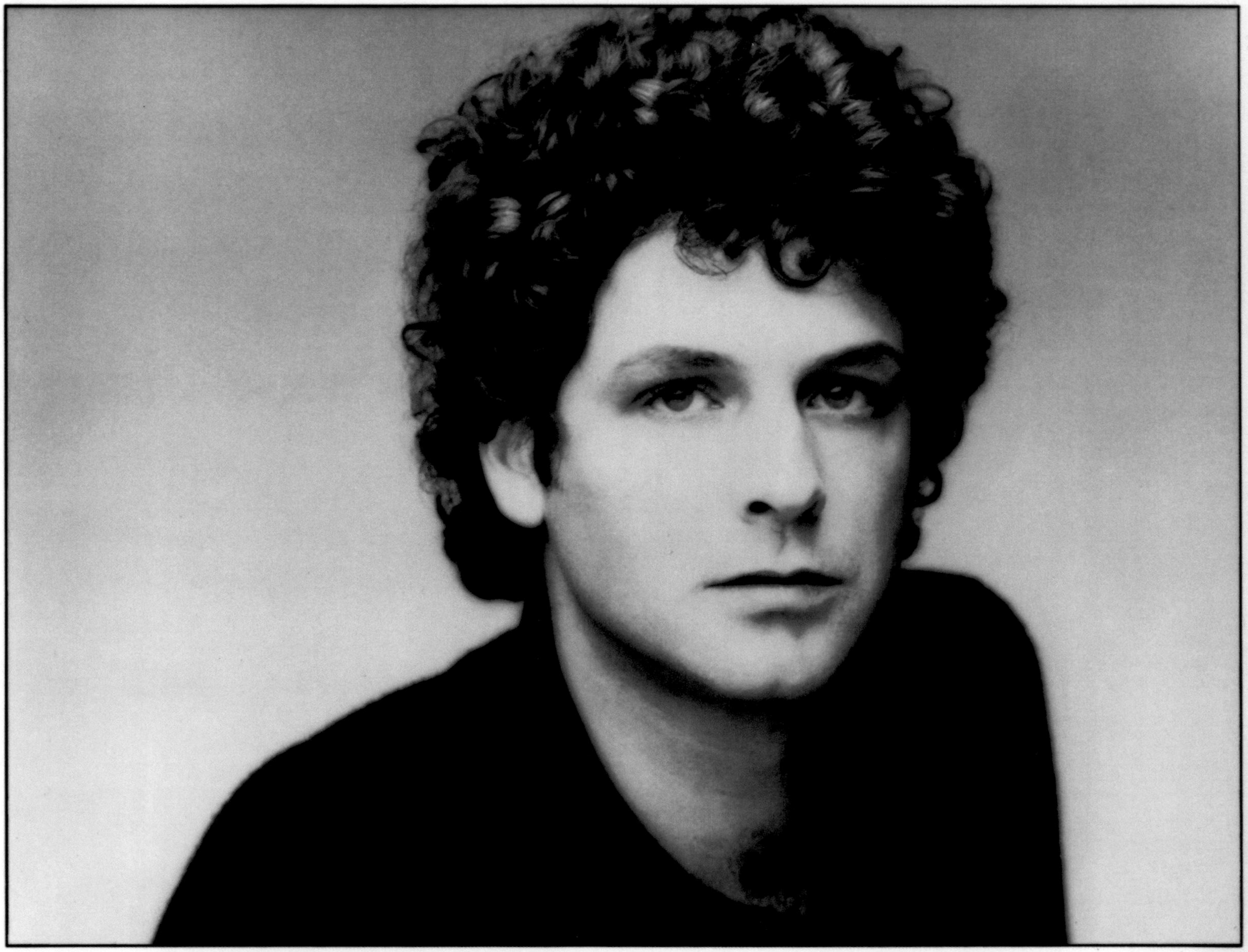

LINDSEY BUCKINGHAM

PHOTO CREDIT: JIM SHEA/1981

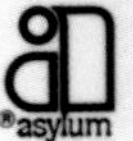

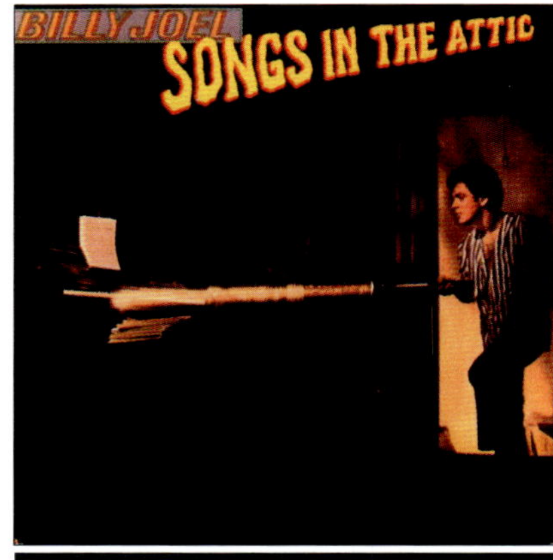

Billboard 200: *Songs in the Attic* (#8)
Billboard Hot 100: "Say Goodbye to Hollywood" (#17);
"She's Got a Way" (#23)

Billy Joel reclaimed some overlooked material from the early period of his career with *Songs in the Attic.*

BILLY JOEL got credit for being unpredictable. Just when folks had him pegged as a late-Seventies balladeer on the strength of *The Stranger* and *52nd Street*, the spunky piano man responded with the rock 'n' roll sound of *Glass Houses.* Hot on its heels came *Songs in the Attic*—his first live album, a not-so-standard reprisal of earlier work that hadn't been heard by the large audience he had won with *The Stranger.* He now had a seasoned backing band that helped reclaim the songs with his signature sound.

"She's Got a Way" was a love song originally released on *Cold Spring Harbor*, Joel's first solo album from 1971. He usually wrote about the struggle in relationships. "It's the yin-yang, the negative and the positive to it, which I'll probably never get away from," he said. "I'll always seek both sides.

"Most of the time when I sit down to write a song, nine days out of ten, nothing happens. But on the tenth day, suddenly ba-***boom***! You go with it, and it feels very spontaneous, but you do have to have discipline and work hard at it. You just can't sit down and wait for the mood to strike. I don't know whether that's spontaneity or inspiration. You have to set yourself up in the mood for it to happen."

And when nothing happened? "I hate it. It's the worst. You're in a desert. There's no water. And there's this piano beast with 88 teeth and you're dueling with this dragon. I kick things and I curse and I drink and I smoke 50 packs of cigarettes and say, 'Don't talk to me, leave me alone!' I walk around in a bathrobe and don't go out of the house. It's the pits!"

Joel was used to his accomplishments as a songwriter being ignored. "People still ask me to this day who writes my stuff. And no matter how many times I put on my album 'Words and music by Billy Joel,' they don't know—they don't read album covers. They don't understand that the writing part is the hardest part, and everything else comes out of that. So a lot of people do think I'm just a rock singer. But it's better than being called a pop star." ■

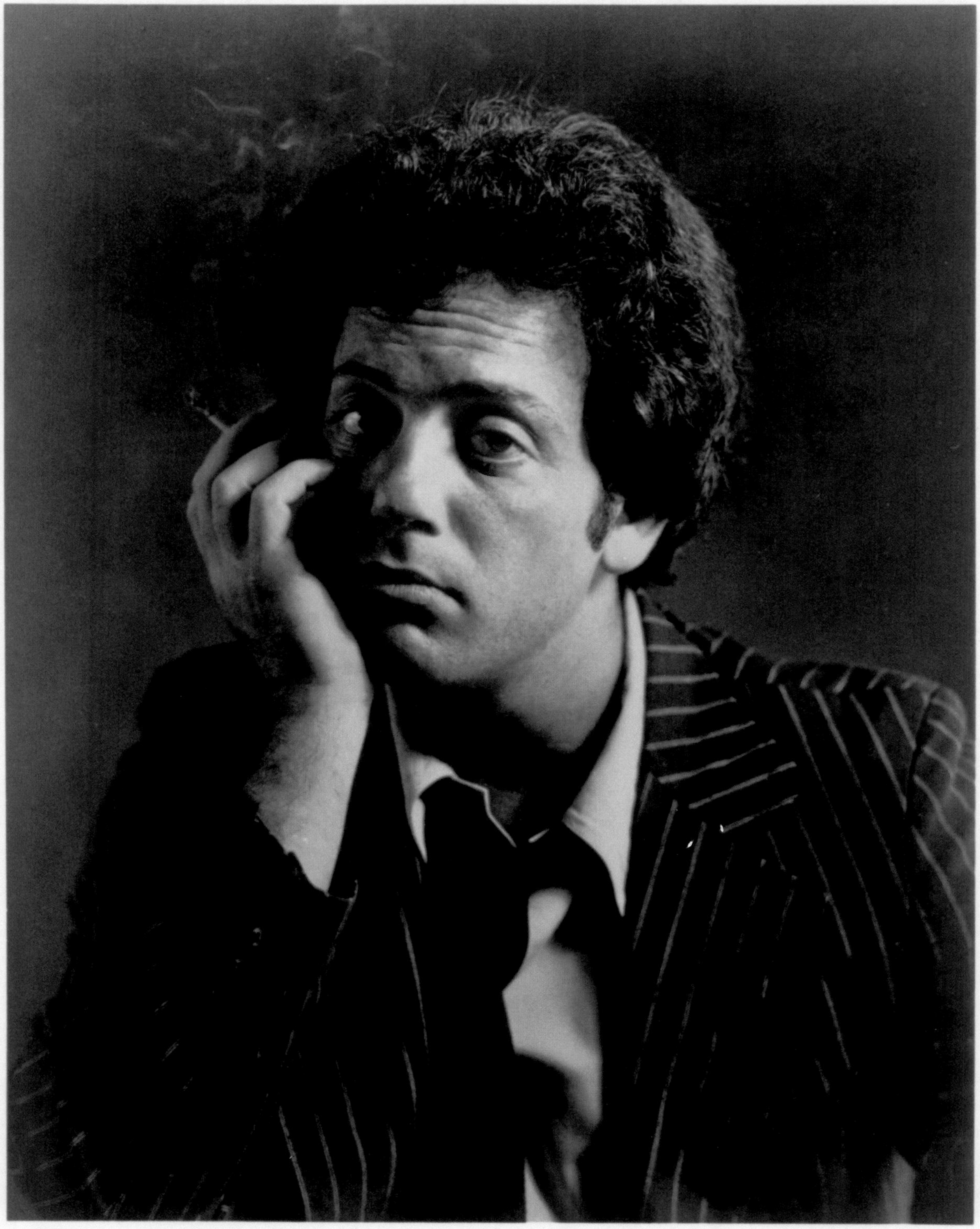

BILLY JOEL

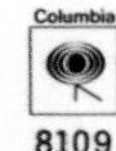

8109

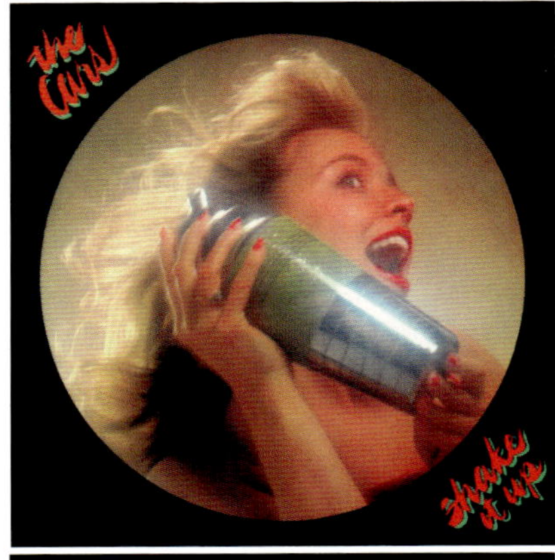

Billboard 200: *Shake It Up* (#9)
Billboard Hot 100: "Shake It Up" (#4); "Since You're Gone" (#41)

The Cars' *Shake It Up* became the Boston band's fourth consecutive album to eclipse one million sales.

SHAKE IT UP was a vindication of sorts for the Cars, returning to the pop roots of the band's 1978 debut after 1980's adventurous *Panorama*.

"Now we're back, it's further proof that we're not insane—we can put out a few pop songs and mid-America will be happy once again," leader Ric Ocasek laughed.

After the success of their first albums, the Cars had enough money to purchase an existing recording studio in Boston and transform it into a state-of-the-art facility, renaming it Syncro Sound.

"We were recording while it was still being constructed—if you listen through headphones, you can probably hear the sawing and the hammering in the background," Ocasek shared. "Now we record when we feel like it for as long as we feel like it."

Shake It Up spawned the band's first Top 10 single with the title track, which was actually written years earlier by Ocasek.

"In fact, the song was in contention for inclusion on *Panorama*," he said. 'There was a lot of crap going on as far as legal hassles and courtroom appearances for months and months (the Cars were involved in a lawsuit with their former management). In retrospect, those things were swimming around in my head, but I can't say that during *Shake It Up* all of a sudden I was happy. I'm no happier or sadder than any human being."

The pensive "Since You're Gone" was another hit. Despite the Cars' exploratory sound and image, Ocasek's lyrics dealt almost totally with love and relationships.

"It's 80 percent of my brain. I see people reacting to other people in detached, alienated ways—afraid to give, afraid to get. I don't get depressed as much as I get in a mood that's noncoherent. I never admit to depression. Anxiety, I'll admit to. People are so afraid of technology, and I can't sympathize with that. I feel we're at the beginning of that age, and you have to make an adjustment to it pretty quick because it's not gonna go away. 'Since You're Gone' has a $29 rhythm machine in it, the cheapest you can get." ■

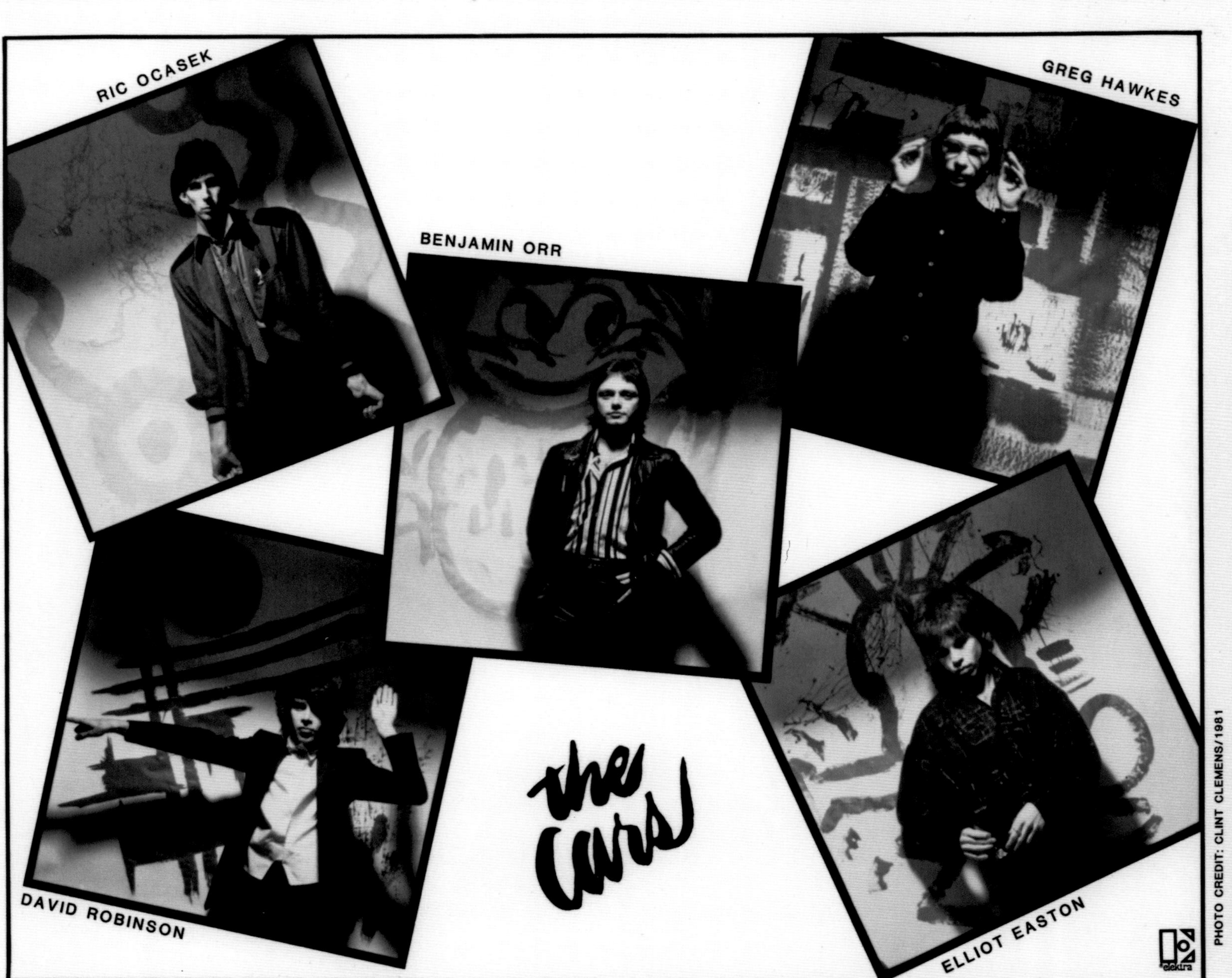
RIC OCASEK
BENJAMIN ORR
GREG HAWKES
DAVID ROBINSON
the cars
ELLIOT EASTON
elektra
PHOTO CREDIT: CLINT CLEMENS/1981

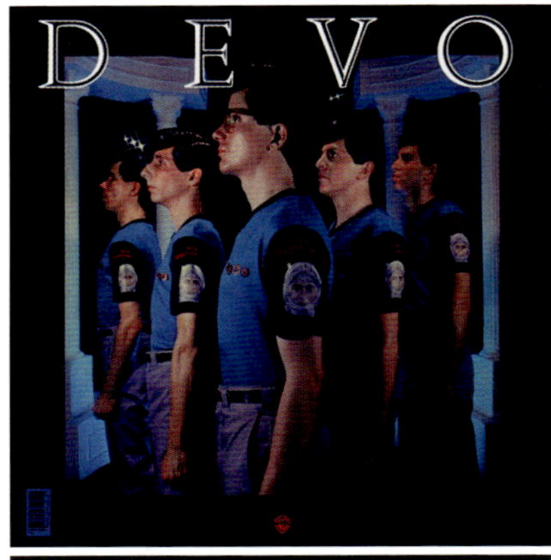

Billboard 200: *New Traditionalists* (#23)
Billboard Hot 100: "Working in a Coal Mine" (#43)

Devo's *New Traditionalists* bore a full measure of the new-wave era's most unexpectedly successful ensemble.

CULMINATING WITH the 1980 hit "Whip It," Devo had represented "the sound of things falling apart." The band's heavily synthesized, bizarre-but-catchy brand of techno-rock was only one component of the conceptual/performance art package; it swirled around in a mix of surreal videos and costumes, delivered in an absurdly provocative philosophy.

"We didn't create the theory of 'devolution'—we read something that we agreed with," frontman Mark Mothersbaugh said. "Devo attempts to cut through the mental grease and grime with techniques of positive mutation designed to protect you from the ninnies and the twits."

A bonus 7-inch single was packaged with initial copies of *New Traditionalists*, an electronically advanced cover of "Working in a Coal Mine" (the Lee Dorsey song, written by Allen Toussaint); Devo's version had been the only charting song on the soundtrack album of the animated film *Heavy Metal.*

"Beautiful World" slipped an oddly disturbing message into the apparently optimistic lyrics ("It's a beautiful world—for you") and was set to a pioneering video linking images from film archives, switching from happy elements to much darker scenes by the end of the song.

It was time to advance the media wizardry. The robotic men of Devo had hung up their red-flower-pot "energy dome" hats and yellow jump suits for plastic pompadour wigs and blue V-neck T-shirts.

"We're still going for all the brains out there that need washing," Mothersbaugh assured. ■

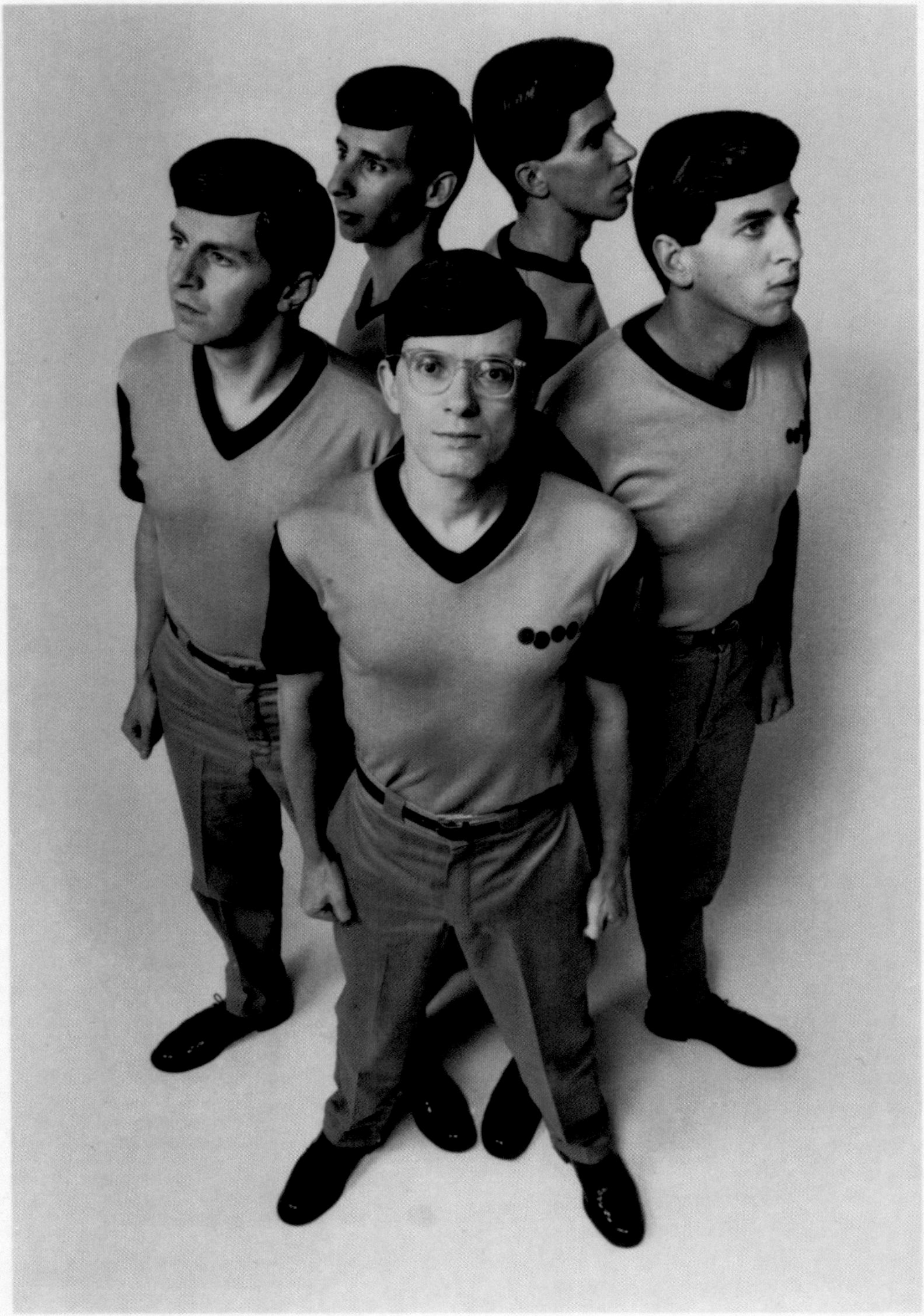

Photo Credit: Robert Matheu September 1981

DEVO

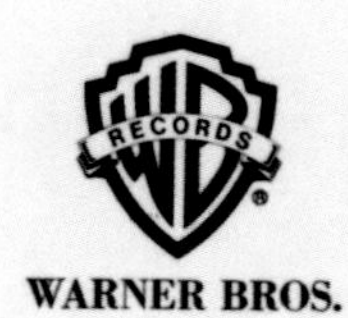

WARNER BROS.

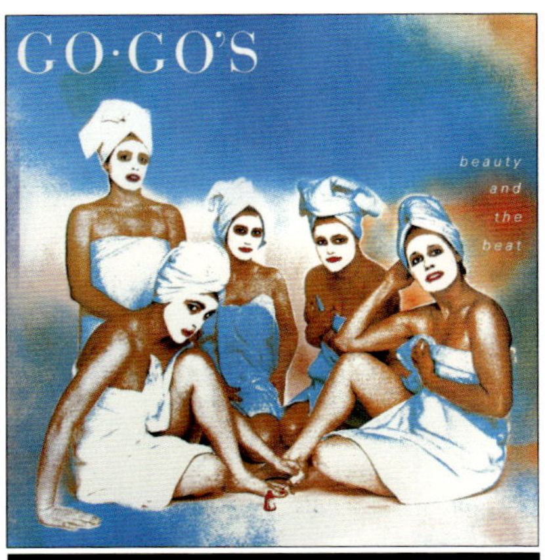

Billboard 200: *Beauty and the Beat* (No. 1)
Billboard Hot 100: "Our Lips Are Sealed" (#20); "We Got the Beat" (#2)

The Go-Go's, an L.A. punk-club band, skyrocketed to fame with "Our Lips Are Sealed" and "We Got the Beat."

WITH A lineup comprised of five female musicians, the Go-Go's started playing together in 1978. When they began selling out punk venues in California, record companies lined up—but the ladies held out for a deal with the small I.R.S. label (headed up by the Police's manager, Miles Copeland, who began the company as a haven for uncommercial artists).

"The other companies had no idea what to do with us," drummer Gina Schock said. "They liked the music, but they couldn't figure out how to market us, which is totally ridiculous—there are uncountable ways to merchandise and promote us."

Richard Gottehrer, a veteran of the Strangeloves (the 1965 hit "I Want Candy") who also wrote the girl-group standard "My Boyfriend's Back," had produced the first Blondie album. He graced *Beauty and the Beat*, the Go-Go's debut, with the same sunny, free-wheeling pop energy (his productions were aptly termed "instant records"), sanding down the pert band's rougher edges.

Beauty and the Beat was a surprise hit, "We Got the Beat" became a signature song, and the music world went gaga over the Go-Go's. The first female band—lead singer Belinda Carlisle, guitarists Jane Wiedlin and Charlotte Caffey, bassist Kathy Valentine and Schock—that wrote its own songs and played its own instruments to top the charts, the Go-Go's paved the way for a host of other new-wave acts.

The ensuing rise to fame was frenetic. No one suffered more stresses than Carlisle, who was barely removed from her upbringing as a Valley Girl and ex-cheerleader. The band endured sexism and overused comparisons to mid-Sixties groups who shared the same sense of sturdy, cheerful pop. Success even sparked a backlash about the album cover, where the gals appeared in cold cream and bath towels.

"Some people have given us a hard time about how we're selling our bodies by appearing that way. Good Lord, we look cute, but I'd hardly say sexy," Schock said. "It's just intended to be fun, the same way our music is." ■

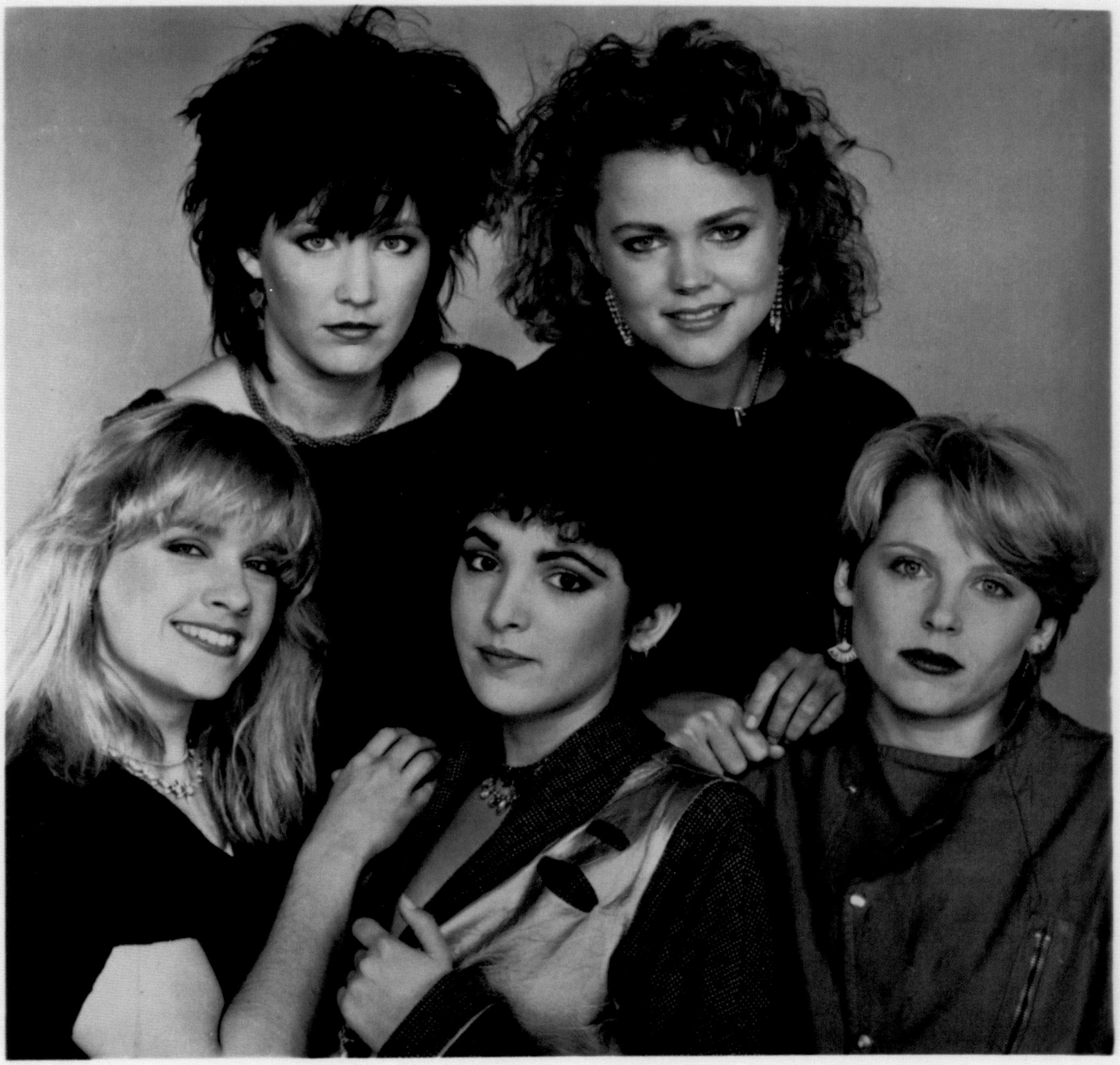

GO·GO'S

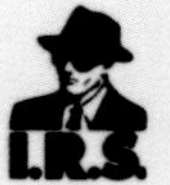

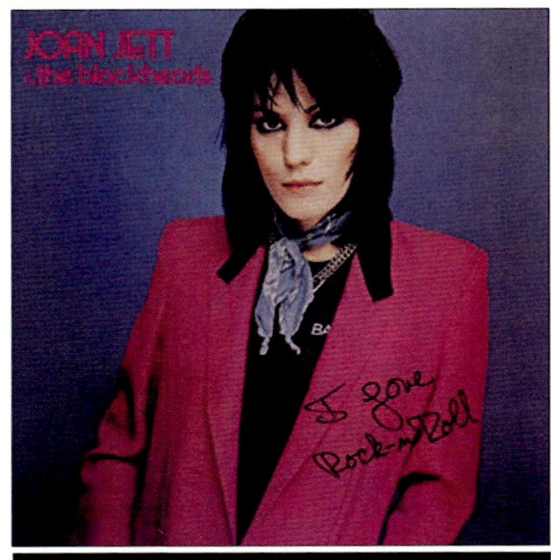

Billboard 200: *I Love Rock 'n' Roll* (#2)
Billboard Hot 100: "I Love Rock 'n' Roll" (No. 1); "Crimson and Clover" (#7)

With *I Love Rock 'n' Roll*, ex-Runaways guitarist Joan Jett emerged as the high priestess of the power chord.

THE TIME had never been better for female performers to reach a rock audience. New release bins were stuffed with contenders, the majority of them subscribing to the same tough-gal pose, sneering out from their album covers just daring a listener to question the authenticity of their street roots and rock 'n' roll capabilities. It was all becoming a blur, but Joan Jett figured that truth would win out.

"I'm not acting; that's just the way I am," the guitarist insisted. "From talking to the girls I meet traveling around, I'm expressing things they can't because they get peer pressure or hassled at school or by their parents. Hey, all girls smoke and drink and swear—that's just a way of life. I'm just a release for them."

Jett, 22, was a veteran of the rock wars by virtue of her stint with the Runaways, the all-girl rock band that she co-founded when she was 16, courting controversy (traced to management's insistence on a sleazy jailbait image) through the legendary glam scene of Seventies Los Angeles.

"When the Runaways ended, I was scared," Jett admitted. "I really thought it was the end of my life. But I finally collected my brains and went to England in 1979, where I hung out with Steve Jones and Paul Cook (the guitarist and drummer for the Sex Pistols)."

Returning to LA, Jett met Kenny Laguna and Ritchie Cordell, men who played seminal roles in the development of bubblegum pop in the Sixties. Laguna and Cordell put Jett in the studio to record enough tracks for an album. With the resulting record, 1980's *Bad Reputation*, Jett was back strong. She formed the all-male Blackhearts band, and with her sassy stage demeanor and no-nonsense hard-rock sensibilities, Jett attained stardom with *I Love Rock 'n' Roll*—the guitar-driven title track was a double platinum single, staying at No.1 for eight weeks, followed by a Top 10 cover of Tommy James & the Shondells' classic "Crimson and Clover."

"I'm having fun now, 'cause writing and recording is hard work," Jett said. "I just try to know enough about the business to get by, but when it comes down to points and percentages, I don't wanna know. I don't understand it in the first place. I just feel like playing." ■

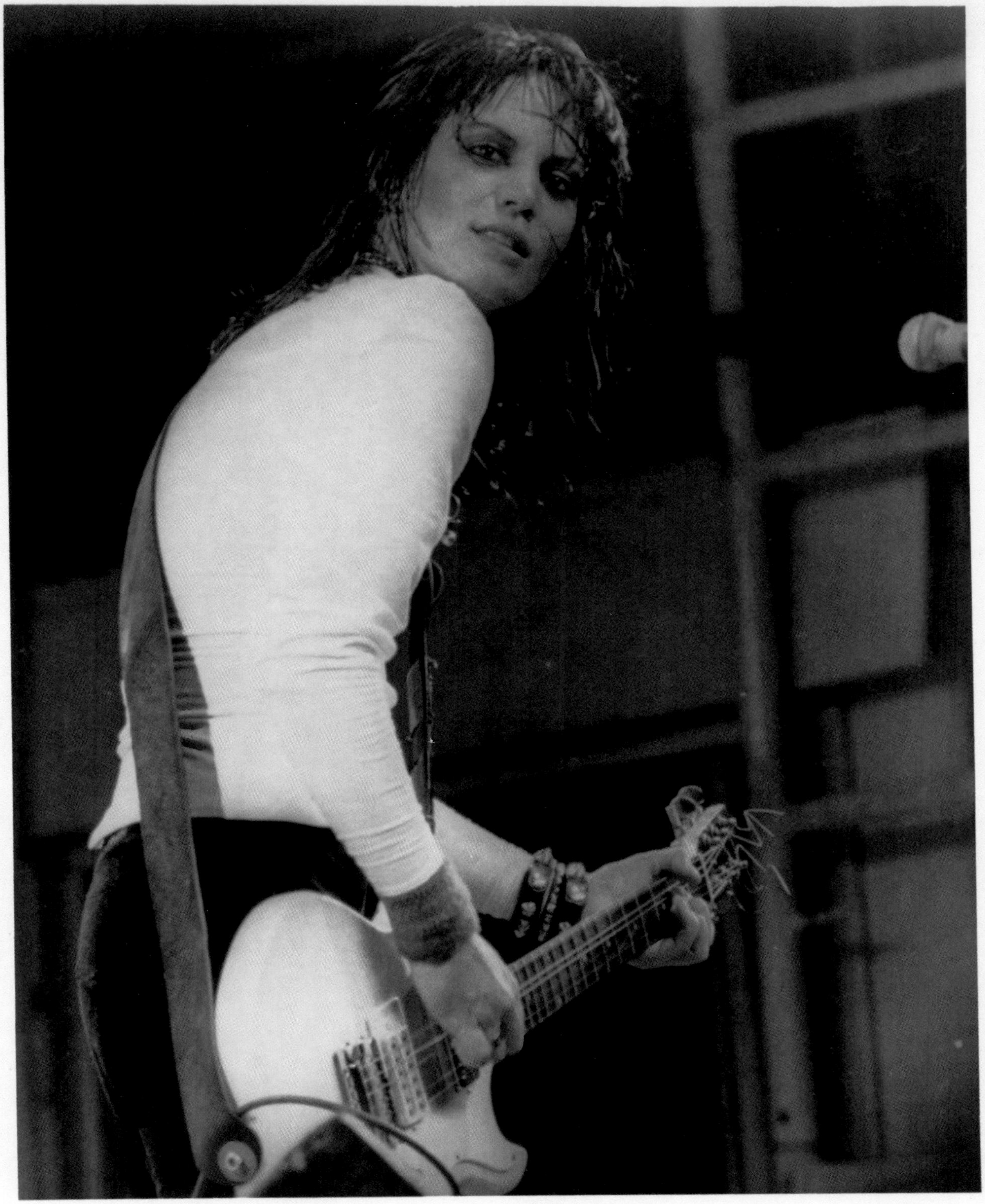

JOAN JETT
AND THE BLACKHEARTS

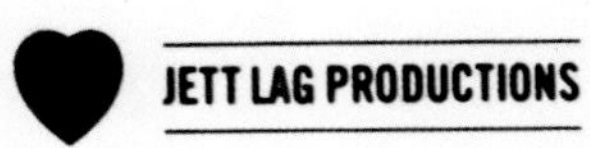

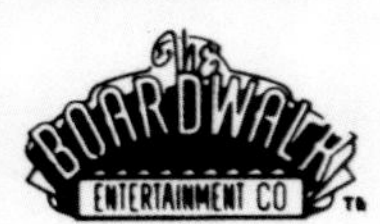

Billboard 200: *Kings of the Wild Frontier* (#44)

Adam & the Ants attempted to galvanize young fans with the adventure-hero theme of *Kings of the Wild Frontier*.

ADAM & THE Ants' homeland credentials were impeccable—six hit singles and a debut album that knocked John Lennon & Yoko Ono's *Double Fantasy* out of the No. 1 spot on the UK charts. America was then subjected to an Ant invasion—the band made the move to conquer the States, with kids lining up to receive the message of lead singer Adam Ant.

Adam & the Ants dressed up in glam swashbuckler garb that was equal parts Native American, pirate and punk. The songs, built around relentless Burundian drum riffs linked with Adam Ant's war whoops and rain-dance chants, were merely advertisements for themselves—"Ant-music" exhorted listeners to "Unplug the jukebox/And do us all a favor/ That music's lost its taste/So try another flavor."

"There's a bigger chance to have fun over here—in England, it's depressing," Adam Ant explained. "Punk music started out as a small group of no more than 60 people in England, but then the press jumped on it and started emphasizing the spitting and the violence—they simply smashed the movement down. Now that attitude is all-pervasive, and if I do one thing, it will be to get rid of that attitude. I don't want to get spit on. Hey, I dress up!"

Ant was well-versed in the punk situation—in the first incarnation of his group, he had worn bondage gear and had his band stolen by the Sex Pistols' former manager (to form Bow Wow Wow) prior to arriving at his Ant concept. "I just decided to label my music before the critics could. Rock 'n' roll is the least of my influences, because most of the bands are dinosaurs. That's why we went to tribal music, because it's very naïve. It's not decadent, it's celebrative. We're just another flavor in a soda shop."

Kings of the Wild Frontier sold well without any major US airplay, an indication of how readily kids accepted the good-natured escapism and swagger of Adam & the Ants.

"Sure, sex plays a part of it," the dapper Ant (born Stuart Goddard) admitted. "But it's innocent sex rather than physical. We dress up because we want people to see a show, to be in fashion. I don't want to wear jeans, I want to surprise myself. It's just showbiz, not a gimmick. My influences run from Alice Cooper to Liberace—anyone who took me out of myself."

It remained to be seen how long the fickle teen audience would be captivated with the adventure-hero theme, but the Ants were unconcerned. "It took four years to get to this point," Ant noted. "Everything we do is a conscious move. I don't like funeral music, I don't want to slash my wrists—I want to have fun. Why Ants? Hey, why Beatles?" ■

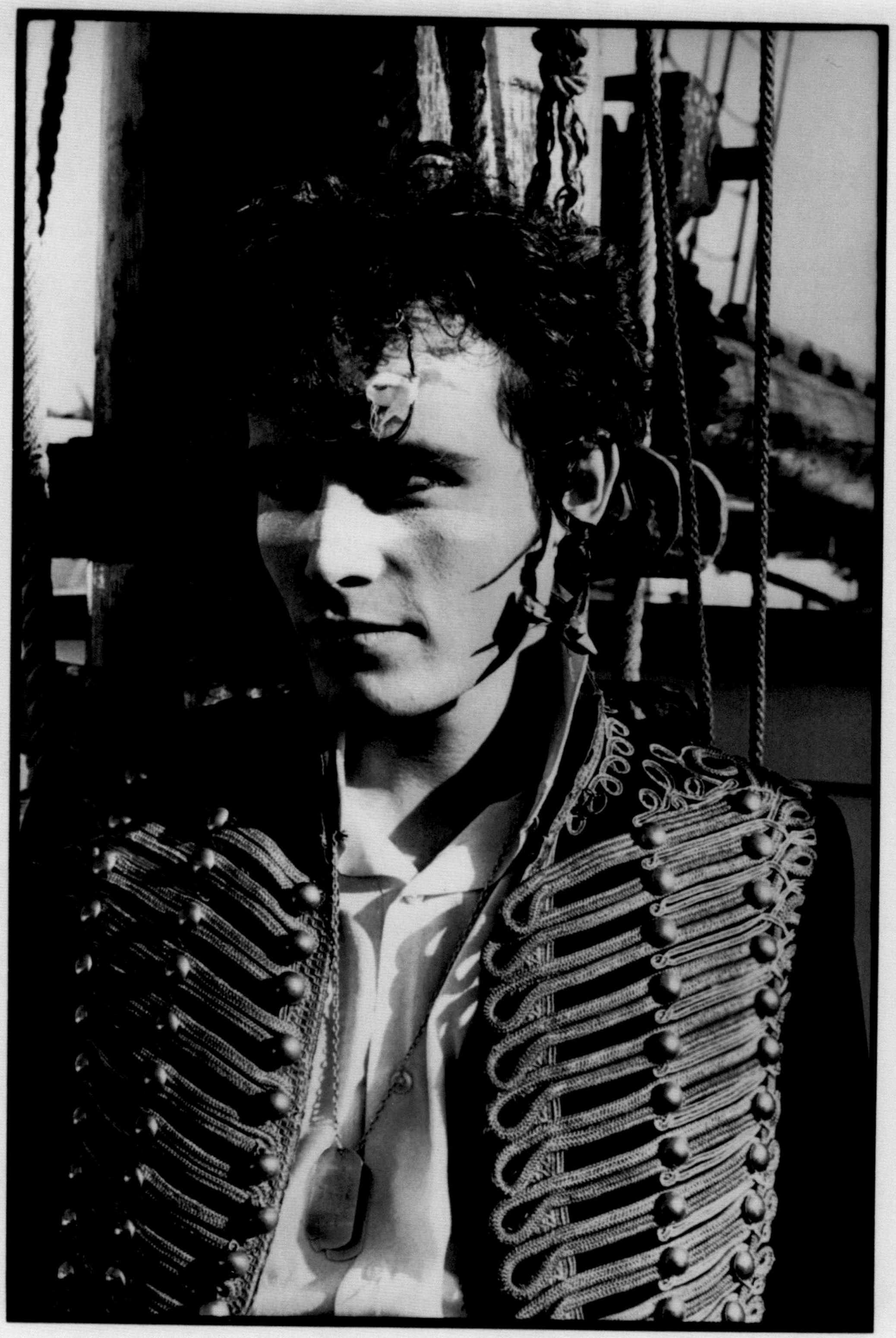

ADAM ANT

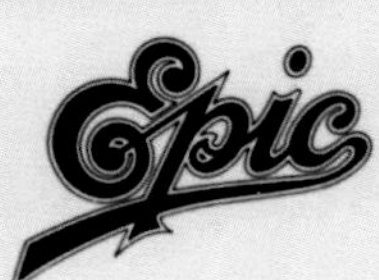

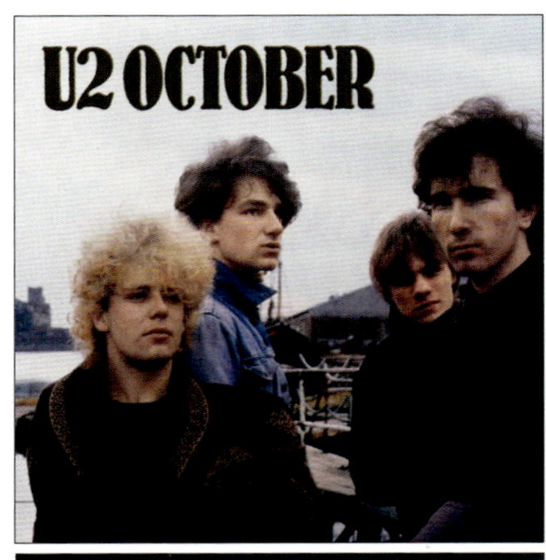

Billboard 200: *October* (#104)

With the release of *October*, U2 left little doubt that the band's success would come on its own terms.

A BAND from Ireland, U2, had released a striking debut album. *Boy* and the song "I Will Follow" heralded the group's innovative approach—the melodies were original, a guitarist named the Edge played all sorts of patterns and harmonics and singer Bono's vocals instilled a sincerity that avoided sappy connotations. U2 established itself as an important new group, but with radio mired in a lowest-common-denominator rut, the band had to make do with word of mouth. Many people felt that a second album making commercial concessions would allow next-big-thing predictions to come true.

But *October* was a difficult, ambitious record, another collection with themes of discord and spirituality, including the transcendent "Gloria." U2 had rendered the deeply emotional songs dramatically (not melodramatically) and artfully (not artily), resulting in work that belied the group's age—U2's oldest member was 21.

The recording sessions were complicated by Bono's loss of a briefcase containing in-progress lyrics. "For *October*, we didn't have the chance to play the songs live, and most of the lyrics just came when I stood at the microphone," he reflected. "I knew what I wanted to say. I just wanted to see how I'd say it."

Bono's technique didn't suggest a lack of preparation or reflect the whims of some kid in a recording studio. Songs such as "Tomorrow" showcased his way with imagery—his protagonist was always forever falling, waking, trying to open doors, to leave, to return, making the tensions in the music all the more gripping. While the record didn't consolidate the band's following—it received mixed reviews and limited radio play—it proved that U2 was committed to its own musical vision, one that wouldn't be dictated by outside forces.

"We canceled our Japanese and Australian tour and some dates in India," Bono explained. "We want to spend more time at home, because if you don't do any living, there's no life to your music. In the last year and a half, I've learned a lot more than most people would at my particular age. I want to go home and recount it. There are a lot of things going on in my hometown Dublin and my country Ireland that I feel very strongly about, and I want to be there.

"I'm bugged by the violence going down, whether it be the physical violence of Northern Ireland or the mental violence of cities like New York. I can't talk about it very well, but I've been writing about it. U2 has never played a plain pop song, or worse, songs about Northern Ireland that some people expect, and that's flipped them. They think they can put *October* on for 40 minutes and everything we want to talk about is just going to become clear to them. U2 demands more than that. We don't fit into a ready-made formula—we're still the square peg trying to fit into the round hole." ■

U2

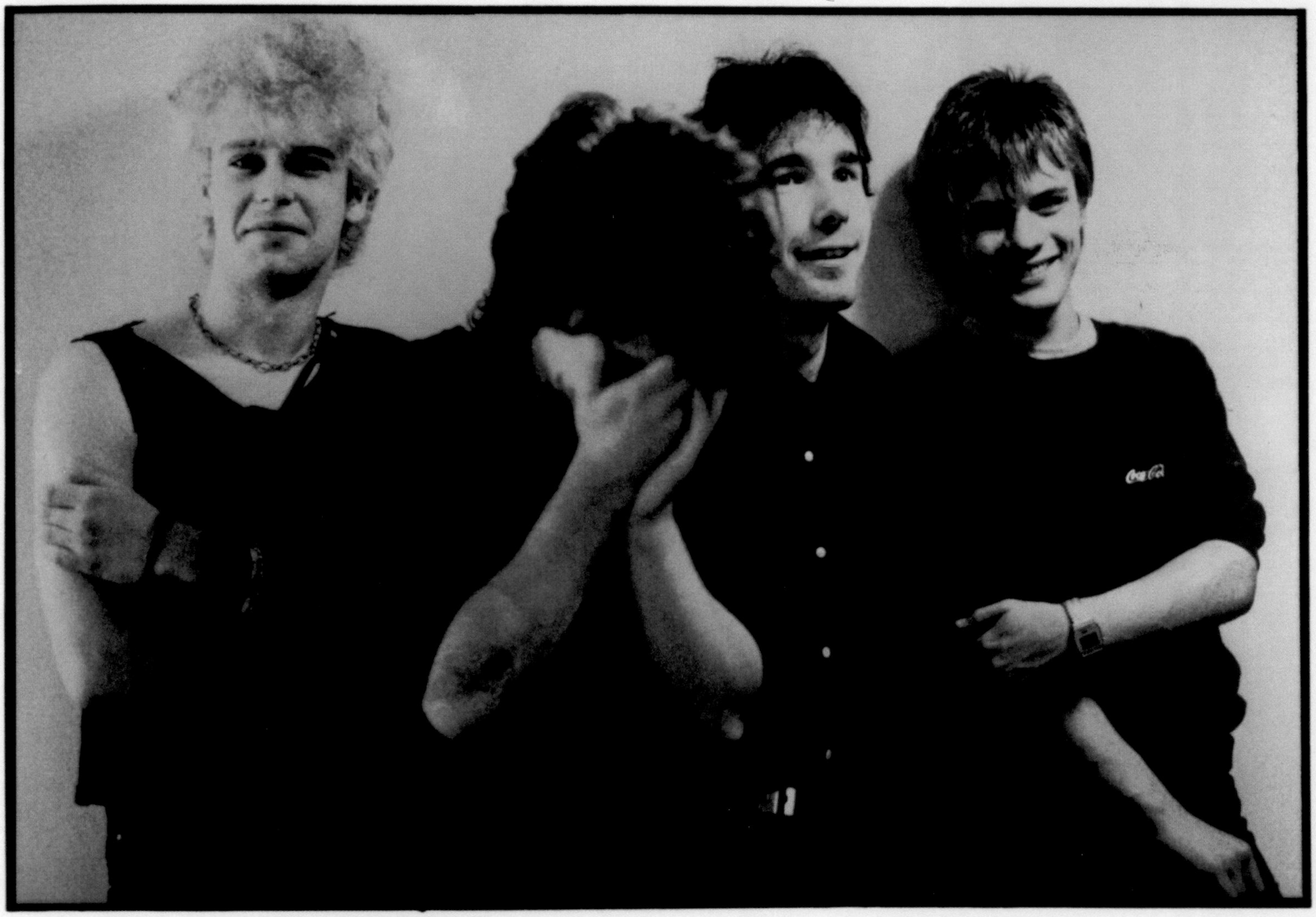

Photo Credit Pennie Smith 1981

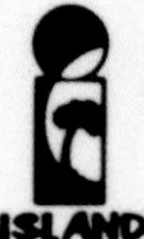

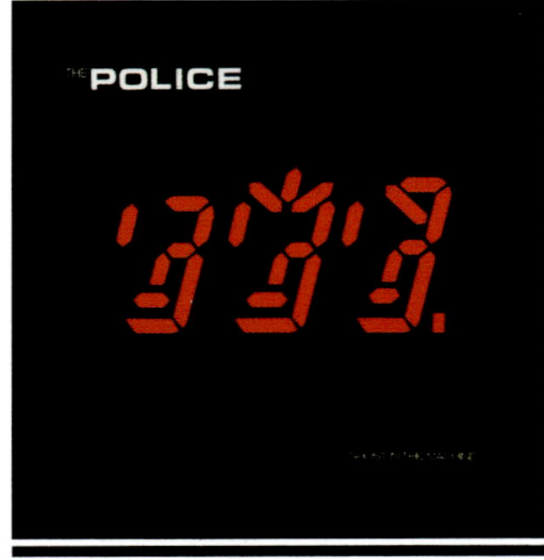

Billboard 200: *Ghost in the Machine* (#2)
Billboard Hot 100: "Every Little Thing She Does Is Magic" (#3); "Spirits in the Material World" (#11); "Secret Journey" (#46)

The Police hammered out an extensive worldwide following with the multihit success of *Ghost in the Machine*.

THE POLICE had managed to transcend the faddish "new wave" labels that had been bandied about since the band's formation in the midst of the punk boom in Britain.

The music received critical and popular acclaim—*Ghost in the Machine*, the fourth album, featured the hits "Every Little Thing She Does Is Magic," "Invisible Sun" and "Spirits in the Material World." A ten-months-a-year touring schedule had allowed the globally popular trio to play in such exotic places as India and Egypt.

"We're selling records all over the world, and we have the statistics to back it up," guitarist Andy Summers said. "Now we're trying to get more time off, because we're all going nuts. Our music has taken on an international appeal, however. I don't think it is such a British or ethnic sound as some groups like Madness or the Specials, for instance. We take our music as a synthesis of really different things."

The Police seemed more than willing to trade in on the mystique that surrounded English rock musicians. "Oh, it's true—I'm very patriotic," Summers noted. "There are great American rock groups, but English groups tend to come out with more original sounds. But some of the world's best music comes from America. The paradox is that most English rock musicians were originally inspired by American music. The Police are inspired by it, but there are other influences, too, like Jamaican music.

"In England, it's much more close-knit—you're closer together and exposed to a lot more variety. People are always moving on and trying to form something else. It doesn't always produce great music, but it's never stagnant—there's always a turnover. There have been so many trends in England in the last few years, but it really doesn't matter how long they last or how valid they are, because at least they keep things fresh."

Several critics had wondered how much longer the band could continue to rework its sound within the framework of a three-piece group. *Ghost in the Machine* was the first Police album to add on keyboard flourishes—"Every Little Thing She Does Is Magic" featured a pianist—as well as a few saxophone riffs contributed by bassist and vocalist Sting. Onstage, however, the group toured with only three horn players to augment its sound on a few numbers.

"I've never found it limiting having only three people in the band," Summers insisted. "It's just a different discipline. It meant that you had to try harder, see what you can get out of it rather than saying, 'Oh, a keyboard can cover that part.' As a guitarist, I enjoy having the space to play with. I don't have to do combat with another harmonic instrument. A three-piece sound gives you a clarity. I do agree with Sting, however—if we get stale and start caricaturing our early albums, then we should finish." ■

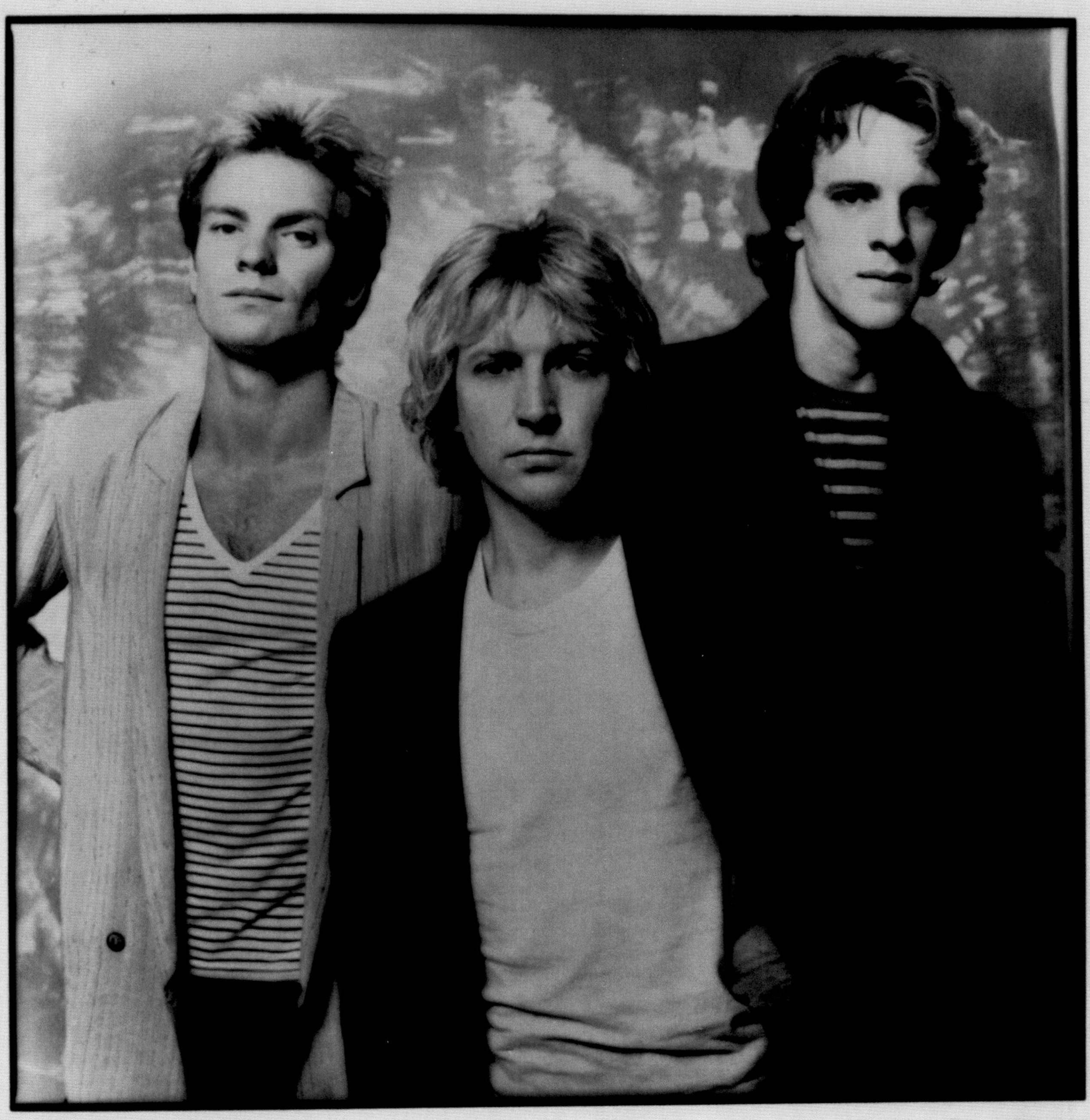

THE POLICE

STING, ANDY SUMMERS, STEWART COPELAND

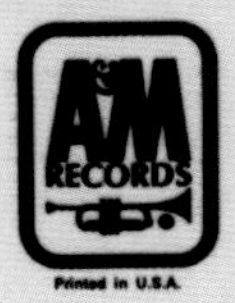

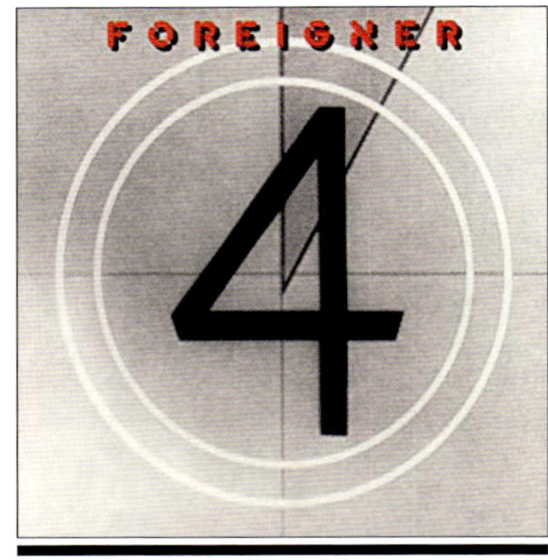

Billboard 200: *4* (No. 1)
Billboard Hot 100: "Urgent" (#4); "Juke Box Hero" (#26); "Waiting for a Girl Like You" (#2); "Break It Up" (#26); "Luanne" (#75)

4 fortified Foreigner's star status, spawning the hits "Urgent," "Waiting for a Girl Like You" and "Juke Box Hero."

IN THE Seventies, Foreigner stood out among all arena-rock acts. Guitarist Mick Jones, born and raised in England, was a hardened veteran of band wars who joined up with Lou Gramm, an unknown American who evolved into one of rock's most distinctive vocalists. The group came to dominate radio, selling close to 16 million records worldwide with the albums *Foreigner*, *Double Vision* and *Head Games* as well as singles like "Hot Blooded" and "Cold as Ice."

Foreigner opened the Eighties involved in a major personnel shift, with the departures of two charter members, multi-instrumentalist Ian McDonald and keyboardist Al Greenwood,

"Things became a little too comfortable, and people became a little jaded and blasé," Jones said. "If we came out with another *Double Vision* or 'Feels Like the First Time,' we'd just be repeating ourselves. What's important is to get better, to do new things."

Produced by Robert John "Mutt" Lange (fresh off his massive success with AC/DC's *Back in Black*) and Jones, *4* was the first Foreigner album featuring the new quartet lineup of Jones, Gramm, Dennis Elliott and Rick Willis. As the architect of Foreigner's "heavy melody" sound, a combination of commercial cunning and hard-rock prowess, Jones added interesting touches—"Urgent," a propulsive piece of heavy-metal funk, featured a stunning solo in the bridge by Motown sax great Junior Walker. "Urgent" hit the Top 5 on the pop charts and, in a surprising development, rode high on the dance music charts as well.

The evocative power ballad "Waiting for a Girl Like You," with a synthesizer theme performed by a young Thomas Dolby, achieved a chart distinction by spending a record 10 weeks in the #2 position on the *Billboard* Hot 100 chart, without ever reaching the top. "It may be a little risky for us to do a ballad, but it is sincere," Jones admitted. "And the thing I want to get across with this album is the feeling and conviction behind it."

4 became the first No. 1 record of Foreigner's career. The magnitude of the band's success astonished Jones.

"When we got together, nobody had any idea Foreigner was going to do what it did," he insisted. "I would have been happy just to make some kind of mark with the first album and keep building." ■

FOREIGNER

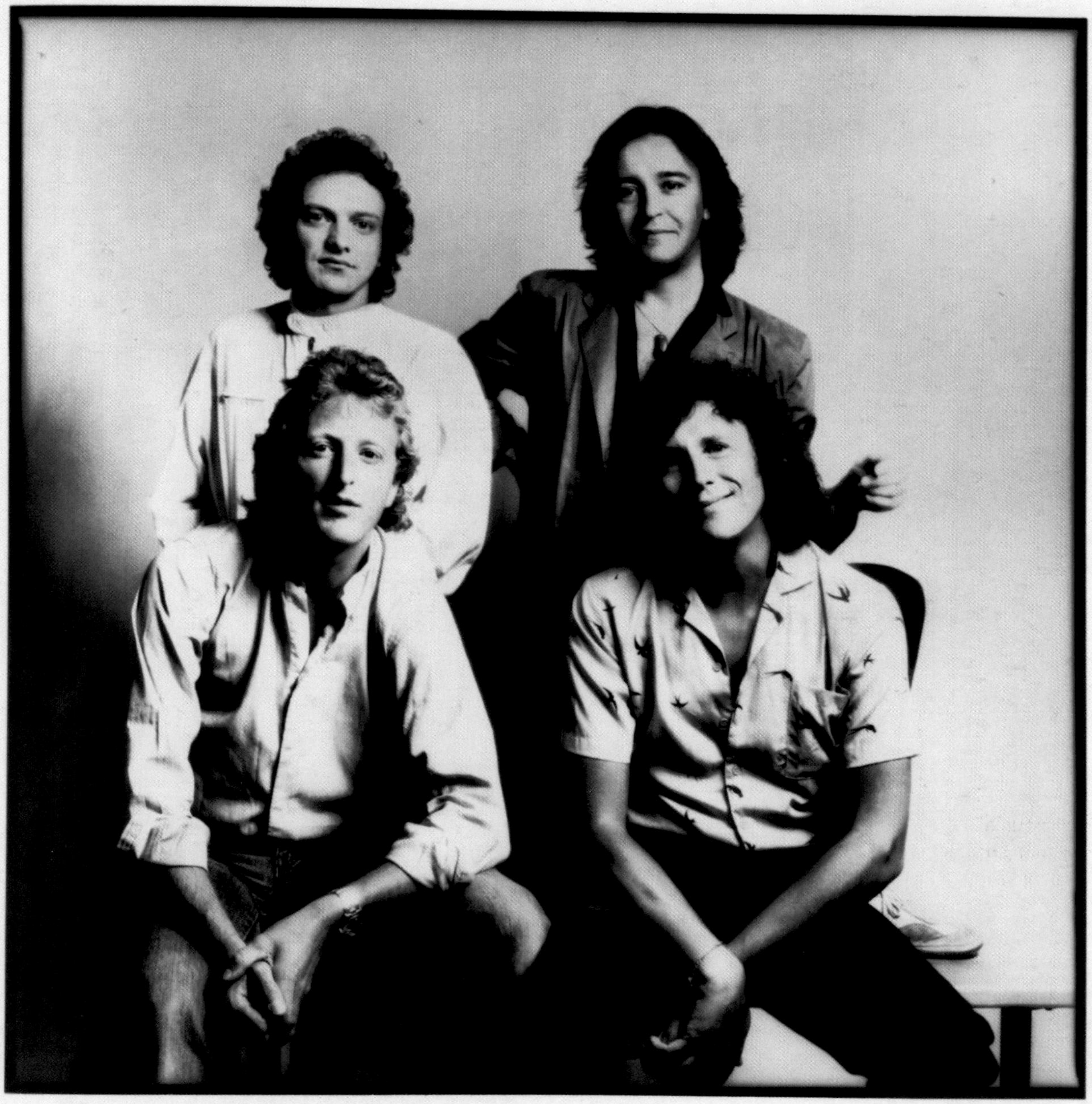

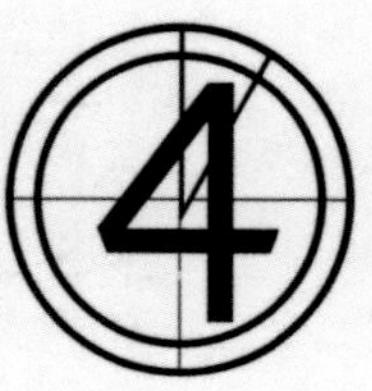

LOU GRAMM
RICK WILLS

MICK JONES
DENNIS ELLIOTT

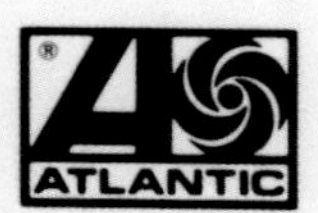

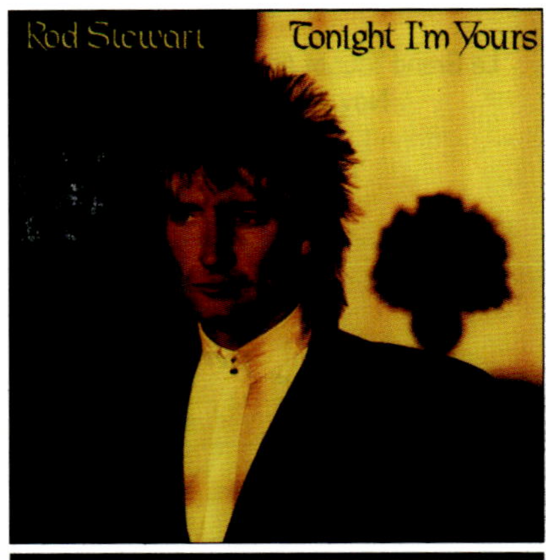

Billboard 200: *Tonight I'm Yours* (#11)
Billboard Hot 100: "Tonight I'm Yours (Don't Hurt Me)" (#20); "Young Turks" (#5); "How Long" (#49)

Introducing a polished new-wave production to his musical form, Rod Stewart rebounded with *Tonight I'm Yours*.

ROD STEWART had lost some credibility. Although his 1980 album *Foolish Behavior* spawned the hit single, "Passion," it didn't come near the Top 10 like past efforts, and where his live performances had always revealed him to be charismatic, his dyed-blonde hair, makeup and foppish costumes had devolved into a self-parody.

But Stewart released *Tonight I'm Yours*, which showed him writing and singing from the gut again. Elements of synth-pop were added to the haunting "Young Turks," a hit concerning teenage pregnancy—"I think it's an important song, a fairly hot subject," he said. Ironically, the record was originally supposed to be a live album, which Stewart's label refused.

"I recorded that whole album out of me own pocket with their approval, and then they decided that they wanted a studio LP. Bloody hell!" Stewart related. "But I was anxious to go back in the studio anyway. I was very disappointed with *Foolish Behavior*—I was embarrassed when it came on the radio. But we all make mistakes. I'm sure there are a lot of people who like that album, but the new one is a lot more honest. That's what I've attempted to do with a different group."

Stewart was working with a revamped band, leaving guitarist Jim Cregan as the only holdover. Tony Brock (drums) and Wally Stocker (guitar) had joined from the defunct Babys, and guitarist Robin Le Mesurier, bassist Jay Davis, saxophonist Jim Zavala and keyboardist Kevin Savigar rounded out the entourage.

"Well, I've never had to look for a musician in me life—God is on my side," Stewart said. "But what I look for in a band is a syncopation, a band that plays totally and utterly together. And now I also have three English guitar players for the first time."

In the mid-Seventies, Stewart had received the blame for the breakup of the Faces—one of Britain's most beloved bands—after he had some success on his own.

"We only had one real hit, 'Stay with Me,'" he reflected. "It was a great band to be in, a drunk's band, but I don't care how much people loved us, it was just diabolical-sounding some nights.

"Ronnie Lane was the drinker, the one who fell over, so it started when he left. I sat down with Woody (Ron Wood), and he said he'd go play with the Stones, even though they were only touring every three years. I wasn't going to be in a group without Woody, 'cause he was and is me best mate. So I had to get my own band. In those days, I didn't have the confidence to do it. I don't mind it now. I'll keep at this until I feel that I'm looking silly or I don't have any music left. I'll do anything to entertain—take off me trousers if I have to." ■

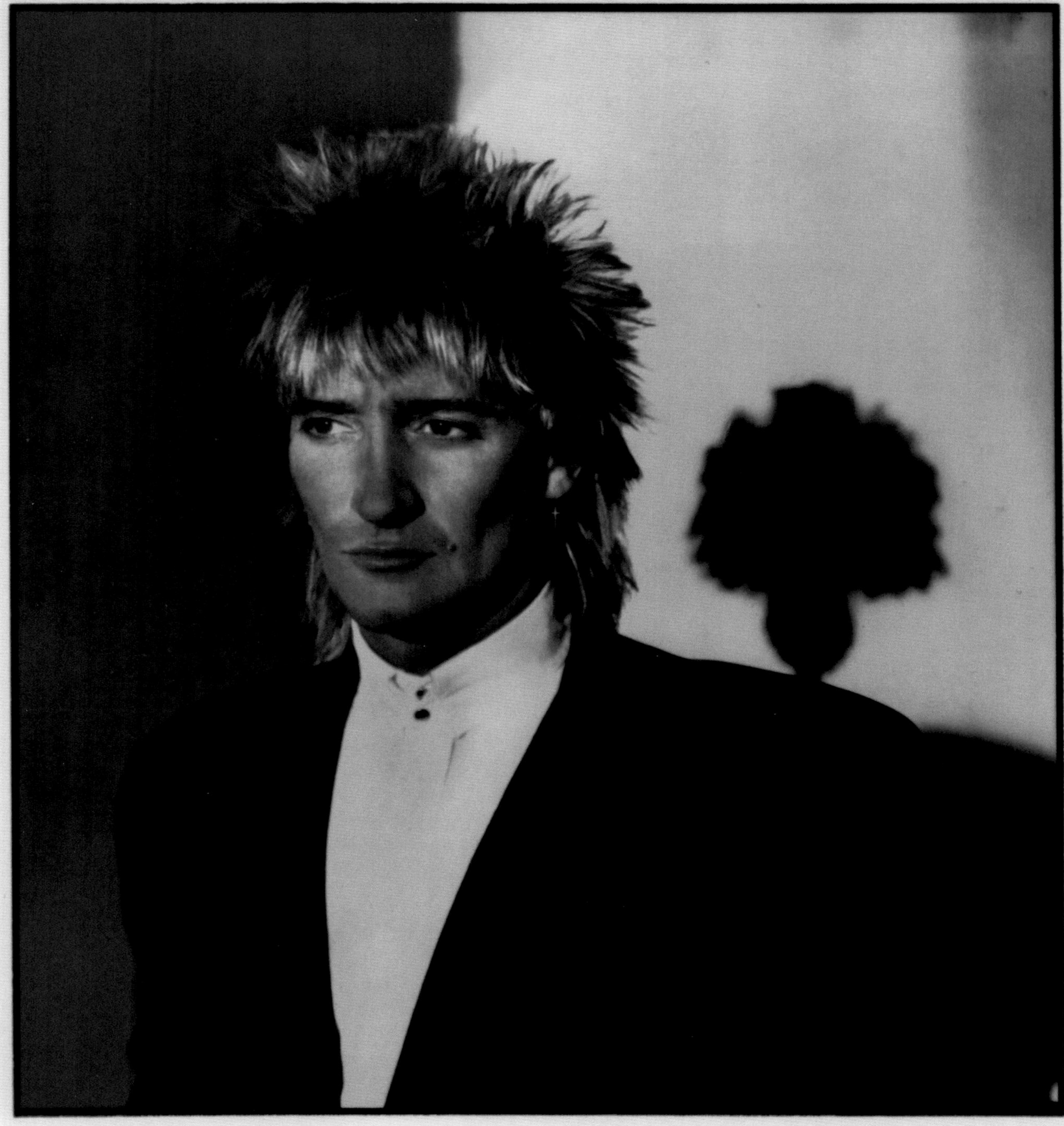

OCTOBER 1981

ROD STEWART

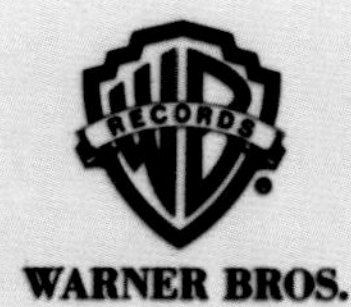

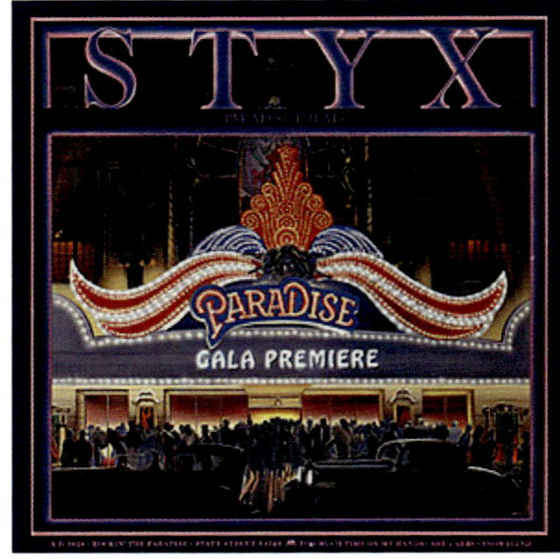

Billboard 200: *Paradise Theater* (No. 1)
Billboard Hot 100: "The Best of Times" (#3); "Too Much Time on My Hands" (#9); "Nothing Ever Goes as Planned" (#54)

Styx's biggest success, *Paradise Theater* yielded the Top 10 hits "The Best of Times" and "Too Much Time on My Hands."

STYX HAD achieved three consecutive multiplatinum albums and for two years had outdrawn everyone else on the road—including such notables as the Who and Bruce Springsteen. Yet Styx was still didn't get any respect from the rock press. Most of the members' energy was directed at their legion of fans rather than at their detractors, but they were willing to try to set the record straight.

"We're still trying to be understood," guitarist Tommy Shaw admitted. "I suppose the biggest rap is that our lyrics are shallow, meaningless, banal and have no social significance. Hey, we live and die with our lyrics—anyone who says that hasn't even bothered to listen. We always try to say something in every song, although I don't think you have to come up with *War and Peace* every time. But our message is always positive, and I think that should mean something to our critics."

The band's battering by the media caused Shaw some personal discomfort. "I'm hearing the same dumb thing that I heard when I joined the band years ago, that Tommy Shaw looks like Peter Frampton. It's pretty hard to take sometimes."

Shaw remained as unaffected by fame as when he joined Styx as a baby-faced whiz out of Atlanta and turned around the group's fortunes.

"There have moments when I could have convinced myself that I was personally responsible for the group's success, but it just isn't that way," he said. "The original members had taken things as far as they could go, and it manifested when the guitarist left. I was just a hungry kid with a wardrobe case full of songs, so joining Styx was like raiding a candy store. Not everything worked—I had never played in a band before—but it was incredible to be with other people who had similar ideas and aspirations."

Envisaged as a culmination of Styx's fame, *Paradise Theater* was a loosely based concept concerning the rise and fall of an old Chicago theater, a cultural metaphor for America. It was the band's greatest commercial triumph, reaching No. 1 on the *Billboard* album chart. The supporting tour was a mammoth undertaking, with seven 45-foot trailers worth of equipment and two tour buses.

"Anybody who has been involved in a big production knows that the crew is the biggest factor in its success," Shaw noted. "We're so happy and excited this time out, because we have so many talented and conscientious people working on it, a big machine that moves from city to city. I haven't yet read a review where the critic stayed for the end of the show, but I'll tell you one thing—it's their loss if they miss it this time." ■

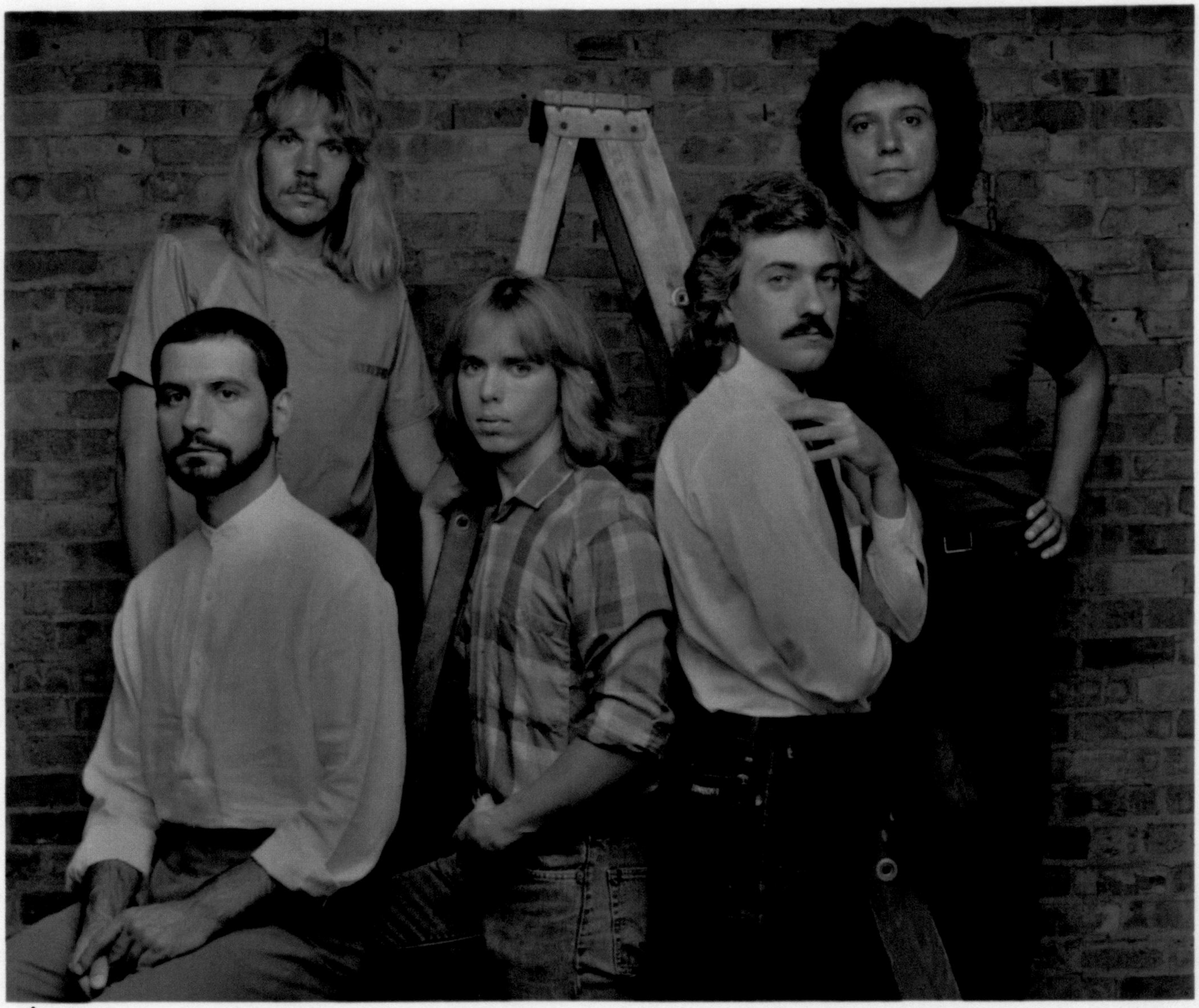

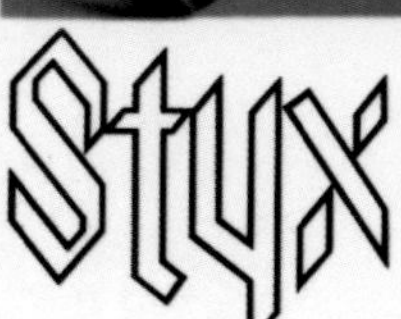

L-R JAMES (J. Y.) YOUNG JOHN PANOZZO
CHUCK PANOZZO, TOMMY SHAW, DENNIS DE YOUNG

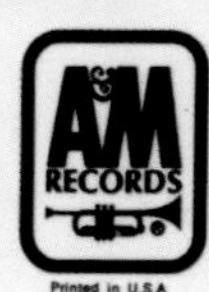

Printed in U.S.A.

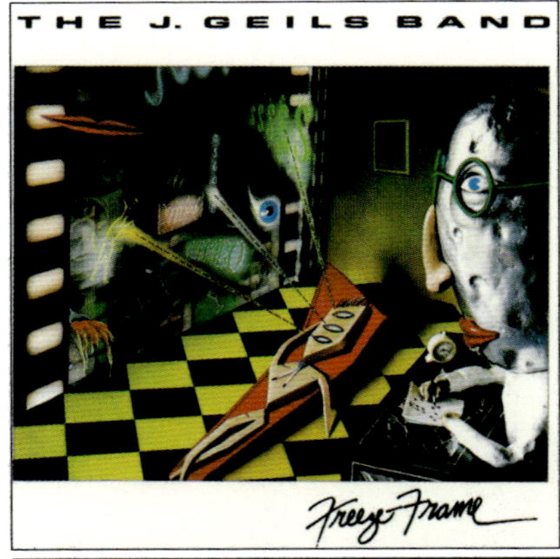

Billboard 200: *Freeze-Frame* (No. 1)
Billboard Hot 100: "Angel in Blue" (#40); "Centerfold" (No. 1); "Freeze-Frame" (#4)

The J. Geils Band broke through with its biggest hits, "Freeze-Frame" and the No. 1 "Centerfold."

R&B STANDARDS and hard-driving blues-rock had fueled the J. Geils Band's years as an energetic opening act, earning the tag "America's best party band" throughout the Seventies. Audiences left the pulverizing live shows with lessons learned in what singer Peter Wolf called "the college of musical knowledge." With his speed-of-light street shuffling and patented triple-tongued jive stage patter, Wolf didn't engage in mere rabble-rousing. He wanted kids to get excited, get involved, or just get mad—any reaction so that they would be moved to find some answers.

"I like the tradeoff," Wolf said. "We feel something up onstage, but I think they're getting something from us, too. I challenge them. I got a rapport with the audience, and I want it to be funny, humorous—not preachy."

The move to a more commercial sound had resulted in the 1980 hit, "Love Stinks." It set the stage for ***Freeze-Frame***, the band's first No. 1 album after a dozen years together. Wolf's passions were expressed on the lyrical lift of the album's themes—turmoil in America, rock-'n'-roll-can-save-your-soul and, of course, love.

Keyboardist Seth Justman, like the rest of the band—Danny Klein (bass), Magic Dick (harmonica), Stephen Jo Bladd (drums) and J. Geils (guitar)—was loving every second of the group's stay at the top. He was largely responsible for that success, having produced, arranged and co-written every Geils album.

"I always did that stuff, but I only got credit for the first time a few albums ago," he shrugged. "If there's one thing we all did to make this happen, it's something all real musicians do—we practiced. Most guys get to a point where it's just style instead of chops. We wanted to be more proficient—that's integral to progressing and expanding."

"We've always had an audience because of our live shows, and they kept us going when we didn't have hits," Wolf summarized. "I look back on all the acts that we used to open for, and it's amazing how many have just dropped from sight. I'm glad we're still out there doing it. A lot of bands complain about how hard the road is, but to me, playing rock 'n' roll is the most exciting thing in the world." ■

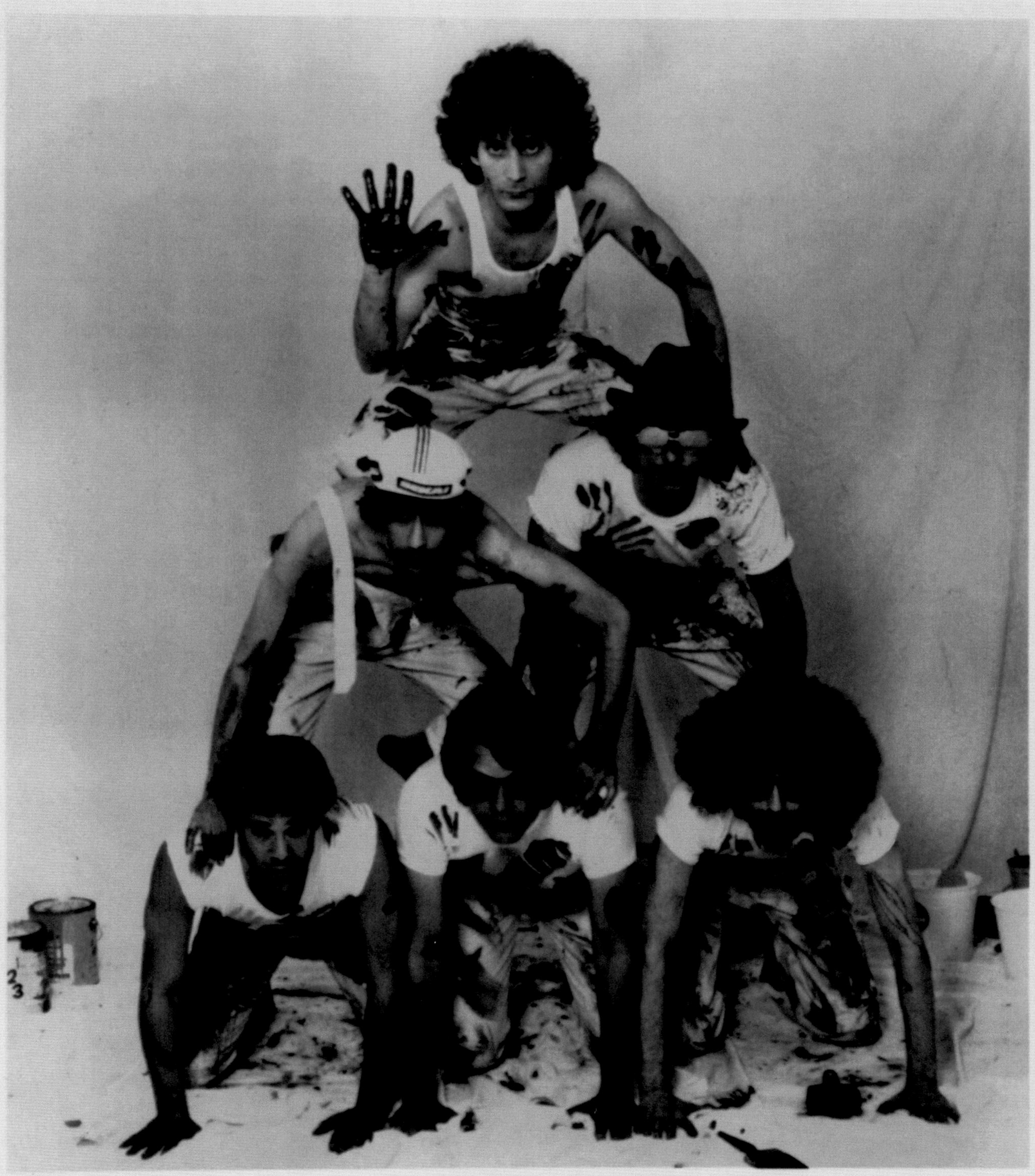

THE J. GEILS BAND

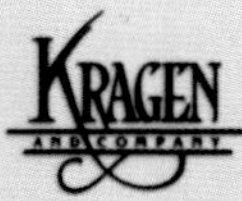

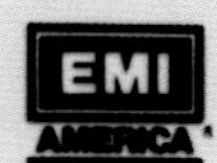

Public Relations
Guy Thomas
Vice President/Creative Services
Kragen & Company
1112 N. Sherbourne Dr.
(213) 854-4400

Billboard 200: *Don't Say No* (#5)
Billboard Hot 100: "The Stroke" (#17); "In the Dark" (#35);
"My Kinda Lover" (#45)

Billy Squier's solo approach reaped immediate advantages, as "The Stroke" became a monster hit around the world.

BILLY SQUIER believed the old adage, "If you want something done right, do it yourself."

"Everybody has certain passions and desires—say, a guy who plays guitar may not have the desire to write songs, or vice versa," he explained. "Me, I was attracted to all of those things. Everything that's happened to me is just the result of realizing that I could do them all."

Two solo albums had granted Squier the power to headline arenas and command more airplay than any of his contemporaries. It wasn't always that way for the guitarist, who paid his dues in two critically acclaimed but commercially ignored groups, the Sidewinders and Piper. Suffering through image control with Piper's management (the same people who foisted Kiss upon the public) gave Squier the impetus to strike out on his own.

"It was the best chance for success," he noted. "When I was in those bands, I didn't have the control or the ability to shape things the way I saw fit. I figured it had to be better to take responsibility for the success or failure of things—and when I developed a more acute idea of what I wanted, it was time."

It didn't take long for Squier to supplement his skills on guitar as a writer and singer. *Don't Say No*, his second solo release, spawned three hit singles—including the Top 10 anthem "The Stroke." "It's a popular, modern-day phenomenon," Squier said. "No matter how distasteful the reality is, some people will always go around stroking other people."

His association with the German producer Mack (previously an engineer for Queen and ELO) gave the material a "heavy guitar rock" edge. Squier initiated a method of writing songs before entering the studio—by locking himself away for three weeks.

"I just find it's a more intensified, spontaneous way to work—I seem to perform better under pressure," he said. "It's like learning a craft—being aware of it doesn't necessarily allow you to accomplish it. It's just a matter of communicating. I write about things in my life as they come up." ■

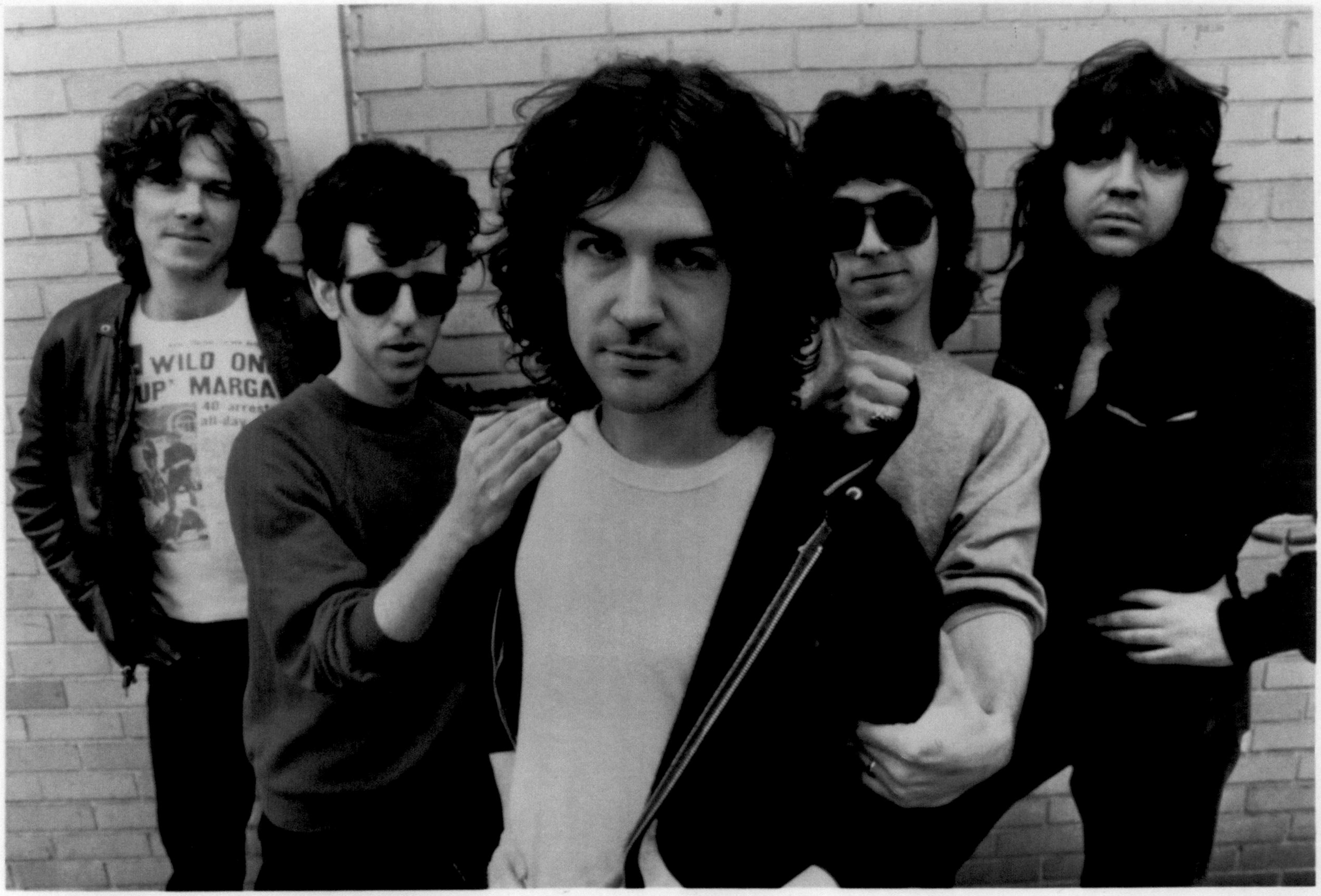

Jeff Golub Kenny Aaronson **BILLY SQUIER** Alan Levi Bobby Chouinard

PHOTO:
GEOFFREY THOMAS / 1981

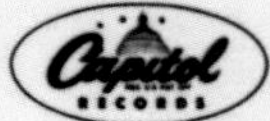

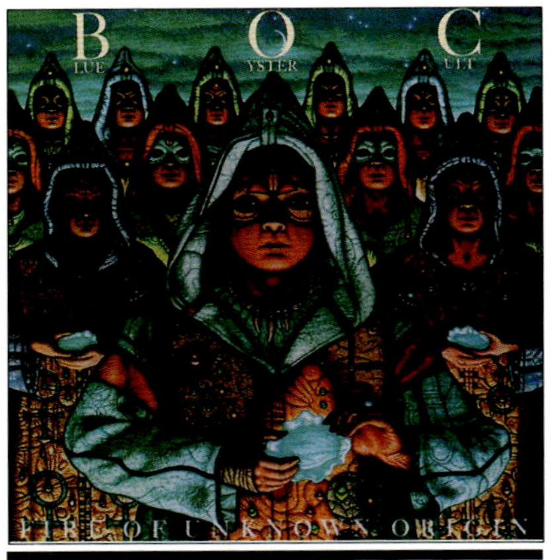

Billboard 200: *Fire of Unknown Origin* (#24)
Billboard Hot 100: "Burnin' for You" (#40)

Fire of Unknown Origin represented the most commercial offering from Blue Öyster Cult in several years.

AFTER RECORDING ten albums and touring the world several times, Blue Öyster Cult should have solidified its credibility in the rock 'n' roll universe. But a couple of Bible-toting brothers were leading a fresh crusade against the band, exhorting teenagers to build bonfires with their copies of the 1976 hit "(Don't Fear) The Reaper." See, any band with the word "cult" in its name…

Guitarist Eric Bloom asserted that the band had dealt with worse situations. "Hey, as long as they buy the albums before they burn them, it's okay with me," he cracked. "Our catalog could use a boost in sales anyway."

A search for a new recording direction had continued since Blue Öyster Cult's split with producer Sandy Pearlman. 1979's *Mirrors* had been suitably tame for the mainstream music market, but producer Tom Werman dabbled too much in the arrangements for the record to be interpreted as a classic BOC product. The following year's *Cultosaurus Erectus* was a backlash of sorts—Martin Birch, who had engineered heavy-metal triumphs by Black Sabbath and Rainbow, returned to the guitar basics that had catapulted the band to fame in the first place, yet the album sold poorly.

Fire of Unknown Origin consolidated the best points of prior releases. Patti Smith concocted the poem-lyric of the title track. British science fiction/fantasy writer Michael Moorcock's newest collaboration with Bloom was "Veteran of the Psychic Wars," a lament for Moorcock's hero Elric the Eternal Champion. And R. Meltzer, a provocateur since BÖC's first album, advanced the lyric of "Burnin' for You," with music and vocal from guitarist Donald "Buck Dharma" Roeser making it as close as the band was likely to get to a romantic love song.

"There are some tunes that are easily the most commercial things that we've done in a while," Bloom admitted. "But we get to stretch out, too. I don't think there's anything too wrong with trying to write a hit—our concerts have always done well, but record sales have been off with the last few albums. A bit of airplay wouldn't hurt at all."

"Burnin' for You" hit the Top 40, and when MTV premiered, the music video received heavy rotation. *Fire of Unknown Origin* achieved gold status while the Blue Öyster Cult concert phenomenon continued unabated.

"A lot of bands make the mistake of trying to push a new album when the fans come expecting something else," Bloom explained. "If we ever tried to walk off a stage without playing 'Reaper' or 'Godzilla,' I hate to think what would happen—but I'm sure it would be a lot more drastic than record-burning." ■

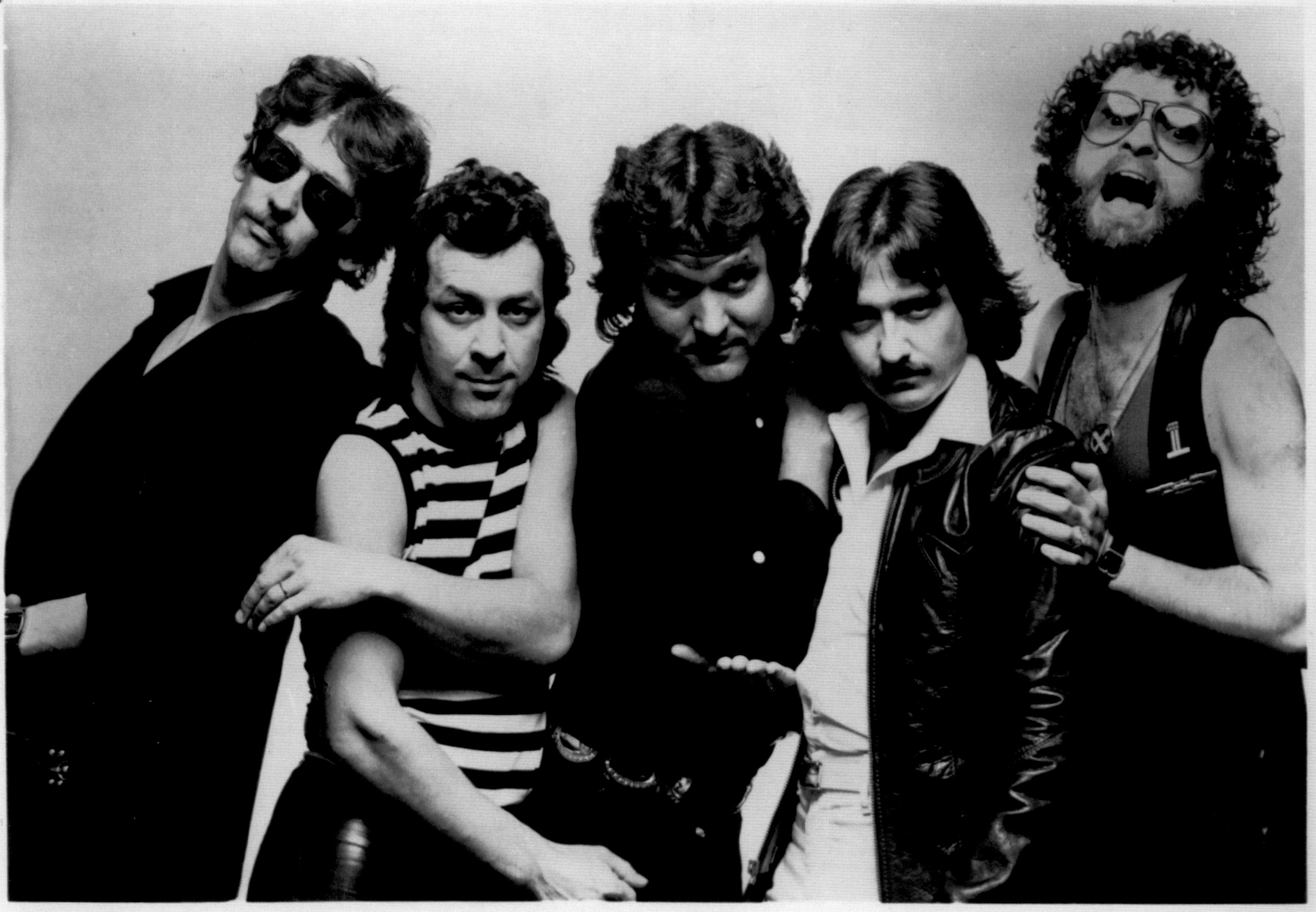

BLUE ÖYSTER CULT

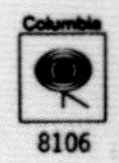

Billboard 200: *Bad for Good* (#63)
Billboard Hot 100: "Rock and Roll Dreams Come Through" (#32)

After penning the songs for Meat Loaf's *Bat Out of Hell*, Jim Steinman stepped into the spotlight himself.

MEAT LOAF came out of nowhere in 1978 with *Bat Out of Hell,* a debut album containing some of the most bombastic, pretentious music ever committed to vinyl—and the record ended up selling more than 8 million copies. Fans had been eagerly awaiting the follow-up, but the beefy singer had been missing in action for some time.

The overblown, operatic style lived on through the album *Bad for Good* by Jim Steinman, the man who had written and arranged all the material for *Bat Out of Hell.*

"Actually, I would have sung those songs myself, but some female biker punched me in the face a few years earlier and I couldn't sing for two years," Steinman explained. "When I found Meat, I freaked—here was this guy with a giant voice who was capable of singing these armor-plated songs I had written. So we teamed up."

Bat Out of Hell got off to a slow start before burning into the public's mind. Steinman's epics of drama and excess meshed perfectly with Meat Loaf's full-throated vocals, but Meat Loaf didn't handle the pressures of stardom well. "When he came off the road, his voice was shot to hell," Steinman said. "There was some physical damage, but a lot of it was mental—he couldn't deal with having to follow such an amazingly successful record. He went to doctors and specialists everywhere, and no one could find anything wrong."

Steinman was left holding the material he had penned for Loaf's second album. "I was singing again, and we had no clue when Meat would be ready. So I started writing more stuff for Meat, and I did *Bad for Good* myself," he said. "It is a very unleashed record!"

Bad for Good held few surprises. The Wagnerian overload of *Bat Out of Hell* was intact—Todd Rundgren once again helped out in the studio, and "Rock and Roll Dreams Come Through" was one of Steinman's most inspirational rock ballads. His unique musical imagination kept him in the public spotlight—he was putting the finishing touches on *Dead Ringer*, the long-awaited second Meat Loaf album.

"Meat finally found this doctor in California who did his voice some good," he said. "The guy is either crazy or a genius, but he took Meat and induced a violent allergic reaction in him—Meat's allergic to a thousand things, but he used cat hair. Then he injected Meat's urine back into his bloodstream. Then he covered him with mats and beat the living hell out of him. It was pretty strange walking into therapy and seeing Meat all swollen and screaming under those mats while this guy pounded on him. He'd stop yelling just long enough to look up and say, 'Isn't this weird?' But I swear to God, it was the only treatment with any results." ■

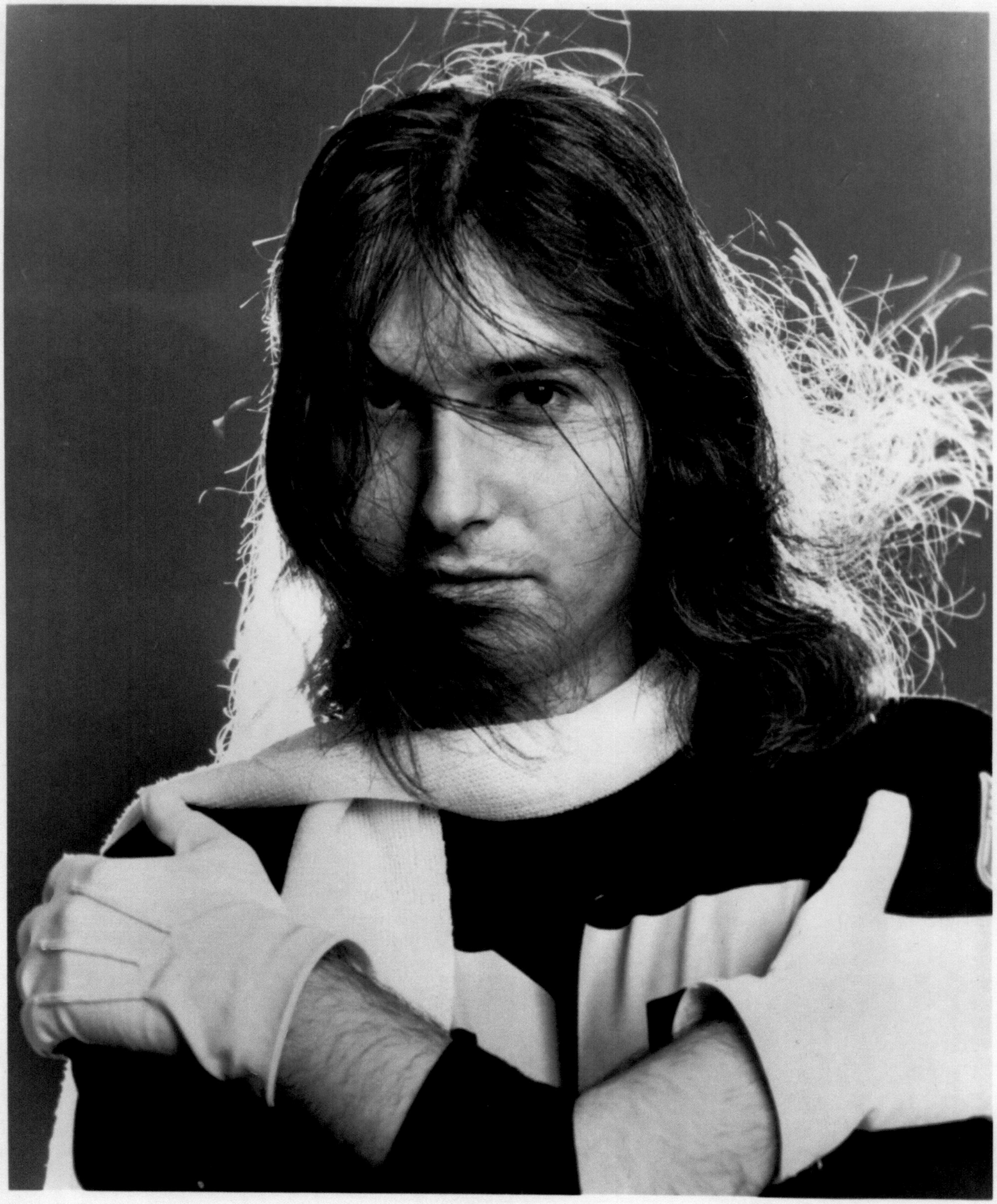

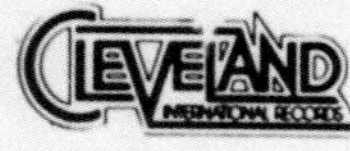

JIM STEINMAN

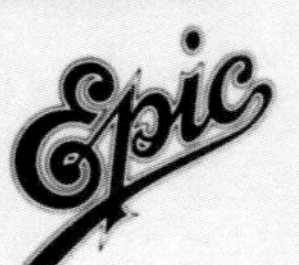

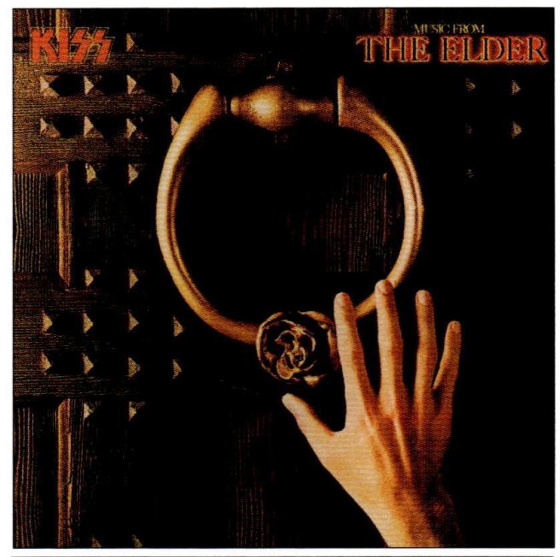

Billboard 200: *Music from "The Elder"* (#75)
Billboard Hot 100: "A World Without Heroes" (#56)

Looking to recapture its US audience, Kiss gambled on its own credibility with *Music from "The Elder"*–and lost out.

TOURS OF Europe, Australia and New Zealand—complete with the notorious makeup and bombastic special effects—had made Kiss an international attraction. By catering to foreign markets, however, the flamboyant hard-rock group had sacrificed its zealous American following. Kiss hoped that *Music from "The Elder"* and a US tour would herald its return.

The lofty concept album, the first recorded work with drummer Eric Carr, created changes in the Kiss philosophy. The storyline revolved around a mystic force that combated evil through chosen mortals. Producer Bob Ezrin added woozy sound effects and stately instrumentation, and the collection contained as many ballads as rockers, and even a short classical piece.

"We had made two passes at recording a 'typical Kiss album,' and it was very good Kiss material—but it wasn't breaking any new ground," bassist Gene Simmons allowed. "*'The Elder'* is something we wanted to do for ourselves, and we're proud of it. Past a certain point of success, you just want to do what you believe in."

An example of the new direction could be heard on the single "A World Without Heroes," the first time Simmons had been allowed to sing a slower song within the confines of Kiss.

"We used to have all sorts of self-imposed restrictions, like I couldn't sing anything but the nasty screamers because that was my character. But if we make the rules, we certainly can change them. *'The Elder'* is the first Kiss record that doesn't have our pictures on it, for example. We felt it would dilute the concept. We could have said, 'Here's another album, and here's what we look like this year.' But the fan magazines will take care of that facet."

Kiss' rabid young audience couldn't keep up. Sales of *"The Elder"* were meager, and the band didn't tour. The ambitious project was presented as a soundtrack to a film, which was never made. It was the final straw for founding guitarist Ace Frehley, who left the group. Regardless, Simmons figured that Kiss would always have a special niche in contemporary music.

"I know that we are responsible for introducing young fetal-aged earth-type people to rock 'n' roll. Imagine being three years old, and the first rock show you see that you'll remember when you grow up is Kiss. Then what are you gonna do, go out and see Atlanta Rhythm Section?" ■

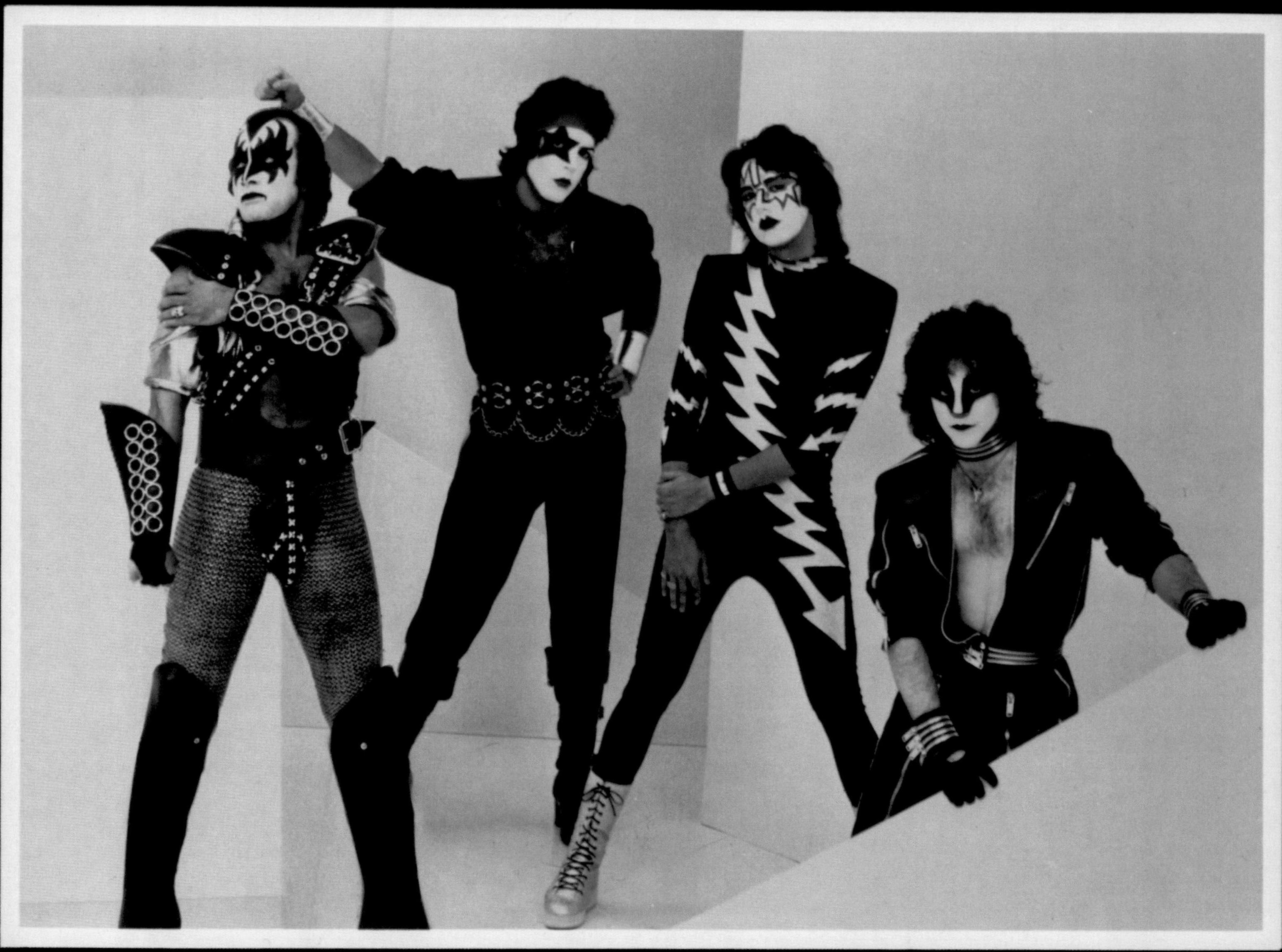
KISS
AUCOIN
PolyGram Records

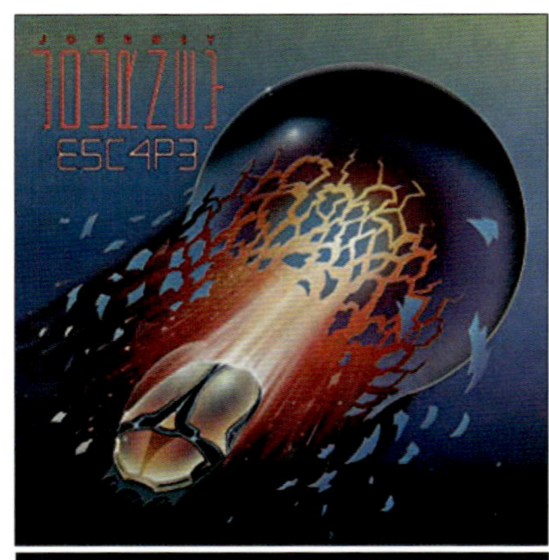

Billboard 200: *Escape* (No. 1)
Billboard Hot 100: "Who's Crying Now" (#4); "Don't Stop Believin'" (#9); "Open Arms" (#2); "Still They Ride" (#19)

Journey's *Escape* spawned three Top 10 hits–"Open Arms," "Who's Crying Now" and "Don't Stop Believin'."

WHEN VOCALIST Steve Perry joined Journey in 1977, it became apparent that his soaring style would become a signature, and that the band would rule the airwaves with his added input. But the anthemic arena-rock outfit continued to evolve. On an ensuing tour, the group took notice of Steve Smith's drumming for opening act Montrose, and his technically precise playing soon added another dimension to Journey's sound. And when the band drafted keyboardist Jonathan Cain from the Babys, the hitmaking machinery was complete—*Escape* reached No. 1.

"If you handpick a band, it's usually a disaster," Cain explained. "With this version of Journey, it's more a matter of the personalities clicking. You can dream of all the success you want, but there's no master plan. I got close to the Journey members when the Babys opened on the road for them. The Babys were a misunderstood band, and we got disenchanted. But I still performed the best I could every night, and it paid off."

Cain replaced founding member Gregg Rolie who, after 12 years of touring and recording with Santana and Journey, had decided to retire.

"They were looking for someone consistent," Cain said. "To their credit, they allowed me input from day one. I was a member of the band, not a sideman—they demanded my equal participation."

Cain's keyboard work added sonic textures that made *Escape* a monster, and he co-wrote many of the songs. The album featured four hit singles—"Don't Stop Believin'," "Who's Crying Now," "Still They Ride" and "Open Arms"—plus the rock-radio staple "Stone in Love." Cain composed and played the potent opening piano riff on "Don't Stop Believin'," and the band felt it had found, as founding member and lead guitarist Neal Schon put it, "an ace reliever. We went to extremes we haven't gone to before—further into hard rock, and further into easy listening. Musically, it appealed to a wider spectrum of fans." ■

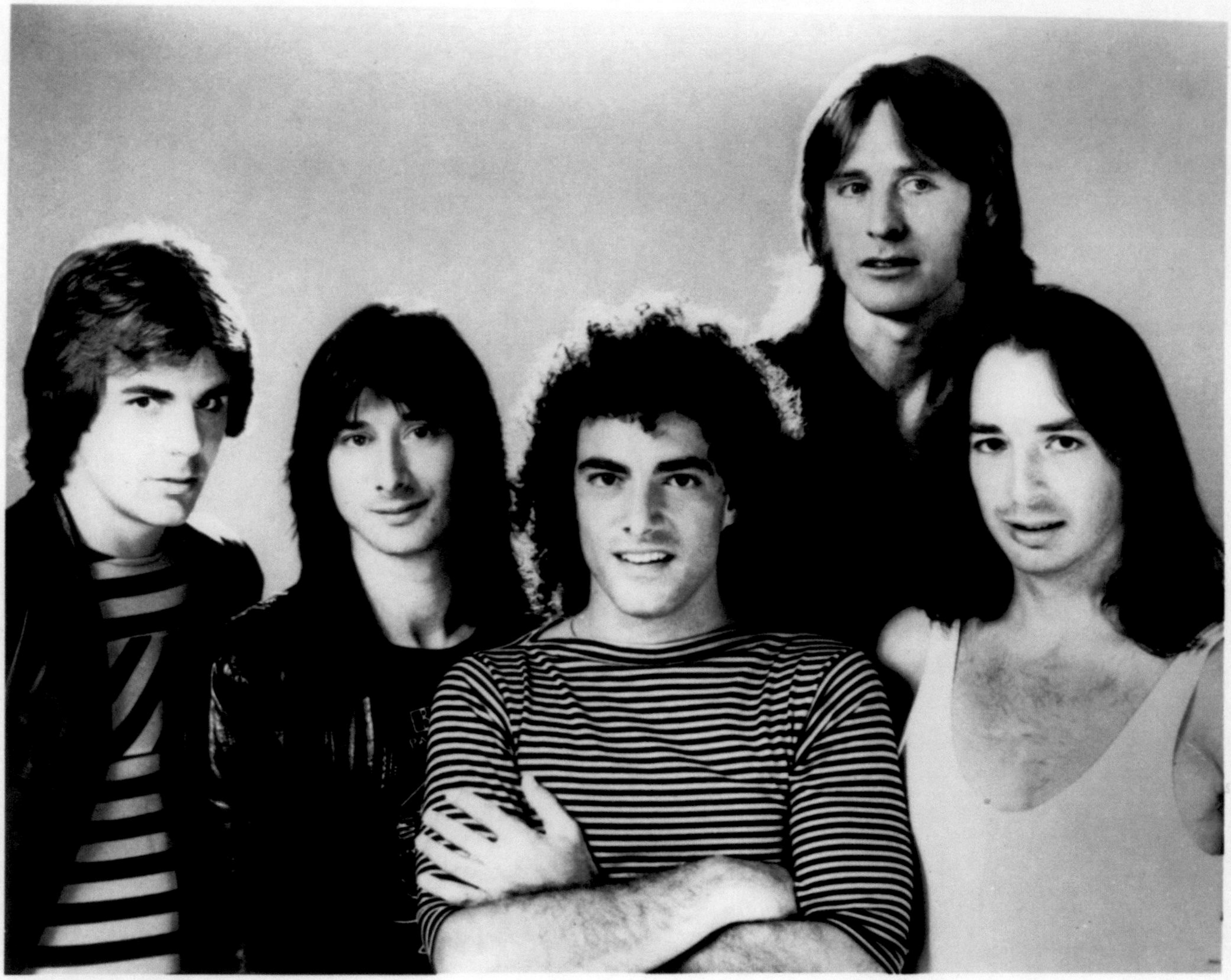

JOURNEY MANAGEMENT·
HERBIE HERBERT
NIGHTMARE, INC.
SAN FRANCISCO, CAL.

JOURNEY

8107

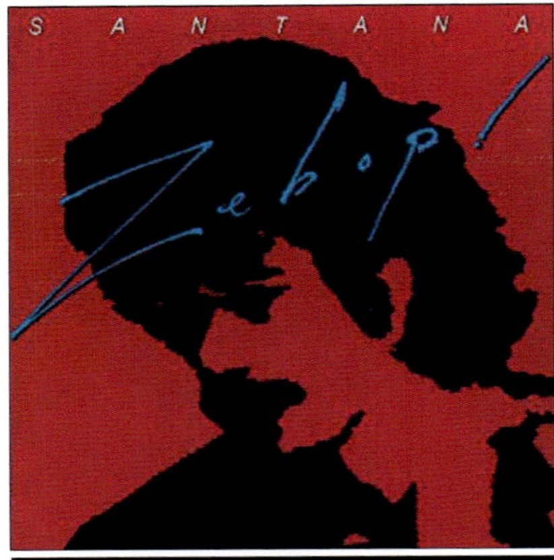

Billboard 200: *Zebop!* (#8)
Billboard Hot 100: "Winning" (#17); "The Sensitive Kind" (#56)

The Eighties started brightly for Santana with changes in personnel and the platinum-selling *Zebop*!

THE GROUP Santana had never slowed down in the decade-plus of its existence. Devadip Carlos Santana, the magical guitarist, had always moved effortlessly from one musical style to the next, taking the original Latin roots of the band into jazz and fusion forays. *Zebop!* continued a move toward a commercial rock sound while including a modicum of the rhythmic framework that marked the early material.

"It's the influx of new people always coming into the band," singer Alex Ligertwood, a two-year veteran of Santana who hailed from Scotland, noted. "We have a new keyboard player and conga player, and Carlos has always looked for the best people to play with. They keep things fresh, even the old material. It's not necessarily better, but it's more pleasing because of the new expertise."

Zebop! reached the Top 10 and featured the Russ Ballard tune "Winning," a hit single.

"Originally, we had used (Fleetwood Mac producer) Keith Olsen on the record, and he is truly an amazing talent, but the sound was just a little too, uh, far for us," Ligertwood explained. "Instead of shopping around for another producer, we ended up using Bill Graham."

The Bay Area concert promoter who had also served as the band's manager for many years, Graham "was like a ninth set of ears, really," Ligertwood said. "He's just been around for a long time. Although he's not a musician per se, he's got so much knowledge and so many ideas after ten years that he was unbelievably helpful. With Olson, we allowed a lot of leeway in the studio. With Bill, the band had a big part in the production."

Devadip Carlos Santana continued to be one of the most lyrical guitarists on the scene. Much had been made of his devotion to his religion, but he was still very much a regular guy—he noted that he took the summer off to "play tennis, meditate and body surf."

He saw the band as "an institution flowing through time and space, ever-changing and exploring musical idioms while retaining the identity of its origins—the driving, incessant Latin percussion foundation and the sound and cry of the guitar at the top. Musicians come into the flowing river, ride through the rapids into calmer water and then move on to be replaced by others who add their own energy and inspiration to its flow."

"We're all basically street people, you know," Ligertwood mused. "We all have various backgrounds and different lifestyles. But that's what keeps Carlos going." ■

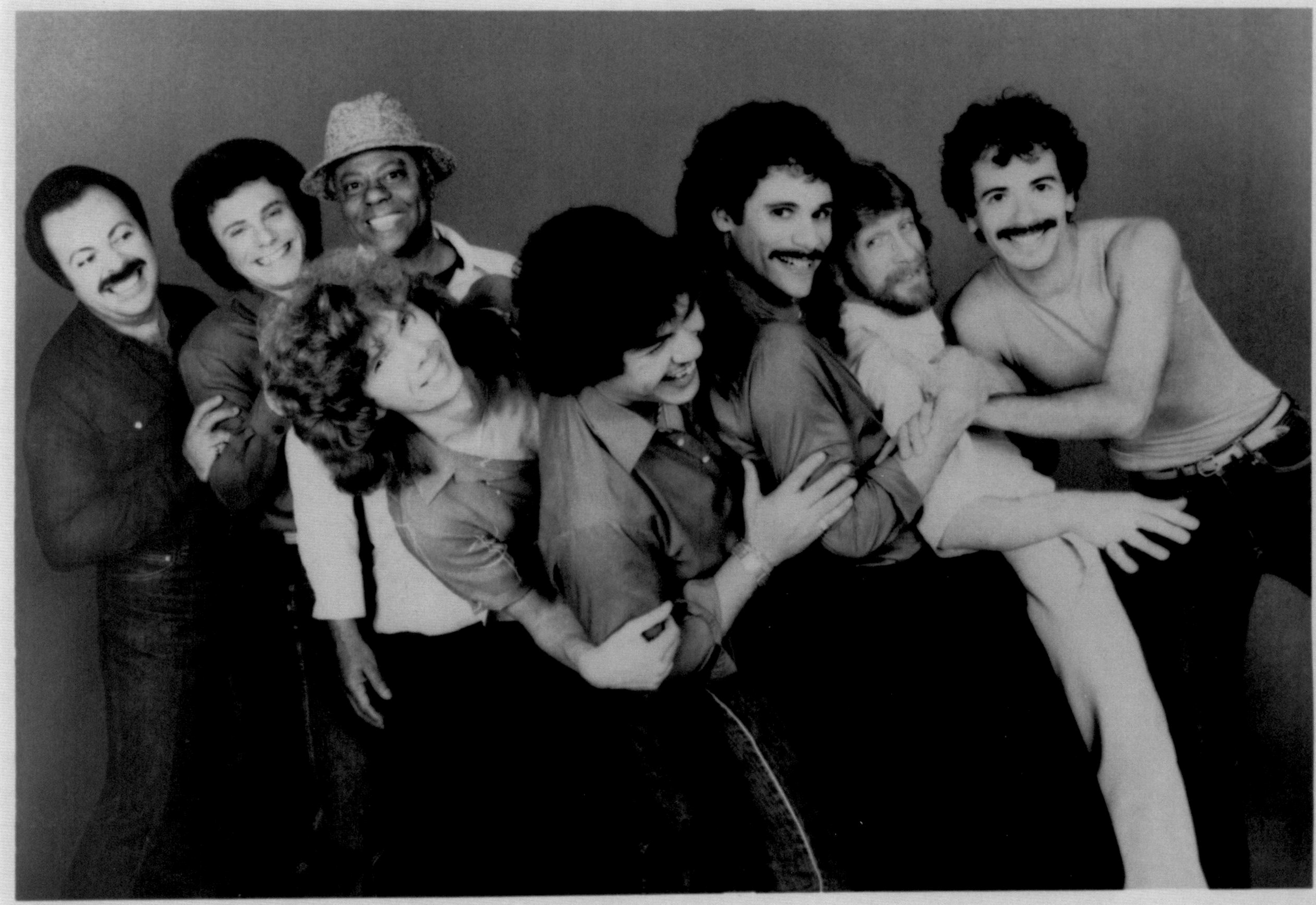

Photo Credit: © ROGER RESSMEYER

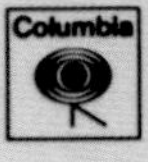

8103

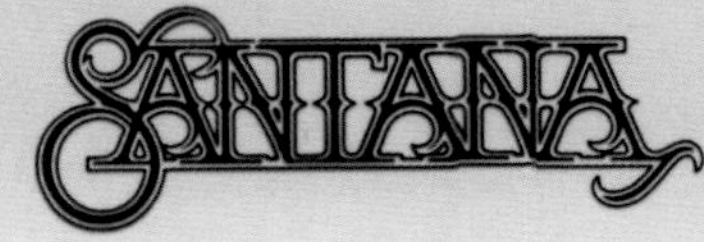

Bill Graham Management

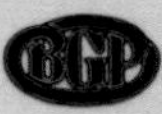

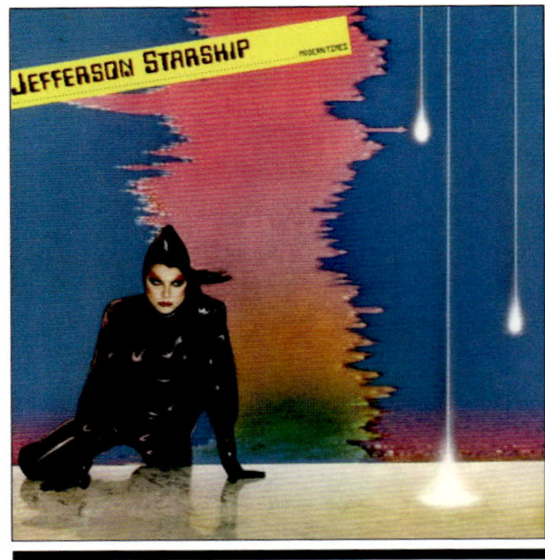

Billboard 200: *Modern Times* (#26)
Billboard Hot 100: "Find Your Way Back" (#29); "Stranger" (#48)

On *Modern Times*, Jefferson Starship welcomed Grace Slick back into the fold after a three-year absence.

EVEN THE most diehard music fan needed a scorecard to keep track of the many twists in the Jefferson Starship's history. Between Grace Slick and Marty Balin using the lead singer position as a revolving door, Paul Kantner's science-fiction excursions and the wavering between a high-energy and mellow style, it had been a dizzying seven years for the band—and that didn't count the nine prior years spent as the Jefferson Airplane.

The latest incarnation was marked by the return of Slick, who had left after the band's 1978 *Earth* album. When she rejoined, the Starship had already completed 90 percent of *Modern Times*. She sang lead on only one song, "Stranger."

In Slick's absence, however, Jefferson Starship had evolved into a top-notch hard-rock outfit. Craig Chaquico emerged as a premier rock guitarist, manifested by his assertive arrangement and solo on the hit single "Find Your Way Back."

An original member of the Starship, Chaquico was in his mid-teens when Kantner recruited him. The band started out playing in the aggressive manner in which Chaquico excelled ("Ride the Tiger"), but when Balin came up with the 1975 smash "Miracles," the band fell into a soft-rock category. Even Chaquico started contributing songs such as "Love Too Good," which he referred to as his "cool Quaalude riff."

"Everything had to sound like 'Miracles,'" Chaquico recalled. "Even if we didn't consciously write anything to sound like it, the record company would pick the one track that came closest to be the single. It really became frustrating—half of the guys didn't want to be active as a band, and the other half really wanted to play for the people."

A succession of personnel changes ensued. Slick left because she got bored, and Balin quit at a later date. John Barbata, the band's precise drummer, knocked himself out of commission with an auto accident. The remaining members linked up with Mickey Thomas (known for his vocal on Elvin Bishop's "Fooled Around and Fell in Love") and drummer Aynsley Dunbar, who wasn't being allowed to stretch out in Journey.

"All of a sudden, I looked around and said, 'Hey, we got a pretty decent hard-rock band here,'" Chaquico noted. The group sought out producer Ron Nevison, who had engineered classic recordings by heavy English bands such as Bad Company and the Who. And with Slick back in the group, the revitalization was in evidence on *Modern Times*.

"We ended up erasing a few vocal tracks to make as much room for her as we could," Chaquico noted. "Grace said, 'Why weren't you guys rocking out when I was in the group? Now you gotta let me back in.'" ■

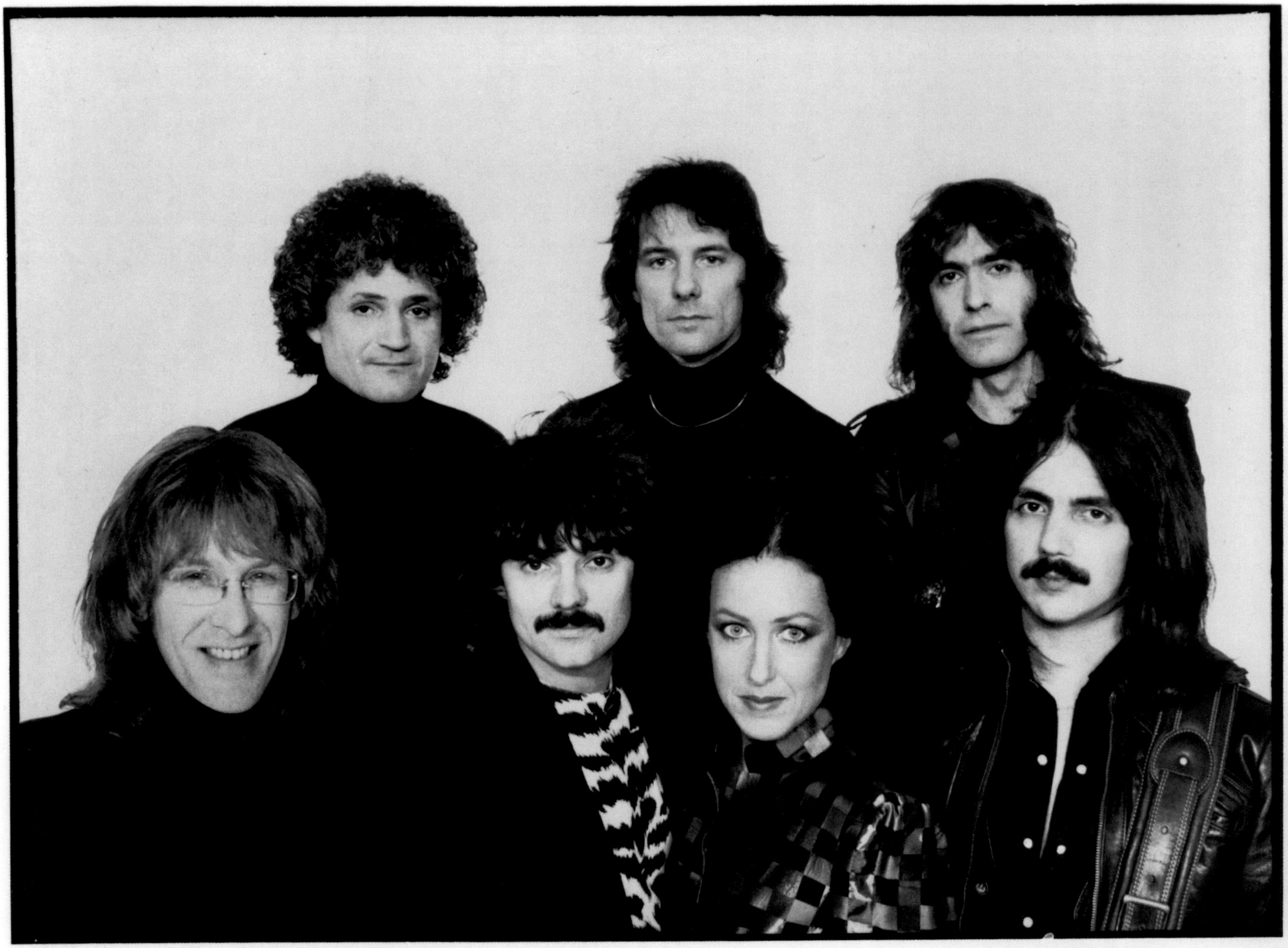

JEFFERSON STARSHIP

Manufactured and Distributed by RCA Records

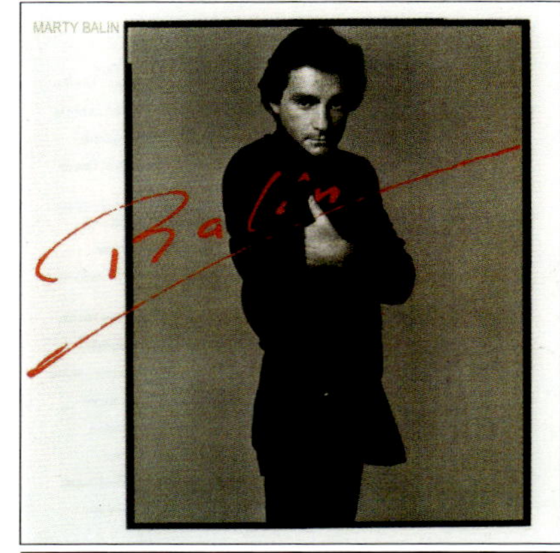

Billboard 200: *Balin* (#26)
Billboard Hot 100: "Hearts" (#8);
"Atlanta Lady (Something About Your Love)" (#27)

Departing Jefferson Starship to mount a solo career, singer Marty Balin scored a Top 10 hit with "Hearts."

DURING HIS stints as a founding member and one of the lead singers and songwriters with the Jefferson Airplane and Jefferson Starship, Marty Balin was depicted as something of a maverick. Rarely granting interviews, he was noted as the ballad singer ("Miracles," "Caroline") in a band with frequent hard-rock tendencies, and he never looked into the camera when photographed with the rest of the group. But since embarking on a solo career, felt the need to step out a bit.

"That reputation of not doing interviews was created by other people," he noted. "Publicists of Grace (Slick) would just jump in front of me, and I wasn't one to fight over that." As far as his balladeer image: "Hey, I've written in a lot of different styles. If you look back at writing credits in the Airplane/Starship days, a lot of it was me." And his penchant for remaining aloof during photo sessions? "I just thought it was funny. Everybody else in the band was posing like a stiff model, and I'd be laughing or turning or talking."

The cover of his album, *Balin*, featured the only eye-contact in memory. "Well, hell, that's a Richard Avedon photo," he explained. "He tells you to hunch your shoulders, to look into the camera—and you do it 'cause you're paying for it."

It was heady stuff for the man who spent most of the Seventies playing musical chairs as lead singer in the Starship. "Now I manage myself and do what I want," he admitted. "I don't have to argue with managers or a band. If I wanna do something, I don't have to call a meeting. That's where I am—handling my own affairs."

The pioneering Airplane was born out of the San Francisco hippie ethic, and Balin's individualistic approach had yielded some unique projects. He put together Rock Justice, a rock opera concerning a musician who dreamed that his music was put on trial by his peers. He hoped *Balin* would establish his versatility, and the hit singles "Hearts" and "Atlanta Lady (Something About Your Love)," both written by longtime friend Jesse Barish, continued Balin's run of sweet love songs.

"I want to be known as much as a singer as a writer," he explained. "I never considered myself a writer—with the old band, I had to write because it was expected of me. Now I'd rather use songs that friends have written for me. Otherwise, it's like eating your own cooking all the time. Writing's lonely—it's a nice sunny day, everyone's outside, and you've got to sit there and figure something out 'cause you're going in the studio that night. I don't really care for it that much—I'm just having a fun time. It's all I ever do." ■

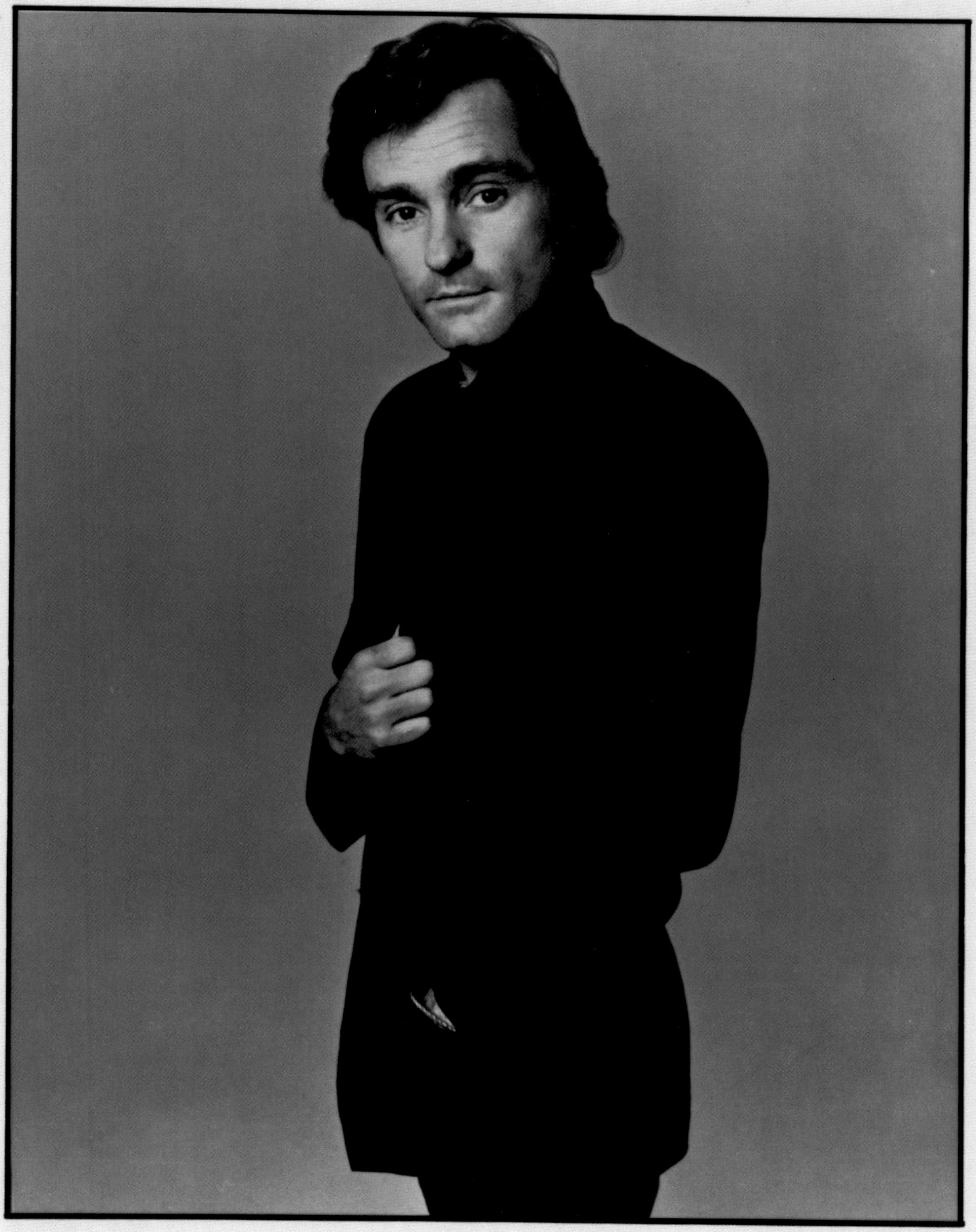

MARTY BALIN

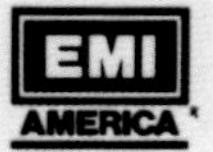

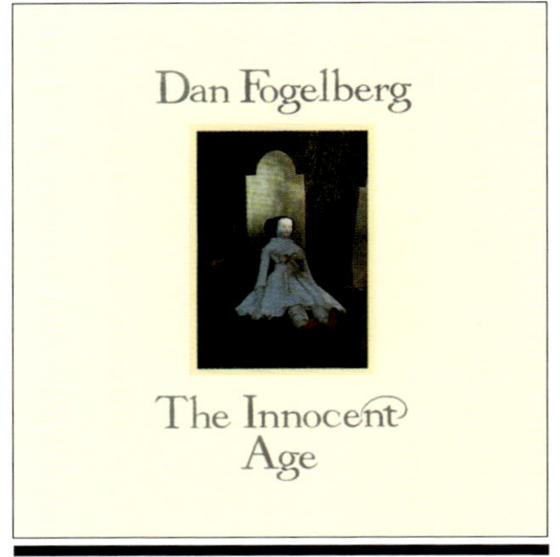

Billboard 200: *The Innocent Age* (#6)
Billboard Hot 100: "Same Old Lang Syne" (#9); "Hard to Say" (#7); "Leader of the Band" (#9); "Run for the Roses" (#18)

Dan Fogelberg's autobiographical *The Innocent Age* included "Leader of the Band," a tribute to his musician father.

DAN FOGELBERG'S heavily sentimental singer-songwriter style—a combination of light harmonized folk-rock, highly dramatic orchestration and introspective lyrics—had endured beyond all critical predictions. He didn't like the star-making machinery of the West Coast, so the "quiet man of music," to borrow one of his lyrics, moved to Colorado in the mid-Seventies and carved out a phenomenally popular and productive career.

The Innocent Age, an ambitious double album, marked Fogelberg's commercial peak and spun off four of his biggest hits—"Same Old Lang Syne" (a story-song about an old girlfriend), "Hard To Say," "Leader of the Band" and the uplifting "Run for the Roses," an unofficial theme for the Kentucky Derby.

The public perceived Fogelberg as a "sensitive balladeer," but he owned up to the lyrical leanings that earned him that tag.

"I've always been in touch with something I write," he allowed. "I feel experiences deeply, and I have an outlet, a place where I can translate those feelings. A lot of people go to psychoanalysts. I write songs. It really isn't a reflection of my total being, though. I've written some sad stuff in my life, but I don't like being called an aching 'heartbreak kid' because I'm just not that way. I've written some sad stuff in my life, but I've written some uplifting songs. 'Leader of the Band' is very positive."

"Leader of the Band" gave a clue as to the variety of Fogelberg's musical influences. The song saluted his father, Lawrence, a bandleader and high-school band director in Peoria, Ilinois, who facilitated and supported his son's musical growth.

"The music has to come from somewhere, and it's certainly no accident that my parents were both trained musicians," Fogelberg stated. "My mother was trained to sing opera, but she decided to have a family, so my dad was the musician in the house. That was great, and music was always around. I was raised on classical music—I didn't understand it, and I didn't necessarily even like it, but I was exposed to it." ■

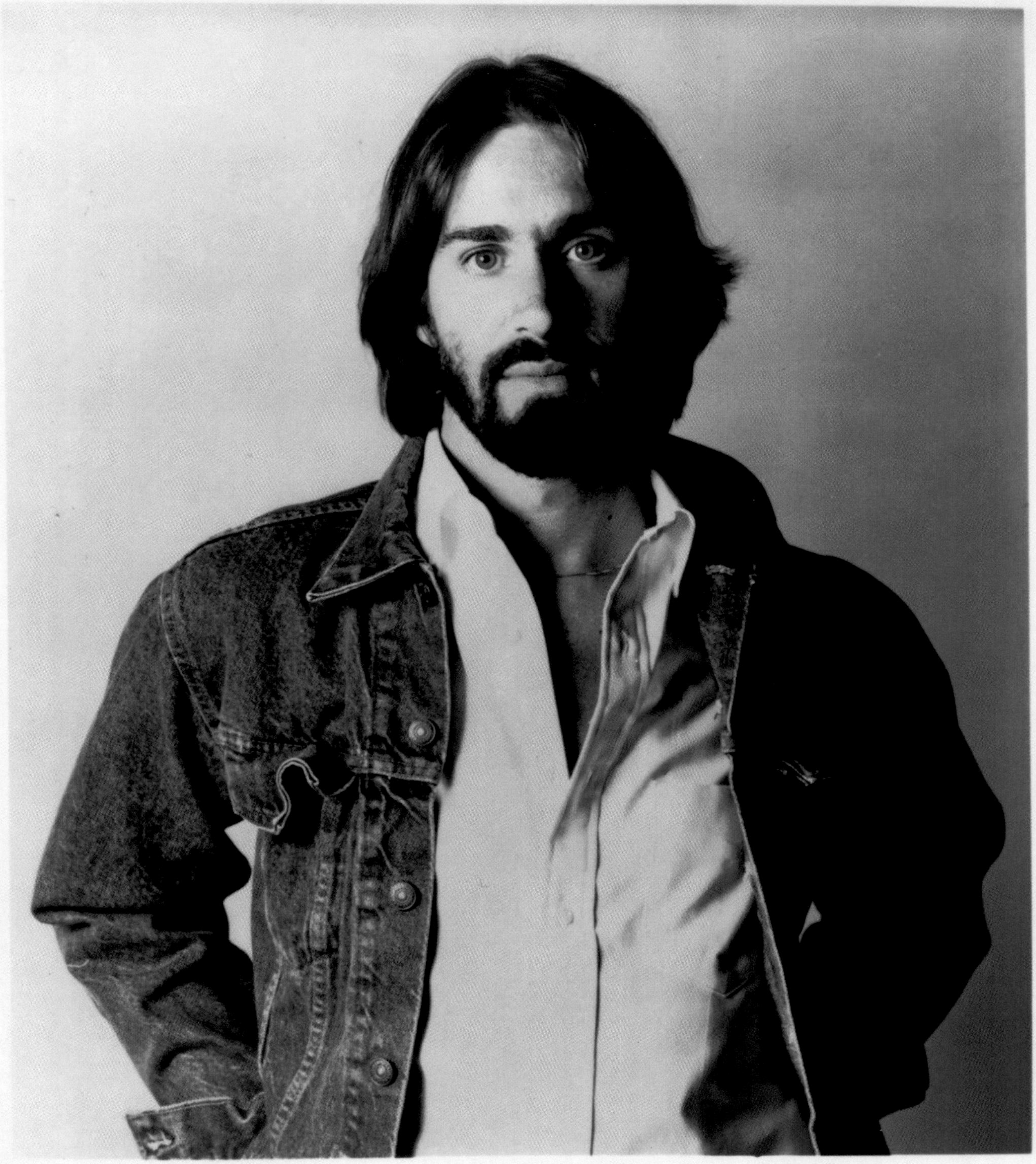

FRONT LINE
MANAGEMENT COMPANY, INC.

9044 MELROSE AVENUE, THIRD FLOOR, LOS ANGELES, CALIFORNIA 90069 - (213) 859-1900

DAN FOGELBERG

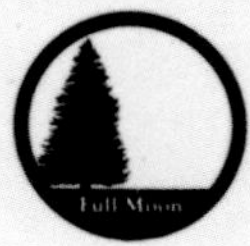

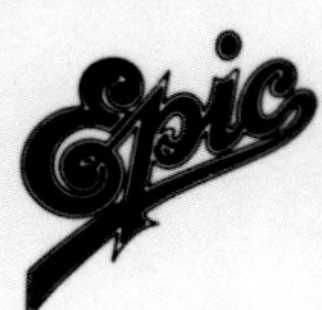

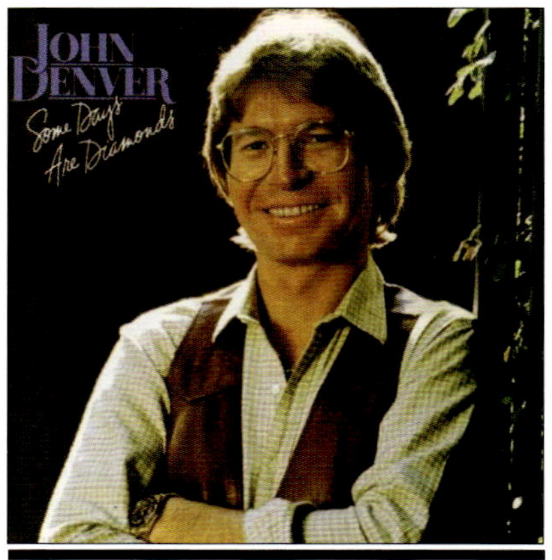

Billboard 200: *Some Days Are Diamonds* (#32)
Billboard Hot 100: "Some Days Are Diamonds (Some Days Are Stone)" (#36); "The Cowboy and the Lady" (#66)

On *Some Days Are Diamonds*, John Denver focused a mature interest on the range of human experience.

ONE OF the top-five-selling recording artists in the history of the music industry, John Denver was distancing himself from the grinning sprite in granny glasses who had been thrust into the world's consciousness with a series of cheery, optimistic songs.

"I think I've appeared to a lot of people as too goody-two-shoes, too nice," the former Henry John Deutschendorf Jr. said. "I'm trying a fresher, more contemporary presentation of my music."

The commercially potent "Sunshine on My Shoulders" phase of the venerable singer-songwriter's career was ending, with his records receiving limited radio exposure.

"There's got to be a place for me," Denver insisted. "The worst things that have ever happened to me have been what people have said about my music—'the Mickey Mouse of pop' or 'the Ronald Reagan of rock.' That's aimed at diminishing not only me, but all the folks whose lives have been touched by my music. I still meet people who use my songs in their weddings, who have played them while they're going through labor. That transcends anything in the paper that's going to be thrown away and burned—or, at best, recycled."

Some Days are Diamonds consisted mostly of numbers gathered from other polished songwriters, including Denver's version of "Some Days Are Diamonds (Some Days Are Stone)," written by Dick Feller. "The Cowboy and the Lady" was a gender-reversed cover of "The Cowgirl and the Dandy," written by Bobby Goldsboro and performed by Brenda Lee in 1980. Many of Denver's songs in the Seventies had tapped into a growing appreciation and concern for the environment. The Aspen resident continued his work with Windstar, a nonprofit organization he founded in 1976 as a research facility to study alternative solutions to food production, energy and land education.

"There are some real concerns in the world that ought to concern us all, but nobody's paying any attention to them," the activist and humanitarian mused. "My philosophy has been as big a part in my success as my songs. Because of my music, I've had opportunities presented to support environmental groups, to help form the presidential commission on world and domestic hunger, to make people understand nuclear power and weapons. These are other expressions of what people hear in my music, what I give myself to. I want to do more than talk about what I believe and feel. I mean to be a good example, the first example." ■

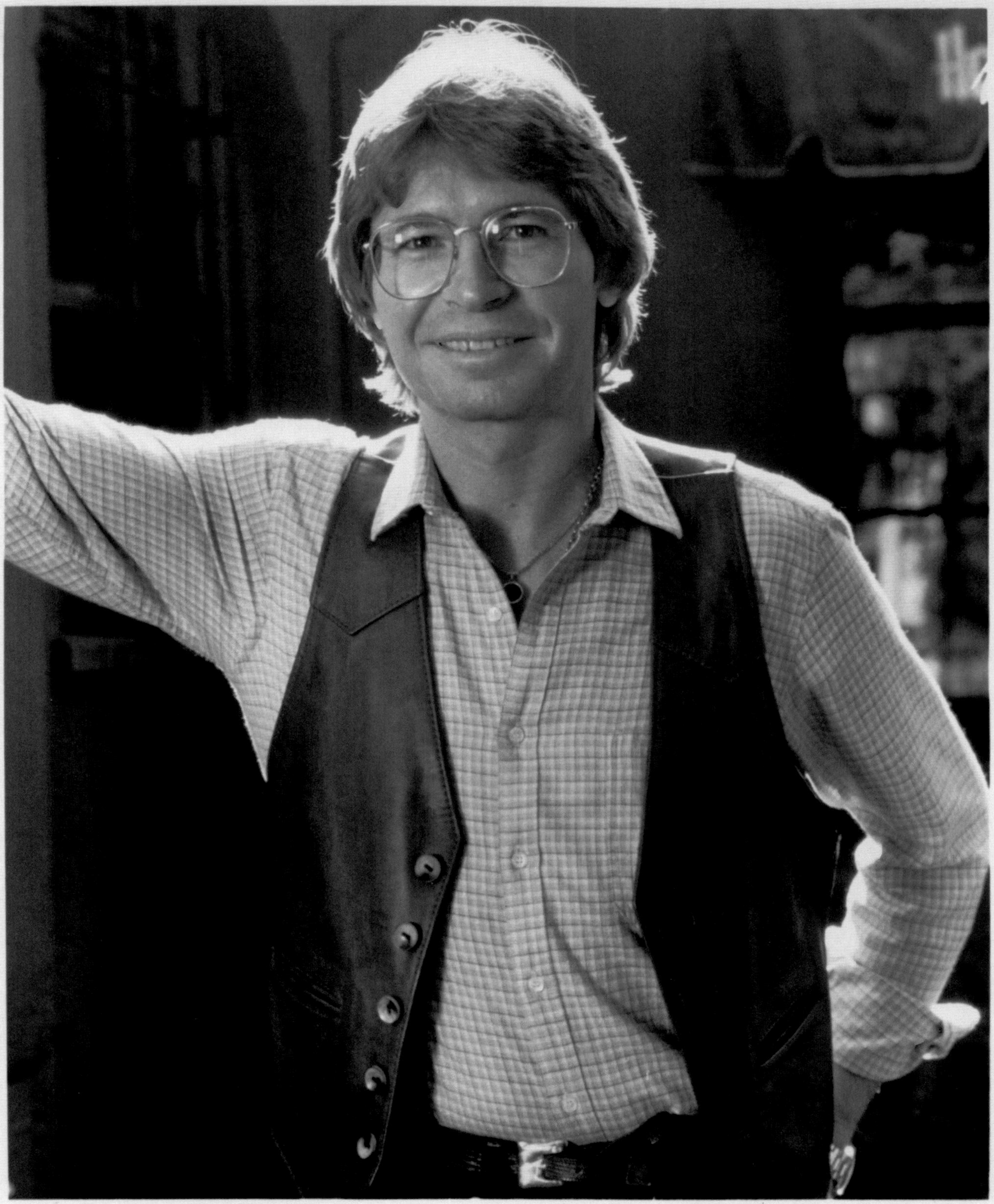

JOHN DENVER

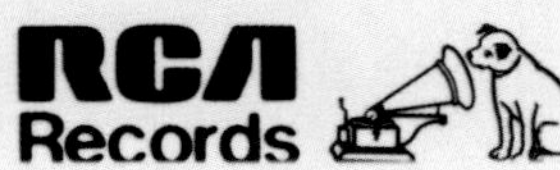

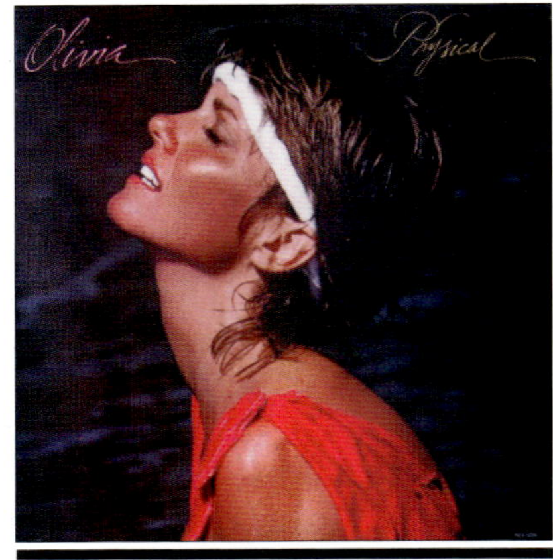

Billboard 200: *Physical* (#6)
Billboard Hot 100: "Physical" (No. 1); "Make a Move on Me" (#6); "Landslide" (#52)

Known for her romantic and lovely ballads, Olivia Newton-John acquired a new image and a huge hit with *Physical*.

OLIVIA NEWTON-JOHN'S gentle voice had made her one of the most successful vocalists of the Seventies. The Australian girl-next-door pop singer scored 16 Top 20 hits, including four No. 1s. "I Honestly Love You" became her signature song, and "Have You Never Been Mellow" also peaked at #3 on the country charts. 1978 brought "You're the One That I Want" with John Travolta from *Grease*, one of the most successful movie musicals in history, in which she played the lead role of the demure Sandy. Though her 1980 film *Xanadu* bombed at the box office, "Magic" also became her biggest adult contemporary hit.

Newton-John had begun departing from her earlier country-pop and soft rock roots, trading those styles for a sexier and more aggressive pop image. *Physical* marked her move from prim to provocative, her first album without any country tracks. Adding a "rock" flavor to the title track and "Landslide" meant a more up-tempo sound, and the album contained considerable use of synthesizers.

"I love all kinds of music, but I never cared much for rock until recently—now I enjoy it more," she said. "If I tried to tackle 'Landslide' five years ago, I probably couldn't have done it. It takes something inside of you."

The suggestive lyrics caused "Physical" to be banned from the playlists of several radio stations. To counter the sexual references, Newton-John filmed an exercise-themed video that reinvented the song as an aerobics anthem. "Physical" became a pop-culture phenomenon, spending ten weeks at No. 1—and its Grammy-winning video made headbands and fitness clothing a fashion style outside of gyms and health clubs. ■

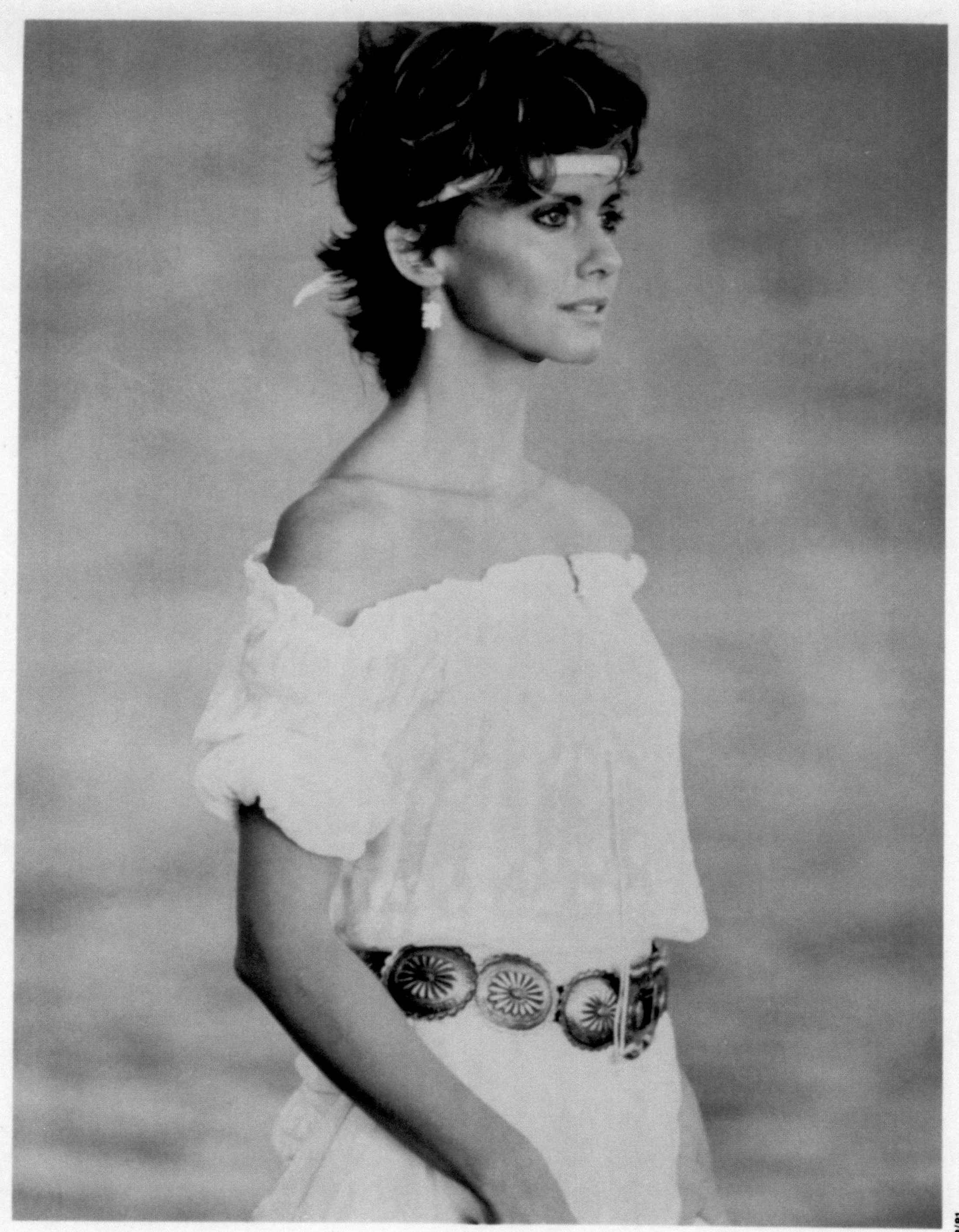

8/81

Olivia Newton-John

.MCA RECORDS

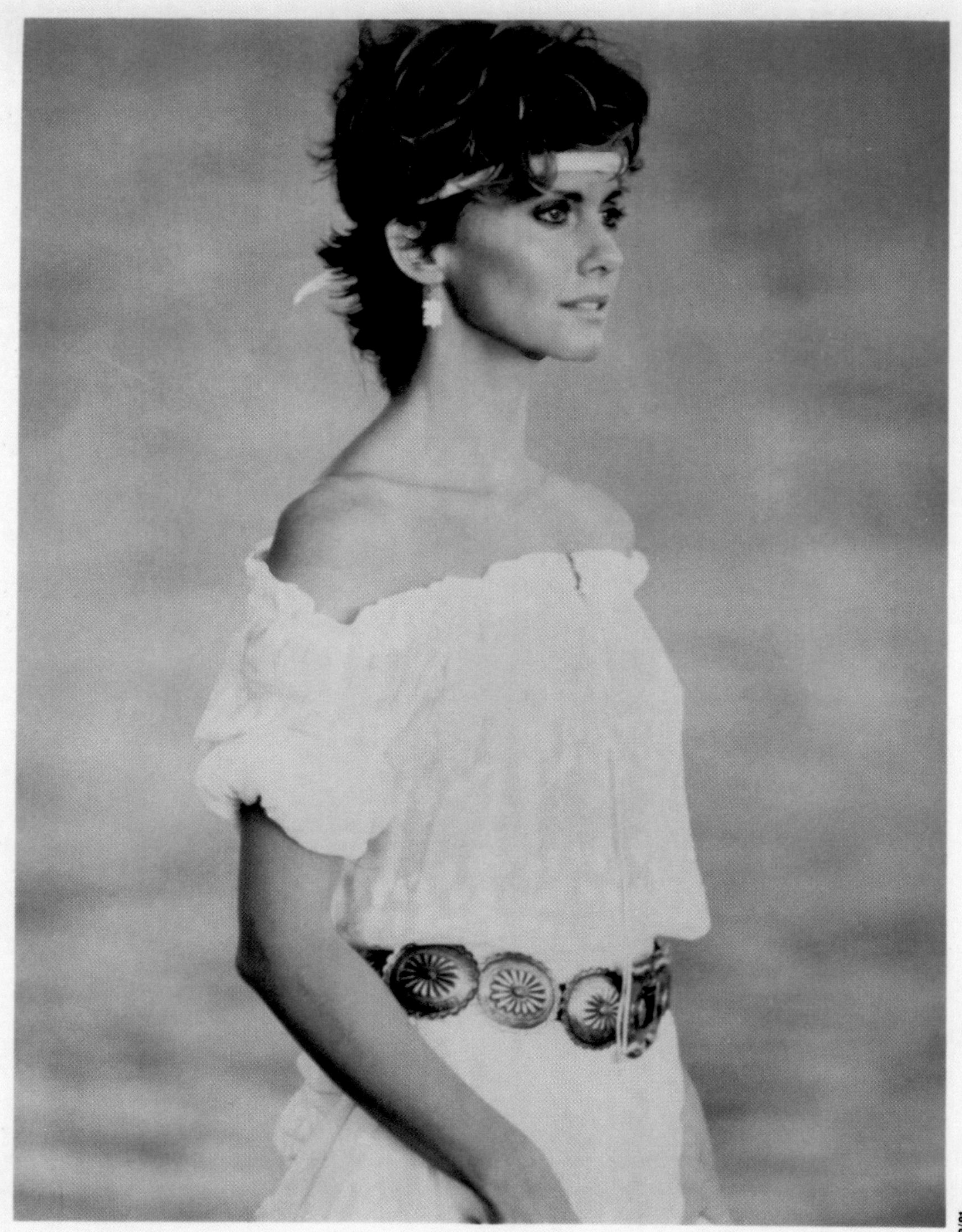

8/81

Olivia Newton-John

MCA RECORDS

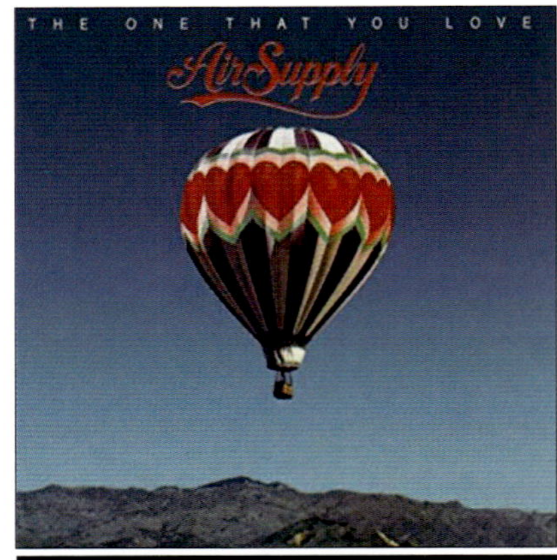

Billboard 200: *The One That You Love* (#10)
Billboard Hot 100: "The One That You Love" (No. 1); "Here I Am" (#5); "Sweet Dreams" (#5)

A zealous international following enthusiastically snapped up Air Supply's impressive *The One That You Love.*

THE AUSTRALIAN group Air Supply was the reigning powerhouse of adult-contemporary music, with three consecutive chart-topping singles from its first international release, 1980's *Lost in Love*. The band got its start in 1976, when Graham Russell and Russell Hitchcock were both acting in a production of *Jesus Christ Superstar*. They started appearing as a pop ensemble, gave themselves the name Air Supply and released four albums that only gained attention in Australia. The band's first international exposure came when the group opened for Rod Stewart on his 1977 North American tours.

Russell's ability to write material that transcended the usual mellow pop offerings led to the breakthrough US singles "Lost in Love" and the million-selling "All Out of Love"—state-of-the-art ballads replete with the finest orchestrations since the late-Sixties heyday of their countrymen, the Bee Gees.

"One of my ambitions has always been to have a Top 10 record in America, and that's happened," singer Hitchcock said. "It doesn't matter how talented you are, you have to have the combination of good songs, the right record company, the right timing, and you still need the extra something to make it work."

Air Supply recorded the follow-up album, *The One That You Love*, and the easy-listening duo's popularity increased—the heart-wrenching title track became a No. 1 hit, and the dramatic "Here I Am" and "Sweet Dreams" were Top 10 singles.

"This is all I do well—music," Hitchcock said. "There's a big place in this world for optimism, especially where love is concerned. Therefore, our songs have meaning for everyone." ■

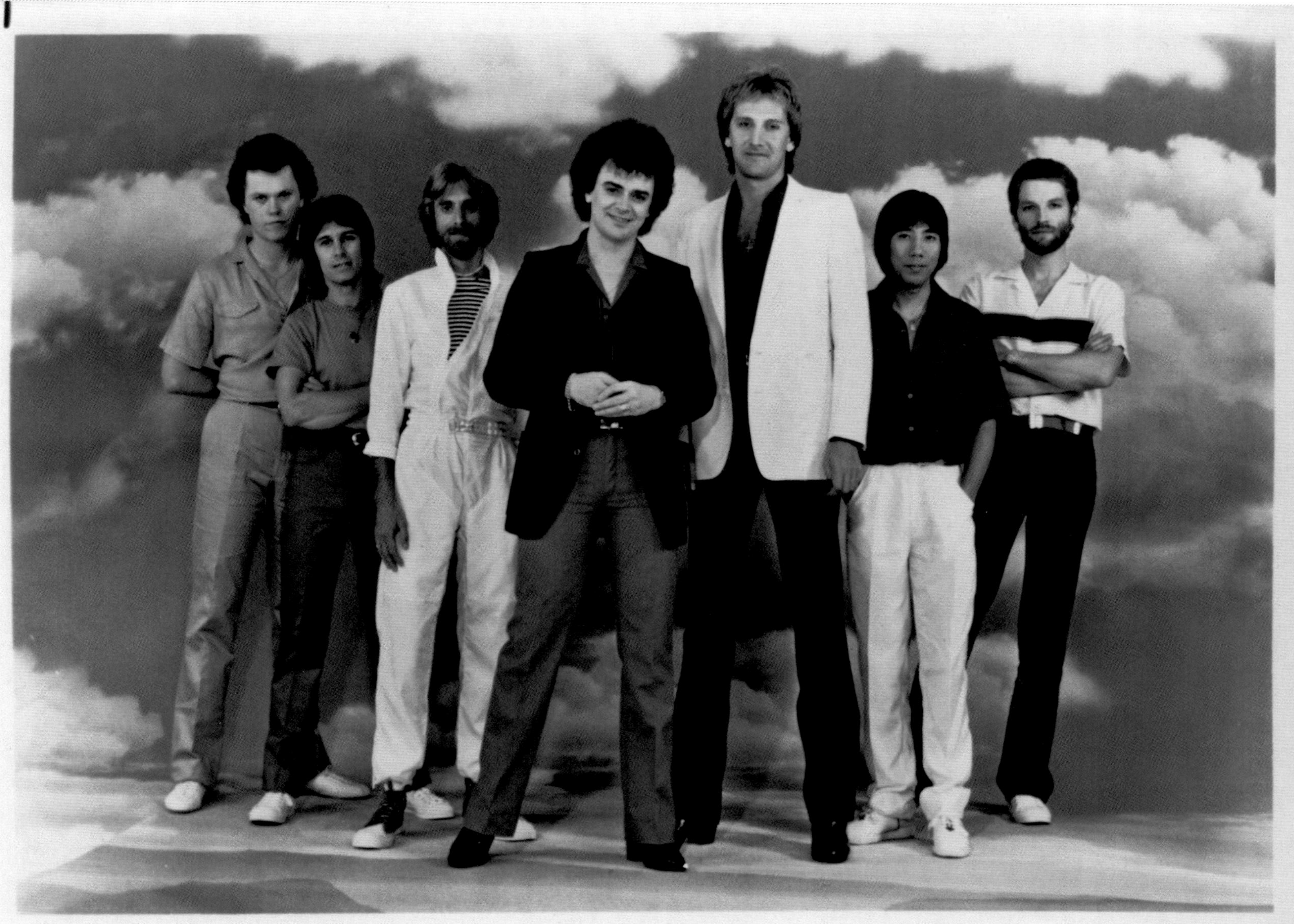

BESTALL AND REYNOLDS, INC.
326 N. LA CIENEGA BLVD.
L.A., CA 90048 (213) 658-7002

ICM

Air Supply

ARISTA™

Billboard 200: *Time Exposure* (#21)
Billboard Hot 100: "The Night Owls" (#6); "Take It Easy on Me" (#10); "Man on Your Mind" (#14)

Little River Band's *Time Exposure* embodied changes, but left intact the well-crafted songs and exquisite harmonies.

THE FIRST Australia-based musical group to establish itself as an international attraction, Little River Band paved the way for an onslaught from Down Under, carting home gold and platinum albums from around the world and headlining concerts in the US since 1979.

On *Time Exposure*, its sixth studio album, Little River Band's creative balance had undergone some revisions. The members worked without longtime producer John Boylan, and the group recorded away from Australia for the first time, on the island of Montserrat in the British West Indies under the direction of revered Beatles producer George Martin.

"We went through all of the names of various people who were in vogue and topical, and finally George Martin came out to see us," lead singer Glenn Shorrock said. "The Beatles were the biggest musical influence on my life, and working with George on an album was quite a thrill—rather strange and rewarding at the same time."

Some finishing touches were completed in Australia, which delayed the album's release by weeks. "The tapes were sent from Montserrat to London to be mixed. After that, they were sent to Australia for our approval and got lost somehow during a customs strike. We finally found them and some songs had to be remixed, but by then there was a telephone strike, and we had trouble making the studio arrangements."

Time Exposure was the first LRB album for bass guitarist Wayne Nelson, an American who had an auspicious start by singing lead on the album's first single, "The Night Owls," which rocked in the band's patented mellow fashion.

"Everyone in the group has proven themselves capable of writing hit songs," Shorrock explained. "We never have had to sit down and figure out what kind of songs we need for an album. Maybe we should, but with four songwriting inputs, we just have never been at a loss for different kinds of songs."

David Briggs, one of the main songwriters, left the band just after the recording of *Time Exposure* to pursue a career as a record producer. His departure had been upsetting, but Shorrock insisted that the Little River Band was still looking forward to the future.

"We've spent the last few years conquering the United States, even at the expense of our following in Australia. Now I guess the changes are inevitable in terms of making things fresh again."

Following the tour, however, Shorrock departed Little River Band, citing the usual "musical differences." ■

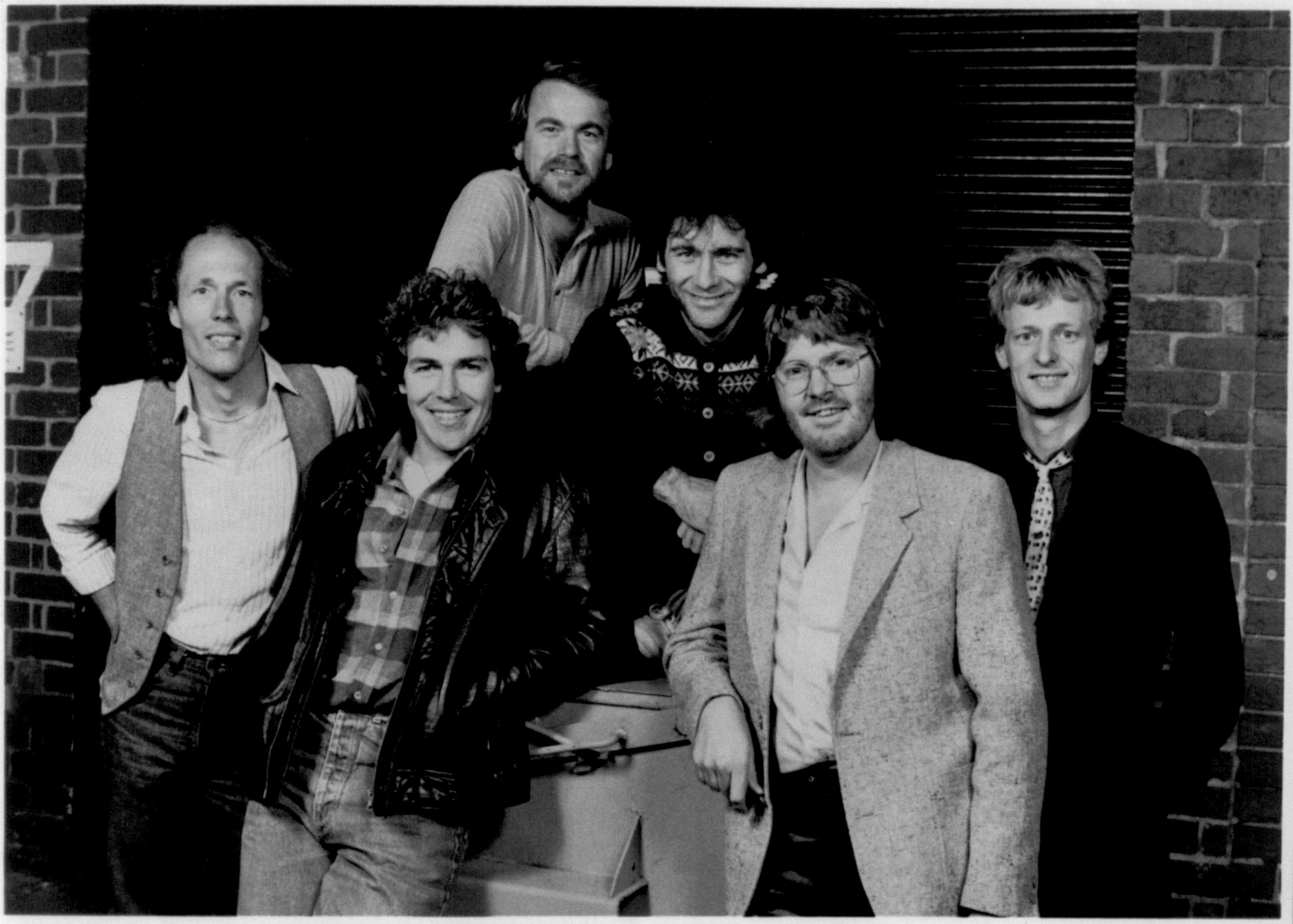

Wayne Nelson Beeb Birtles Glenn Shorrock Derek Pellicci Graham Goble Steve Housden

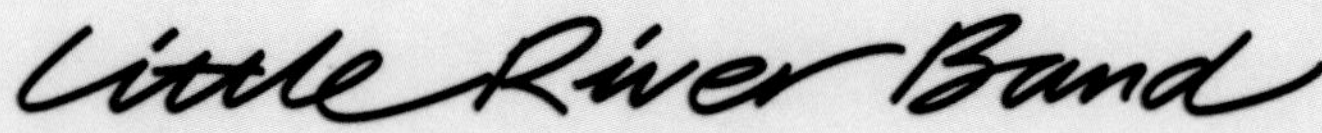

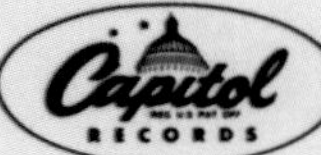

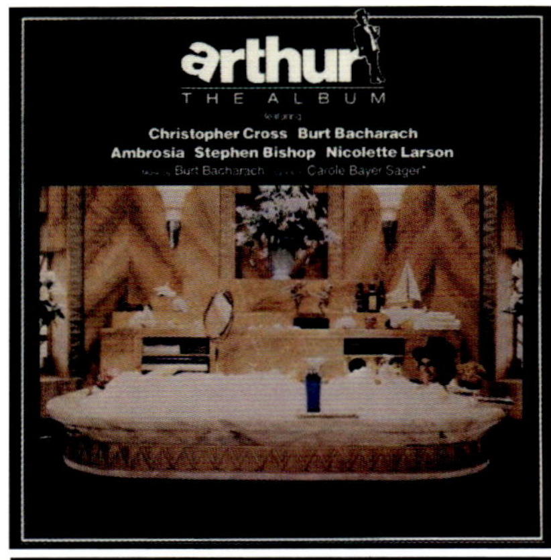

Billboard 200: Arthur - *The Album* (#32)
Billboard Hot 100: "Arthur's Theme (Best That You Can Do)" (No. 1)

Christopher Cross' "Arthur's Theme (Best That You Can Do)" from the film *Arthur* shot to No. 1 and won an Oscar.

CHRISTOPHER CROSS' success story was potent stuff in a day of music marketing. Out of nowhere, his eponymous 1980 debut recording had sold millions of copies and included several hit singles, including a smooth pop classic in "Sailing." Things came to a peak when the newcomer walked off with five Grammy awards.

Cross showed no signs of letting up—his theme song from the movie *Arthur* was all over the radio. The humble Texan was aware of the immense pressure to maintain his sudden popularity, but his quick ascent up the charts hadn't left his perspective in the lurch.

"It's something to deal with, but it's also what I've worked for all these years to attain," he explained. "I'm a pretty normal guy with the usual phobias and insecurities, so I try not to think about it and just stick with what got me here. If I sit around and contemplate a lot, I'd probably be a lot more worried than I am."

The contributions of such luminaries as Michael McDonald of the Doobie Brothers, Valerie Carter and guitarist Larry Carlton helped spur interest in Cross' debut recording. The *Arthur* theme provided a similar foundation for Cross's enthusiasm for name-dropping—not only did it keep him on the airwaves while he recorded his second album, but it enabled him to collaborate with such traditional songwriting heavyweights as Burt Bacharach, Carole Bayer Sager and Peter Allen.

"I've always liked albums that have a bunch of names listed in the credits because it infers a kind of kinship," Cross shared. "When I was getting started, I always thought it was neat to pick up a Jackson Browne album and see the names of the Eagles and other people on there, so I like that same feeling."

Whether Cross would continue to top himself remained to be seen, but he felt secure in the niche he'd found in popular music.

"I think I've attracted an audience that's more serious and sophisticated than most," he mused. "They all bought the first album, and they'll be looking for the second. And if they want to like me, they'll try to like the record. I don't think I could ask for any more than that." ■

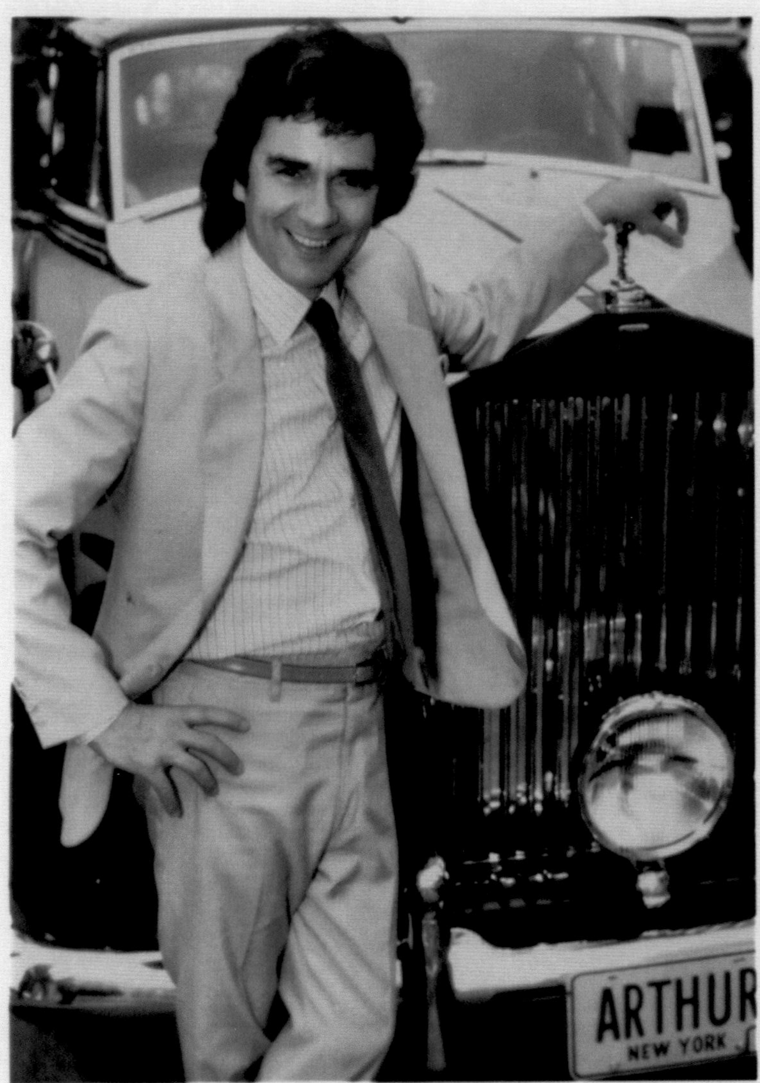

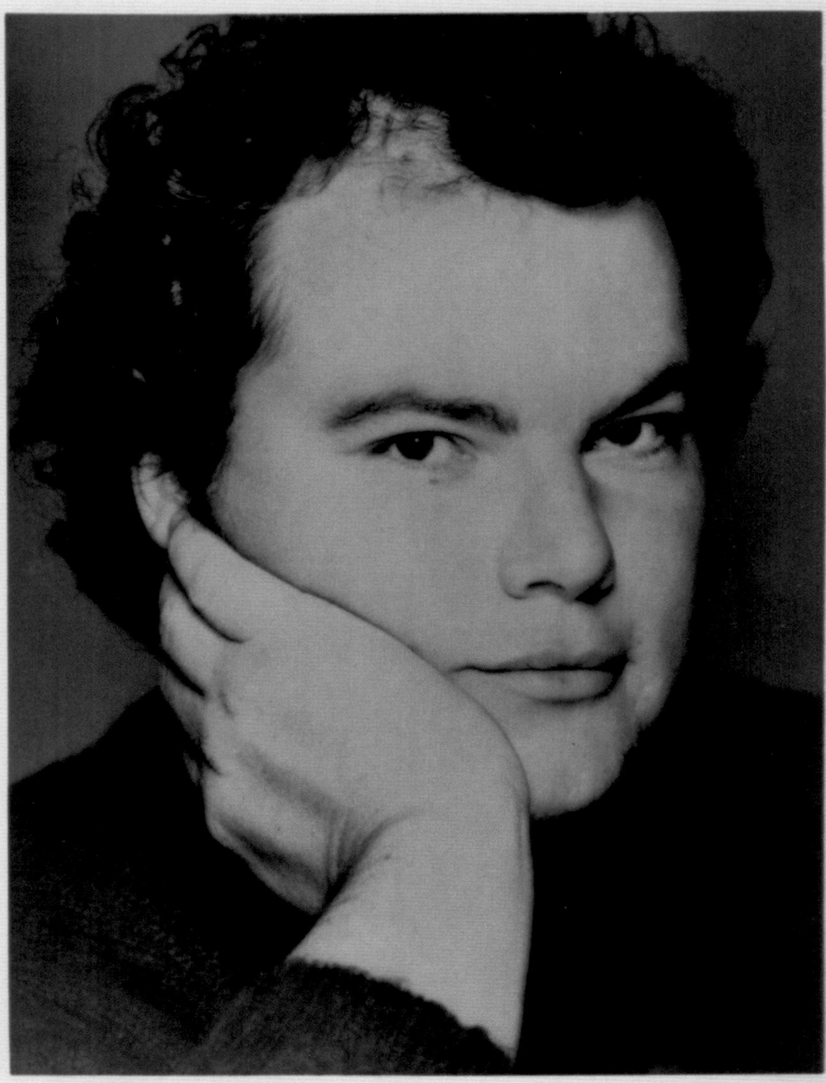

Dudley Moore (left) has the title role in ARTHUR, an Orion Pictures release through Warner Bros Five time Grammy winner Christopher Cross (right) sings "ARTHUR s Theme (Best You Can Do)" on ARTHUR The Album, now available on Warner Bros Records and tapes The album includes new songs from Nicolette Larson, Ambrosia, Stephen Bishop as well as music from the original score composed by Burt Bacharach

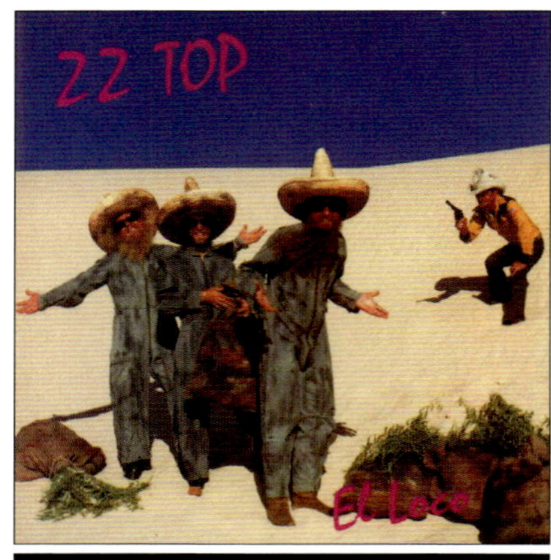

Billboard 200: *El Loco* (#17)
Billboard Hot 100: "Leila" (#77)

With the release of *El Loco*, ZZ Top cemented its status as one of America's most popular and enduring bands.

FOR YEARS, many dismissed ZZ Top as a faceless boogie troupe, but grassroots support for the famed "little ol' band from Texas" eventually won out. Billy Gibbons earned respect as one of the world's most inventive guitarists, and he was rightfully proud of the *El Loco* album. The work showed a marked progression beyond the band's patented blues-cum-boogie sound with the first appearance of synthesizers on a ZZ Top record.

"It's funny—as much as we try to make a different sound, it's always ZZ Top," Gibbons insisted. "There are probably a few offerings on *El Loco* that would make the average fan stop and say, 'Hey, where are you cats headed?' But we aren't doing anything that much different from when we started, and after 10 years, nobody thinks we're faking it. We've seen so many changes in musical styles—we're just getting patted on the back for something we always did."

The songs were among the most ambitious Gibbons had ever written, stretching from the double entendres on "Tube Snake Boogie" and "Pearl Necklace" to the steel guitars and pleasant harmonies of the ballad "Leila."

"I love the Beach Boys," Gibbons admitted. "I think Brian Wilson is a genius—frankly, I tried to sound like him on that cut." And what did he accomplish? "I thought that Leila would come back to me, but she never did," he laughed. "I'm just working out girls' names now, trying to find ones that fit the meter until I get some action."

Nobody toured as much as ZZ Top. The group rated as a superstar concert attraction, playing over 300 shows a year for fans all over the world. "It's real nice to get back and spank the plank," Gibbons laughed. "We're not actually a theatrical band. I know we've pulled some stunts in the past, like the 1976 Worldwide Texas Tour (where the group had buffaloes, cacti and snakes right on stage) and the Lone Wolf Horns on the *Degüello* tour (the three members learned how to play saxophone and accompanied themselves via tapes and video). But, heck, this is showbiz, innit?" ■

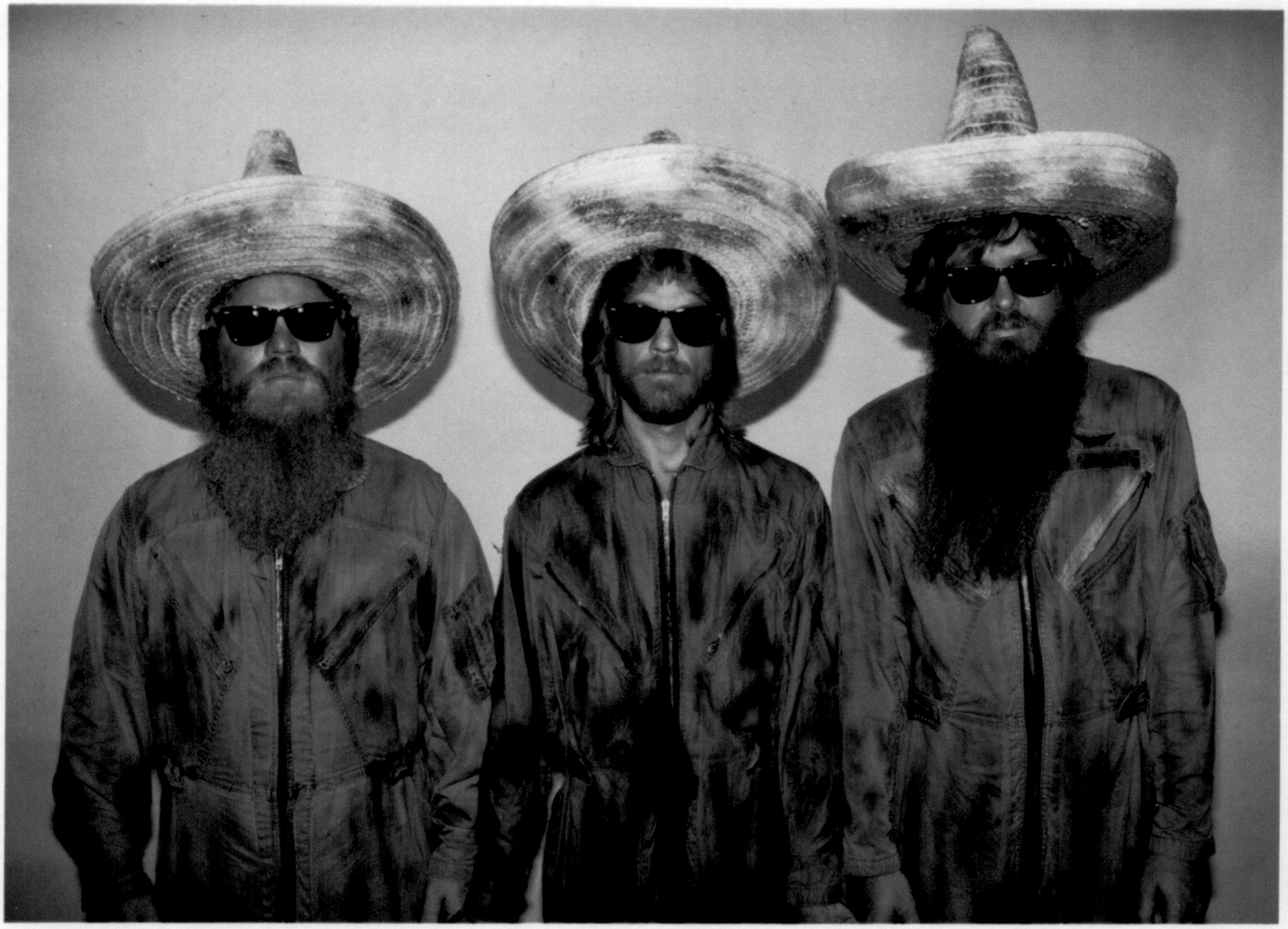

JULY 1981

ZZ TOP

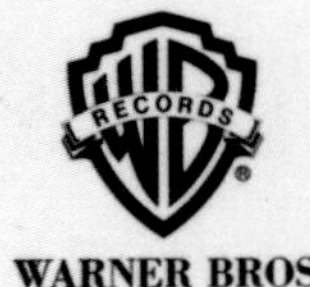

WARNER BROS.

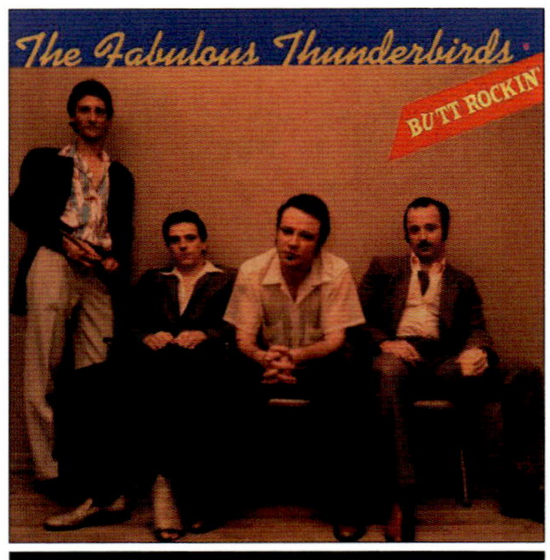

Billboard 200: *Butt Rockin'* (#176)

The Fabulous Thunderbirds helped popularize roadhouse Texas blues with the rollicking *Butt Rockin'*.

PERHAPS IT was a direct reflection of the mood of the country, but the musical idiom known as the blues was enjoying a revival of sorts. All across America, bar bands were slugging out steamy versions of blues classics, giving the best groups in each area—such as the Lamont Cranston Band in the Great Lakes region and the Nighthawks in the Northeast—the benefit of strong regional appeal.

But the Fabulous Thunderbirds were making the biggest inroads. The T-Birds had constantly toured outside of their native Texas in hope of breaking through to the big time.

"I guess we've been able to nationalize the trend a little bit," lead singer and harmonica player Kim Wilson admitted. "Since we're just a four-piece, we're a lot more portable than the bands that have horn sections. That's enabled us to get out to the East Coast and Los Angeles, where some other groups have had to stay at home."

In fairness, the Fabulous Thunderbirds' repertoire didn't exclusively consist of blues material—the band covered R&B, rockabilly and other American roots music forms. But Wilson did feel a special responsibility to the blues.

"A lot of the older blues artists who blew me away when I was growing up are dead or too old to perform," he noted. "So I do feel it's up to us to get the word out to kids who might be as impressed as I was. People are pretty fed up with the junk that passed as music in the Seventies. Now they're looking for something honest, and that's where R&B and blues come in—a lot of performers are turning to that music for inspiration. Bruce Springsteen does a medley of R&B for his encore these days, and he's working with Gary U.S. Bonds. Even Tom Petty is writing his own songs in that vein. There are capable songwriters out there who can work in that tradition."

Wilson was one of them. His "One's Too Many (And a Hundred Ain't Enough)" from the *Butt Rockin'* album—which marked the first time the band had used keyboards and sax on several tracks—became an underground hit. Co-written with Nick Lowe of Rockpile fame, the song captured the flash that marked the T-Birds' best performances.

"I met Nick when we toured Europe with Rockpile a couple of years ago," Wilson said. "It's amazing that we remembered the chords for that long!" ■

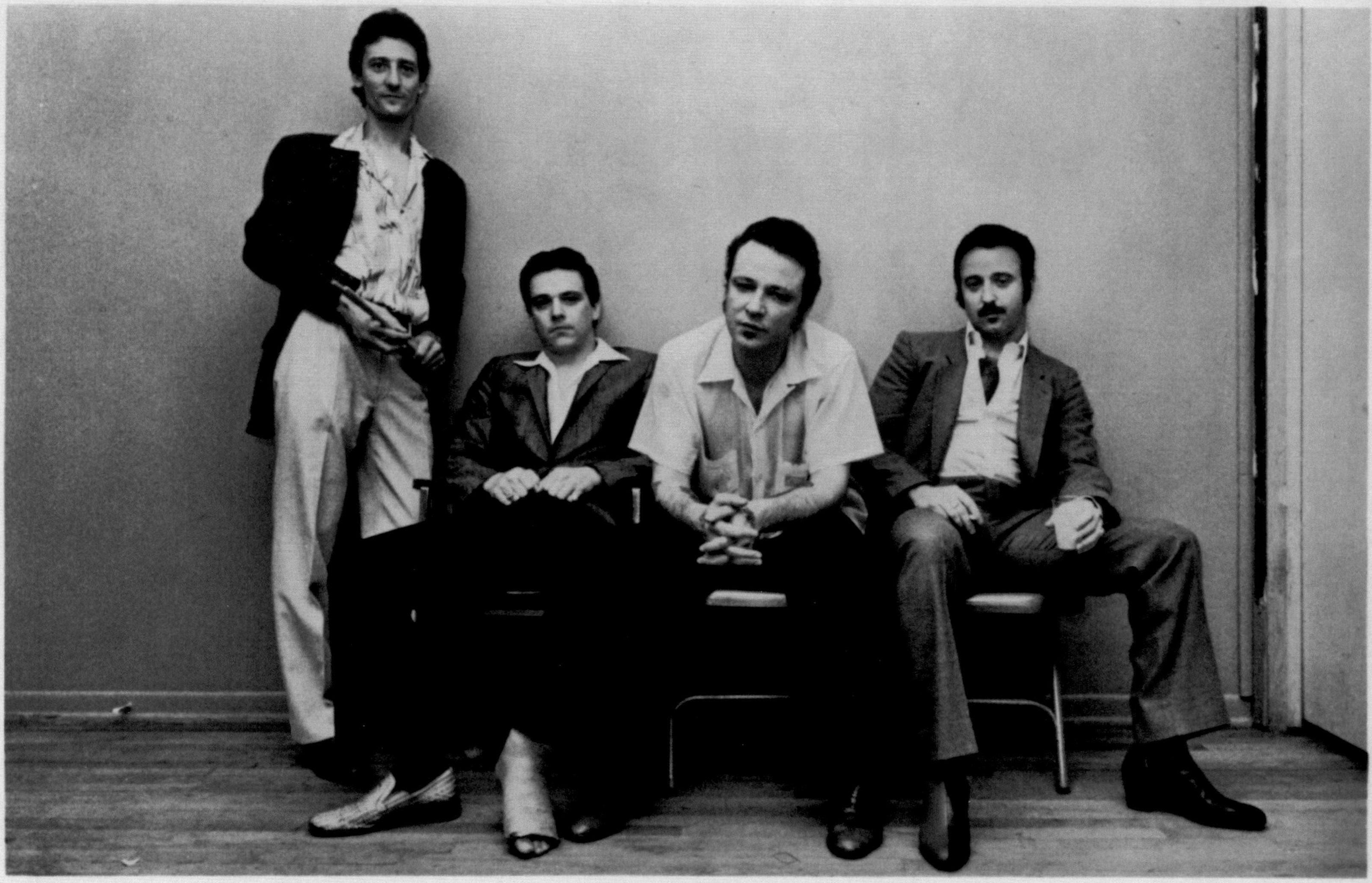

The Fabulous Thunderbirds

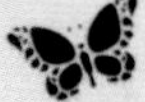

Chrysalis™

Billboard 200: *Musta Notta Gotta Lotta* (#135)

Befriended by the Clash, Texan Joe Ely gained international notoriety as a country-rock crossover performer.

JOE ELY'S abilities as a songwriter had sustained him on a critical and cult level. He grew up in Lubbock, Texas, where the combined talents of Buddy Holly and Waylon Jennings had resulted in some of rock and country's first experiments together. Critics agreed that Ely embodied the promise of country and rock music fulfilled, but his music defied any simple categories or labels. New-wave country? Punkabilly? Crazed cowboy?

"I don't care too much for definitions," Ely grimaced. "If I could get my guitar, play a song and talk at the same time, I might be able to tell you how I feel when I play. But to me, it's something I've always done—hard to talk about, because music happens in the process of doing it."

It was Ely's acceptance in England that kept him working hard. He had toured with the likes of the Clash and other bands who didn't quite share the same countrified roots.

"Yeah, sometimes it's funny-looking out on the dance floor when I play," Ely said. "Either it's hardcore country or some fella with his hair dyed green and yellow. It makes things interesting, that's for sure."

Musta Notta Gotta Lotta expanded Ely's rock and country fusion into a bigger scope that reflected his hard-living attitude. "The last few years on the road came together on this record," he said. "It shows in the titles—'I Keep Gettin' Paid the Same,' 'Musta Notta Gotta Lotta.' It's all reflective of a working man's rocking attitude. It's a higher energy, a little tougher record."

Ely's label had tried to break him as an outlaw country artist in the vein of Butch Hancock and Jimmie Dale Gilmore, his former bandmates in the Flatlanders. But America was on the verge of discovering him as a genre-crossing musician. "Hitting the road with Linda Ronstadt, we played places we'd never been before—Salt Lake City, Denver, Tucson," he said. "It was a completely different kind of audience."

But Ely's popularity had burgeoned in England. "Playing with the Clash was a big eye-opener—big crowds. They look at everything upside down over there. They love music like rockabilly and Carl Perkins, and they just latched onto me as someone who was maintaining some sort of tradition. I try not to make distinctions. If people like what they hear—critics or kids on the street, English punks or cowboys—then that's all that matters. 'Cause that's all I'm gonna be doing anyway—makin' people jump." ■

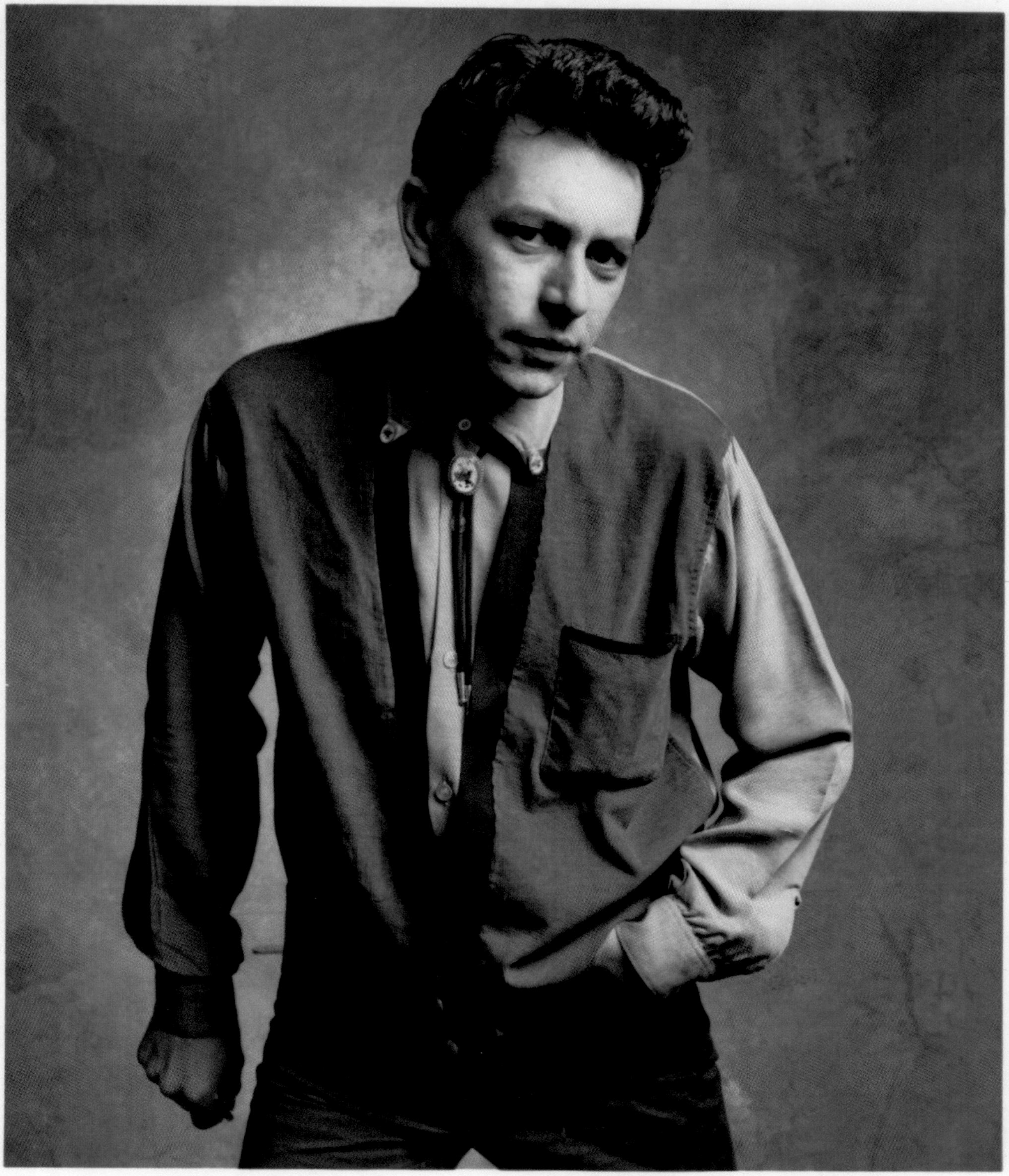

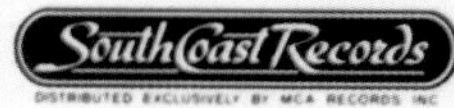
SouthCoast Records
DISTRIBUTED EXCLUSIVELY BY MCA RECORDS INC

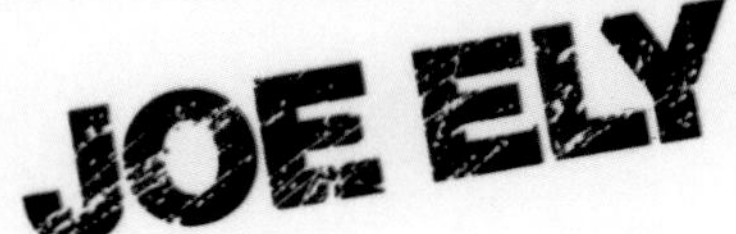
JOE ELY

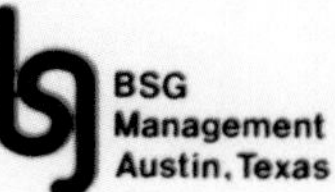
BSG
Management
Austin, Texas

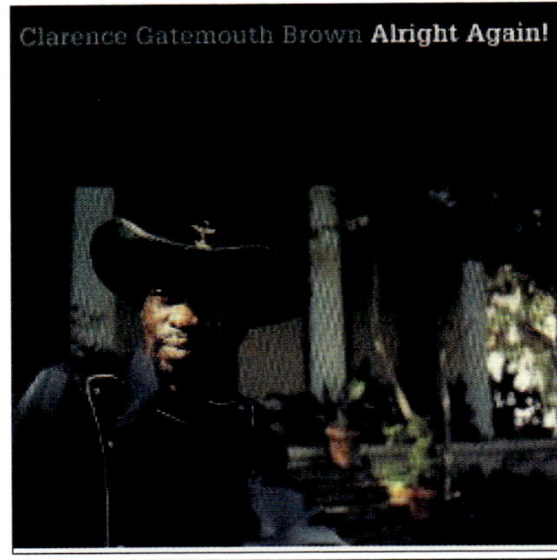

Clarence "Gatemouth" Brown's stellar *Alright Again!* proved that the versatile veteran wasn't just about the blues.

DURING THE late Forties and Fifties, Clarence "Gatemouth" Brown became a huge star in Texas by developing a distinct picking style, pulling and snapping his guitar strings for a twanging, staccato sound.

"I wanted to do two things playing guitar," he explained. "I didn't want it to sound like a guitar, and I wanted it to sound more like horns. And I was able to achieve that."

By the Eighties, though he was widely acknowledged as a Texas bluesman, Brown was steadfastly pursuing his own musical vision, weaving arcane influences into his sound.

"I played country, Cajun and bluegrass all my life—that's what my dad played, so that's what I played," he said. "I didn't know anything about the blues until I grew up some. Then I found roots in jazz and everything else.

"Some guys play one line all night long and pump it as hard as they possibly can, and they pound it into the brains of the public and keep making money off of it. But as far as history goes, they ain't doing nothing I'd want to write. No one can copy what I do. That's made my career much harder, but I tell you what, I'm giving my best to the public."

Adorned with swinging, horn-abetted blues, the acclaimed album *Alright Again!* was credited with revitalizing Brown's career. He won a Grammy award for Best Traditional Blues Album and received nominations for five more. During his joyful concerts, he was as likely to be sawing on his fiddle as blistering his guitar, and he sang with a hard-edged passion, revealing why he was regarded as one of the finest purveyors of pre-rock R&B.

"Now I can give young musicians advice," he said of those just discovering the charms of his "American and World Music, Texas Style." "I tell them to stay off of heavy drugs and booze, and to develop their own style. It may not sound good to start with, but if you keep at it, sooner or later it will sound great rather than sounding like everybody else." ■

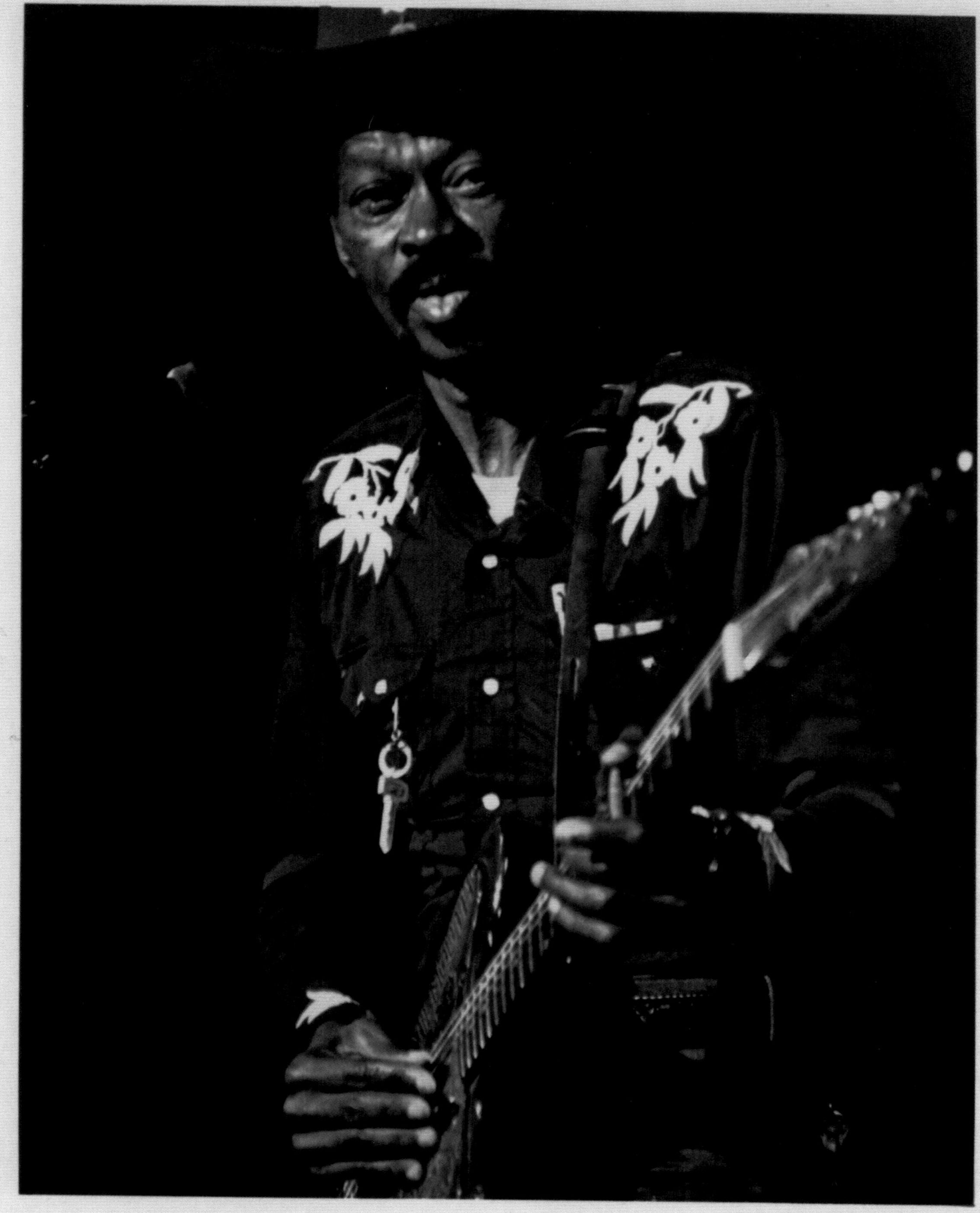

PHOTO CREDIT: MILT CLAYDON

CLARENCE GATEMOUTH BROWN

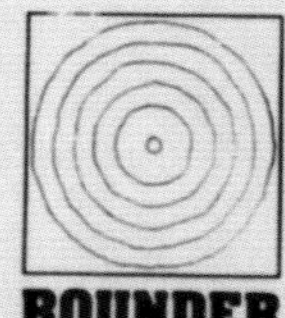

Rounder Records
186 Willow Avenue
Somerville, Mass. 02144
617-354-0700

Empire Booking
P O Box 514
Marietta, GA 30061
404-427-1200

NEVILLE BROTHERS

FIYO ON THE BAYOU

The Neville Brothers took the New Orleans sound a giant step forward with their exceptional *Fiyo on the Bayou*.

THE SURNAME Neville had a long and distinguished history in New Orleans music. As a teenager, Art, the oldest Neville brother, sang lead vocal on 1954's "Mardi Gras Mambo" with a band called the Hawketts. He had solo regional hits in the Fifties before forming the Meters in 1969. The Meters rapidly became New Orleans' equivalent of Memphis' Booker T. & the MG's, playing as house band for many Allen Toussaint productions and recording as an R&B instrumental group in their own right. In 1966, singer Aaron scored a million-selling pop hit with "Tell It Like It Is."

The Neville Brothers—Art, Aaron, Charles (sax) and Cyril (percussion)—merged their talents in 1977, but superstar reputation at home in Louisiana only translated to a cult status everywhere else.

"For years, we were told we were the hottest act in the industry not to have a record deal," Art said. "Everybody knew about the buzz, but no one knew how to handle us. We couldn't get out of New Orleans—it wasn't that we didn't want to, we just couldn't afford to do it. No promoter was willing to take a chance. It just took time."

The album *Fiyo on the Bayou* was a brilliant updating of the Neville Brothers' native city's rich R&B sound, a gumbo of syncopated rhythms—particularly the backbeat of Mardi Gras parade music called "second time"—and soulful singing that was guaranteed to arouse excitement. Aaron's angelic tenor illuminated standards like "Mona Lisa" and "The Ten Commandments of Love," and renditions of "Sitting in Limbo" and "Brother John/Iko Iko" advanced the heavy influence of their uncle, George Landry, one of the great Mardi Gras Indian leaders who, by the time of his death in 1980, had become a folk hero known as "Big Chief Jolly."

Fiyo on the Bayou garnered rave reviews but poor sales, because the Nevilles' Crescent City advocacy didn't mix with mainstream pop. The situation had the brothers hungry for success, however belated.

"We're gonna keep trying," Art said. "Music is just in our blood, something we have to do." ■

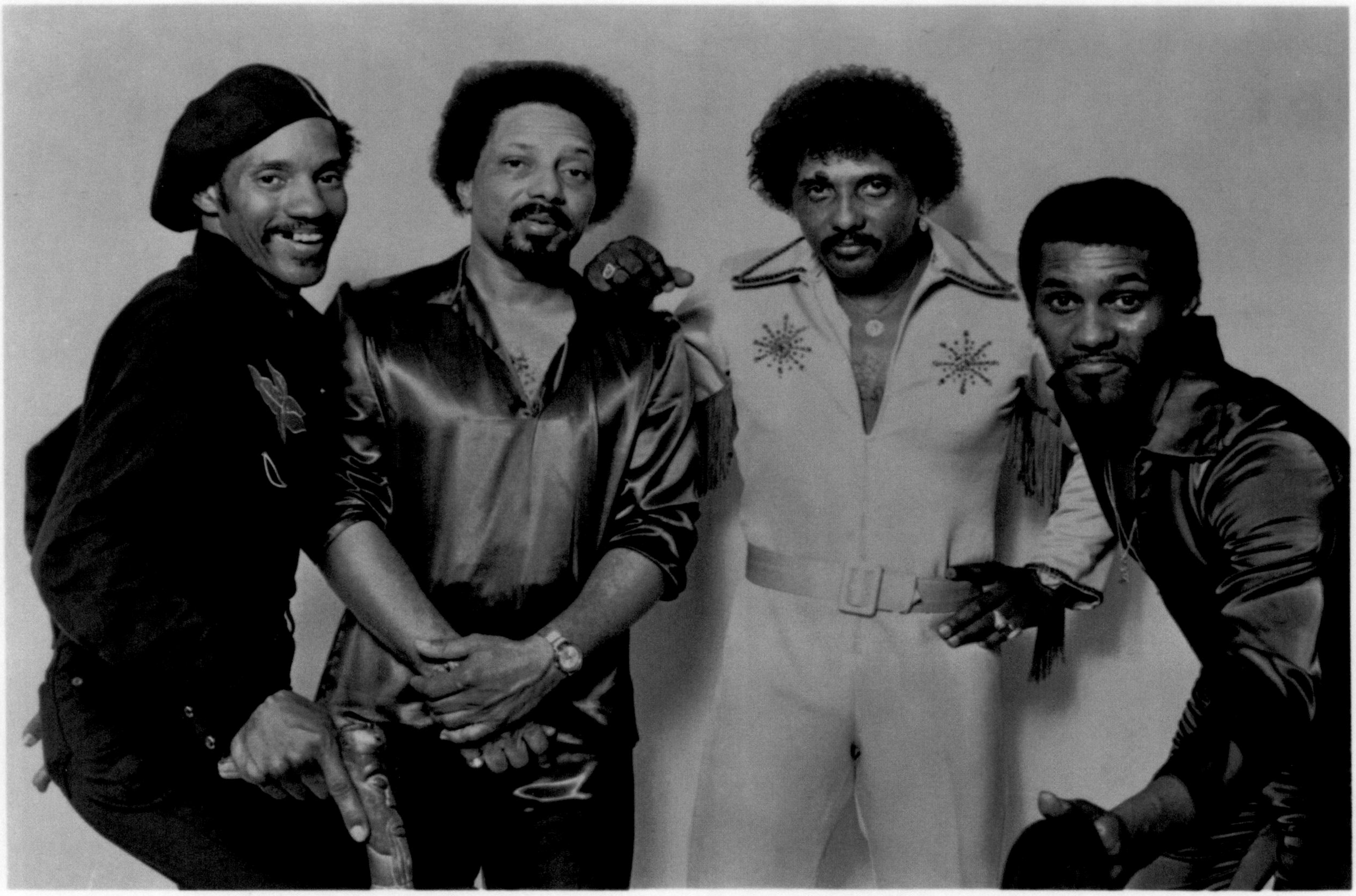

CHARLES NEVILLE ART NEVILLE AARON NEVILLE CYRIL NEVILLE

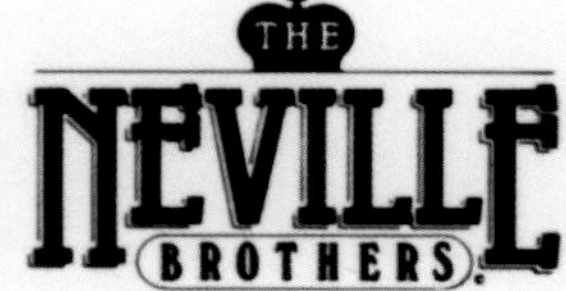

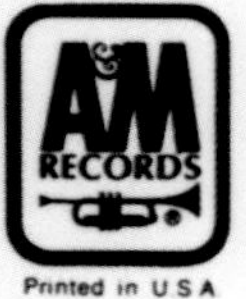

Printed in U.S.A.

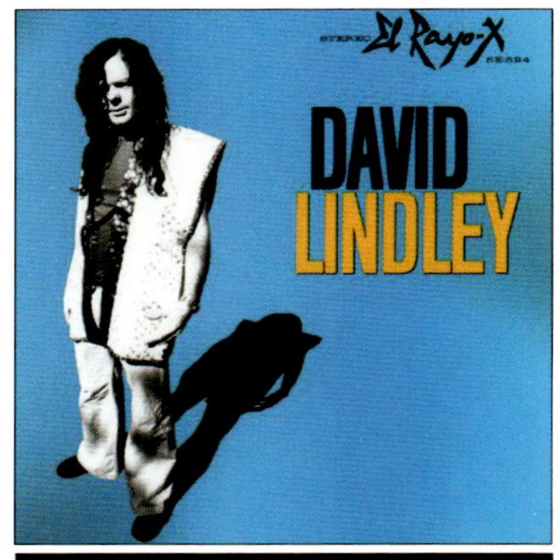

Billboard 200: *El Rayo-X* (#83)

With *El Rayo-X*, multi-instrumentalist David Lindley launched a solo career fashioned by musical cross-pollination.

WITH HIS encyclopedic knowledge of traditional forms, his arsenal of odd-shaped and stringed foreign instruments and his deft touch in every melodic style, David Lindley had pursued a peculiar path of music making.

The founder of Kaleidoscope, a semi-legendary California rock group of the late Sixties, Lindley was probably best known for his role on Jackson Browne's recordings and concert performances throughout the Seventies—immortalized by his impressive slide solo on "Running on Empty" and marvelous falsetto on the live version of "Stay." He also toured as a member of the bands of Crosby & Nash and Linda Ronstadt, and his diverse musical talent had put him at the top of everyone's list of most sought-after sidemen.

"That was all good work, but it's been an albatross," the celebrated multi-instrumentalist reflected. "Unfortunately, people approach my own music with a preconception—'Gee, he's well off, is he doing this for a lark?' They're primed to come to my shows and see the teacup as full, no room for anything else. But it's empty, there's more room for stuff that's interrelated."

Lindley formed his own reggae-rock band, El Rayo-X, and Browne produced the first album. *El Rayo-X* yielded an unlikely mixture of guitar wizardry, rollicking humor and exotic arrangements. Lindley's imaginative slide-guitar performance of "Mercury Blues" became an FM radio staple.

On top of his virtuosity, Lindley was amusing—"the prince of polyester" was invariably garbed in something loud and tacky from his vast collection of Seventies leisure wear. Like his friend Ry Cooder, Lindley got labeled an "archivist"—a term he dismissed as lazy, unimaginative and inaccurate. "If I was a scholar or historian, it would apply," he argued. "But it's different as a musician. I get ahold of something like Zaire drummers as a fan, and it fascinates me—I listen and march around the house like anyone else. But my tastes are weird, and I assimilate everything I can, so my records are called 'ethnic.'

"Maybe the way to look at it is, split up the music of the word into two categories—traditional world music and then world music 2 percent, like milk. When you look at it, it's notes and spaces, sound and no sound. People everywhere react to music in the same way. So maybe we'll see that we're all really similar, and things will change—but probably not! At least we're making a good try at it!" ■

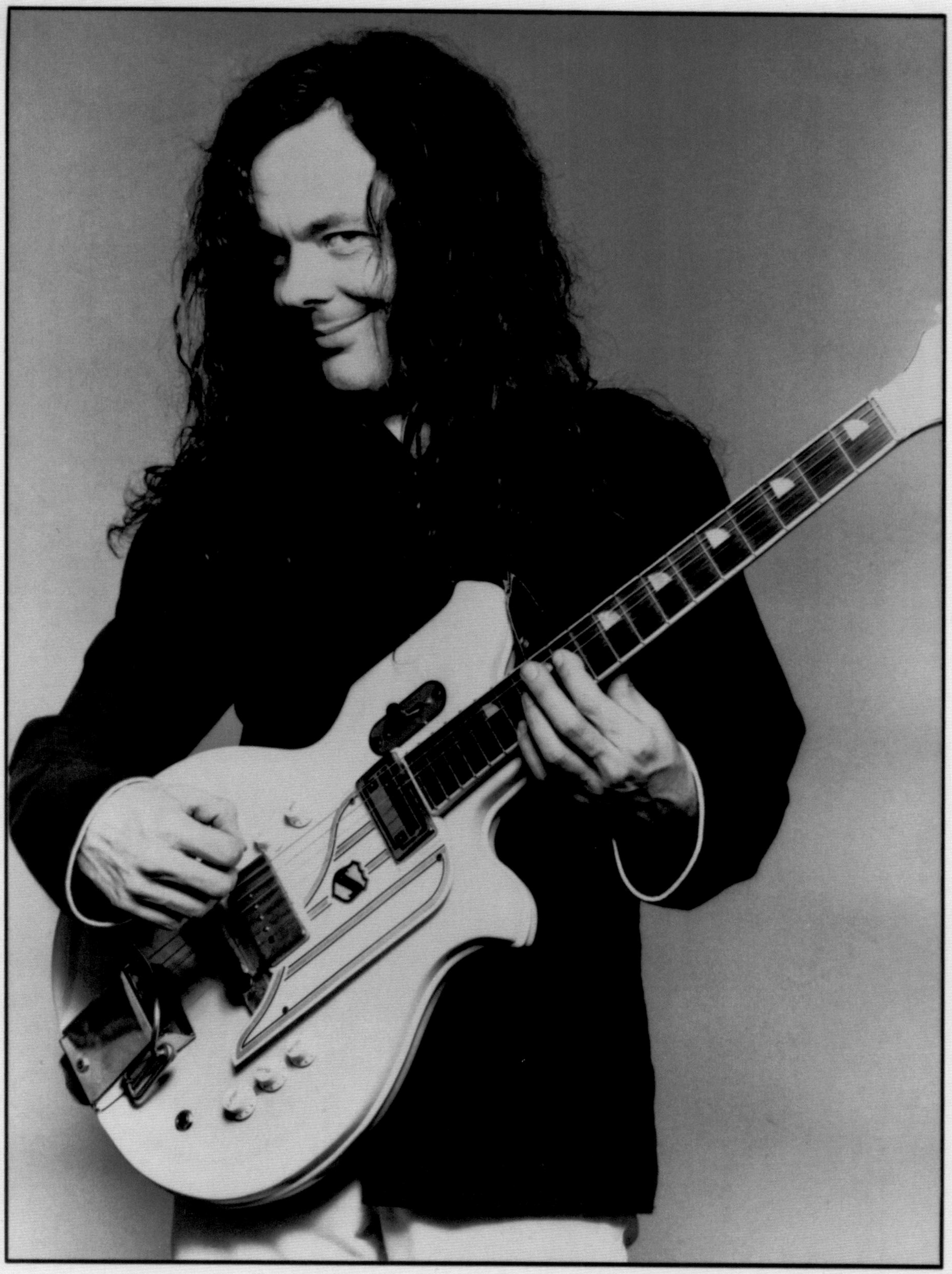

DAVID LINDLEY

PHOTO CREDIT: RANDEE ST NICHOLAS/1980

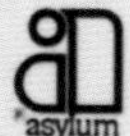

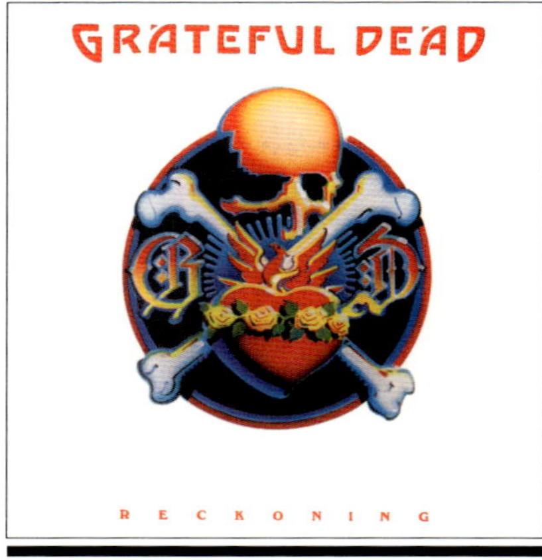

Billboard 200: *Reckoning* (#43)

The Grateful Dead continued to connect with its legions of devoted fans, treating them to two live double albums.

FOR 15 YEARS, the Grateful Dead had toured constantly, playing marathon sets and promoting a sense of community among Deadheads, many of whom followed their tours for months or years on end. As a cultural institution, the Dead had a reputation, as guitarist Bob Weir said, of "putting on a helluva live show." The band members never went onstage knowing what they were going to play, and their vast repertoire guaranteed that their confederacy of loyalists could go to a concert three or four consecutive nights and not hear a song repeated.

"We've tried to keep a fresh approach to our music and life in general," Weir said. "We've got lots of fans in their forties, and I like to think our music maybe has less of an age barrier than other presentations. But as far as how we generate so many new fans, I still don't know how that happens. It's a mystery to me."

The Dead had long forgotten how to answer charges of excess. In 1981, the band released two live double albums within months of each other. April brought *Reckoning*, featuring acoustic tracks culled from a series of shows at the Fox Warfield Theatre in San Francisco and Radio City Music Hall in New York in the fall of 1980. Those same concerts also yielded the electric performances that appeared in August on *Dead Set*.

"The original concept was to release a double album with one acoustic and three electric sides," guitarist Jerry Garcia said. "But there were so many good performances from Radio City that we couldn't do it justice. We really couldn't whittle it down, because our songs are so long anyway. An acoustic side of just three songs seemed ridiculous."

Showing affection for the Dead's folk and country roots, the *Reckoning* material was the most varied of live Dead releases, but the recordings captured Garcia in poor voice. "I did have a cold, and the singing is a bit weaker for it," he admitted. "But I still think the songs stand up instrumentally. Really, I think of *Reckoning* as a novelty record—playing acoustic is not what we do, and you can't even do it in most rooms. It was a change in texture, just a neat thing to do live—an intimate thing between us and the crowd."

Garcia professed more enthusiasm for *Dead Set*. "On *Europe '72* and the other live albums, we were basically playing one-nighters in a different venue every night—the realities of touring keep you from playing more than three nights at any one place," he explained.

"We play better with more nights in the same place. It's a cumulative thing as we adapt to the environment. At Radio City, we fulfilled a dream of playing a theater for a long run in one room, just like on Broadway. It gave us fine-tuning possibilities that we couldn't do before." ■

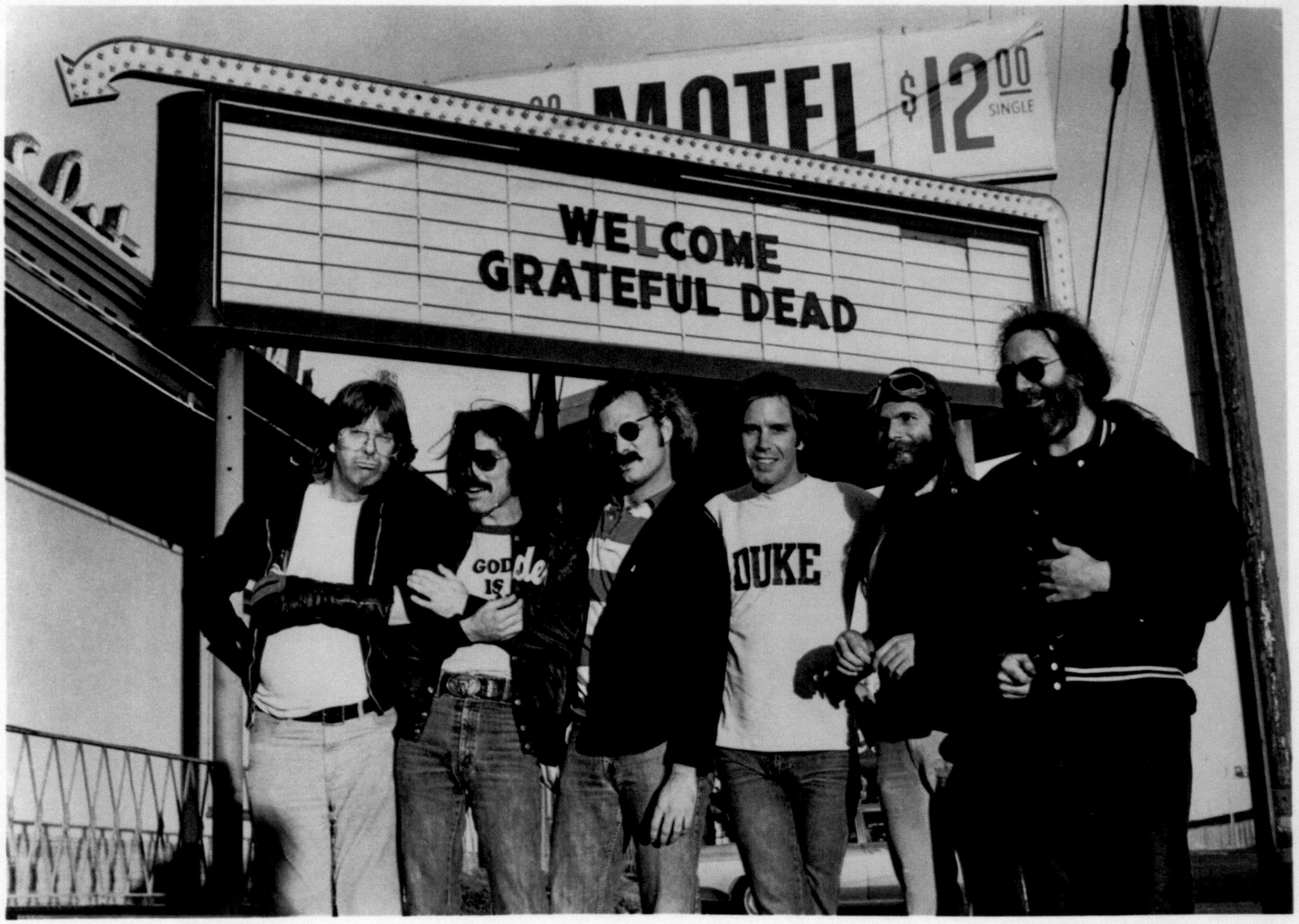

National Tour Management:

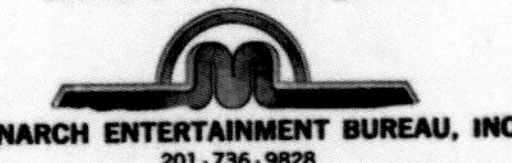

MONARCH ENTERTAINMENT BUREAU, INC.
201-736-9828
412 PLEASANT VALLEY WAY, WEST ORANGE, N. J. 07052

THE GRATEFUL DEAD

ARISTA™

Public Relations:

REN GREVATT ASSOCIATES

200 West 57th St. • Suite 807 New York City, N.Y. 10019 • Tel.: 212-582-0252

Billboard 200: *Mondo Mando* (#174)

Virtuoso mandolinist David Grisman finally got his due as a creative musical innovator with *Mondo Mando*.

FOR SEVERAL years, mandolinist David Grisman had taken his instrument and freed it entirely from its traditional bluegrass role. He created a new style of acoustic music that, in his words, blended "the excitement of rock 'n' roll, the improvisational interplay of jazz, the precision of classical music and, coming full circle, the joyful spontaneity of bluegrass."

Not bad for a guy who originally thought he'd wind up playing on other people's sessions forever.

"Yeah, I just got motivated through unemployment," Grisman admitted. "I spent the mid-Seventies playing on records by James Taylor and Dolly Parton and Linda Ronstadt, but I wasn't making any money. So I decided to do it myself, and lo and behold—now I'm considered a virtuoso of sorts."

Without doubt, Grisman kept busy—he worked on film scores and was the editor of his own mandolin magazine, *Mandolin World News*. His all-instrumental album *Mondo Mando* continued to showcase his sense of innovation—the title track utilized a classical string quartet, while "Dawg Funk" perpetuated his notorious "dawg music" sound.

"Some people have said that the album leans a bit too much toward country, but I don't see it that way at all," Grisman noted. "There's plenty of expansion on those themes. To go someplace, I don't think I have to leave anywhere else. My whole trip is to expand the role of the mandolin in various musical genres, but bluegrass and country are things I don't want to ignore."

Grisman's touring unit, the David Grisman Quintet, had become a quartet—Mark O'Connor, the group's violinist and guitarist, had left to join the Dregs. The remaining members—Darol Anger (violin, cello and violectra), Mike Marshall (mandolin, guitar and violin) and Rob Wasserman (bass)—were notorious for stretching Grisman's musical boundaries in concert.

"See, I don't think there any limitations on what I can do—even something I played 15 years ago, I can play better now," Grisman explained. "A lot of jazz musicians have this feeling that they have to be 'evolving' towards something to have artistic credibility. I don't see it that way at all—I can keep my roots and still feel that I've come up with something different to say." ■

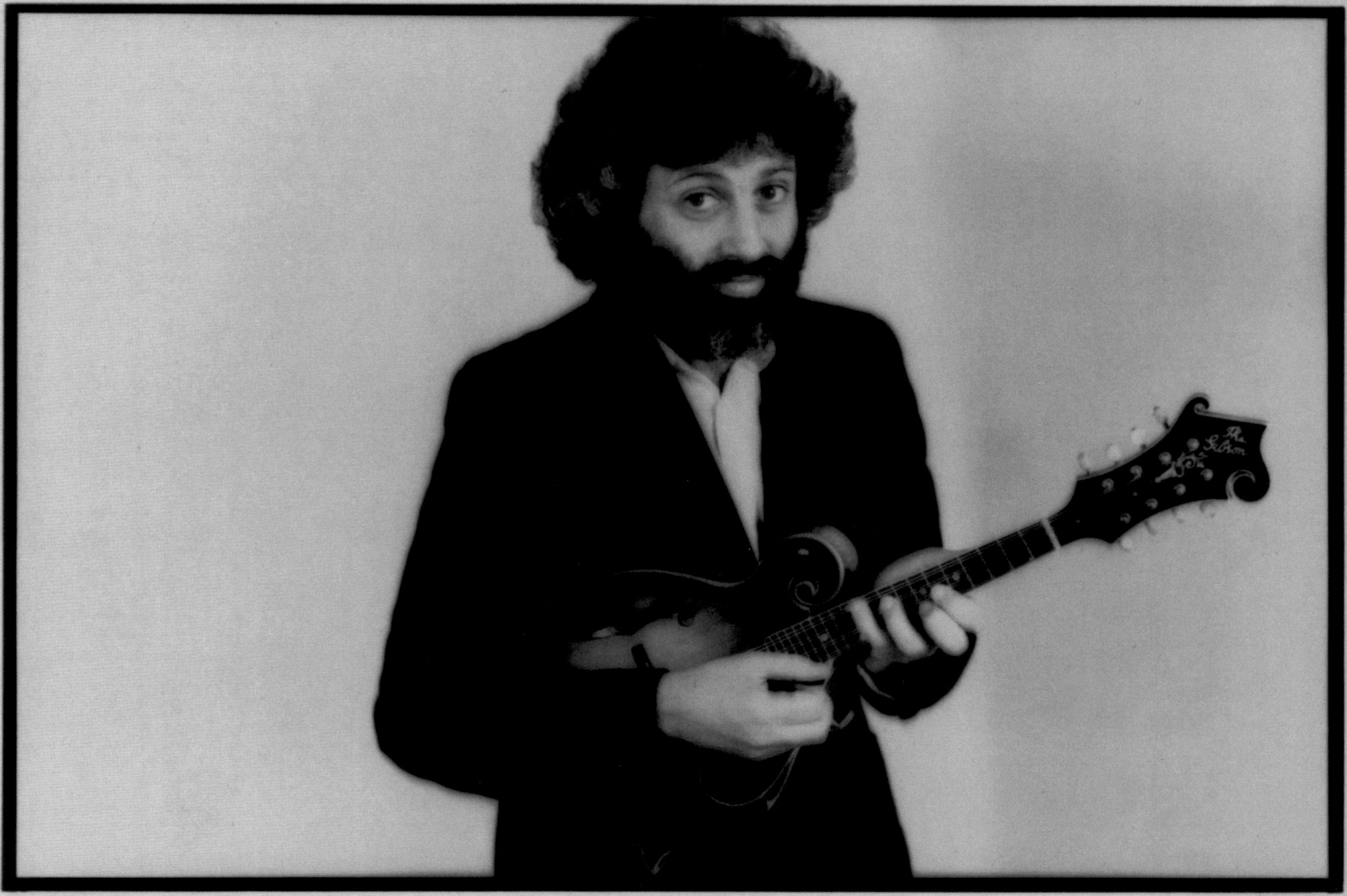

September 1981

DAVID GRISMAN

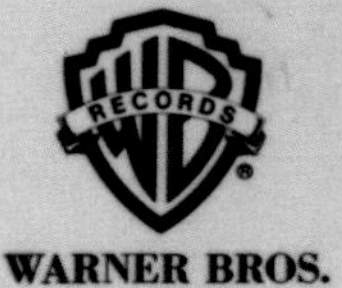

WARNER BROS.

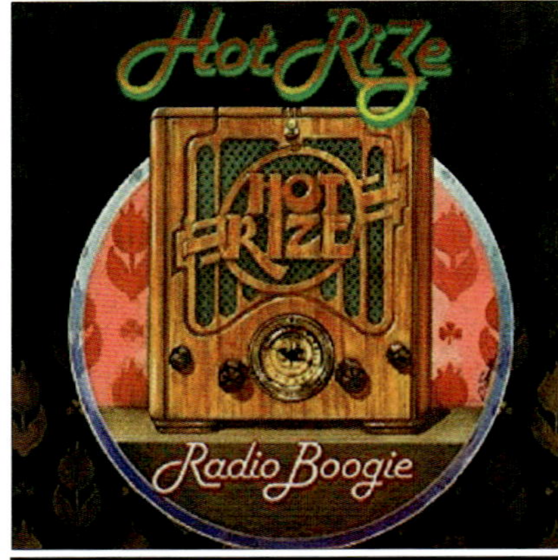

A talented, innovative quartet, Hot Rize became the most talked-about bluegrass aggregation in the nation.

NAMED AFTER the secret ingredient of Martha White Self-Rising Flour (for years a leading sponsor of bluegrass music on the Grand Ole Opry), Hot Rize formed in 1978. Four stellar musicians made up the progressive bluegrass band—Tim O'Brien on lead vocals, mandolin and fiddle; Pete Wernick (aka "Dr. Banjo"); acoustic guitarist Charles Sawtelle; and Nick Forster on bass.

"There was a band based at the Denver Folklore Center called the Rambling Drifters, basically a bluegrass pickup band," Forster explained. "Charles and Pete were at the core, and they had a revolving cast of guests. Tim and I were two of those guys. We were about 10 years younger than Pete and Charles. They had the wisdom and experience that really helped us. We set attainable goals—whatever we dreamed of, we got to do it very quickly."

An eponymous debut album, recorded for Flying Fish Records in 1979, fueled the rise of the contemporary bluegrass scene. *Radio Boogie*, the band's second album, met with universal critical acclaim.

"We were different from other bands," O'Brien said. "Colorado was friendly to all kinds of music, a great place to learn our craft. We were looking to make records, and it seemed like a good idea to write songs. Lester Flatt's advice was, 'If you sing something no one else sings, then they have to hire you to do it.'"

The musicians traveled in a black-and-silver '69 Cadillac, their equipment behind them in an old U-Haul trailer that matched. Mix tapes recorded by Sawtelle for the band's road trips provided an education.

"They were incredibly diverse," Forster said. "Traditional bluegrass, then Freddie King and Blind Willie Johnson, then a Jimi Hendrix cut. We listened to a lot of country blues. We agreed on certain qualities that songs either had or didn't have."

Hot Rize took those special song traits and infused them into a unique and exciting style, playing straight bluegrass as well as a quirky mix of folk, jazz and rock elements. "I was one of the first troublemakers in the world of bluegrass during the Seventies," Forster said. "We'd play the long-established festivals, and I'd walk out on stage with my electric bass and get boos and catcalls from the audience. But we weren't Mister Bluegrass kind of guys. I went to Swiss boarding school. Pete had a doctorate in sociology from Columbia. Tim had gone to a military academy and private college in Maine. That's not exactly the same background that Earl Scruggs had." ■

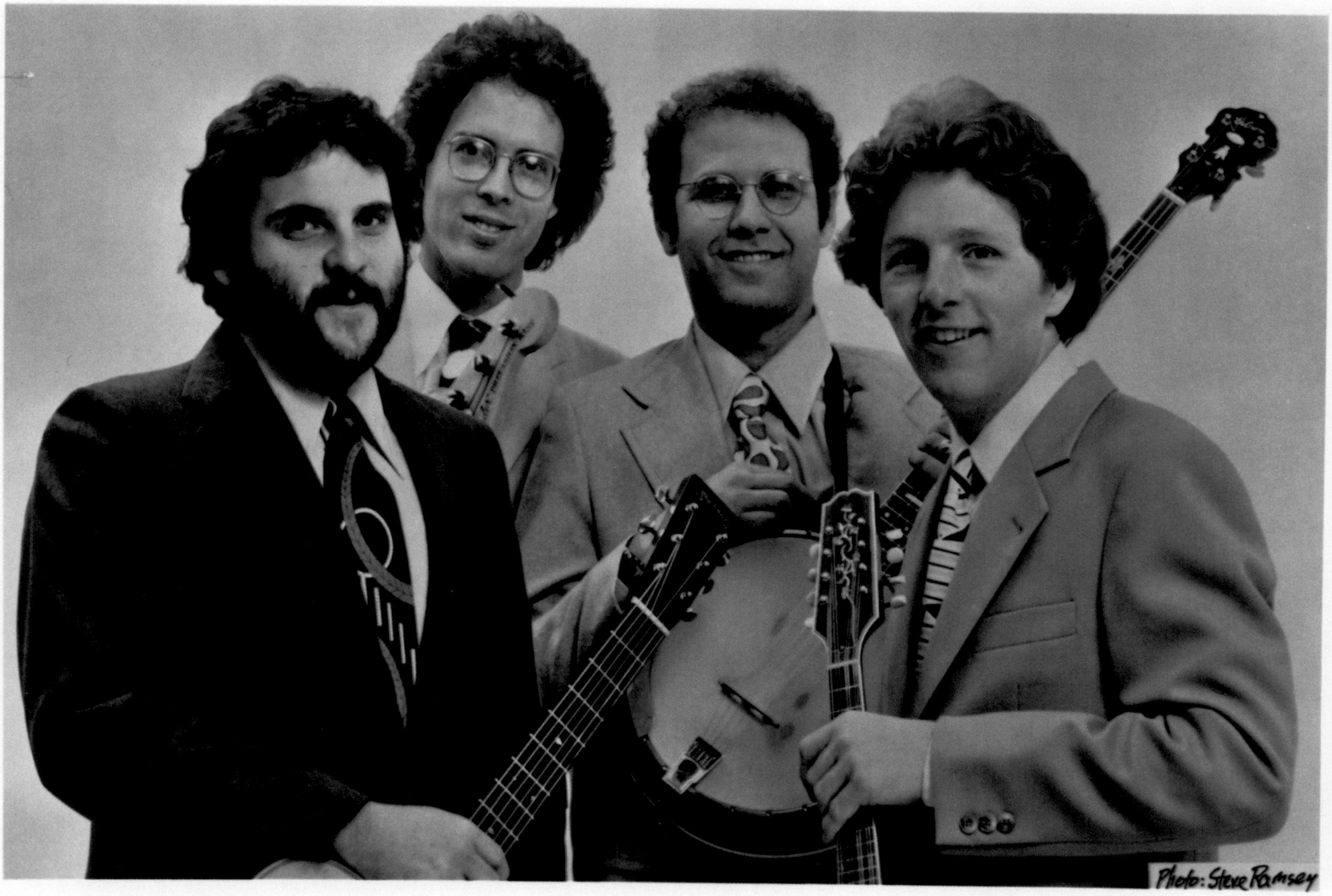

Photo: Steve Ramsey

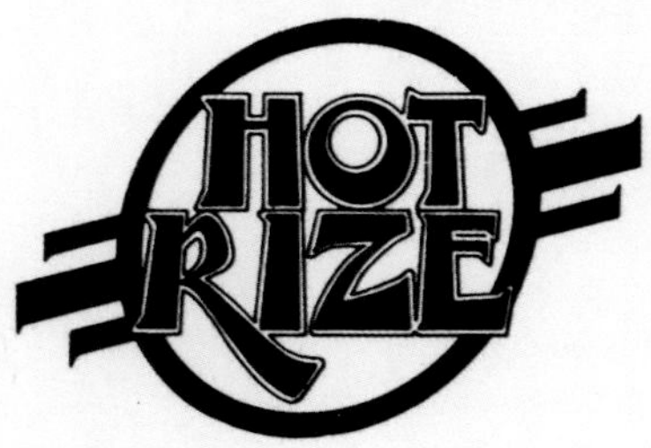

(l. to r.) Charles Sawtelle, Nick Forster, Pete Wernick , Tim O'Brien

(303) 444-4537
7930 Oxford Road Longmont, Colorado 80501

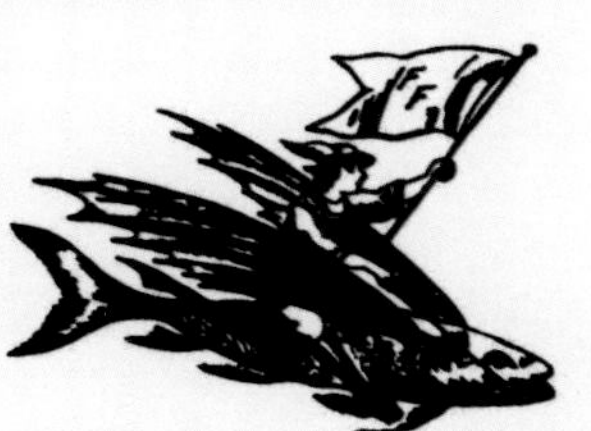

on *Flying Fish* records

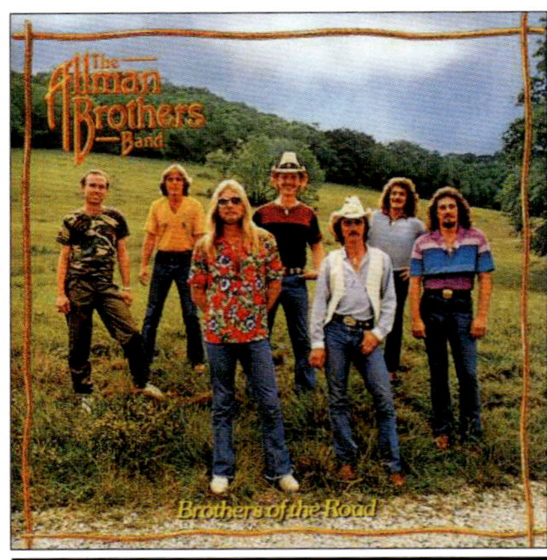

Billboard 200: *Brothers of the Road* (#44)
Billboard Hot 100: "Straight from the Heart" (#39)

The Allman Brothers Band recaptured some of its early glory with the radio-friendly hit, "Straight from the Heart."

DURING THE Allman Brothers Band's halcyon days at the forefront of early Seventies rock, tunes such as "Whipping Post," "Melissa," "Blue Sky" and "Ramblin' Man" became radio staples. But internal turmoil overtook the group, and the ABB dissolved in 1976. If fans wanted to know the latest scoop on the members, they had to pick up *People* magazine instead of *Rolling Stone*. The drug conviction of road manager Scooter Herring was a downer, and Gregg Allman's much-publicized marriage to Cher didn't do much for his musical credibility. Nor did reports of him taking a snooze face down in a plate of spaghetti at an awards banquet.

By the end of the Seventies, however, the band showed signs of becoming a hard-working musical force once again with additional personnel changes. Drummer Butch Trucks insisted that the group's recorded work took a back seat to the commitment to live performances that had served the ABB through the good and bad times.

"My analogy is recording is a craft like building a house, and playing a concert is more of an art form like sculpting," Trucks said. "In the beginning, concerts were the only place we were comfortable. I think it's taken us about ten years to get used to a studio."

For its second album with Arista Records after the bankruptcy of Capricorn Records, the group made a few concessions to commercialism. In order to grab the record-buying public between doses of REO Speedwagon and Kenny Rogers, the Allmans collaborated with John Ryan, a "name producer" (Styx, Pure Prairie League) who balanced traditional-sounding Allman tunes with some new directions. "Straight from the Heart" became a minor hit, the group's last appearance on the Top 40 charts and the most blatantly pop track it had ever conceived.

"We put a little more conscious effort into it," Trucks admitted. "and this was the first time we took a tune—Dickey (Betts, guitarist) wrote it— and produced it that way. We could have loosened it up and added solos and stuff, but we decided that this time around, with the market the way it is, it's really hard to get exposure without some kind of AM or Top 40 play. We thought, 'What the hell, give it a shot'—times are a-changin'." The group subsequently decided to hang it up again. ■

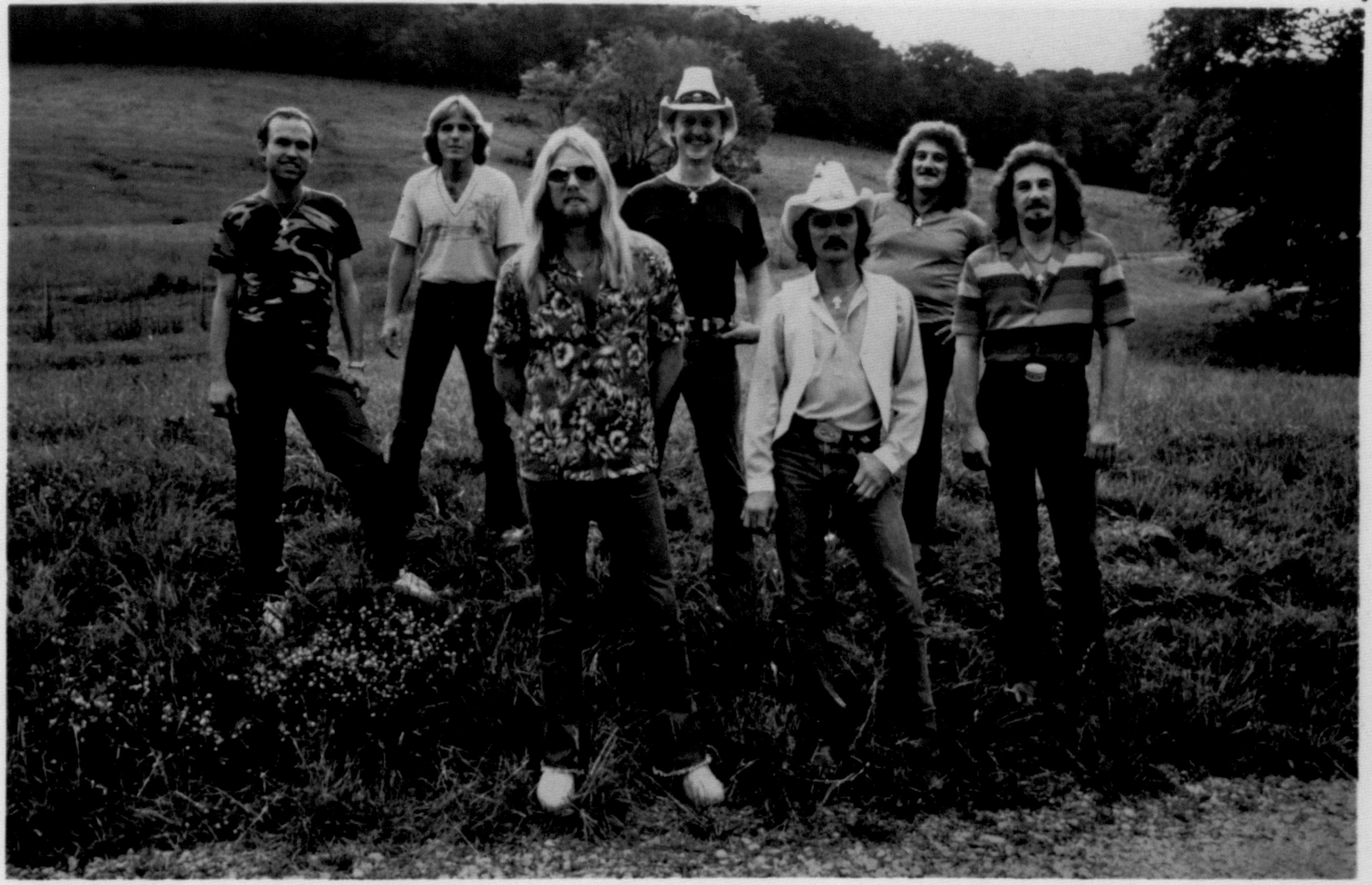

Left to Right: Mike Lawler, Dave Goldflies, Gregg Allman, Butch Trucks, Dickey Betts, Dan Toler, Dave Toler

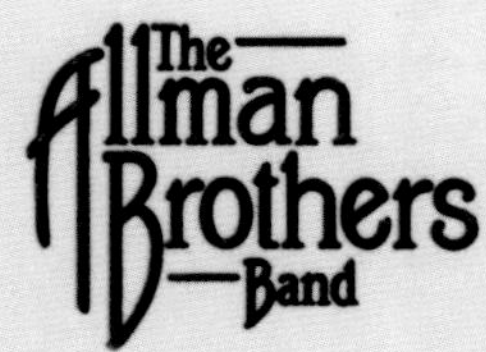

Management:

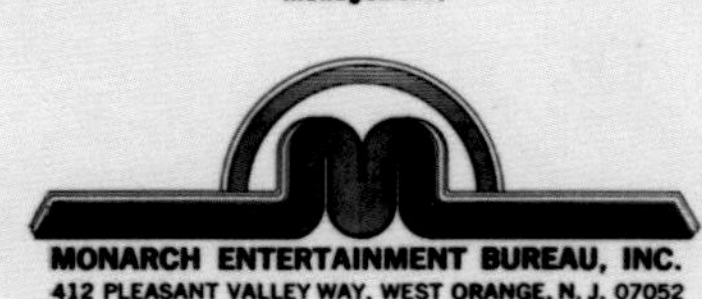

empire agency, inc.
P.O. BOX 514
MARIETTA, GEORGIA 30061
TELEPHONE (404) 427-1200

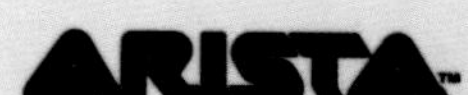

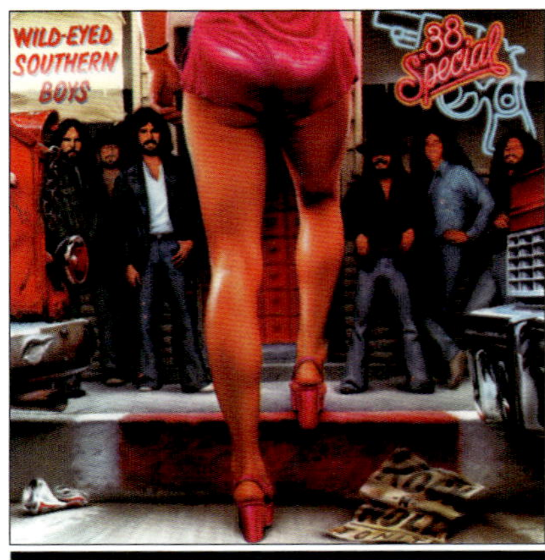

Billboard 200: *Wild-Eyed Southern Boys* (#18)
Billboard Hot 100: "Hold On Loosely" (#27); "Fantasy Girl" (#52)

38 Special hit a bulls-eye with the platinum-selling *Wild-Eyed Southern Boys* and the enduring hit, "Hold On Loosely."

MANY ROCK bands from the South were identified with the considerable fury of triple-lead guitar attacks and overused "whiskey and women" clichés. 38 Special avoided being lumped into the same category.

"We don't consider ourselves a Southern-style boogie band, even though we have to deal with that image," singer Donnie Van Zant admitted. "We're a little different from the rest—a little more sophistication in a rock 'n' roll sense."

Wild-Eyed Southern Boys set matters straight. Producer Rodney Mills let the band's Southern roots shine through, while incorporating the inflections of British heavy metal and contemporary pop hooks. The approach created two bona-fide smash singles—"Hold On Loosely" tossed in a little Cars influence, and "Fantasy Girl" was catchy, approachable guitar rock. Mills' efforts were supported by the production assistance of guitarists Jeff Carlisi and Don Barnes.

"They co-wrote those songs with Jim Peterik, who helped write our first national hit last year, 'Rockin' into the Night,'" Van Zant explained. "He's from Chicago and he gives us a good outside influence—he's definitely not from the south."

With *Wild-Eyed Southern Boys*, 38 Special scored a platinum album and made its mark on music, the only path out of the west side of Jacksonville, Florida—the same tough, heavily industrial community that spawned the Allman Brothers, Lynyrd Skynyrd, Blackfoot and Molly Hatchet. "There's a lot of camaraderie and less ego with Southern bands, and it's because most of us grew up together," Barnes added. "People say, 'How long have you known each other?' Well, all of our lives. That carries through all of the groups—you've all come up at the same time and you're all friends. It all works out." ■

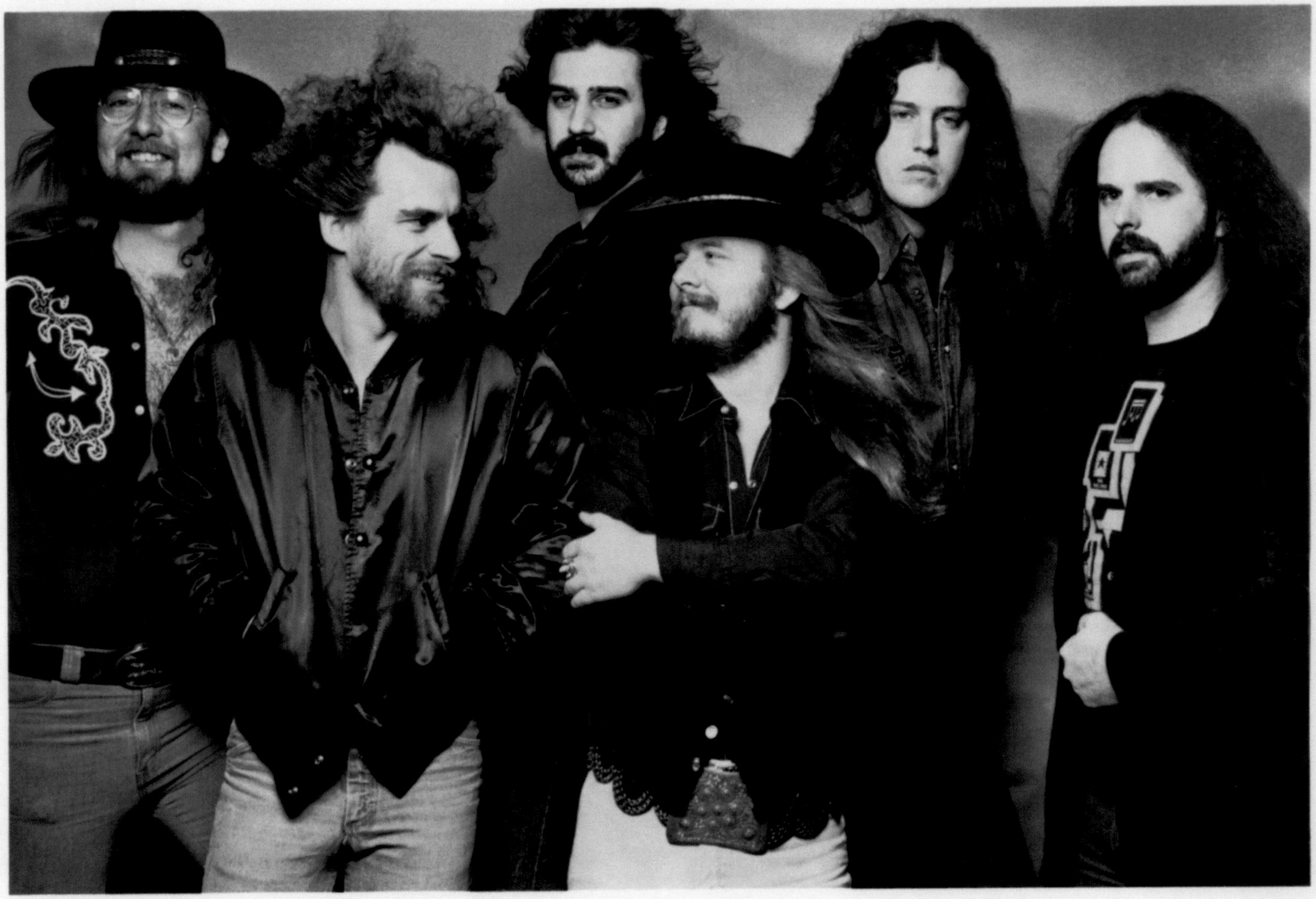

.38 SPECIAL

L-R: LARRY JUNSTROM, JACK GRONDIN, JEFF CARLISI, DONNIE VAN ZANT
STEVE BROOKINS, DON BARNES

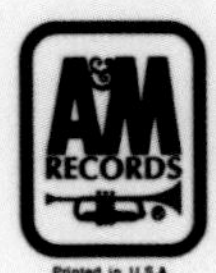

Printed in U.S.A.

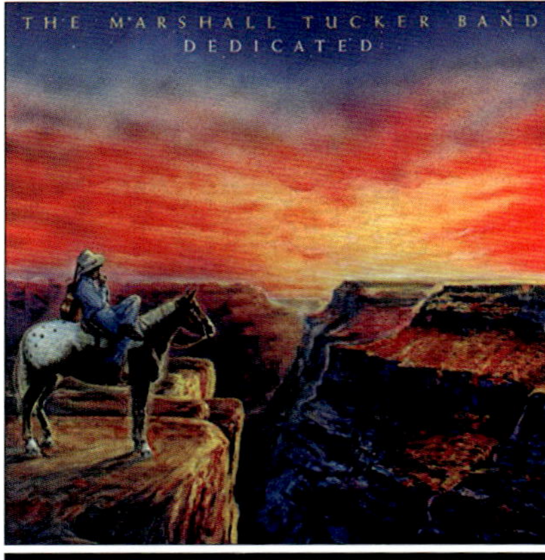

Billboard 200: *Dedicated* (#53)

The Marshall Tucker Band, following the loss of bandmate Tommy Caldwell, came back strong with *Dedicated.*

WHEN BASSIST and founding member Tommy Caldwell died from injuries sustained in a car accident in the summer of 1980, many observers predicted the demise of the Marshall Tucker Band, one of the major Southern rock outfits of the Seventies. But the group's positive attitude prevailed. The remaining members added longtime pal Franklin Wilkie to maintain their familial character, and MTB came back with *Dedicated,* the band's eleventh album.

The recruitment of Wilkie was more natural than outsiders could imagine. He was a lifelong friend of Tommy Caldwell and his older brother Toy, as well as the rest of the band's members—all of whom had remained close to their roots despite MTV's international notoriety. They'd all grown up and still lived within a few miles of Spartanburg, North Carolina, a foothills community of 50,000 hard-working souls.

"Yeah, we all went to kindergarten together," Wilkie noted. "We were all together in our first bands in junior high, me and Toy and George (McCorkle). There was no such thing as a bass until 1962, so we all played guitar and cut our teeth on the same copy music."

Wilkie would have undoubtedly been a charter member of the Marshall Tucker Band, except that a stint in the military interfered. Upon his release from the Air Force in the late Sixties, he moved to Atlanta, where he got involved with such minor bands as Garfeel Ruff. But upon Caldwell's death, the band brought him back into the fold. "It's been the most natural progression of my life, just rehashing what we'd missed over the last few years," Wilkie reflected.

Dedicated was the first album on which Wilkie had contributed in the studio, and the live feel of the recording reflected some changes in the band's attitude. On the prior two MTB albums, producer Stewart Levine had the group experimenting with jazz arrangements and horn charts. The results, while artistically fulfilling, didn't translate to the live show. For *Dedicated*, producer Tom Dowd (Eric Clapton, Allman Brothers, Rod Stewart) steered the band back to a mainstream sound. "We had to get back to playing the way we play in concert," Wilkie admitted. "The idea is to keep the basic song framework and let each guy take a longer ride. It's kinda 'structured unstructured' music—if one of us doesn't feel good, he just takes a shorter turn."

Dedicated featured McCorkle's "Silverado," and the most poignant composition was Toy Caldwell's "Ride in Peace," dedicated in part to "all lost loved ones." ■

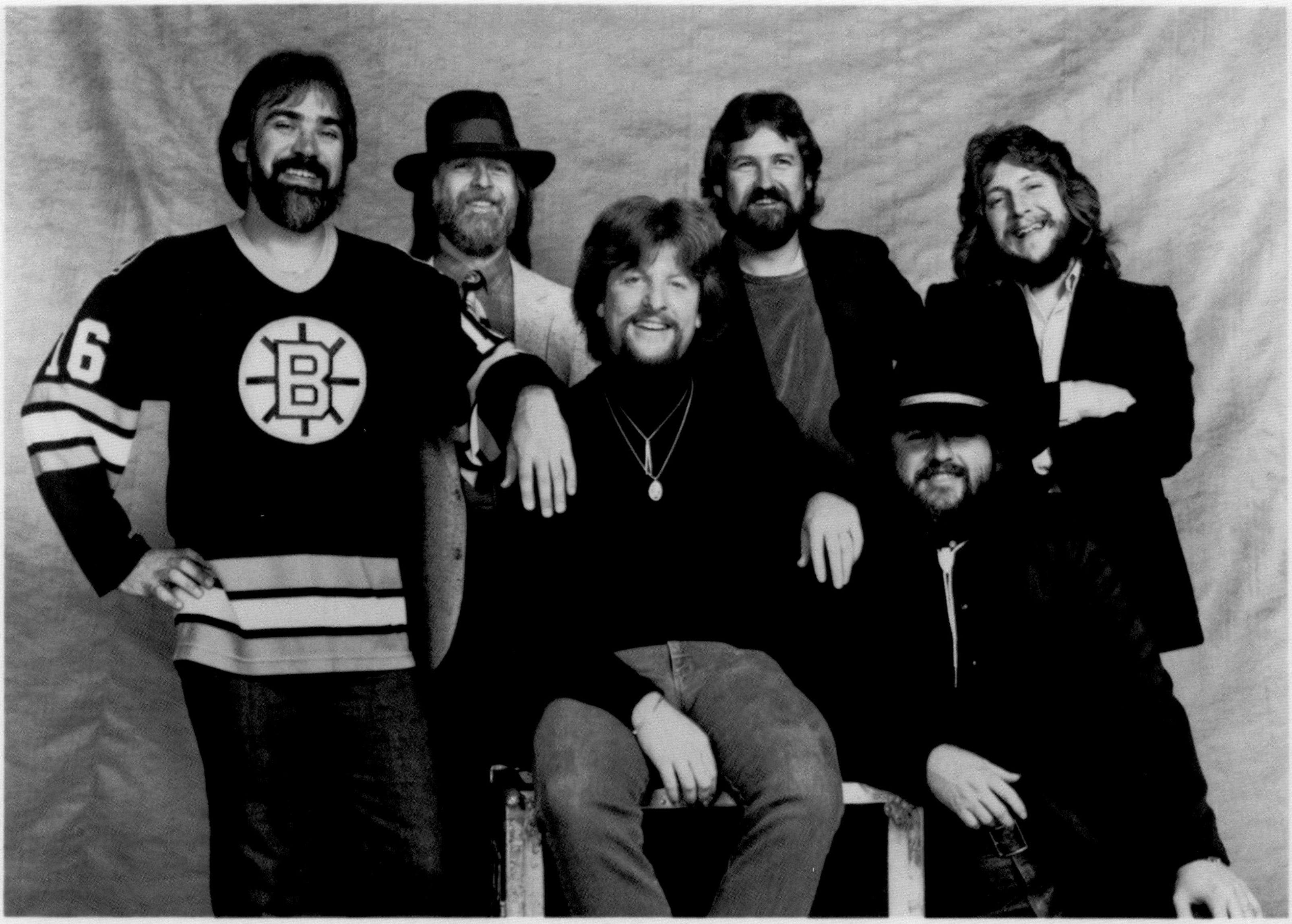

THE MARSHALL TUCKER BAND

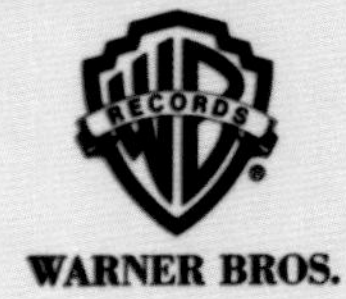

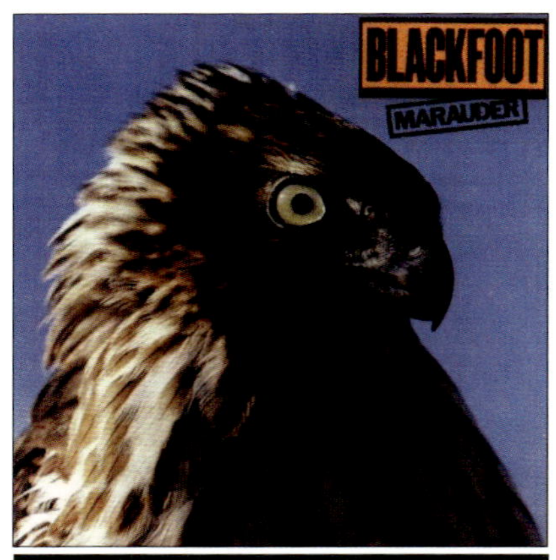

Billboard 200: *Marauder* (#48)
Billboard Hot 100: "Fly Away" (#42)

With *Marauder*, the Southern hard rockers Blackfoot fancied having "one foot in England and one foot in Florida."

JACKSONVILLE, AN industrial city tucked into Florida's far northeastern corner, had spawned an impressive list of groups since the late Sixties—the Allman Brothers Band, Lynyrd Skynyrd, Molly Hatchet and 38 Special. Rick Medlocke had made the acquaintance of all of them and developed his own blend of southern blues and Anglo-heavy metal with Blackfoot.

Blackfoot's breakthrough album, 1979's *Strikes*, struck a chord with "Train Train" (written by Medlocke's grandfather, blues and bluegrass musician Shorty Medlocke) and "Highway Song." The band was suddenly an "overnight sensation" after nearly ten years of struggling.

"Sure, we're from the South, and we're proud of it, but we've never believed in letting our heritage dictate the type of music we could play," Medlocke said. "Our roots are just as much in Free as they are in southern boogie."

Since that first success, Blackfoot had been searching for a follow-up hit. "Fly Away," a track from the *Marauder* album, made the charts with its juxtaposed dynamics of an acoustic verse and raucous chorus, but it failed to make the band a staple of the airwaves.

"We stayed off the road for the longest time in our career just to make sure we got everything sounding just the way we wanted," Medlocke noted. "We're just not a Top 40 commercial group—I don't think we're ever gonna have a No. 1 single, although we might make a No. 1 album. We're just the type of band that writes the way we feel—that's how 'Highway Song' came about."

Instead, Blackfoot concentrated on touring, spreading its message through direct contact with fans. Medlocke was well-known for his charismatic approach, and Blackfoot's Who-meets-Lynyrd-Skynyrd sound found receptive audiences in Britain and Europe.

"I'm from the street and our fans are still street kids—I speak their lingo, in other words. I'm gonna stay in the streets, too—we'll never get too polished or slick. Mass appeal will come in time, but for now I'm in my element." ■

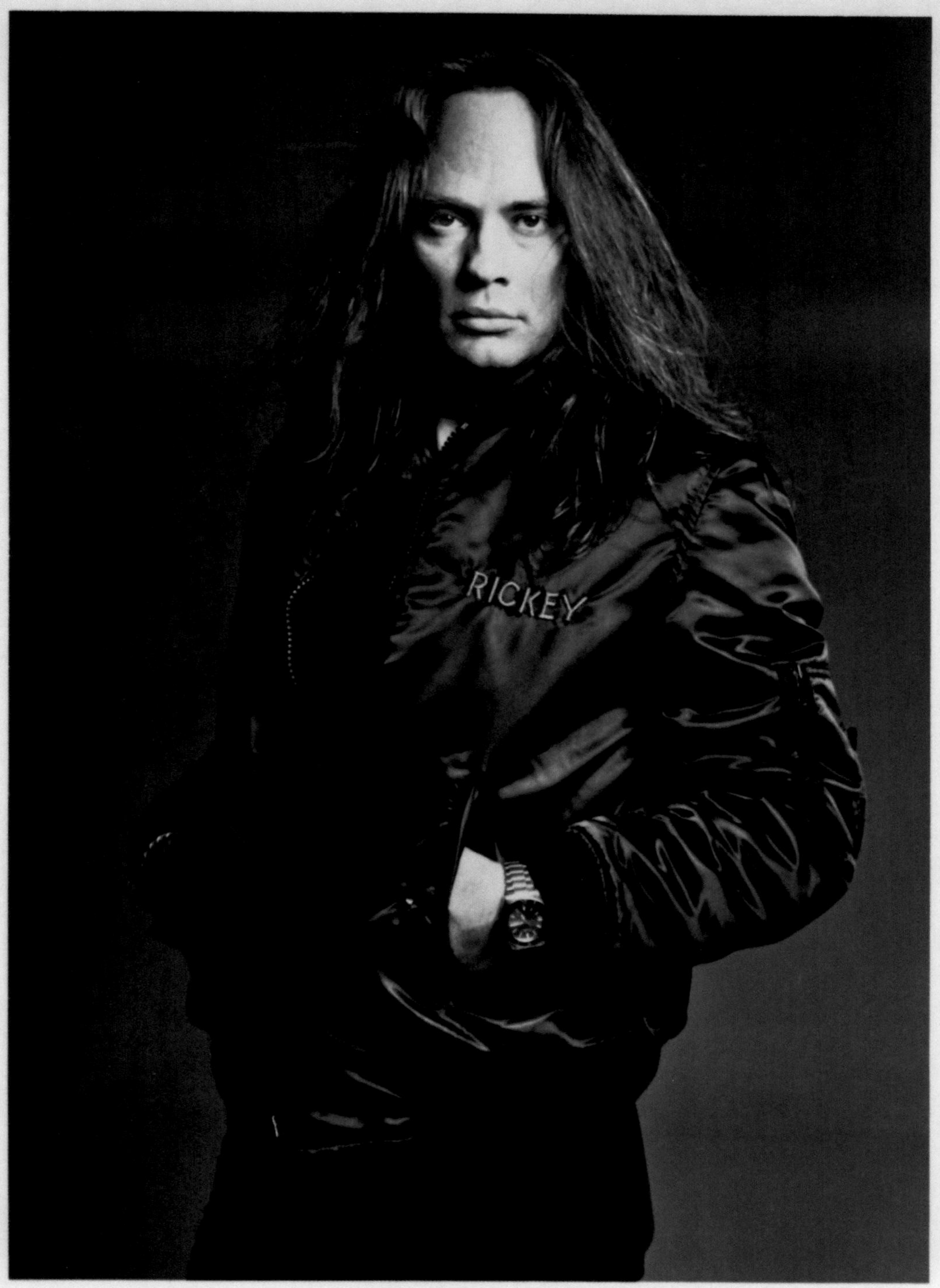

Rick Medlocke

BLACKFOOT

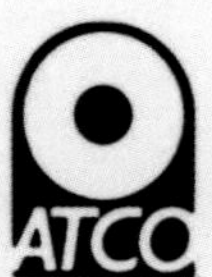

Billboard 200: *Go for the Throat* (#154)
Billboard Hot 100: "Tin Soldier" (#58)

Go for the Throat marked Humble Pie's tenth album and the final embodiment of the British band's enduring charm.

STEVE MARRIOTT couldn't be accused of holding a grudge. While other bands broke up amidst vows never to play again, the talented guitarist and vocalist spearheaded drives to reunite his previous groups, including a short-lived resurrection of Small Faces circa 1977.

"Hey, mate, it's not that big of a deal," Marriott enthused. "You don't see the guys for four or five years, because you never meet out on the road. And then, when you finally meet up with 'em, the first thing you wanna do is play—or at least that's what I wanna do."

Marriott had reformed Humble Pie, an English blues-based hard-rock band that found success on both sides of the Atlantic with such songs as "30 Days in the Hole" and "I Don't Need No Doctor." The rejuvenated group had scored a hit with 1980's "Fool for a Pretty Face." Marriott was candid about his role in the rock music circus.

"Hey, it's not a bad time to be out there, 'cause all the good English bands are dropping like flies," he reasoned. "There's no one out there save a few new groups, but the rest is just noise. We're still capable of fitting into the mainstream. Besides, I don't know what else I'd be doing if I wasn't in a band. I'm an old fucker and I still don't know how to do anything else, even how to use a screwdriver. I'll be trying to do rock 'n' roll until there's no other alternative."

The revived Humble Pie released a second record, *Go for the Throat*, with the same lineup—Marriott, original drummer Jerry Shirley, and newcomers Anthony "Sooty" Jones (bass) and former Jeff Beck Group member Bobby Tench (guitar). The album's significance derived from Marriott's one-of-a-kind rasp of a voice and a cover of "Tin Soldier," one of Small Faces' best-known songs written by Marriott.

"It's funny about bands," he noted. "It takes a year or two to start playing well together, and by the time you get good, you break up. It's when you can't cope with the day-to-day things that you go, 'Fuck it, I've had it.' It's happened in every group I've ever been in. We're doing okay this time, though. We're good mates, and if the road doesn't drive us crazy, we'll do another album easy."

At the beginning of the promotional tour for *Go for the Throat,* Marriott crushed his hand in a hotel room door, delaying the band's scheduled appearances. He then fell victim to an ulcer, forcing the cancellation of all further tour dates. The group soon disintegrated. ■

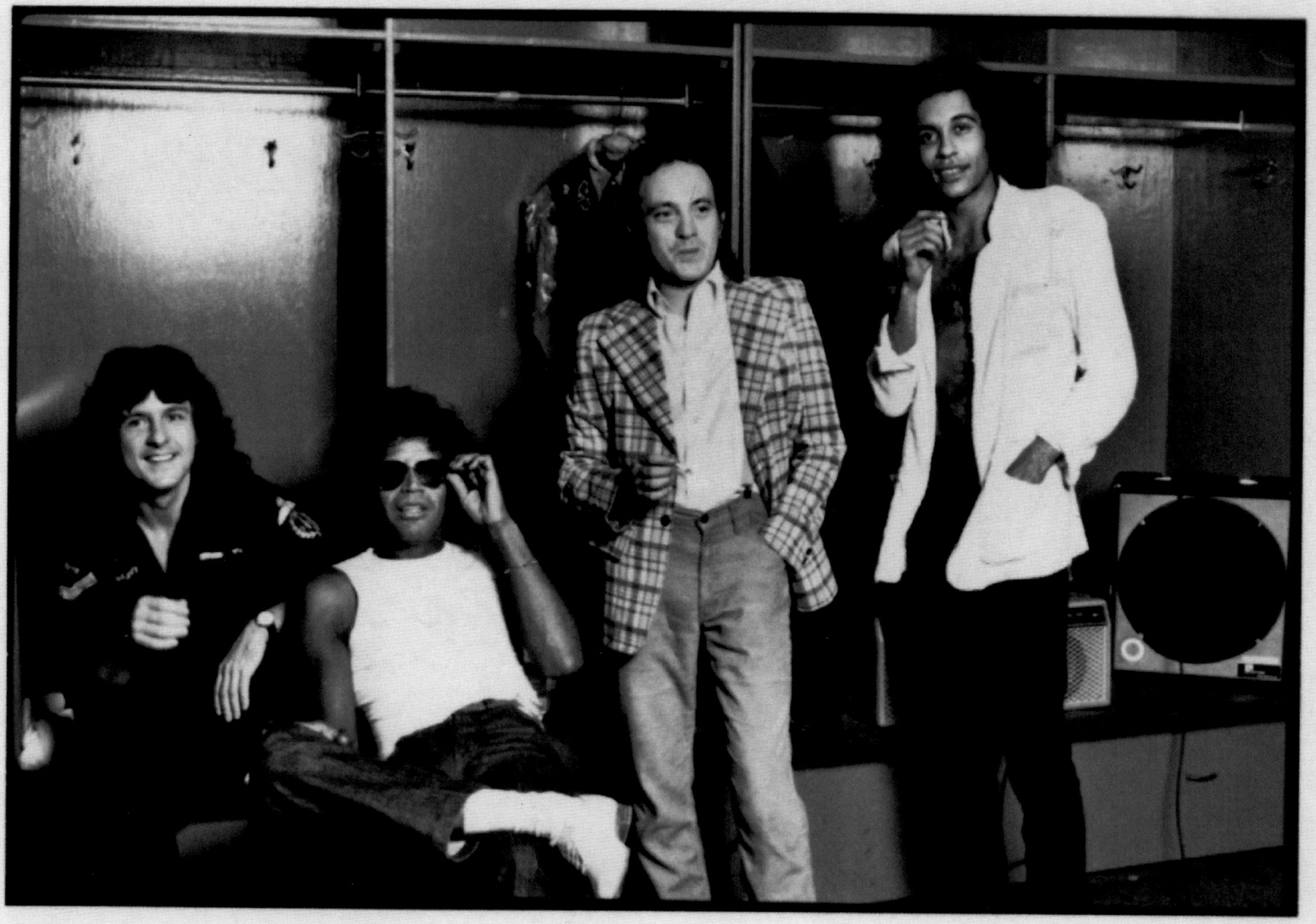

JERRY SHIRLEY BOBBY TENCH STEVE MARRIOTT ANTHONY "SOOTY" JONES

HUMBLE PIE

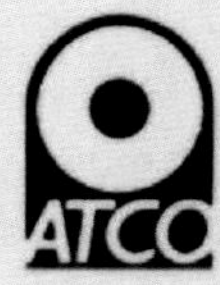

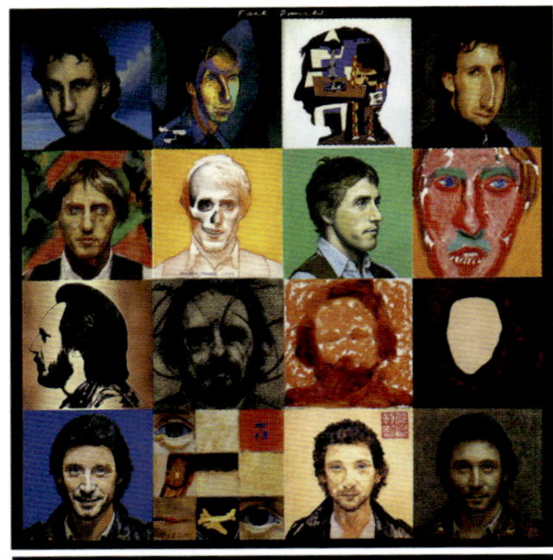

Billboard 200: *Face Dances* (#4)
Billboard Hot 100: "You Better You Bet" (#18);
"Don't Let Go the Coat" (#84)

The Who released *Face Dances*, the veteran British band's first studio album with Kenney Jones as drummer.

THE WHO was slowly falling apart. Each member grappled with the aftermath of drummer Keith Moon's 1978 death and the following year's concert tragedy, when 11 people were trampled to death before a Cincinnati show. Lead singer Roger Daltrey starred in the film *McVicar* and released the soundtrack as a solo album. Guitarist and principal songwriter Pete Townshend's third solo album, *Empty Glasses*, spawned "Let My Love Open the Door," a transatlantic hit.

Work began on *Face Dances*, and an important factor in the musical equation was drummer Kenney Jones, a longtime friend who had replaced the late Moon. Jones had previously played with the Small Faces and the Faces. "We went in the studio without much material," Jones said. "Pete came in with unfinished demos and we all got to pounce on it and join in as a whole, to say what we wanted individually. It was presented very much on a workshop basis, and it was fantastic—just the four of us, a very healthy way of working."

Face Dances was the Who's first outing with producer Bill Szymczyk, renowned for his work with the Eagles, among many others. The album received mixed reviews but was a hit. The sharply written "You Better You Bet" came to be one of the band's most popular songs, and "Don't Let Go the Coat" was a fine Townshend devotional to his spiritual teacher, the late Meher Baba.

"When Keith died, my problem was learning the old songs—the Who library—in a week," Jones mused. "But I feel more comfortable and relaxed because time has gone on, y'know? I think I've established my own level in the group. I just refused to change for the people who wouldn't forget Keith. I'm me. Sod it." ■

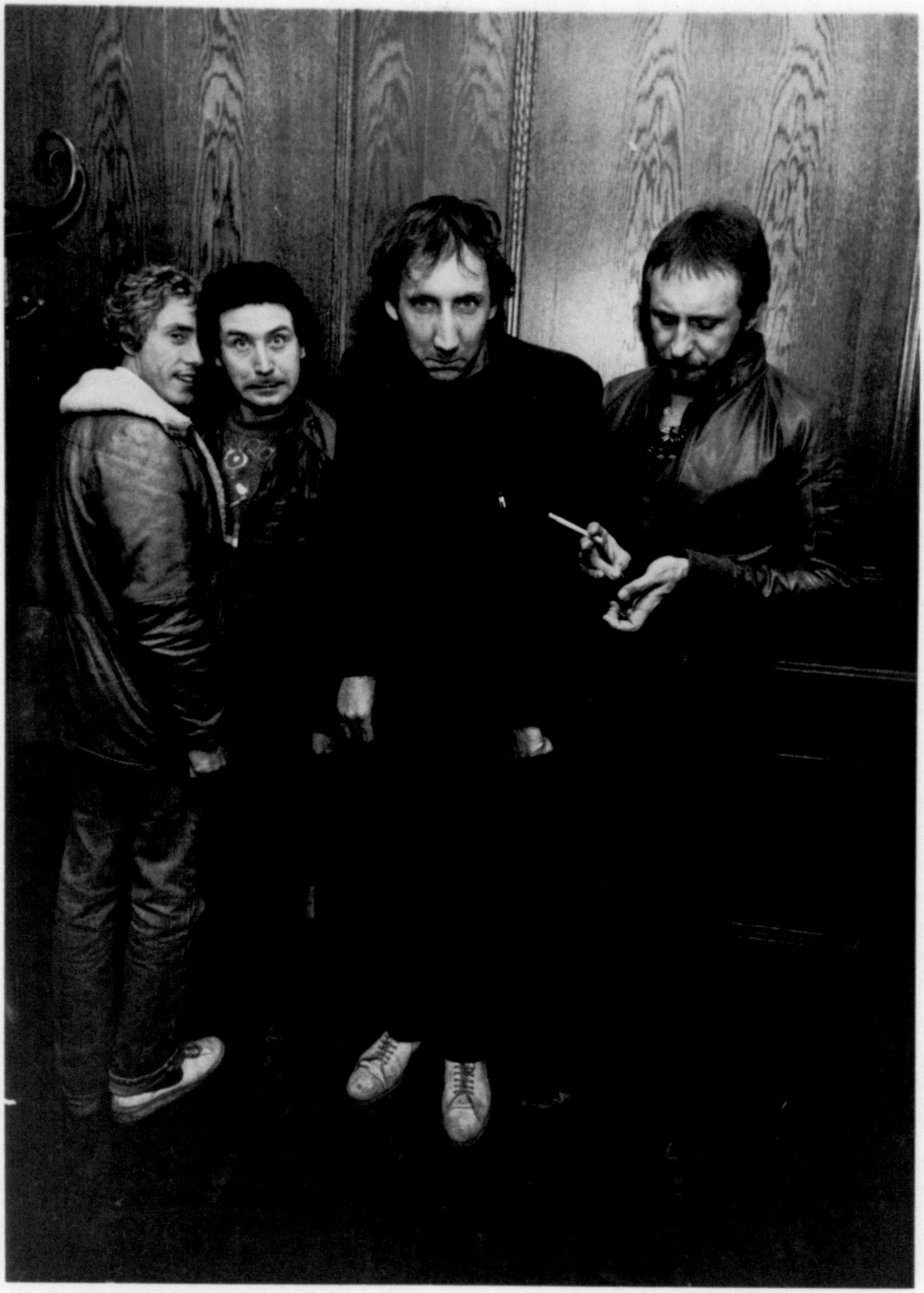

THE WHO

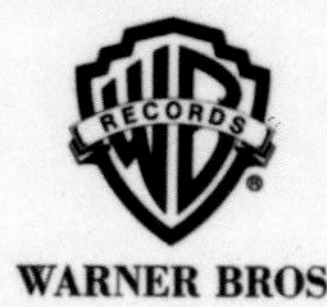

WARNER BROS.

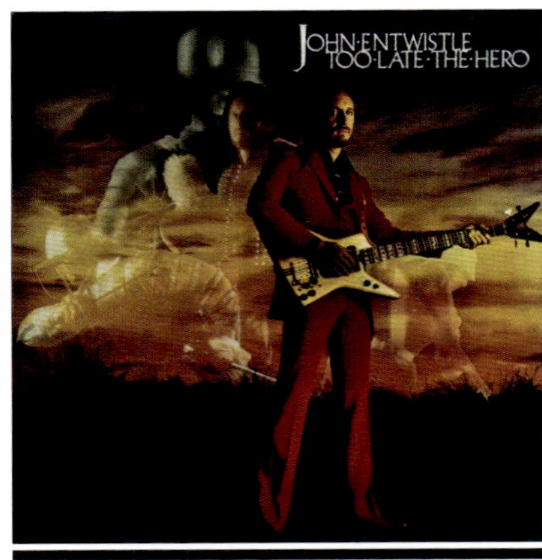

Billboard 200: *Too Late the Hero* (#71)

Too Late the Hero, John Entwistle's fifth and most successful solo album, spotlighted the Who bassist's musical range.

LONG TYPECAST as the "quiet one" in the Who, John Entwistle had developed a reputation as a retiring bassist with an affection for the macabre. That image, however, obscured the range of his musical contributions.

Starting with his twangy solo on 1965's "My Generation," Entwistle had redefined the role of bass guitar in rock music. On stage with the Who, he provided the sonic bottom of the band's sound as well as playing lead-style counterpoint to Pete Townshend's guitar work, preferring complex melody lines to rock's traditional blues progressions. When Townshend incorporated classical elements in his writing, he used Entwistle's French horn playing to add an extra dimension. And Entwistle's dark, whimsical songwriting credits on Who records ("Boris the Spider," "My Wife") provided contrast to Townshend's compositions.

Who trivia buffs noted that Entwistle even drew the humorous cover art of the group in dots on the 1975 hit album, *The Who by Numbers*.

"We all took turns doing the album covers," Entwistle explained. "The cover of the previous album, *Quadrophenia*, cost something like £16,500, which was the price of a decent-sized house back then. It was my chance to do one, so I decided I was gonna do mine cheaper. I'd been drawing bits and pieces of cartoons of the band—the original title of the album was going to be *Car Tunes*, a play on tunes to play in the car. But the way *The Who by Numbers* turned out, if you played it in the car, you'd drive into a wall—it's a pretty depressing album. So I got the idea from one of my son's coloring books—'Well, it's just a collection of numbers…'"

Between 1971 and 1975, Entwistle had released four solo albums. *Too Late the Hero* was his first effort of the Eighties, though he'd sown the seeds in 1975, when guitarist Joe Walsh invited Entwistle's own band, Ox, to be his special guest on a series of shows (Walsh's James Gang toured extensively with the Who in the early Seventies), and drummer Joe Vitale's Mad Men were supporting the bill. The three musicians discussed the possibility of recording an album when schedules allowed.

Too Late the Hero was the highest-charting album of Entwistle's solo career. The Who had passed its prime—drummer Keith Moon had died in 1978, and the group was in the midst of a reassessment. "I'm trying to channel my energy elsewhere—I'm concentrating on me," Entwistle noted. "Writing is such a learning process. I always felt restricted in the past, trapped in that black-humor vein. I feel a lot freer now." ■

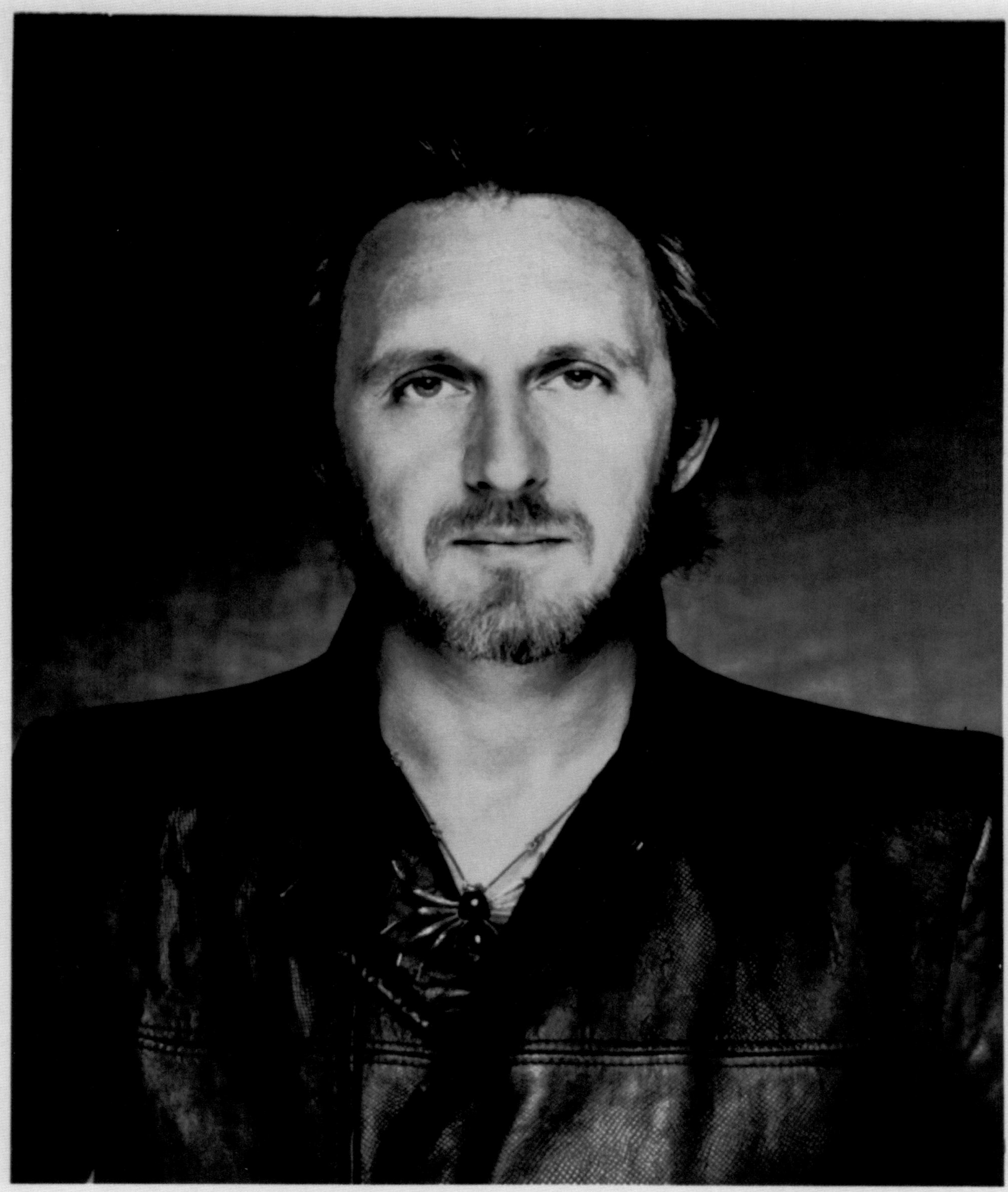

JOHN ENTWISTLE

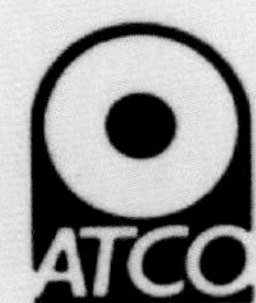

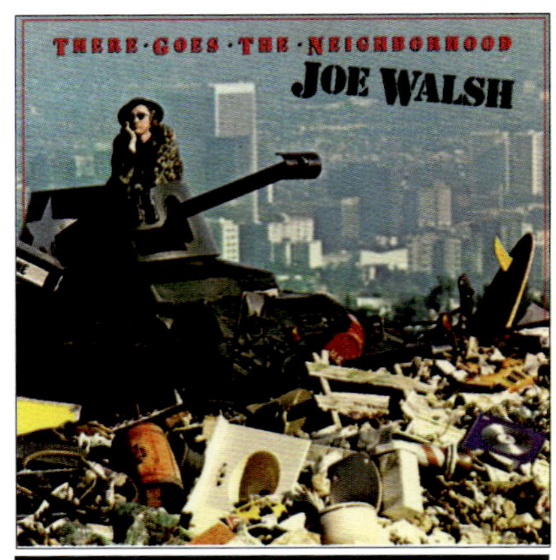

Billboard 200: *There Goes the Neighborhood* (#20)
Billboard Hot 100: "A Life of Illusion" (#34)

Eight years after co-writing it, Joe Walsh released the hit "A Life of Illusion" on *There Goes the Neighborhood.*

KNOWN AS rock music's consummate cynic, Joe Walsh built his reputation on hotel-room demolition and goofy wordplay. "Life's Been Good," his riotous hit single from 1978, epitomized his sarcastic perspective.

"I broke through with 'Life's Been Good'—that was a good joke," the former James Gang and Eagles guitarist said. "Everybody thinks this lifestyle we lead is so extravagant, and it ain't—it's a pain in the ass. But now it's gotten to the point where peers in the industry are calling and saying, 'Oh, Joe, you're so funny! What are you gonna call the next one? What stupid ideas you got?'"

There Goes the Neighborhood was Walsh's first solo album since the demise of the Eagles, one of the most influential bands of the Seventies. The comical cover picture showed him looking bored while sitting atop a military tank surrounded by a city turned to rubble. He co-wrote "A Life of Illusion" with bassist Kenny Passarelli, a member of Walsh's first solo band, Barnstorm. The group had recorded a basic track for 1973's *The Smoker You Drink, The Player You Get*, but never completed it.

"I couldn't find the master tapes of the song," Walsh explained. "So (producer) Bill Szymczyk took a 2-track mix of the original basic track, we cleaned it up and overdubbed over that to complete it."

"Joe called me and said, 'Hey, remember that track that we did?'—I think it was called 'Garlic Prawns,'" Passarelli recounted. "Joe had written lyrics, and he sent me a cassette. God, this was seven years later. I'd gone on to play with Elton John and Hall & Oates, and Bernie Taupin (John's collaborator) and Sara Allen (who contributed to Hall & Oates) had written lighthearted lyrics to that same melody. Then Joe sends me this apocalyptic, really dark version.

"Then Joe said, 'By the way, do you still play trumpet?' I said, 'No, but I'm sure I can.' In the studio, after a couple of tequilas, he said, 'I want mariachi trumpets on there.' I have to thank my father for all those music lessons. So you've got this bizarre tune—the lick that I'd written, Joe's brilliant lyrics, I played drunken trumpet—and it was a hit."

"A Life of Illusion" topped *Billboard*'s Mainstream Rock Tracks chart. "At this point, I'm an old-timer, a second-generation rock 'n' roller," Walsh shrugged. "I've had a chance to be famous, not be famous, get a big royalty check, spend it all, play on a lot of people's albums…" ■

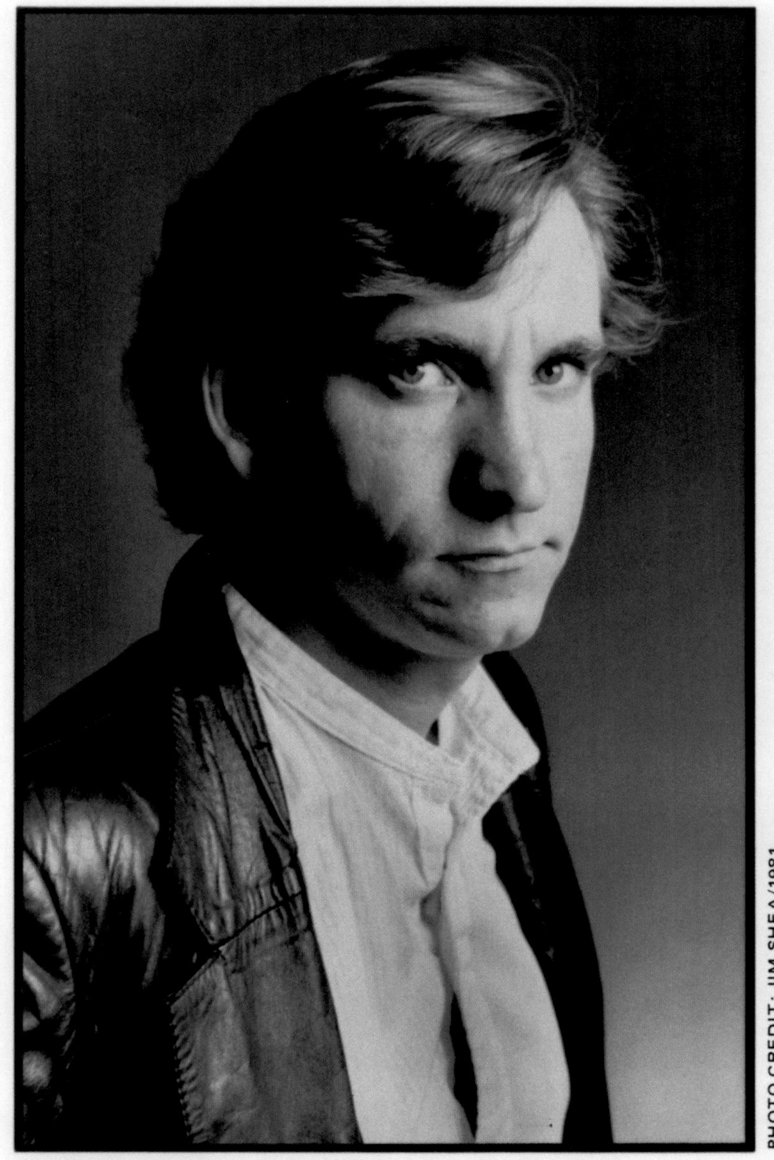

PHOTO CREDIT: JIM SHEA/1981

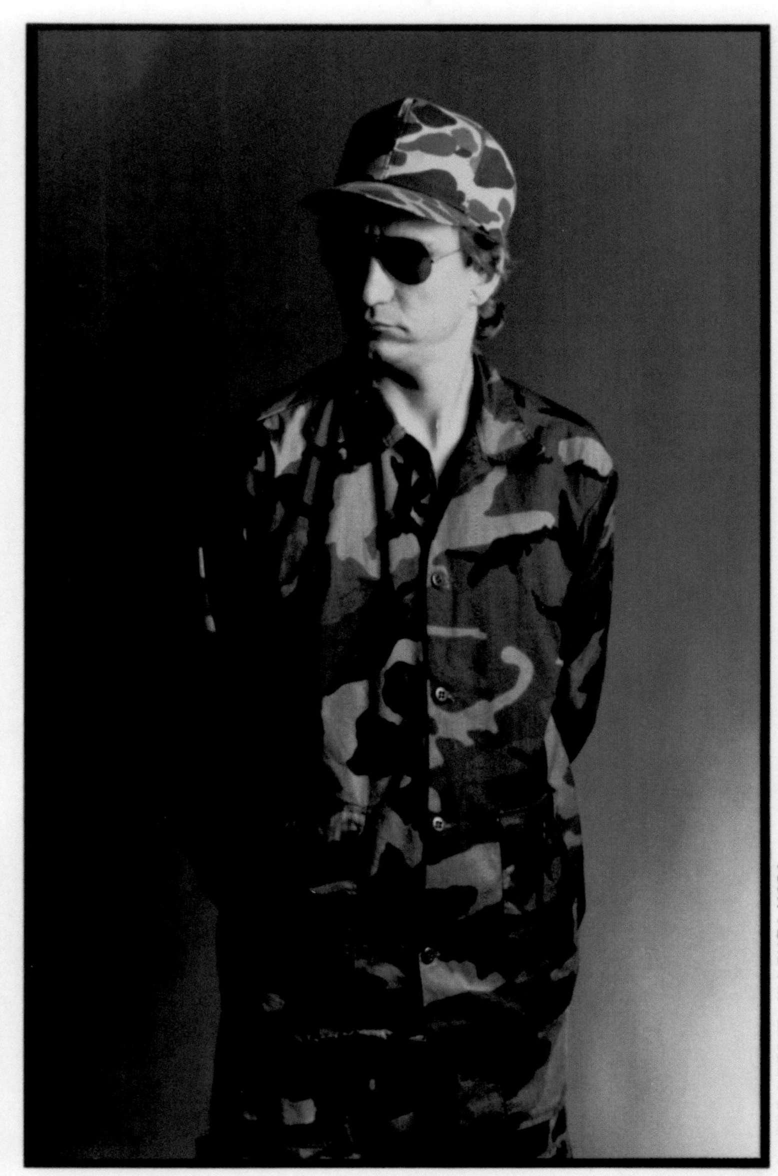

PHOTO CREDIT: JIM SHEA/1981

JOE WALSH

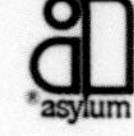

Billboard 200: *Plantation Harbor* (#181)

Having played with many of the top names in music, multi-instrumentalist Joe Vitale released *Plantation Harbor.*

JOE VITALE'S life had been a whirlwind of tours and studio dates as an in-demand drummer and keyboardist. The beginning of 1972 found Vitale and Joe Walsh moving to Boulder, Colorado, to form the band Barnstorm, initially rounding it out with bassist Kenny Passarelli. Barnstorm brought Vitale's drum work to a mass audience, both on record and onstage, and he and Walsh began a longtime partnership.

After recording a solo album in 1974, Vitale linked up with Stephen Stills and joined the Stills-Young Band, and later backed Crosby, Stills & Nash on the trio's reunion album and subsequent tours. He also sat in with the Eagles on tour dates backing *The Long Run.*

Bill Szymczyk, whose work with Walsh and the Eagles, Bob Seger and the Who had made him one of rock's most sought-after producers, asked Vitale if he'd be interested in working on a second solo project. Longtime cohorts Walsh, Stills, Don Felder, Timothy B. Schmit and Graham Nash all put in appearances on *Plantation Harbor*, adding their talents in the same way that Vitale had lent his to their projects. "Lady on the Water," a single about the Statue of Liberty, received airplay on album-oriented rock radio and helped the album chart.

"I was watching the American hostages coming home from Iran on television, and that really got me going," Vitale said. "I'm really patriotic, and I thought, 'All the anthems ever written are either country or tearjerker ballads. I want something that Americans can grit our teeth to.' I had some help with the lyrics from Stephen when I got stuck—the second verse is mostly his. Joe Walsh really got behind the song in the studio—he even throws in a little of 'The Star-Spangled Banner' on slide guitar." ■

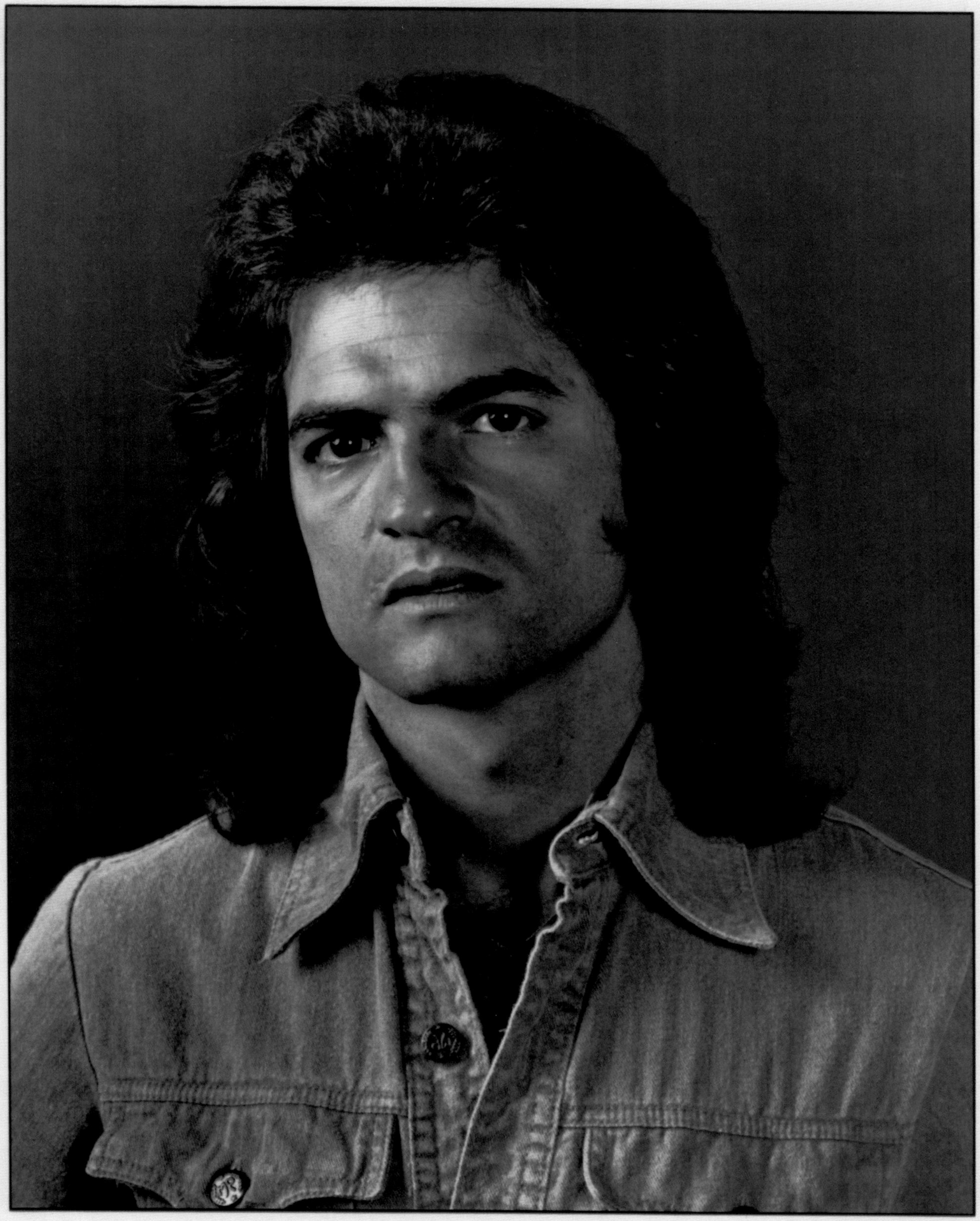

JOE VITALE

1981

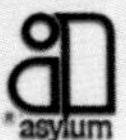

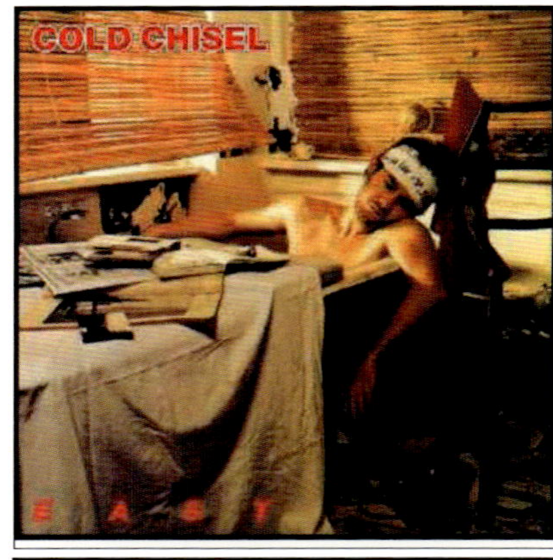

Billboard 200: *East* (#171)

Conquering America with *East* topped the list of priorities for Cold Chisel, the No. 1 group in Australia.

COLD CHISEL'S music was new to America, but the pub rock band arrived with a "bad boy" reputation from a recent incident in its native Australia. During a televised music awards ceremony, the members refused to appear on camera until the end of the show—despite being named the country's favorite band and taking seven awards out of 11 nominations. When the group finally appeared, singer Jim Barnes ranted at the music industry moguls in the audience, saying that he had never seen them at the band's early performances. A few smashed guitars and amplifiers later, Cold Chisel had a whole new slew of publicity.

"It's one of the first times that we've had a good time," Barnes said, laughing. "We had won over our fans, and then the establishment figured it was okay to step in and sanction our popularity. I'm not sure how they feel now."

Having grown accustomed to across-the-board acceptance—its new Australian release, *Swingshift,* a live double album, entered the Australian charts at No.1—Cold Chisel focused on having the same impact on America with *East,* its third Australian album and first US release. The group embarked on its inaugural tour of the US.

"Our live show will do it," Barnes predicted. "We've done heaps and heaps of support billings to American bands down in Australia. Now it's time to turn the tables and get things happening here."

America was slow to pick up on the record, although certain markets supported the single "My Baby." Credited to bass player Phil Small, the song featured a pop sound different from the band's hard-edged rock. "I would have preferred one of the Australian singles to be released first," Barnes admitted. "I'm the frontman, but I don't sing 'My Baby.' I would have liked 'Cheap Wine' (the band's first Top 10 single in Australia). But it had a drug reference in it—not pro or con, just a reference—and we were advised heavily against making it our first single."

Exercising that type of caution was completely out of character for Cold Chisel, whose first Australian single, "Khe Sanh" (included on the US version of *East*), had been a cynical description of a Vietnam War veteran's experiences. Although Australian radio stations refused to play it—keyboardist and main songwriter Don Walker said, "They told us they objected to the line, 'Their legs were often open'"—the song went Top 20 in 1978. ■

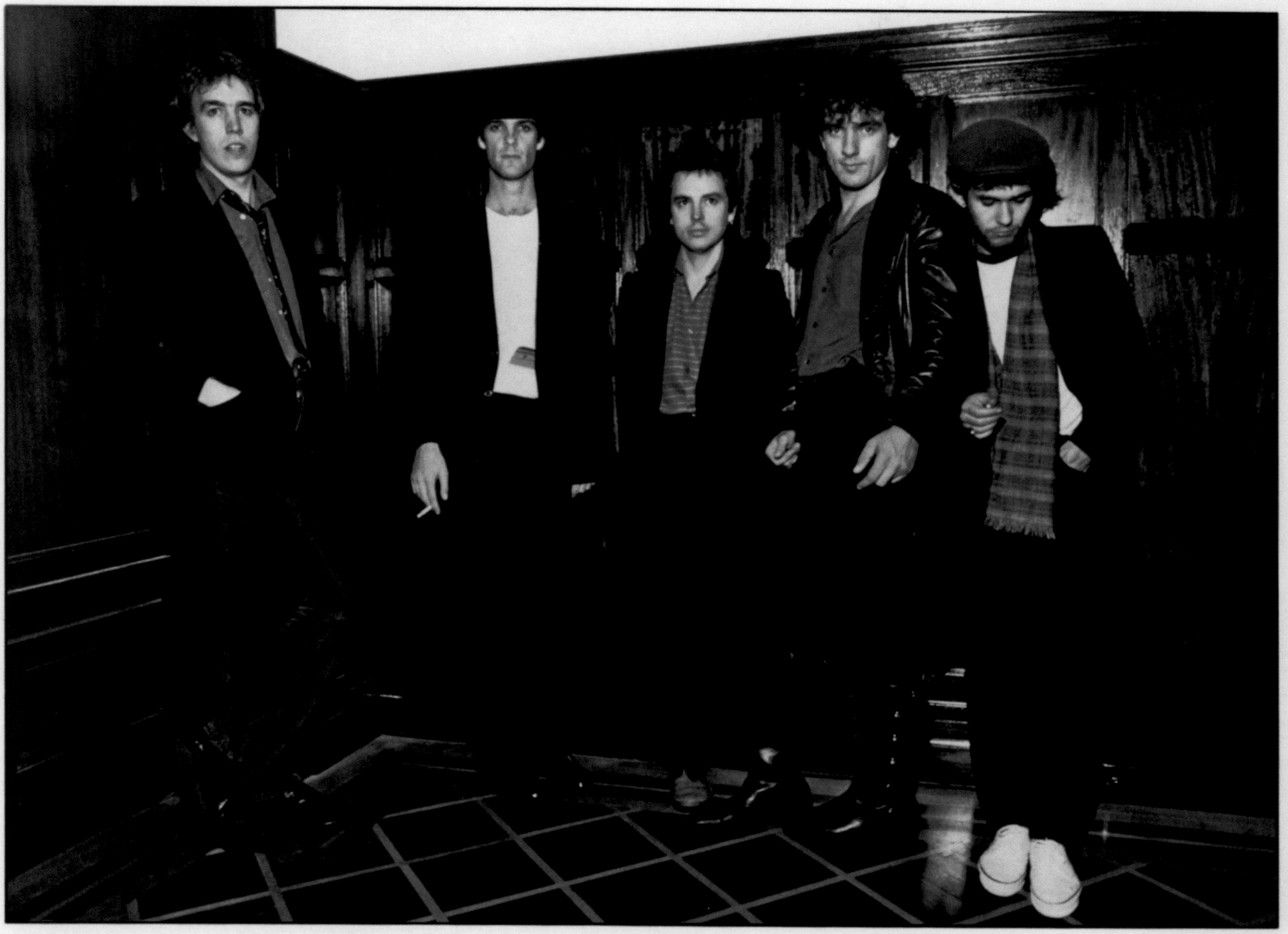

STEVEN PRESTWICH DON WALKER PHIL SMALL IAN MOSS JIM BARNES

COLD CHISEL

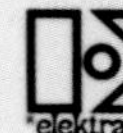

Billboard 200: *Waiata* (#45)

The first New Zealand band to achieve international success, Split Enz continued growing its popularity with *Waiata*.

FOUNDED BY singer Tim Finn and guitarist Phil Judd, Split Enz hailed from New Zealand, hardly the rock capital of the world. The members played a distinctly uncommercial brand of progressive rock, made all the more inaccessible by their wild costuming, odd hairstyles and makeup. The band's sole American tour in 1977 lasted only a couple of weeks and almost split up Split Enz.

One great song turned around the group's fortunes. Following the contentious tour, Finn's brother Neil had joined the group, and in 1980, his alluring "I Got You" showcased Split Enz's new streamlined approach and became a worldwide smash, making the band a hot property.

"We never gave it a thought to make our music consciously commercial," Tim Finn said, "but it was definitely put-up-or-shut-up time. We're not exactly Tin Pan Alley songwriters, but we have a strong sense of melody. When we brought in Neil, no one knew how good he was as a songwriter—he was just to be an extra singer and guitarist. 'I Got You' was only the third song he'd ever written—not too bad for a novice."

Waiata proved that the group's command of pop stylings was no flash in the pan. "History Never Repeats" and "One Step Ahead"—notable in that it set up a repeating pattern rather than the standard verse/chorus structure—climbed the charts in several countries and became among the first music videos to air on MTV in the US. Live, the band had made similar strides in presenting its material.

"I've always been into theater and the English music hall tradition," Tim Finn allowed. "And my mom's Irish, and they're great raconteurs. In the old days, we took great pains to maintain a distance from the audience, and that got us nowhere. Now our show is more of a direct conversation, although it's formally presented—I'm rather like a master of ceremonies. We used to be detached, but now we invite participation." ■

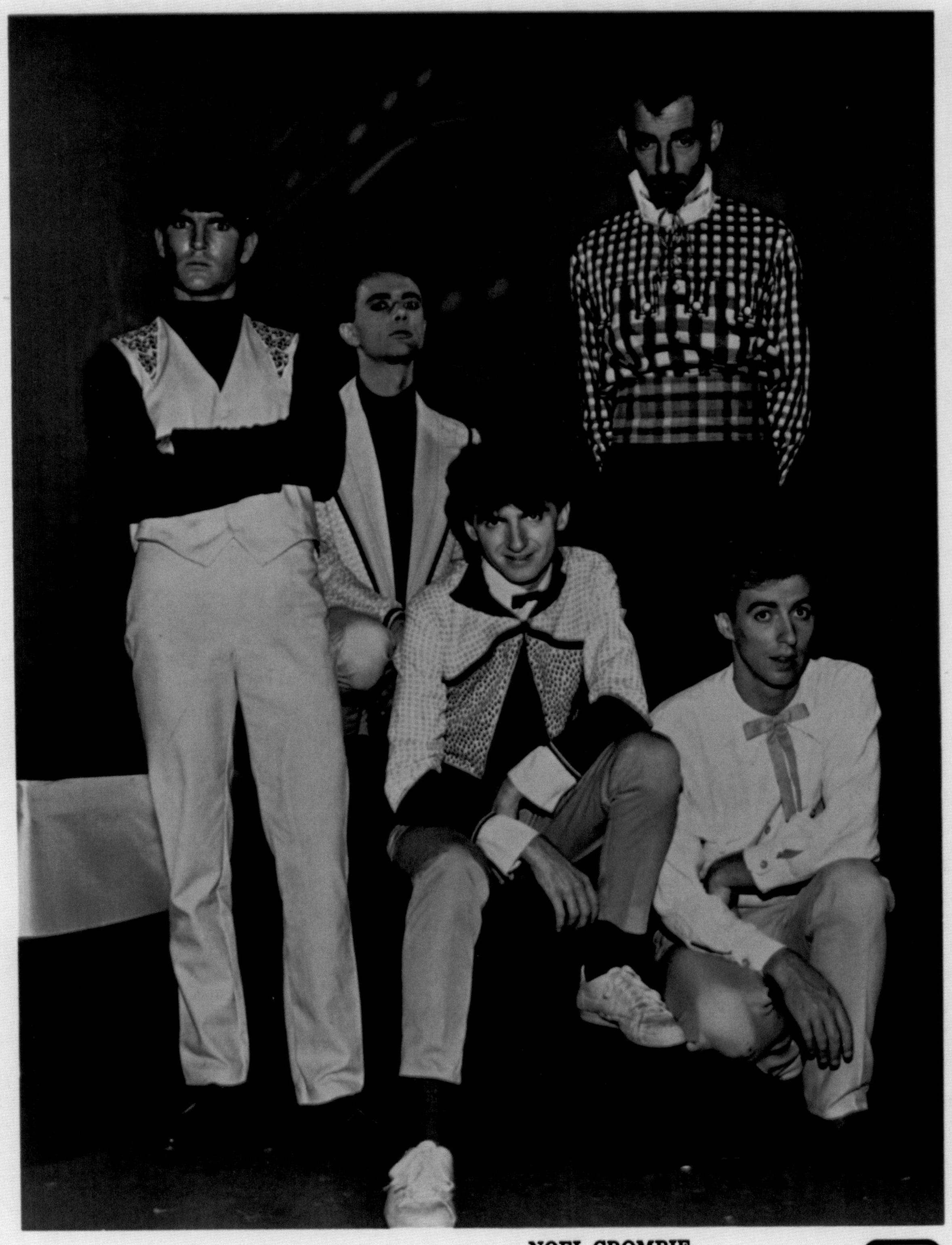

NOEL CROMBIE

TIM FINN   NIGEL GRIGGS   NEIL FINN   EDDIE RAYNER

SPLIT ENZ

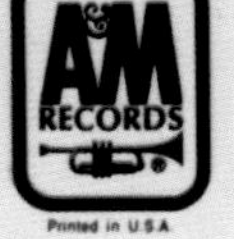

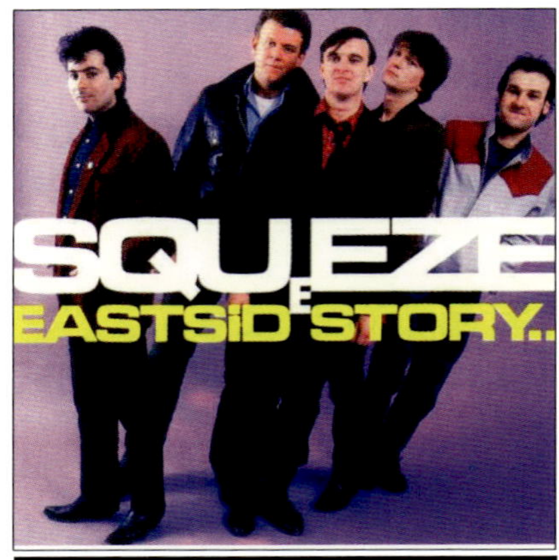

Billboard 200: *East Side Story* (#44)
Billboard Hot 100: "Tempted" (#49)

The post-punk English band Squeeze attained mainstream American airplay with the soulful sway of "Tempted."

BROUGHT TOGETHER in 1974 by an ad in a shop window, musicians Chris Difford and Glenn Tilbrook founded Squeeze, releasing a self-titled debut record in 1978 when the hardcore British punk movement was in high gear.

"The record company was just as confused as we were," guitarist Tilbrook admitted. "Our first press release described us as 'five angry young men roaming the streets of England.' We were labeled a new-wave band because we came out of that time, but we never had anything to do with it."

Difford and Tilbrook quickly developed into a crack composing team, and Squeeze made a move for recognition in England as intelligent purveyors of post-punk irreverence. But the group didn't catch on commercially the way people predicted, and another tribulation occurred when keyboard player Jools Holland, a fast-talking cigar-chomping extrovert, left to form his own band. His absence left the other members—Tilbrook, Difford, drummer Gilson Lavis and bassist John Bentley—to pick up the slack.

"He just got frustrated," Tilbrook said of the amicable split. "He was developing into a frontman, but he was only getting to sing a couple of songs."

Holland's departure seemed to serve as a catalyst for better things, however. After interminable auditions for a replacement, Pete Thomas of Elvis Costello's Attractions recommended Paul Carrack, who wrote and sang the hit "How Long" with the group Ace in 1975. With *East Side Story*, Squeeze delivered a testament that perfectly captured its wit and fine melodies. Tillbrook credited Costello, who produced the album.

"We'd always taken three or four months to record an album prior to this, trying to get things perfect—and we never had any fun," Tillbrook admitted. "This time we got the feel, and it's apparent in the sound."

Although Tilbrook handled vocals on the majority of songs, keyboardist Carrack took the singing spotlight on "Tempted," the band's first charting US hit. "In terms of songwriting, that was a big step forward for us," Tilbrook said.

Squeeze's aptitude for classic songcraft was never in question. "I don't know why people get turned off when you're referred to as a pop band," Tilbrook allowed. "If you think of Rupert Holmes as pop, then I guess it's understandable. But we're not rubbish pop—the Beatles were a pop group, if people can remember that far back." ■

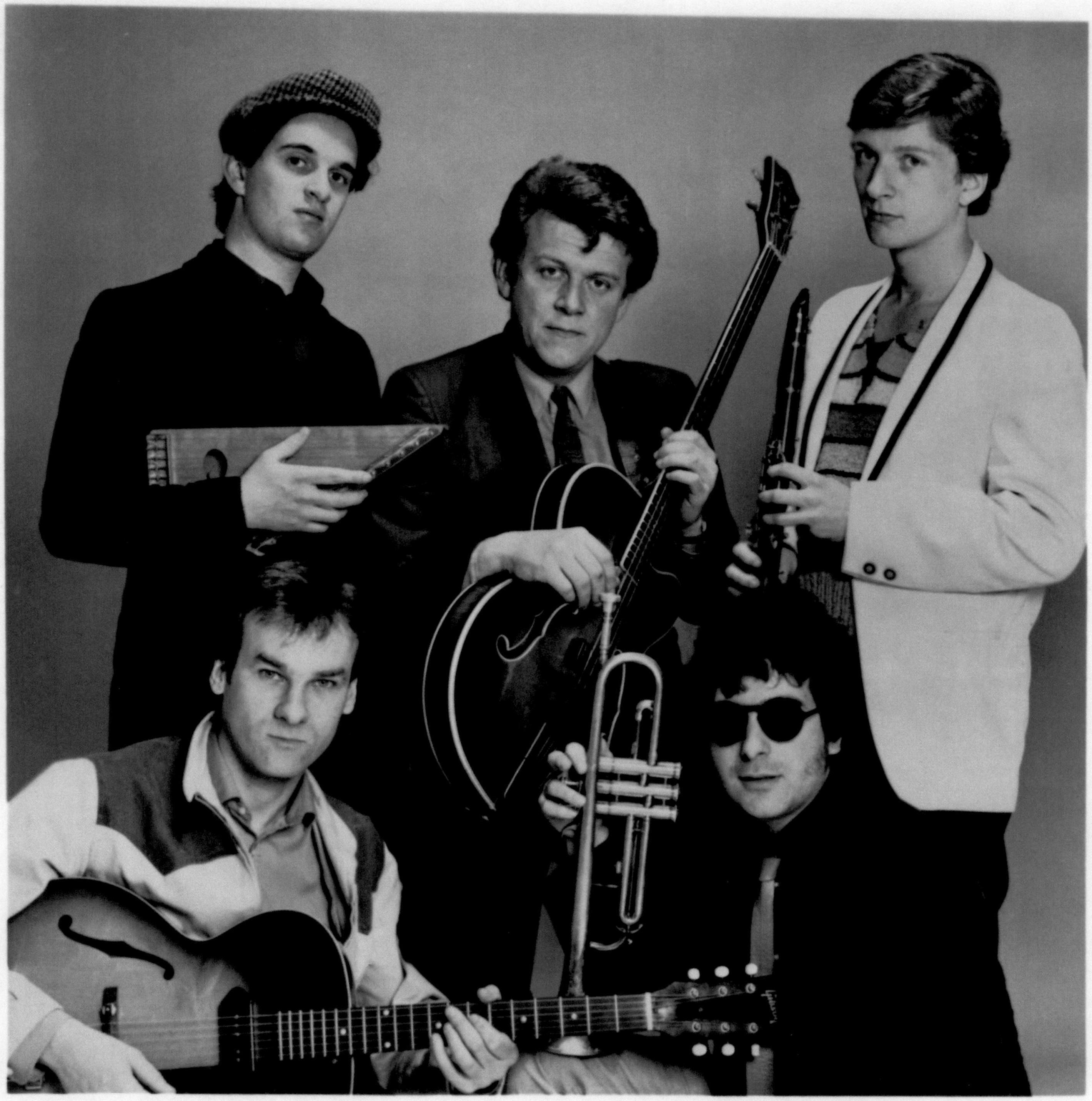

CHRIS DIFFORD
PAUL CARRACK

GILSON LAVIS

GLENN TILBROOK
JOHN BENTLEY

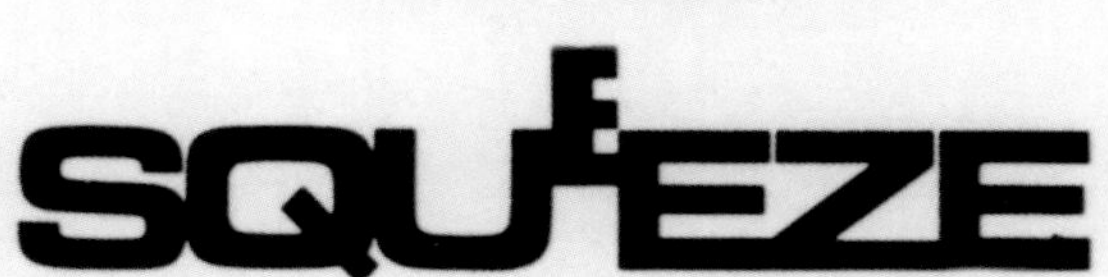

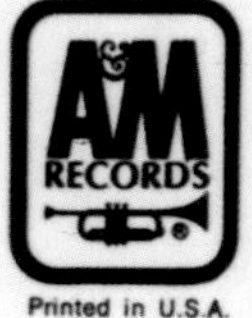

Printed in U.S.A.

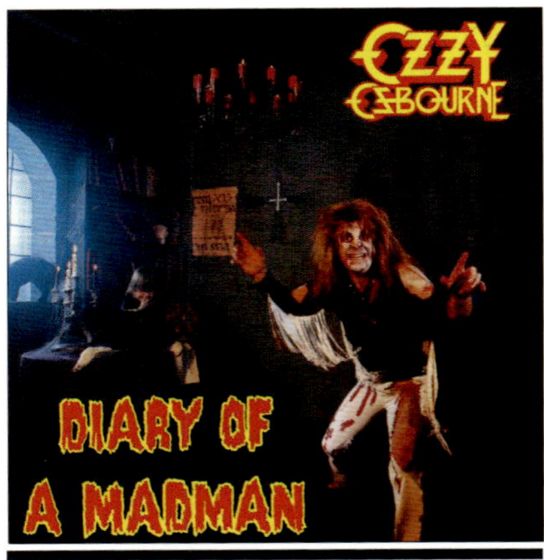

Billboard 200: *Diary of a Madman* (#16)

Ozzy Osbourne continued the madness with the release of his second post-Sabbath effort, *Diary of a Madman.*

THE MOST outrageous, controversial and outspoken rock hero in the music world, Ozzy Osbourne's name created a fervor in the general public. "I'm the guy your mother likes to hate," the former Black Sabbath lead singer said. The success of 1980's *Blizzard of Ozz* had ensured Osbourne's future, and his energetic young guitarist, Randy Rhoads, had become one of heavy metal's most acclaimed players.

Immediately after the album's release, Osbourne revamped his band, canning the rhythm section to include drummer Tommy Aldridge and bassist Rudy Sarzo. But he had already recorded and readied for release his second solo album, *Diary of a Madman*, with his old unit.

"I had to get something out right away—I was frightened that people would forget me," Osbourne explained. "See, you could put four dummies up on a stage, call them Black Sabbath, and they'd fill a hall. Black Sabbath always had this weird cult following—we had black magic stuff thrown on stage perpetually. I'm definitely glad to be away from that. I'm a bit of a crazy fucker, but that's all."

Rhoads ended up providing the musical muscle of "Flying High Again" and "Over the Mountain." The giant theatrical rock tour in support of *Diary of a Madman* was the most ambitious undertaking in Osbourne's career, as he gleefully conceptualized macabre props and effects.

"It's the grossest show ever, and only I could think it up," Osbourne said. "I hang midgets and throw meat into the audience. There's gallons of pig's blood—and at the end of the show I explode!"

Not surprisingly, Osbourne's life was a series of crazy occurrences. During the tour, in Des Moines, Iowa, he sought treatment for rabies at two hospitals after a concert in which he reportedly bit the off the head of a bat thrown from the audience, supposedly thinking it was fake.

Shortly afterward, as the band headed to a concert in Orlando, Florida, Rhoads died in a bizarre and sadly avoidable accident that also nearly killed the rest of the entourage, as a Beechcraft F35 with Rhoads aboard struck the tour bus where the band members—including Osborne and his manager and wife, Sharon—were sleeping. ■

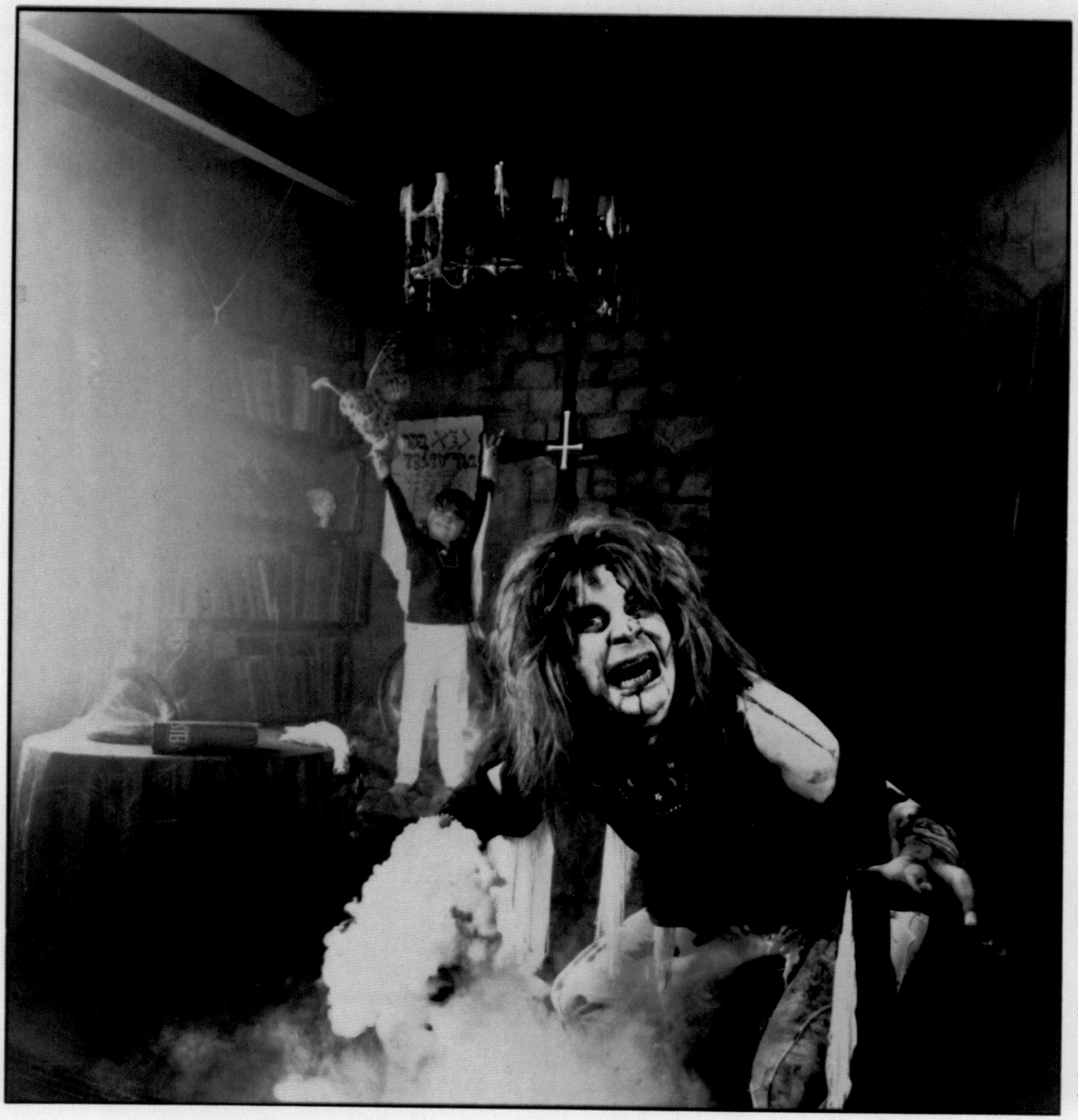

photo credit: FIN COSTELLO

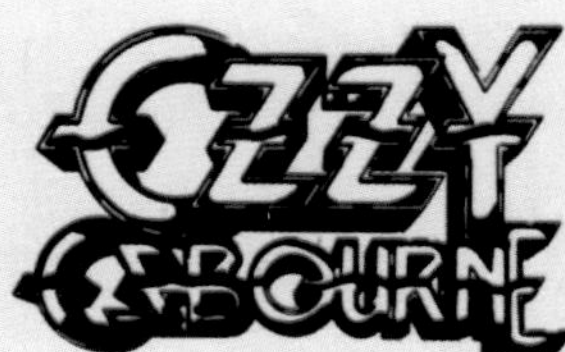

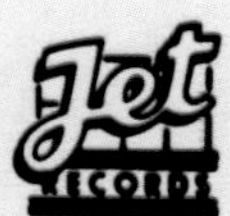

Billboard 200: *Mob Rules* (#29)

Mob Rules, the second album to feature Ronnie James Dio's powerful vocal style, reenergized Black Sabbath.

HEAVY-METAL singer Ronnie James Dio inherited quite a responsibility when he joined Black Sabbath, filling the shoes of the departed Ozzy Osbourne. Fronting the band was easy enough compared to the expectations of devotees who would run onstage to present the group with boa constrictors or carry upside-down crosses in hopes of getting the members to join their satanic cults.

Dio played down Black Sabbath's mythos. "The band has never preached what these fans say they have—we've always played music," he insisted. "If anyone's done it, it's Ozzy through the publicity he's generated in the past and in what he's doing now. If kids come up with the idea of black-magic-evil-baby-sacrificing, it's all of their own making. We run into weirdos who want us to touch them or give them the evil eye, but we're not hassled by it."

Dio had aligned with Black Sabbath after getting kicked out of Rainbow when he couldn't shoehorn his ego into the same act as guitarist Ritchie Blackmore. 1980's *Heaven and Hell* marked his recruitment, and *Mob Rules*, featuring "Turn Up the Night," "Voodoo" and the thundering title track, expanded the new lineup's musical evolution, which also included the addition of former Derringer drummer Vinnie Appice. Dio expected the latest version of Black Sabbath eventually to make its own mark, unhesitatingly calling the group "second to none, what I consider the greatest rock 'n' roll band on the road."

"We've remained popular on the road because of the original mystique that was built up," he mused. "People want to come and see what's going to happen—maybe they think goats are going to be blown up or something. But maybe it's because Black Sabbath has always been a people's band, a street-level band. And we were the first heavy-metal group—people want to go see the legend and keep it alive."

But Dio still wanted to be accepted as something more. Although the rest of the band wasn't too thrilled about it, the diminutive frontman had plans to record his first solo album.

"The biggest part of the band's revitalization has been myself," he noted in precise, clipped tones, "and I don't say that to pat myself on the back. A vocalist is the one that's going to be seen and heard in a group. Ozzy had extreme character, but as far as sparking another musician onstage with him to greater heights, that was an impossibility." ■

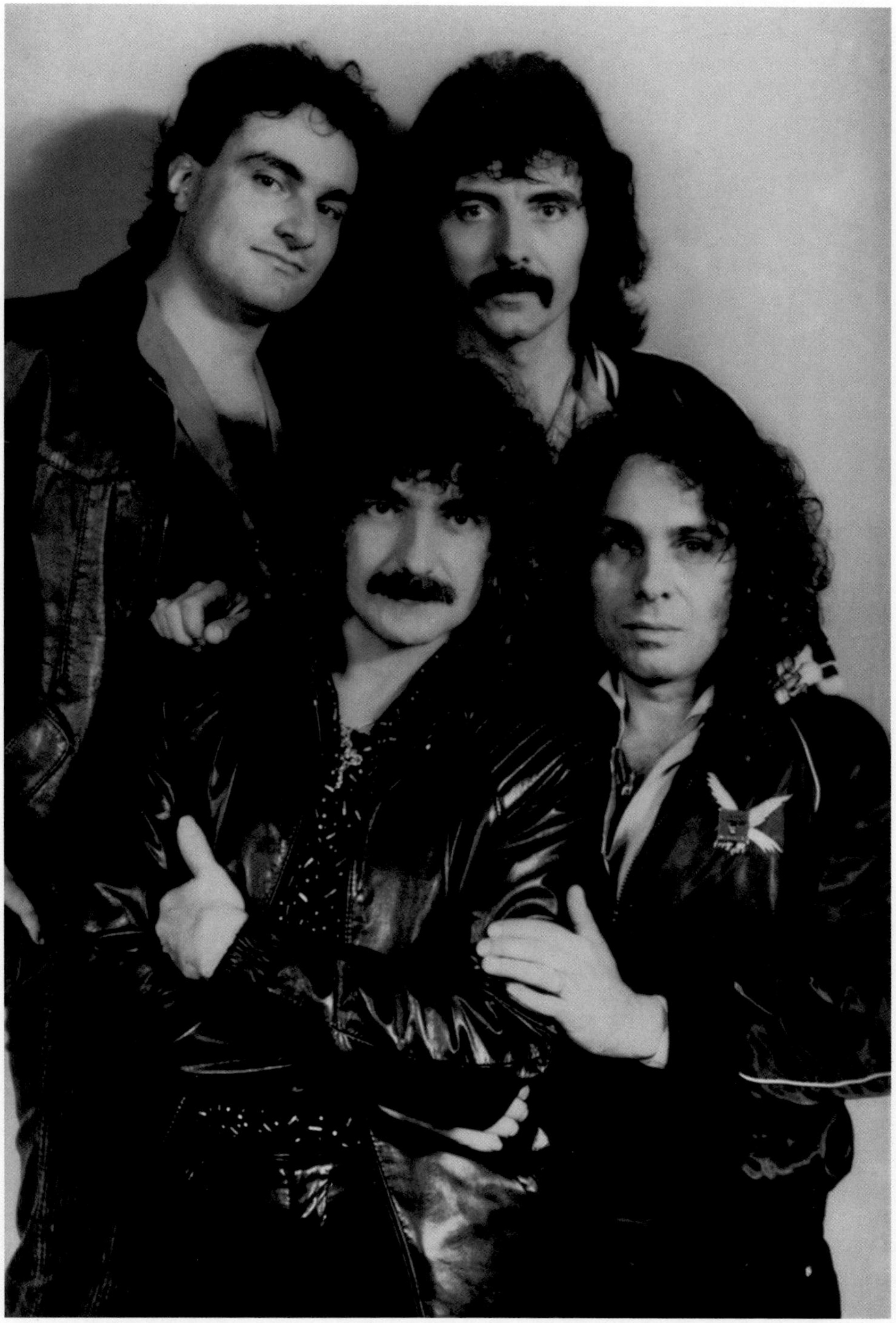

BLACK SABBATH

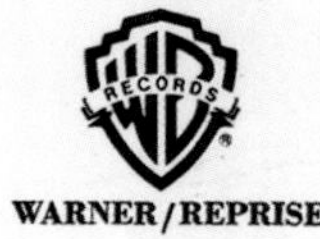

Billboard 200: *High 'n' Dry* (#38)

On *High 'n' Dry*, its second album, Def Leppard took its British bombast beyond basic heavy-metal tastes.

A GROUP of enthusiastic kids from the industrial confines of Sheffield, Def Leppard emerged in the late Seventies as part of the "New Wave of British Heavy Metal." The group's "throat" (as he described himself) Joe Elliott explained how the band got its name.

"At school, I used to draw posters for imaginary gigs and I made the name up. The rest of the guys were up in the bedroom one day and saw the poster and took to the name—it could have been anything." Initially, the moniker was spelled in its proper form, which, for some reason, attracted a lot of punks to gigs. Needing to appeal to a more appropriate audience, the band decided to modify it. "Everyone said we did it because it looked like Led Zeppelin," Elliott said. "We didn't mind. It was better to look like them than the Boomtown Rats."

Signing up with a management company that negotiated a recording deal and a rigorous touring schedule supporting AC/DC, Def Leppard was almost instantly regarded as the cream of the crop of new metal groups. "I agree that other bands have had time to evolve and grow up in the small clubs," Elliott put it. "We're making our mistakes in front of thousands of people, but I still wouldn't have wanted it any other way."

For *High 'n' Dry*, Def Leppard worked with AC/DC producer Robert John "Mutt" Lange, whose meticulous approach in the studio helped the band begin to define its style, toning down the heavy riffs and emphasizing melody. The standout track "Bringin' On the Heartbreak," an unabashedly dramatic rock ballad, became one of the first videos played on MTV, and the strong rotation brought the band increased visibility in the US.

The youthful members, just nearing the legal drinking age, learned the ropes of touring America through on-the-job training. "It's tired us out," Elliott admitted. "Tempers get flared when you have a bus that sleeps nine and there's fourteen guys in the band and crew. We can't afford separate buses. But we're committed to touring. We'll always be out six to eight months a year."

Where other groups such as Iron Maiden and Saxon contented themselves with perpetuating a heavy-metal tradition, Def Leppard saw room for its "melodic hard rock" within the genre.

"We're looking to be heard in a commercial sense," Elliott said. "Bands like REO Speedwagon, Led Zeppelin, Thin Lizzy and UFO have all played hard rock and cleaned it up so more people could enjoy it. We're trying to go much in the same direction." ■

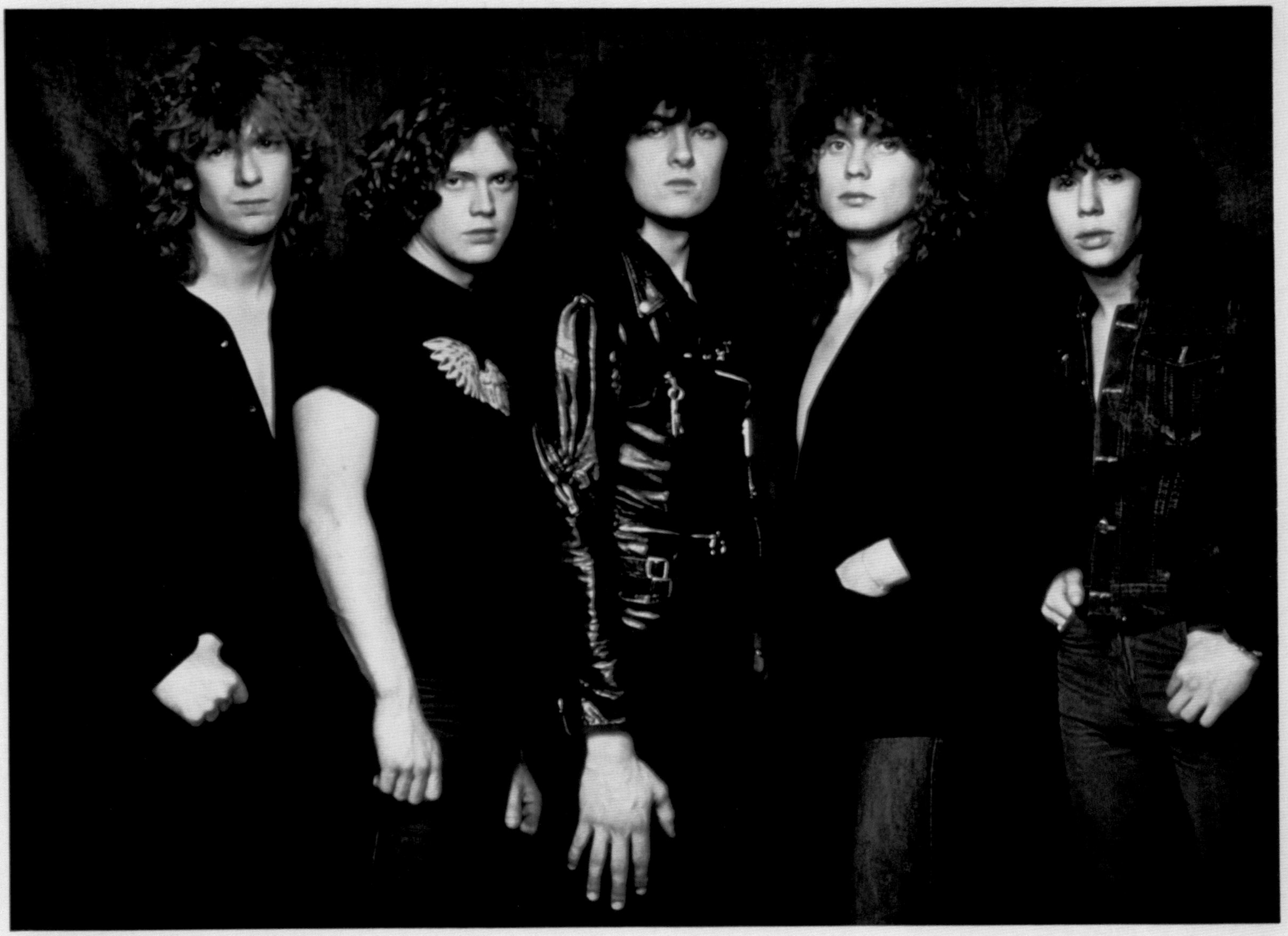

DEF LEPPARD

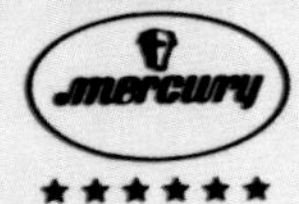

PolyGram Records

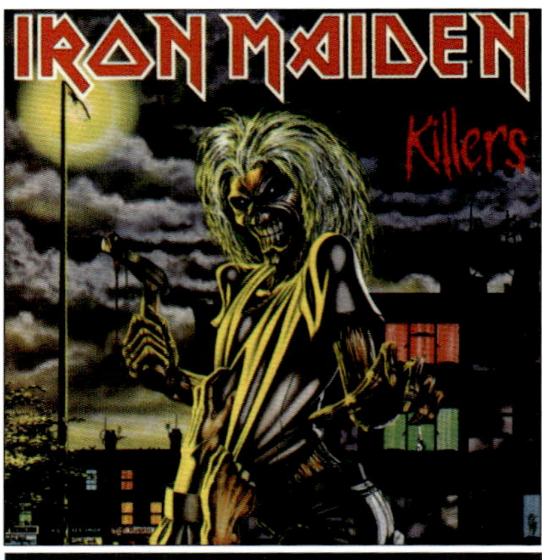

Billboard 200: *Killers* (#78)

The success of the sophomore album *Killers* propelled British metal band Iron Maiden's maiden tour of the US.

NAMED AFTER the medieval torture device, Iron Maiden made its way from the seamy working-class pub scene of London's East End. Releasing a debut album in 1980, the group came to prominence along with Motörhead, Def Leppard and Saxon, spearheading "the New Wave of British Heavy Metal"—a movement peddled by the British press encouraging new bands and replacing Deep Purple and other tax exiles.

"Just a year before, we'd been on the verge of total collapse, not through any musical doubts or problems, but simply because the money it was costing us all in loss of day-job work threatened to stop the band in its tracks," bassist Steve Harris said. "And now we've got EMI saying to us, 'We want to sign you lads up to a long-term worldwide deal.' We'd only ever dreamed of something like that being said to us."

Iron Maiden released a second studio album, *Killers*, produced by Martin Birch (renowned for his work with Deep Purple, Rainbow and Black Sabbath). The band's zombie-like mascot, Eddie, appeared in the iconic cover art wielding a bloody axe as his dying victim clawed at his shirt. The illustration for "Twilight Zone," a single included on the US version of *Killers*, depicted Eddie's spirit reaching towards a young woman through a mirror.

"The artwork goes along with the music and lyrics—it gives fans a bit more to hang on to," guitarist Dave Murray said. "People can get into heavy metal and go with it. It's not a fickle type of music; it's black and white—you either love it or hate it."

Killers was followed by Iron Maiden's first world tour, featuring shows in America as guests of Judas Priest.

"You've got to keep things in perspective," vocalist Paul Di'Anno reasoned. "I don't want people to start muttering, 'Oh, look, there's so-and-so from Maiden, shall we talk to him or shan't we?' Bollocks! They should be able to say, 'Hello, mate, how you going? I thought you played like a twat the other night!'"

The rigors of touring brought on drugging and drinking by Di'Anno. After the tour, he was dismissed for his increasing unreliability and replaced by Bruce Dickinson. ■

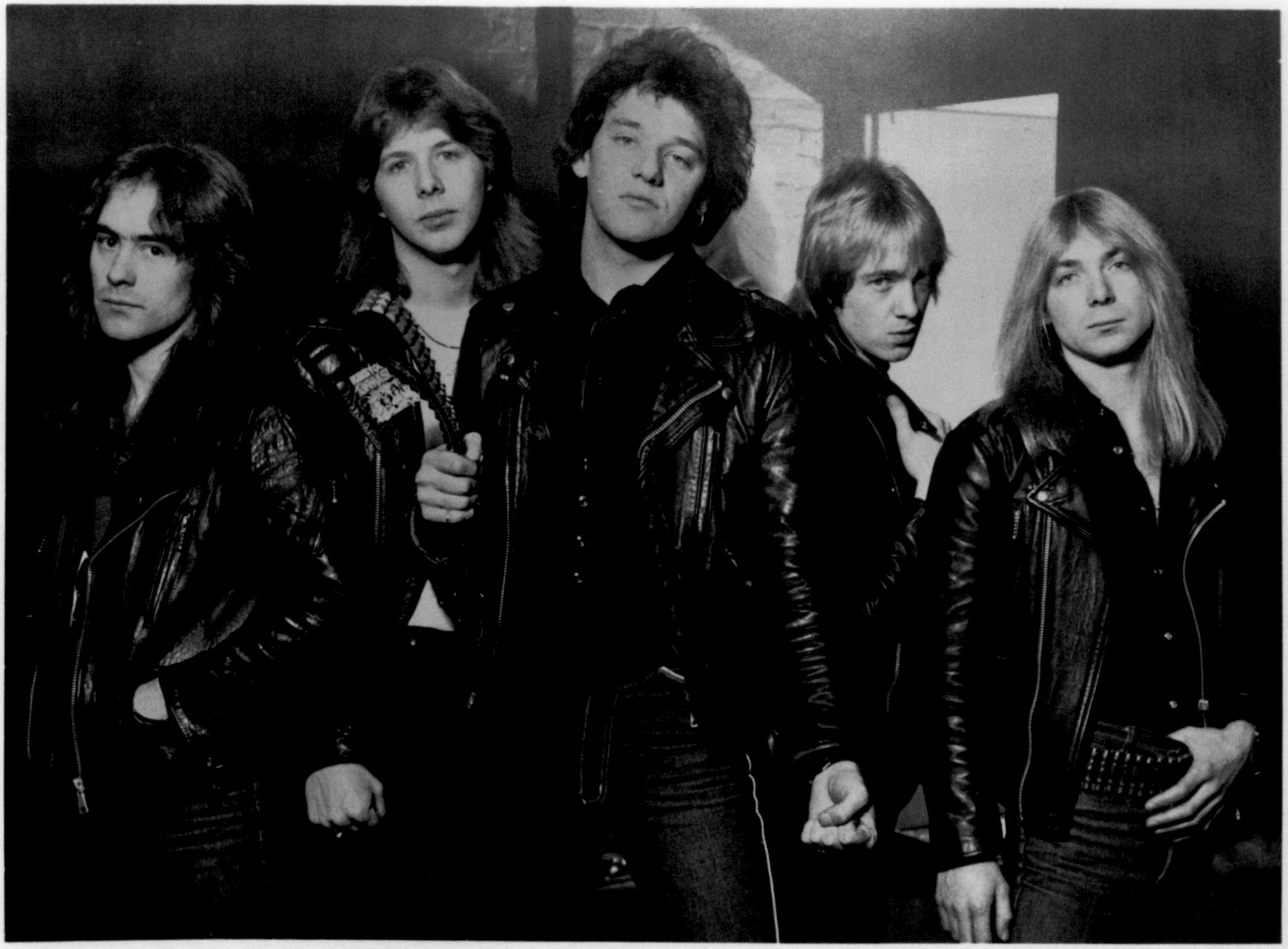

Steve Harris Clive Burr Paul Di'anno Adrian Smith Dave Murray

IRON MAIDEN

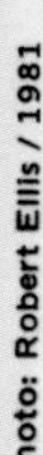

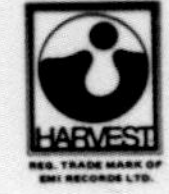

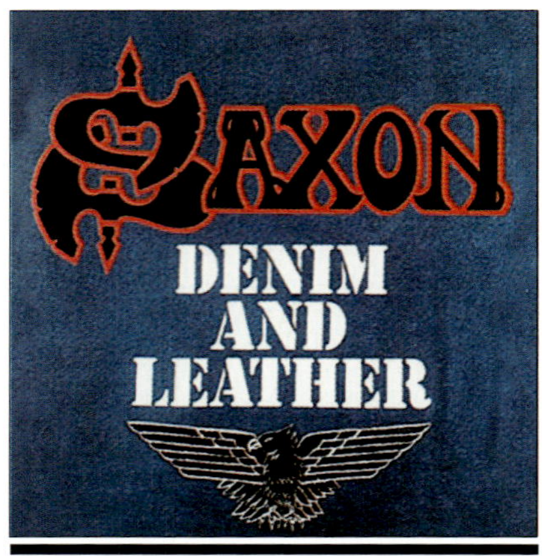

Heavy-metal standout Saxon aimed to ride its ear-splitting European momentum into the American market.

WHEN SAXON started out in 1977, punk groups such as the Sex Pistols and the Clash were the rage. But the five band members, who hailed from South Yorkshire, stuck to their guns.

"At first they told us to piss it—the press simply wanted something to sell papers," Biff Byford, the band's lead vocalist, stated. "Then the new wave was sensational enough to do just that. The movement is pretty dead now. And now the press is turning its attention to something else, and it just happens to be heavy metal this time."

The media generated hype and established Saxon as a leading force in the "New Wave of British Heavy Metal" movement with Iron Maiden and Def Leppard. Slogging the British club circuit, Saxon had acquired the reputation of a tireless, barnstorming band and built a loyal following with its musical thunder. *Denim and Leather* featured the title track, a metal anthem inspired by metalhead culture.

"We're the loudest band in Britain, and eventually we had to get noticed," Byford asserted. "After a while, it got to the point where bands were posting decibel counts. I think the ultimate goal was to see who'd be the first band to kill someone with sound!" ■

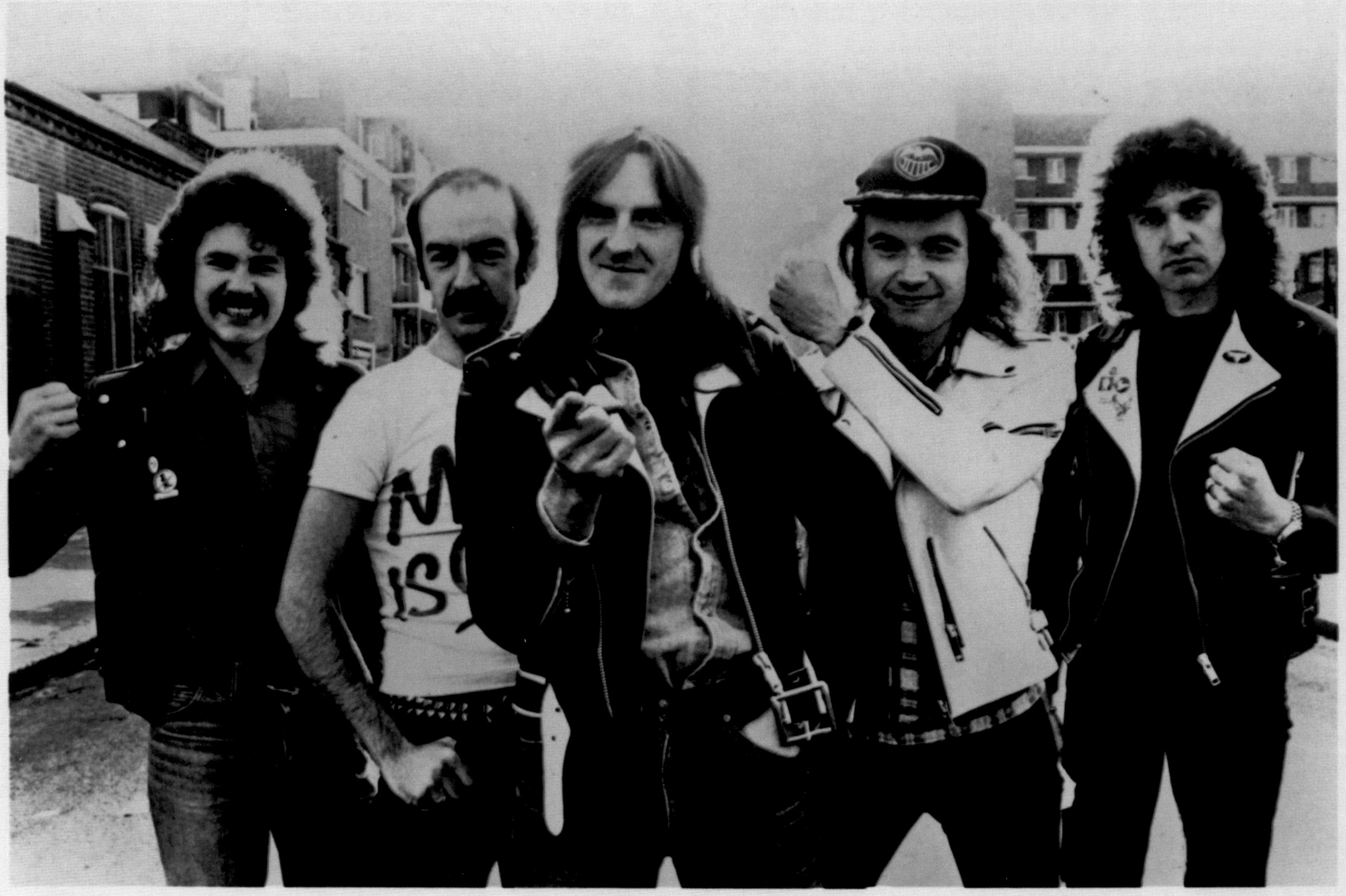

CARRERE
RECORDS

Saxon

MICHAEL SCHENKER GROUP

Billboard 200: *MSG* (#81)

The heyday of Michael Schenker Group's short career was brilliantly encapsulated on the album *MSG*.

BY WAILING on his trademark black-and-white Gibson Flying V guitar, Michael Schenker was held in high esteem by in-the-know hard-rock fans. As a 15-year-old, the German guitarist joined Scorpions (the band co-founded by his elder brother Rudolf Schenker) in 1971, and he propelled UFO during its 1974-1978 glory days. He remained an undeniable guitar talent who combined blazing speed with a rare clarity of structure and style, but he had become notorious for disappearing from UFO without any notice, leaving the rest of the group helpless and abandoned in the middle of tours.

The intense Schenker started a solo career, beginning with the studio album *The Michael Schenker Group*, and got off to a promising start. During tours of America, Europe and Japan, crowds warmly welcomed him and his touring band of Gary Barden (vocals), ex-UFO rhythm guitarist and keyboard player Paul Raymond, former Sensational Alex Harvey Band bassist Chris Glen and veteran drummer Cozy Powell, who'd recently departed from Rainbow.

That lineup recorded the second album, *MSG*, with Ron Nevison's elevated production skills guiding the release. His fans regarded it as Schenker's finest hour. But the album went over budget, and Schenker continued to have problems communicating. He didn't speak much English, a hurdle with his British-American bandmates.

"I think the songs are better than last time," he said, coached by his publicist. "The group is working well after the past year's tour, and the musicians fit my music."

The band continued touring in Europe and Japan, but personality conflicts and incidents followed. ■

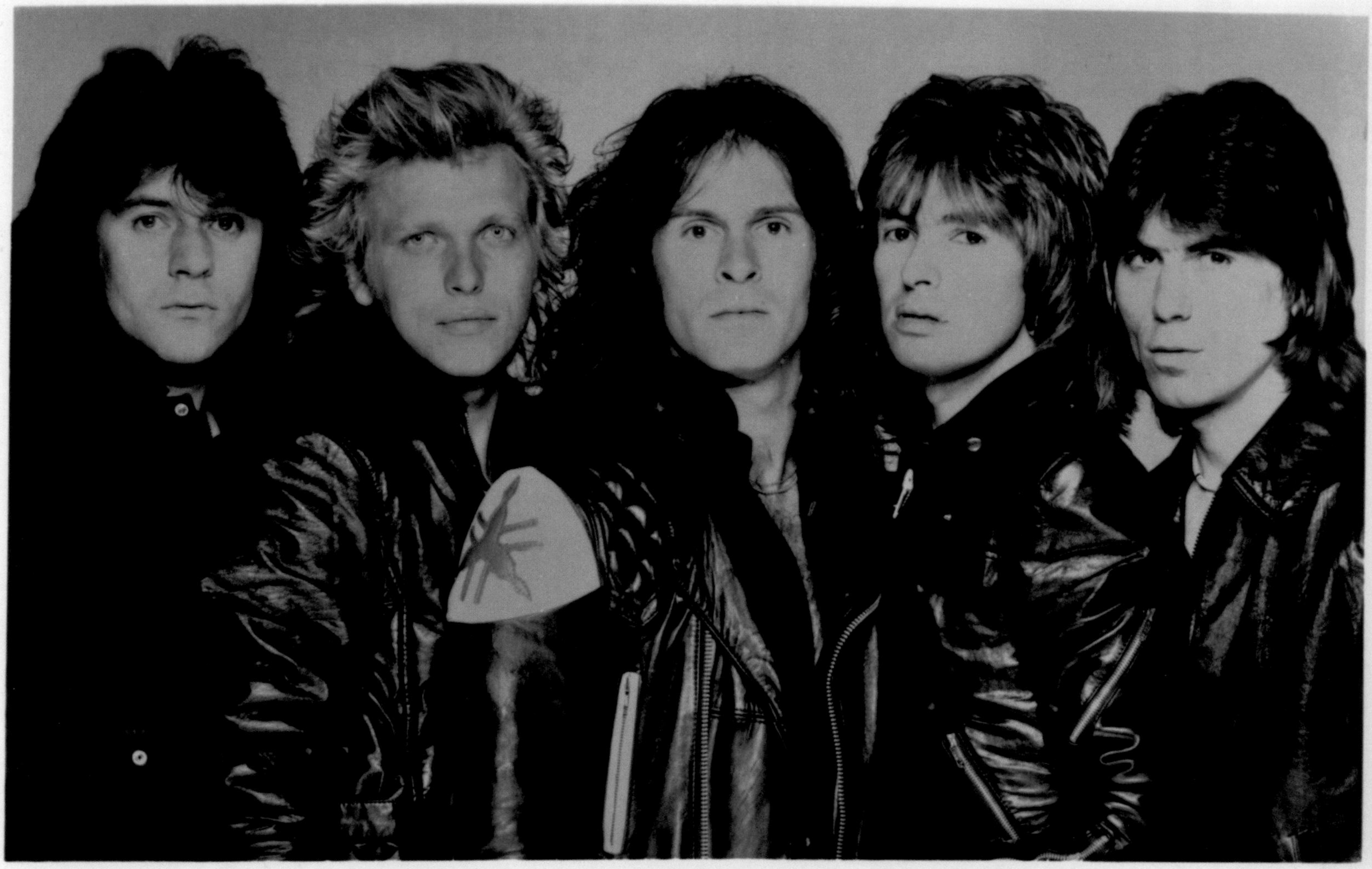

MICHAEL SCHENKER GROUP

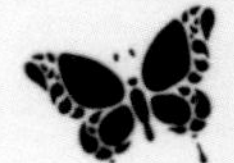

Chrysalis

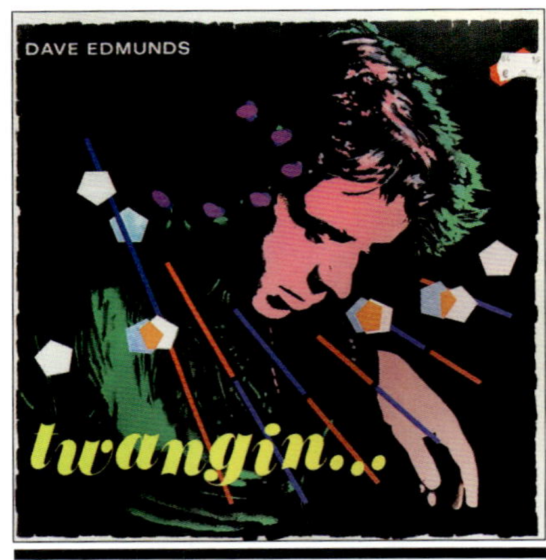

Billboard 200: *Twangin...* (#48)
Billboard Hot 100: "Almost Saturday Night" (#54)

Dave Edmunds' cover of "Almost Saturday Night," penned by John Fogerty, attained more success than the original.

ONE OF Britain's musical heroes, Dave Edmunds stayed true to the roots of Fifties and Sixties rock 'n' roll. His love of rockabilly yielded "I Hear You Knocking," a gigantic American hit in the early Seventies, and his stylized updating of stock Chuck Berry riffs established him as an artist and as a producer.

In 1976, he signed with Swan Song Records and formed Rockpile, which existed as some kind of mythical ideal rock band. Comprised of Nick Lowe on bass, Edmunds and Billy Bremmer on guitars and Terry Williams on drums, the four Englishmen played as a unit on Edmunds' records through the Seventies and on two of Lowe's solo albums. But Rockpile had to wait until its 1980 "debut" album, *Seconds of Pleasure*, to record under its own name. Basically, Edmunds and Lowe were under separate recording contracts, with Edmunds especially trapped by his circumstance.

With Rockpile on the verge of major success shortly after the release of its first bona fide album, an unexpected rift between band members developed, and they issued a joint statement announcing their demise. Most observers figured that Lowe would have the edge over Edmunds in the commercial potential of their ensuing solo careers.

But Edmunds emerged with the upper hand. His last solo piece for Swan Song, *Twangin...* was recorded as Rockpile was in the process of breaking up.

"It does seem to be working out," Edmunds said with a chuckle. "If I attribute it to anything, it's that I didn't sit around and mope when Rockpile split. There wasn't any sense in thinking about what had happened. I just wanted to move on."

Edmunds, who had recently produced the debut effort by the Stray Cats, asked them to perform on *Twangin...* The album generated a hit cover of John Fogerty's "Almost Saturday Night," putting Edmunds in the musical mainstream.

"Well, it's nice," Edmunds allowed. "But I've always enjoyed what I'm doing anyway." ■

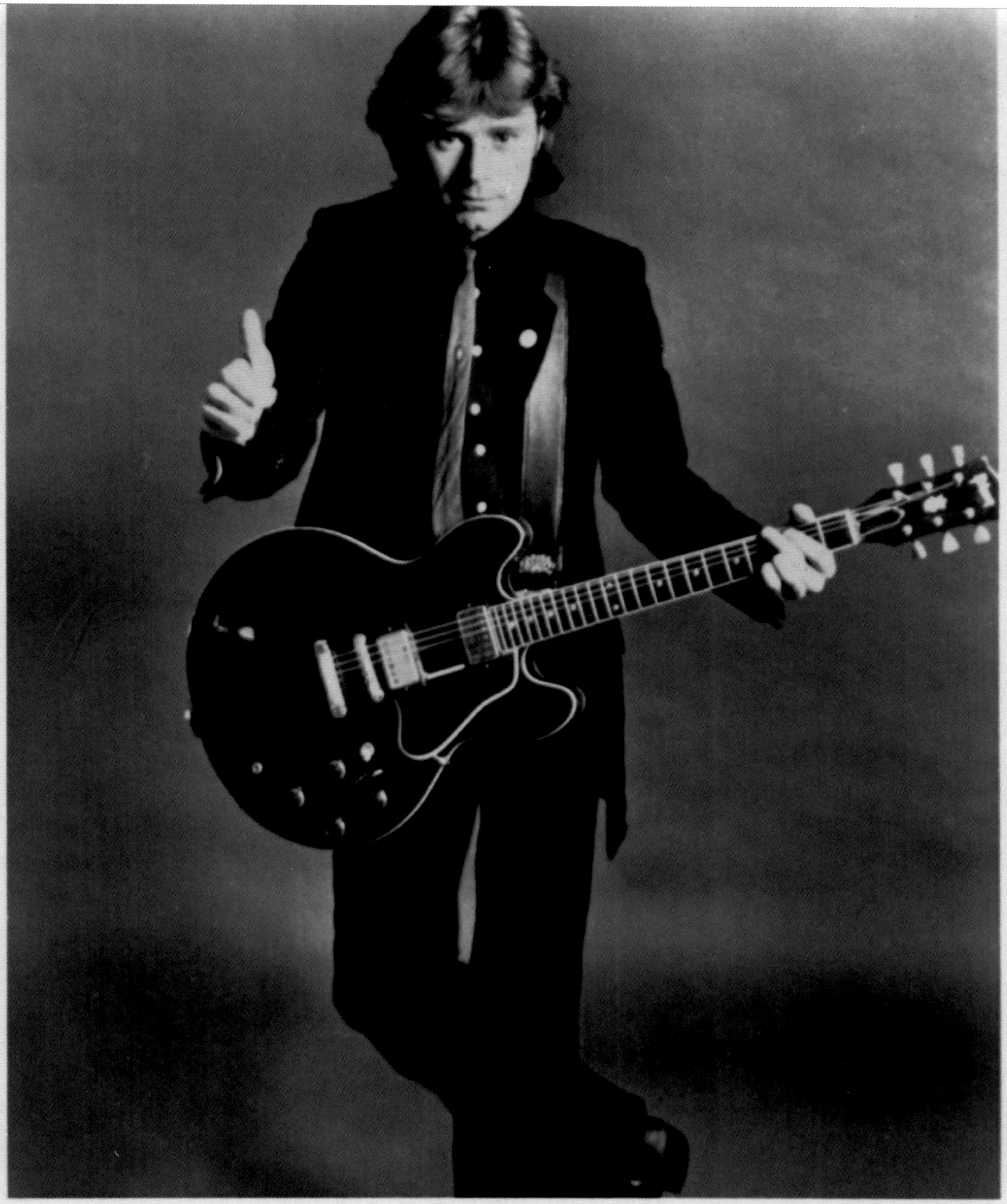

DAVE EDMUNDS

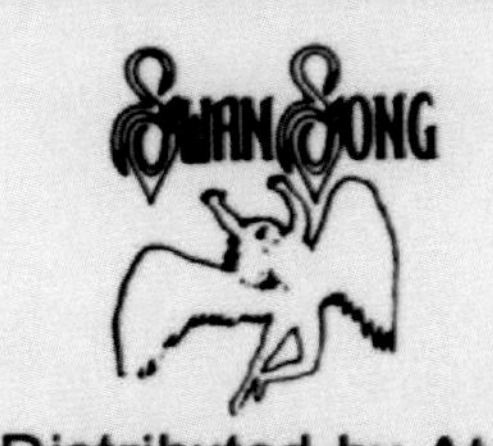

Distributed by Atco

Billboard 200: *Moving Pictures* (#3)
Billboard Hot 100: "Limelight" (#55); "Tom Sawyer" (#44)

Rush's popularity reached its pinnacle with *Moving Pictures* and the singles "Tom Sawyer" "Limelight" and "YYZ."

RUSH HAD started to improve its songwriting, featuring tighter structures with more radio-friendly lengths compared to the early prog-rock albums. The change in the Canadian power trio's direction emerged while on tour in support of 1980's *Permanent Waves*. During sound checks, new songs developed that interested the members enough to perform them live.

"In a short tour, mainly the eastern seaboard of the United States, we rehearsed the five completed songs whenever possible, and introduced 'Tom Sawyer' and 'Limelight' into our shows," drummer Neil Peart said. "Both underwent some changes before being committed to tape."

Fully prepared, Rush then recorded *Moving Pictures,* the most elaborate venture yet. Extending the instrumental acumen that helped thrust the band into the spotlight, Peart, guitarist Alex Lifeson and bassist and vocalist Geddy Lee investigated new sound textures on synthesizers and sequencers, increasing the band's capacity to arrange material.

"We were painfully aware of the ambitious nature of our project, as we had to work long and hard," Peart said. "It took relentless grinding to capture the right sounds and performances for each track—'Tom Sawyer,' 'Limelight' and 'YYZ.'"

The studio had been recently outfitted with a digital 48-track machine, which necessitated the band members to spend time familiarizing themselves with the equipment. *Moving Pictures* was producer Terry Brown's first digitally-produced album.

"The tracks were eventually finished when the disasters began," Peart explained. "In a massive electronic freak-out revolution, the digital mastering machine, the mixdown computer and one of the multitrack machines gave up their collective ghosts one after the other, setting us two weeks behind. After much technical tearing of hair and gnashing of teeth, the machine maladies were finally put right. It's a curious sensation, when listening back to a completed album for the first time, how quickly all those months and difficulties go racing by. Suddenly you're listening without analyzing, feeling the responses that you hope the listener at home will feel."

The lead track, "Tom Sawyer," became Rush's most renowned song, and "Limelight," which examined the pros and cons of stardom, received a gratifying response from listeners and radio stations. The instrumental "YYZ" received a Grammy Award nomination for Best Rock Instrumental Performance. ■

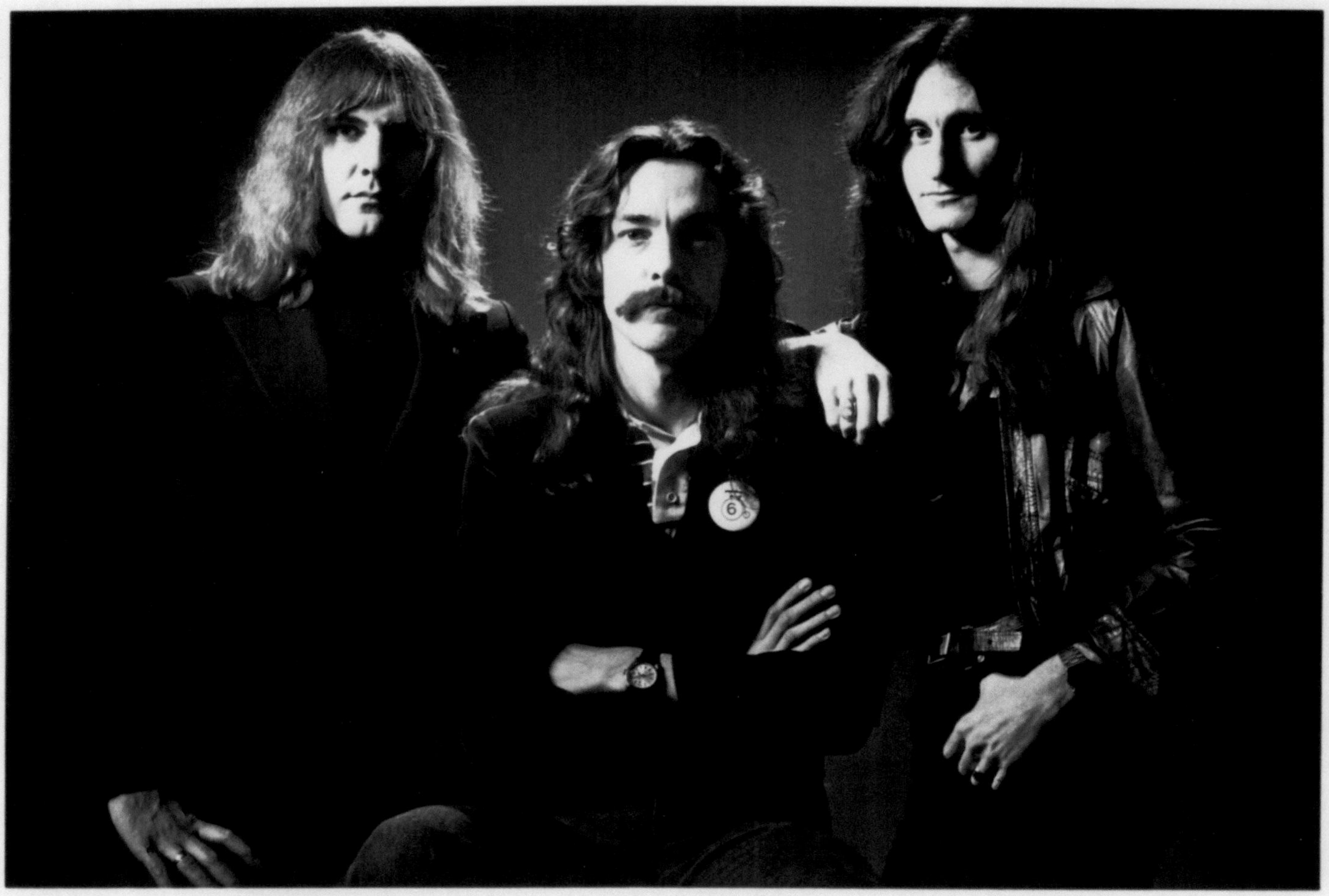

ALEX LIFESON NEIL PEART GEDDY LEE

RUSH

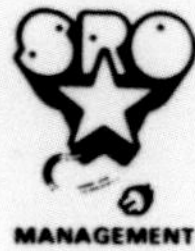

Recording Exclusively For

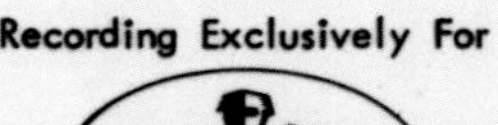

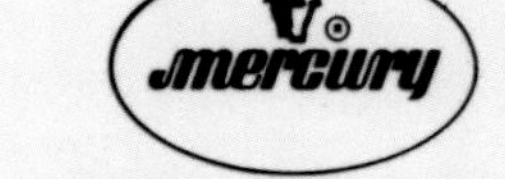

A product of Phonogram, Inc.

Billboard 200: *Great White North* (#8)
Billboard Hot 100: "Take Off" (#16)

Bob & Doug McKenzie's brand of Canadian lunacy became a comic phenomenon, earning them an *eh* for effort.

NOTORIETY STARTED for Bob & Doug McKenzie when the producers of *SCTV*—the syndicated Canadian comedy show and NBC's late-night hit—asked the cast to add two minutes of "Canadian content." In Canada, government regulations required a specific amount of radio airtime, films and TV programming to be devoted to native material. Two cast members, Rick Moranis and Dave Thomas, decided to fight politics with satire. They created Bob & Doug McKenzie, two fictional Canadian brothers who hosted their own two-minute talk show, "The Great White North," on every episode of *SCTV*.

Moranis and Thomas were both graduates of the Second City improvisational troupe based in Chicago (the nation's "Second City" and the SC in *SCTV*), which also boasted John Belushi, Dan Ackroyd, Bill Murray and Gilda Radner among its alumni.

Although the *SCTV* shows were rigidly scripted, the "Great White North" segments were totally improvised. The formula was simple, playing on Canadian stereotypes. Dressed in their parkas, flannel shirts, blue jeans, work boots and knit stocking caps, they sat behind a coffee table filled with empty beer bottles ("cold ones"), ended every sentence in "eh," fried up slices of back bacon and tried to come up with a topic—for example, the lack of parking spaces at take-out doughnut shops, or how to put mice in beer bottles to scare breweries into springing for a free case.

The filler material was dumb, funny and fairly predictable. It also exploded into a pop culture phenomenon—the duo's first comedy album, *Great White North,* became a sensation in Canada and in the States. "Take Off," the single, featured fellow Canadian Geddy Lee of Rush on vocals and was a novelty hit on US airwaves, and the duo's improvised version of "The Twelve Days of Christmas" was hugely popular around the holidays. Teenagers all across the continent picked up on catch phrases such as "G'day," "Take off, you hoser" and "How's it goin', eh?"

The comic creations showed up in America to promote their record. They played innocent games of Beerhunter, a sort of Canadian version of Russian roulette, where one beer from a six-pack was shaken up, hidden amongst the other five, and the participants took turns opening the cans next to their heads. But Bob and Doug ran into a communication breakdown when they tried to order breakfast—back bacon and eggs in particular.

"They stared calling us hosers," a hurt Bob said. "So we said, 'Take off! We're from the Great White North and we have back bacon up there.' The waitress goes, 'Oh, you mean *Canadian* bacon.'" Doug continued, "So we figured, like American cheese, eh? You probably call it *back* cheese here, eh?" ■

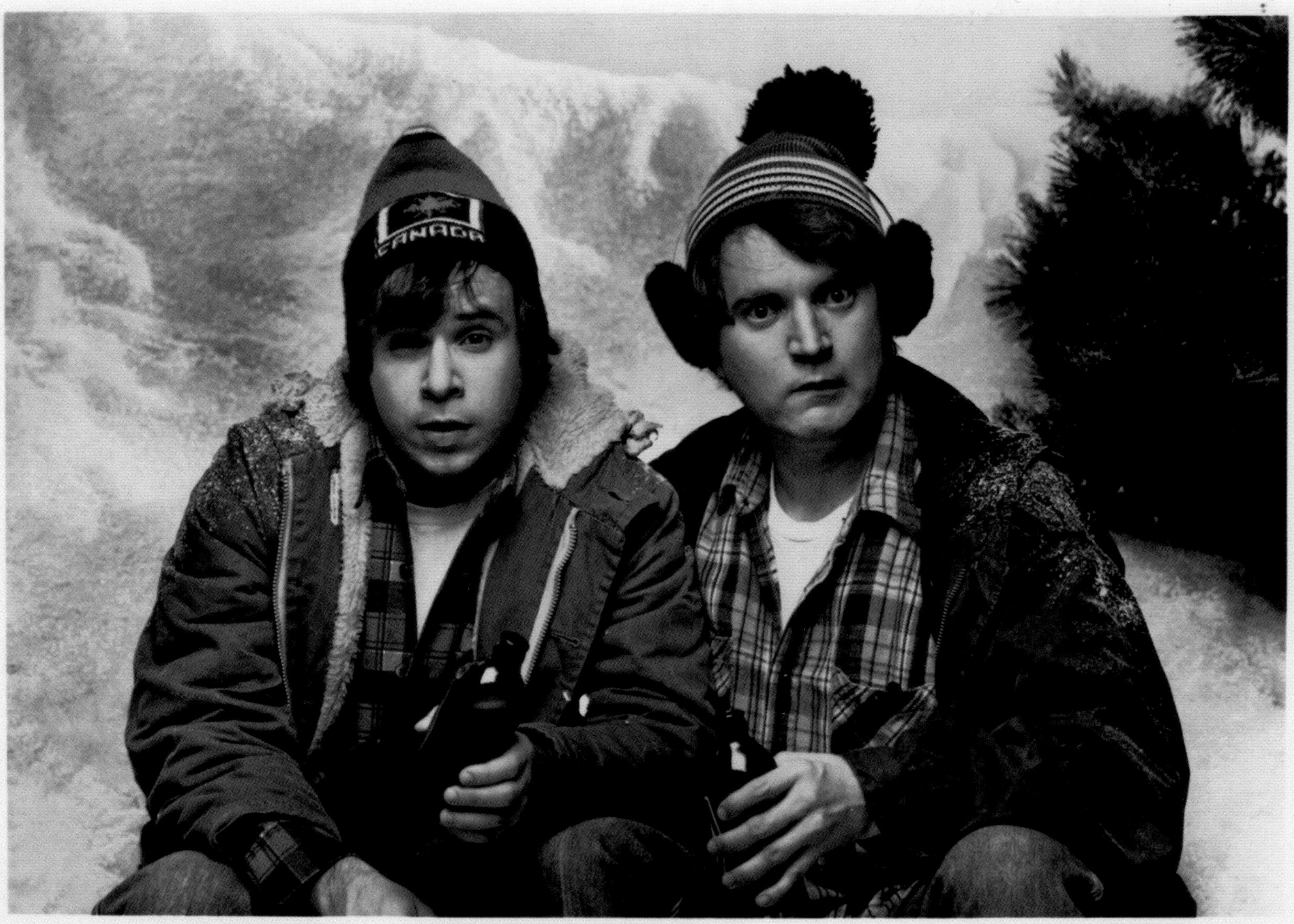

BOB & DOUG McKENZIE

PolyGram Records

Billboard 200: *Get Lucky* (#7)
Billboard Hot 100: "Working for the Weekend" (#29); "When It's Over" (#26)

"Working for the Weekend" again demonstrated Loverboy's stranglehold on the rock 'n' roll mainstream.

LOVERBOY'S DEBUT album and single "Turn Me Loose" had broken big in America, and the five-piece band from Vancouver went on a touring spree, putting on more than 200 shows.

"It's funny," vocalist Mike Reno noted. "We've always tried to work a crowd as best we can, and that almost worked against us when we were trying to get a record deal—most people said that we were 'too clubby,' that we involved the audience too much to be able to succeed in big arenas. So the fact that we are now involving 14,000 people at a time is vindication of sorts—fuck those people who didn't grab us when they could!"

The band hit pay dirt with its follow-up, *Get Lucky*, when "Working for the Weekend" became a signature tune. Paul Dean, the group's lead guitarist from its inception, played the riff and co-wrote the party anthem.

"In our live show, that cowbell intro never fails to get the crowd on its feet," bassist Scott Smith noted. "When Paul first played us the song, I remember we all rolled our eyes—'You really missed the boat here, pal.' But I guess he was right!"

Loverboy scored an additional hit with "When It's Over," a power ballad that boasted an emotive performance from Reno. Critics were the last people to appreciate Loverboy, since they didn't find the Canadian export all that interesting—there was no overwhelming angst or truly obnoxious habit that distinguished the group. But that didn't keep consumers from supporting the hard-touring unit, and Reno wasn't worried.

"Hey, we all have curly hair, we give everything we have to the audience, we are dripping with sweat after three numbers, and we like girls," he said. "That's the only image I care about." ■

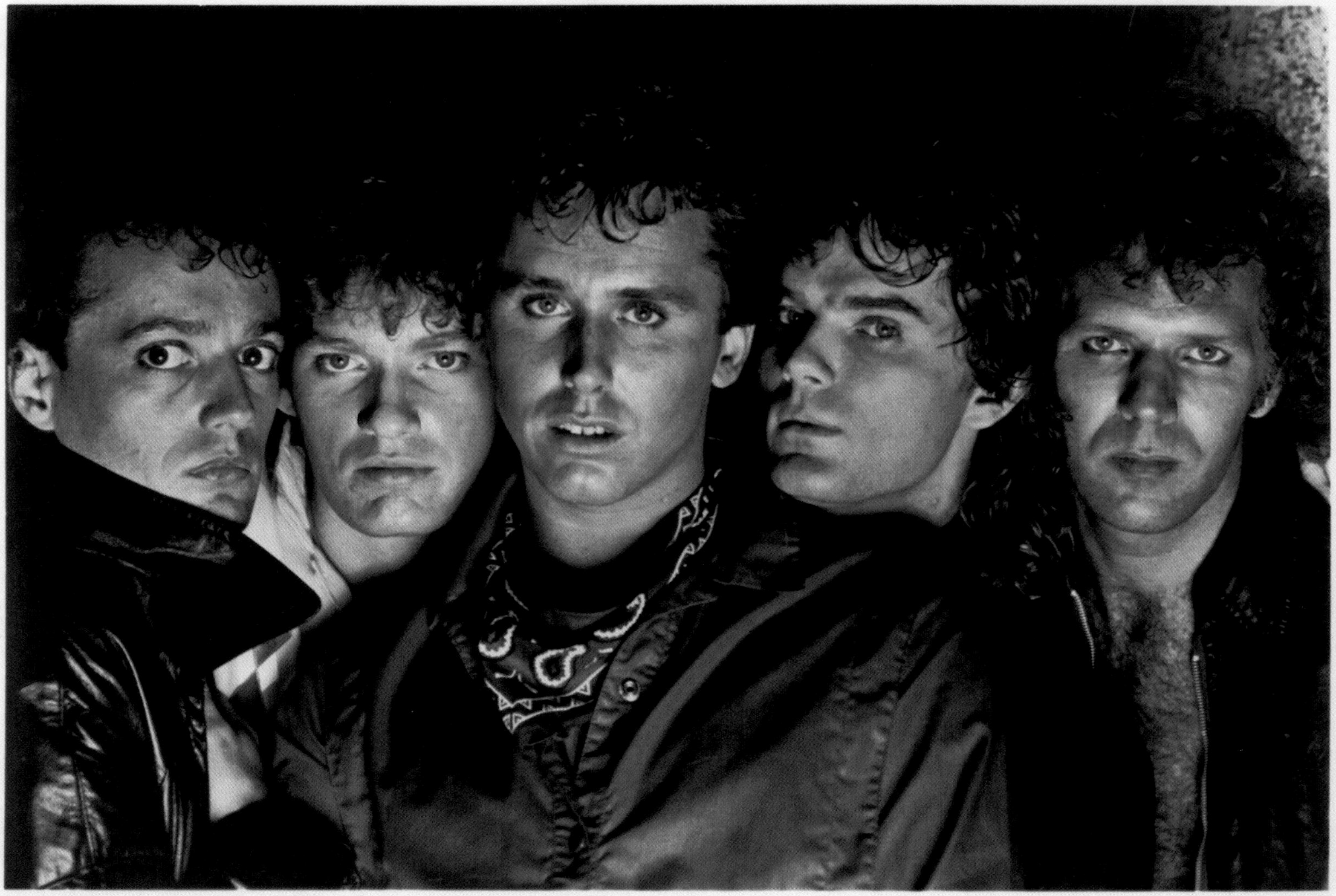

LOVERBOY

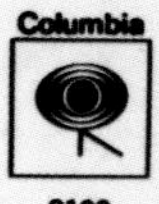

Billboard 200: *The Nature of the Beast* (#21)
Billboard Hot 100: "Just Between You and Me" (#22); "Sign of the Gypsy Queen" (#57)

"Just Between You and Me" became April Wine's biggest hit and thrust the Canadian band into the spotlight.

SUCCESS IN America had been a long time coming for April Wine, a band from Nova Scotia whose members had been superstars in their native country for nearly a decade. The hit single "Just Between You and Me" did for April Wine what "Keep on Lovin' You" had done for REO Speedwagon—delivered a ton of radio airplay via a power ballad for a hard-rock group.

Ironically, April Wine had a lot of practice cranking out pop hits up north while maintaining its in-concert edge.

"The problem we had up in Canada was that AM radio was the only outlet," guitarist Gary Moffet explained. "Only the softer, more poppy songs got airplay, so we always bastardized our albums to get on the radio. Then we'd play live and didn't even play our hits, because we were a loud bang-it-out band."

Lead singer and guitarist Myles Goodwyn had always showcased a knack for composing melodic songs in both genres, and several April Wine albums in the late Seventies deserved a better break stateside. But the group's succession of American record companies was never able to figure out what to do with the band.

"We always figured that America would come to us if we had a good record, rather than us touring," Moffet noted. "When we saw that it wouldn't work that way, we rethought our strategy. We had to establish an identity right off the bat as a touring, hard-rock band—that's how we broke in Canada. When we signed with our current label, we committed to being on the road for the next few years."

April Wine's seventh and eighth albums—1979's *First Glance* and 1980's *Harder ... Faster*—started breaking down barriers with the tunes "Roller," "Say Hello" and "I Like to Rock," and the group's members paid their apprenticeships all over again as the opening act on several big-name tours.

In 1981, the band finally busted loose in America—"Just Between You and Me," "Sign of the Gypsy Queen" and "All Over Town" made April Wine a staple of the airwaves, and the album *The Nature of the Beast* became one of the year's biggest success stories.

"People think we should be really tired of the road at this point of our career," Moffat said. "But it's actually the most ideal situation we've ever been in. In the past, we had to create the energy by playing when the records came out. Now, our record is selling and the buzz from the audience provides all of the excitement we need." ■

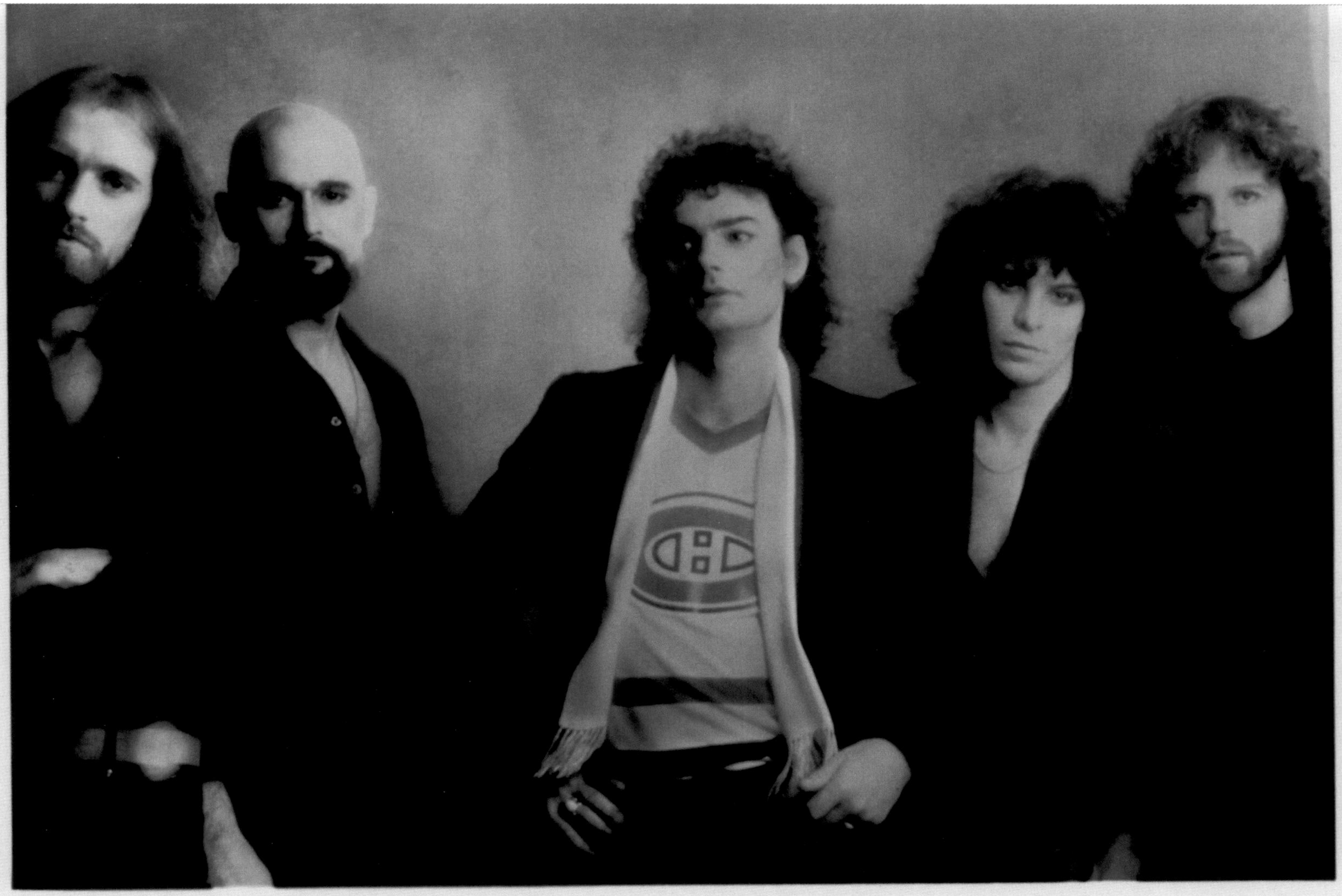

Steve Lang Jerry Mercer Myles Goodwyn Brian Greenway Gary Moffet

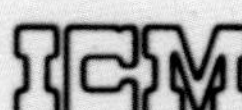

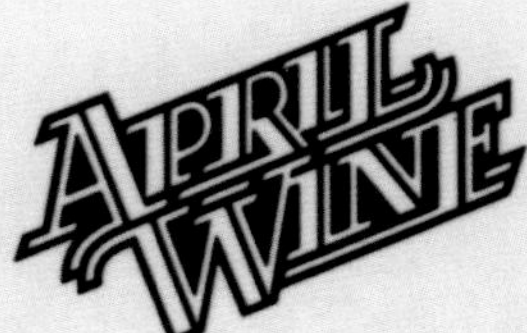

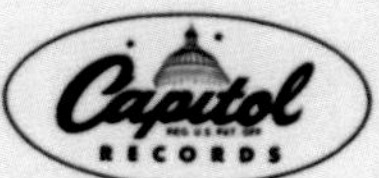

Billboard 200: *Allied Forces* (#23)
Billboard Hot 100: "Magic Power" (#51)

Known for its extravagant shows, Canada's Triumph reached its height of popularity in the US with *Allied Forces*.

FROM ITS inception in Toronto in 1975, Triumph had made performances a virtual war on rock concert boredom. The group was frequently banned by club owners as "too explosive."

"Right from the beginning, we used to build our own stage props and effects, even though we were told by everyone that we would never be successful, that we were crazy for doing such an elaborate show," guitarist Rick Emmett said.

"We went into hock" was how bassist Mike Levine explained Triumph's decision to develop an arena-sized rock production. ""We never hurt anyone—we'd just burn a few curtains here and there. We were the only band with a tractor-trailer parked outside these clubs. Every time we played, it was a big extravaganza, and people would line up around the block for it."

Headlining concert halls in cities where few had ever seen an elaborate rock production before, Triumph arrived with rows of computerized lights, smoke machines, sudden geysers of flames and fountains of sparks.

The excitement earned the Canadian power trio thousands of fans. *Allied Forces,* the group's fifth album, helped expand its following in the US, with "Magic Power" and the anthem "Fight the Good Fight" receiving wide airplay on FM rock radio. Staking its reputation on a flashy stage show—including lasers and indoor fireworks—the members looked to conquer the Midwestern "boogie belt."

"We're not exactly subtle onstage, but it's the type of music we like to play," Levine said. "The new-wave bands have tried to strip things down a bit and rely on a basic intensity, but we still believe in giving the kids a big show when they come to see us." ■

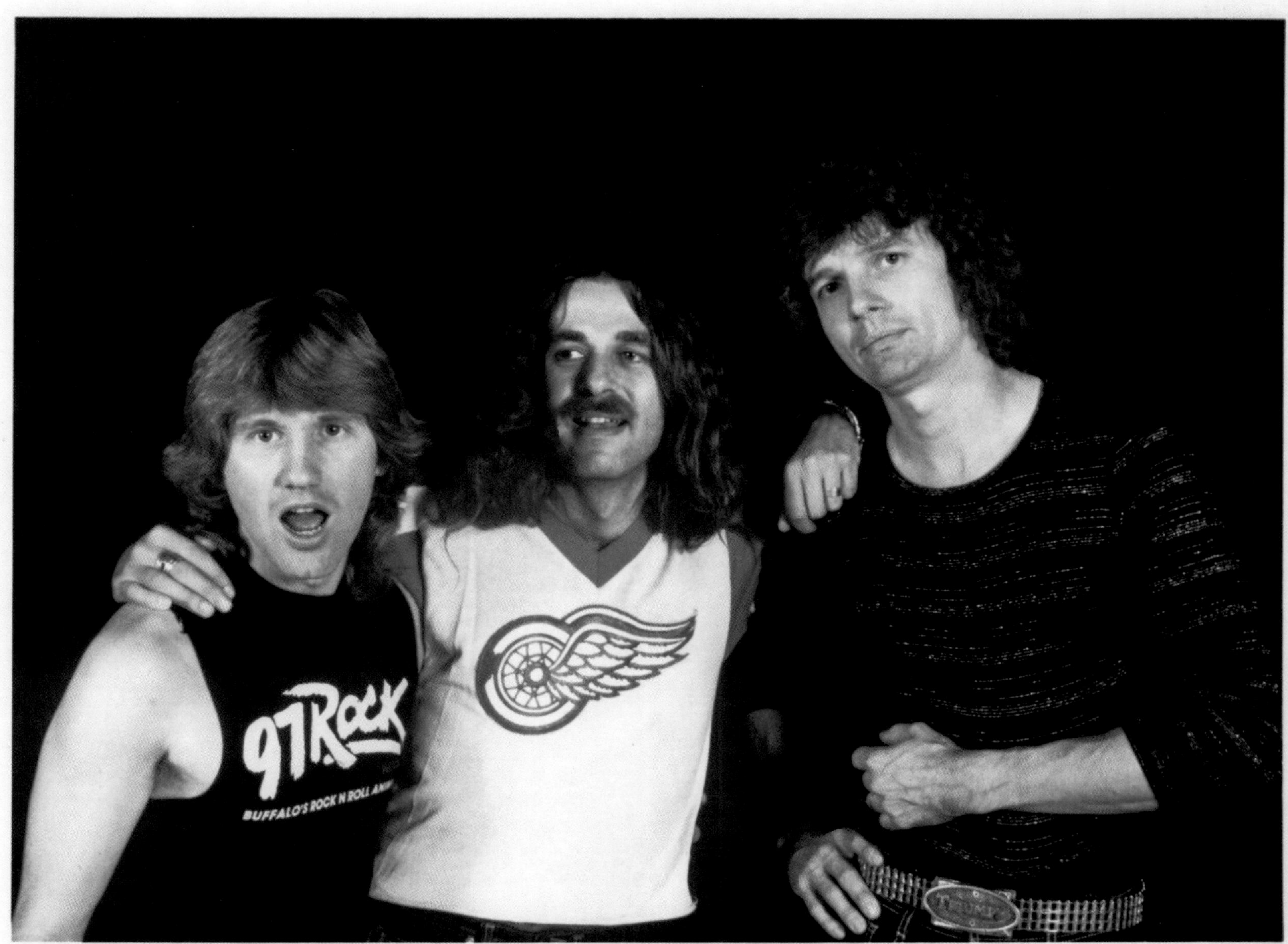

TRIUMPH

RCA
Records and Tapes

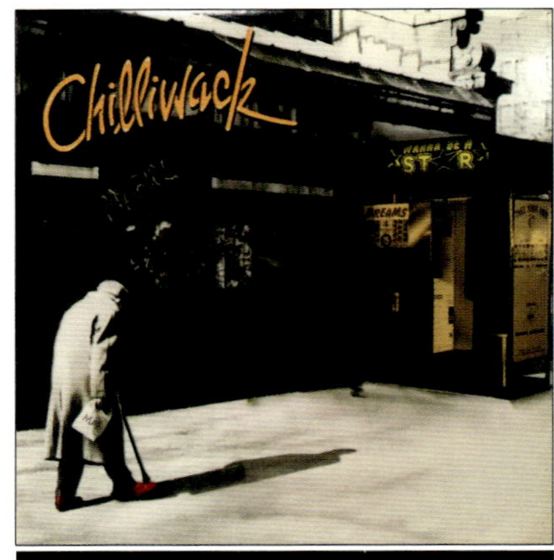

Billboard 200: *Wanna Be a Star* (#78)
Billboard Hot 100: "My Girl (Gone, Gone, Gone)" (#22); "I Believe" (#33)

Vancouver rock band Chilliwack achieved an international upturn with the hit "My Girl (Gone, Gone, Gone)."

CHILLIWACK STARTED out as the Collectors, playing cafes and cabarets in Vancouver. The band toured the west coast of North America and officially adopted Chilliwack as its name in mid-1969. In the Seventies, the group's five albums generated several Canadian hit singles as its style evolved towards a straight-ahead rock-pop sound, but the act suffered multiple changes in labels and band members.

"Then, Mushroom Records out of Vancouver was just starting to have enormous success with Heart," singer and guitarist Bill Henderson said. "They were interested in signing us. We agreed, and *Dreams, Dreams, Dreams* became our most popular album up to that time. At the height of our next release, we received word that Shelly Siegel, the driving force behind Mushroom, had died unexpectedly. Soon the label's promotion began to falter, and consequently our next album was never released in the US."

After a lengthy legal battle to get out of its contract, Chilliwack recorded *Wanna Be a Star* for Millennium Records as a trio (Henderson, Brian MacLeod on drums, guitar and keyboards, and Ab Bryant on bass) and enjoyed its greatest success. Chilliwack's best-selling song, "My Girl (Gone, Gone, Gone)," reached the top of the charts in Canada and gave the band its breakthrough in the US, where "I Believe" was also a Top 40 hit. The rest of the songs on *Wanna Be a Star* formed a concept of sorts about rock 'n' roll glory.

"The album turned out to be thematic," Henderson said. "Jimmy Ienner, president of Millennium, described it as 'a rock 'n' roll fantasy, the dreamer's guide to stardom and the avoidance of boredom.' That's an apt statement." ■

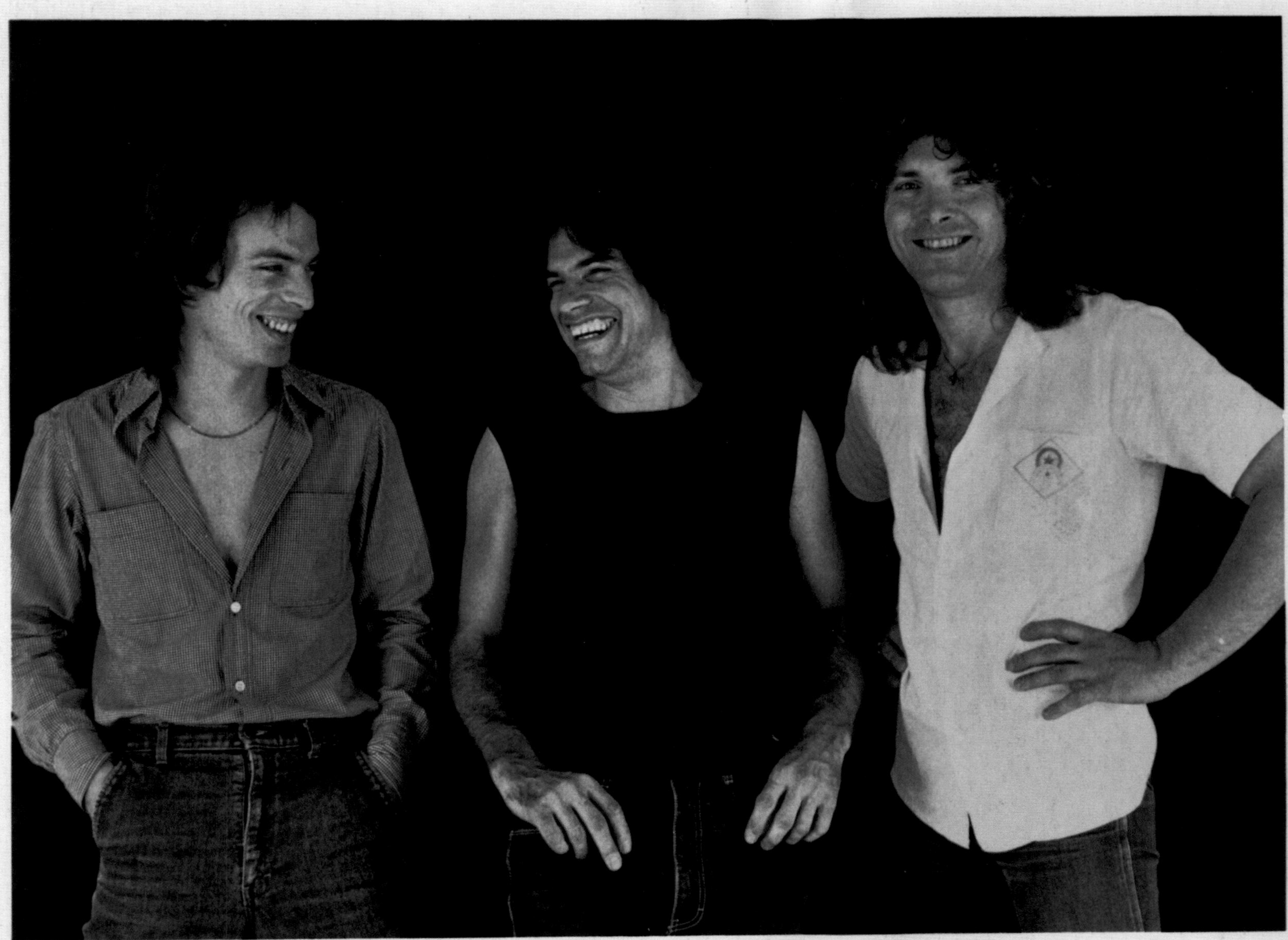

CHILLIWACK

Direction: DIXON—PROPAS PRODUCTIONS.

Millennium RECORDS
Manufactured and Distributed by RCA Records

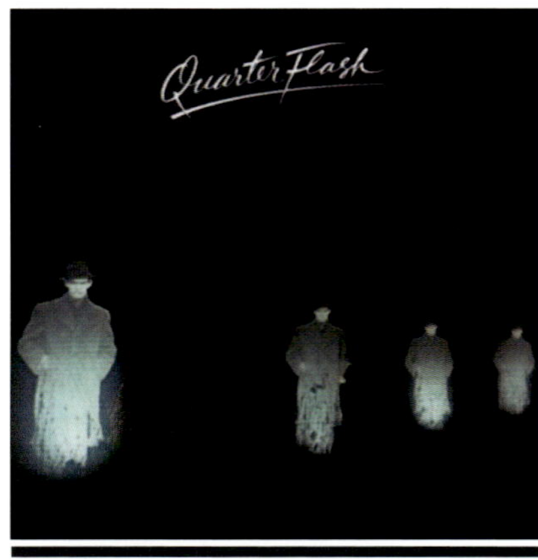

Billboard 200: *Quarterflash* (#8)
Billboard Hot 100: "Harden My Heart" (#3); "Find Another Fool" (#16); "Right Kind of Love" (#56)

A creamy sax riff, striking female vocal and slick production shot Quarterflash's "Harden My Heart" into the Top 10.

QUARTERFLASH, A new band out of the Northwest, became the first unknown group to sign with Geffen Records, a label that had concentrated on signing such big name artists as Elton John, John Lennon and Donna Summer. The album *Quarterflash* was produced by John Boylan, who had supervised recordings for Boston, Little River Band and Linda Ronstadt.

Quarterflash centered around Rindy and Marv Ross, ex-schoolteachers who "didn't even play music seriously before we were married ten years ago," Rindy explained. "It was eight years ago that we finally got into it enough to form a band on the side while we were teaching school."

In 1977, the couple decided to forego their initial careers and pursue music full-time. "It was a little bit scary to leave the security of our jobs," Rindy admitted, "but we realized we were living for the weekends instead of the week. We saved our money and played in Portland clubs and bars. The Northwest music scene has always been very supportive—there are many places where you *have* to play originals instead of covers."

With the diminutive Rindy singing and wielding a saxophone onstage while husband Marv played guitar and composed most of the material, the Rosses led several different bands over the next few years, each getting more and more rock-oriented. "There were a lot of country and folk influences in our music early on. Our last group, Seafood Mama, was very eclectic—we'd do a salsa tune, then some country, then some rock. It worked great in bars, but it wasn't too good for a specific recording sound."

However, the band recorded one tune written by Marv, "Harden My Heart," as an independent single.

"We were going to appear on an hour-long television special in Portland, and we thought it would be foolish not to have any product out," Rindy recalled. "We recorded the song on an 8-track machine in a basement and pressed it up. When the TV show came on, we peddled it out of our car."

The tune ended up hitting the No. 1 slot on three regional radio stations and sold 10,000 copies in Oregon, enough to push the song onto some national charts. Interest from several major labels resulted, with Geffen Records winning the battle to sign the band. The Rosses had dissolved Seafood Mama and linked up with another Portland club band, Pilot, to form Quarterflash. *Quarterflash* was an auspicious debut—besides "Harden My Heart" being all over the radio, the driving "Find Another Fool" proved that the band was capable of some exuberant material. ■

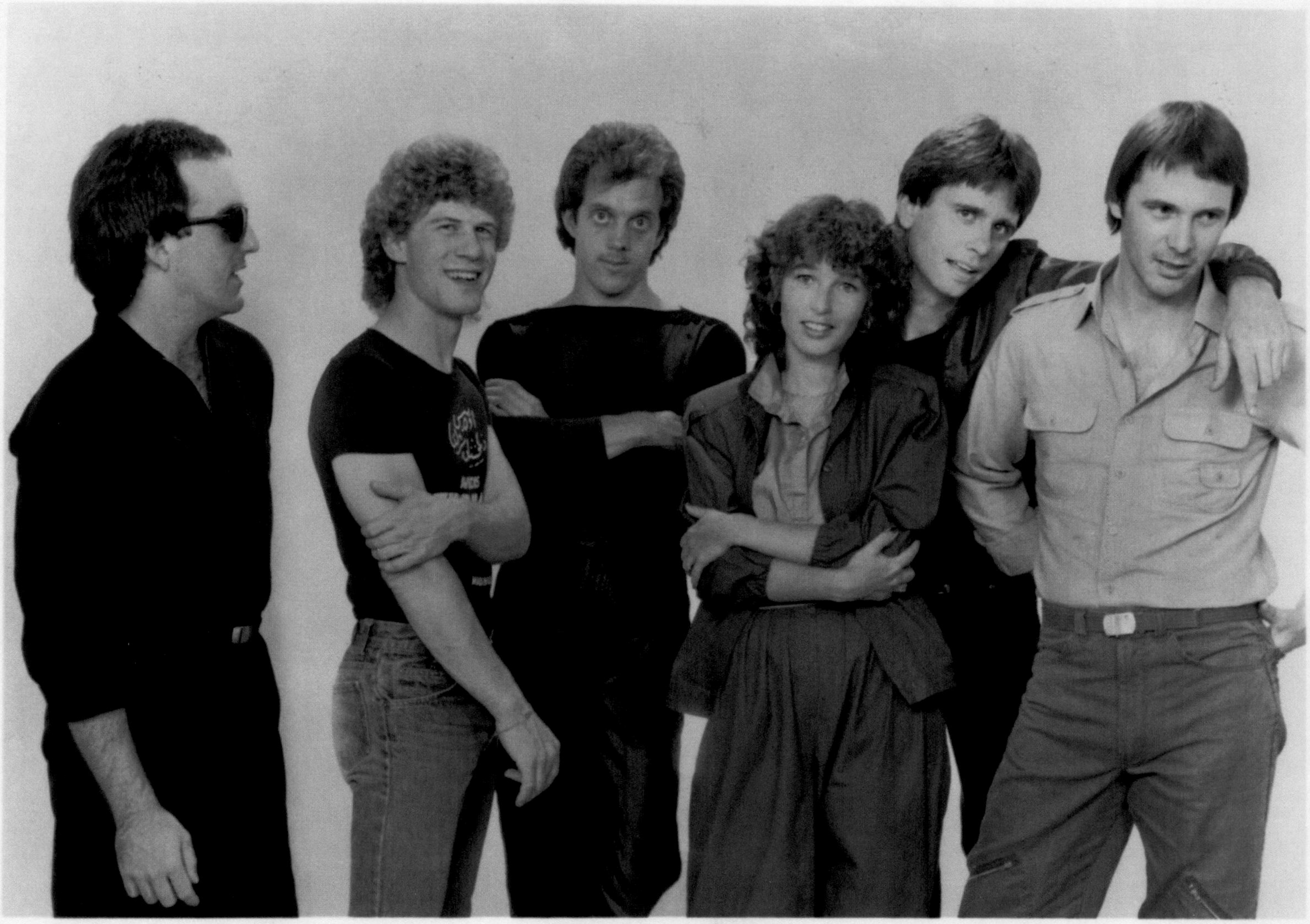

QUARTERFLASH

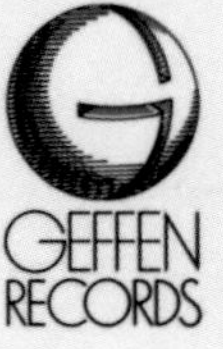

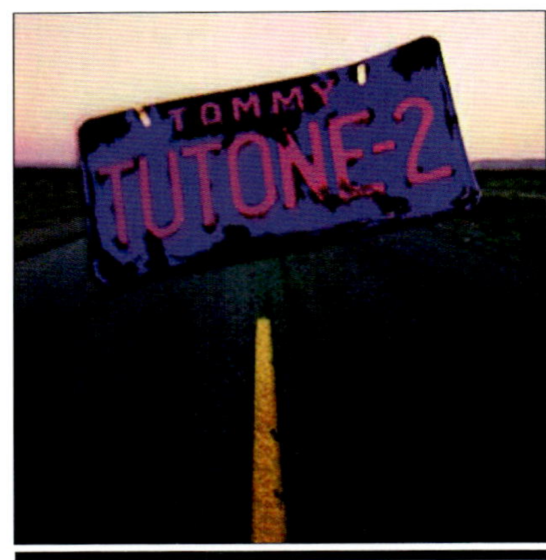

Billboard 200: *Tommy Tutone 2* (#20)
Billboard Hot 100: "867-5309/Jenny" (#4)

For a good time, people were calling for "867-5309/Jenny," the Tommy Tutone hit song ensconced in the Top 5.

TOMMY TUTONE wasn't a guy with a cutesy-pie name; it was a group from California with a cutesy-pie name. The band's first album had received a push from Columbia Records.

"They spent some dough on the first one—we kinda got the hype treatment," guitarist Jim Keller said. The debut spawned "Angel Say No," which cracked the Top 30 with the benefit of the promotional muscle, and "Cheap Date" became an FM favorite in some markets.

Like most major record labels, Columbia issued a slew of product every month and waited to see what stuck. If an album didn't make an impression within a few weeks, it usually got lost in the shuffle. That was the company's attitude on Tommy Tutone's second release. But the unassuming band immediately went out on the road and started a groundswell. When the album *Tommy Tutone 2* showed up on critics' "best of" lists, Columbia finally started taking notice.

With the renewed interest, the group continued its relentless touring. "We've seen direct results—every place we've been, we've picked up sales and key airplay," Keller noted.

The video of "867-5309/Jenny" was shown on cable TV networks for visual identification, and voila—Keller and co-leader Tommy Heath watched the punchy power-pop song come from nowhere to give them newfound notoriety.

Tommy Tutone had a smash record, plus a lot of silly publicity—it seemed that any place in the United States with an 867 phone prefix had someone getting prank calls.

The coast-to-coast club dates had polished Tommy Tutone's live act to match its recorded excellence. "We work hard," Keller said, "And we hope we're doing something of lasting value. The only word I can muster about the momentum of '867-5309' is 'astounding.'" ■

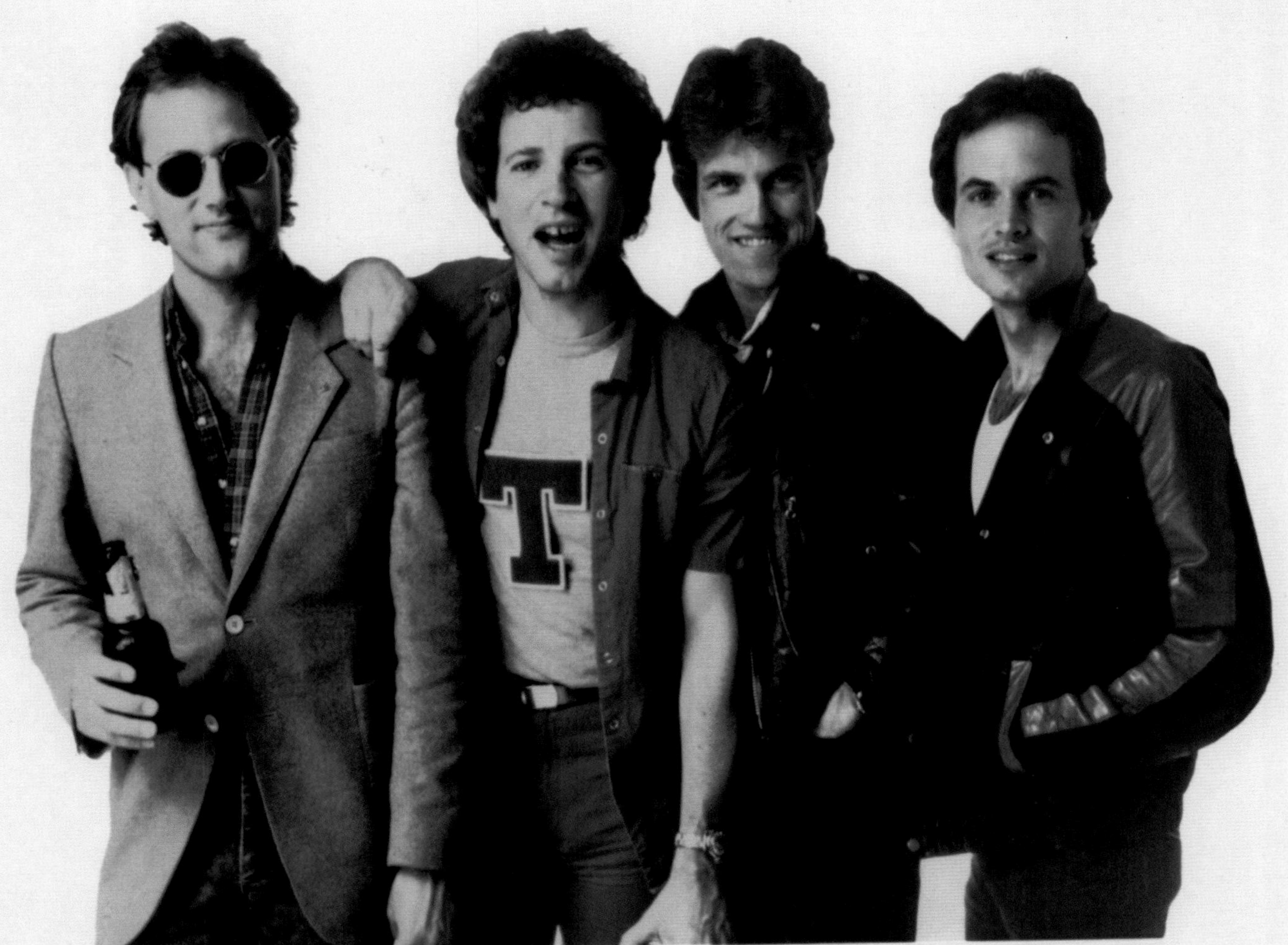

TOMMY TUTONE

JIM KELLER TOMMY HEATH JON LYONS VICTOR CARBERRY

Columbia

8109

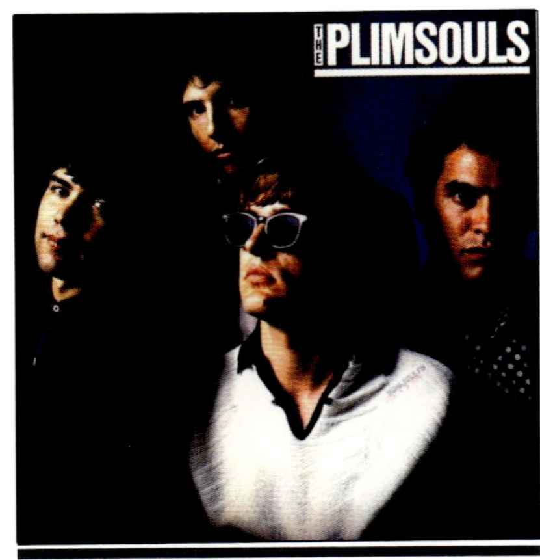

Billboard 200: *The Plimsouls* (#153)

The Plimsouls, one of the top-drawing bands on the Los Angeles club circuit, recorded a promising debut album.

THINGS HADN'T always looked promising for Peter Case, the Plimsouls' co-founder, guitarist and chief writer.

"I had a hard time finding people to play with," he allowed. "I always wanted a band—guys you could work with, bounce off of, relate to. It's easy to find people who can play, but people who share your enthusiasm are hard to get. I didn't want a bunch of clock-punchers."

Case's previous group, the Nerves, had broken up in 1978. The punk-pop band included Jack Lee (author of "Hanging on the Telephone," a hit for Blondie) and Paul Collins (who then led the Beat), but the group never managed to transcend a California cult following. "I learned everything not to do," Case said of the experience. "We were great, but there was no future—we were writers, not performers."

Case hung out for a while, painting houses and writing songs, patiently waiting for the right players to surface for a band. "I ran an ad that said, 'Wanted: musicians, influences Elvis Presley, the Who'—I changed it every week because I have a lot of influences," he recalled. "And I'd get these piano players from Malibu, jerks who couldn't play, guys with beards down to their knees who wanted work right away, always something wrong."

Finally, he began to rehearse with drummer Lou Ramirez and bassist David Pahoa, and the threesome sustained an attack on the local club circuit in 1979. During the recording of an EP entitled *Zero Hour*, guitarist Eddie Muñoz joined up. Several magazines voted the Plimsouls the best unsigned band in Los Angeles. Albums by skinny-tie power-pop groups had glutted the L.A. market since the success of the Knack's debut, but Case held out for the right deal.

The Plimsouls featured a healthy dose of rough-edged pop, with Case turning in several excellent songs—"Zero Hour," "Hush, Hush" and "Now" received strong local airplay. Yet the record couldn't capture the manic energy that permeated the Plimsouls' live shows, which Case accepted.

"I can't wait to get out and play other places," he said. "It's real basic stuff, but I know that people everywhere will dig it. The sooner we can make new fans and disassociate ourselves from the L.A. BS, the better." ■

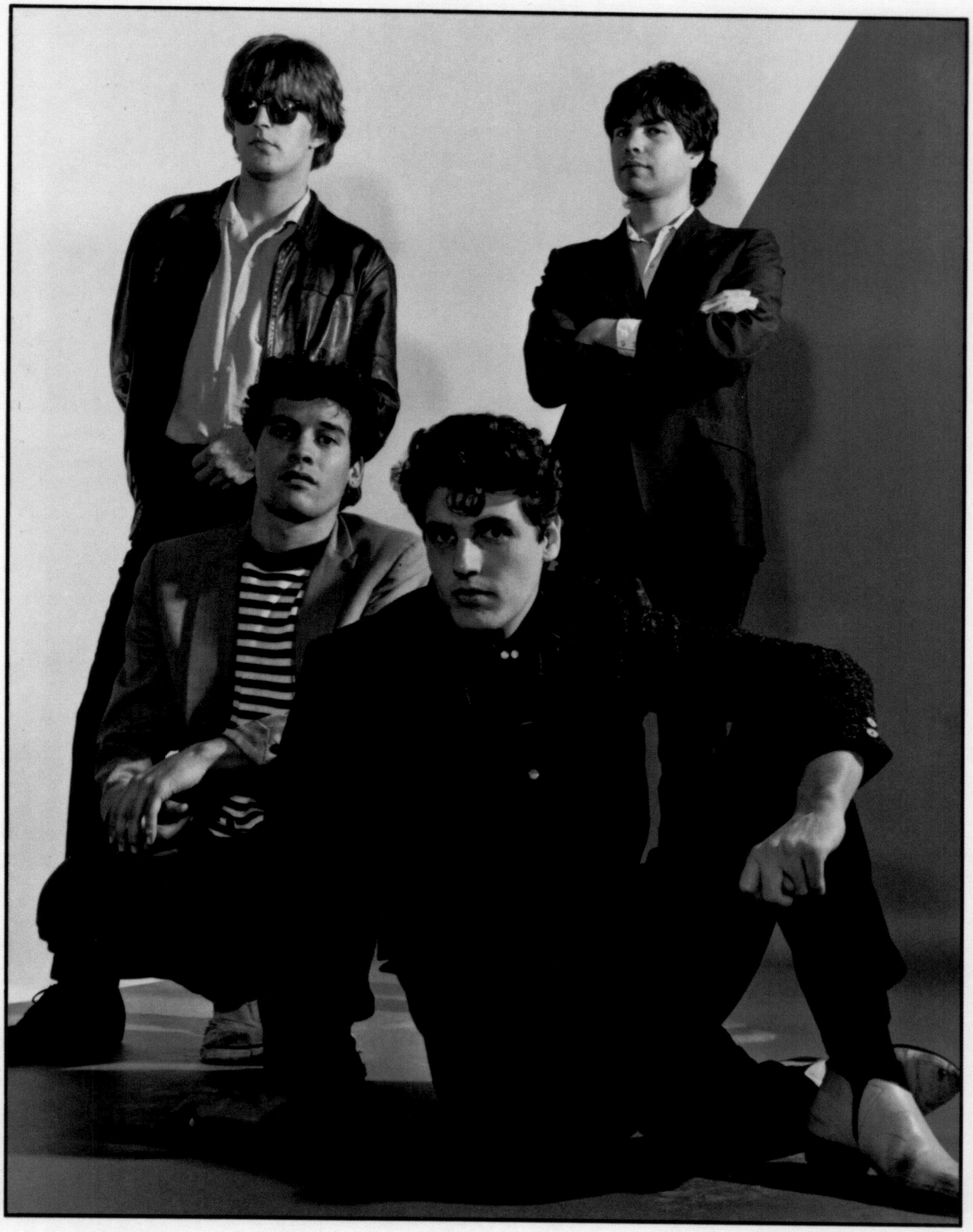

PETER CASE DAVID PAHOA LOU RAMIREZ EDDIE MUNOZ

THE PLIMSOULS

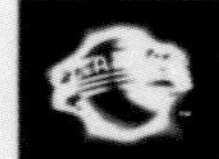

PHOTO CREDIT: CRAIG DIETZ/1981

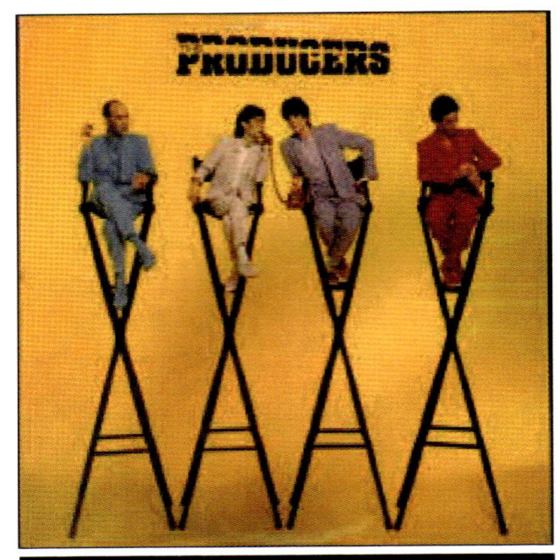

Billboard 200: *The Producers* (#163)
Billboard Hot 100: "What She Does to Me (The Diana Song)" (#61)

The Producers became an MTV favorite, receiving airplay with the video for the buoyant track, "What's He Got?"

THE PRODUCERS called Atlanta home, but the quartet's debut album bore little resemblance to the sound of standard Southern rock.

"Atlanta has produced at least two major modern bands," bassist and vocalist Kyle Henderson said. "The B-52's are from Athens, but they played Atlanta constantly, and the Brains, who didn't sell as well but met with great reviews, are from Atlanta."

The members of the quartet had honed their chops in the usual assortment of original and cover groups on the club circuit. Forming the Producers, they wrote and rehearsed new material. The band's manager contacted producer Tom Werman, who had worked with Cheap Trick. Werman agreed to audition the band if it could come to New York, so the Producers hopped into a van.

"We drove 17 hours straight to play a 45-minute set for him," Henderson recalled. "We were all hoping he would say, 'Sounds good, let me hear a tape.' We would have considered that a positive statement."

Werman responded more enthusiastically than that. He signed the Producers to Portrait Records, a CBS subsidiary, and his crisp, crackling production on *The Producers* captured the catchy pop-rock craftsmanship of "What She Does to Me (The Diana Song)," "What's He Got?" and "Who Do You Think You Are?" Getting in on the ground floor of the MTV experience, the band promoted the album with energetic performances, opening for Cheap Trick and others. ■

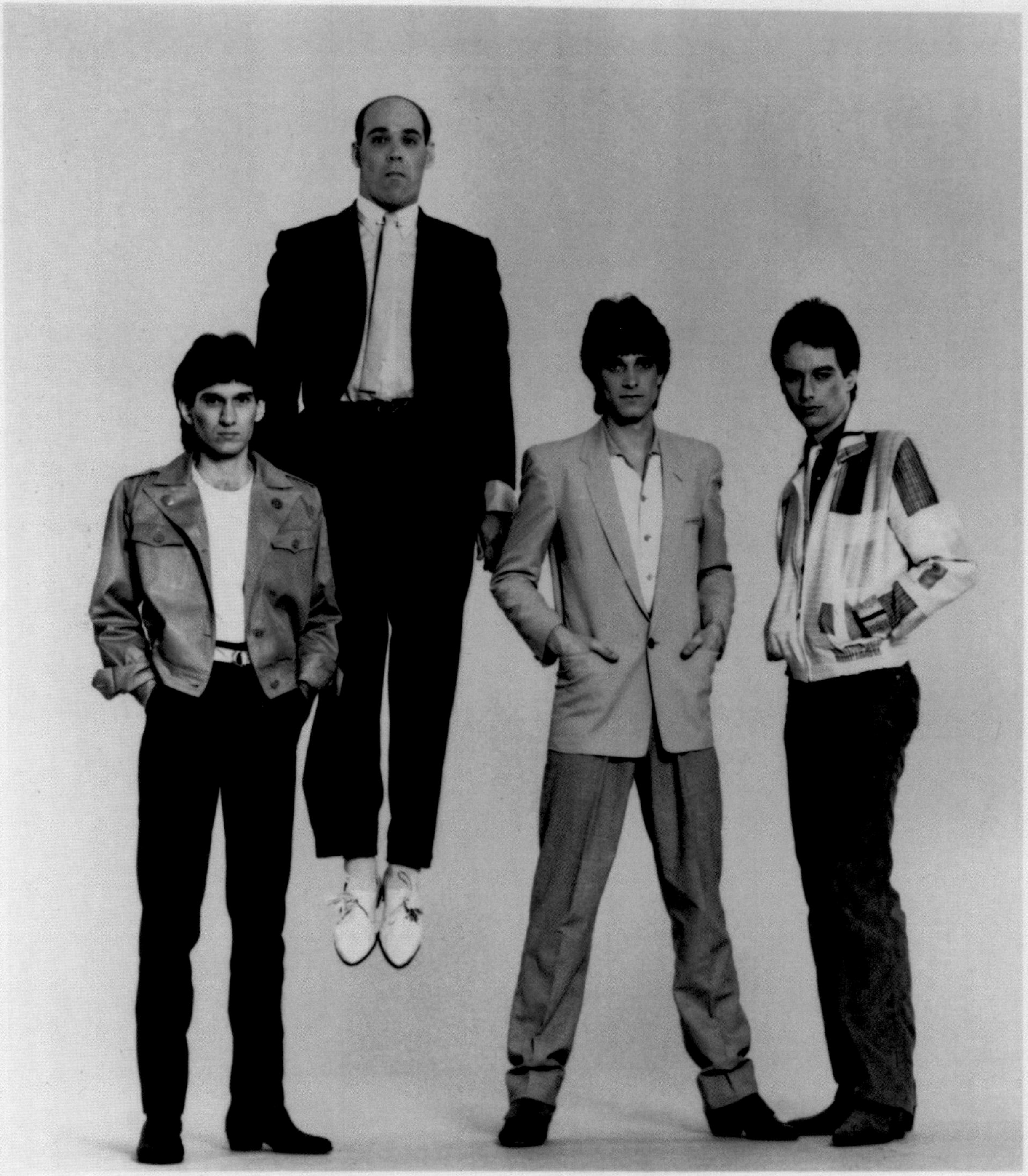

VAN TEMPLE   WAYNE FAMOUS   KYLE HENDERSON   BRYAN HOLMES

THE PRODUCERS

HUGH RODGERS
(404) 992-1050

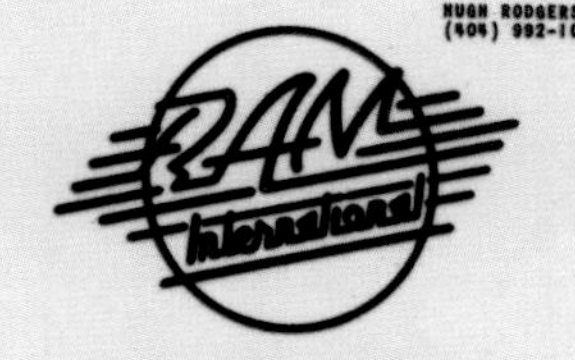

RODGERS ARTISTS MANAGEMENT
BOX 76640; ATLANTA GEORGIA 30328

Billboard 200: *Novo Combo* (#167)

The skilled musicians of Novo Combo incorporated decades of experience into a high-spirited debut album.

WHEN PEDIGREED rock musicians with technical expertise got together to form a band, turgid albums filled with boring albeit precise solos too often resulted. But Novo Combo was striving to be the exception.

The group's nucleus was formed by drummer Michael Shrieve and bassist-singer Stephen Dees, who'd met in New York in the late Seventies. Shrieve, a founding member of Santana, was ready for new challenges, while Dees had just extricated himself from the Hall & Oates camp. Their newspaper ad attracted veteran guitarist and singer Pete Hewlett (who'd played with Carly Simon among others), and with guitarist Jack Griffith also joining, the Novo Combo lineup was established.

"From the beginning, the concept was to put everything under the Novo Combo umbrella," Hewlett explained. "Besides Santana, Michael had gone through the progressive-rock mill with Automatic Man (with German synthesizer composer Klaus Schultze) and Go (with percussionist Stomu Yamashta and Stevie Winwood), so he was willing to start from the bottom again with another group."

Some gigs around New York garnered a recording contract, and *Novo Combo* spawned the compelling mainstream rock singles, "Up Periscope" and "Tattoo." The debut album showcased all four members of the band, who could write and sing as well as play their respective instruments with taste or abandon.

"I think we can contribute a new sound by sublimating all of our skills within the group," Hewlett noted. "We don't want to be constantly compared to the past, the things we've already done. We're trying hard to put that aside." But critics and radio programmers focused on similarities to the Police's sound, and Novo Combo never got a crack at the big time. ■

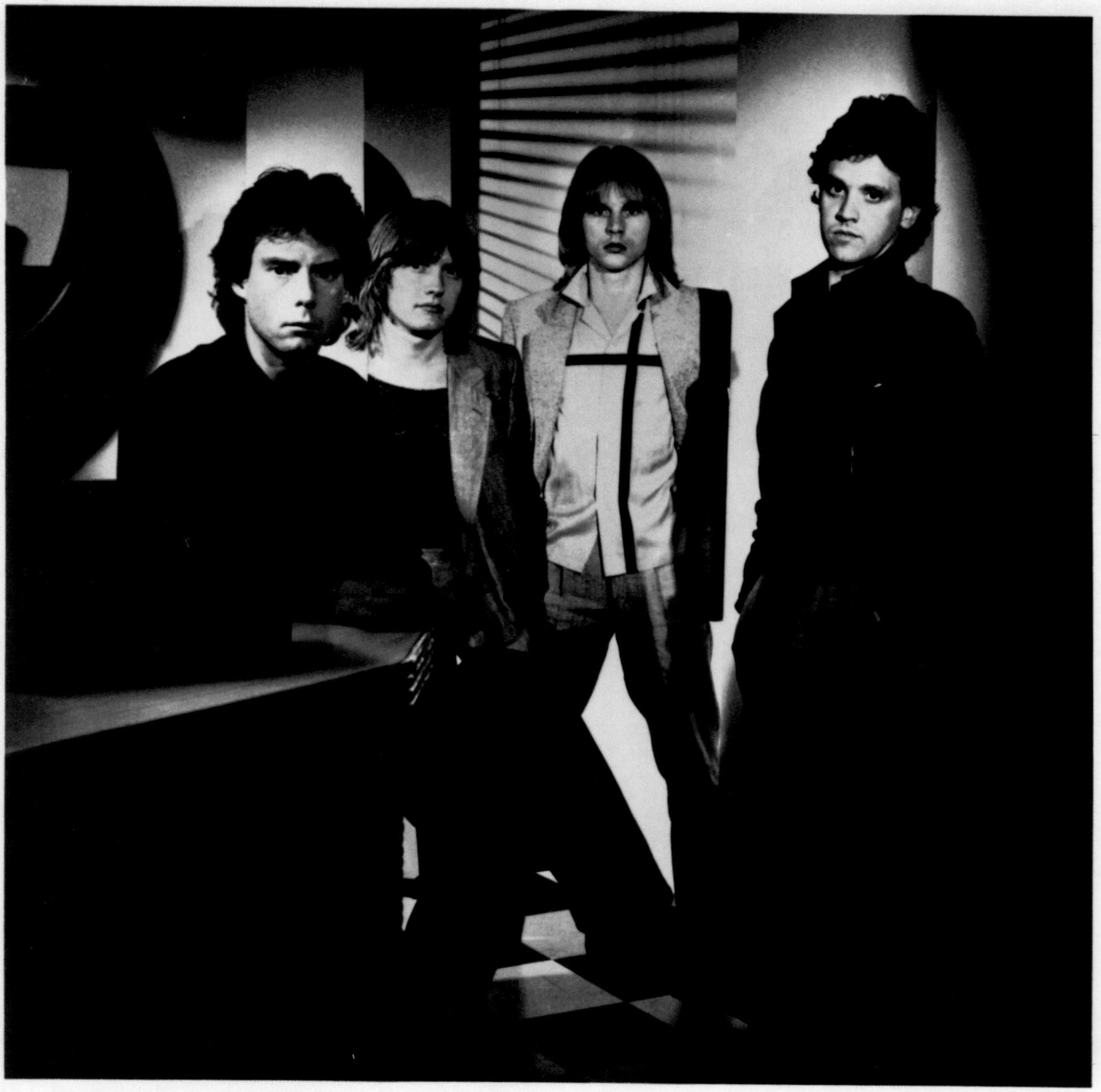

NOVO COMBO

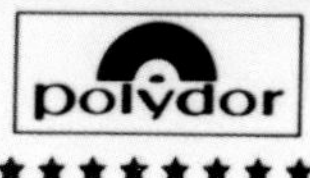

MANAGEMENT:
Sanford Ross Management, Ltd.
Sandy Ross/ Glenn Orsher
1700 Broadway
New York, N. Y 10019
212/245—8228

PolyGram Records

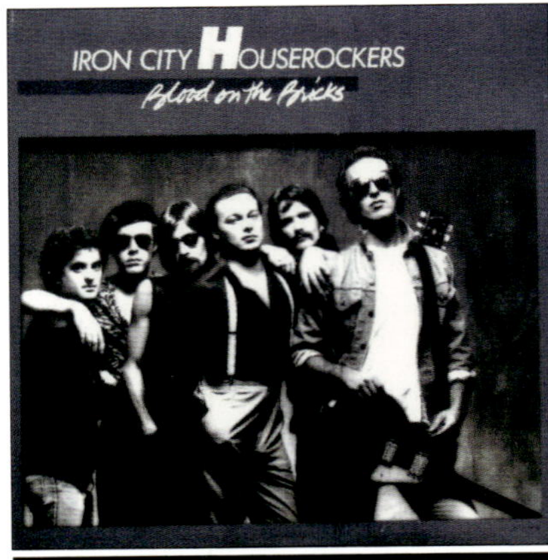

Critical acclaim for *Blood on the Bricks* gave Joe Grushecky and his Iron City Houserockers renewed energy.

CRITICS HAD heralded the Iron City Houserockers, a blue-collar bar band out of Pittsburgh, as one of America's best new groups. Much had been made of the Houserockers' sound—tough, serious and street-smart—but they hadn't been able to take their show west of Chicago. Singer-guitarist Joe Grushecky and his cohorts rolled with the punches, contenting themselves with a spirited East Coast sound nurtured by growing up with AM radio and soul music.

"I thought about doing music when I was younger, but when David Bowie and Yes became popular in the early Seventies, I couldn't relate," Grushecky explained. "It was in 1975 that I decided to give it a serious shot. We just played R&B and rock 'n' roll, which we never really separated in the first place."

Teaming up with bassist Art Nardini and other friends, Grushecky started playing every bar and club in Pittsburgh until they signed to a record deal in 1977. "Until then, our routine was pretty tough," he said. "I'd get up at 7 a.m. to go to work (as a special education teacher), get home at 4 p.m. and try to get to sleep until 8 p.m. Then we'd get up and load our equipment, head to a club and set up ourselves, since we couldn't afford a roadie. Then we'd play from 10 p.m. to 2 a.m., break down the stage, load the truck and get home by five in the morning."

Despite two critically acclaimed albums, *Love's So Tough* and the outstanding *Have a Good Time but Get Out Alive!*, lack of management and experience kept the band from capitalizing on its cult reputation.

"It was pretty frustrating," Grushecky admitted. "Here we were reading this great endorsement in *Rolling Stone* and we couldn't even afford to be out on the road."

Grushecky and the band had their work cut out for them with *Blood on the Bricks*. Produced by Steve Cropper (of Booker T. & the M.G.'s), the album featured another batch of terse anthems dealing with the working class. But like previous records, it was praised by reviewers but ignored by the public.

"We started out as a bunch of guys who were fans, who wanted to go out and play in bars because we like the songs. We never had a grip on the music business as such, because it doesn't exist in Pittsburgh. We got signed to a bad deal, and no one was there to help us—we've learned everything from the bottom up," Grushecky explained. "Our goal right now is just to be seen—I get the feeling we're not known, period. I hope I'm wrong." ■

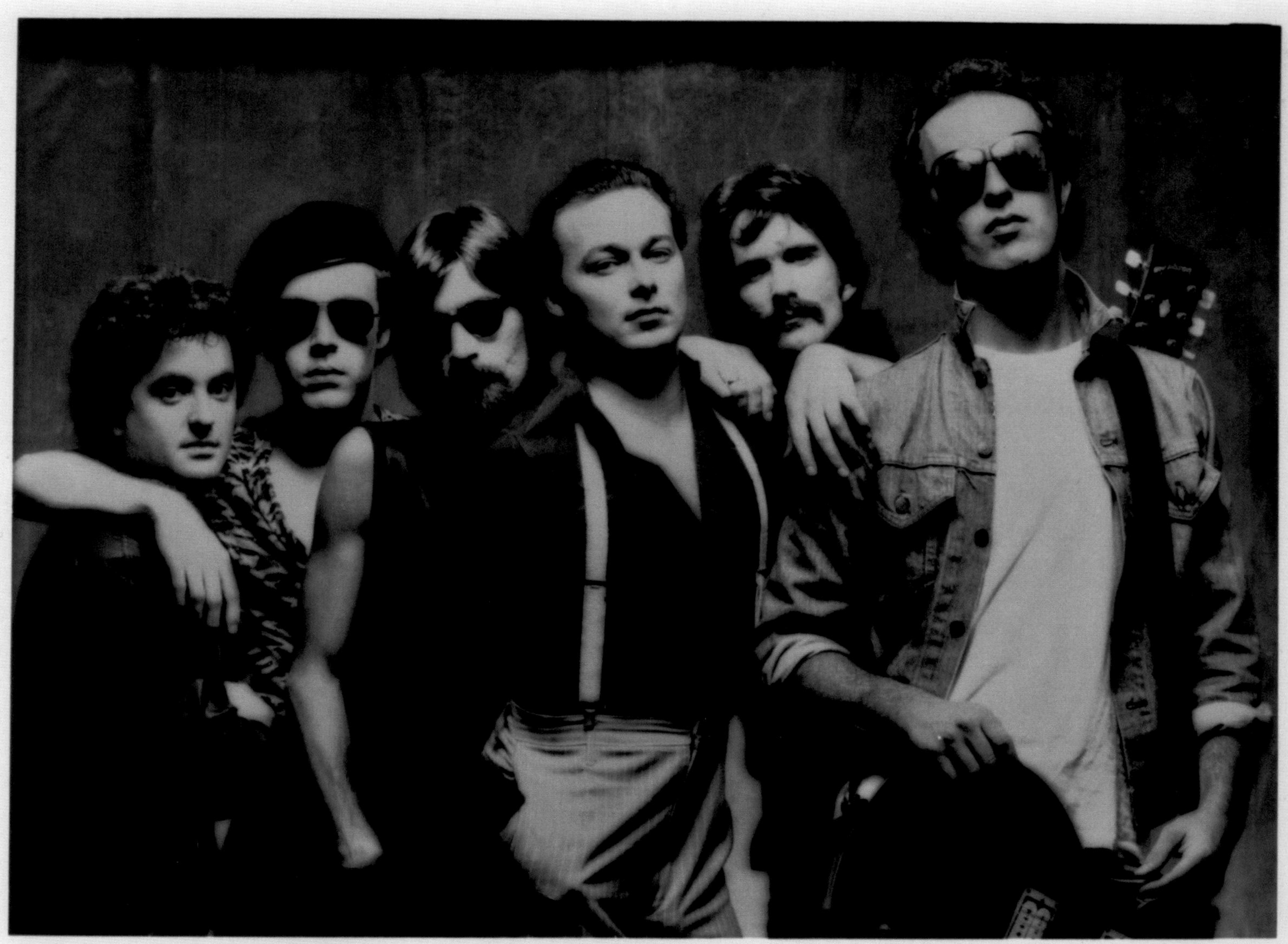

8/81

Iron City Houserockers

MCA RECORDS

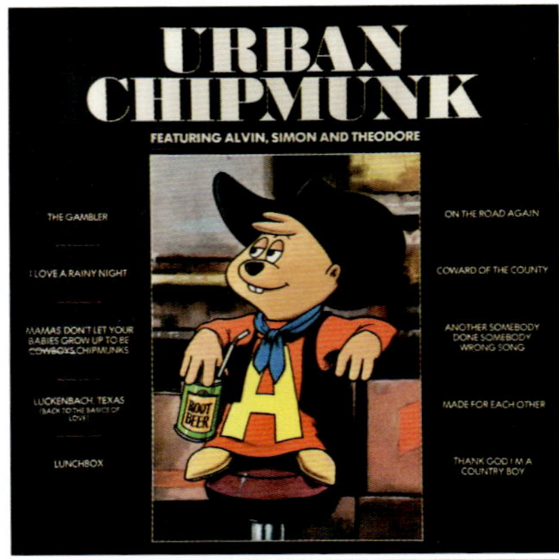

Billboard 200: *Urban Chipmunk* (#56)

Singing country favorites on *Urban Chipmunk*, **Alvin & the Chipmunks** remained a popular kids' recording act.

ROSS BAGDASARIAN Sr. created the Chipmunks, three singing animated anthropomorphic rodents—Simon and Theodore and the impetuous Alvin. A novelty record, "The Chipmunk Song (Christmas Don't Be Late)," became a success in 1958 and turned into a holiday staple. Bagdasarian (who appeared in the product as David Seville) achieved the Chipmunks' helium vocal stylings by recording at half the normal audiotape speed while also talking or singing at half the normal speaking rate. Played back at normal speed, the voices would sound a full octave higher in pitch, at normal tempo. The technique wasn't new, but the Chipmunks' popularity was linked to it.

After Bagdasarian's death from a heart attack in 1972, his son Ross Jr. carried on the concept, reviving the Chipmunks in a subsequent incarnation for the Eighties. A new album, *Chipmunk Punk* (and Saturday-morning reruns of *The Alvin Show*, an animated cartoon series from the Sixties) proved popular enough to warrant another new record. *Urban Chipmunk*—the title parodied the 1980 movie *Urban Cowboy*—was the first country album by Alvin & the Chipmunks, recording favorites with guest stars Brenda Lee and Jerry Reed and producer Larry Butler. "The country is in the mood for something like the Chipmunks," Don Johnson, the general manager of Pickwick Records, said. "It's a novelty—it's cute, it's fun and it's musically sound."

Two out of three wasn't bad. Despite scathing reviews from irritated adults, the album ended up going gold (as had *Chipmunk Punk*) and managed to break into the country charts. ■

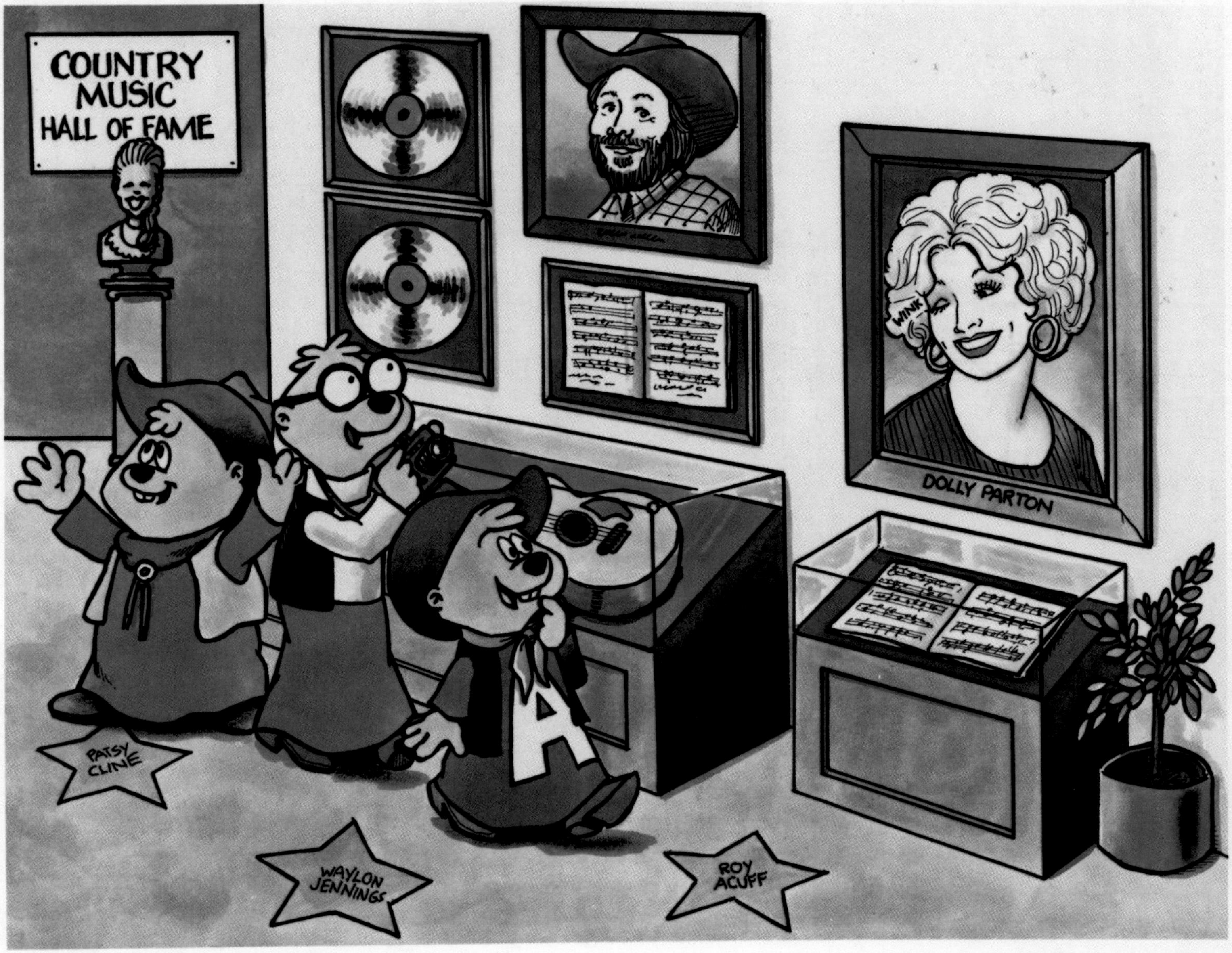

COUNTRY MUSIC HALL OF FAME

WINK

DOLLY PARTON

PATSY CLINE

WAYLON JENNINGS

ROY ACUFF

THE CHIPMUNKS

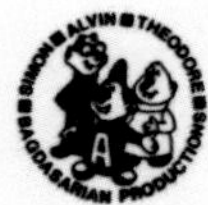

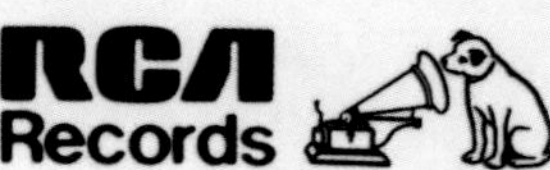

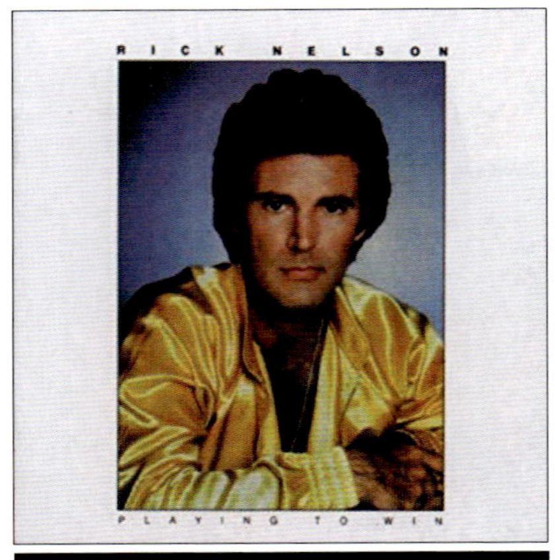

Billboard 200: *Playing to Win* (#153)

Returning to his rock 'n' roll roots, Rick Nelson bid for yet another commercial comeback with *Playing to Win.*

RICK NELSON was the first teen idol to use television as a way to promote records. In 1948, he joined his parents' radio program, *The Adventures of Ozzie and Harriet*, which moved to television for a 14-year run. Five years into the show, Nelson became an "overnight success" by parlaying his clean-cut parent-pleasing image into a recording career and a slew of hit singles.

Nelson's career foundered for a few years after the Beatles' invasion, but during the late Sixties he helped pioneer the country-rock sound with his Stone Canyon Band (whose alumni included the Eagles' Randy Meisner and others). The Seventies were uneventful, save for Nelson's refusal to play "nostalgia" shows. After being booed for his lack of an oldies repertoire during a 1972 Madison Square Garden concert, he came up with "Garden Party," which became one of that year's biggest hits.

There was little of interest on the albums he recorded over the rest of the decade. But with *Playing to Win*, Nelson again concentrated on his roots. The album showcased his revitalized interest in tight, snappy rock 'n' roll.

"Rock 'n' roll is what I first started out doing," he noted. "I feel fortunate being around back then, because I can look back and utilize my knowledge of what works. The only thing that has changed is recording techniques—when I started, people didn't even know what tape echo was."

Assembling a four-piece band, Nelson recorded with producer Jack Nitzsche, who had worked with legendary studio wizard Phil Spector during his heyday. They came up with some fine songs to cover, including selections from cult favorite John Hiatt ("It Hasn't Happened Yet"), Graham Parker ("Back to Schooldays") and John Fogerty ("Almost Saturday Night"). Nelson insisted his return to basics was not just a whim.

"Things have come back around to musicians who know what to do with three chords and don't have to be overly produced. I can appreciate that, because that's just how I started—with just a handful of musicians to work with. Heck, I got to play with James Burton (legendary guitarist who played on Elvis Presley's classics) for ten years. I've managed to span three generations of listeners with my music, and I'm planning on continuing. I'm even learning my fourth chord!"

Playing to Win would be Nelson's last album of original material to be released during his lifetime. He would die in a private plane crash in 1985 on his way to a New Year's Eve gig. He was 45. ■

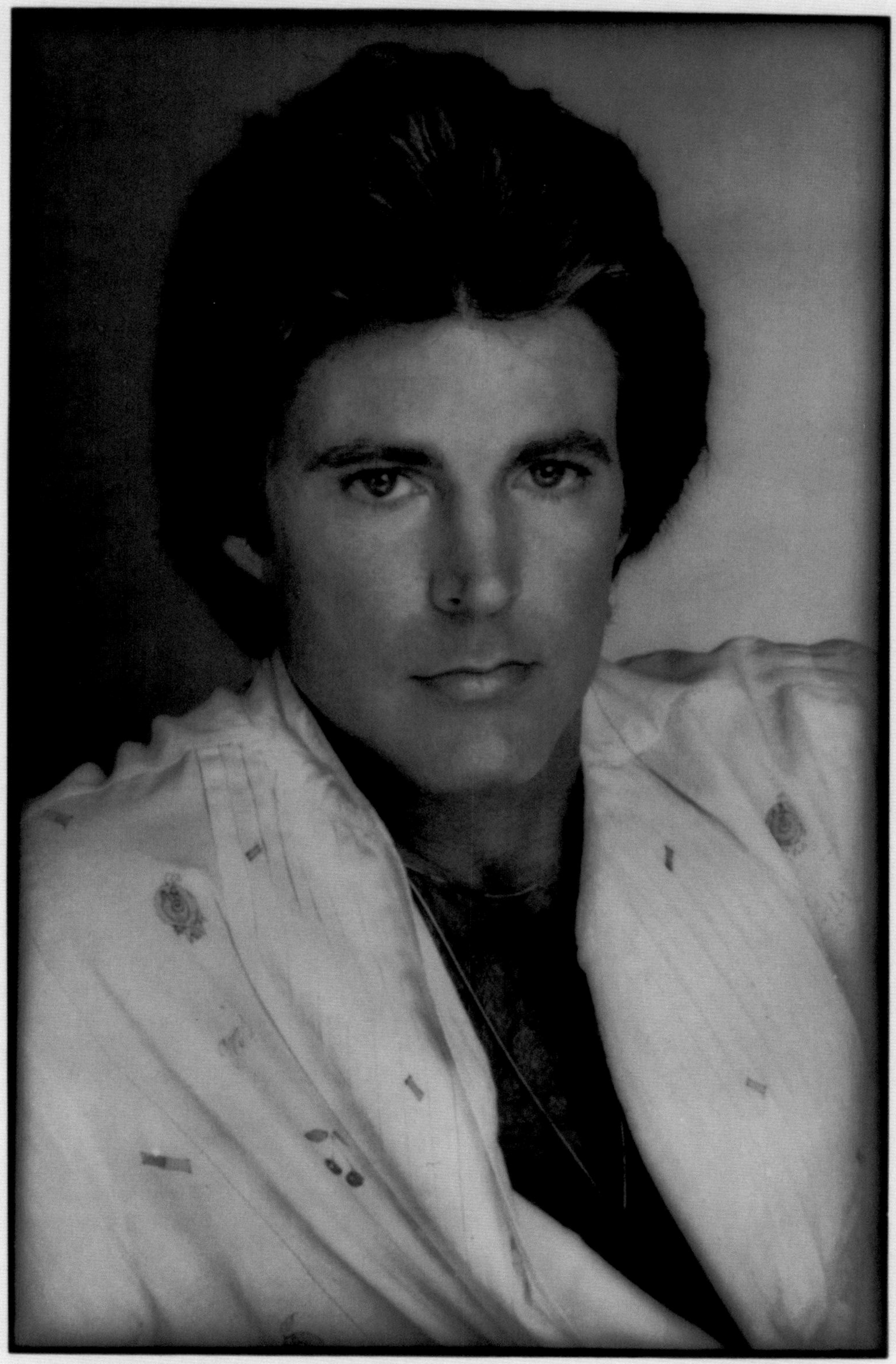

Photo: Susan Rothchild

RICK NELSON

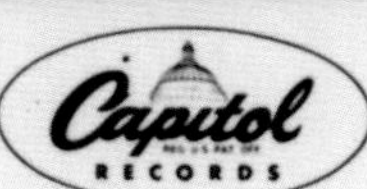

Billboard 200: *Dedication* (#123)
Billboard Hot 100: "This Little Girl" (#11); "Jolé Blon" (#65)

With the help of Bruce Springsteen, Gary U.S. Bonds was the biggest and most unlikely comeback story of 1981.

IN THE early Sixties, Gary U.S. Bonds churned out the charting hits "Quarter to Three" and "New Orleans." On the basis of those rowdy classics, the R&B singer perpetuated his career, spending the Seventies doing many of Dick Clark's oldies tours—"Hey, that's a real lucrative circuit," he noted—and waxing nostalgic in nightclubs, colleges and Holiday Inn lounges until a guy named Bruce Springsteen caught his act one night.

"No, I didn't even know who he was," Bonds admitted. "But I didn't feel bad. Some people don't know who he is, either."

Drawing inspiration from his roots, Springsteen had encored with "Quarter to Three" on his last several tours. He had also recorded a song called "Dedication," which he thought would be perfect for Bonds to sing. They made a record with Springsteen's E Street Band—and Bonds soon found himself climbing the charts again after almost two decades, with the brisk-selling *Dedication* album and the Springsteen-penned hit single, "This Little Girl." A cover of the Cajun standard, "Jolé Blon," featured a duet between Bonds and Springsteen.

Springsteen was the obvious catalyst to bringing Bonds back into the public eye, but the talented E Street guitarist "Miami Steve" Van Zandt also played a considerable role. Both gentlemen were equally capable of reworking the galvanizing energy of early rock 'n' roll—they had contributed fantastic songs early in the career of Southside Johnny & the Asbury Jukes—and with Bonds they found another gravelly-voiced singer to do their tunes justice.

Bonds became a rock story with a happy ending. He had no special arrangement made with Springsteen, but he would get to record a second album.

"This has been a project where everyone got to be in charge, combining to make a big, happy sound," Bonds said. "It takes a lot of people to make happiness. I'm just glad to be here." ■

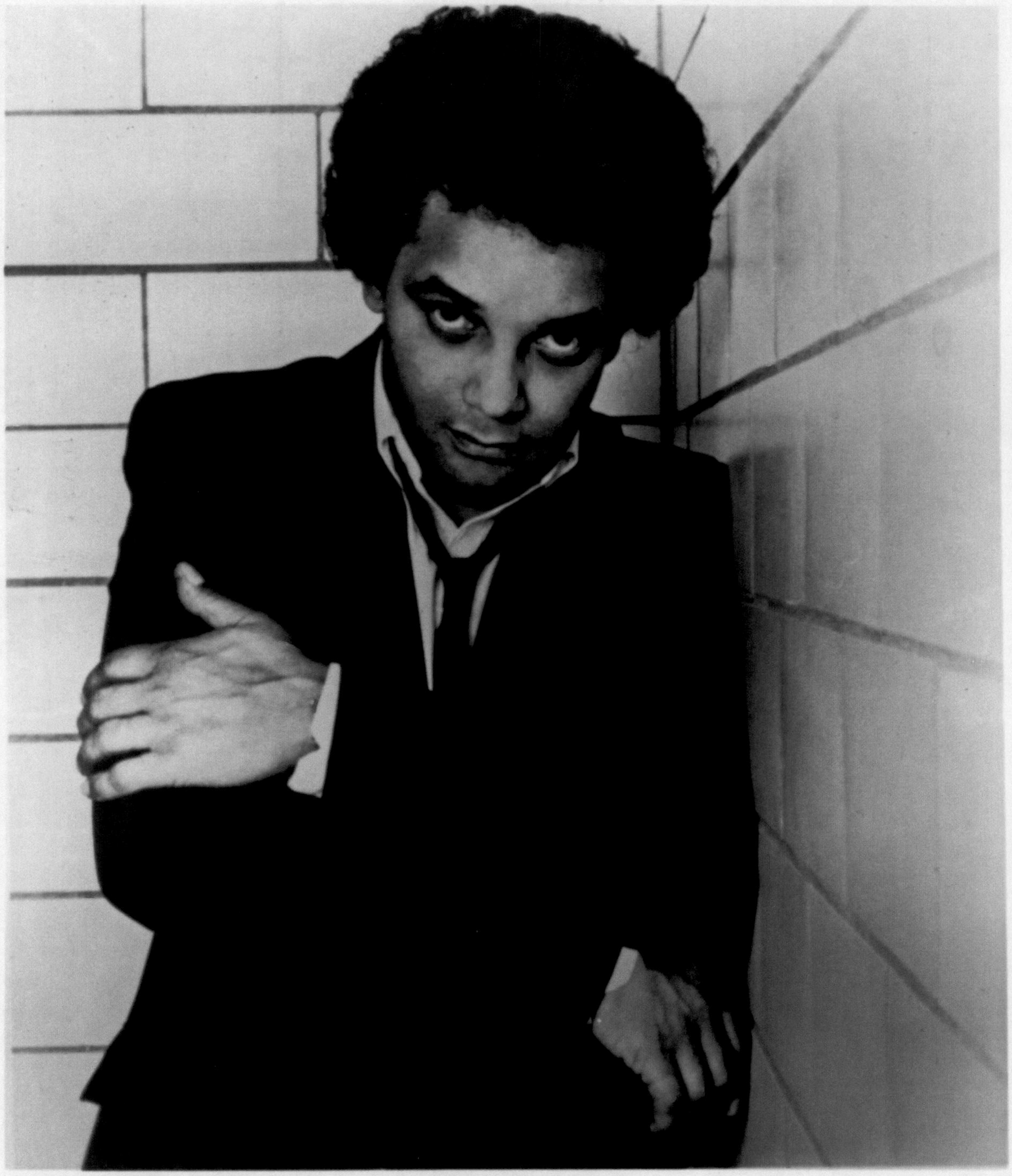

GARY U.S. BONDS

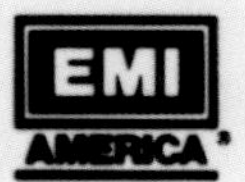

MANAGEMENT/DIRECTION
APOSTOL ENTERPRISES, LTD.
NYC., NY-(212) 399 • 0090

DEL SHANNON

Billboard 200: *Drop Down and Get Me* (#123)
Billboard Hot 100: "Sea of Love" (#33)

Del Shannon, twenty years removed from his immortal "Runaway," returned with *Drop Down and Get Me*.

BORN CHARLES Westover, Del Shannon earned his place in rock 'n' roll history in 1961, when "Runaway," his first record, went to No. 1. Seven Top 40 hits would follow for the Michigan native, who wrote his own material—dark tales of loneliness, heartbreak and revenge, notably "Hats Off to Larry" (where he thanked his ex-girlfriend's new love for breaking her heart), "Keep Searchin'" (a classic lover-as-outlaw song) and "Stranger in Town."

"It was all new and great," Shannon said. "I had some pretty-boy competitors like Fabian, but I did it with music. Maybe it seemed there was a lull with Elvis in the Army carrying a gun, but, man, I loved it."

Shannon was one of the few to survive the initial "British Invasion"—his cover of the Beatles' "From Me to You" charted in America before any Beatles record did, and he supplied Peter & Gordon with a hit, "I Go to Pieces." "But by 1966 it got to the point that if you didn't talk with an English accent you couldn't get anywhere," he lamented. "Guys like the Animals could come over with one hit and tear up the place. I knew I had to get out for a while."

He ended up getting into production, working with Smith ("Baby It's You") and Brian Hyland ("Gypsy Woman"), but he had his share of bad career experiences, and by the mid-Seventies he was also an alcoholic and pill-popper. His lack of direction continued with an aborted attempt at recording with Jeff Lynne of Electric Light Orchestra.

"It sounded more like ELO than me, but Jeff gave me confidence," Shannon recollected. "I was hitting the juice pretty hard back then, and he'd say, 'Do you really need that drink at noon?' It embarrassed me. I went out and got some help and my life totally changed. I gave up the juice, started running and lost 50 pounds. It was a whole new start."

Shannon received a big boost when Tom Petty expressed an interest in producing an album. "I was going to go to Nashville and record country, but he rescued me and got me back into rock 'n' roll," the singer explained. "Him being younger than me made me grow up musically all over again."

Legal complications prevented Petty from speedily completing the album, but with *Drop Down and Get Me*, Shannon returned to the rock mainstream. Featuring members of the Heartbreakers as backing musicians, the album showcased Shannon's powerful voice and still-limber falsetto, and his version of Phil Phillips' classic "Sea of Love" got him his first Top 40 hit in 16 years.

"When you're not on the charts, you're not an artist, you're just an entertainer," Shannon said. "Now that I've got confidence, I know what I want." ■

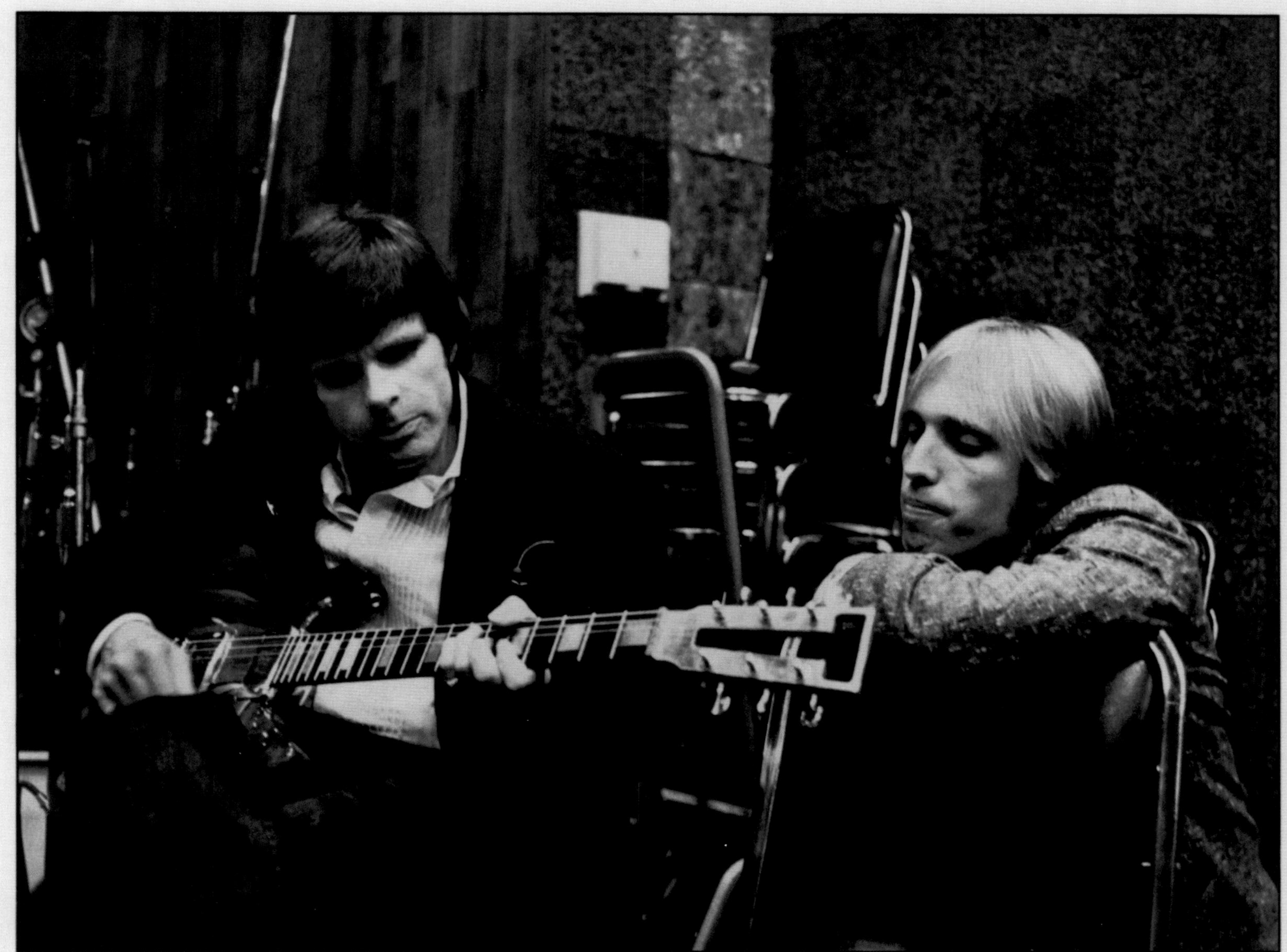

PHOTO CREDIT: DENNIS CALLAHAN/1981

DEL SHANNON & TOM PETTY

NETWORK RECORDS

Distributed by Elektra/Asylum Records.

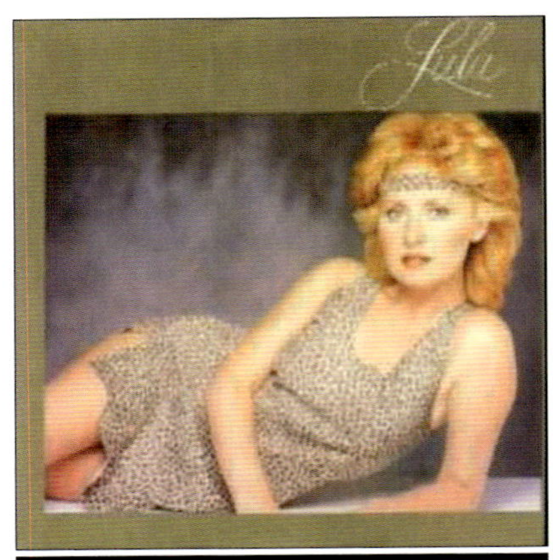

Billboard 200: *Lulu* (#126)
Billboard Hot 100: "I Could Never Miss You (More Than I Do)" (#18); "If I Were You" (#44)

After a 14-year absence, Lulu returned to the US charts with "I Could Never Miss You (More Than I Do)."

SINCE CUTTING her first record at age 14—"Shout," an instant hit in her native UK—Lulu was known as a rock vocalist. Wanting to make her mark as a ballad singer, she starred in the 1967 film *To Sir with Love* with Sidney Poitier and performed the movie's title song. It sold more than 4 million copies worldwide and was a No. 1 hit in America for five straight weeks, a feat unequalled by any foreign female singer.

"Since I was three years old, people were always telling me that they were going to make me a star," Lulu recalled, "because I could sing before I could talk."

That same year, Lulu married Maurice Gibb of the Bee Gees and, after the release of *To Sir with Love*, made her first and only tour of America. Saying she wanted to stay with her husband in England, she limited her touring to Europe until their divorce in 1973. "He objected to my working much at all, actually," she clarified. "I always vowed someday to return to America." Her chart success waned in the US, but she stayed in the public eye in the UK, maintaining her upbeat attitude in a full-time career in pop music, on television, on the stage and in the movies.

In 1981, with the release of *Lulu*, she fulfilled her pledge of coming again to the American music scene. She had been hosting *Let's Rock*, a Fifties rock 'n' roll show being distributed in America. "I Could Never Miss You (More Than I Do)," produced by Mark London (songwriter of "To Sir with Love"), marked a triumphant return to the US charts, a Top 20 pop hit that reached #2 on the adult contemporary chart.

"My roots are really rock 'n' roll with a slice of country," Lulu enthused. "So I've always considered America important. In fact, the whole country's always been like a family to me, like a big, warm blanket." ■

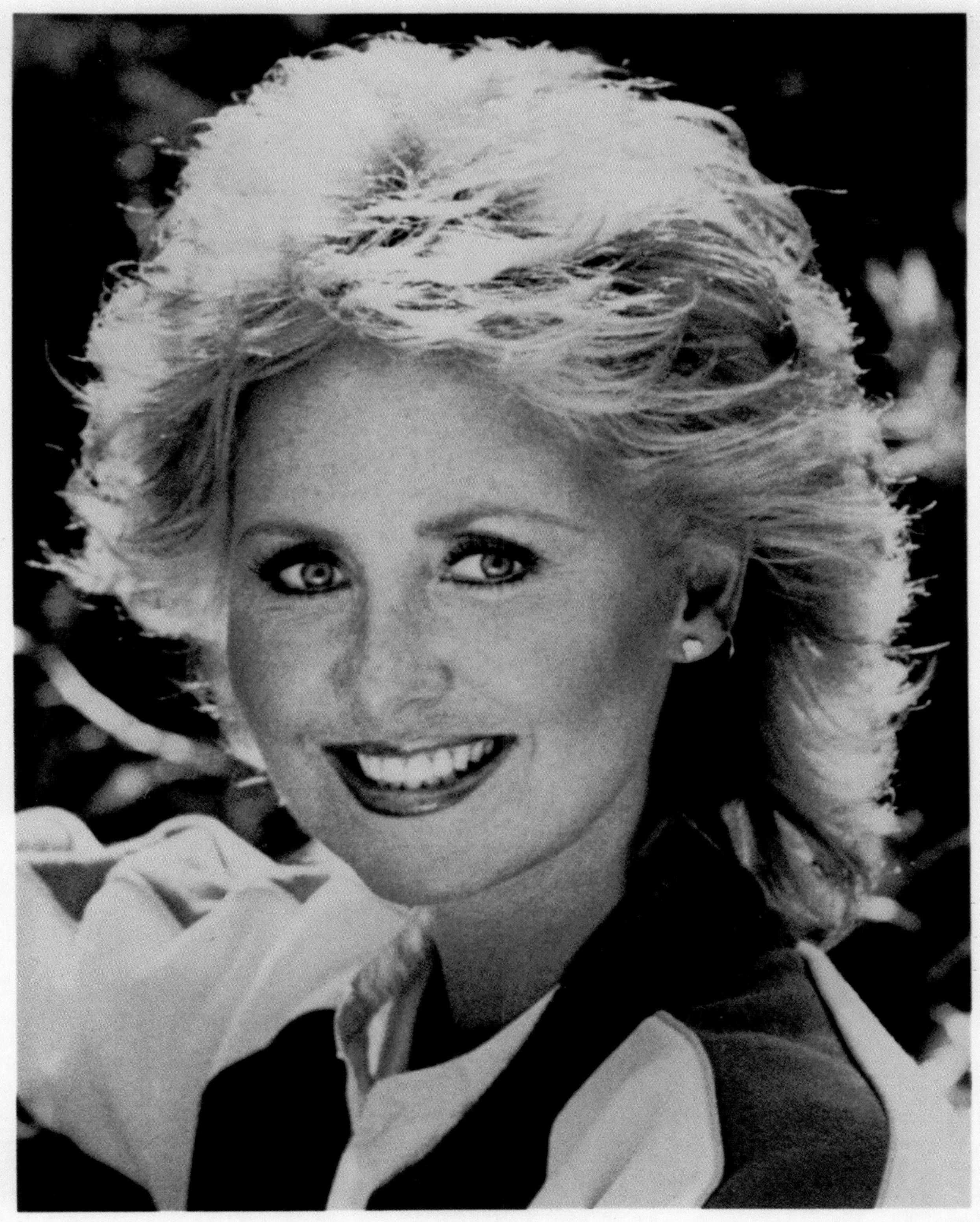

Lulu

Alfa™

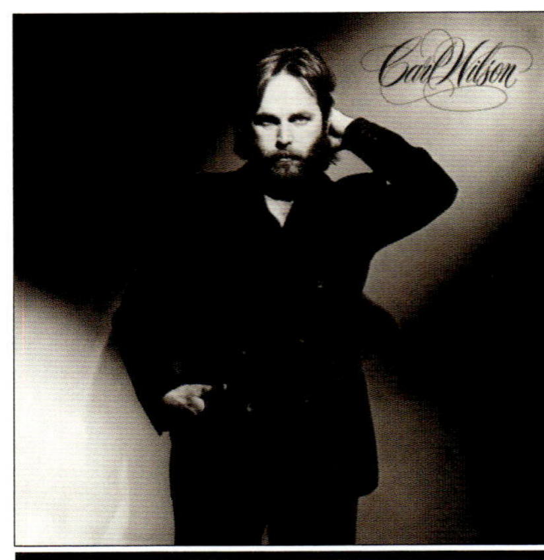

Billboard 200: *Carl Wilson* (#185)

Carl Wilson, the lead guitarist of the Beach Boys, released his self-titled solo debut for Caribou Records.

DURING THE Sixties, the Beach Boys' ability to surf the waves of commercial success and artistic development made them America's preeminent pop group. By the late Seventies, however, the venerable band was threatening to splinter. Carl Wilson, the man who many people credited with keeping the group together all those years, ventured out on his own.

"I never pushed to do a solo record because my first responsibility had always been to the Beach Boys," he explained. "But they had mostly just done concerts for the last couple of years. The group can't really provide me with an outlet for the other music I love to play—good, straight-ahead rock 'n' roll. I just wanted to get some of that off my chest."

Carl Wilson differed substantially from the Beach Boys' cool harmonies and odes to fun in the sun. Myrna Smith, formerly of the Sweet Inspirations, co-wrote all of the songs with Wilson and supplied vocals; the two met at manager Jerry Schilling's house, where, Wilson said, they "hummed melodies and took it from there." When it came time to choose a producer, Wilson gravitated to Jim Guercio, who had mentored the band Chicago and ended a three-year absence from the studio to undertake the project at his home base, Colorado's Caribou Ranch, where Wilson had lived for several years.

Wilson's album was full of raw vocals and thundering guitar tracks. "What You Gonna Do About Me?" featured a new wave-ish chanted chorus, and "The Right Lane" emphasized a chunky rhythmic edge that could have been borrowed from Kiss. "Heaven" was the song that manifested the magic and passion of a Beach Boys work.

"I have always wanted a situation where I could be free and loose to just sing as hard as I could," Wilson explained. "I've been involved with all kinds of stuff, like the *Holland* album—that was as homey and artistic as you could get. I just had to see the other end."

Carl Wilson charted for two weeks on the *Billboard* Top 200. Wilson embarked on the first solo tour by a member of the band that he and his brothers had started 20 years earlier. "It's a chance to see what folks are willing to accept from a Beach Boy," he said. "I feel like a lucky dog—we always have been. Gosh, it's been a wonderful run." ■

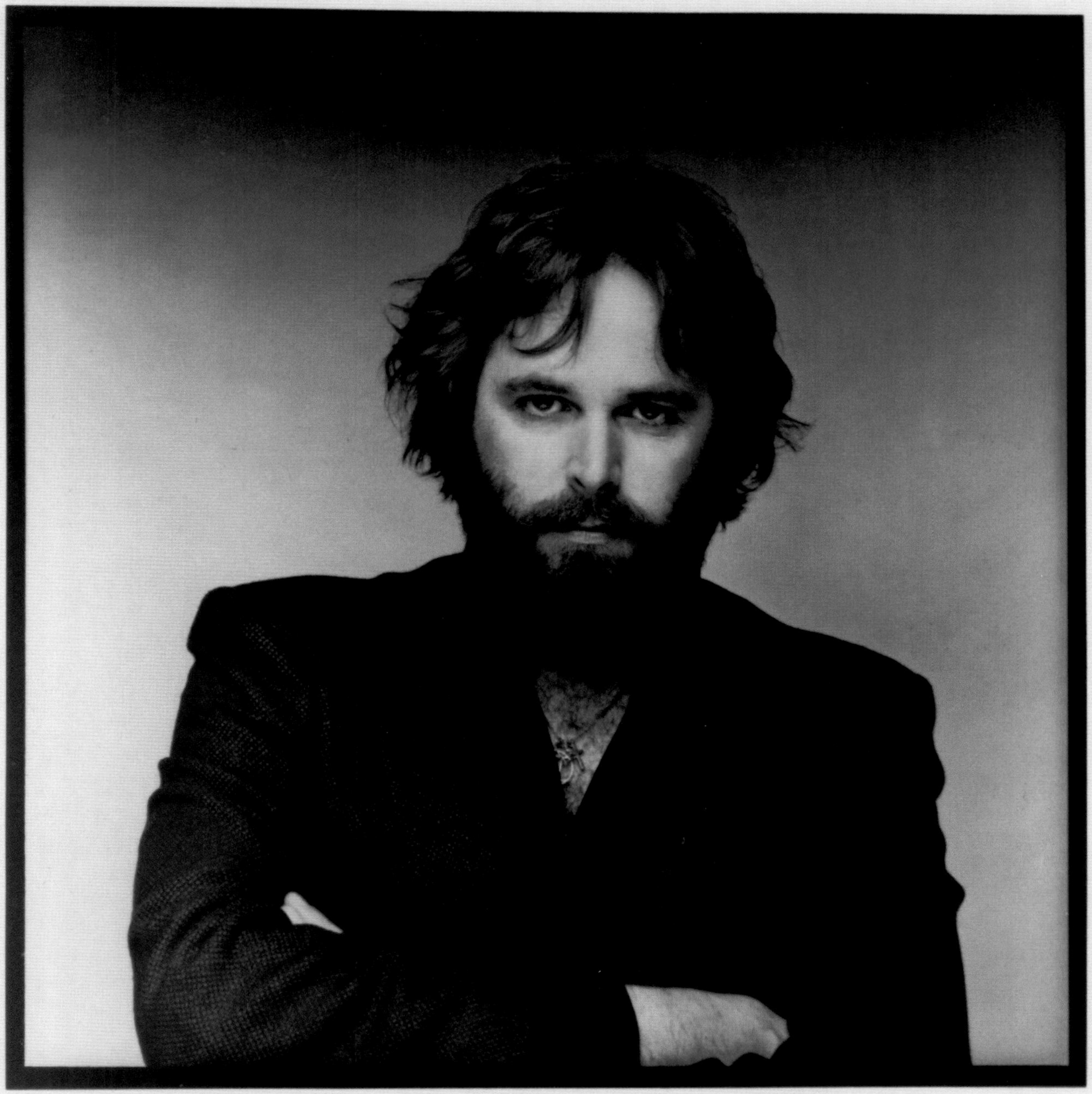

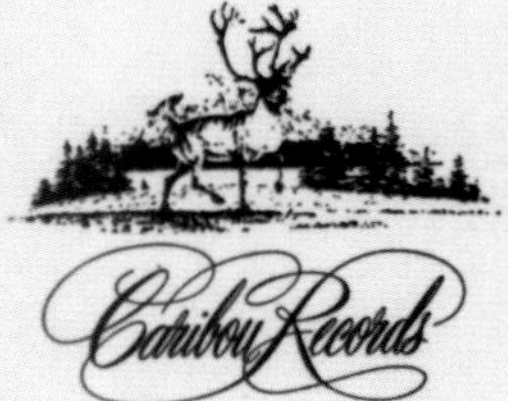

CARL WILSON

Jerry Schilling
MANAGEMENT

10880 Wilshire Blvd
Suite 306
Los Angeles, CA 90024
(213) 475-9629

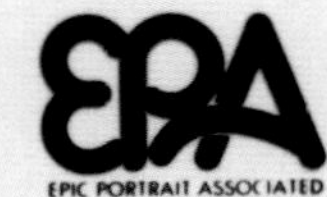

Billboard 200: Honi Soit (#154)

His place in rock history secured, Velvet Underground co-founder John Cale shaped various moods and images on *Honi Soit*.

JOHN CALE was revered in rock music circles as an individual of overwhelming influence, if for no other reason than being an original member of the Velvet Underground. A classically trained Welsh musician who arrived in New York during the early Sixties, Cale linked up with Lou Reed to form the Velvets under the patronage of pop artist Andy Warhol. The Velvets went on to become a seminal cult group whose uncompromising stance became the source of most new-wave, post-punk music. Cale's "modern" sensibilities—screeching viola, throbbing bass and repetitive keyboard work, evident in such seminal recordings as "Heroin" and "Sister Ray"—defined the Velvets' avant-garde vision.

Since those halcyon days, Cale had been a peripheral albeit adventurous composer, with records ranging from the introspective classical recital, *Paris 1919*, to the aggressive, deranged rock 'n' roll tirade of *Fear*. At the same time, the visionary producer had worked with the Stooges, Velvets alumni Reed and Nico, Brian Eno, Phil Manzanera, Jonathan Richman & the Modern Lovers, Patti Smith and Squeeze. In other words, Cale had built up one of rock's most imposing résumés.

"I've said over and over again that I'm a ham, a classical composer disheveling my musical personality by dabbling in rock 'n' roll," Cale mused. "What's most important is the work. If you can do some good work, it's there for a while."

Cale reached a new level of frenzy during one British show circa 1977—he sacrificed a chicken on stage voodoo-style, prompting half of his vegetarian band to quit. *Honi Soit* represented a pleasant creative upswing, a move in a more commercial direction and his only album to chart in the US. Cale was often forced to confront his past work due to the enduring legacy of the Velvet Underground, whose white-noise symphonies continued to be scrutinized by rock archivists.

"I can't think of a single thing that hasn't been covered, except maybe our nose hairs," he muttered. "The record company is pretty shameless, they'll put anything out. But I'm reminded of some pleasant moments in those times, some giggling going on—we did have fun in the studio."

What else could Cale do to add to his legend?

"You mean to assume my rightful position?" he grunted. "That's a pleasant thought. But I'm just busy getting things done. That's all I can do, try to get on with it." ■

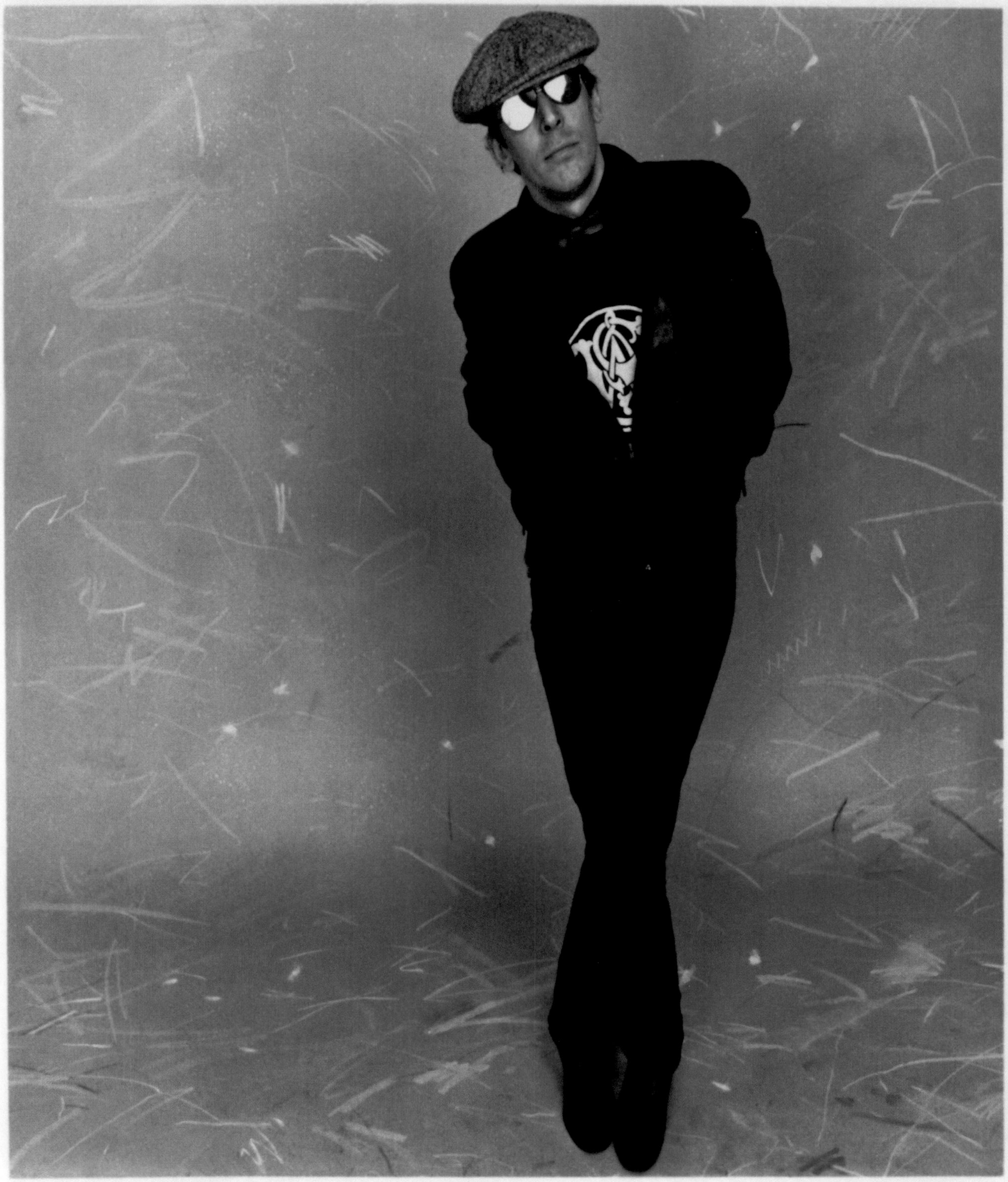

PHOTO: LARRY WILLIAMS

JOHN CALE

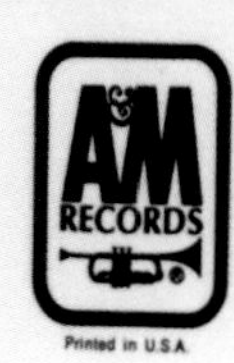

Printed in U.S.A.

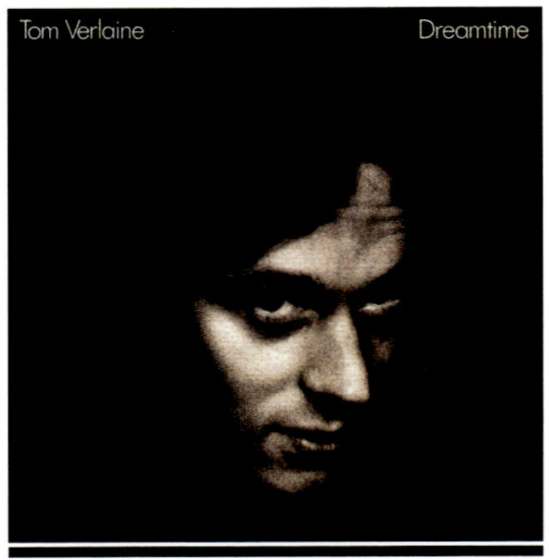

Billboard 200: *Dreamtime* (#177)

Dreamtime, Tom Verlaine's second solo effort, picked up where his influential and erstwhile group, Television, left off.

BACK IN the fabled 1977 summer of punk, while the majority of New York-based bands were recycling the venom of various English counterparts, the group Television surfaced to rave reviews. The band was doomed to cult status, but Tom Verlaine's angst-ridden vocals and circular guitar style distinguished two excellent albums—*Marquee Moon* and *Adventure*—before the band disintegrated.

Verlaine released a self-titled solo album in 1979 before dropping out of sight. The following year, David Bowie recorded Verlaine's "Kingdom Come" for his *Scary Monsters* album. A new music audience had developed, and Verlaine was in a strange position—fans who dropped up-and-coming names such as the Cure and Human Sexual Response weren't aware of Television's groundbreaking role.

Verlaine resurfaced with *Dreamtime*, a weighty album that showed he hadn't been twiddling his thumbs during his break. Tunes such as "Always" and "Penetration" retained the best kinetic factors from the Television albums, while Verlaine's ringing guitar work remained among the most compelling in rock—an amazingly clean, trebly sound that was at once dissonant and dynamic. His solos verged on drifting to all the wrong places, almost like Jeff Beck trying to play a Charlie Parker riff on guitar. But the lanky, pale artiste framed his excursions with choppy rhythms and some solid band interplay, and the result was hypnotic.

"I dunno much about my style," he explained. "It's just the way I play that comes out. I listened to a lot of Roland Kirk and jazz when I was a kid, and I guess I'm trying to do some of the same things in a rock context. All I know is that I play my solos on a Jaguar—a lot of surf groups used to use them, but I can't play on anything else." ■

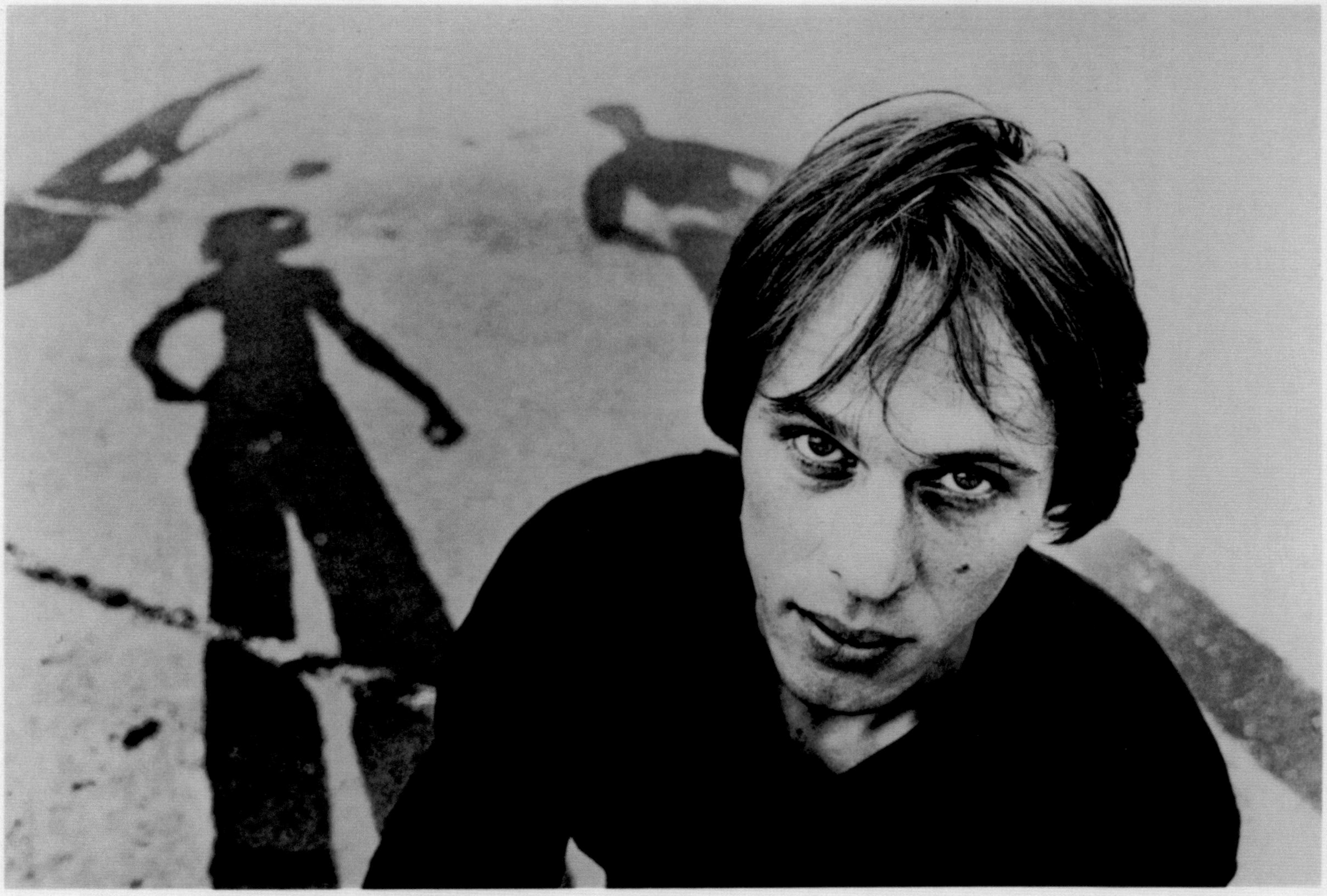

TOM VERLAINE

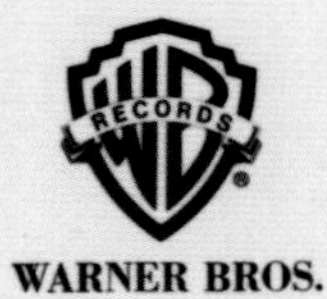

WARNER BROS.

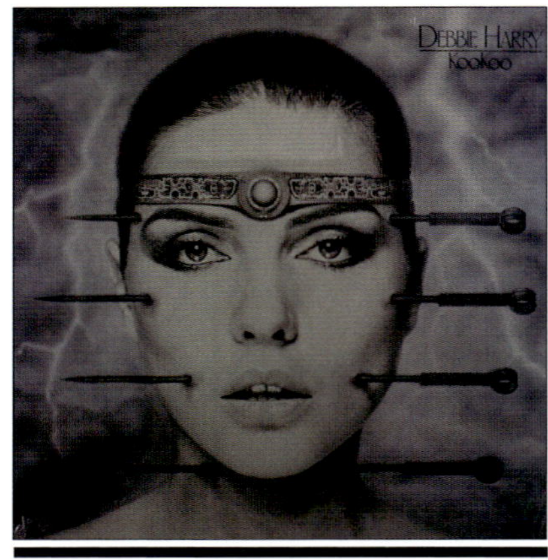

Billboard 200: *KooKoo* (#25)
Billboard Hot 100: "Backfired" (#43); "The Jam Was Moving" (#82)

In an attempt to expand her creative horizons, Blondie's Debbie Harry released her first solo album, *KooKoo*.

AFTER FIVE years of garnering acclaim with the new-wave band Blondie—including the No. 1 singles—"Heart of Glass," "Call Me," "The Tide is High" and "Rapture"—lead singer Debbie Harry decided to branch out on her own separate project. She asked Bernard Edwards and Nile Rodgers of the R&B band Chic to produce and cowrite *KooKoo*, a union of rock, funk and dance music.

"I hope people like the music whether they are dancing or listening while driving, at home or at work," Harry said. "They ask me if the lyrics mean such-and-such, but anything deeper than what the words say is merely a personal interpretation by the listener."

"Backfired," the first single taken from *KooKoo*, failed to make a significant impact on the charts, but the stunning cover art gained plenty of media attention. Created by Swiss painter and designer H.R. Giger—whose visual design for the 1979 sci-fi suspense film, *Alien*, had earned him an Academy Award—the album featured an image of metal skewers going through Harry's face and neck, Many stores refused to stock the album.

"I see the cover as projecting energy and vitality," Harry stated. "The album title stems from the 'cu' syllable in acupuncture. Eventually, I came up with *KooKoo*." ■

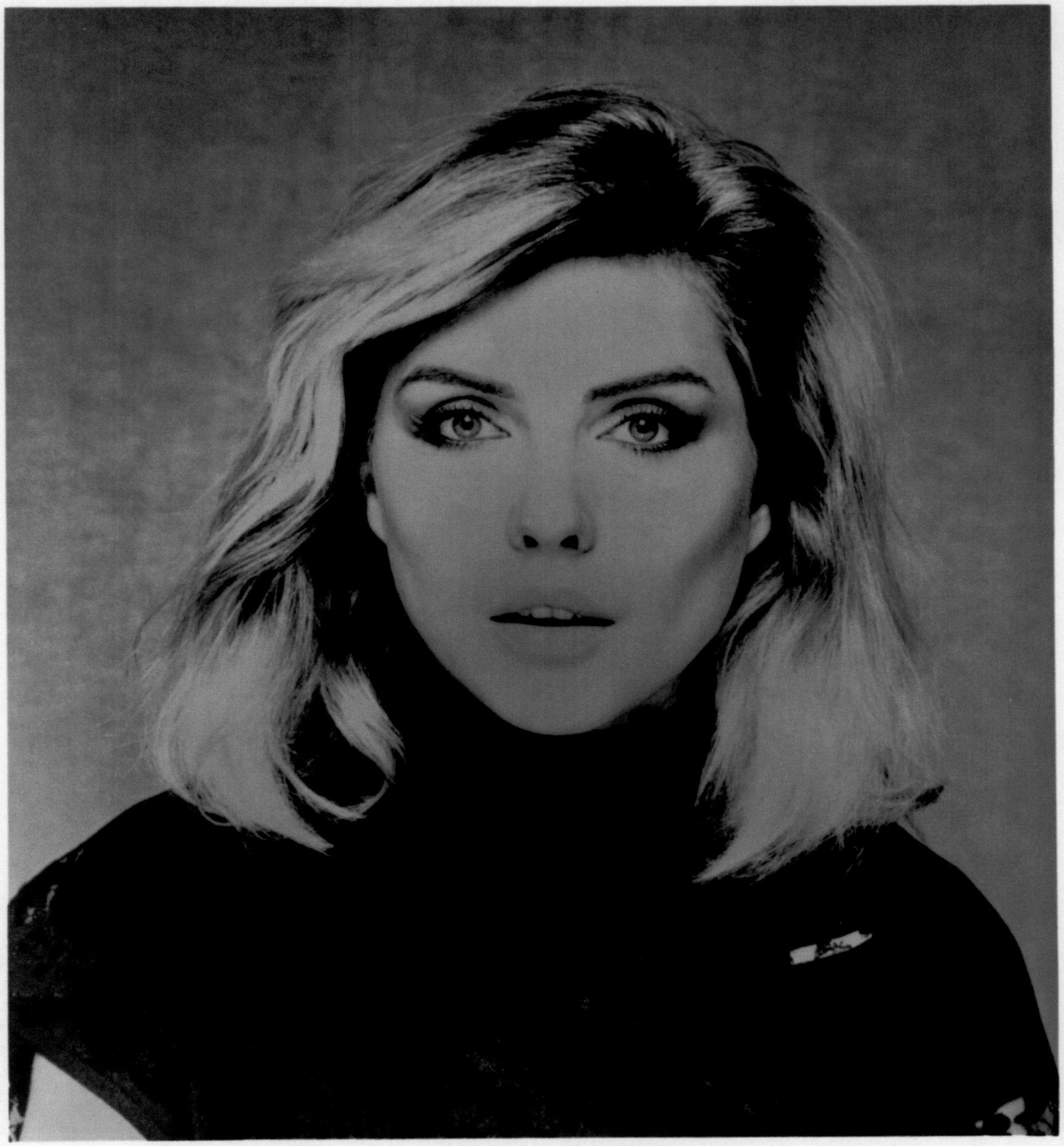

DEBBIE HARRY

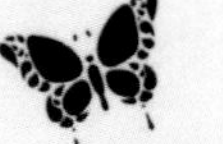

Chrysalis

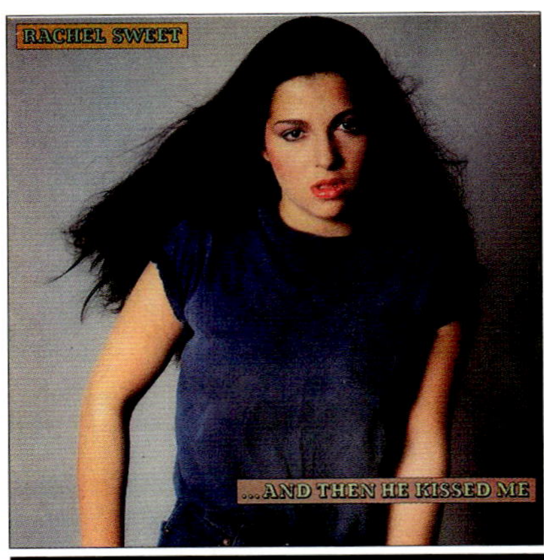

Billboard 200: ...*And Then He Kissed Me* (#124)
Billboard Hot 100: "Everlasting Love" (#32)

"Everlasting Love," a duet with Rex Smith, was the featured hit from Rachel Sweet's ...*And Then He Kissed Me.*

A GIRL with decent rock 'n' roll sensibilities seemingly needed two noses to stand out in the overcrowded recording and touring markets. But some smart money was being placed on Rachel Sweet, a "spunky" 18-year-old who had acted in commercials as a child before trying her hand as a country singer at age 11. Three years later, she switched to rock.

"There were no kids doing it—that was the main inspiration," she explained. "In country music, the whole audience was filled with 50-year-old women who just clapped politely when I was done. I knew I was missing something."

The precocious Sweet's first major venture into the recording industry occurred when Liam Sternberg, a friend of her father's, had her record a demo of his songs for Stiff Records, the oddball English record label famous for launching the careers of Elvis Costello, Nick Lowe and Ian Dury. Stiff ended up calling the then-16 Sweet at her Ohio home, asking her to fly to London to record (she agreed on the stipulation that she could bring her sister). Her debut record, *Fool Around*, included a version of Carla Thomas' Sixties hit "B-A-B-Y." *Protect the Innocent*, her second album, went largely ignored.

Unfortunately, some of the connotations of Sweet's affiliation with the unorthodox Stiff left the wrong impression about her very real talents. Attention centered on her hometown of Akron, the city that gave the world Devo, and her age was an obvious point of discussion, as Stiff pushed a statutory-untouchable image for her. Sweet had a gift to transcend her years and her competition. Her voice possessed just enough squeak to reap benefits when the right material came along. "I sound like Mickey Mouse," she exaggerated, but her instantly identifiable vocal sound was rooted in the Sixties tradition that was enjoying a renaissance.

...And Then He Kissed Me found Sweet refining her own writing ability, but the album's Top 40 hit turned out to be a remake of Robert Knight's 1967 "Everlasting Love," a duet with Rex Smith.

"I wanna get away from any sort of soft image—I'm no female Barry Manilow. There's a tendency to label girls as doing mushy love songs," she said. "You either come in on the crest of a wave or you get buried by it. I'm offering personality." ■

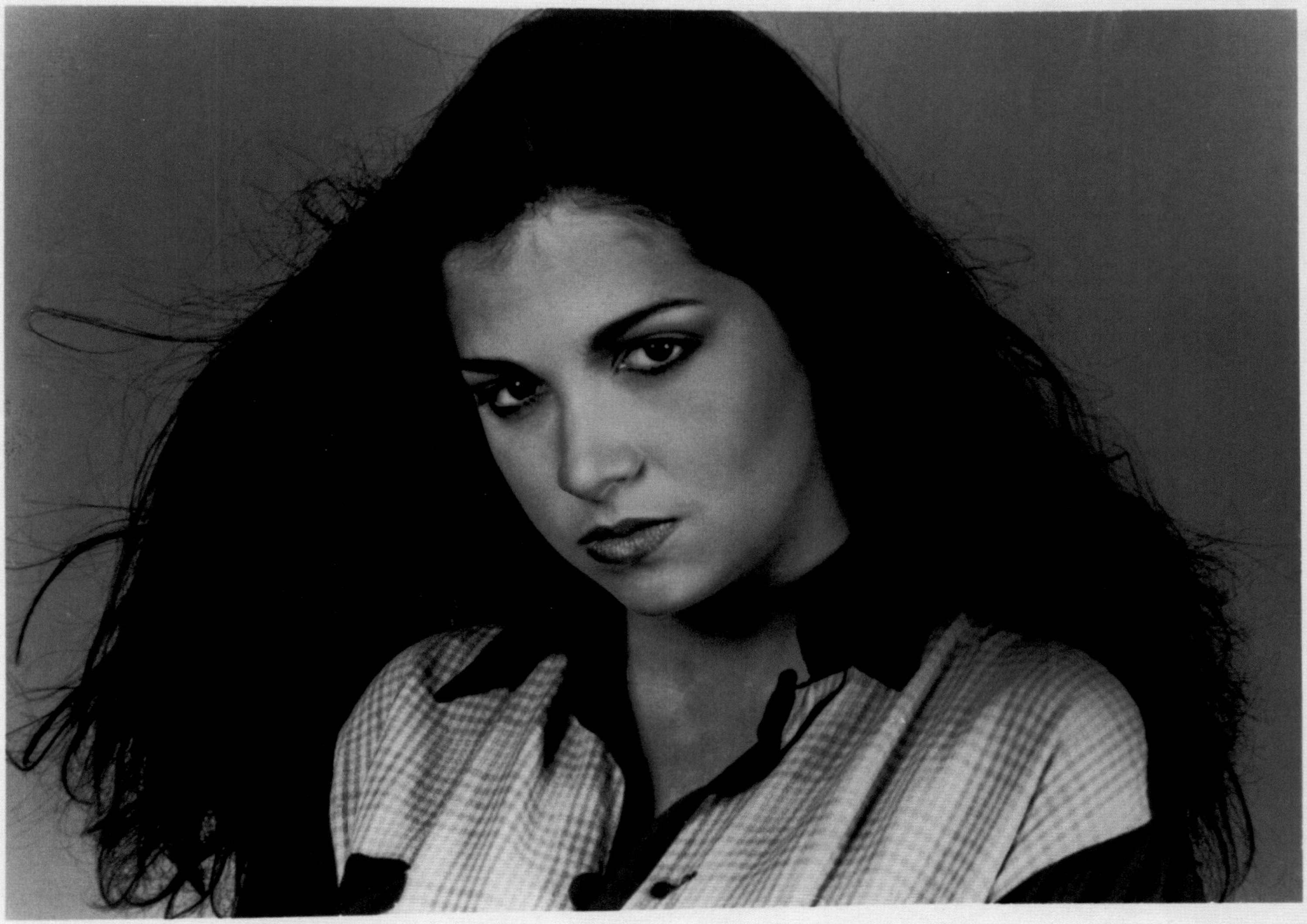

Photograph: Lynn Goldsmith/LGI

RACHEL SWEET

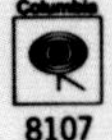

8107

New wave diva Lene Lovich yelped her way through "New Toy," a dance tune written by synth-pop artist Thomas Dolby.

LENE LOVICH made a trendy splash in the late Seventies with her eccentric vocal improvisations—chirping like a bird, or swooping like a siren (or, more precisely, "*eek*," "*wowp*" and "*hhkak*"). On her early albums, there was no telling the difference between a synthesizer droning and her provocative vocal trills. Her melodies had a distinctly Slavic flavor, combined with her penchant for dressing like a peasant queen from Mars.

She enjoyed moderate success in Europe. In 1978, Stiff Records signed her after hearing her first demo, a remake of Tommy James & the Shondells' "I Think We're Alone Now." It appeared on her first album, *Stateless*, which was released in the UK and produced three Top 30 hits, led by "Lucky Number," which made the diminutive nonconformist a leading figure on the new-wave scene.

Released in 1981, the six-song mini-LP *New Toy* featured the title track, a satire of consumer culture penned by new band member Thomas Dolby, a synth-pop pioneer.

Lovich saw a hint of irony as she returned to the US as a European artiste—she was born in Detroit and moved to England when she was 13. "But I don't feel very American," she noted. "My memories of America are those of a child." Thus the imaginative effects and bewitching textures that Lovich and her guitarist-boyfriend Les Chappell concocted in the studio were far removed from the mainstream of American music.

"People think that I write those brooding European melodies because I have a foreign-sounding name, but I don't know about that," she said. "There just seems to be some sort of ethnic attraction." ■

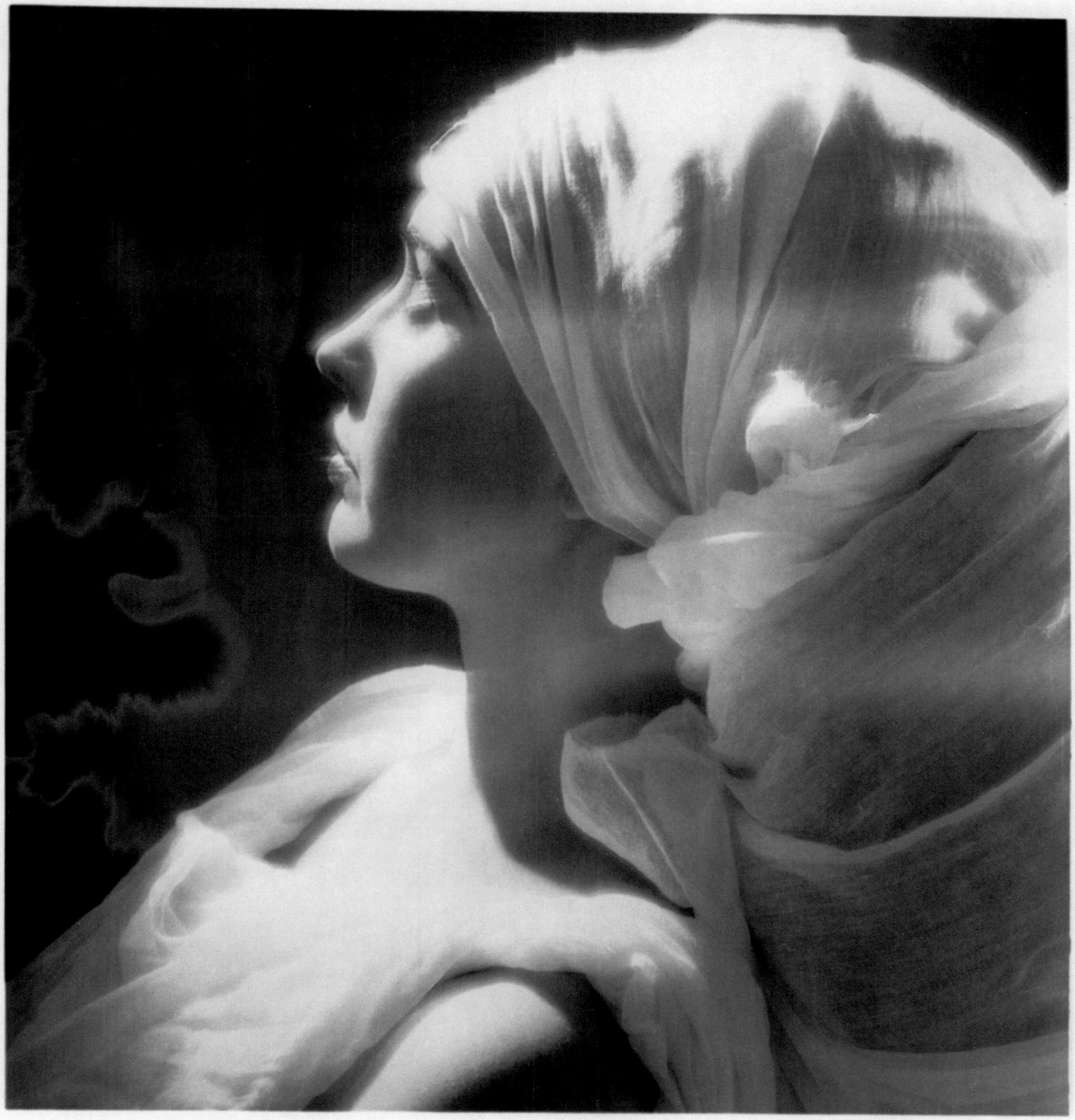

LENE LOVICH

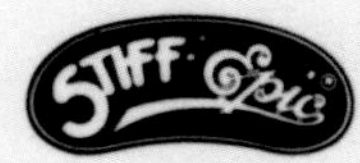

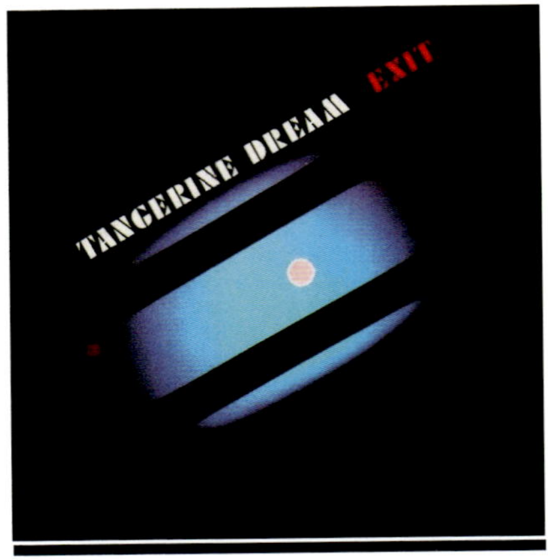

Billboard 200: *Exit* (#195)

Exit marked a new phase in the innovative, often-imitated electronic music of Germany's Tangerine Dream.

ROCK'S NEW wave had brought to the fore a myriad of synthesizer-based bands—all of which derived a degree of inspiration from Tangerine Dream. The German group began recording in 1970 with the advent of the very first electronic keyboards, starting out as a hippie space ensemble that made Pink Floyd sound like a bar band, as the musicians used entire album sides as canvases to paint their atmospheric aural imagery.

But Tangerine Dream's pioneering days had set the stage for a wider acceptance. The moody creations no longer sounded inaccessible, and the group found itself reaching a larger audience. The band supplied the soundtrack to *Thief,* a film starring James Caan that owed much of its success to the terse background music.

"Writing for movies necessitates composing in shorter segments," group leader Edgar Froese admitted. "But our music has always had a cinematic scope—almost a soundtrack without the film."

And with *Exit,* Tangerine Dream hoped its compositions would take on a worldwide scope. Most of the attention centered on the track "Kiew Mission," which featured only the second vocal in the group's history. The song was not standard Top 40 fare—the uncredited vocalist sang in Russian, an unorthodox approach designed to spread the message of world peace.

"In Europe, young people are much more aware of the possibility of global war than their American counterparts are," Froese explained. "Everything that happens over in Europe is done with the feeling that another war is imminent. We felt that our music could help spread a message and act as an emissary in itself—so 'Kiew Mission' utilizes a subliminal approach that hopefully will get the attention of world leaders."

Tapes of the song had been sent behind the Iron Curtain, and Froese reported that the nine-minute number had found a large degree of acceptance. "It is important to try and say something in the context of music," he maintained. "Especially now, when so many other bands are using the techniques that we pioneered several years ago. Kraftwerk has stopped being innovative, and Giorgio Moroder gets an award for the soundtrack to *Midnight Express* using musical themes we developed. We have to be careful what we say when we talk to these people, because we find our ideas getting used." ■

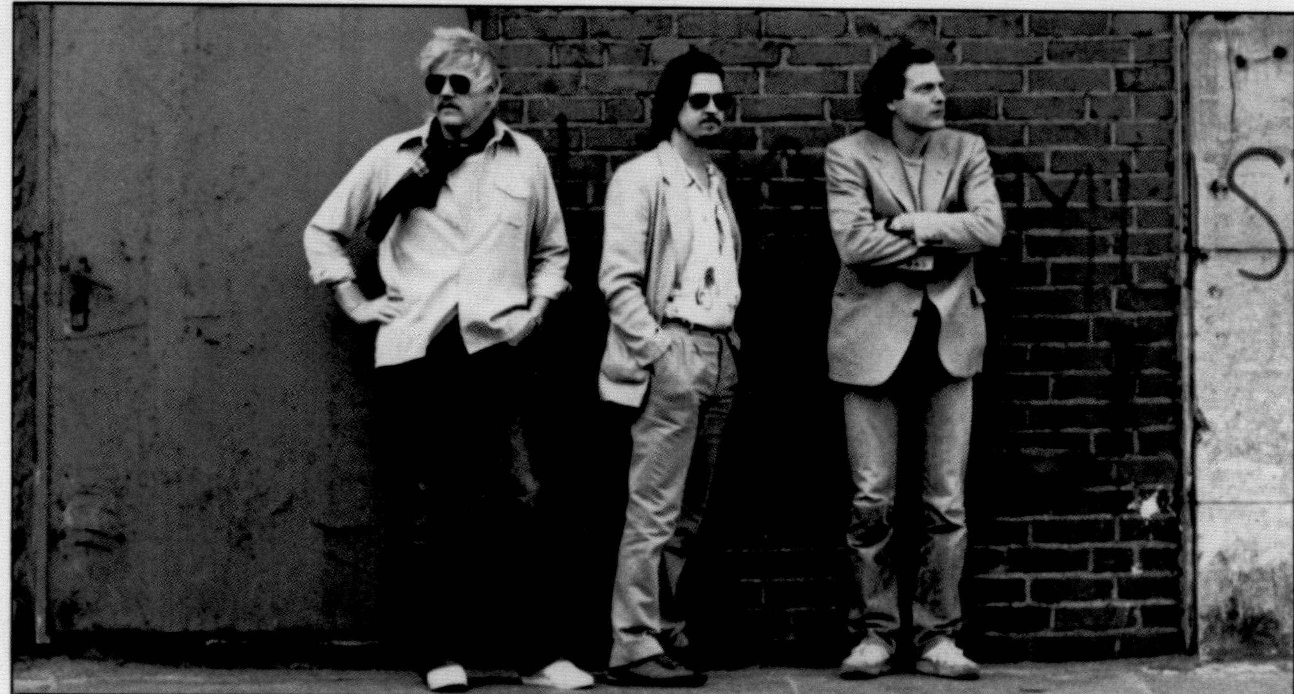

EDGAR FROESE CHRIS FRANKE JOHANNES SCHMOELLING

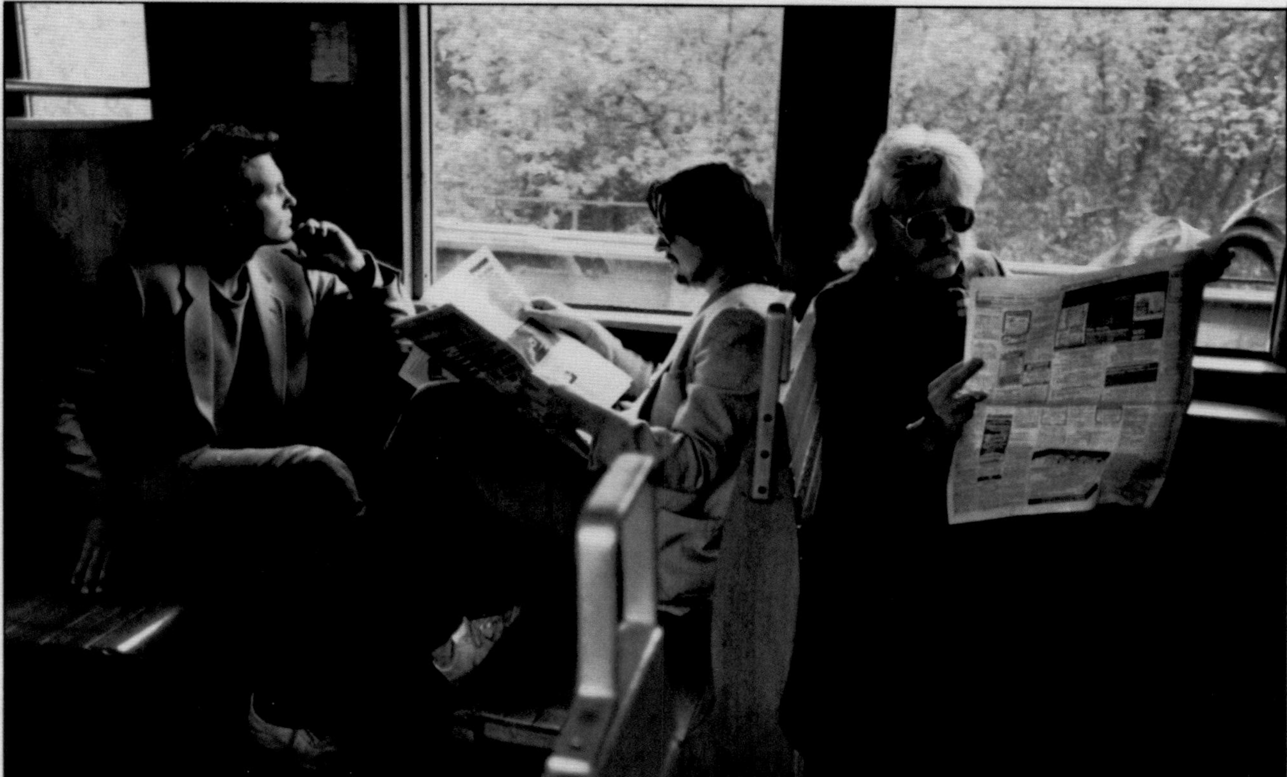

JOHANNES SCHMOELLING CHRIS FRANKE EDGAR FROESE

PHOTO CREDIT: MONIQUE FROESE/1981

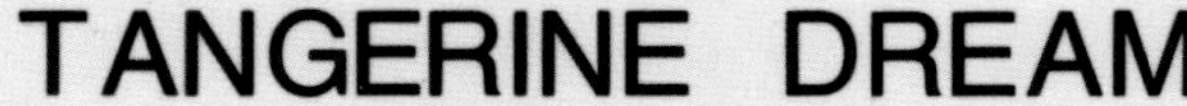

TANGERINE DREAM

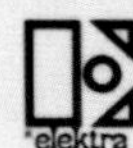

Billboard 200: *Breakin' Away* (#9)
Billboard Hot 100: "We're in This Love Together" (#15); "Breakin' Away" (#43); "Teach Me Tonight" (#70)

Breakin' Away consolidated the talented Al Jarreau's position as a favorite and enduring "vocal musician."

BORN IN Milwaukee, Grammy-winning jazz vocalist Al Jarreau had been singing with his family since the age of four.

"My older brothers were singers and brought a lot of jazz music into the house—they would rehearse at home and I would listen," Jarreau said. "I can remember hearing Daddy-O Daylie out of Chicago when I was eating my oatmeal in the kitchen. I learned to harmonize in the second and third grade—simple harmony to simple songs. It was that early stuff that developed my ear for improvised sound."

Jarreau received an education in psychology and earned a master's degree in vocational rehabilitation from the University of Iowa before moving west—first to San Francisco, where he did counseling work, and later to Los Angeles. In both cities, he began performing in local clubs on a part-time basis.

"I had been grooming myself towards a music career for a long time. The turning point was in 1968, when I began to have some real misgivings about my place as a rehabilitation counselor. I wasn't as effective as I should have been, and I didn't really fit the mold—a round peg in a square hole."

Talent scouts spotted Jarreau and signed him to a recording contract. His debut album, *We Got By*, met with international acclaim. By his sixth album, he had moved into the realm of sleekly produced pop—*Breakin' Away*, his most commercially successful effort, spent two years on the album charts and hit No. 1 on both the jazz and R&B charts. "We're in This Love Together" was his first pop Top 40 entry, and "Teach Me Tonight," a standard from the Gene DePaul/Sammy Cahn songbook, received a new life.

At the Grammy Awards, *Breakin' Away* received the prize for Best Pop Vocal Performance, Male. "(Round, Round, Round) Blue Rondo à la Turk," a version of Dave Brubeck's classic with words added by Jarreau, earned the award for Best Jazz Vocal Performance, Male.

"Winning awards is wonderful, but the main thing is doing the music and getting response from the audience," Jarreau maintained. "That's happening more and more—I love it!" ■

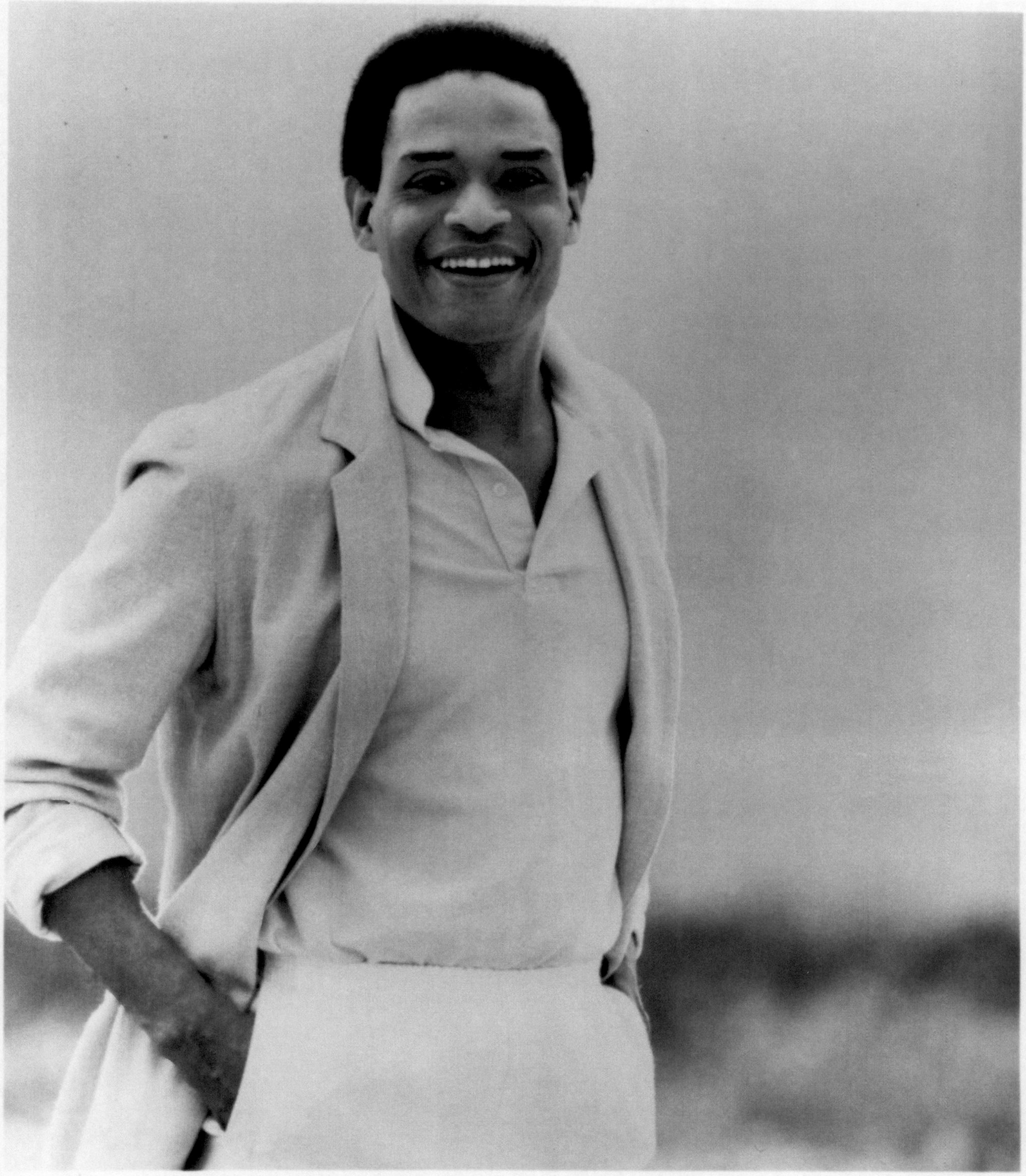

AL JARREAU

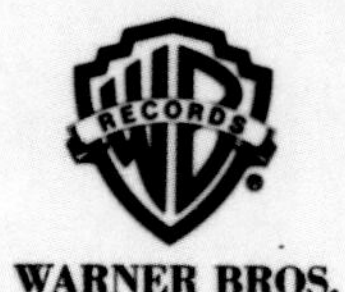

WARNER BROS.

Billboard 200: *The Clarke/Duke Project* (#33)
Billboard Hot 100: "Sweet Baby" (#19)

The Clarke/Duke Project aimed for an atypical audience for jazz musicians Stanley Clarke and George Duke.

AT THE 1971 Pori Jazz Festival in Finland, the singer-songwriter, keyboardist and record producer George Duke spotted a gangly player in the lobby of his hotel. The young bassist walked up to Duke and made his simple introduction with the point of a bony finger—"Stanley Clarke."

"I knew then he was someone a little strange," Duke recalled. "Ever since then we've tried to make a record together."

For most of the Seventies, Clarke had been recognized as the premier jazz bassist, thanks to his spectacular work with Chick Corea and Return to Forever. Since leaving that group, he had released several solo works that were respected but kept him pigeonholed in the jazz virtuoso category. Clarke made a concerted effort to expand his audience in a 1979 stint with Ron Wood and his New Barbarians, where his bass solo spot and inspired interaction with Keith Richards proved to be a memorable part of the show.

"People have locked me into this 'Best Bleeping Jazz Bassist in the World' category, and I know that I'm capable of much more," Clarke remarked. "I'm a good composer, a good performer, even a good husband and father. People should give me a chance to prove myself on other horizons."

Clarke teamed with Duke on *The Clarke/Duke Project*, finally succumbing to pressures from friends, record companies and fan mail. "Sweet Baby," a slick attempt at pop-soul, found its way up the pop singles charts and made the two more famous as a duo than as solo artists. A bizarre remake of the standard "Louie Louie" was one of the loosest jams to be associated with either musician.

"Stanley wanted to rework an old song that everybody knew—something that would cross racial barriers, that wouldn't put us in an R&B or rock bag exclusively," Duke noted. "After a couple of glasses of wine late at night, we did it in one take."

Such an attitude might have offended jazz perfectionists, but Duke said the majority of flak had died down.

"We've done so many different things that the purists have forgotten about us," he declared with a laugh. "We wanted to do an album nobody expected us to do, such as trying our hand at pop with "Sweet Baby"—why not do an album that will reach people that we don't usually reach?" ■

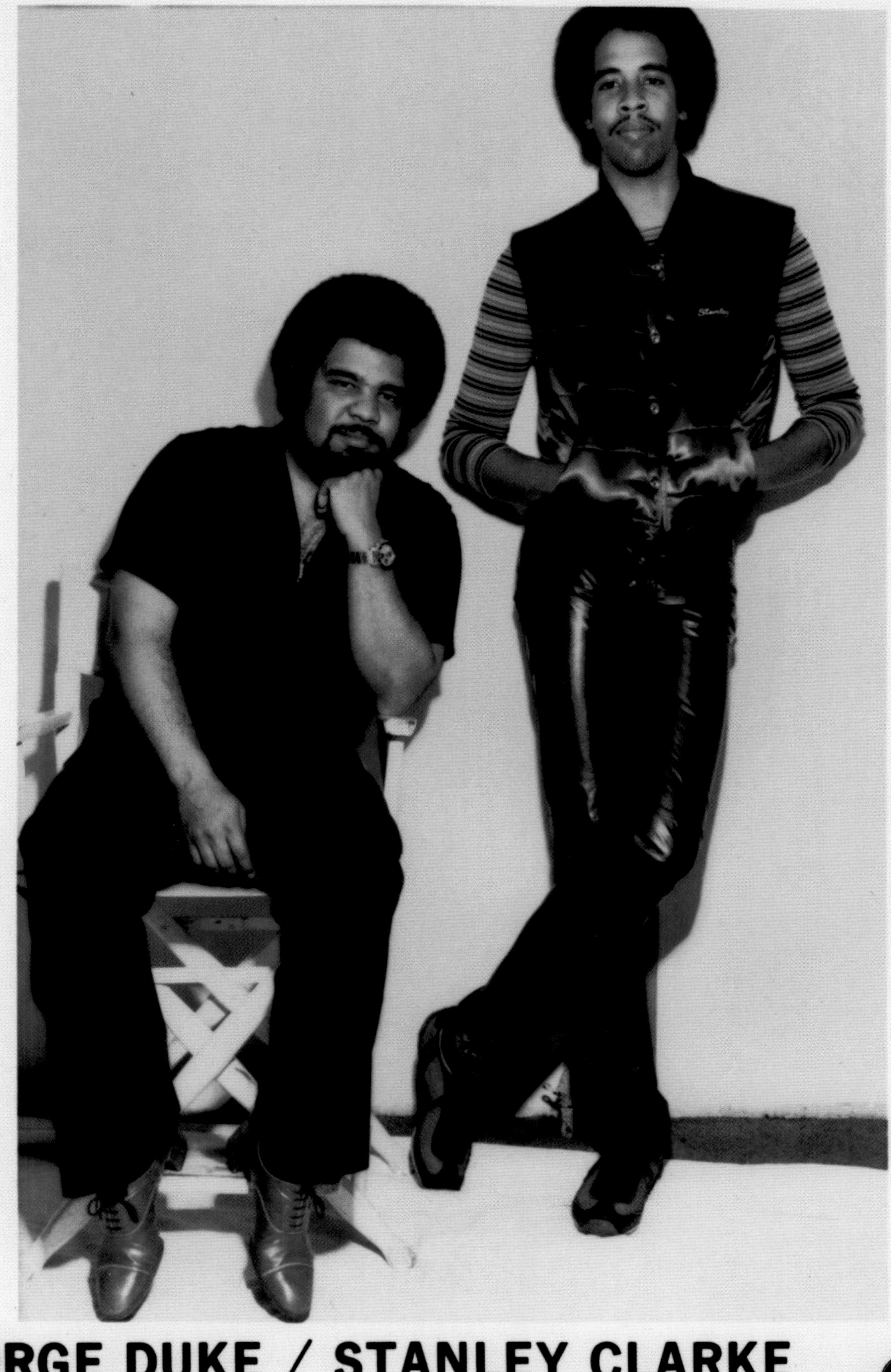

GEORGE DUKE / STANLEY CLARKE

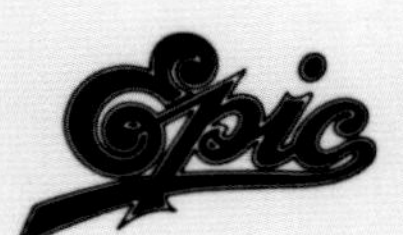

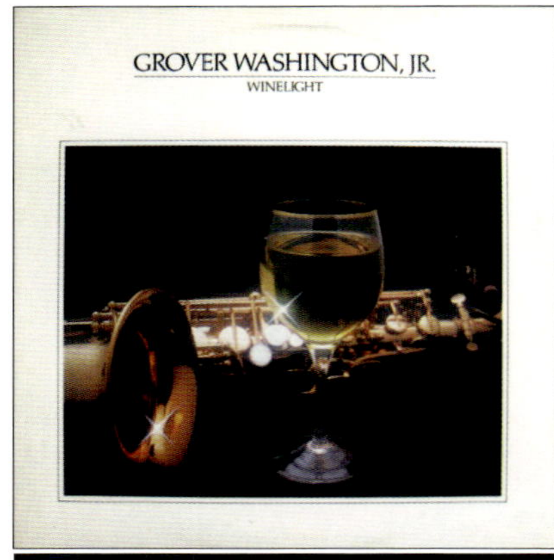

Billboard 200: *Winelight* (#5)
Billboard Hot 100: "Just the Two of Us" (#2)

Grover Washington, Jr.'s "Just the Two of Us," exposed the jazz superstar to a whole new range of listeners.

LIKE MANY successful musicians, Grover Washington, Jr. had weathered a protracted period of dues-paying before a run of six solo LPs held the No. 1 slot on the jazz albums charts. The seventh, *Winelight*, reached the top for a record-breaking run of more than six months. Sparking its penetration into the pop and R&B charts was "Just the Two of Us," the one track with vocals. Sung by soul artist Bill Withers, the hit dominated radio during the spring and summer of 1981.

"It's something with the old feel of the islands, the kind of two-step thing they do in Trinidad," Washington said. "I needed someone who could both speak and sing the words, and I realized Bill would be perfect. I've delved into vocal tracks because I've been writing songs that are personal. I've been making good music for years—that's the only thing that has to remain constant."

When the young Washington stopped growing just shy of 5 feet 9 inches, he decided music held more promise as a career alternative than basketball, his first love. He contented himself with being a Philadelphia 76ers season ticket holder; he also played the national anthem at many 76ers home games. He had become good friends with the team's star, Julius Erving, and he dedicated the track "Let It Flow (For 'Dr. J')" to him.

"After last year's playoff game with Los Angeles (Game 4 of the 1980 NBA finals), I told Doc that for that one shot he made—where he was behind the backboard and flipped the ball all the way to the other side of the basket and it went in—he had a tune coming."

Winelight reached the platinum sales mark, and "Just the Two of Us" won a Grammy Award for Best R&B Song. Jazz purists painted Washington as someone who had sold out, but his integration of R&B and pop with jazz—a melodic, slick and structured sound—was his recognition of a larger world.

"Music should describe life, and be about communication," he said. "You're always going to have the old-line jazz guy who says, 'If it's not acoustic, it's not jazz.' But that's basically being pissed off about how much I sell. What else could it be? The music is good." ■

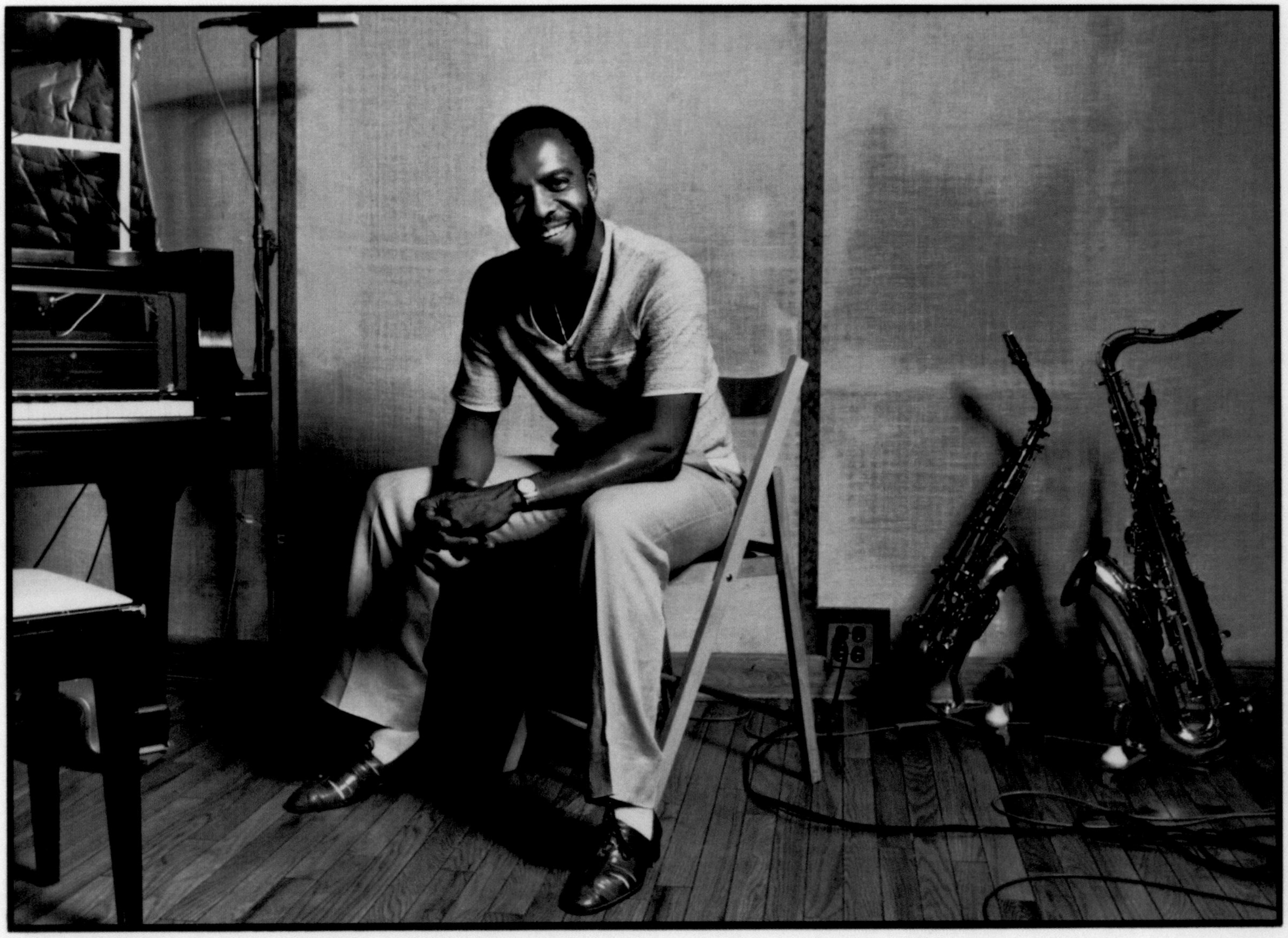

PHOTO CREDIT: DON HUNTSTEIN/1980

GROVER WASHINGTON JR.

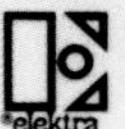

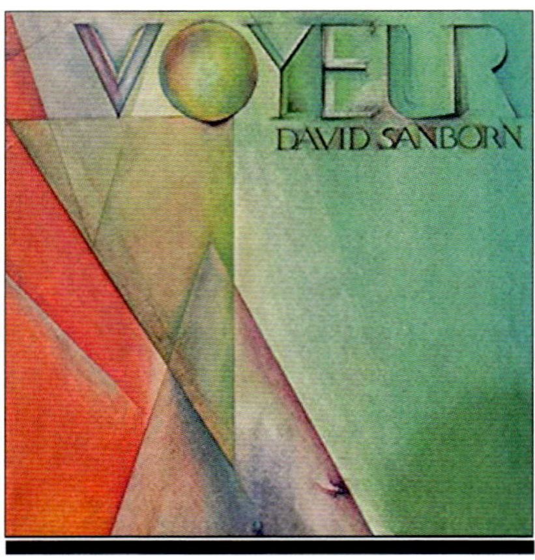

Billboard 200: *Voyeur* (#45)

With *Voyeur,* saxophonist David Sanborn emerged as a leading purveyor of the smooth-jazz genre.

DAVID SANBORN'S passion with the alto saxophone went back to grade school. In his youth, he started playing gigs around his native St. Louis area, frequenting downtown clubs where he would listen and sit in. "My musical roots go back to the R&B I heard in those clubs," he remembered. "I always was greatly influenced by Hank Crawford and the old Ray Charles band."

Sanborn studied music theory more formally at Northwestern University and later at the University of Iowa. But he first earned recognition as a rocker, performing with Paul Butterfield's band in the late Sixties before linking up with the musical establishment. Among other performers, he recorded and toured with Stevie Wonder (the *Talking Book* album), David Bowie (*Young Americans*), Paul Simon (*Still Crazy After All These Years*) and played the solo on James Taylor's charting cover of the Marvin Gaye hit, "How Sweet It Is (To Be Loved By You)."

"I don't know how much of my past my audience is aware of," he said. "Actually, as a soloist, you're fulfilling someone else's idea of what you're supposed to sound like. Very rarely will they let you just blow. Afterwards in the studio, they can drastically alter what you've done and change the impact of what you played."

Sanborn came into his own as a solo artist and composer with 1980's *Hideaway,* a sophisticated blend of jazz and pop elements which marked the beginning of a long association with bassist Marcus Miller. He followed it with *Voyeur*, the first of his albums to hit the top spot on the jazz charts. He netted his first Grammy Award for the track "All I Need is You," which won Best R&B Instrumental Performance, but the renowned instrumentalist had to deal with dismissal by jazz purists.

"They have an ax to grind and I'm an easy target—'This guy is masquerading as a jazz artist.' I never called myself a jazz musician," he fumed. "I don't happen to think I'm a real innovator. What I play is a synthesis of different styles I've heard over the years. Some of it comes from jazz, but most of it comes from R&B. I've played in enough idioms to have the respect of the people I work with." ■

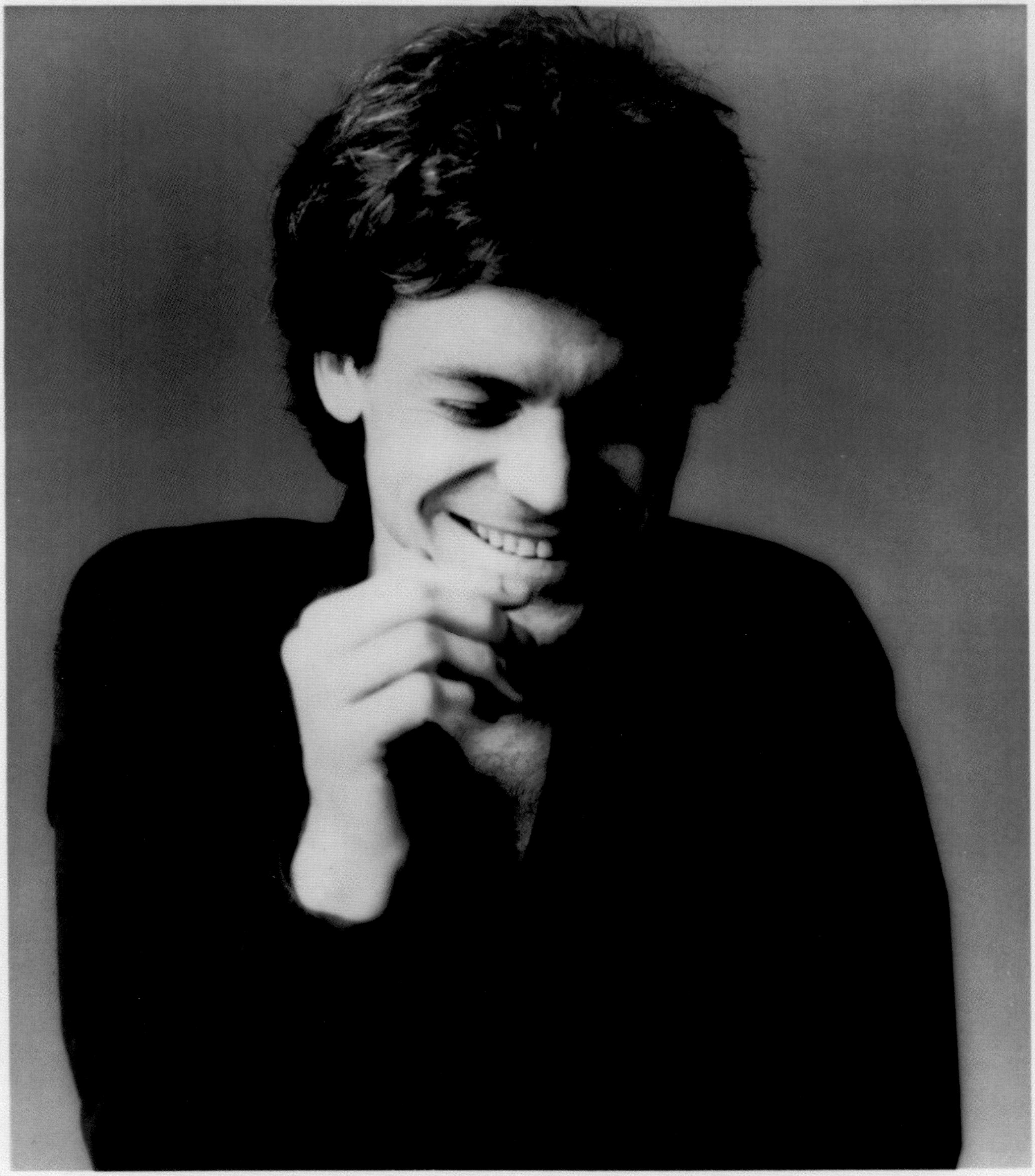

DAVID SANBORN

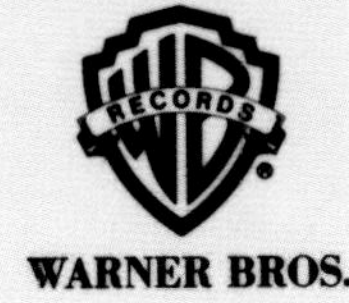

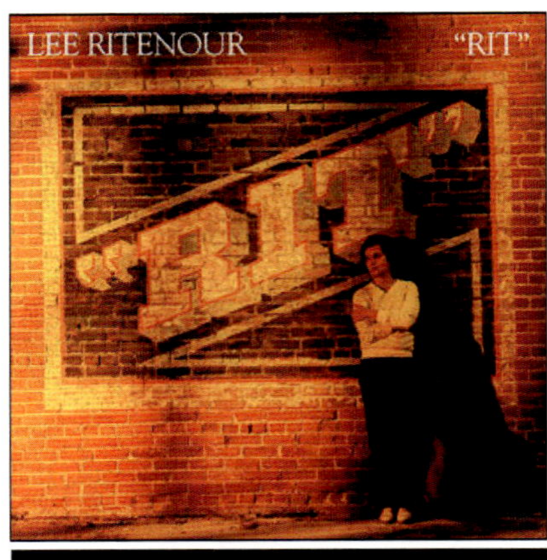

Billboard 200: *Rit* (#26)
Billboard Hot 100: "Is It You" (#15)

Rit represented the breakthrough album jazz guitarist Lee Ritenour had worked long and hard for.

LEE RITENOUR, known among his admirers as "Captain Fingers" for his exceptional nimbleness, had been a noted jazz artist and session musician since the early Seventies. After studying classical guitar at the University of Southern California, he quickly became a phenomenon in the Los Angeles area. By his own conservative estimation, at one point he was regularly hired for a norm of 15-20 studio gigs a week. He played a key role on albums by Quincy Jones and Pink Floyd (*The Wall*), and he emerged the two-time winner of *Guitar Player* magazine's Best Studio Guitarist award.

Eventually, however, Ritenour found the musical connection during sessions was different. "People felt almost obligated to give me a solo or some important part," he said. "It was very flattering but inappropriate to the anonymous role of the session man. I began to feel that I shouldn't be there anymore. It was time to move on."

Making the transition from musician's musician to solo artist, he won acclaim with models of the prevalent jazz-funk sound. As the Eighties began, he started adding what he characterized as a more "pop-oriented message," beginning with *Rit*. "When I realized the kind of album I wanted *Rit* to be, I called Eric Tagg, an old friend from Dallas—a lyricist, writer and singer—and invited him to come work on the album," Ritenour said.

"Is It You," the first single, was co-written by Ritenour, Bill Champlin and Tagg, with lead vocals by Tagg. "I originally planned it for George Benson and Quincy Jones because I was working on their album at the time I wrote it," Ritenour commented. "But then I decided to hold it for my own album."

"Is It You" enjoyed sweeping popularity on the charts—Top 15 pop and adult contemporary, Top 30 R&B. Combined with album-oriented radio airplay of the track "Countdown Captain Fingers," it sent *Rit* into the pop Top 30, the R&B Top 20 and the jazz Top 5. ■

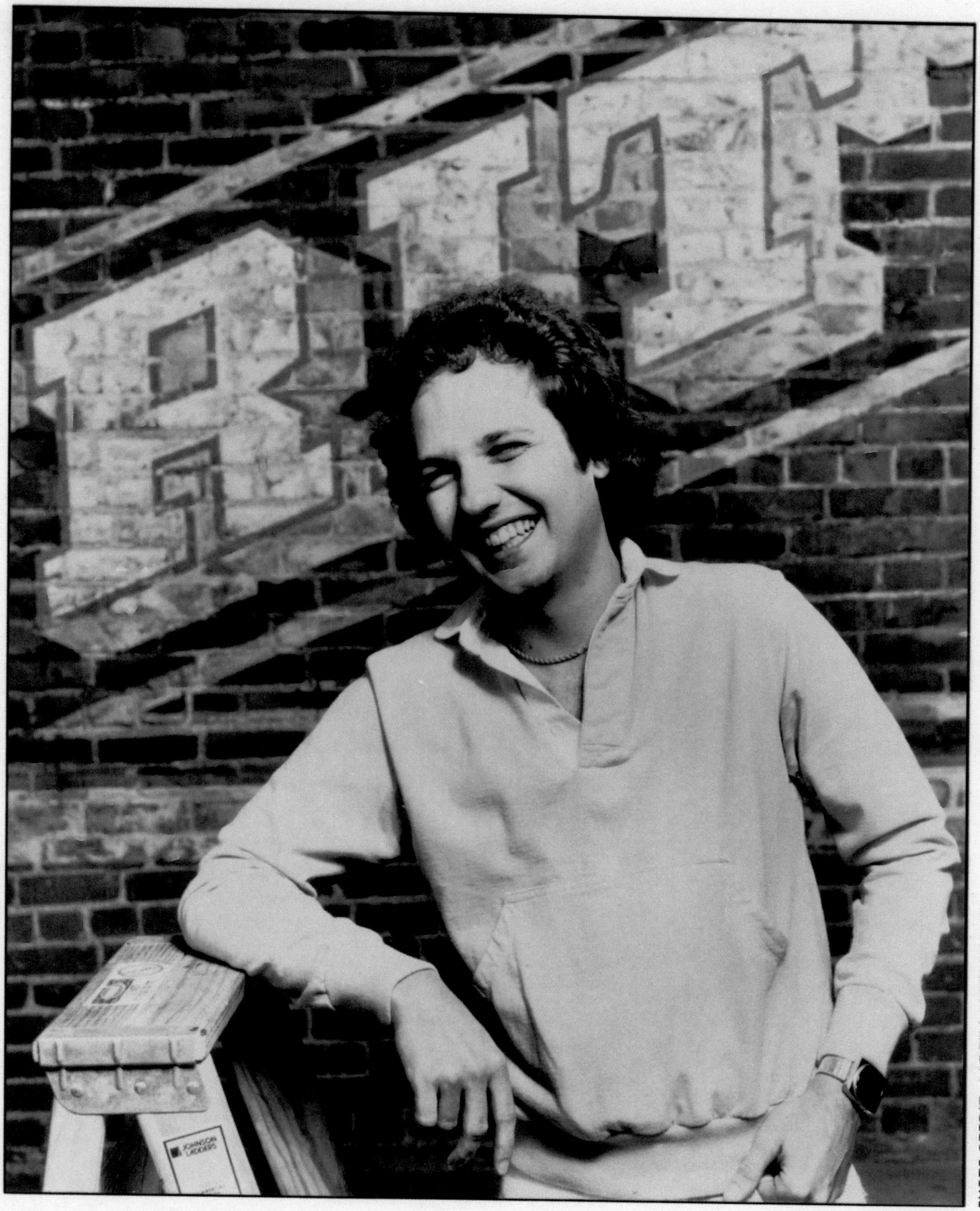

PHOTO CREDIT: AARON RAPOPORT/1981

LEE RITENOUR

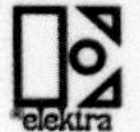

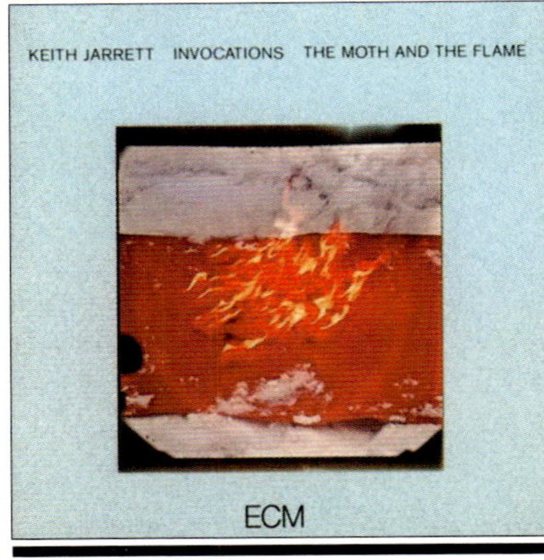

Exploding the narrative in solo jazz improvisation, Keith Jarrett introduced a new aesthetic during his concerts.

WHEN KEITH Jarrett gave a solo piano performance, it wasn't the somber, stuffy occasion suggested by the word "recital." He considered each of his concerts a one-of-a-kind experience in which he filtered through himself such variables as the hall, the audience and the instrument. He completely improvised everything.

Jarrett's visual antics were as much a part of the event as his spontaneous composing. He came onstage and sat at the keyboard for minutes on end before the muse struck him. He stomped his tennis shoes on the floor, hovered over his piano and moaned and grunted as he played. He was also totally impatient with noisy crowds, giving pat lectures about coughing or loitering in the aisles.

There was no doubting Jarrett's artistry, but he cut a controversial figure. Admirers couldn't decide whether to idolize him as a jazz or classical artist, and detractors felt he tainted his obvious talents with a massive ego. Yet Jarrett remained impulsive.

"I never know what I'm going to focus on until I get to a show," he admitted. "There's only one thing I need from an audience, and that's their openness. I don't need their understanding. People's understanding is almost a negative force sometimes, because they come in thinking they understand what's going to happen, and then they expect it instead of being open."

Jarrett was known for his prolific output, intermittently recording solo piano albums in the studio. *Invocations/The Moth and the Flame* was a double album of improvised music. He performed "Invocations" on the massive pipe organ at the Imperial Abbey in Ottobeuren, West Germany (bracketed with some meditations on soprano saxophone), and "The Moth and the Flame" on grand piano.

"In concert, the music happens just in that one place in time. On a recording, the music has to have a certain validity in my absence," he explained. "Making a record is a plan in itself. Considering that you have to show up at the address, you're already planning more than if you just wanted to play. Performing and recording are not two different things for some people—they have some product that they present ad nauseum. But my product changes with every place I play." ■

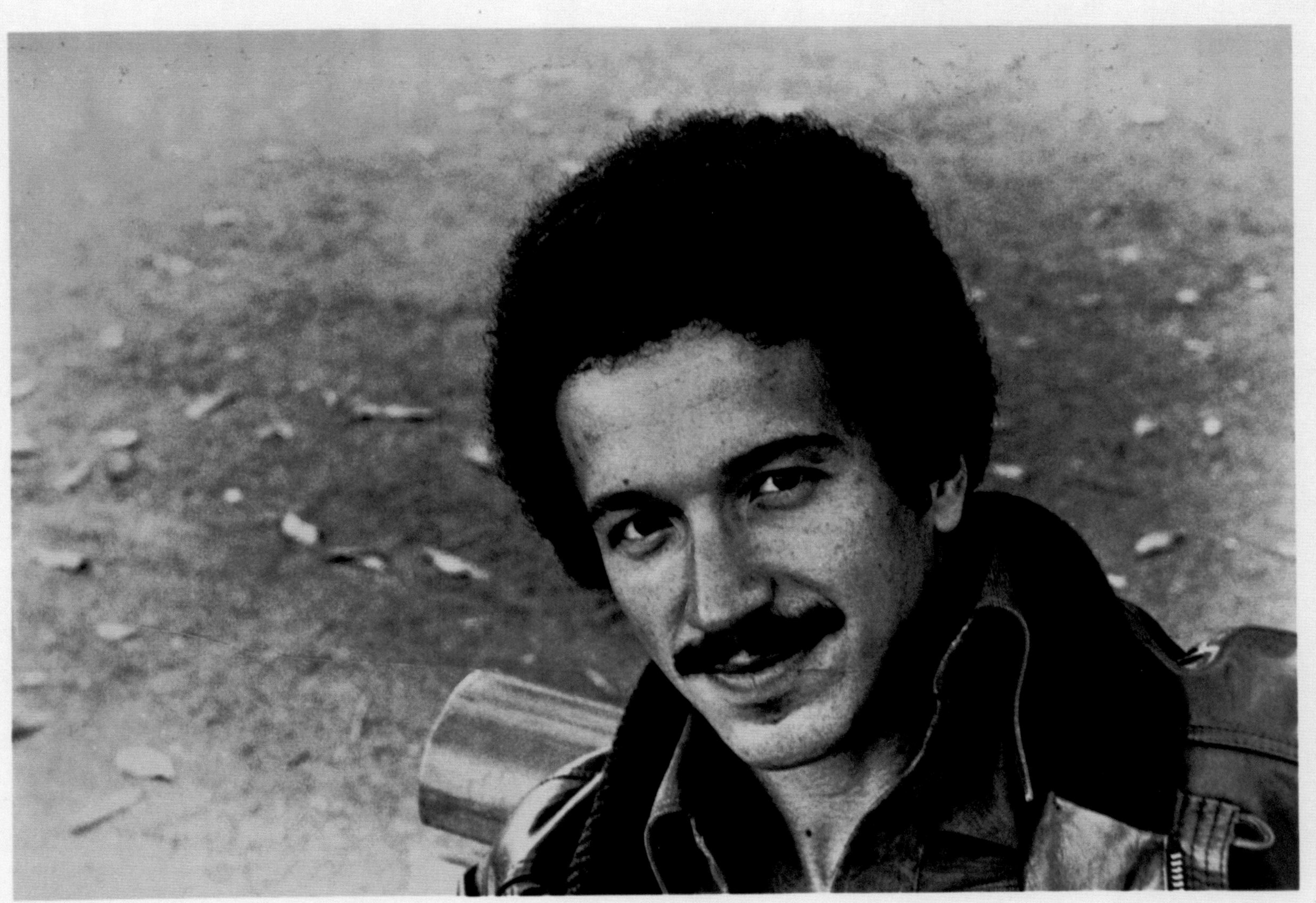

KEITH JARRETT

ECM RECORDS

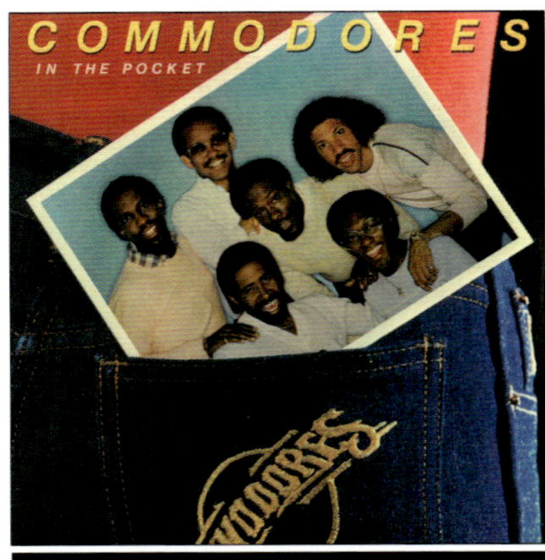

Billboard 200: *In the Pocket* (#13)
Billboard Hot 100: "Lady (You Bring Me Up)" (#8); "Oh No" (#4); "Why You Wanna Try Me" (#66)

In the Pocket marked the last Commodores album before Lionel Richie departed for a solo career.

THE COMMODORES were riding a wave. Each new album sold millions, and each new song—"Three Times a Lady," "Sail On," "Still"—got played constantly on the radio. Leader Lionel Richie had success with everything he touched—production of Kenny Rogers' *Share Your Love* album, the "Endless Love" duet with Diana Ross—and everyone from Bad Company to Little River Band had solicited songs from the group.

"When everyone becomes so excited about the possibility of working with you, you have to think, 'Yeah, maybe we have arrived as songwriters and innovators," guitarist Thomas McClary admitted. "I wish we had a tape of the conversation we had in Richie's grandma's basement 13 years ago. We thought of doing everything back then, but we are just now getting the chance to reach so many people. There are all races and ages at our concerts, and we've never had a single bad incident."

Originally forming while students at Tuskegee Institute in Alabama, the Commodores signed with Motown Records in 1972, but they spent two years hassling with staff producers until they began writing material. An eventual team-up with producer James Carmichael also proved fruitful. The band's first albums were straight funk workouts, yielding a dance ("The Bump") and several Black-oriented hits—"Machine Gun," "I Feel Sanctified," "Slippery When Wet."

Then came the blockbuster ballad "Easy," which garnered the band a pop following as well. "We didn't want to lose our old audience, but we still wanted to get new people," McClary explained. "'Easy' was a brilliant synthesis, with the groove and melody of a pop song and a touch of country in the delivery, performed with the soulfulness of a Black group."

From *In the Pocket*, the upbeat "Lady (You Bring Me Up)," sung by Richie, ventured into sophisticated funk.

"There's something different about us," bassist Ronald LaPread admitted. "Maybe it's just a feeling, but six little country boys have evolved into a pretty fantastic musical force. The people we once looked up to are now looking up to us."

"We have serious demands on us all over the world, and trying to take on new responsibilities is fun—but it takes more time to keep track of the eight corporations we have," McClary added. "If in ten years we haven't taken over the entire musical spectrum, we won't have reached our goal."

In the Pocket ended Richie's association with the band. ■

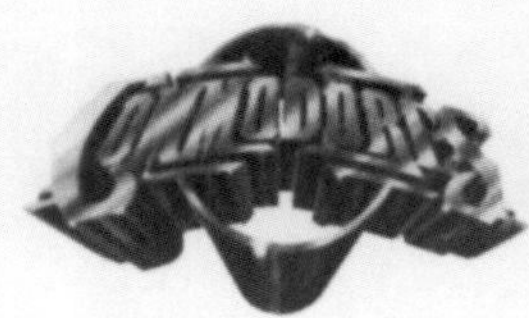

MOTOWN

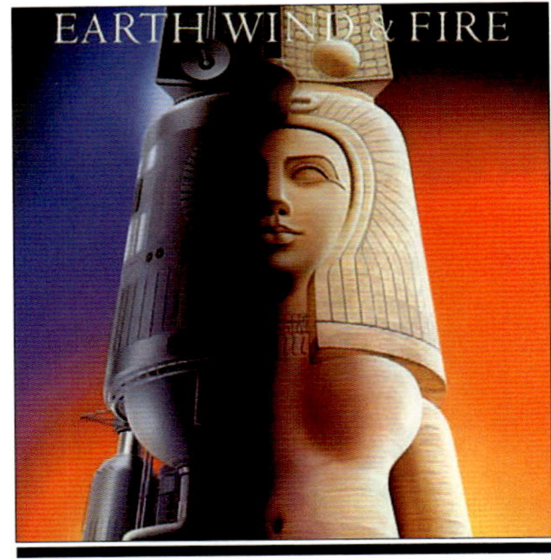

Billboard 200: *Raise!* (#5)
Billboard Hot 100: "Let's Groove" (#3); "Wanna Be with You" (#51)

Earth, Wind & Fire's "Let's Groove" ranked as one of the most joyous moments in the music world.

EARTH, WIND & Fire had secured its place in the annals of pop music. The band had racked up 14 Top 40 hits since 1974 with the elements that made it perhaps the greatest big band of Black music's golden era: crisp horn arrangements, soaring harmonies, African-accented percussion and the starkly contrasting lead vocals of the group's two principals—founder and producer Maurice White's charming baritone and Philip Bailey's pure, sweet and impossibly high falsetto.

"I came in at age 20, straight from a year of college and getting married, and there were guys younger than me," Bailey said. "We literally grew up in Earth, Wind & Fire, and Maurice was our elder. So it was more than a band, it was a family."

Raise!, Earth, Wind & Fire's eleventh album, featured the band's distinctive funk and love ballads. "Let's Groove" revived disco music and reached No. 1 on *Billboard's* Top R&B Singles chart, and "Wanna Be with You" won the band a Grammy for Best R&B Vocal Performance by a Duo or Group. Rhythm guitarist Roland Bautista returned, and his playing added a bit of a hard-rock feel.

The album also addressed the changes in the musical landscape, as White decided the band needed to incorporate more of the popular new electronic sound.

"It's trying to find that perfect match, what's actually you and what's actually in vogue at the time," Bailey explained. "Comparing yourself with work that you've done before, trying to remain current but not getting too far ahead—all of those factors are challenges that you run into, especially with the amount of music we have out."

The group's sense of purpose and exuberance had always been best conveyed in live performance, where members displayed their shrewd sense of theater, visual dress and elaborate stage productions. Bailey promised more—"We'll always do some hands-are-quicker-than-the-eyes things." ■

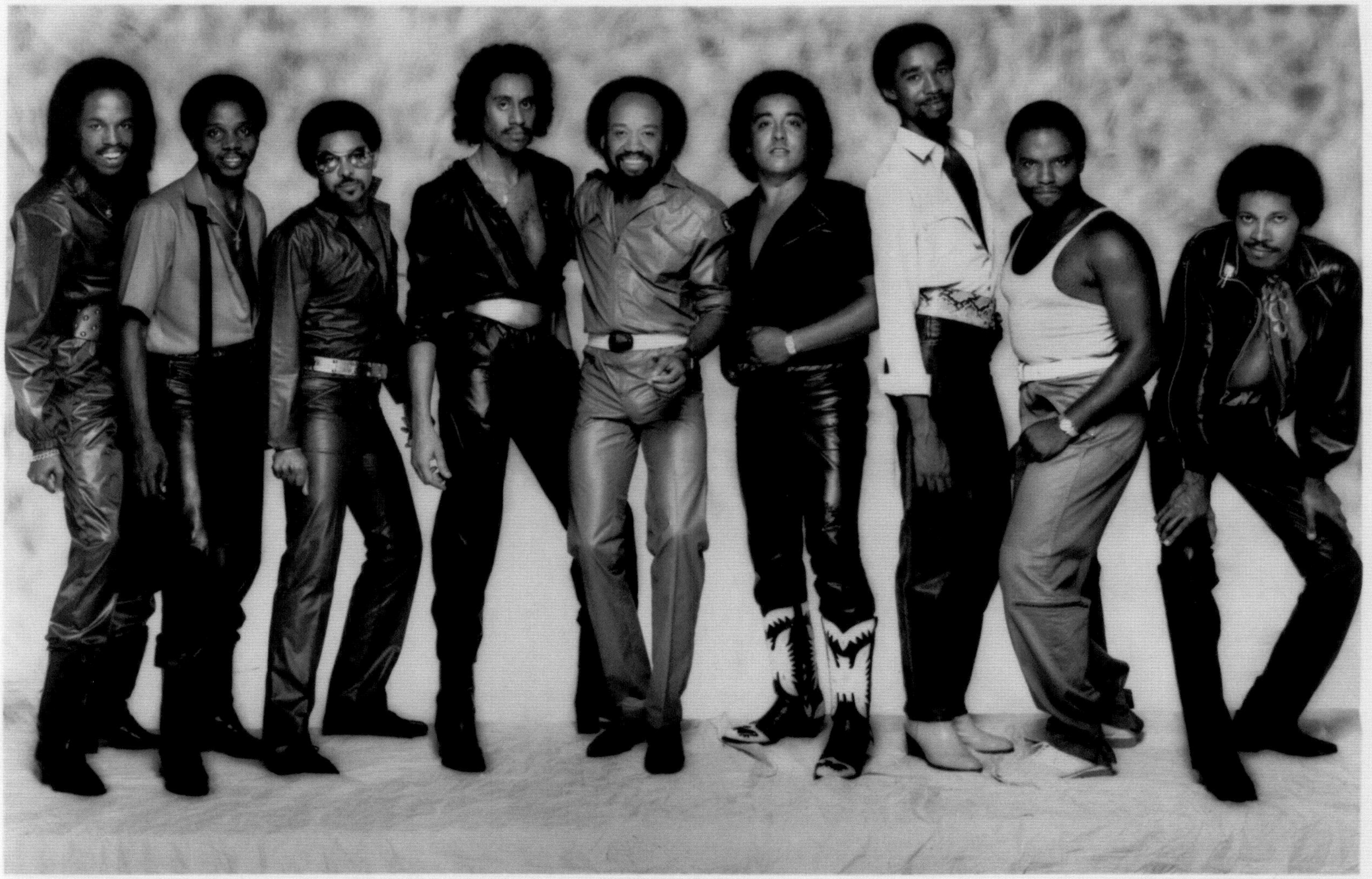

ARC

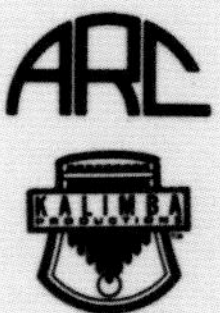

EARTH WIND & FIRE

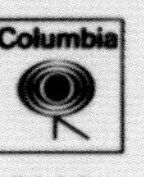

8110

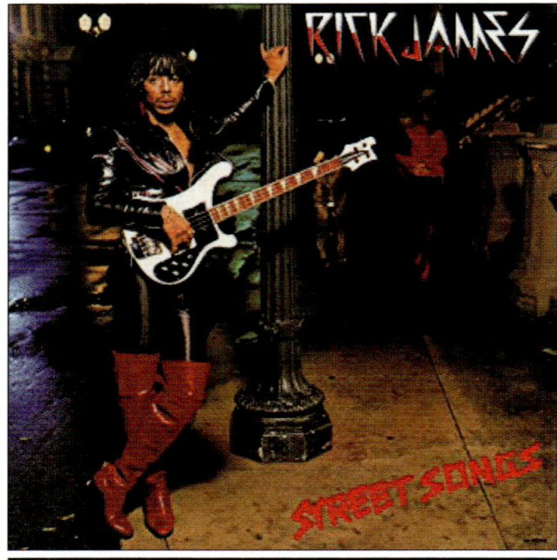

Billboard 200: *Street Songs* (#3)
Billboard Hot 100: "Give It to Me Baby" (#40); "Find Another Fool" (#16); "Super Freak" (#16)

Releasing the seminal *Street Songs*, Rick James became the self-proclaimed master of music he called "punk funk."

BORN IN Buffalo, New York, Rick James weaved a tale of enculturation into ghetto life, referring to his childhood and early teens as "delinquent." But music was always going to be the vehicle to legitimize his dreams. In 1964, he ran away from the Navy and escaped to Toronto, where he helped form the Mynah Birds with a young Canadian singer-songwriter by the name of Neil Young (the band signed with Motown Records and recorded an album that was not released).

After returning to the States and doing time for military desertion, he began nurturing his craft, playing bass in various groups before signing again to Motown as a staff writer and developing his talents as a producer.

By 1978, it was time for James to step into the studio. The flashy image he developed—spandex and sequin stage costumes, shoulder-length braids—concealed a sharp and inquiring mind.

"The whole Rick James trip was thought up, planned out," he said. "From the braids to the costumes to the writing—everything."

Nobody was quite doing funk 'n' roll like the outrageous James. "You and I," which topped the R&B charts, and the double-entendre of "Mary Jane" highlighted *Come Get It,* his debut album on Motown in 1978. Three more successful album releases followed, and James also found time to produce two albums for his 13-piece Stone City Band and promote his one-time protégé Teena Marie's debut album.

"No matter how much I appreciated Parliament-Funkadelic and Bootsy Collins' crafty Jimi Hendrix/James Brown cross-breeding, I wanted to go even further," James revealed. "I wanted to play everything I heard in my head."

Street Songs included James' career-defining masterstrokes, the No. 1 R&B hit "Give It to Me Baby" and "Super Freak," his biggest pop single—"about girls who just enjoy life and havin' a great time ***all*** the time." The album's stint on the charts—it reached the highest position by any Black artist in 1981—catapulted James into national prominence.

"Freedom, man," he said. "Just to be able to do what I want to do, say what I want to say and not have it condemned. The only thing I put down is somebody who's hung up on what somebody else is doing or looking like. A lot of the people who come to my concerts live through me, and I'm glad about that." ■

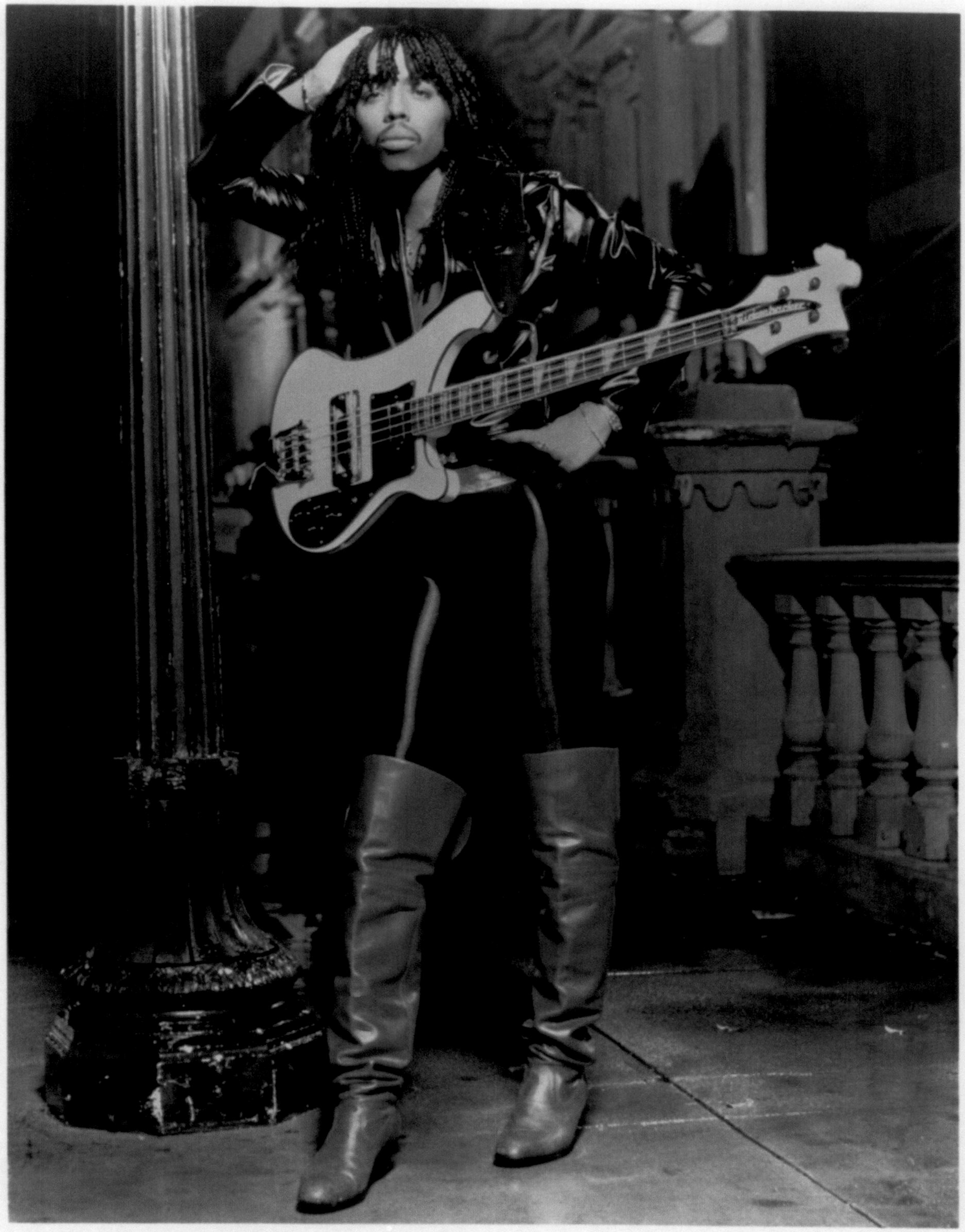

RICK JAMES

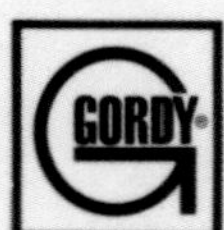

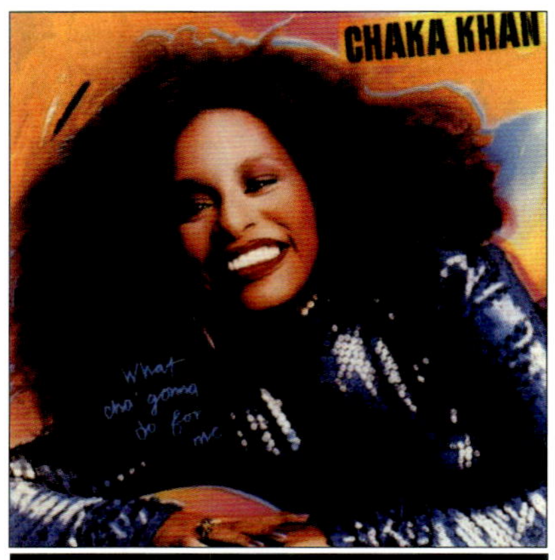

Billboard 200: *What Cha' Gonna Do for Me* (#17)
Billboard Hot 100: "What Cha' Gonna Do for Me" (#53)

Reuniting with producer Arif Mardin, Chaka Khan achieved the grand and glorious *What Cha' Gonna Do for Me.*

WITH RUFUS, Chaka Khan had become a world-class vocalist and performer. In 1972, the group released its first album, containing "Tell Me Something Good," a tune written for her by Stevie Wonder that went on to sell more than 3 million copies and earn a Grammy. Khan recorded six gold and platinum albums with Rufus before stepping out on her own.

Khan issued two albums in 1981. She and Rufus reconvened for *Camouflage*, but she was concentrating on becoming her own entity with her third solo album, *What Cha' Gonna Do for Me.*

"If I could record with them every three years, it would be perfect," she allowed, her lack of enthusiasm apparent. "But I have to fulfill a contractual obligation. I can't say that it will be the last time we'll work together, but it will be for a while."

The sassy singer showed far more passion for the *What Cha' Gonna Do for Me* material. "I can't imagine working with anyone else but Arif Mardin," she said of her renowned producer. "He's the most amazing catalyst I've ever worked with."

A bold reworking of the Beatles' "We Can Work It Out" and the No. 1 R&B title track were released as singles, but the highlight was "And the Melody Still Lingers On (Night in Tunisia)."

"I've always wanted to do jazz, so we collaborated on some lyrics to put with Dizzy Gillespie's music," Khan enthused. "Not only did Arif get Dizzy himself to play a solo as well as Herbie Hancock, but he dubbed in Charlie Parker's 1946 solo from his version."

The result was Khan's finest work, as her vocal wizardry added a new element to the jazz standard. Her energy seemed boundless—besides her record, suporting tour and the Rufus project, she also worked with famed keyboardist Rick Wakeman on his concept album, *1984.*

"My goals keep changing day to day," she admitted. "I want to go farther and learn more. If I have a goal, it's to be remembered as the best singer, like a Michelangelo. Now all I need is a little patience—I've already had a little luck." ■

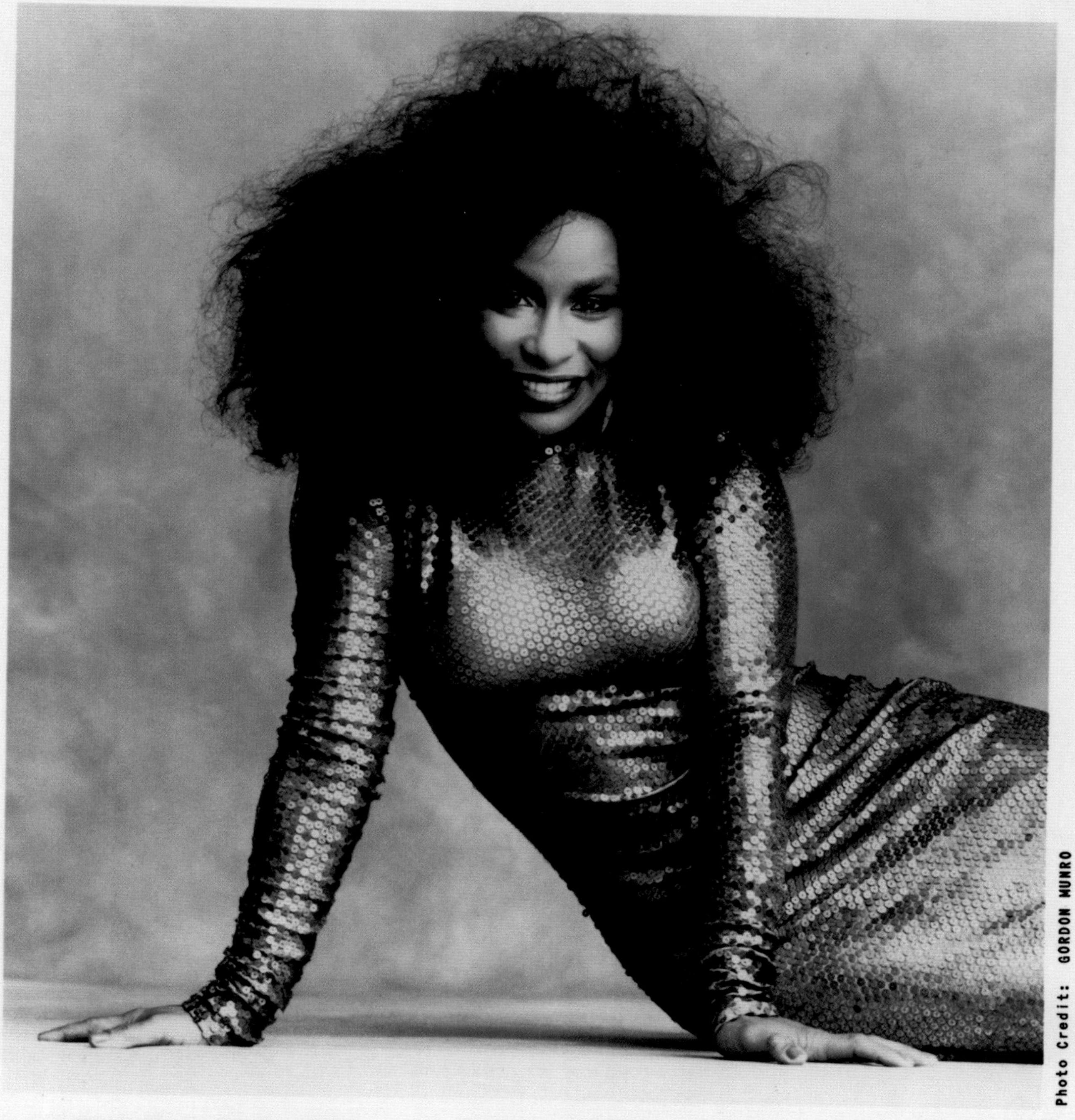

Photo Credit: GORDON MUNRO

CHAKA KHAN

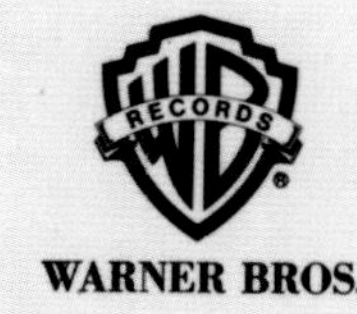

WARNER BROS.

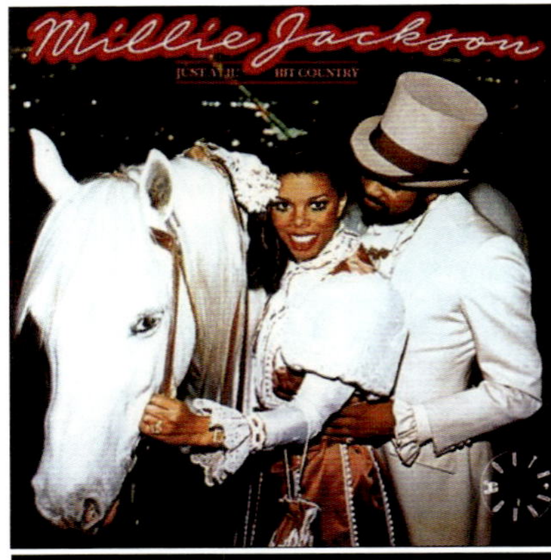

No stranger to controversy, soul singer Millie Jackson tackled country music with *Just a Lil' Bit Country*.

FOR A decade, Millie Jackson had developed a reputation for her furious, velvety gospel-blues vocals and outrageous shows—raunchy, sexual tours de force distinguished by X-rated stage patter. Jackson would invariably start rapping in the middle of her songs about how to handle a man or gripe about how she'd been done wrong. Her libido-liberating tirades had kept her from gaining mainstream acceptance, but her albums were a guilty pleasure for countless fans.

Recording in Nashville for the first time, Jackson pulled another trick out of her hat with *Just a Lil' Bit Country*. "A country album is something I wanted to do for a long time, but it never seemed to be the right timing," the Georgia-born singer explained. "Shoot, country music and soul music have the same lyrics—all I did was take the twang out of the guitar and bring up the bass. My record company had no faith in the idea, which I guess was understandable. But after *Urban Cowboy* came out and everyone started wearing rhinestones, they gave me my shot."

"I Can't Stop Loving You," a riotously funky version of Ray Charles' standard, was offered as a single, but the country-styled album didn't sell well, a fact that Jackson attributed to a lack of foresight on her record label's part.

"What I record is my business—I work hard to get feedback, a feel for what is right," she steamed. "My company refused to market my record in a different way, so now I guess it's back to the drawing board."

Uninhibited bawdiness remained Jackson's trademark. "I know my audience well," she stated, citing the song "Anybody That Don't Like Millie Jackson," a suitably bawdy version of Kris Kristofferson's classic "Anybody That Don't Like Hank Williams" ("...can kiss my ass")—substituting, of course, her own name. ■

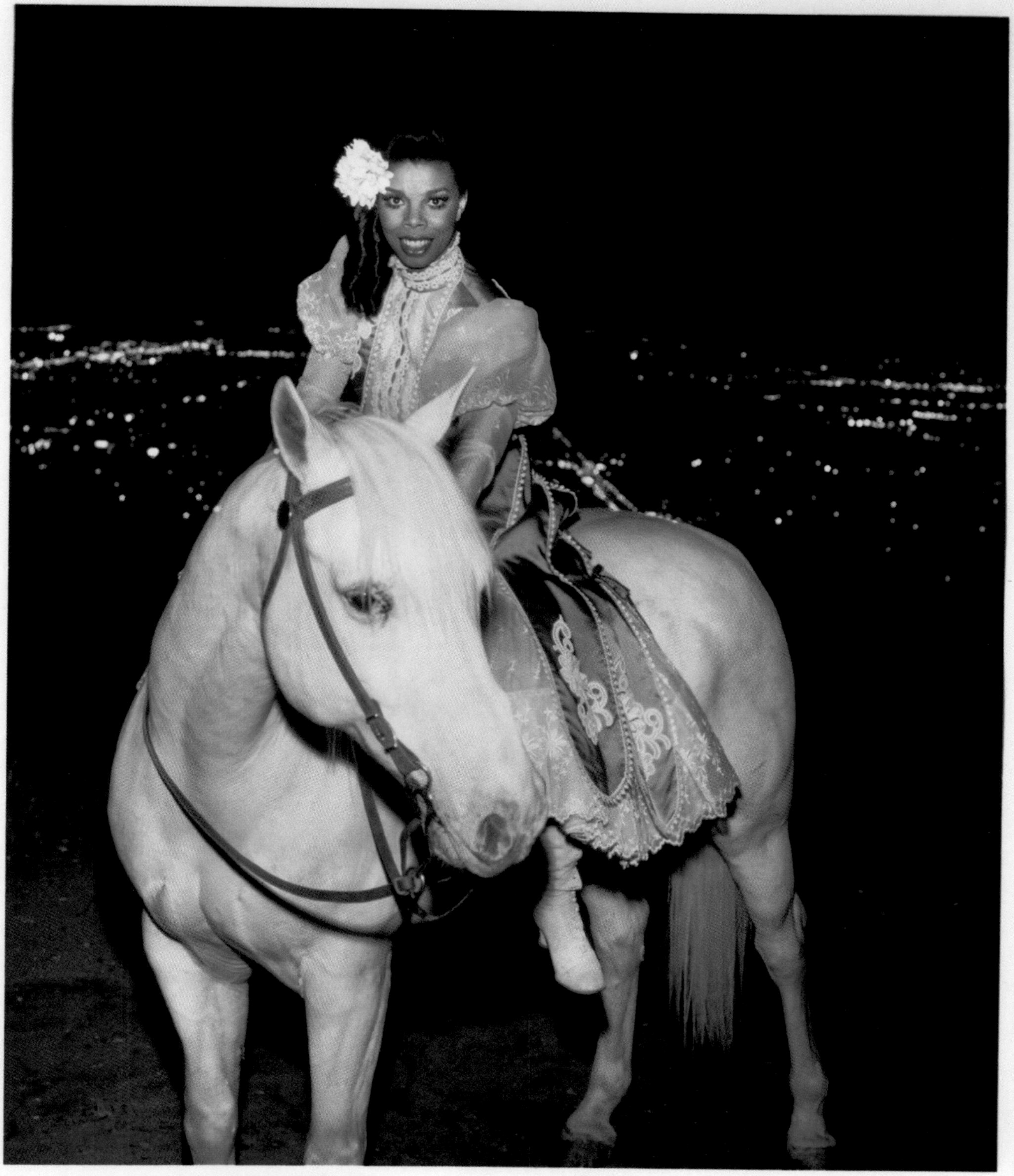

MILLIE JACKSON

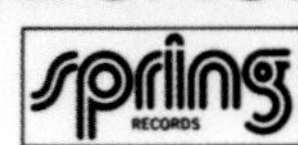

PolyGram Records

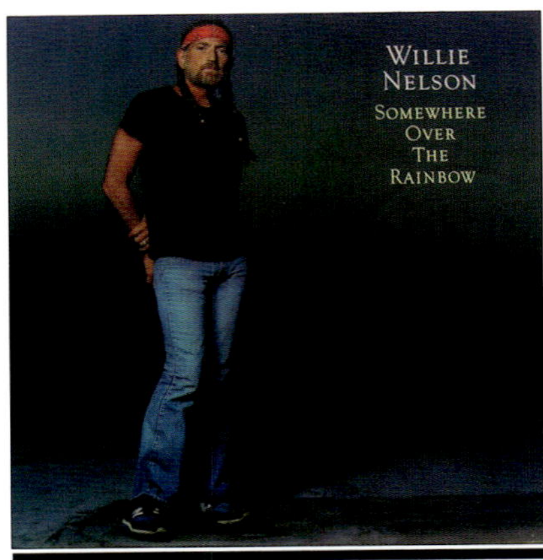

Billboard 200: *Somewhere Over the Rainbow* (#31)

Somewhere Over the Rainbow surpassed platinum status, but Willie Nelson had ventured into a more visible medium.

HE WAS still "just a singer" to some folks, but Willie Nelson had become a commodity, balancing two careers—his music and movies, such as the neo-noir crime film, *Thief*.

Nelson didn't appear overworked by his double duty. Despite his cinematic ambitions and his nothing-left-to-prove status among country singers, he professed a continued commitment to recording. His *Somewhere Over the Rainbow* album included Nelson's all-acoustic arrangements of such pop standards as "Mona Lisa," "Twinkle, Twinkle Little Star," "I'm Gonna Sit Right Down and Write Myself a Letter," "Who's Sorry Now?" and the immortal title song.

"There's always a challenge when you make a record, to come up with something you like that everyone else will like, too," he noted. "It's the same thing with going out on tour. Even though you've been through a town before, things can change since the last time you were there."

Nelson explained that his entrance into acting was typically casual. "Robert Redford and I met and became friends, and he told me he'd like to see me get into movies one day. When *Electric Horseman* came along, he came after me. My role in *Thief* came about the same way—James Caan had come along on one of the tours."

Nelson readily admitted that his roles hadn't exactly been a departure from his scruffy down-home image. His film experiences, he said, "were all pretty much me playing myself. In *Honeysuckle Rose* I was a band manager, and in *Electric Horseman* I was a cowboy—and I could certainly play the role in *Thief*." He portrayed a jailed criminal.

He found Hollywood to be what he had figured. "I had been around Kris (Kristofferson) when he was making movies, so I pretty much knew what to expect. There's a lot of just waiting and sitting around—but, you see, I like that." ■

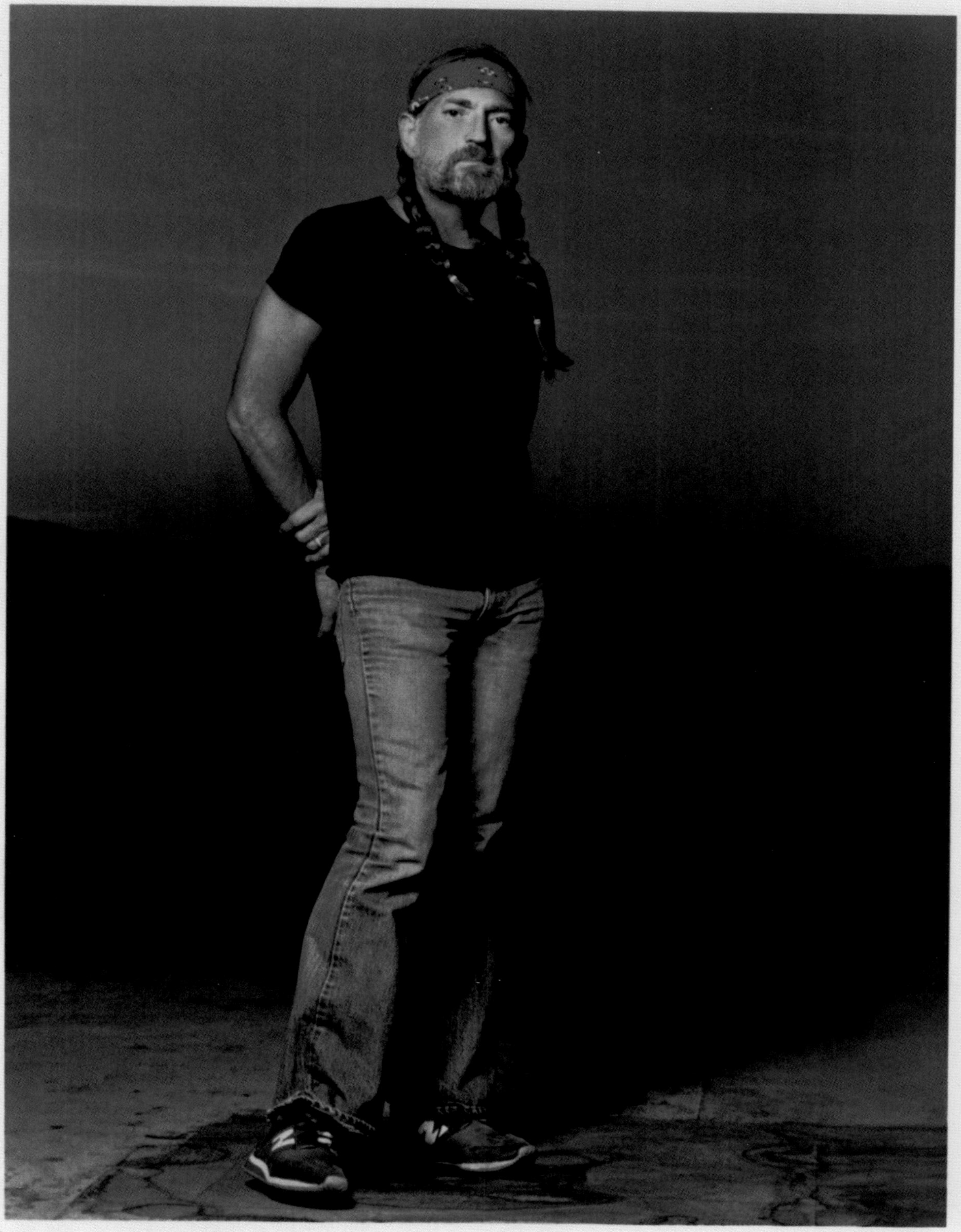

photo credit: Norman Seeff

WILLIE NELSON

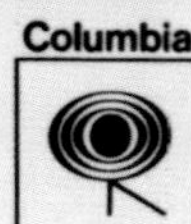

Billboard 200: *Big City* (#161)

Backed by his band the Strangers, hardscrabble country legend Merle Haggard released the critically acclaimed *Big City*.

MERLE HAGGARD'S weather-beaten face, homemade tattoos and the soft sense of pain in his eyes were testimonials to the places he had been and the things he had seen. Born in a tiny suburb of Bakersfield, California, Haggard lost his father to a brain tumor when he was nine. He spent a total of nearly six years in confinement at various reformatories and penal institutions; the charges against him ranged from burglary and suspicion of armed robbery to escape and auto theft. His life of crime came to an end one night when he and some friends got drunk on wine and attempted to burglarize a tavern that was still open.

"It was only 11:00 p.m.," Haggard recalled, "but we were so drunk, we thought it was three in the morning."

On account of that caper, Haggard ended up serving nearly three years at San Quentin State Prison, where he watched Johnny Cash perform the first of his legendary prison concerts. The experience inspired Haggard, who'd occasionally sung in bars when he wasn't robbing them, to join the inmate band. At one point, however, he ended up in solitary confinement for making home brew. He had conversations through the ventilation system with the condemned murderer Caryl Chessman (the "Red Light Bandit"), who was awaiting his fate on Death Row. The experience prompted an about-face on Haggard's outlook on life. He became a model inmate and served out the rest of his term working in the penitentiary's textile mill. "I'm not sure it works that way very often, but I'm one guy the prison system straightened out," Haggard said. "I know damned well I'm a better man because of it."

After being paroled in 1960, at age 22, he managed to turn his life around and launch a successful country music career, gaining popularity with his songs that identified with the working man. Since 1966, he'd had 25 No. 1 hits on the US country charts, including "Okie from Muskogee," which he recorded in 1969 during the height of the domestic unrest brought on by the Vietnam conflict.

In 1981, the bona fide country legend left his long association with MCA Records and signed with Epic, where he began producing his own records, giving the music a leaner sound. He wrote or cowrote almost every song on *Big City*, including two No. 1 singles, the title track and "My Favorite Memory." "Are the Good Times Really Over (I Wish a Buck Was Still Silver)" won the Academy of Country Music Song of the Year.

"I'm not in the music business for glamour," Haggard said. "I'm in it to play music, to be in a band, to be around people I've admired for years." ■

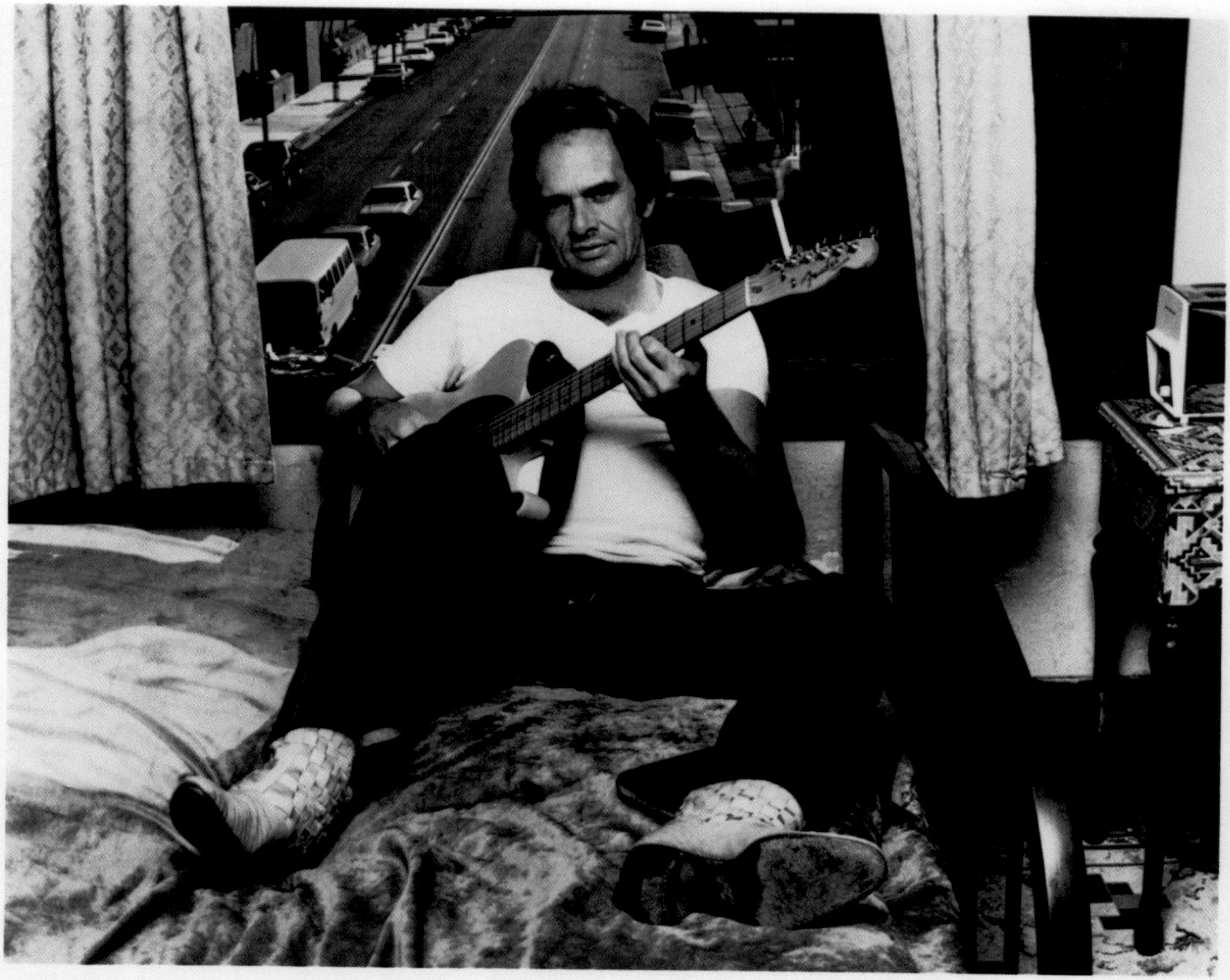

MERLE HAGGARD

photo credit: Norman Seeff

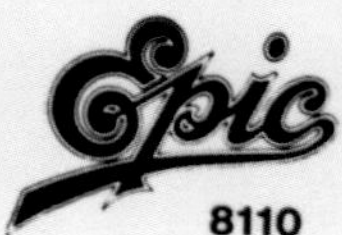

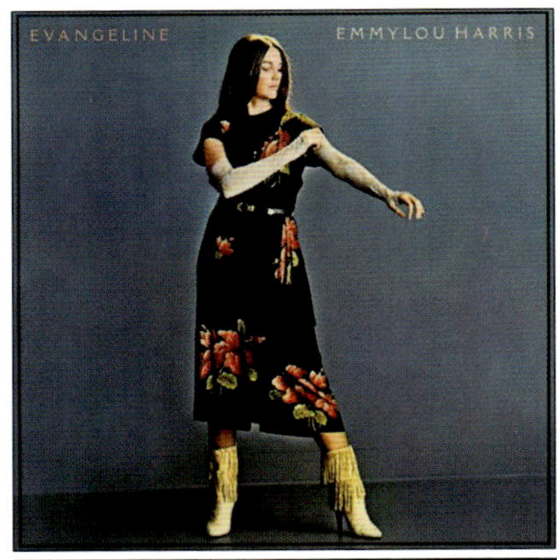

Billboard 200: *Evangeline* (#22)
Billboard Hot 100: "Mister Sandman" (#37)

Evangeline found country singer Emmylou Harris exploring a broader musical spectrum and wider audience.

THE BUILDING of Emmylou Harris' career had been casual. After nine albums, the prospect of "crossing over" to mass appeal hadn't been a priority for the singer and her black Gibson guitar.

Whereas earlier albums such as *Blue Kentucky Girl* and *Roses in the Snow* defined her interest in bluegrass and traditional country material, *Evangeline* boasted swing music, rock 'n' roll and oldies—all linked by her acclaimed voice—and a cover of the classic "Mister Sandman" featuring Harris, Dolly Parton and Linda Ronstadt that reached the Top 40 on the *Billboard* pop chart.

"Gee, I think I've been pretty radical with the records I've been making—it's true that I've always worked with Brian Ahern and a lot of the same musicians, but we felt *Evangeline* was a departure of sorts," she noted. "I can feel that we've made progress towards growing together as a team making records."

Parton and Ronstadt had already taken on an allure by putting pop trimmings to the true country style. With *Evangeline*, Harris moved further in that direction. "I do think country music should take pride in its roots," she asserted. "But I'm not Loretta Lynn. It would be nice to say I'm a coal miner's daughter, and I really admire Loretta for who she is and the music she does. But I'm not that, and I can't pretend to be." ■

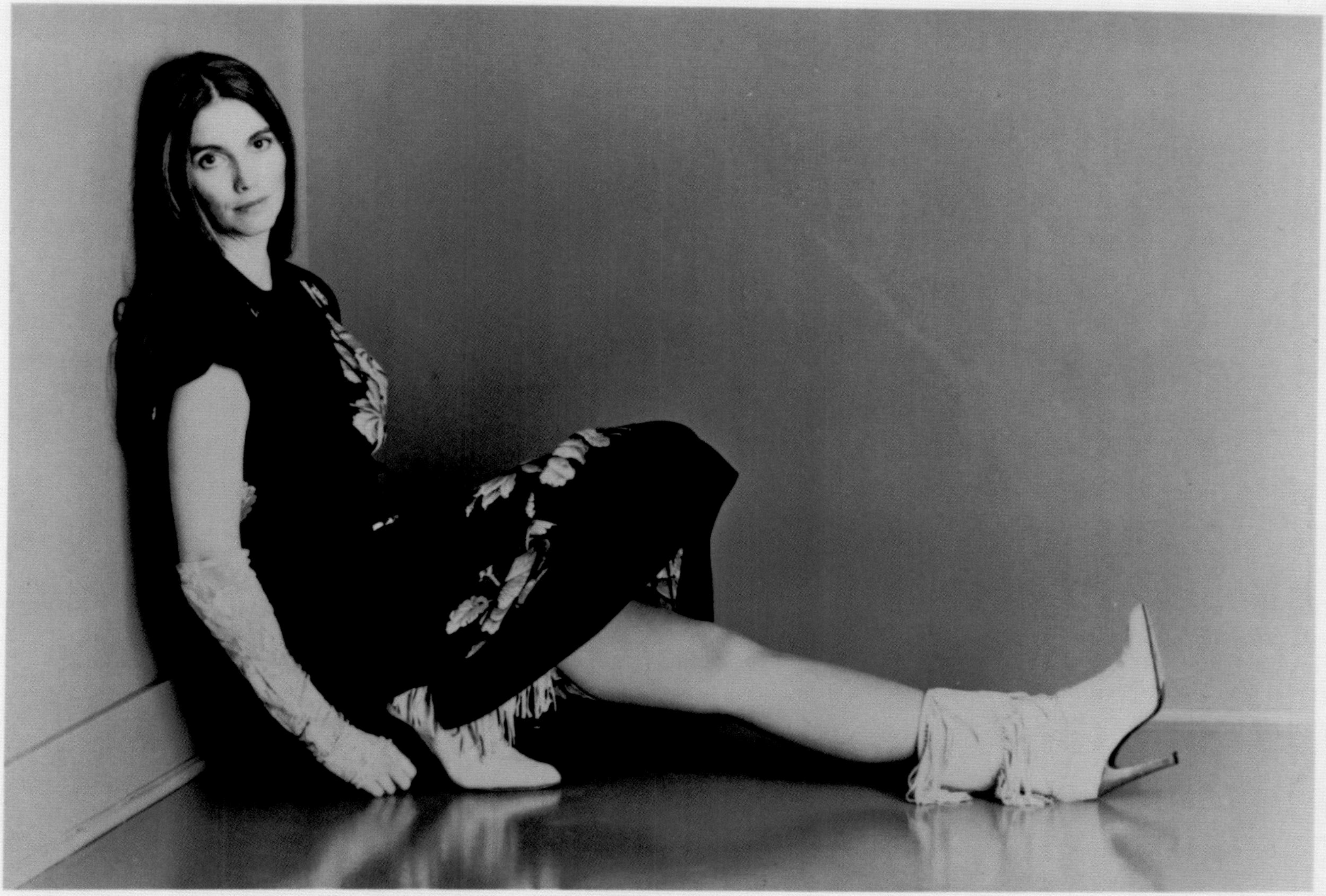

EMMYLOU HARRIS

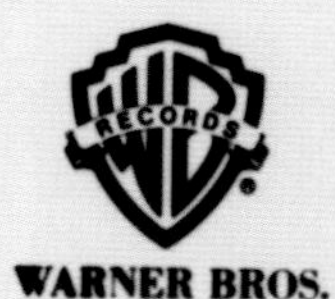

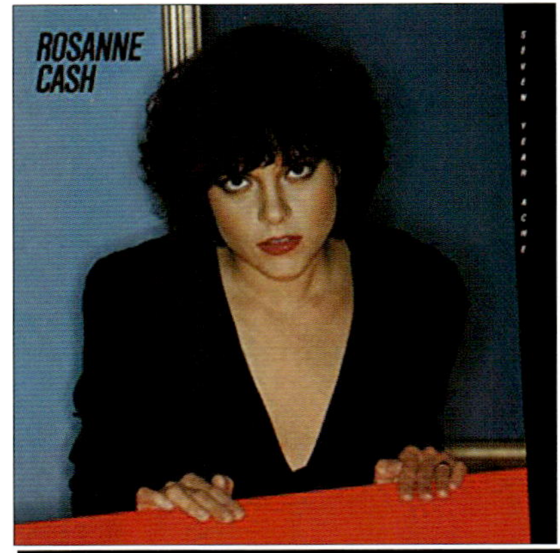

Billboard 200: *Seven Year Ache* (#26)
Billboard Hot 100: "Seven Year Ache" (#22)

Achieving critical raves and solid sales, Rosanne Cash's *Seven Year Ache* reached No. 1 on the country album charts.

ROSANNE CASH received a great deal of media attention with the release of her debut album, *Right or Wrong*, in 1980. Yes, she was the eldest daughter of country music legend Johnny Cash, and her husband, Rodney Crowell, had established himself as an artist, writer and producer of merit. Beyond that, however, Rosanne distinguished herself as a refreshing talent who communicated a self-possessed poise through her music.

She was born in Memphis in 1955, the same year her father released his first single. After her parents' divorce in 1966, she lived with her mother in Ventura, California, and following her graduation from high school, she joined her father's road show and handled wardrobe duties until he promoted her to singing backup. An interest in acting eventually prompted her to study at the Lee Strasberg Theatre Institute in Hollywood, but after going to Germany to cut a self-titled album that was never released, she became a singer.

Right or Wrong earned acclaim without the benefit of any promotional tours, due to Rosanne's pregnancy. With the release of *Seven Year Ache*, produced by Crowell, Cash attained major success when three tracks peaked at No. 1 on the *Billboard* country chart. "Seven Year Ache," one of two songs she penned, also crossed over to the pop chart and defined her place in the music world.

"I was talking to a girlfriend, and she said she hadn't been out of L.A. for seven years and, oh god, how she wanted to get out, so I just came up with that line. I wrote the song about Rodney, because he was being a butt—he left me outside a French restaurant on Ventura Boulevard," Cash laughed. "He loves the song."

"My Baby Thinks He's a Train" was written by Asleep at the Wheel's Leroy Preston. "At first, I didn't think I could sing that because of the octave changes, but I love it. Me and Rosemary (Butler) and Emmylou (Harris) did the harmonies like the Andrews Sisters going rockabilly."

Cash also wrote the shattering ballad "Blue Moon with Heartache." "I like sad songs—that's what I was reared on," she said. "It's like keeping a journal and there's some gratification in somebody reading it. I wrote that song while Rodney was on the road. In my mind, this is a subtle concept record. It's a story about relationships and the sometimes painful changes they cause. It was a hard record to make, a lot more difficult than the first one. Because we knew more. A little knowledge is a dangerous thing." ■

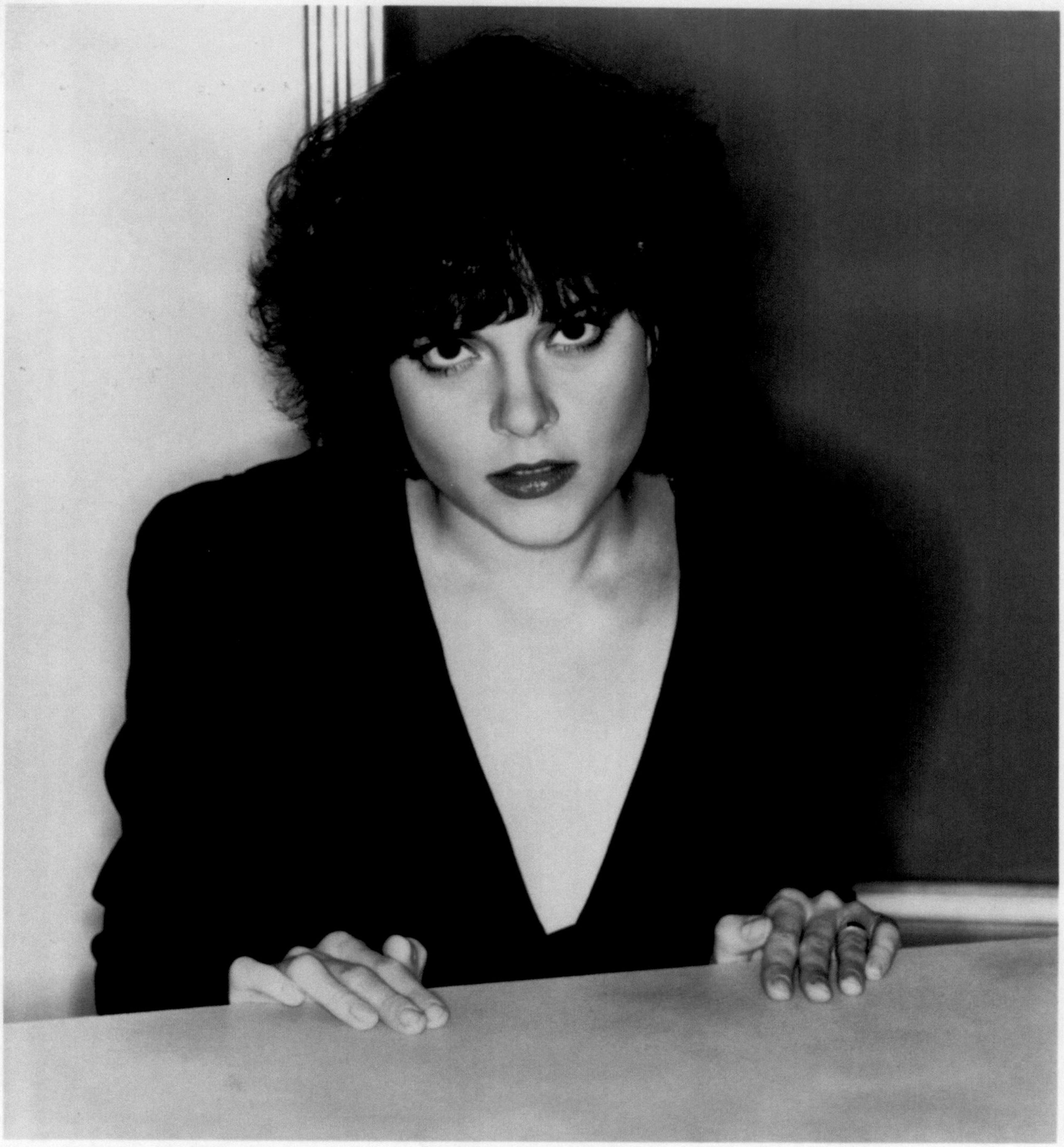

photo credit: Beverly Parker

ROSANNE CASH

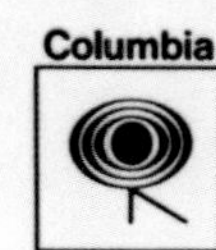

8102

Billboard 200: *Waitin' for the Sun to Shine* (#77)

As the hottest new star in country music, the multitalented Ricky Skaggs prompted a back-to-basics movement.

UNTIL RICKY Skaggs left Emmylou Harris' Hot Band to launch a solo career, he was heralded as the member with the heartfelt tenor who could play mandolin, fiddle—anything with strings.

"My goal was to put together my own band at some point," Skaggs said. "But I wanted to produce my own records, which is a big responsibility for a new, unproven artist. (Epic Records) checked me out with reputable people such as Brian Ahern (Harris' producer) and Rodney Crowell, and they backed me up. Several other labels showed some interest, but they ended up with the attitude of 'You're too country, you'll never sell.' I have to laugh at those folks now."

Skaggs' debut album *Waitin' for the Sun to Shine* spawned four successful country singles, with "Cryin' My Heart Out Over You" and "I Don't Care" reaching No. 1. Skaggs was tabbed New Artist Entertainer of the Year by the Country Music Association, and folks in the industry described him as "the genius of country music in terms of bluegrass."

The phenomenal success could be attributed to two factors. The most obvious was Skaggs' unique sound—a blend of acoustic and electric instruments that Skaggs coalesced in the studio. "I used to just play acoustic instruments, but with a good engineer you can get the sound levels right up there with the electric sounds," he explained. The second factor was his choice of tunes. The affable singer wasn't a songwriter, merely an interpreter of traditional and historical material. After years of stockpiling various standards and refining his skills as an arranger, he'd managed to strike a responsive chord among the dichotomized country audience.

"I won't do drinking or cheating songs," he noted. "I don't live that way, and I ain't gonna sing that way. I'm a Christian, and that's where I get much of my strength from. I was raised in eastern Kentucky on old mountain music, gospel from Flatt & Scruggs, Bill Monroe and the Stanley Brothers."

Kentucky proved to be fertile ground for Skaggs, both musically and personally. "I had a group called Boone Creek in Lexington for two years, and I learned how to front a band—plus the headaches and heartaches of having people on payroll," he recounted. "I got to see mistakes, things I let swell out of proportion—like drugs. I've never done any, but there were people in my band doing things that I didn't want any part of. It scared me to death because it was illegal, and if they got caught, I was there with them. Now I can set down rules for everyone from the road crew on down—*ix-nay* on the *ugs-dray*. I've got too much responsibility to jeopardize things now." ■

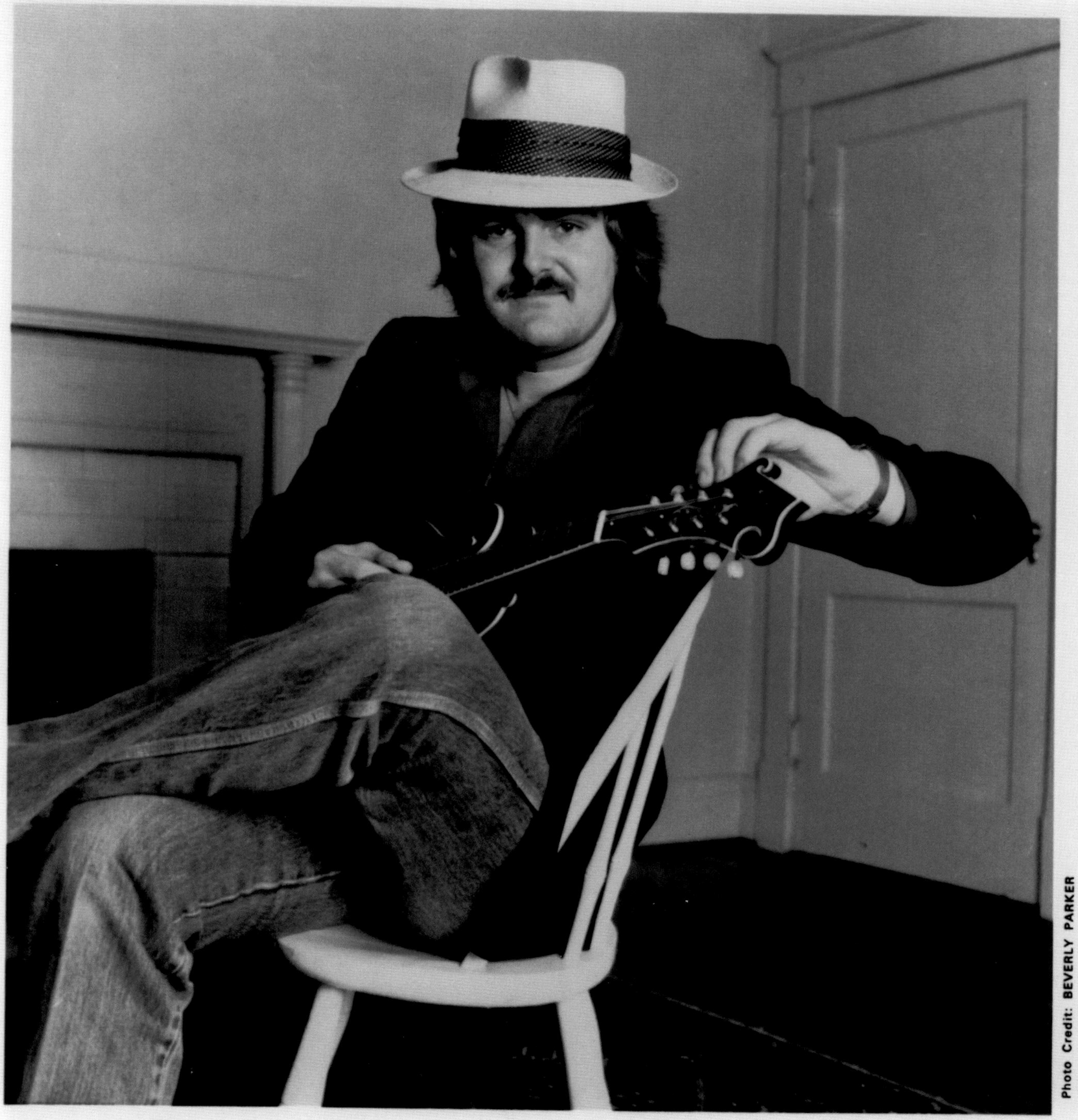

Photo Credit: BEVERLY PARKER

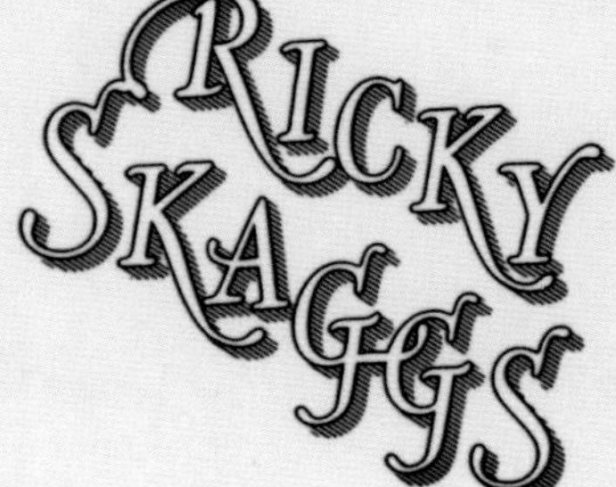

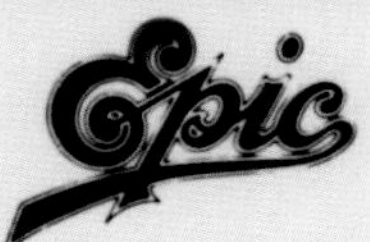

8105

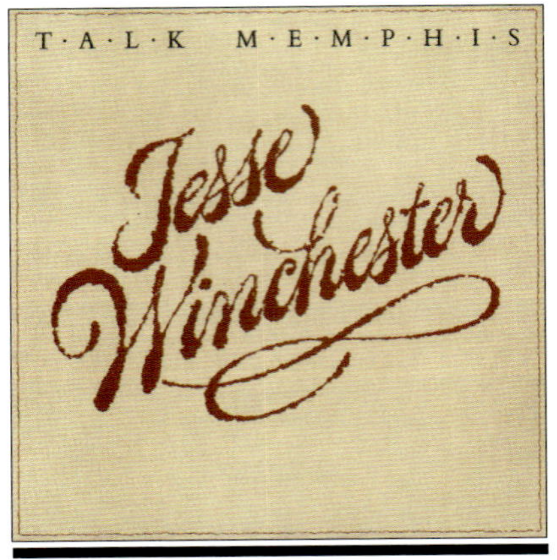

Billboard 200: *Talk Memphis* (#188)
Billboard Hot 100: "Say What" (#32)

Talk Memphis, expat Jesse Winchester's "homecoming" album, contained the singer-songwriter's biggest hit, "Say What."

JESSE WINCHESTER attained near-legendary status after issuing his galvanizing debut album in 1970. Produced by Robbie Robertson of the Band, *Jesse Winchester* emphasized a bygone America. The classics "Biloxi," "The Brand New Tennessee Waltz" and "Yankee Lady" made astonishingly mature statements, but the artfulness was heightened by a sense of the poet-in-exile—Winchester was the most prominent musician to have chosen banishment over conscription in the Vietnam War circa 1967.

Winchester's feelings suggested neither bitterness nor cynicism. He was simply weary of having his image irrevocably linked with "being a draft dodger."

"I have to admit that if I had a magic wand that could make that whole issue go away, that it never happened, I would wave it without hesitation," he reflected. "But there is no magic wand, and there's no point in regretting things like that. I'm one of these people who knows what his obituary is going to read like already, and I don't like that very much. It's a trite thing to say, but I'd rather that my songs be what people focus on."

Winchester hadn't spent much time looking backward. In the Seventies, he continued to record in a mild country-rock vein and released a string of impressive albums, his Southern roots resonating through his melodies and lyrics. But he was unable to tour in the US, and he became a Canadian citizen in 1973. President Jimmy Carter's declaration of blanket amnesty allowed him his first legal entry to the United States in a decade, and he returned to his hometown of Memphis in what he called "a very emotional moment."

The appropriately titled *Talk Memphis* was Winchester's first joint effort with famed Memphis producer Willie Mitchell, best known for his Al Green records. The Winchesters were one of the great founding families of the city.

"The title song is about growing up in Memphis," Winchester explained, recalling barbecue, University of Memphis football and baseball games, and the R&B station WDIA. He had a Top 40 hit with the lighthearted "Say What," written in the wry, closely observed style he was known for, and his soulful, flexible voice hit every high note perfectly.

The album gave Winchester a presence on the charts, but sales remained low.

"I'm only a marginal artist," Winchester shrugged. "There's very little interest in me on the part of record companies." ■

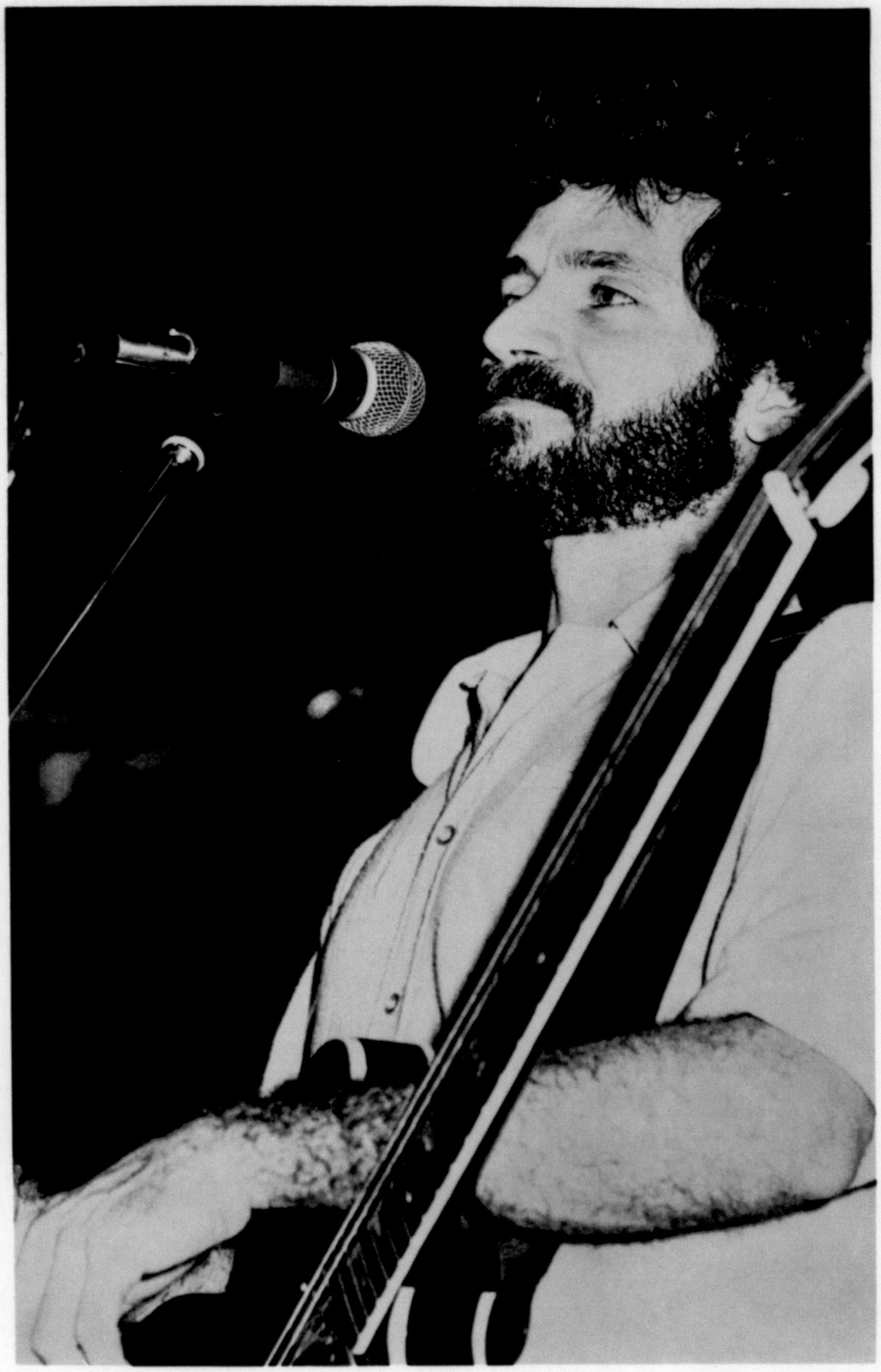

JESSE WINCHESTER

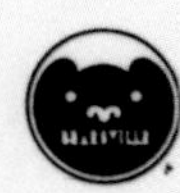

An ode to the joys of fast food held **Commander Cody**'s position as "America's most certifiable rock 'n' roll lunatic."

COMMANDER CODY, alias George Frayne, had been a fixture on the American music scene for almost a decade. His brand of good-time boogie-woogie rock 'n' roll—notably the gonzo barroom country classic "Hot Rod Lincoln" and a breakneck reading of "Daddy, Beat Me Eight to the Bar"—had endeared him to audiences throughout the world.

But Commander Cody was just another character to Frayne, a talented individual in many areas. After graduating with honors from the University of Michigan with a degree in fine arts, he discovered that the straight world held no charms for someone with diverse interests. He invented the Cody character to conquer the world of rock 'n' roll, but as he tried to promote himself as an author and painter, he had found that he was pigeonholed. He reemerged with *Lose It Tonight*, featuring the single "2 Triple Cheese (Side Order of Fries)."

"I wrote and produced it myself, and that's the last thing that record companies want from me," Frayne explained. "They think of hicks, drunken cowboys and fiddle music. All it takes is for someone to say, 'Hey, listen, George, you're more than a stoned hippie that doesn't know what he's doing, you're a stoned hippie that *knows* what he's doing. But screw trying to figure things out. That's something I've learned over the last couple of years—just relax. I have no financial goals other than to pay the rent, eat regularly, and buy enough pot so I can smoke it all the time and think of songs."

Frayne hoped "2 Triple Cheese (Side Order of Fries)" could top "Seven Eleven," his infamous hymn to shoplifting.

"I did pretty good with that one," Frayne boasted. "In San Francisco, a guy went through a store's aisles grabbing stuff whistling that song. He then punched out the owner and split. Every radio station in the Bay Area dropped the song from their playlists within a half-hour. I've got a lot of stuff that is out-and-out controversial. I've got a nasty song about John Wayne because I don't like John Wayne. Stuff like 'Under that tan he was a helluva man/He tried to send me to Vietnam.' And 'In the end, of course/He got off on his horse.' They don't wanna hear that in Nashville.

"With me, you really expect something different. I mean, Frank Zappa can do it because people believe in him. What's the difference between Frank Zappa being a schmuck and a genius? It's that a whole bunch of people *think* he's a genius. If people thought I was a genius, I'd be making some funny fricking albums." ■

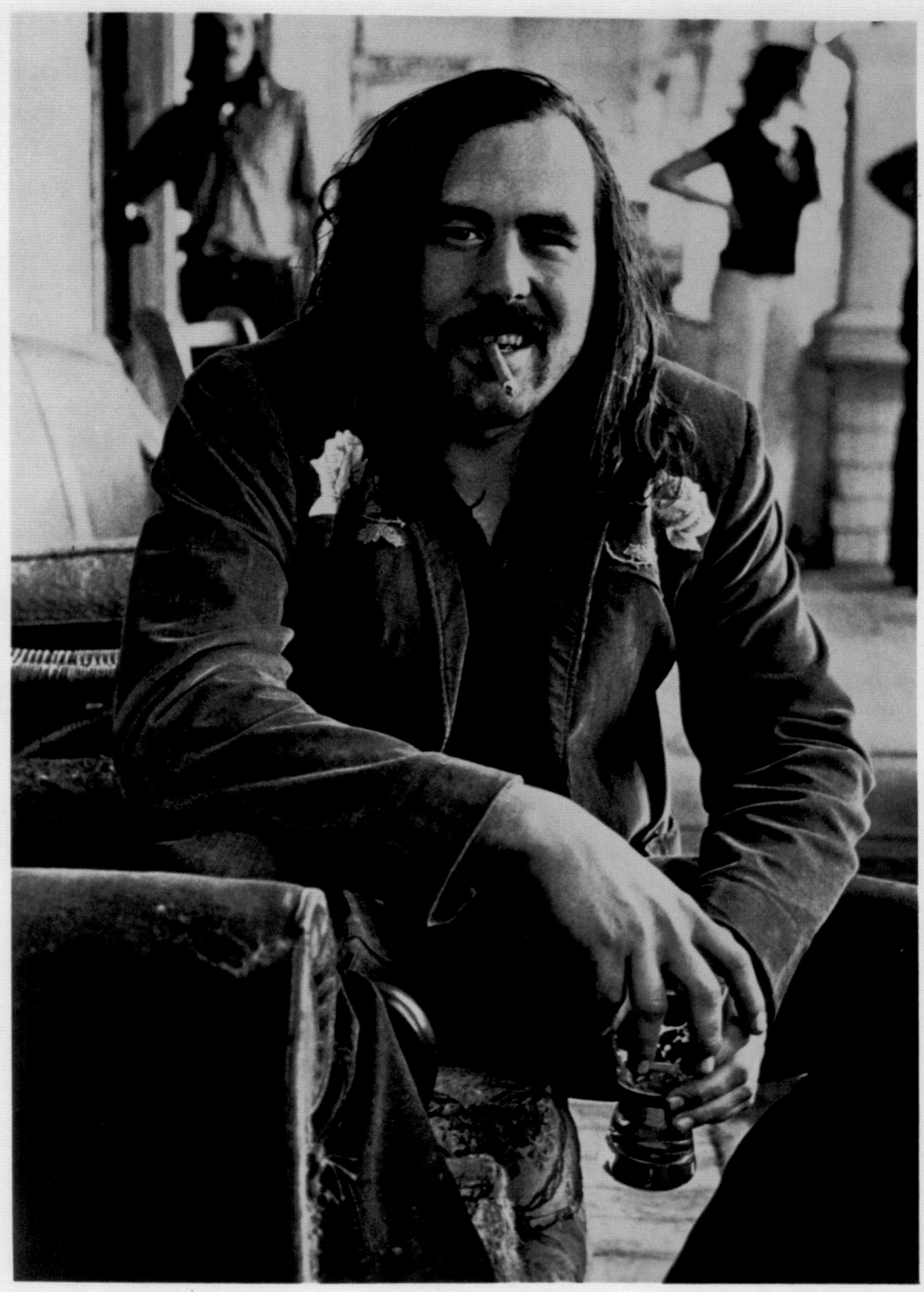

MANAGEMENT:
JOE KERR

P. O. BOX 273
SAN RAFAEL, CALIF 94902
(415) 457-6660

COMMANDER CODY

MAGNA ARTISTS CORP
9200 Sunset Blvd., Los Angeles, Ca. 90069
(213) 273-3177

Billboard 200: *Pirates* (#5)
Billboard Hot 100: "A Lucky Guy" (#64)

Two years after her wildly successful debut, Rickie Lee Jones resurfaced with her follow-up album, *Pirates*.

BORN IN Chicago, Rickie Lee Jones settled in Los Angeles in 1973. She played in dive bars and small clubs for $10 for four sets before she scored a Top 5 hit with 1979's snazzy "Chuck E.'s in Love," making her the reigning queen of street-sleaze to an adoring audience. The wise, wild waif with the red beret and beatnik affectations won the Grammy Award for Best New Artist.

Her poetic imagination and gritty swagger led to comparisons to everyone from Joni Mitchell to Tom Waits. Jones and Waits had been lovers at the outset of her career; a break-up occurred in late 1979. She wrote and recorded *Pirates* partly in reaction to their relationship, and Waits inspired "A Lucky Guy," the album's only charting pop single.

Jones made it known that her music would advance, drawing upon longer and more intricate song structures.

"My music is really personal," she allowed. "I think that's what will make it noticed. Most artists aren't very secure, but now that I know I don't have to fight to make my songs heard, I can feel a lot more confident about writing and performing."

"Pirates (So Long Lonely Avenue)," another ode to Waits, and the bebop tribute "Woody and Dutch on the Slow Train to Peking," with its finger snaps and jive talk beat, were minor hits.

"Remember that we are in a creative business," Jones said. "Those two words need not cancel each other out. Don't go bananas over new ideas that come your way simply because you've never tried them before. It is your business to be creative." ■

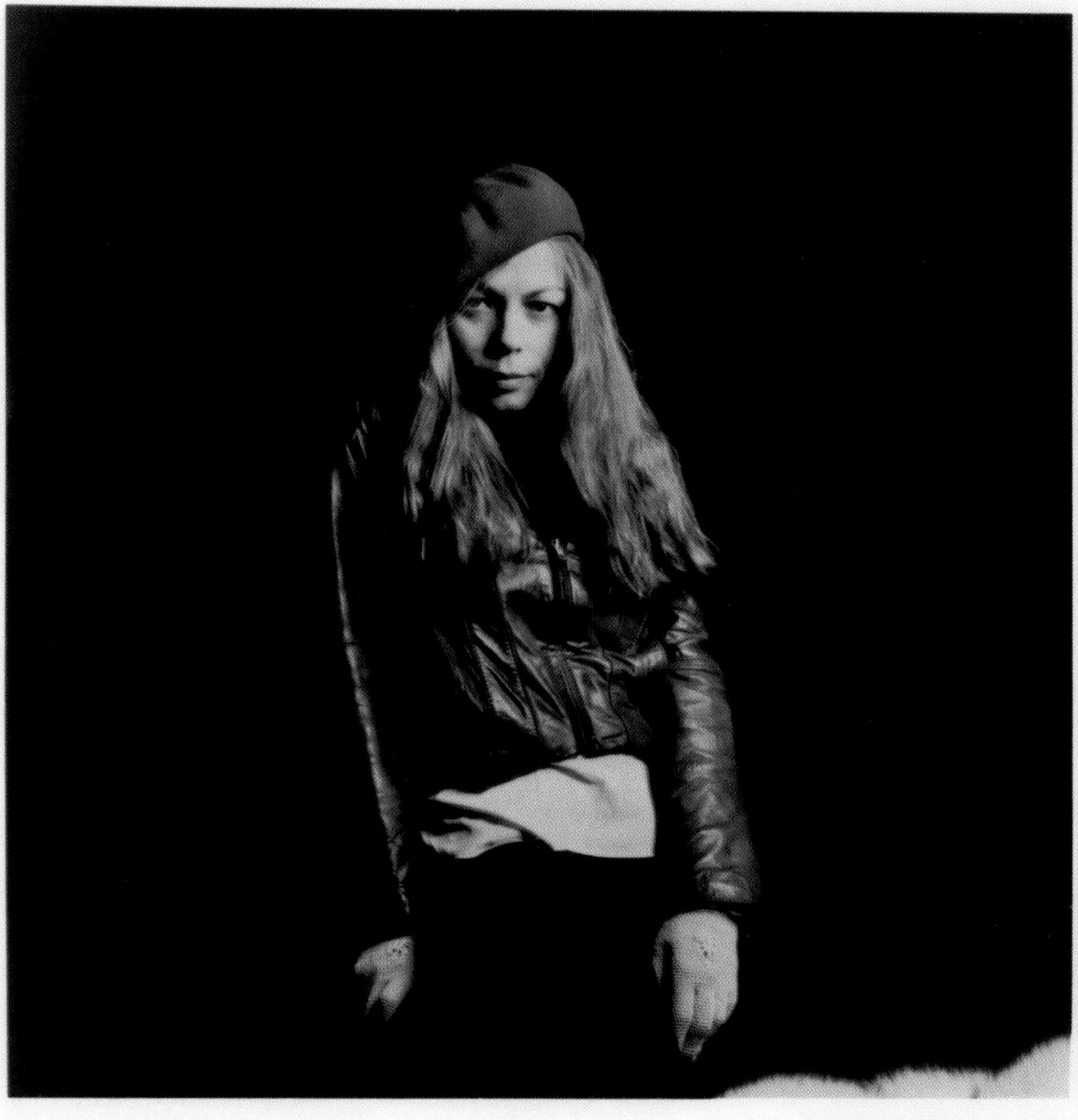

Photo Credit MICHAEL HALSBAND July 1981

RICKIE LEE JONES

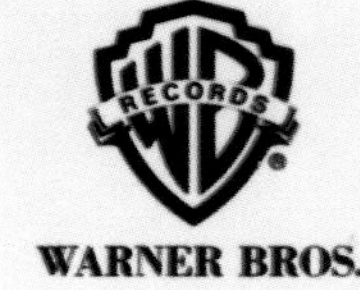

WARNER BROS.

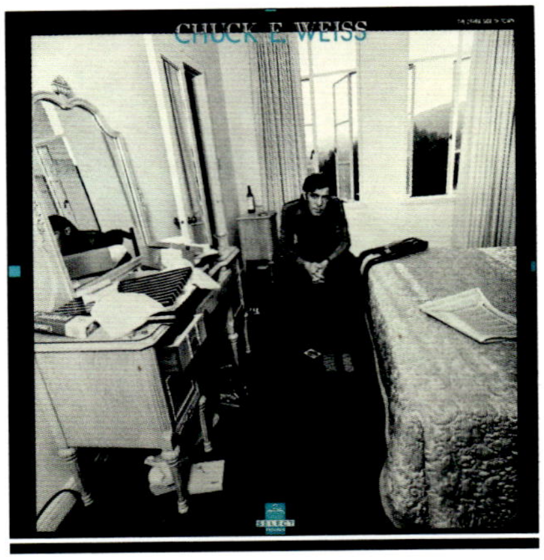

One of the L.A. scene's coolest cats, Chuck E. Weiss explored his offbeat blend of Americana on *The Other Side of Town.*

WHAT CHUCK E. Weiss described as "twisted jungle music"—inspirations ranging from New Orleans dirge jazz to demented electric country-blues, brazenly mixed with boozy attitude and jive poetry—bristled with both cultural and historical value. The synthesis represented the breadth of experience he gained growing up in Denver in the Fifties and Sixties, where his aura (his idea of awesome was gold pointed-toe shoes and black cut-off t-shirts) gave him a reputation for being a little offbeat—but right on the beat.

"I was the only Jew for a hundred miles—I felt like a Ubangi dropped in Times Square on New Year's Eve," Weiss recalled with a laugh. "Denver was a hub for the railroads. Hence you had that huge skid row downtown that's now been yuppified. The con was born there. All the grifters came in the early part of the century and they'd get their training and then they'd go to Chicago and other cities. That gave rise to all the bohemians coming to Denver. When (Jack) Kerouac discovered the place, it was already wide open. As a kid, I caught the tail end of that.

"People were different. The place had a lot of soul. There was a jazz station. There were so many little coffeehouses and clubs. We used to take the bus to go find stuff in pawnshops. You could hear a million great Mexican rock 'n' roll bands. There were always little things like that happening. I don't think anybody ever took it seriously. Naturally, it molded me, so I took it seriously."

Weiss learned to drum, and circa 1970, he was asked to sit in during an appearance by Lightnin' Hopkins at a Boulder nightclub. The gig went well, and Weiss persuaded Hopkins, one of the last great exponents of Texas blues, to take him on tour. Weiss then hit it off with singer-songwriter Tom Waits at Ebbets Field, a Denver club where Waits was performing.

"We were both sitting at the counter of the coffee shop next door. I was wearing a chinchilla coat and three-inch platforms, and I thought he was just some bum folksinger. I remember bragging to him about all the people I knew."

The pair cultivated a lasting friendship. Weiss subsequently moved to California, and in the late Seventies he joined Waits and an up-and-coming female artist named Rickie Lee Jones at the vanguard of an "alternative singer-songwriter" trend based out of West Hollywood's famed Tropicana Motel. Jones later immortalized Weiss in her Top 5 hit "Chuck E.'s in Love," and Waits sprinkled Weiss' likeness around a lot of his music. Perhaps that encouraged the perception of Weiss as some sort of hipster novelty artist, but his music retained a life-learned authenticity. He launched his recording career with the release of *The Other Side of Town*, a collection of demo tapes.

"I did a session with Dr. John and a lot of New Orleans cats. We were just screwing around in the studio, trying to get some songs together to convince the record company to give us money to make a real album. They sent me an easy-to-read contract and I signed it hoping I had a record deal. I did—but they never gave me money! I sent them the demo tape and they put it out as the record. But I'm so proud to have been with the New Orleans guys—that overshadows the shame I have." ■

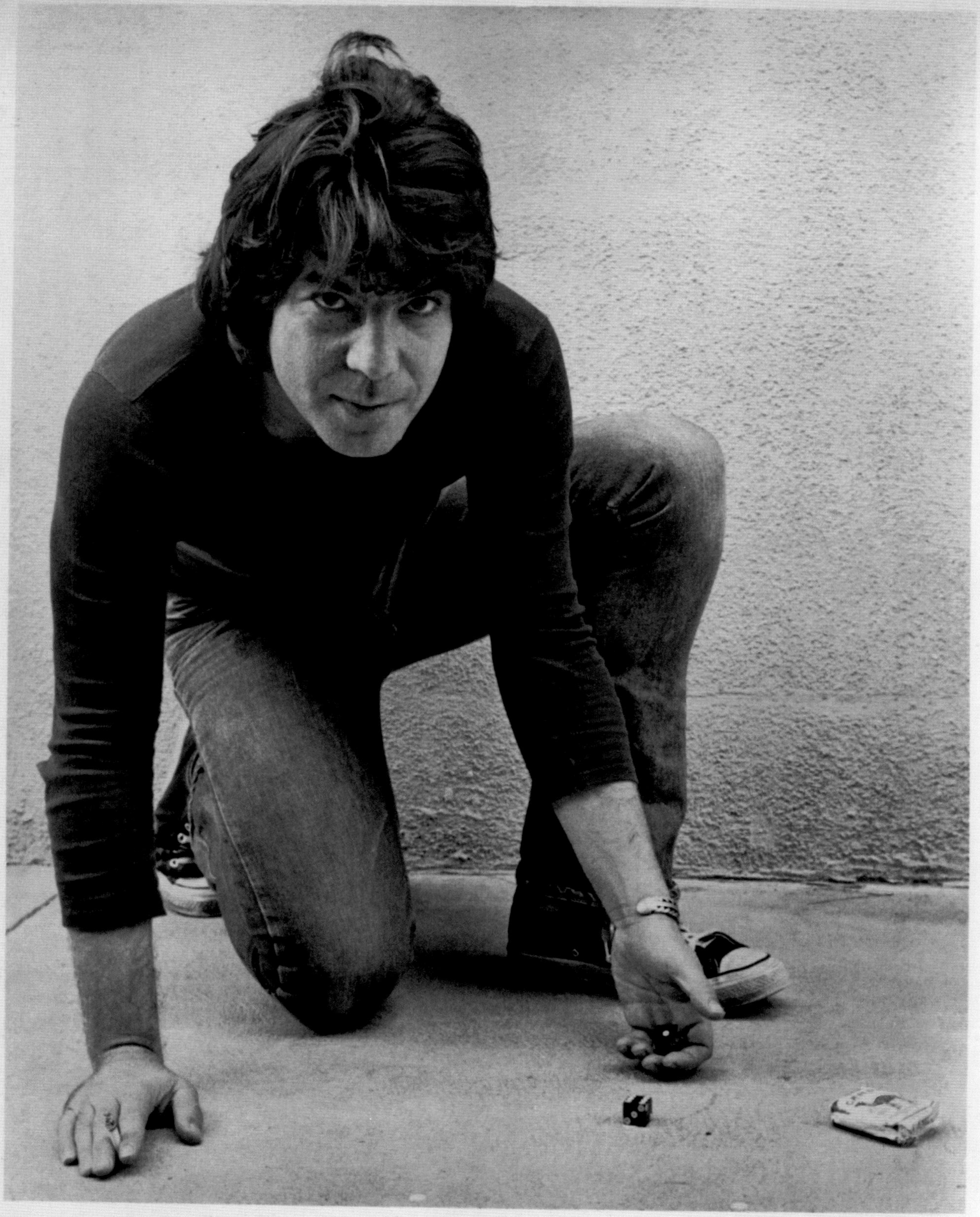

CHUCK E. WEISS

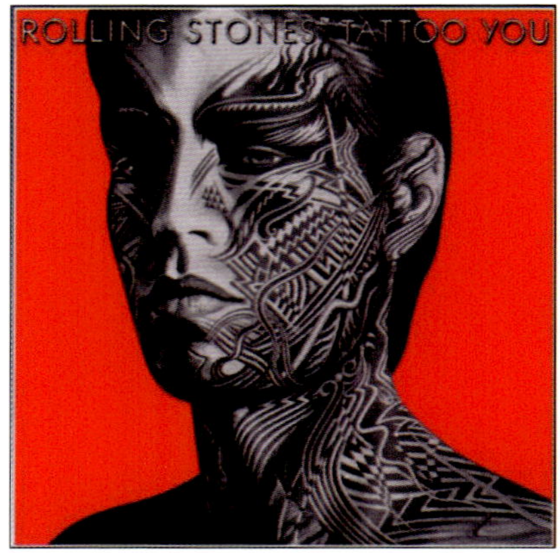

The Rolling Stones released *Tattoo You* to wide acclaim, as the infectious "Start Me Up" and "Waiting on a Friend" helped the album dominate the charts.

Billboard 200: *Tattoo You* (No. 1)
Billboard Hot 100: "Start Me Up" (#2);
"Waiting on a Friend" (#13); "Hang Fire" (#20)

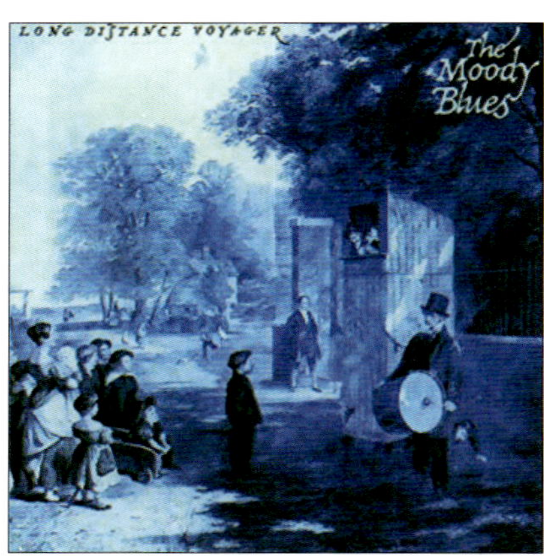

The Moody Blues' *Long Distance Voyager* was a huge success, reaching No. 1 on the album chart and yielding two hits, "The Voice" and "Gemini Dream."

Billboard 200: *Long Distance Voyager* (No. 1)
Billboard Hot 100: "Gemini Dream" (#12);
"The Voice" (#15); "Talking Out of Turn" (#65)

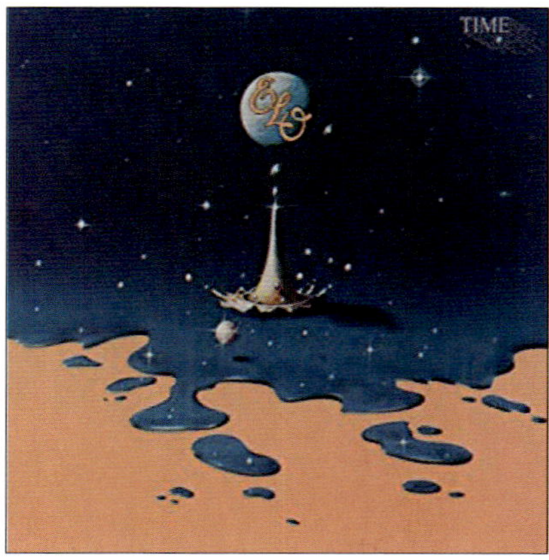

With the three-man string section departed, bandleader Jeff Lynne emphasized synthesizers on *Time*, ELO's concept album dealing with time travel.

Billboard 200: *Time* (#16)
Billboard Hot 100: "Hold On Tight" (#10);
"Twilight" (#38)

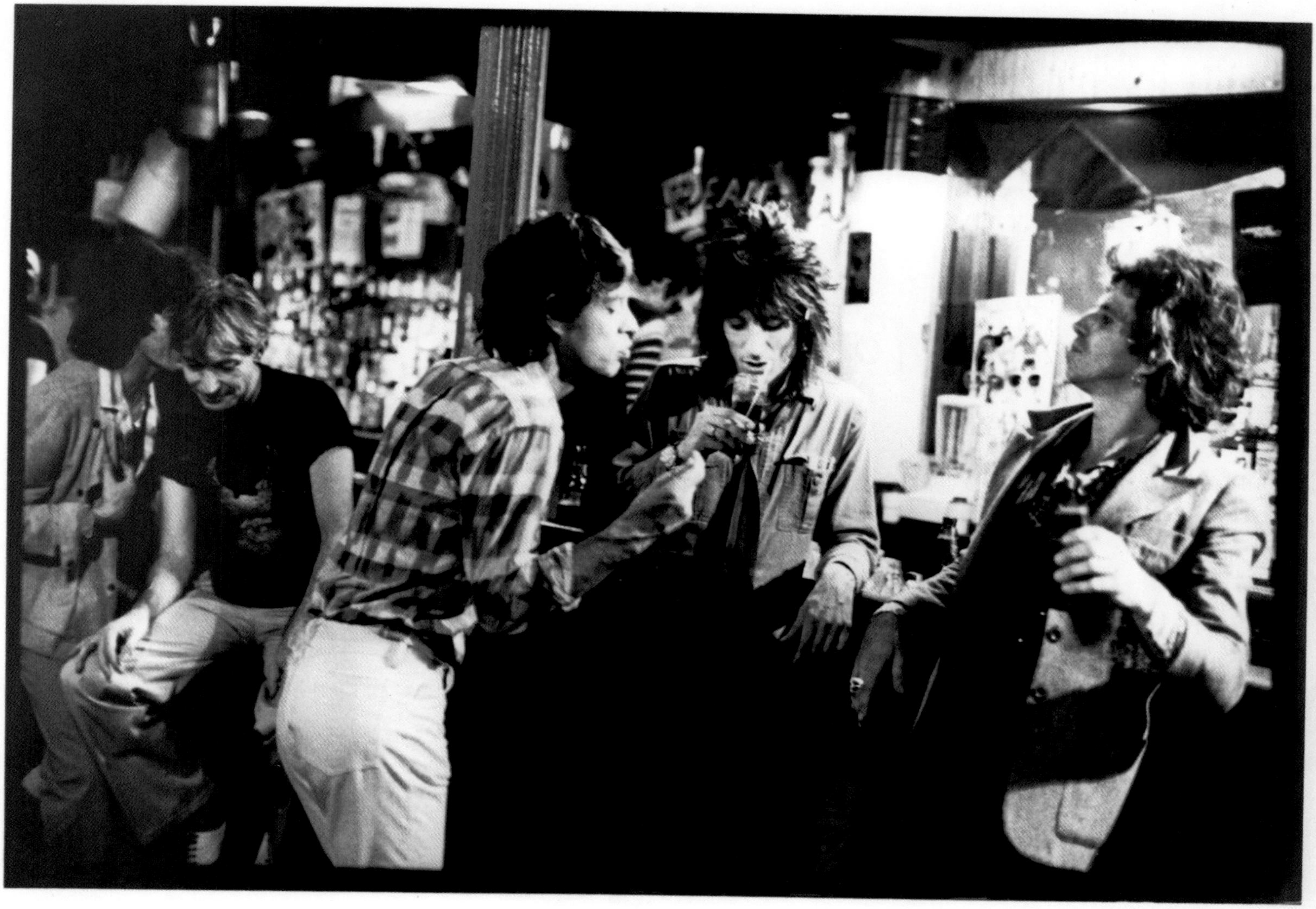

THE ROLLING STONES

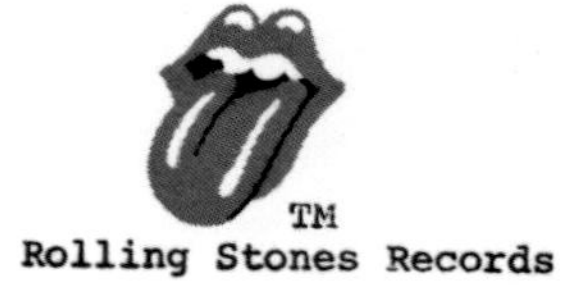

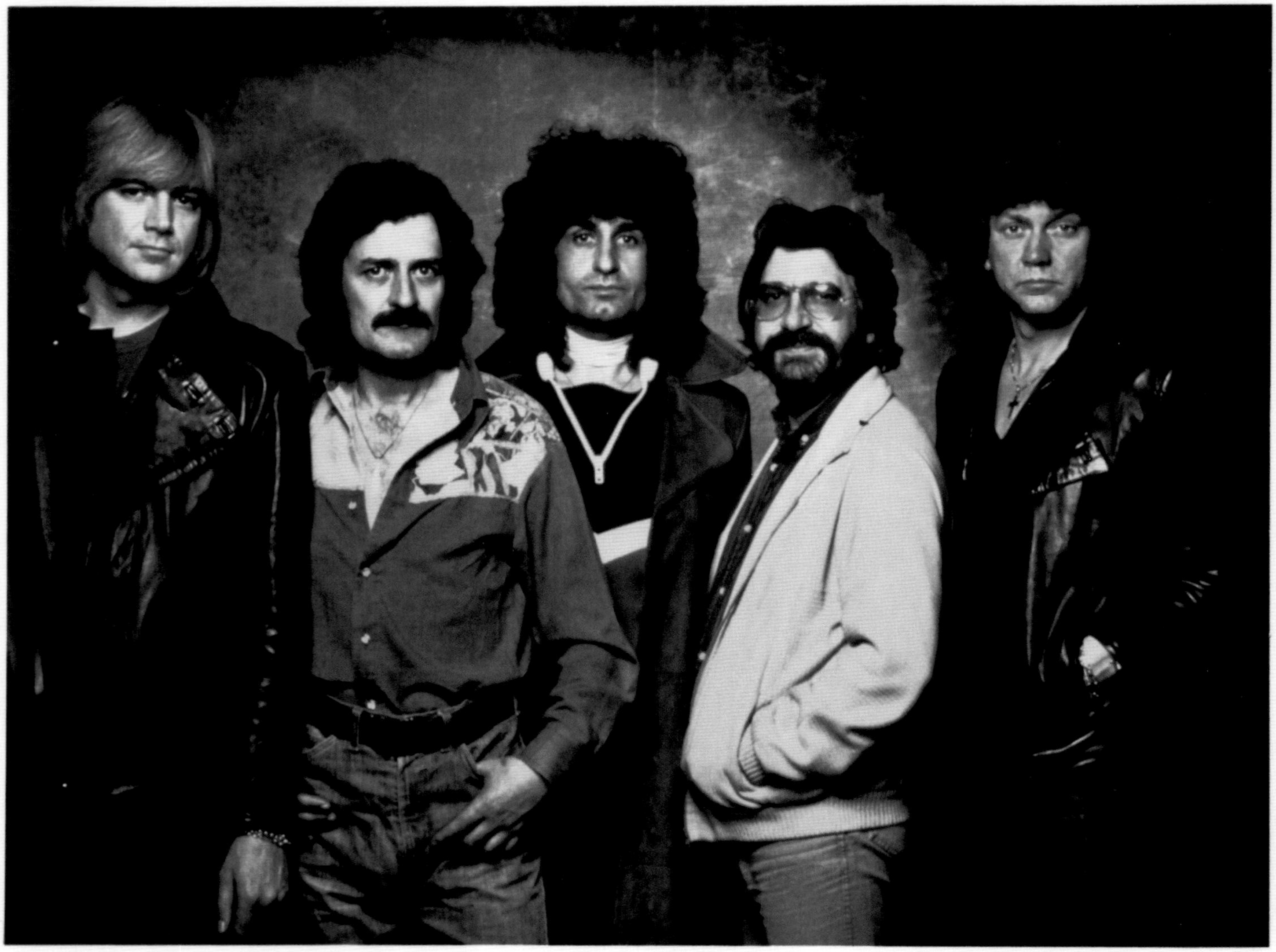

THE MOODY BLUES

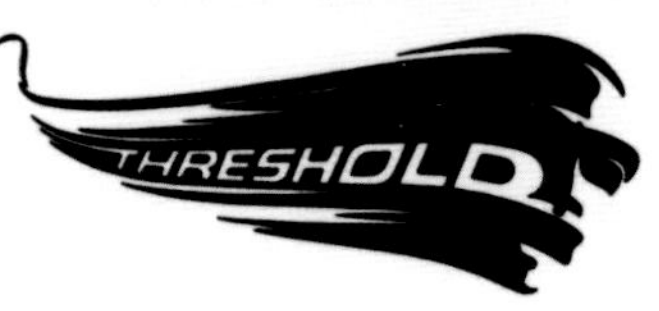

PolyGram Records

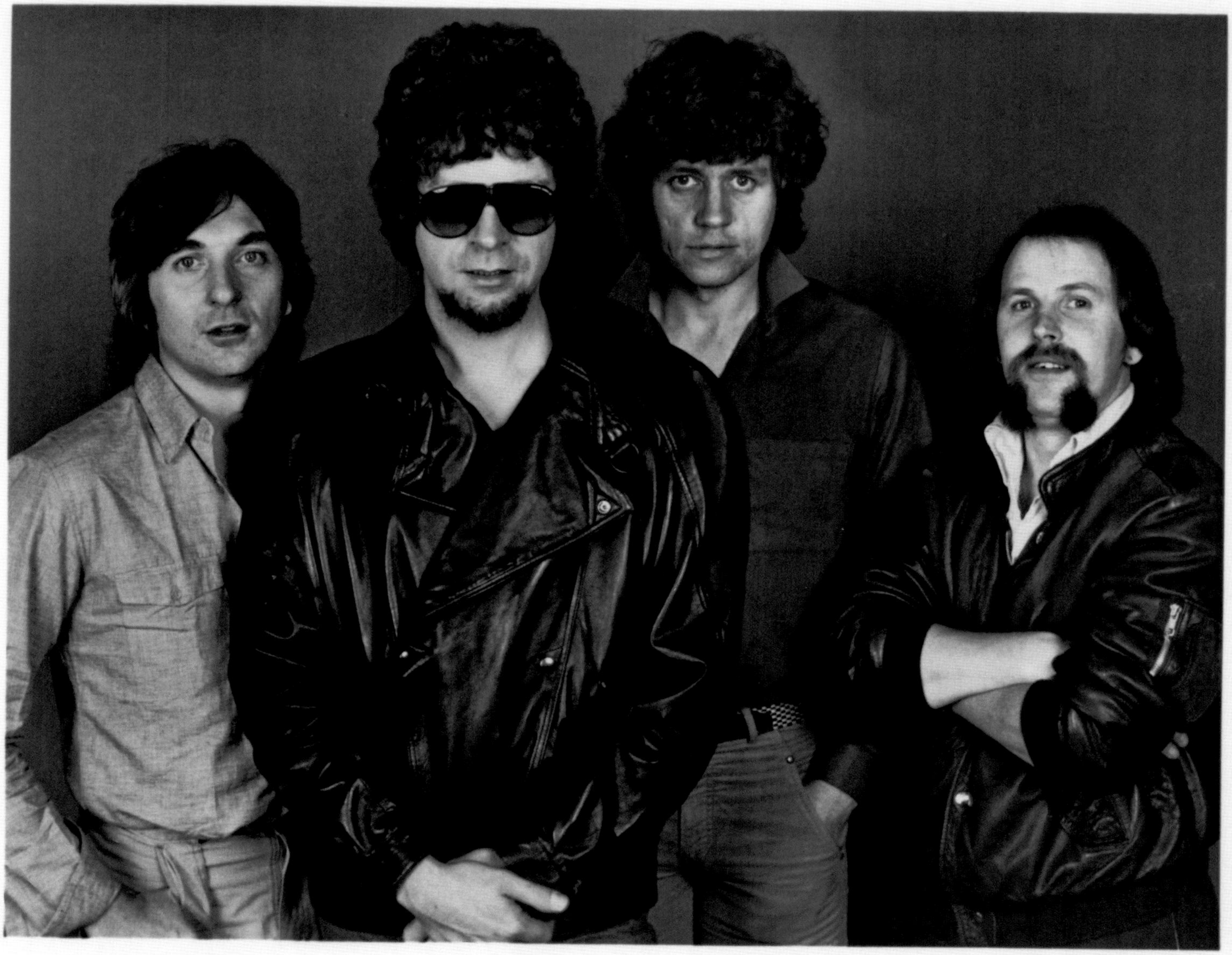

RICHARD TANDY JEFF LYNNE BEV BEVAN KELLY GROUCUTT

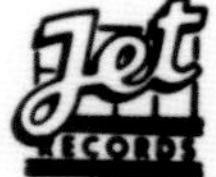

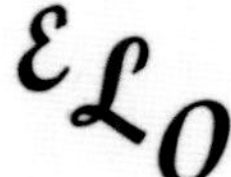

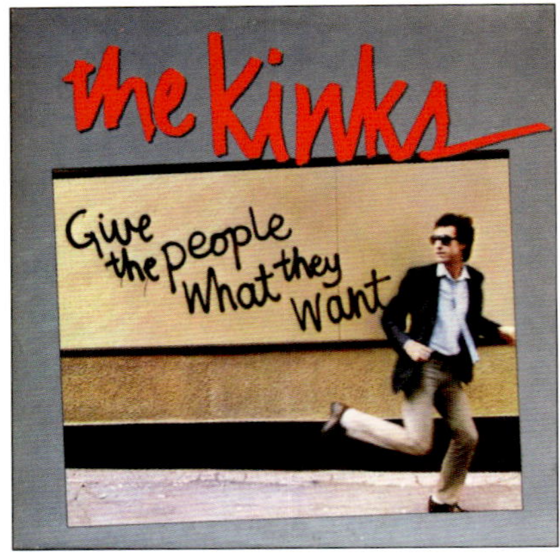

The Kinks' *Give the People What They Want* featured the paranoid "Destroyer," a rock hit distinguished by references to the influential English band's earlier hits.

Billboard 200: *Give the People What They Want* (#15)
Billboard Hot 100: "Better Things" (#92); "Destroyer" (#85)

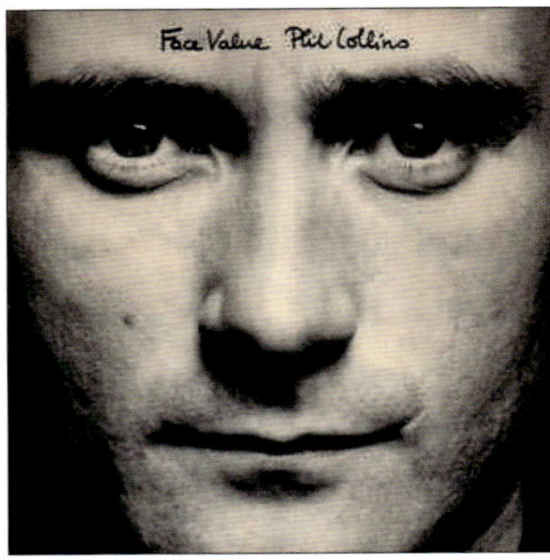

Genesis drummer and singer Phil Collins cited his divorce as the main inspiration for *Face Value*, his first solo album, and the international hit, "In the Air Tonight."

Billboard 200: *Face Value* (#7)
Billboard Hot 100: "In the Air Tonight" (#19);
"I Missed Again" (#19)

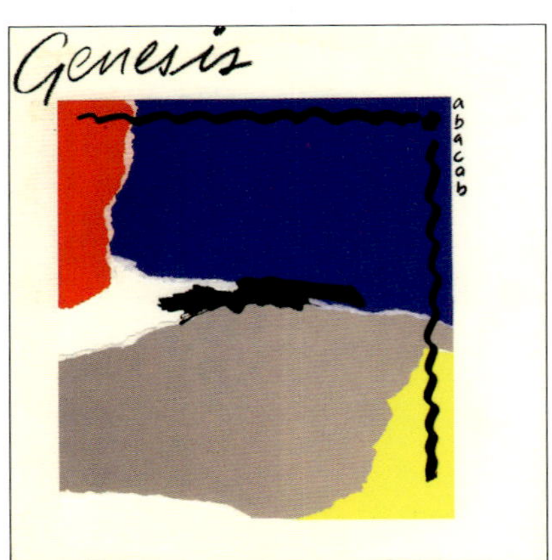

British art-rock band Genesis continued to achieve accessibility with *Abacab*, powered by three Top 40 singles—the title track, "No Reply at All" and "Man on the Corner."

Billboard 200: *Abacab* (#7)
Billboard Hot 100: "Abacab" (#26); "No Reply at All" (#29);
"Man on the Corner" (#40)

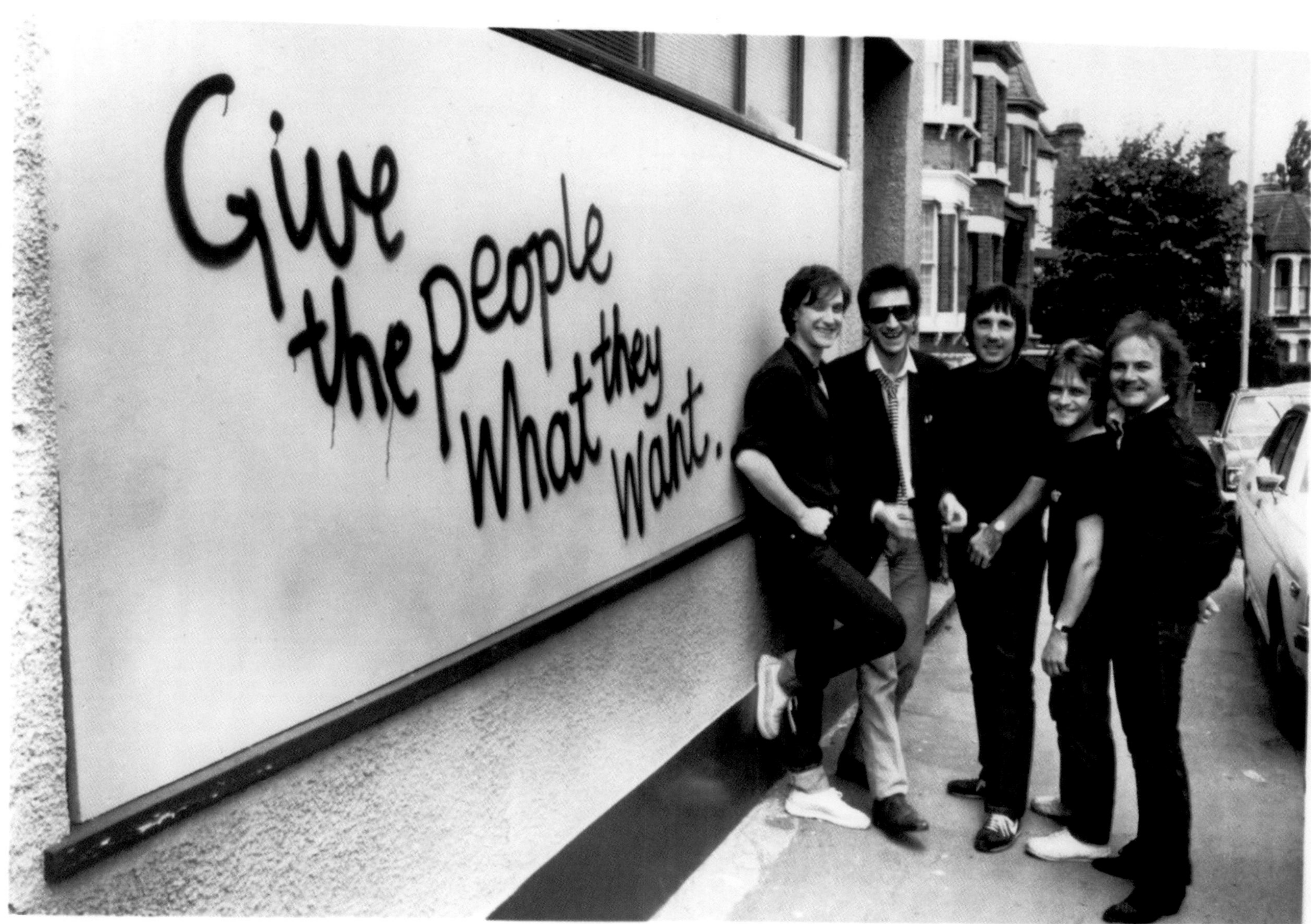

Renaissance Management
433 North Camden Drive
Beverly Hills, CA 90210
213-273-4162

ICM **THE KINKS** ARISTA™

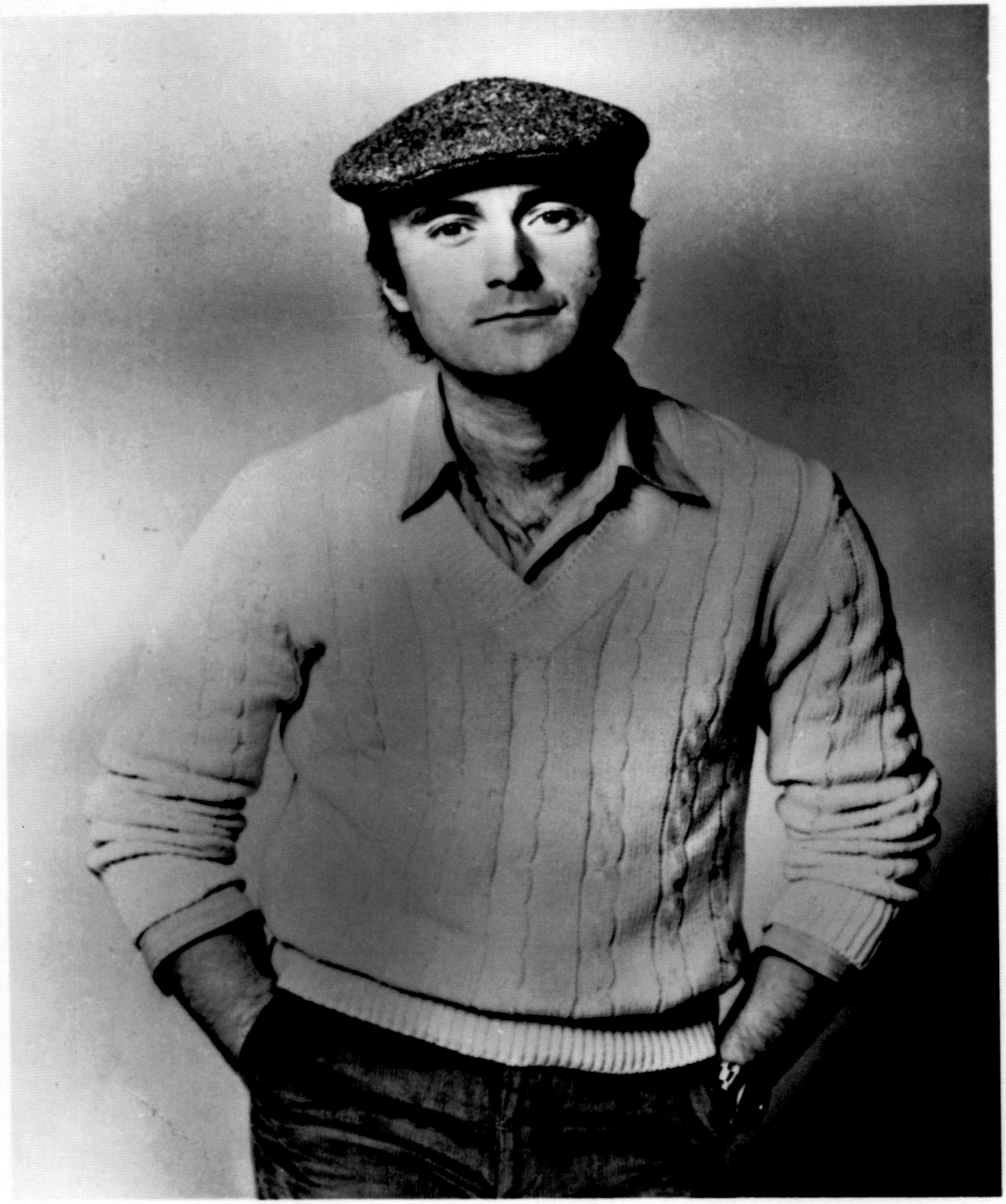

PHIL COLLINS

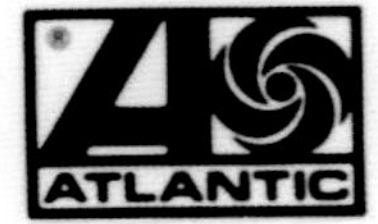

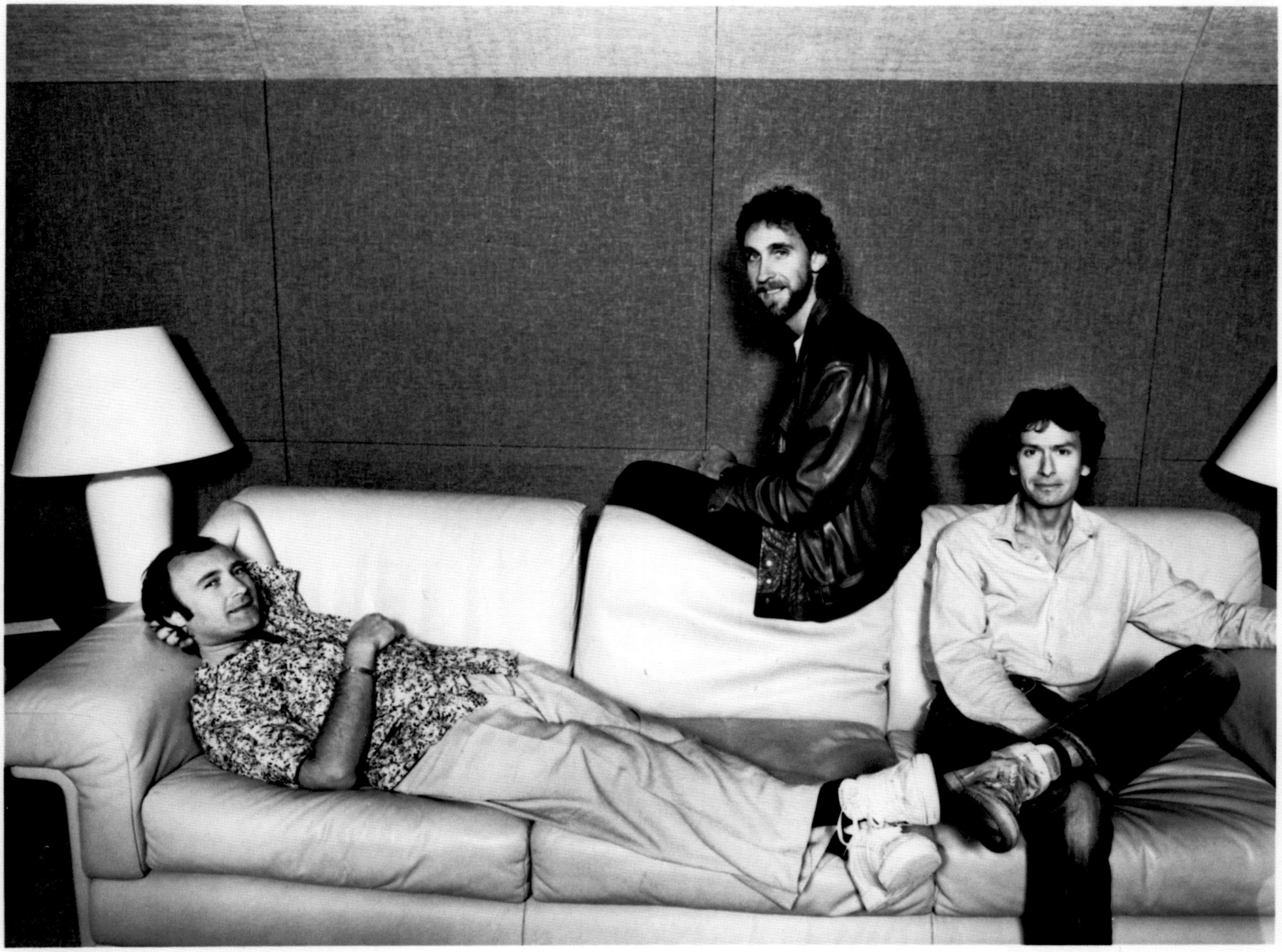

PHIL COLLINS MIKE RUTHERFORD TONY BANKS

GENESIS

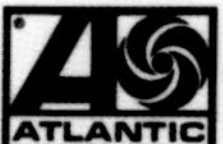

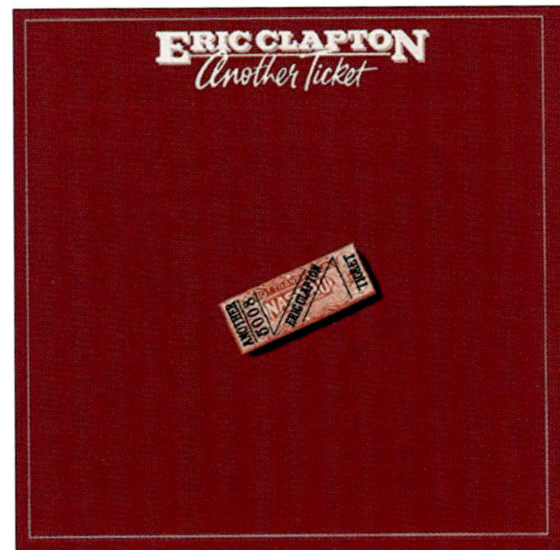

"I Can't Stand It" from **Eric Clapton**'s *Another Ticket* was the first No. 1 song on the Top Tracks chart, introduced by *Billboard* to measure the airplay of rock album tracks.

Billboard 200: *Another Ticket* (#7)
Billboard Hot 100: "I Can't Stand It" (#10);
"Another Ticket" (#78)

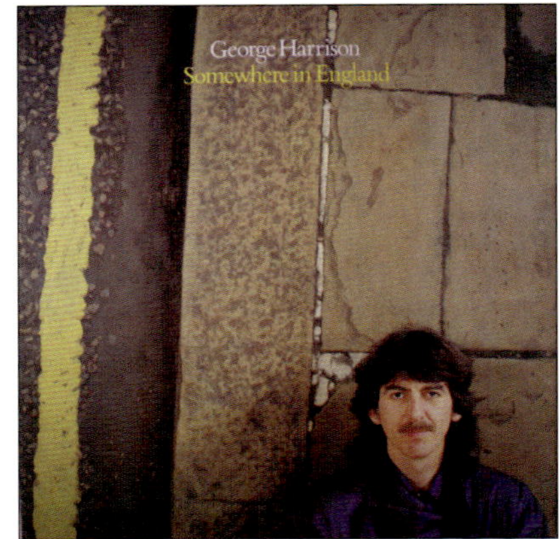

Following John Lennon's murder, **George Harrison** recorded "All Those Years Ago" with Paul McCartney and Ringo Starr as a tribute to their former Beatles bandmate.

Billboard 200: *Somewhere in England* (#11)
Billboard Hot 100: "All Those Years Ago" (#2)

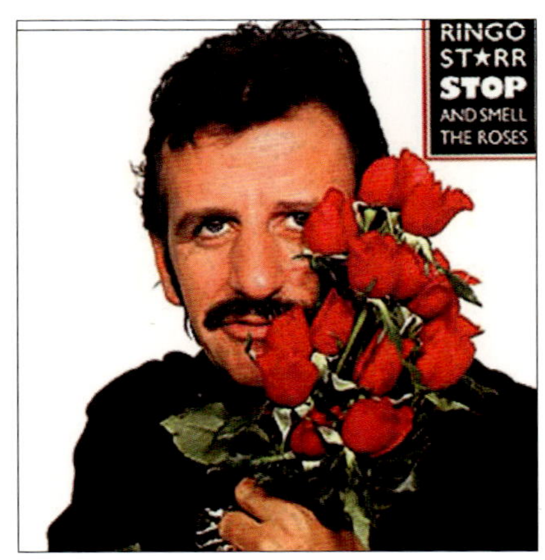

From the album *Stop and Smell the Roses*, "Wrack My Brain," written and produced by fellow Beatle George Harrison, gave **Ringo Starr** a Top 40 hit.

Billboard 200: *Stop and Smell the Roses* (#98)
Billboard Top 100: "Wrack My Brain" (#38)

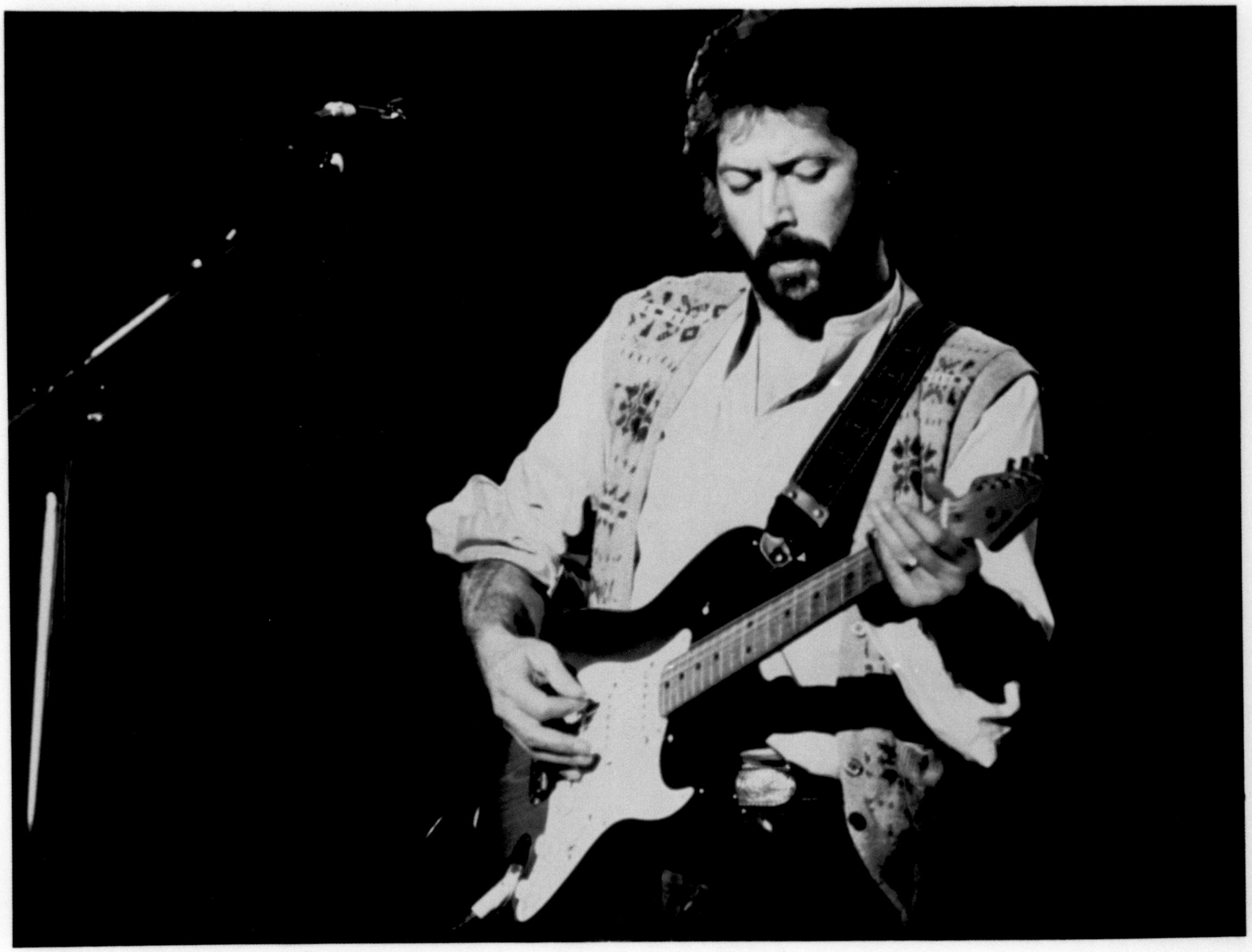

Management:
Roger Forrester
67 Brook Street, London W1Y 1YD.
Tel: 01-629 9121

ERIC CLAPTON

Another Ticket

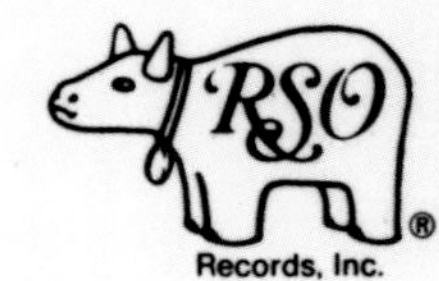

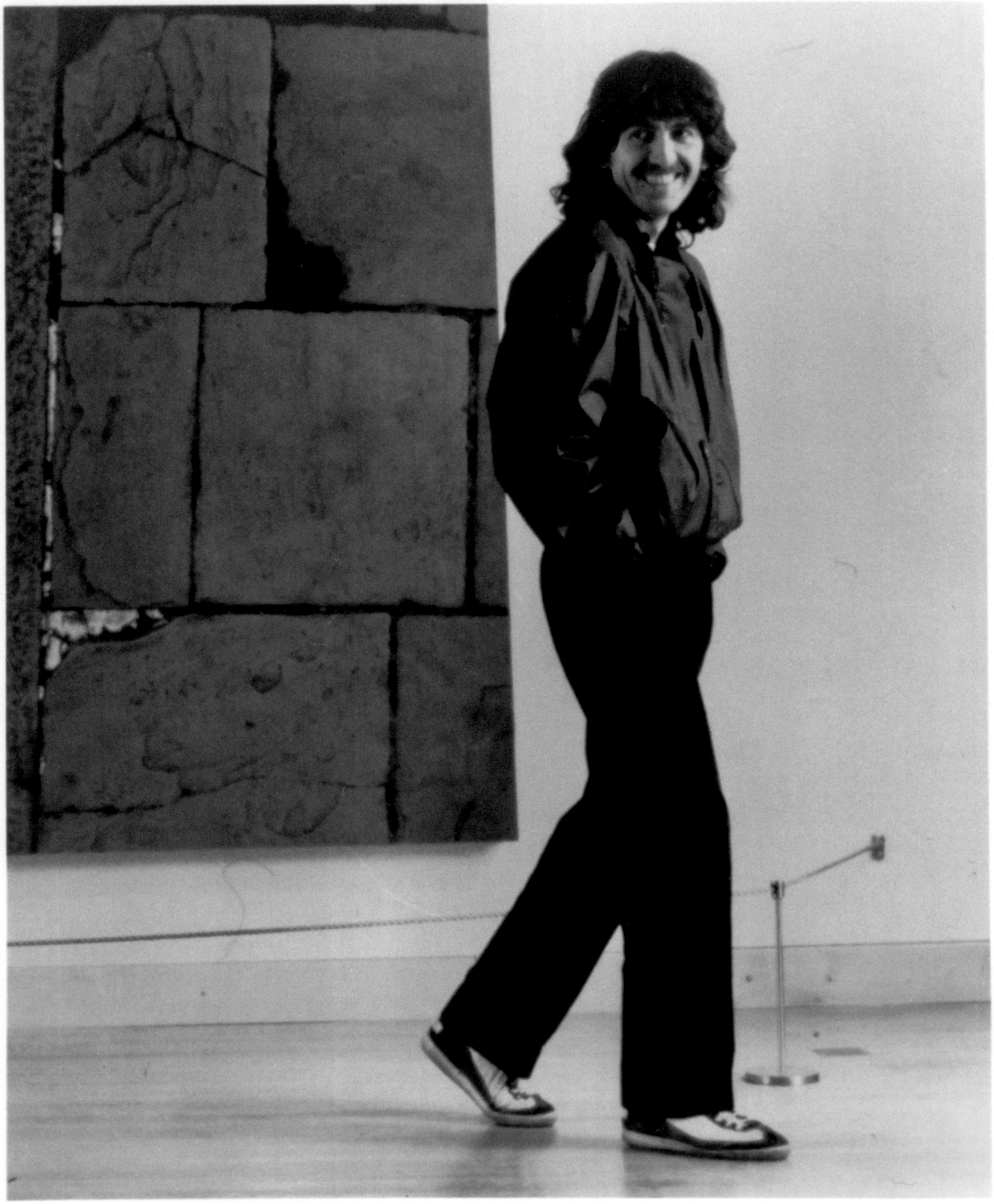

GEORGE HARRISON

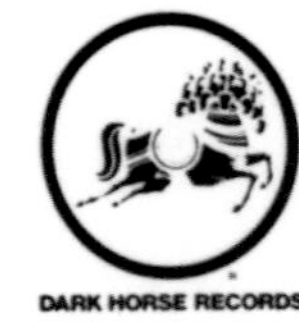

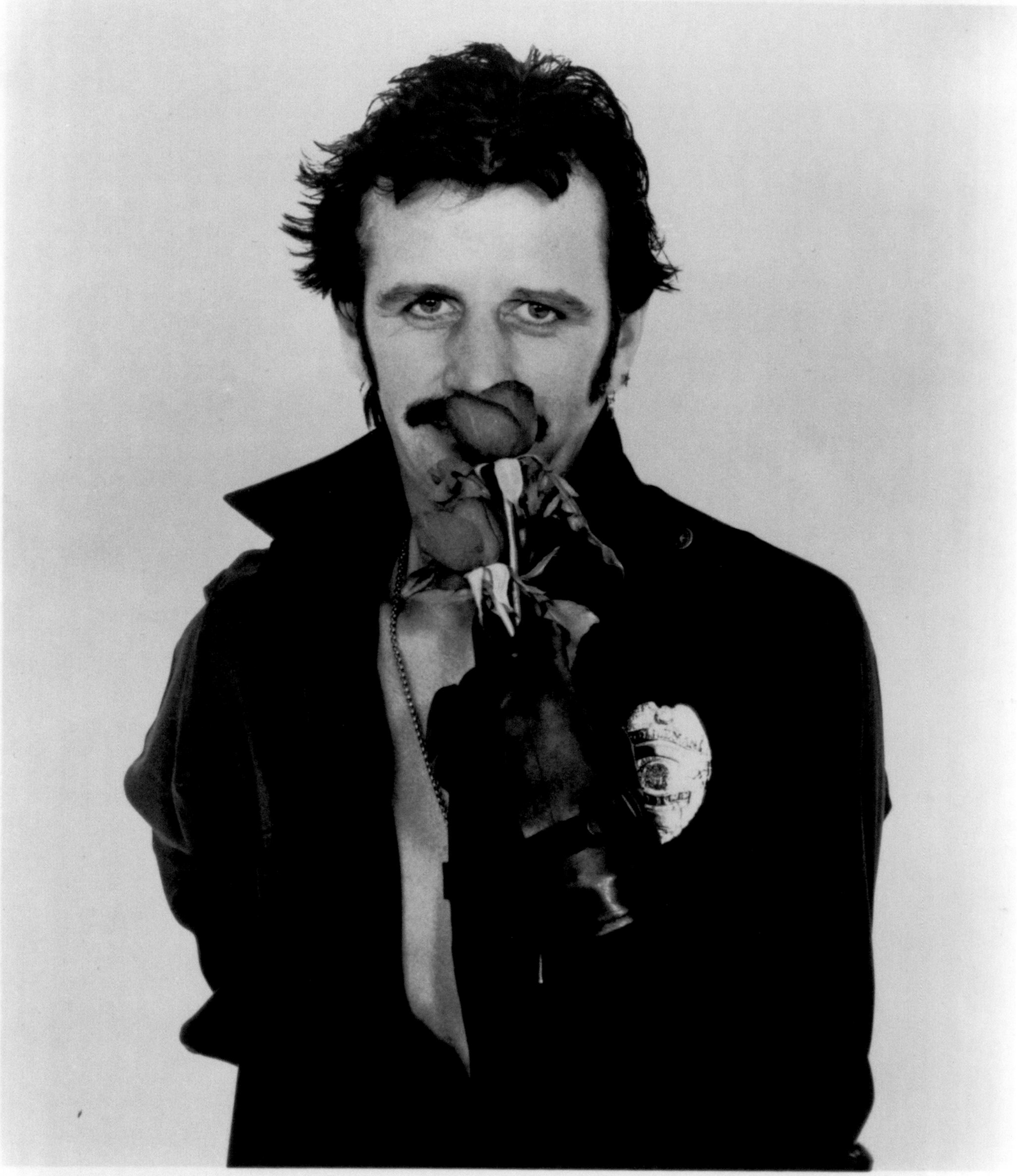

RINGO STARR

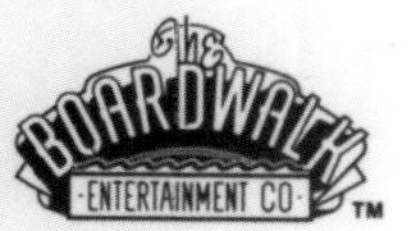

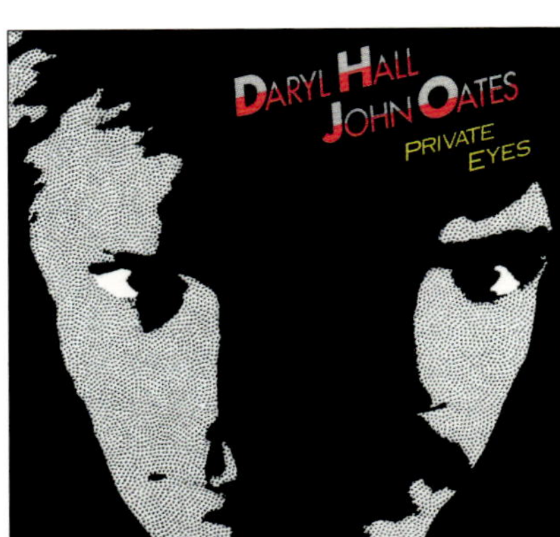

Daryl Hall & John Oates' hot streak continued with two No. 1 singles, "Private Eyes" and "I Can't Go for That (No Can Do)," as well as the Top 10 hit, "Did It in a Minute."

Billboard 200: *Private Eyes* (#5)
Billboard Hot 100: "Private Eyes" (No. 1); "I Can't Go for That (No Can Do)" (No. 1); "Did It in a Minute" (#9); "Your Imagination" (#33)

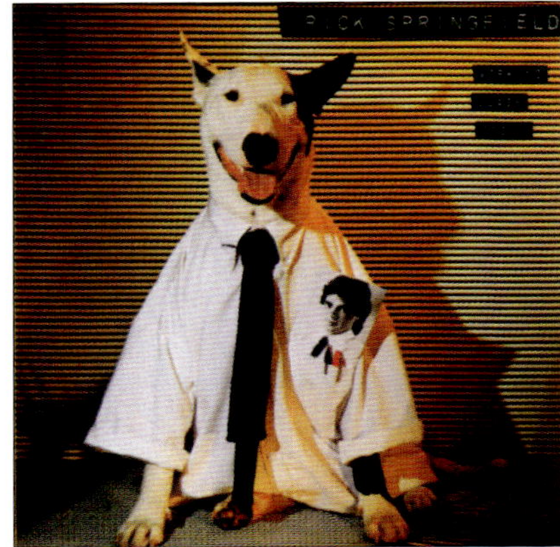

Working Class Dog, Rick Springfield's fourth album, spawned the power-pop classic, "Jessie's Girl," and the Sammy Hagar-penned "I've Done Everything for You."

Billboard 200: *Working Class Dog* (#7)
Billboard Hot 100: "Jessie's Girl" (No. 1); "I've Done Everything for You" (#8); "Love Is Alright Tonight" (#20)

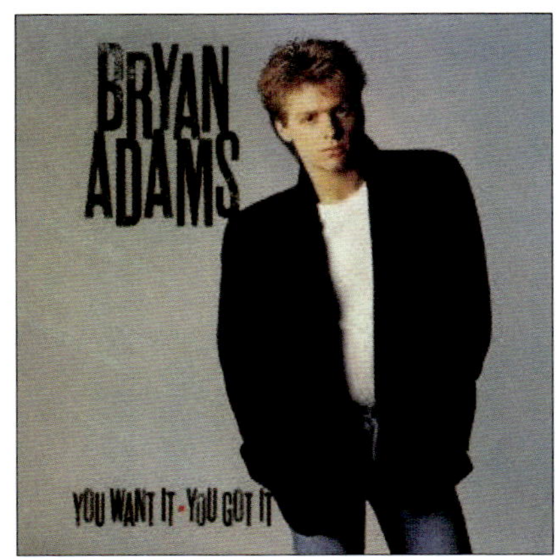

Bryan Adams' first radio hit, "Lonely Nights," peaked at #3 on *Billboard's* Mainstream Rock Tracks chart and established the Canadian singer-songwriter's sound.

Billboard 200: *You Want It - You Got It* (#118)
Billboard Hot 100: "Lonely Nights" (#84)

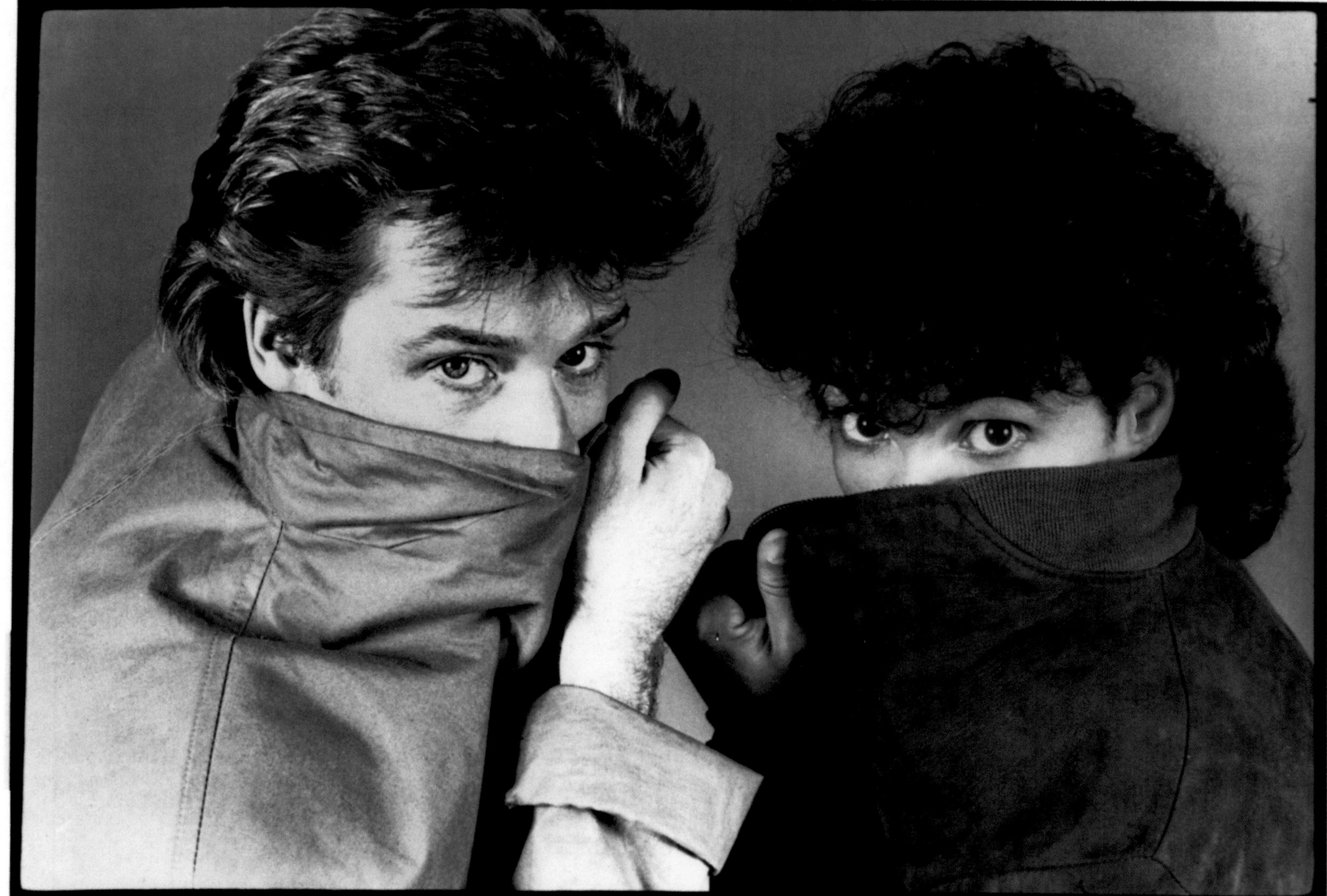

DARYL HALL JOHN OATES

RCA
Records and Tapes

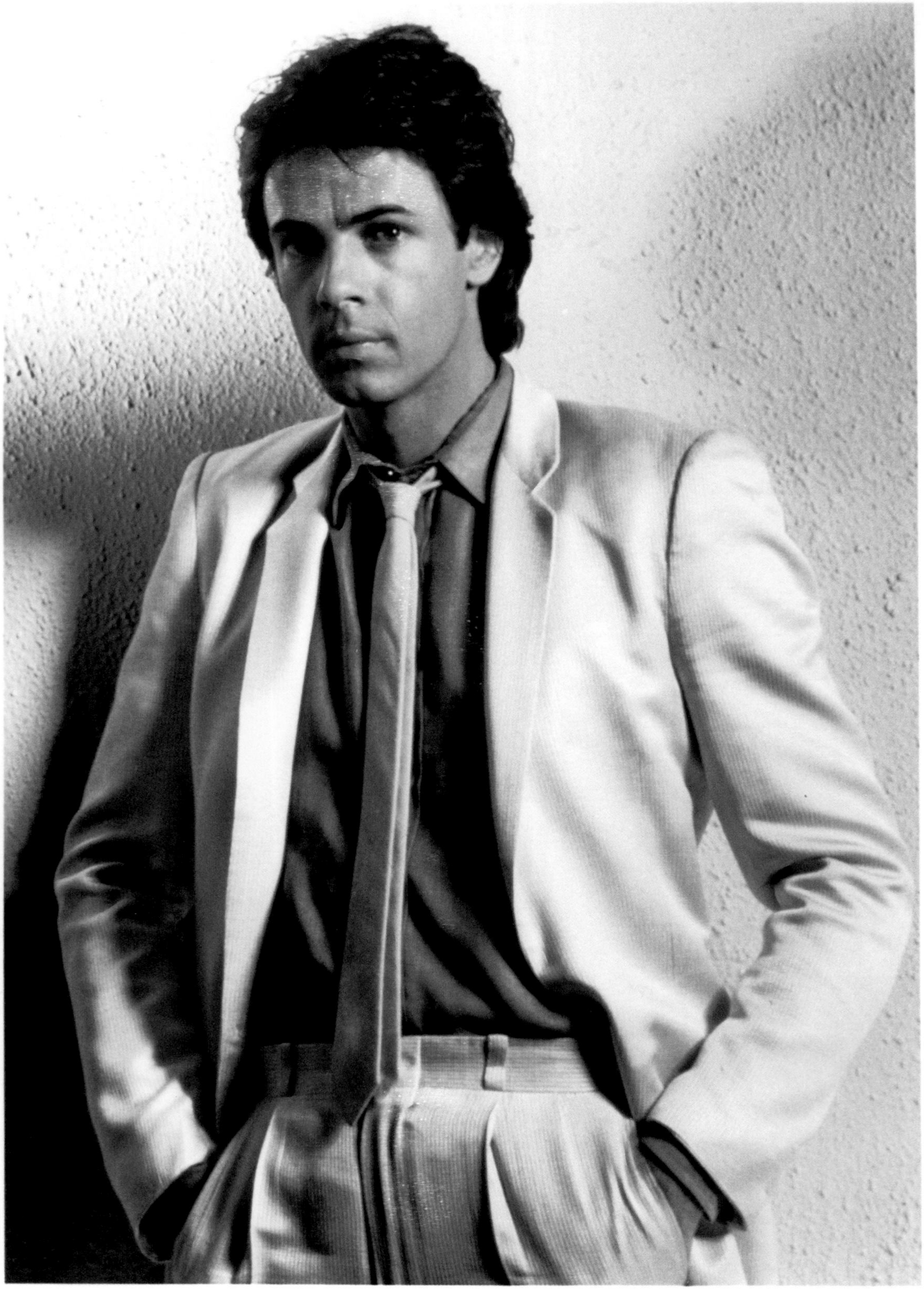

RICK SPRINGFIELD

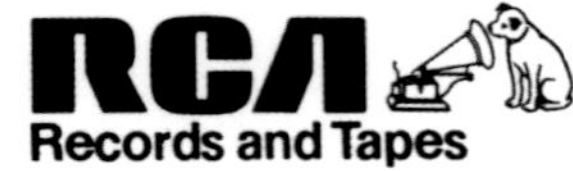

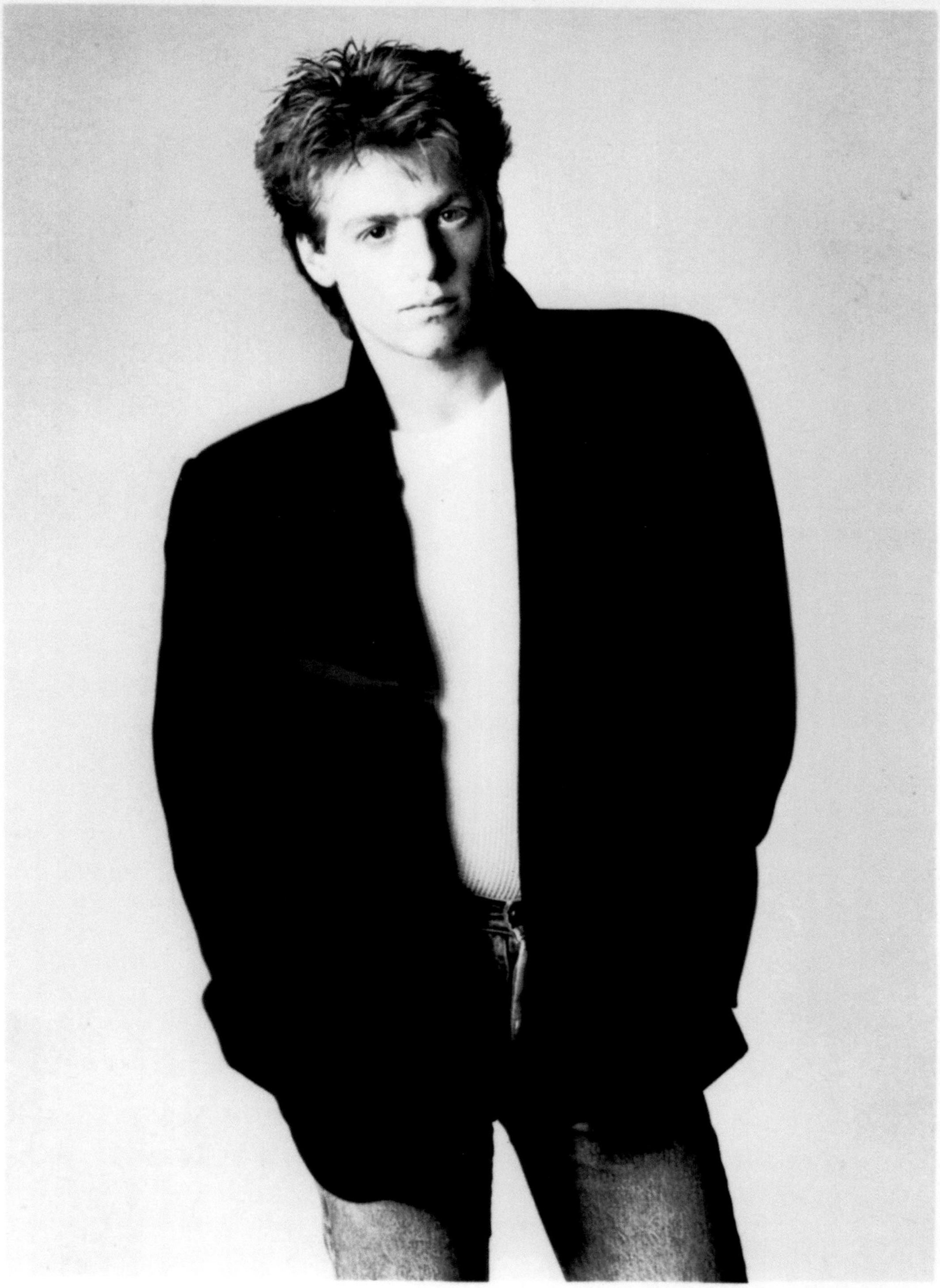

BRYAN ADAMS

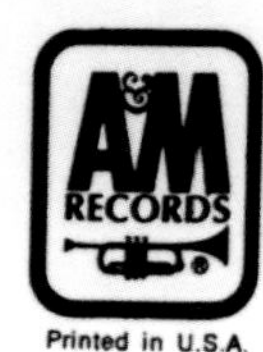

Printed in U.S.A.

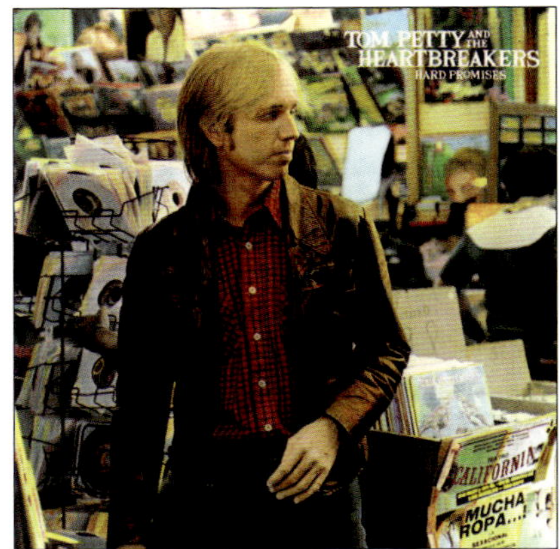

Tom Petty & the Heartbreakers successfully challenged their record company's price increase, then delivered *Hard Promises*, featuring the hit, "The Waiting."

Billboard 200: *Hard Promises* (#5)
Billboard Hot 100: "The Waiting" (#19);
"A Woman in Love (It's Not Me)" (#79)

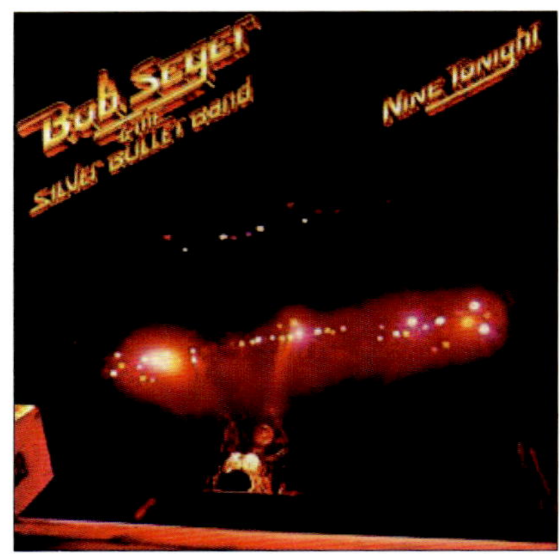

From their second live album, *Nine Tonight*, **Bob Seger & the Silver Bullet Band**'s take on Otis Clay's "Tryin' to Live My Life Without You" became a Top 5 hit.

Billboard 200: *Nine Tonight* (#3)
Billboard Hot 100: "Tryin' to Live My Life Without You" (#5);
"Feel Like a Number" (#48)

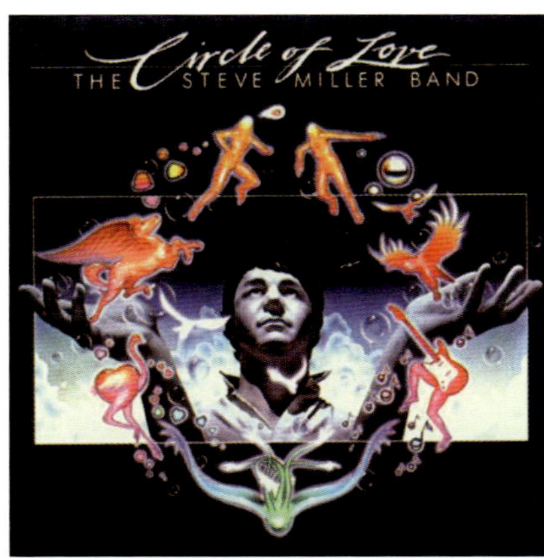

The Steve Miller Band's *Circle of Love*, the first album of new material since the 1977 multiplatinum release, *Book of Dreams*, was a commercial disappointment.

Billboard 200: *Circle of Love* (#26)
Billboard Hot 100: "Heart Like a Wheel" (#24);
"Circle of Love" (#55)

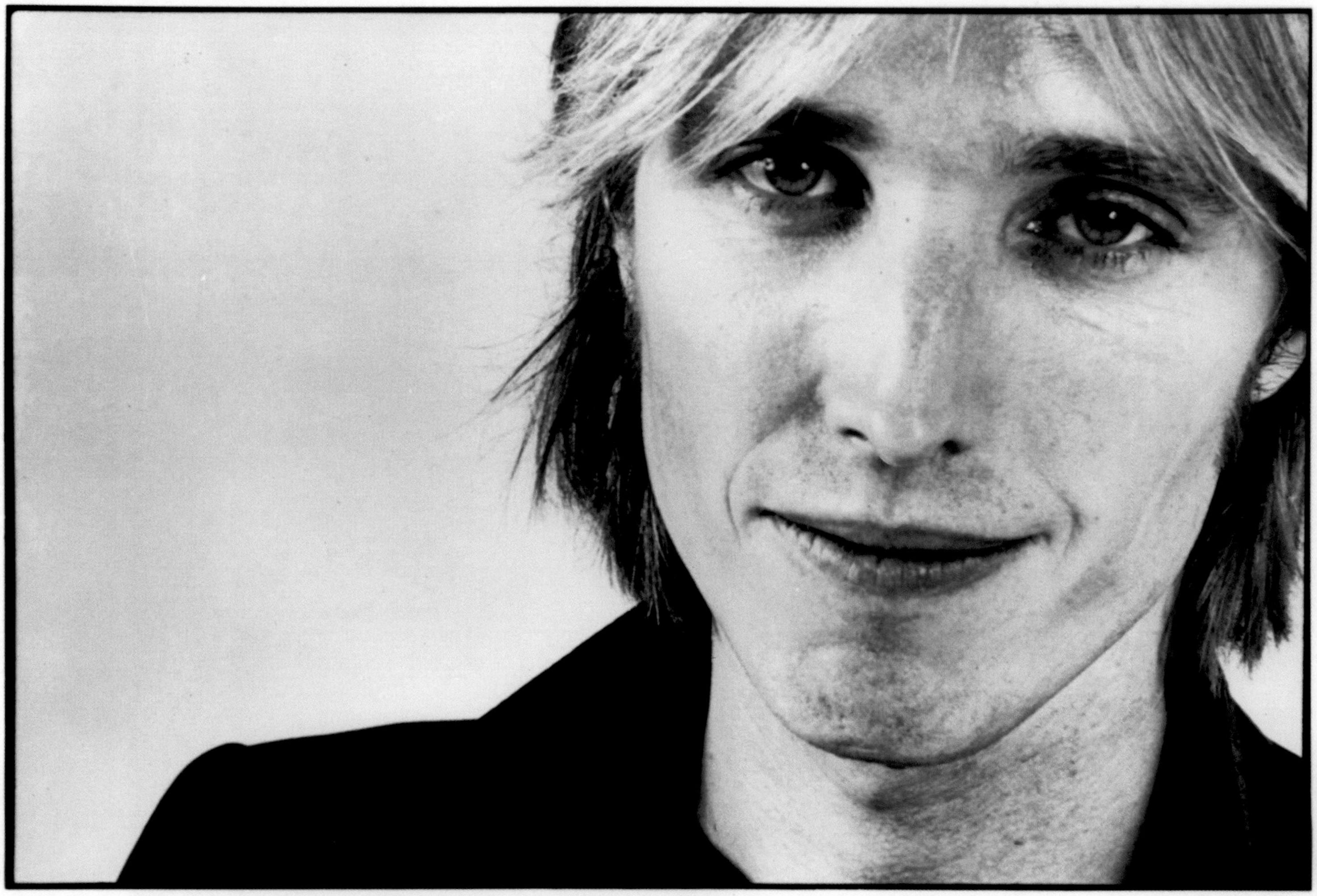

Photo: Lynn Goldsmith

4/81

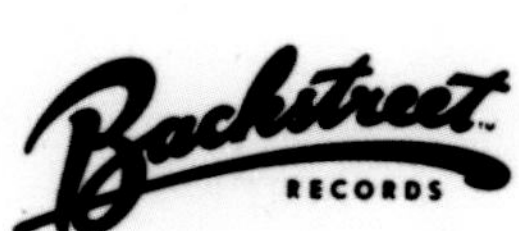

Management: Lookout Management

MAHONEY/WASSERMAN & ASSOCIATES
PUBLIC RELATIONS
117 N. Robertson Blvd., Los Angeles, California 90048
(213) 550-3922
510 Madison Avenue, New York, New York 10022
(212) 751-2060

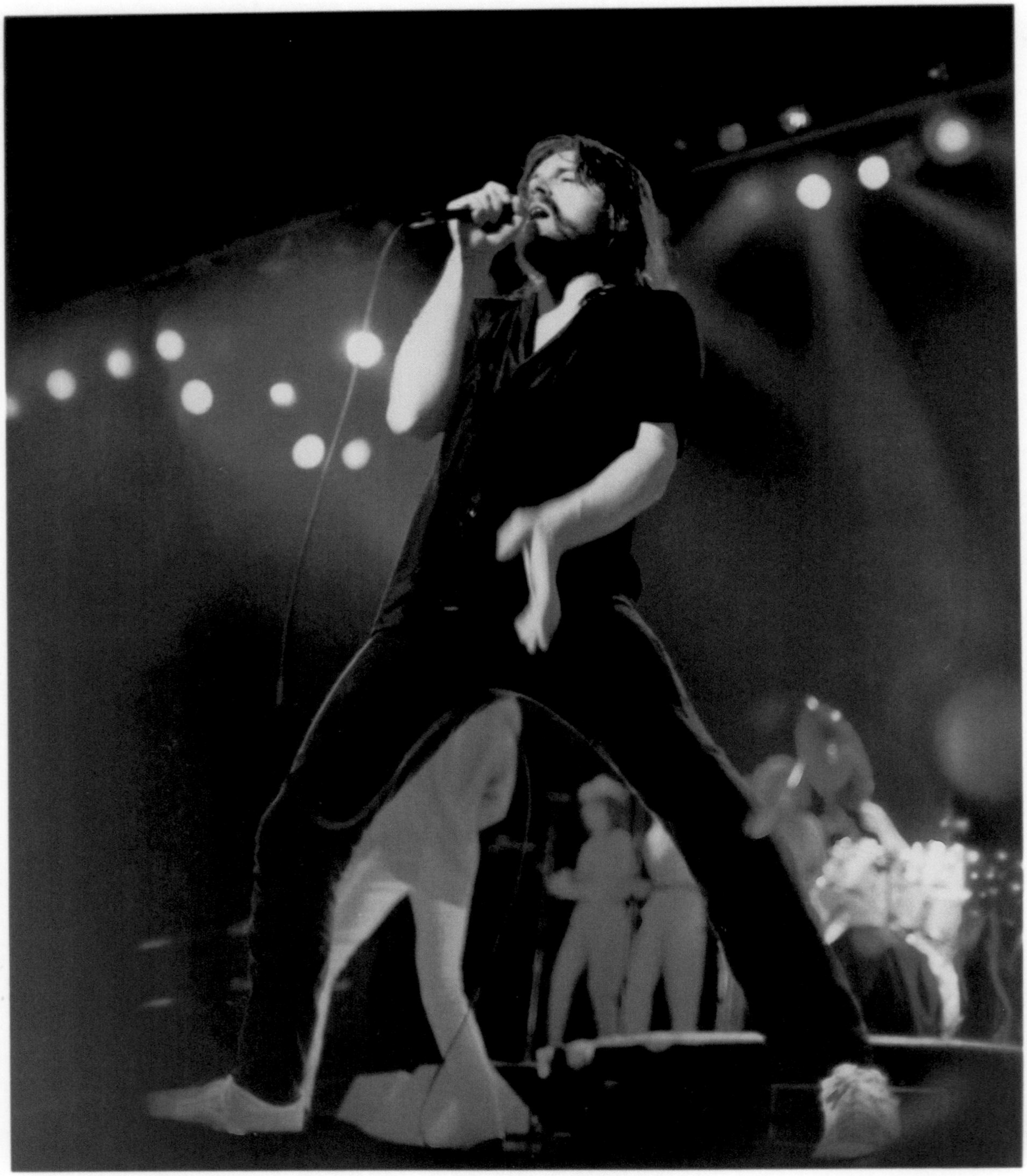

Photo: Michael Marks / 1981

BOB SEGER

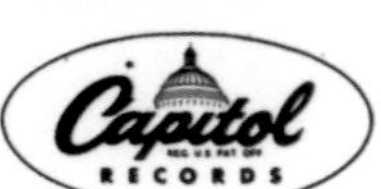

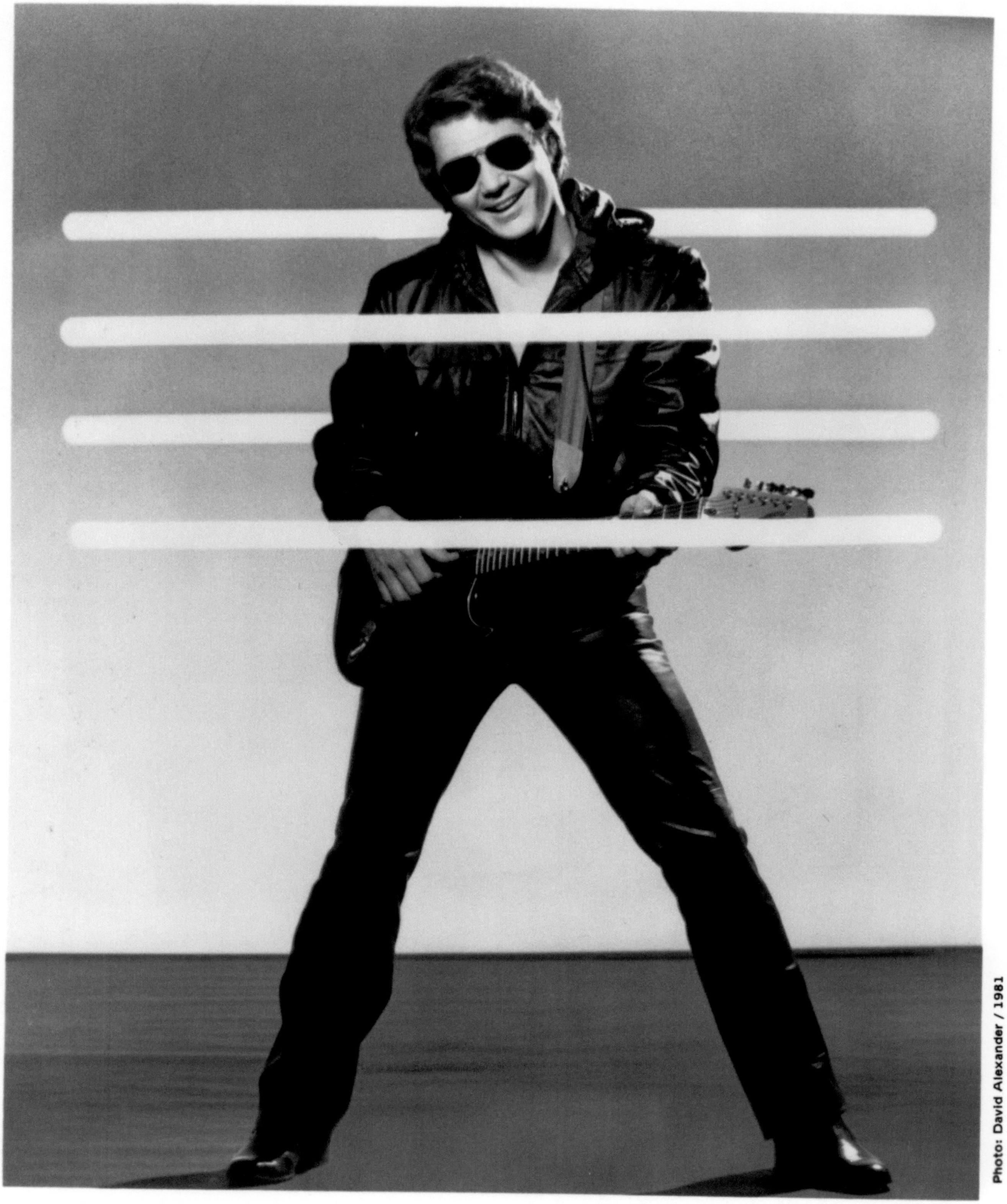

Photo: David Alexander / 1981

STEVE MILLER

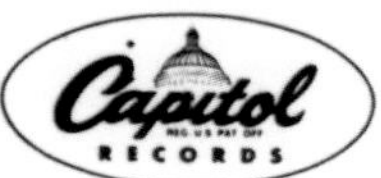

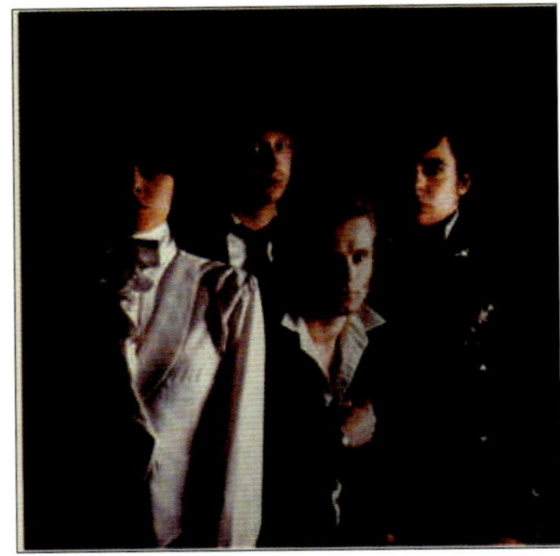

Containing two previously released singles, "Talk of the Town" and "Message of Love," **Pretenders**' second album was the final release from the band's original lineup.

Billboard 200: *Pretenders II* (#10)

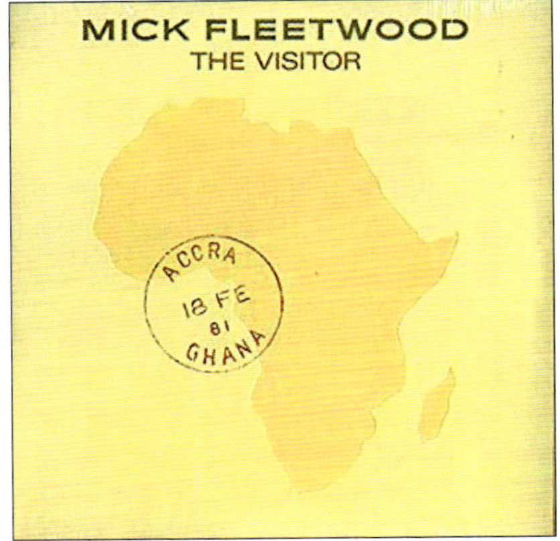

Drummer **Mick Fleetwood** led *The Visitor*, a solo project recorded in Ghana that featured a remake of Fleetwood Mac's "Rattlesnake Shake" with original guitarist Peter Green.

Billboard 200: *The Visitor* (#43)

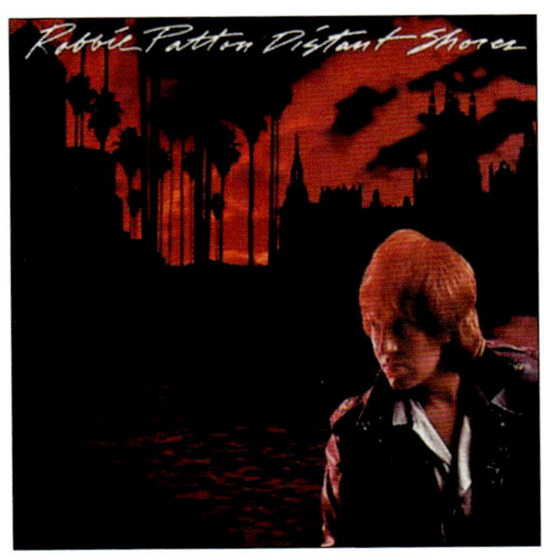

Fleetwood Mac's Christine McVie co-produced and Lindsey Buckingham added guitar to the English singer-songwriter **Robbie Patton**'s hit, "Don't Give It Up."

Billboard 200: *Distant Shores* (#162)
Billboard Hot 100: "Don't Give It Up" (#26)

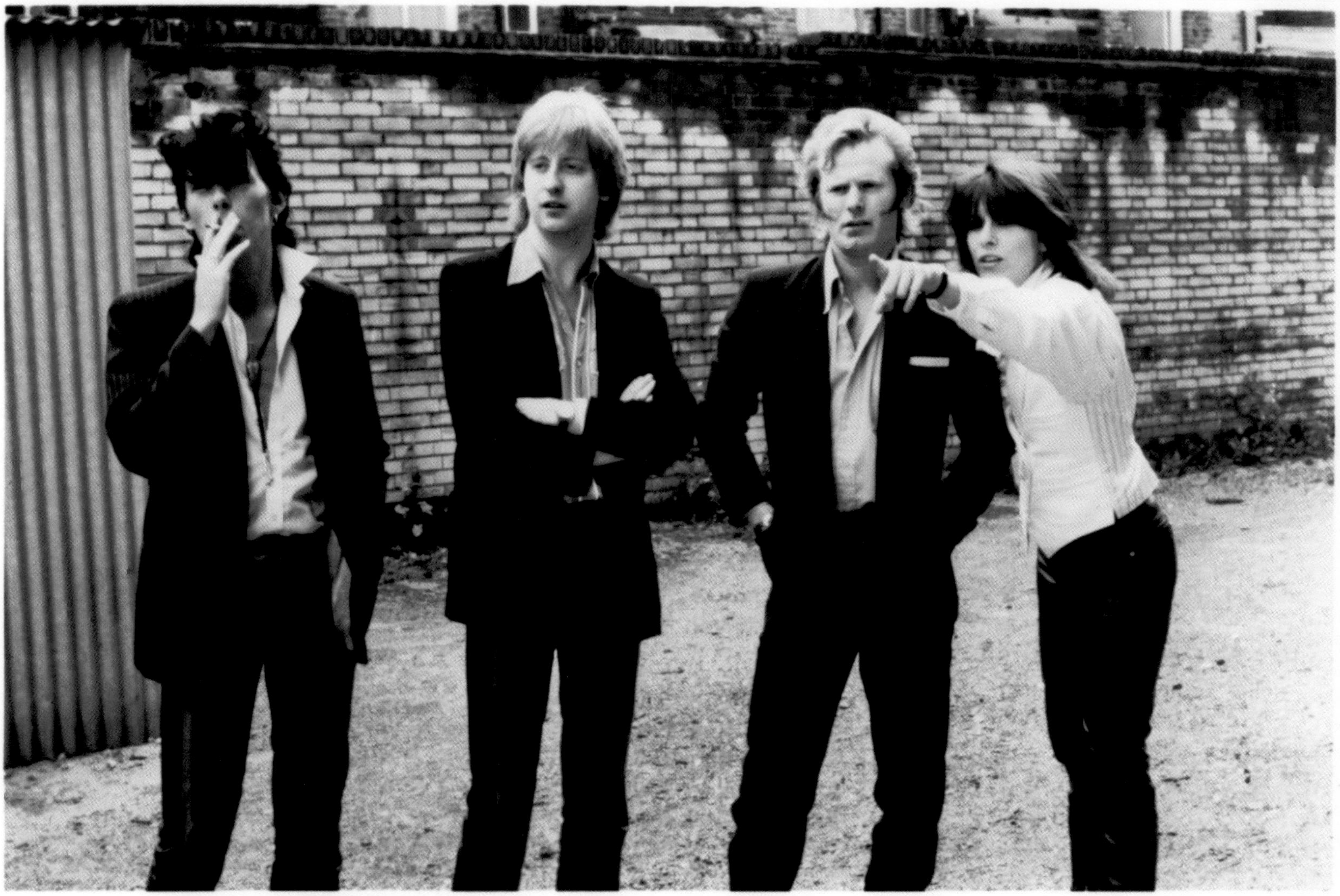

PETE FARNDON JAMES HONEYMAN SCOTT MARTIN CHAMBERS CHRISSIE HYNDE

PRETENDERS

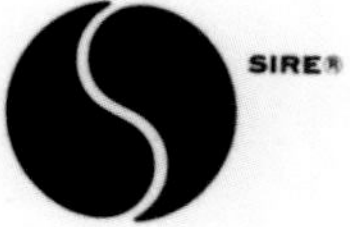

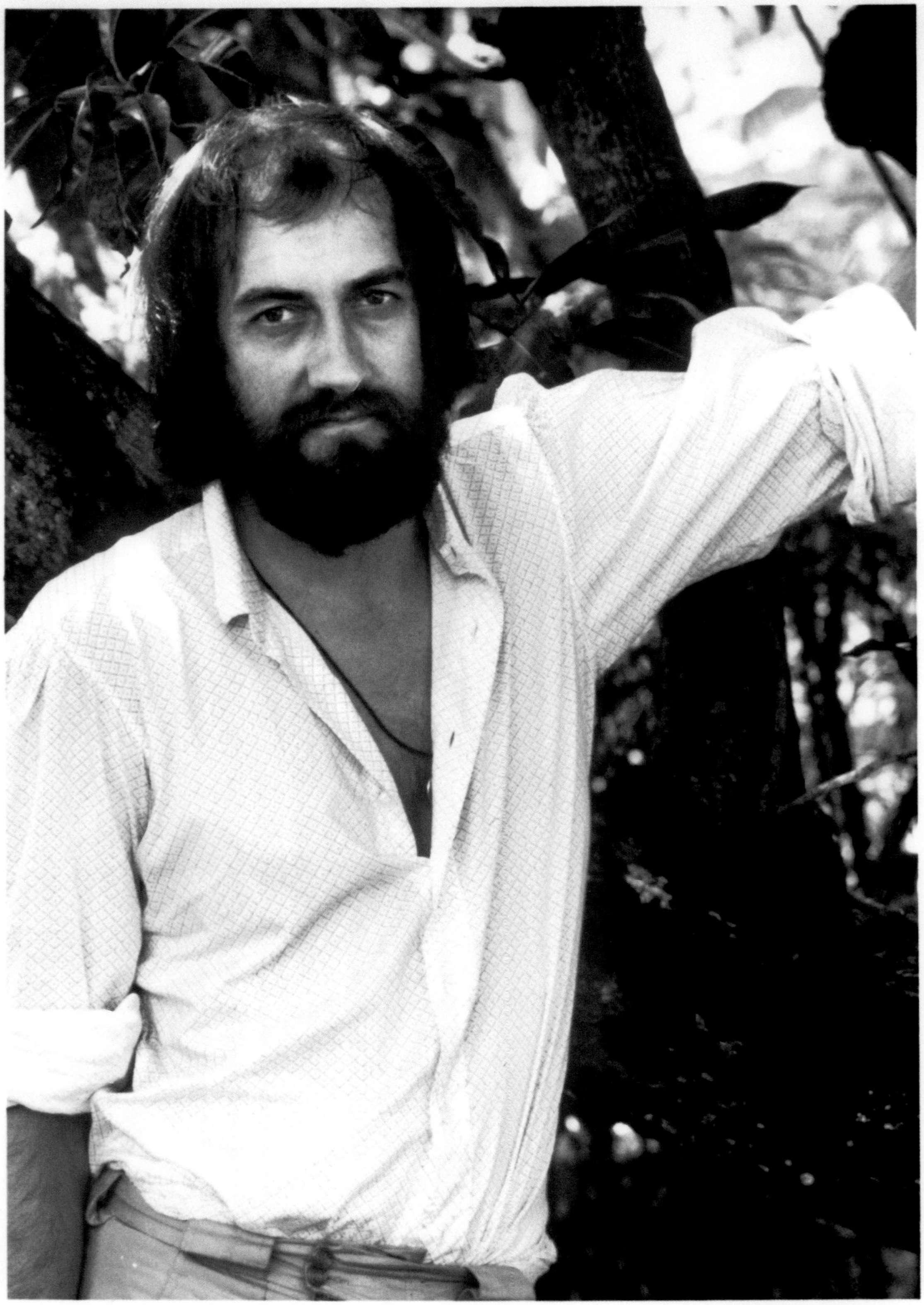

MICK FLEETWOOD

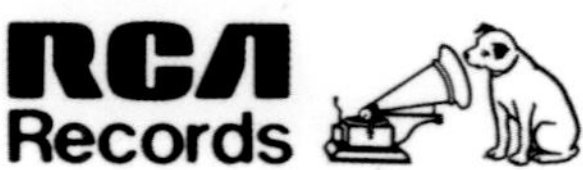

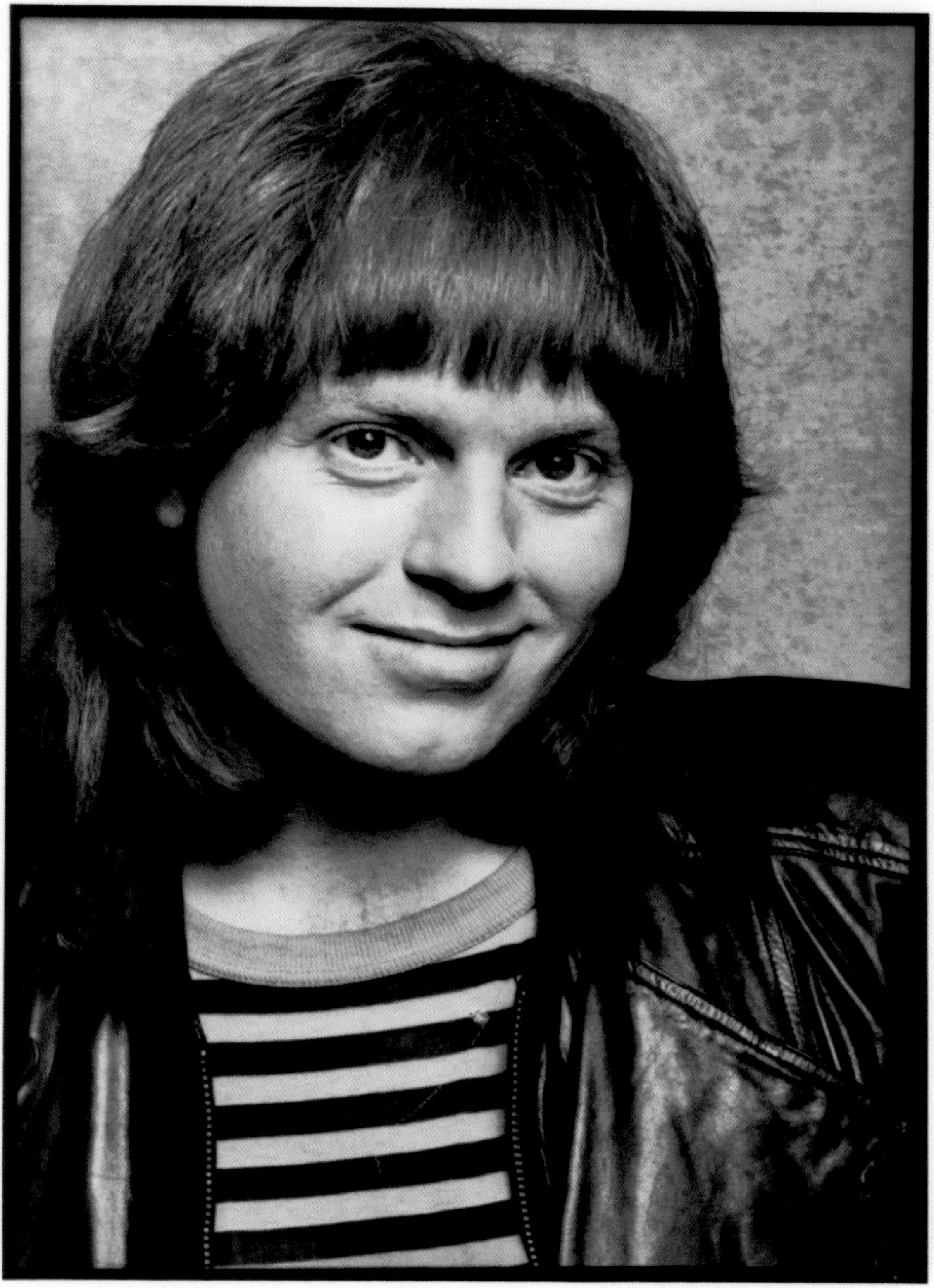

ROBBIE PATTON

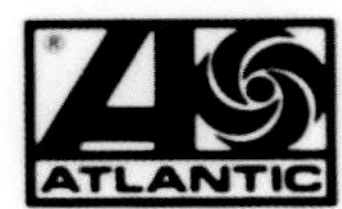

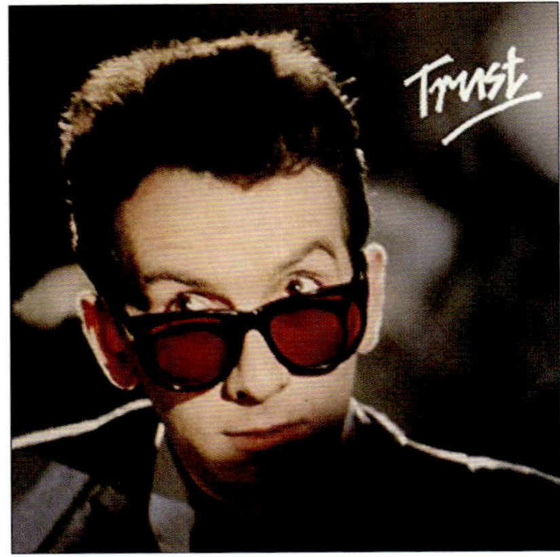

Elvis Costello & the Attractions released the eclectic *Trust*, which included the popular tracks "Watch Your Step," "Clubland" and "From a Whisper to a Scream."

Billboard 200: *Trust* (#28)

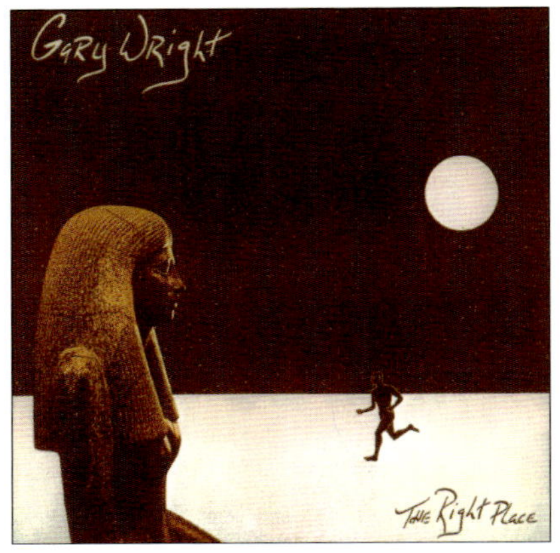

Gary Wright notched his last chart success with "Really Wanna Know You," his third biggest single after two 1976 hits, "Dream Weaver" and "Love Is Alive."

Billboard 200: *The Right Place* (#79)
Billboard Hot 100: "Really Wanna Know You" (#16)

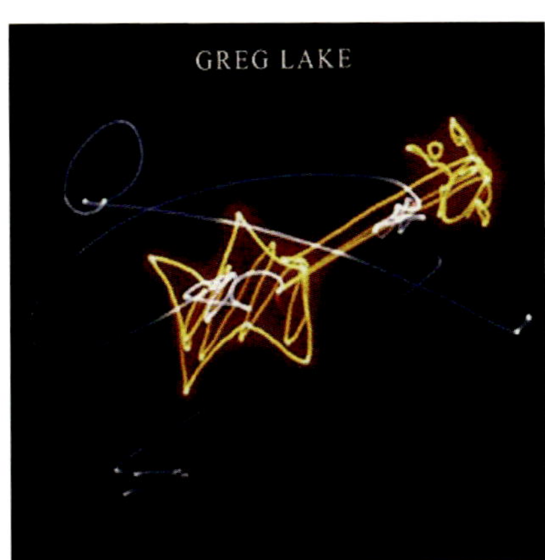

Singer and guitarist **Greg Lake**, a founding member of the progressive-rock bands King Crimson and Emerson, Lake & Palmer, recorded his first album as a solo artist.

Billboard 200: *Greg Lake* (#62)
Billboard Hot 100: "Let Me Love You Once" (#48)

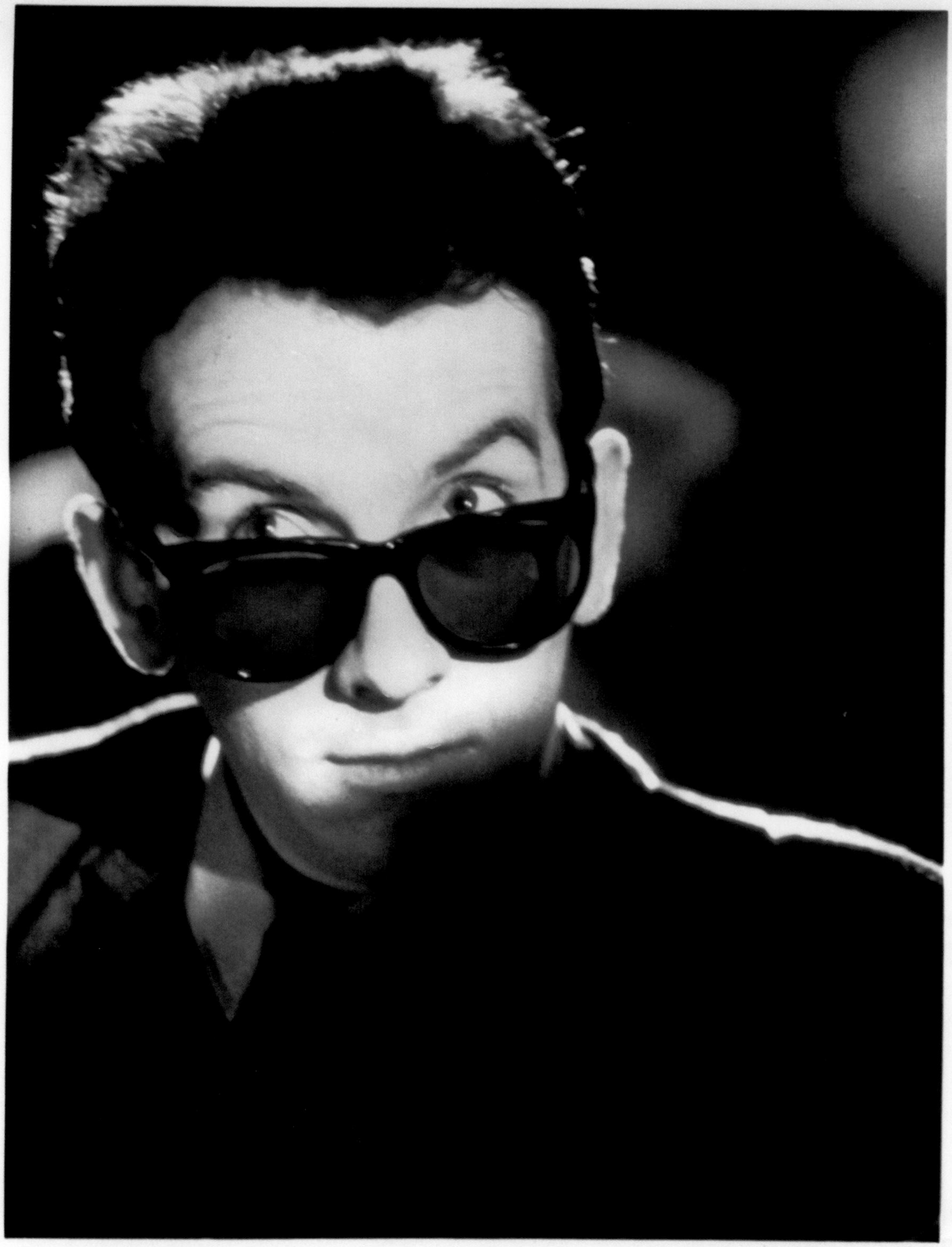

ELVIS COSTELLO

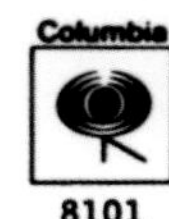

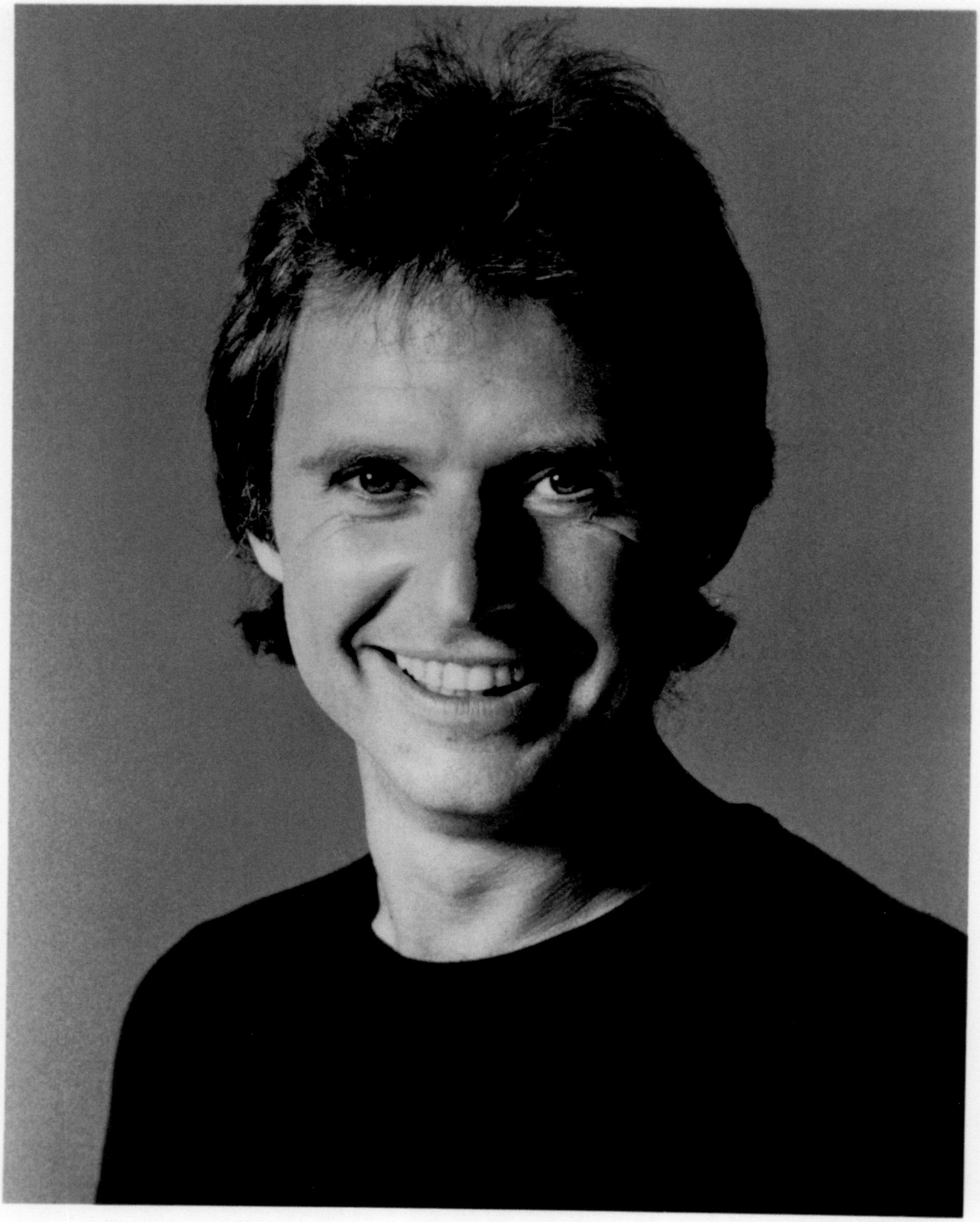

GARY WRIGHT

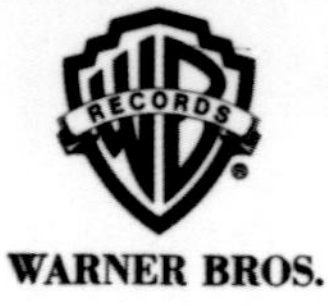

WARNER BROS.

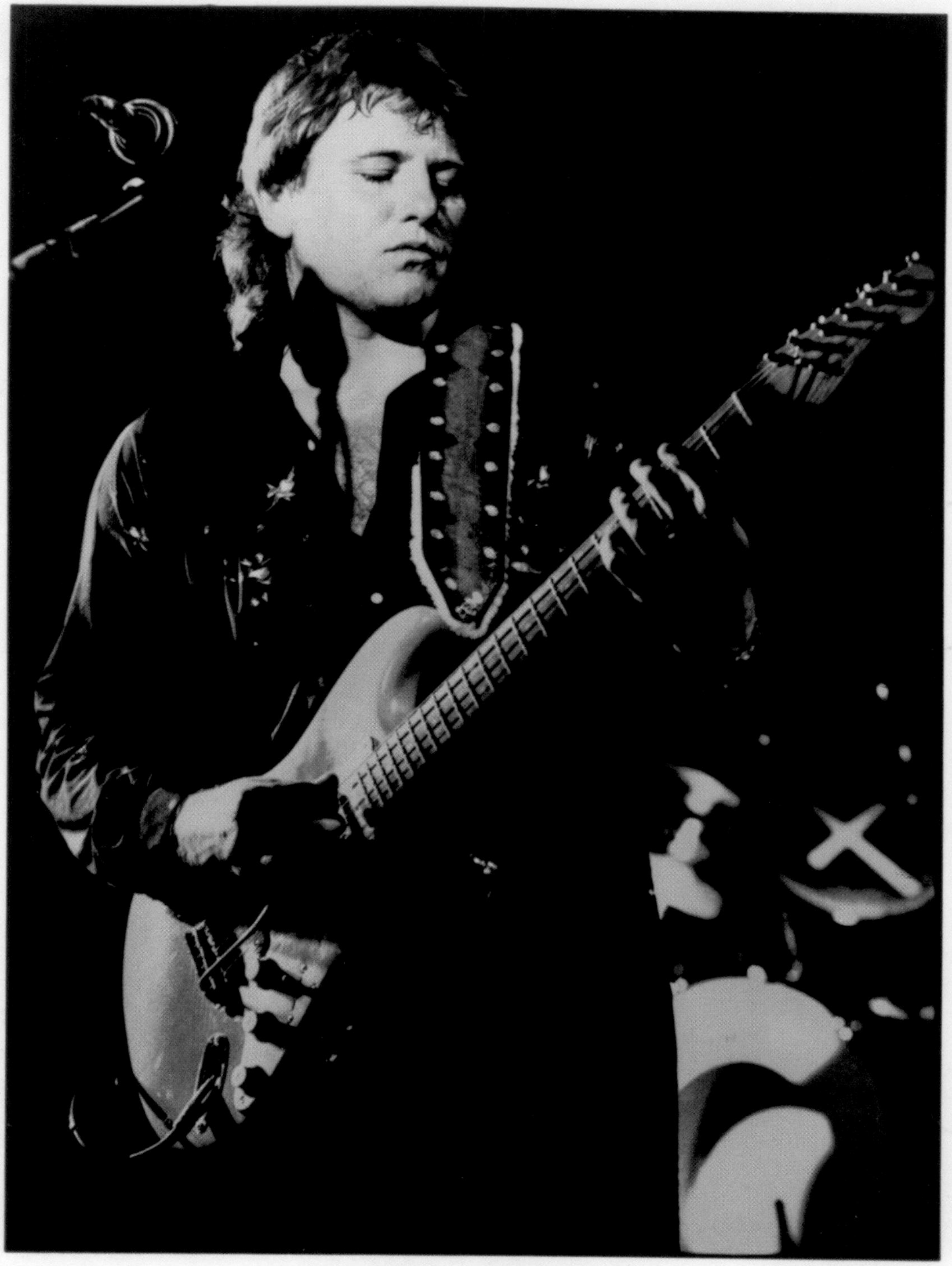

GREG LAKE

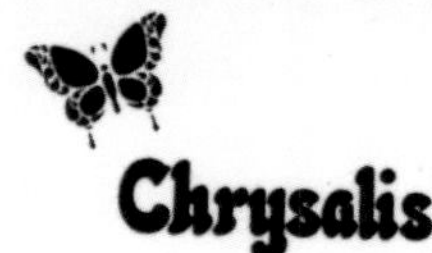

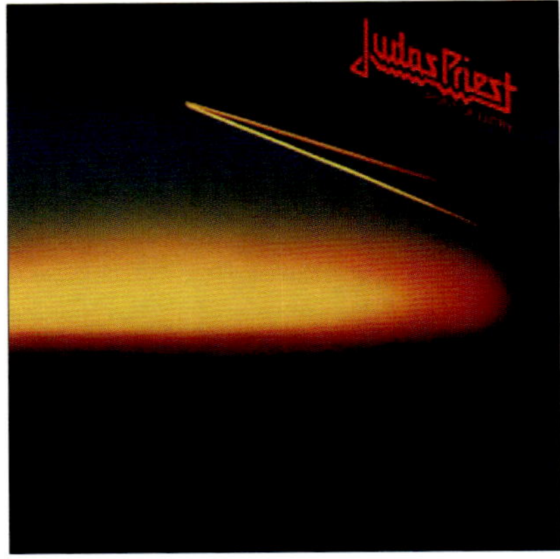

Judas Priest stayed the course on *Point of Entry*, with the song "Heading Out to the Highway" pursuing the rumble of heavy metal but with a radio-friendly bent.

Billboard 200: *Point of Entry* (#39)

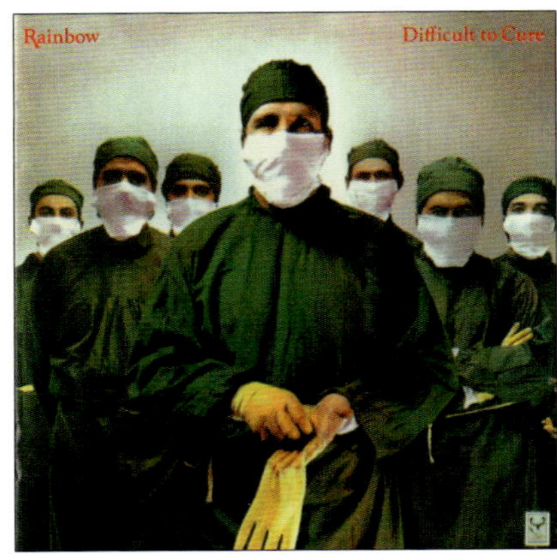

Guitarist Ritchie Blackmore's desire to commercialize **Rainbow**'s heavy-metal sound resulted in significant airplay for the UK-charting single, "I Surrender."

Billboard 200: *Difficult to Cure* (#50)

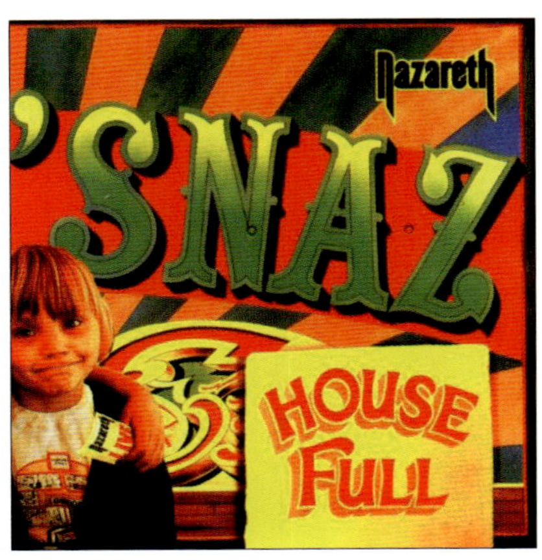

With its commercial power dwindling, **Nazareth** issued *It's Naz* (also known as *'Snaz*), a live double album that rated as a highlight in the Scottish hard-rock band's career.

Billboard 200: *It's Naz* (#83)

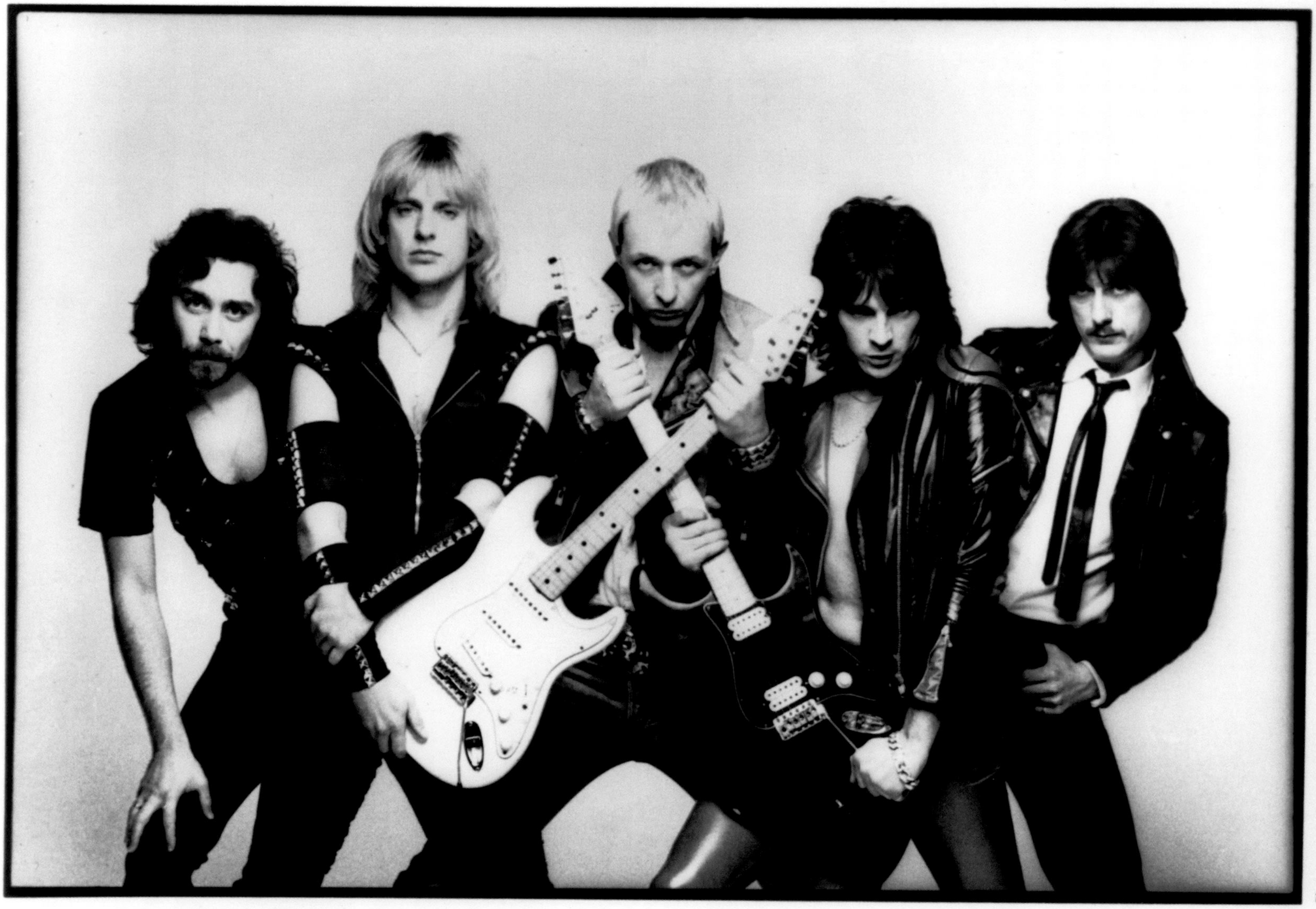

Photograph: Lynn Goldsmith

JUDAS PRIEST

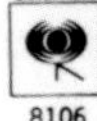

8106

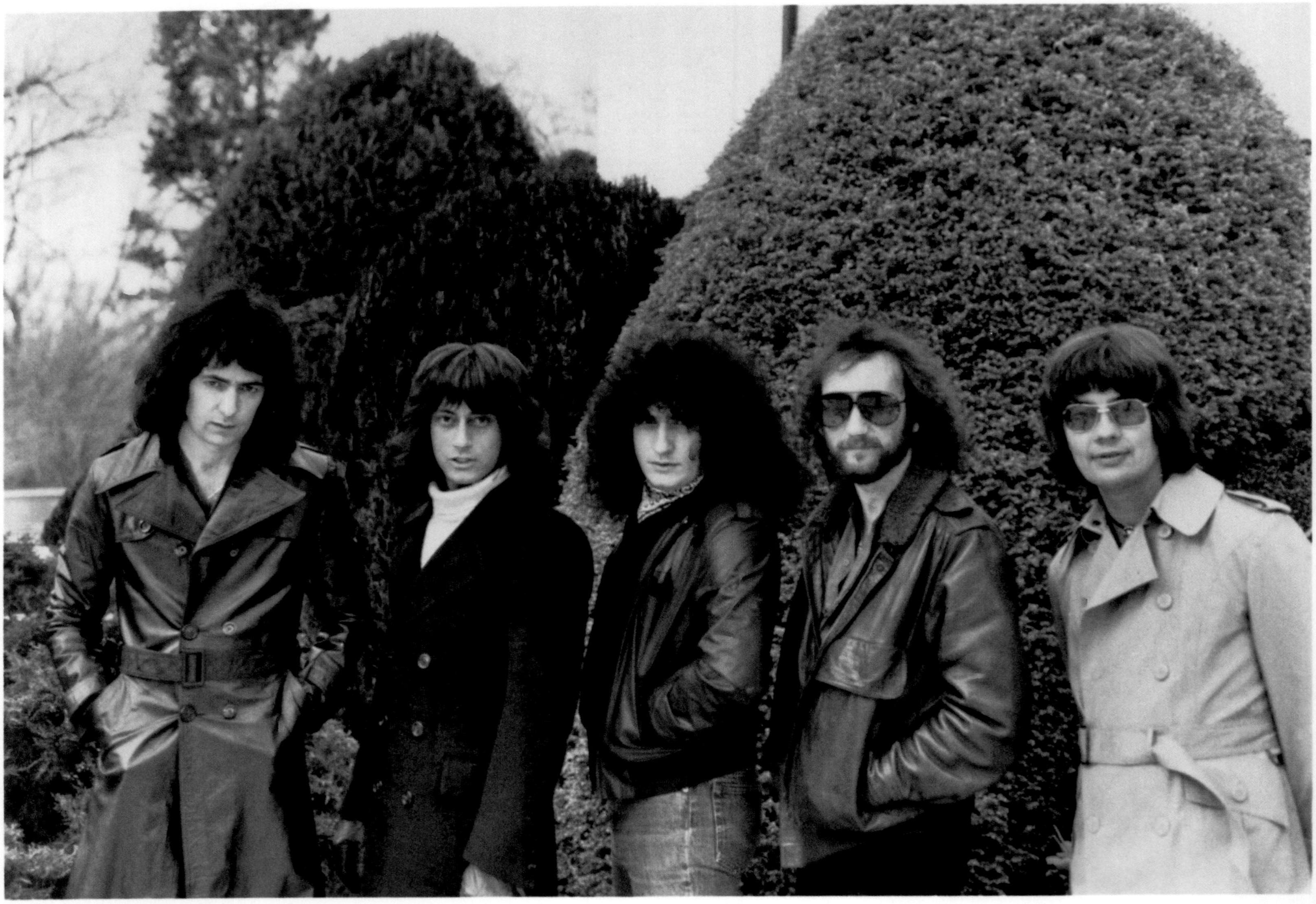

RAINBOW

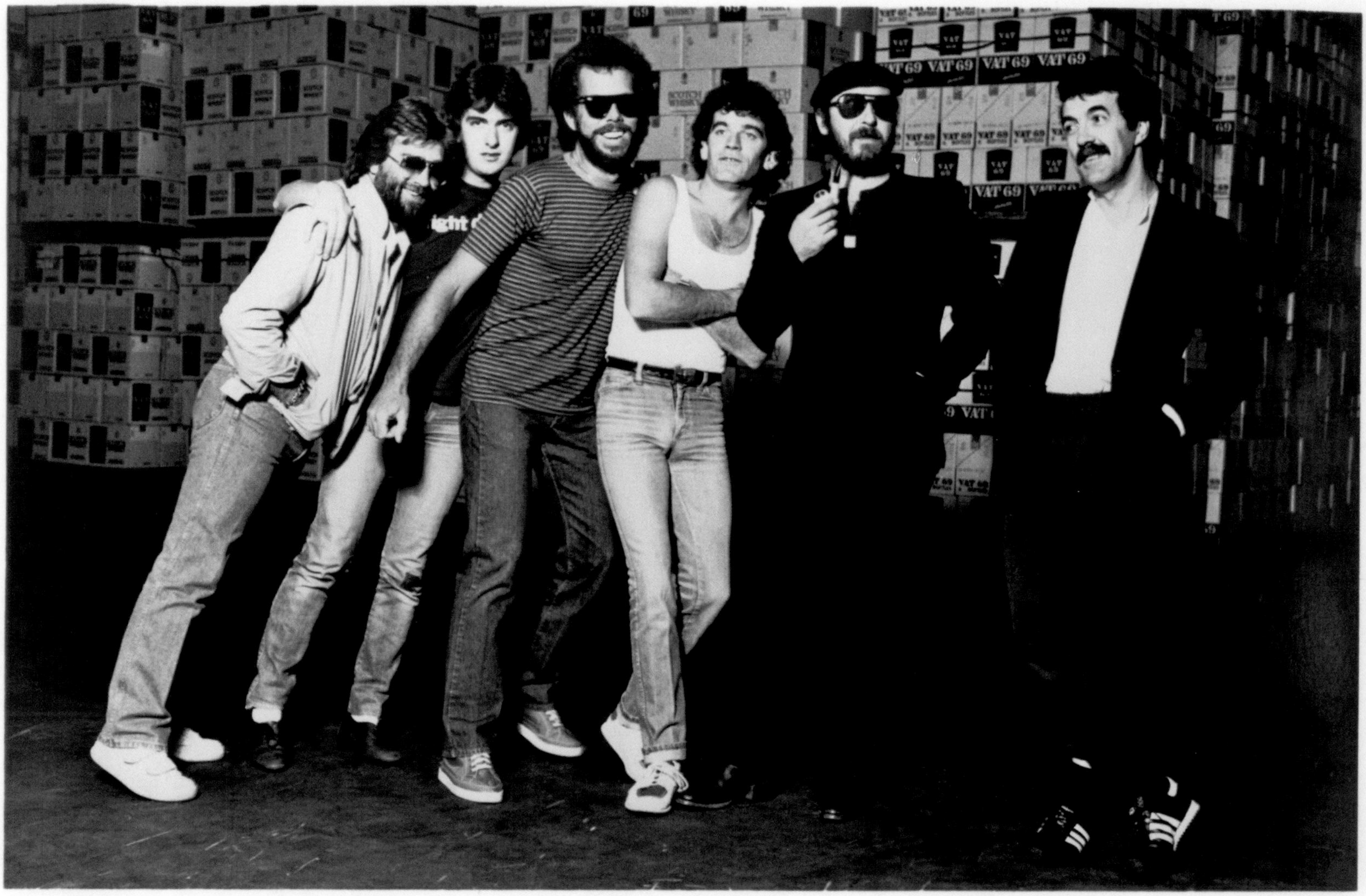

DARRELL SWEET | BILLY RANKIN | JOHN LOCKE | DAN McCAFFERTY | PETE AGNEW | MANNY CHARLTON

NAZARETH

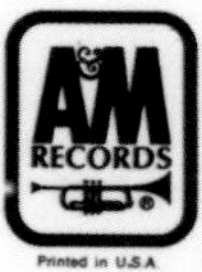

Printed in U.S.A.

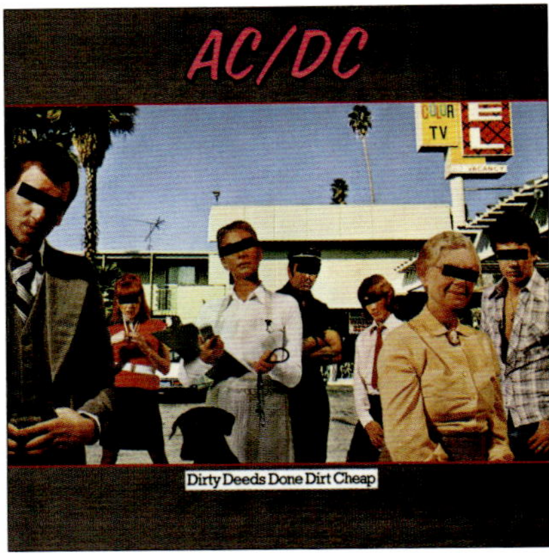

Released in **AC/DC**'s native Australia in 1976, *Dirty Deeds Done Dirt Cheap* was issued in the US in 1981, a year after lead singer Bon Scott's death at age 33.

Billboard 200: *Dirty Deeds Done Dirt Cheap* (#3)

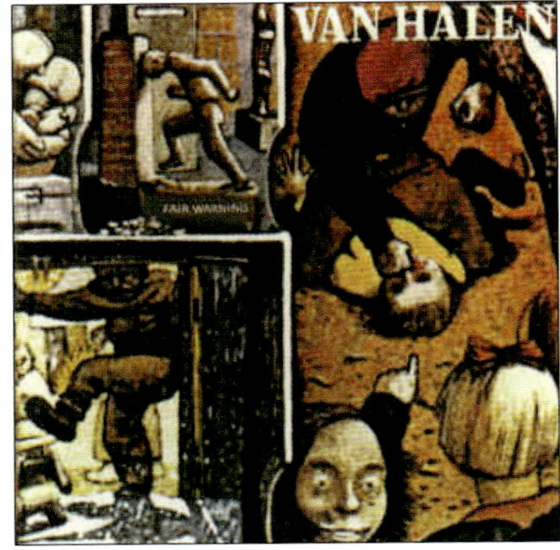

Dominated by Eddie Van Halen's heavy guitar wizardry, *Fair Warning* lacked the radio friendliness and commercial viability of previous **Van Halen** albums.

Billboard 200: *Fair Warning* (#50)

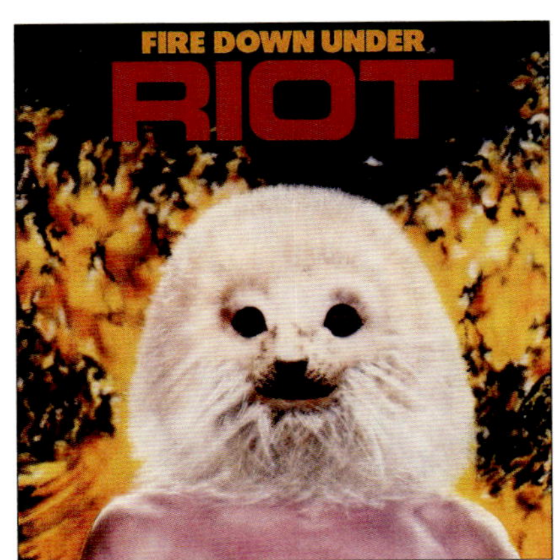

New York-based **Riot** arrived with the raucous *Fire Down Under*, the heavy-metal outfit's most successful album and the last with original vocalist Guy Speranza.

Billboard 200: *Fire Down Under* (#99)

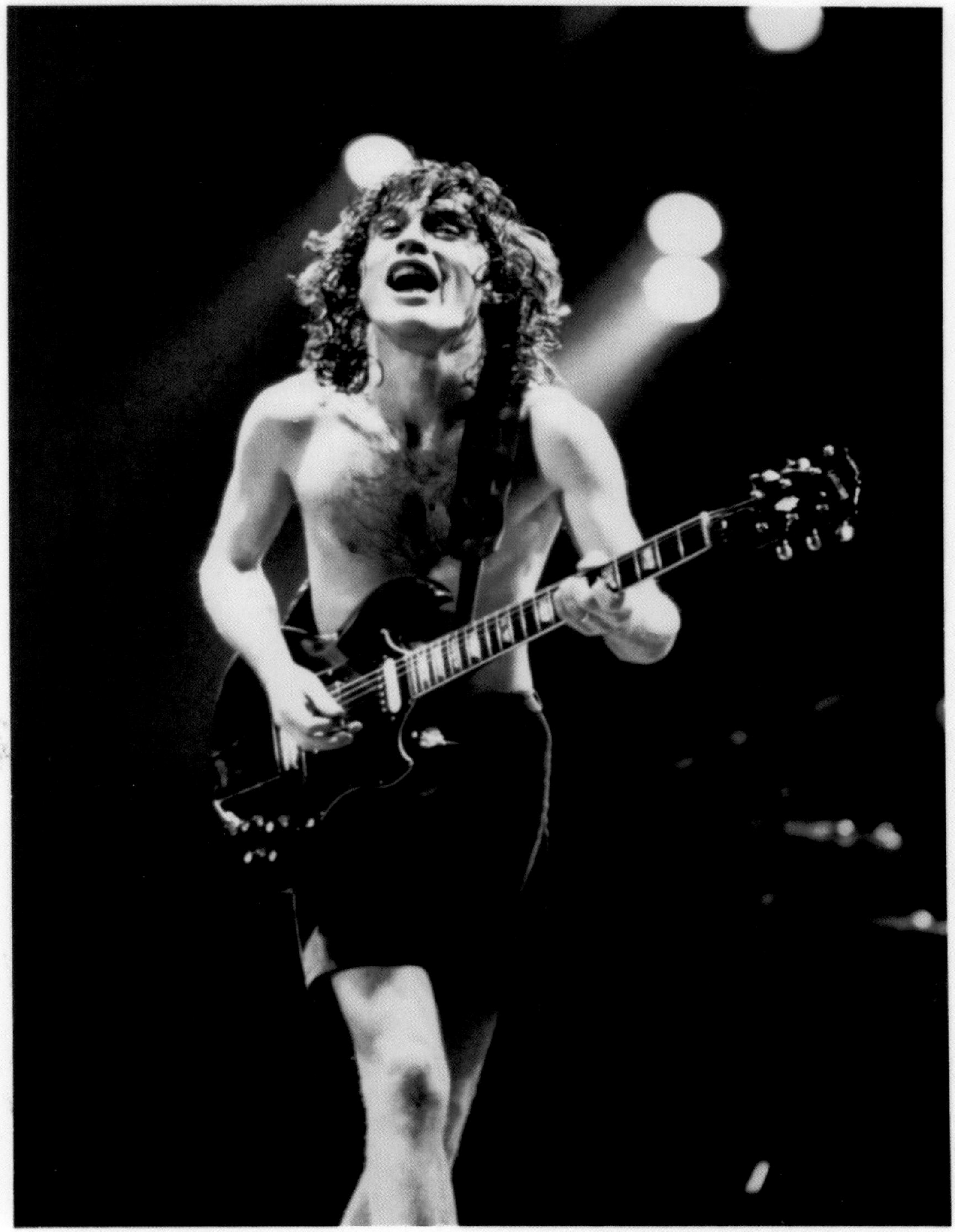

Angus Young

AC/DC

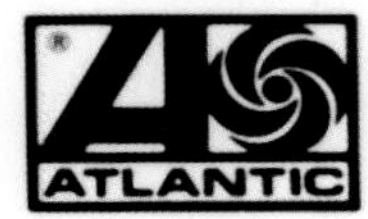

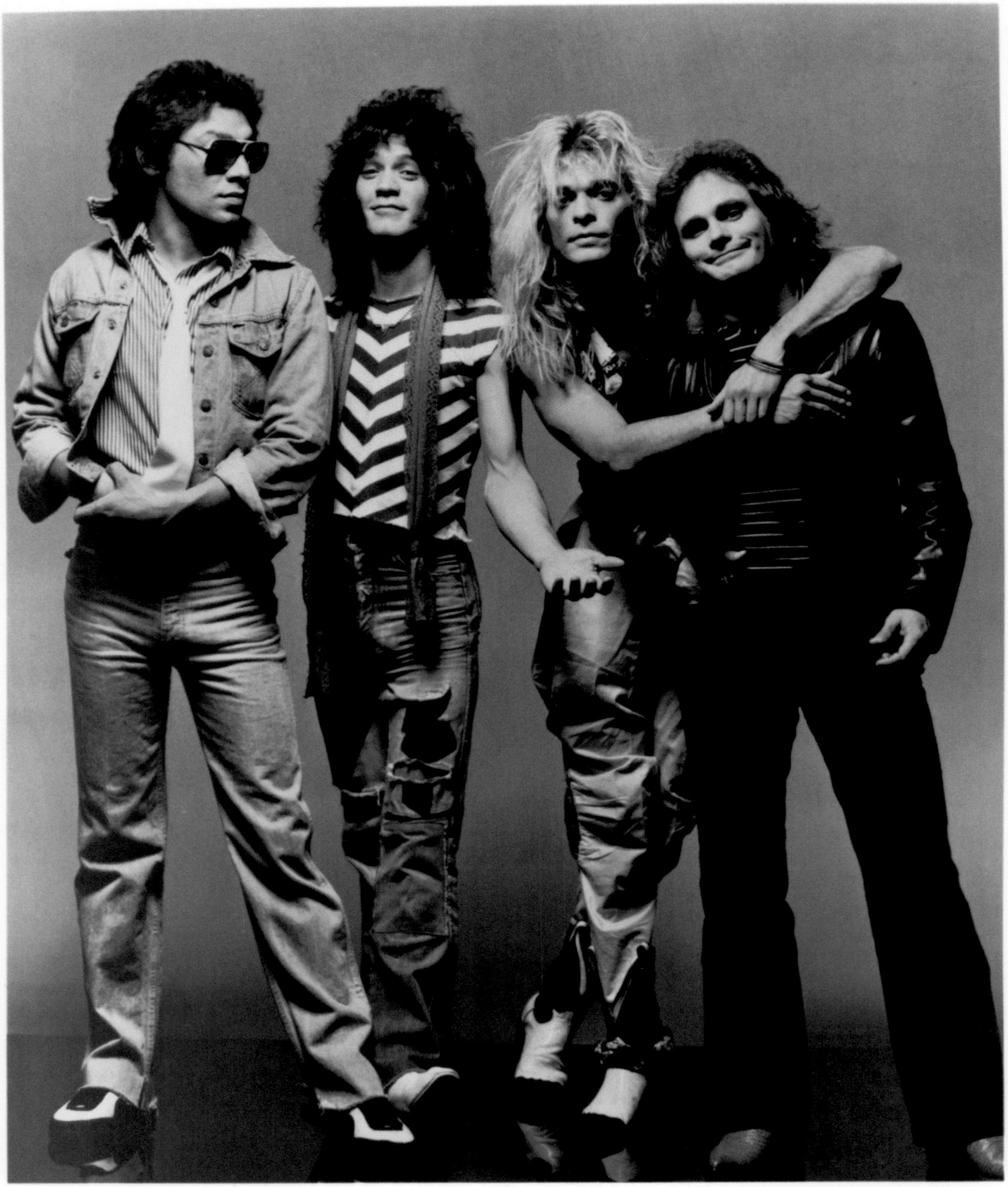

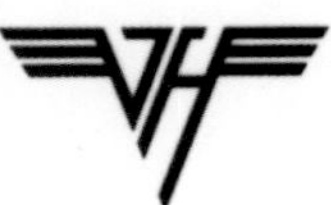

VAN HALEN

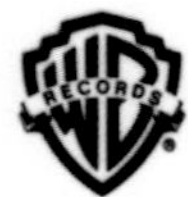

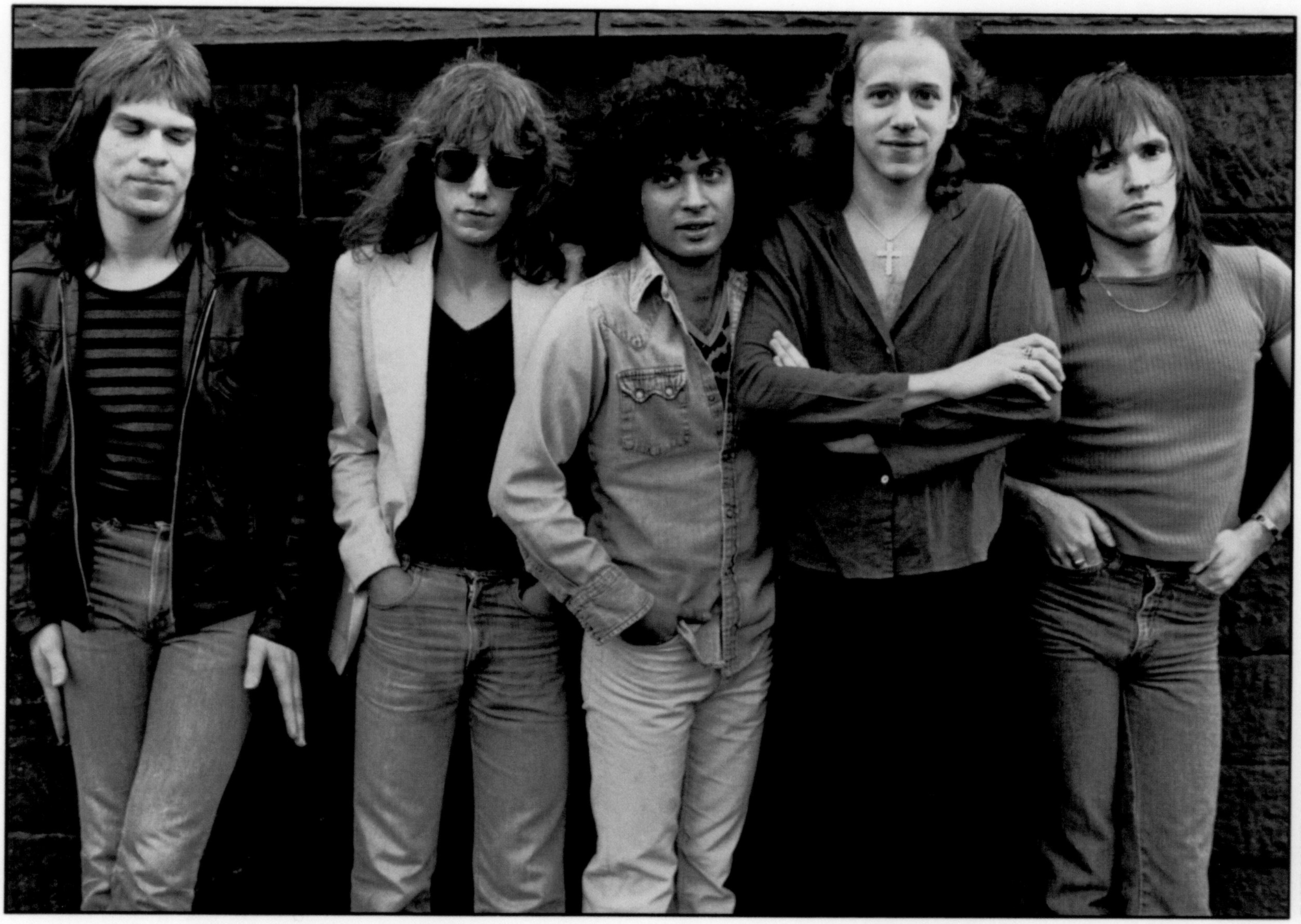

RICK VENTURA KIP LEMING GUY SPERANZA MARK REALE SANDY SLAVIN

PHOTO CREDIT: ROSS HALFIN/1981

RIOT

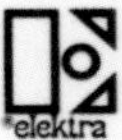

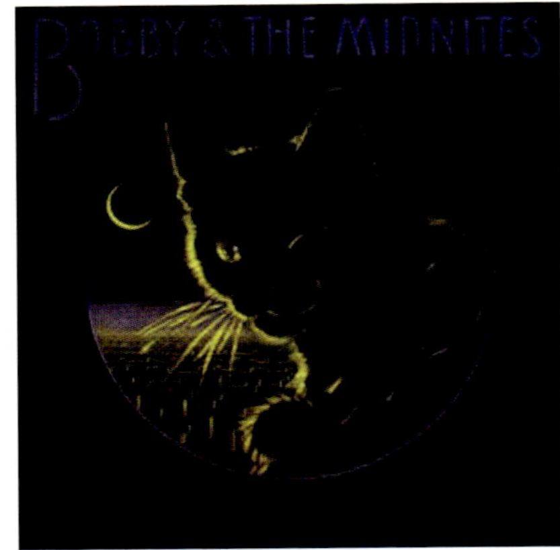

Bobby & the Midnites, a side project led by the Grateful Dead's Bob Weir, also featured the talents of the Dead's Brent Mydland and jazz fusion drummer Billy Cobham.

Billboard 200: *Bobby & the Midnites* (#158)

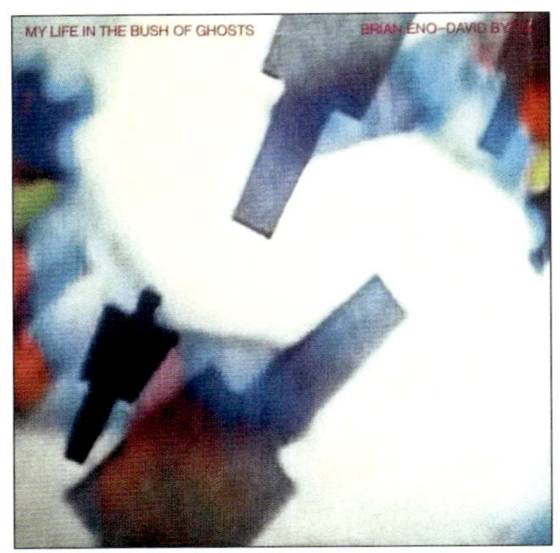

David Byrne & Brian Eno's landmark *My Life in the Bush of Ghosts* coalesed vocal samples and found sounds from around the world with African and Middle Eastern rhythms.

Billboard 200: *My Life in the Bush of Ghosts* (#44)

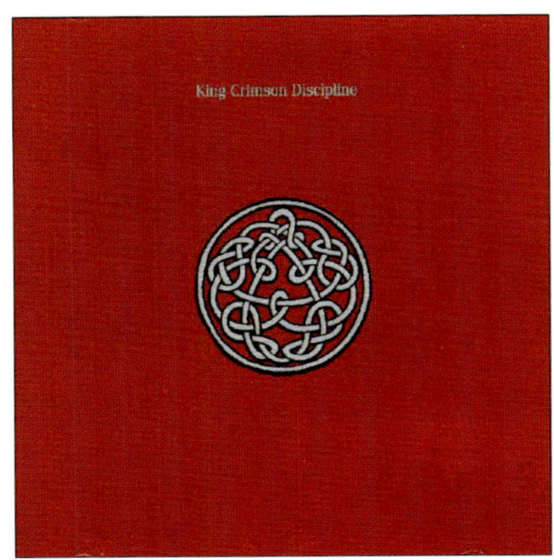

After a seven-year hiatus, **King Crimson** reconfigured, as Robert Fripp enlisted drummer Bill Bruford, bassist Tony Levin and guitarist-vocalist Adrian Belew to record *Discipline*.

Billboard 200: *Discipline* (#45)

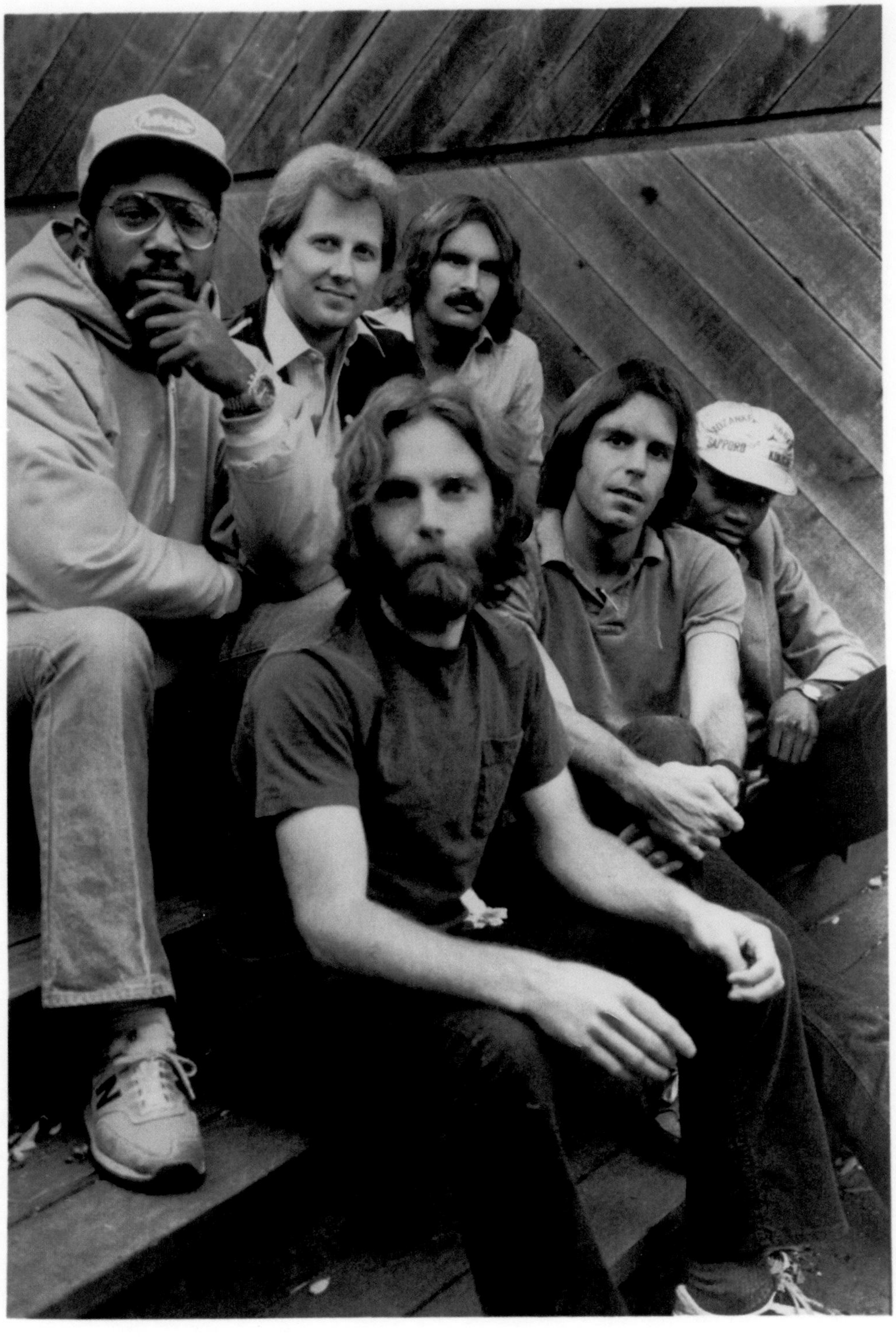

(Top row left to right) Billy Cobham, Bobby Cochran, Matthew Kelly
(Bottom row left to right) Brent Mydland, Bob Weir Alphonso Johnson

Management:
(415) 459-5877

BOBBY AND THE MIDNITES

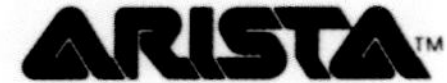

BRIAN ENO

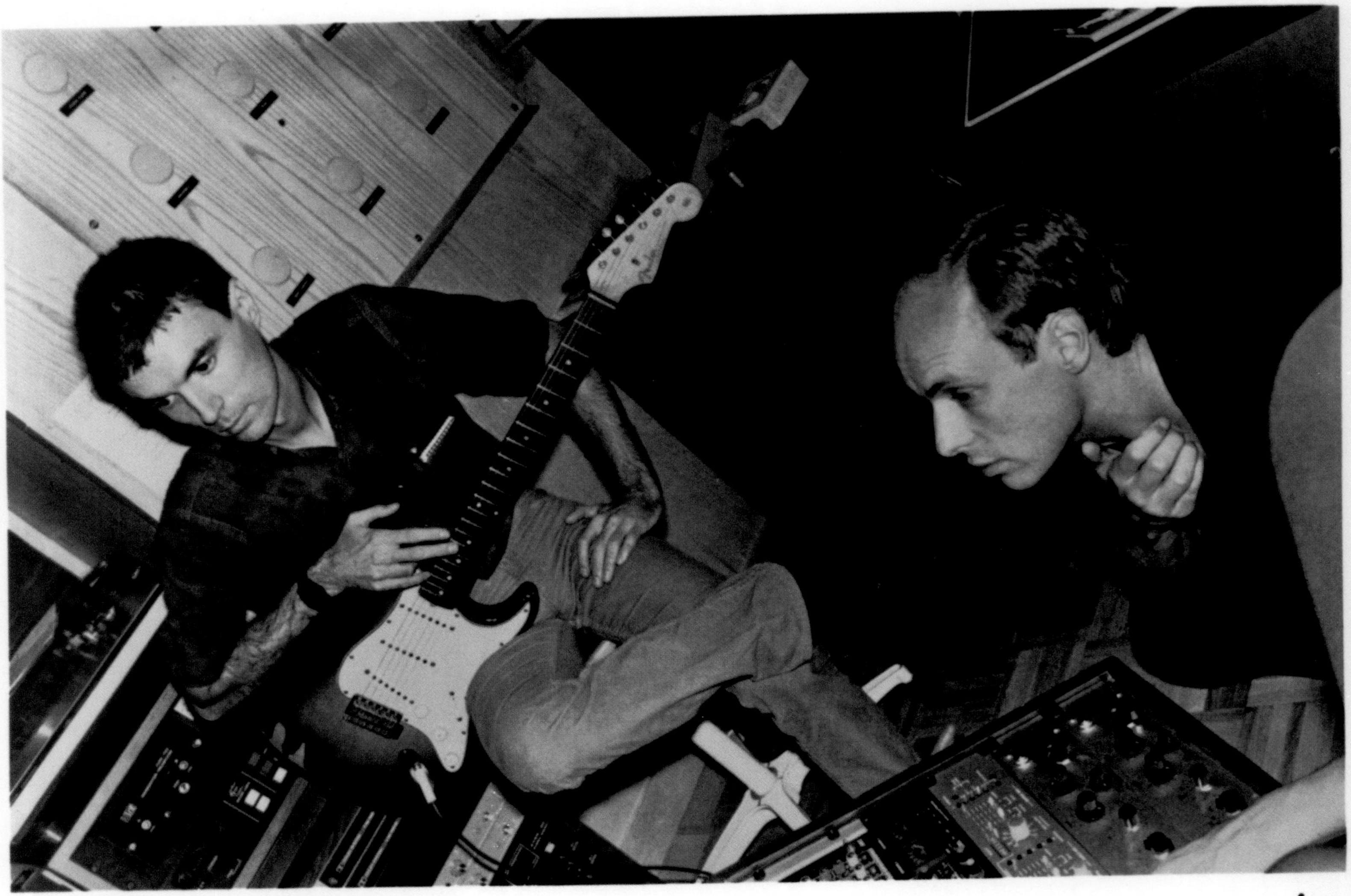

DAVID BYRNE

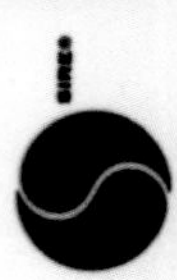

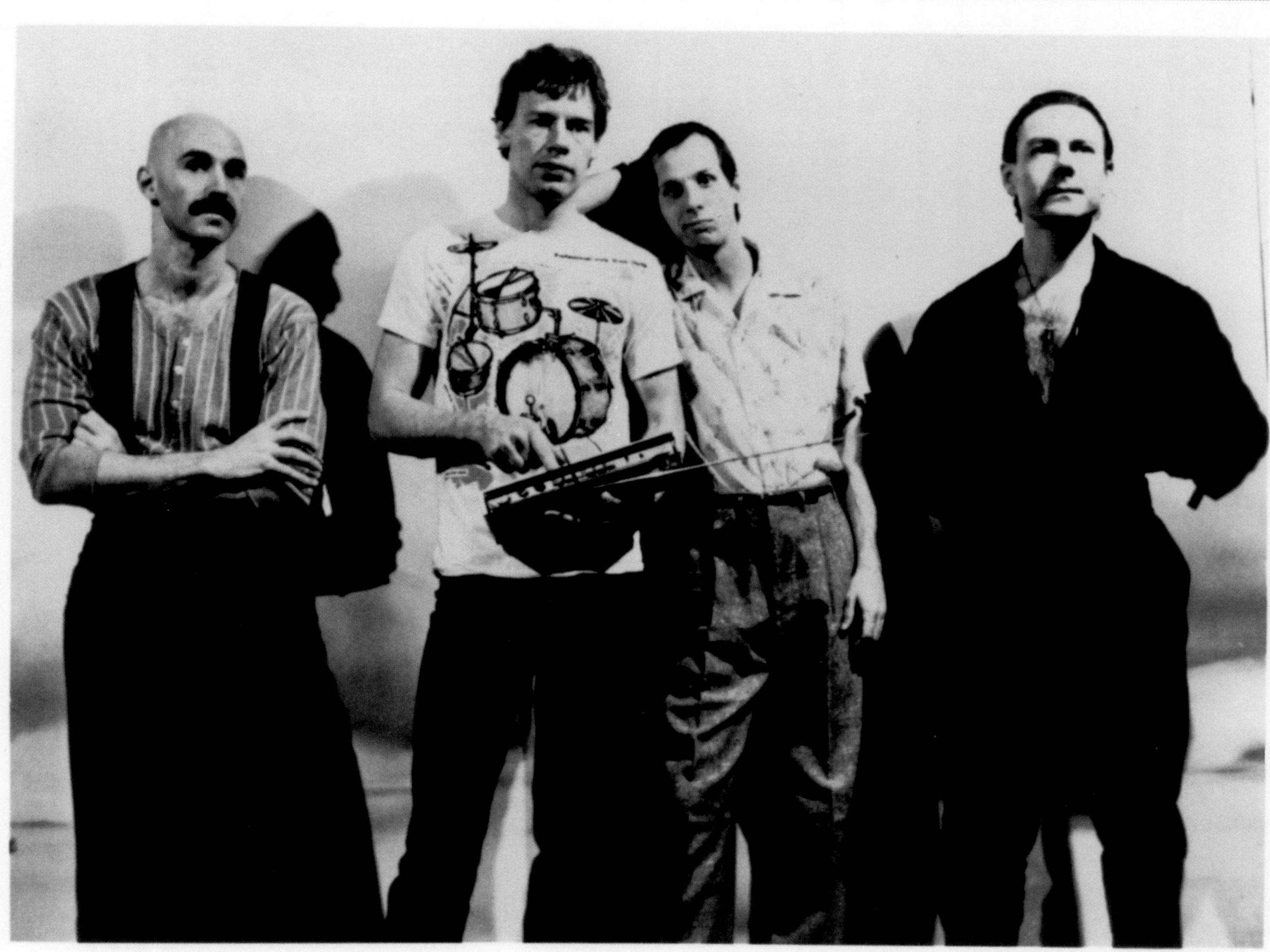

Philippe Hamon — Paris, May 1981.

King Crimson

eg

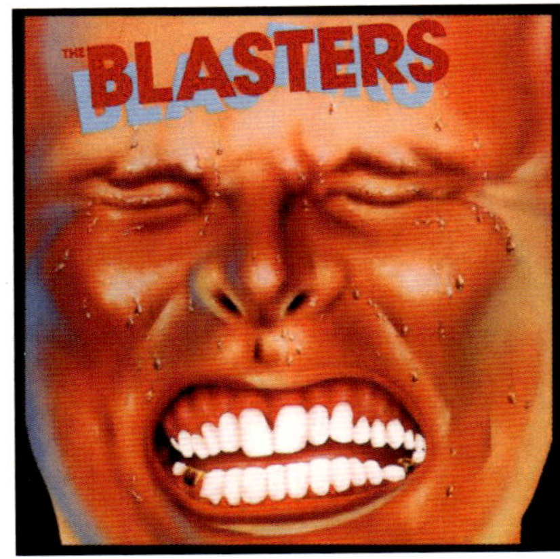

The Blasters' self-titled second album earned a nationwide following for the California band's vigorous stylings of "American Music"—rockabilly, early rock 'n' roll, punk and blues.

Billboard 200: *The Blasters* (#36)

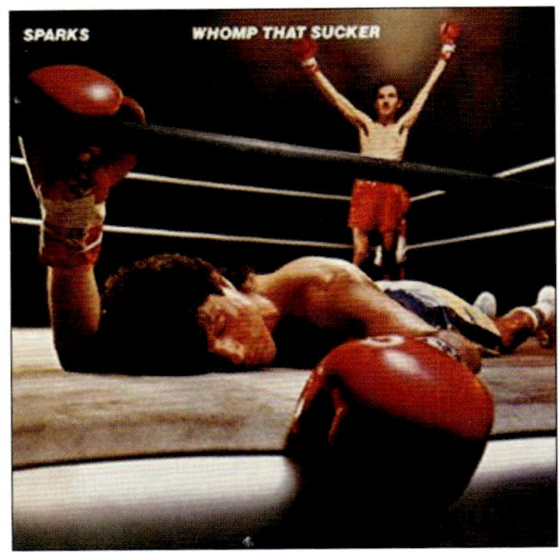

After veering in an electronic dance-pop direction for two records, Sparks reverted to a rock band, as *Whomp That Sucker* heralded a return to the album chart.

Billboard 200: *Whomp That Sucker* (#182)

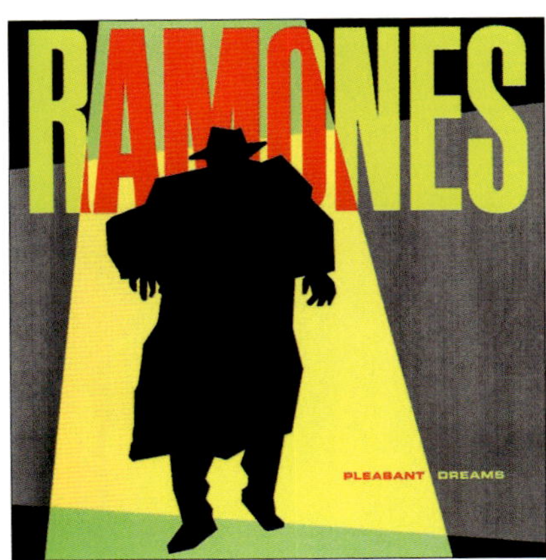

Resuming the direction established by the previous Ramones album, *Pleasant Dreams* took the seminal punk rockers further from the raw sound of their early records.

Billboard 200: *Pleasant Dreams* (#56)

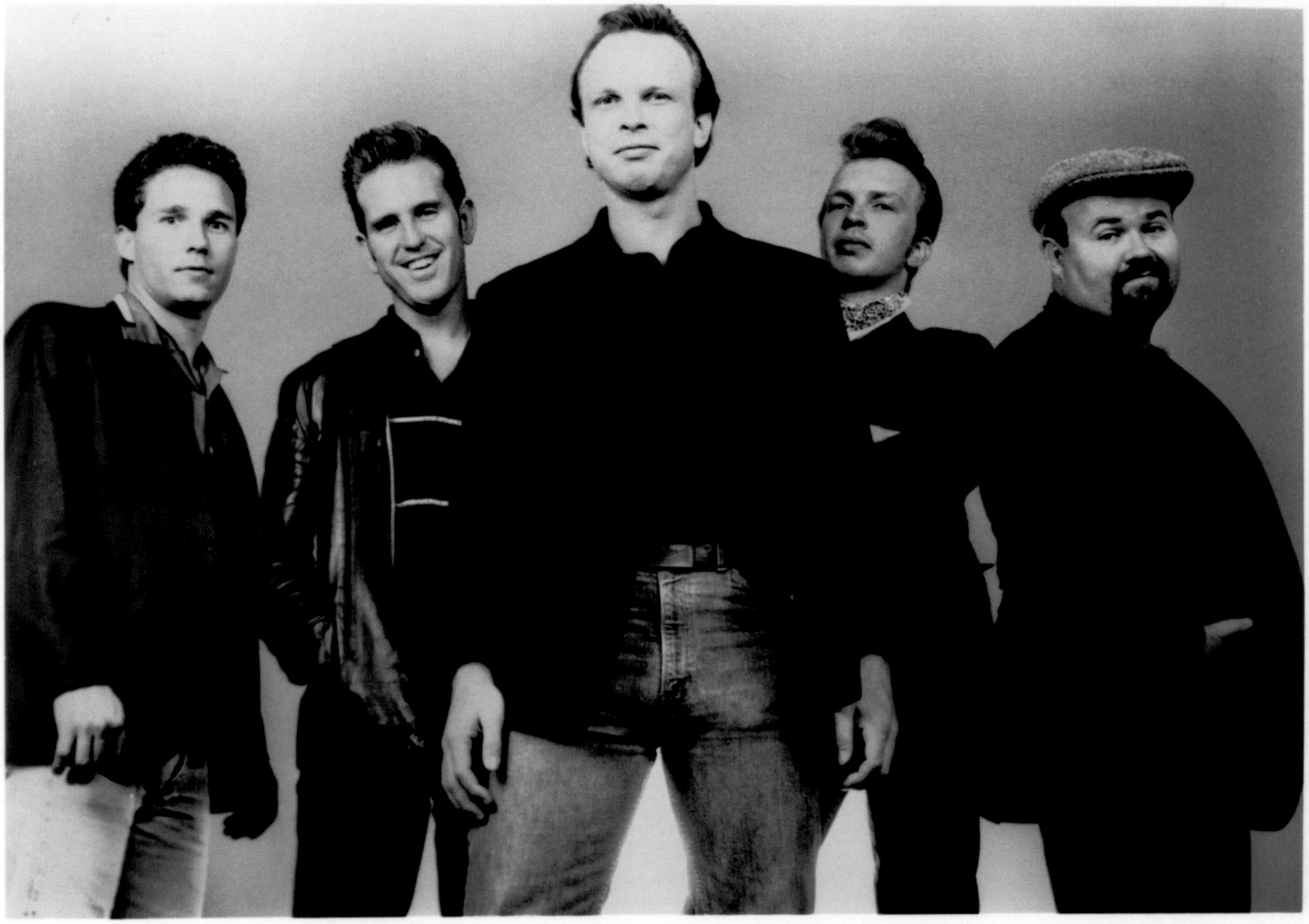

JOHN BAZZ   BILL BATEMAN   PHIL ALVIN   DAVE ALVIN   GENE TAYLOR

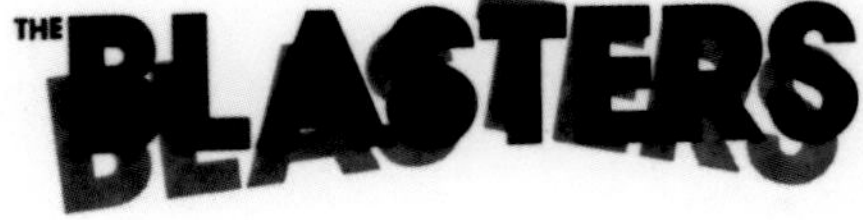

Management:
Vision Management
6565 Sunset Suite #400
Hollywood, Ca 90028
(213) 464-8341
Contact: Shelly Heber

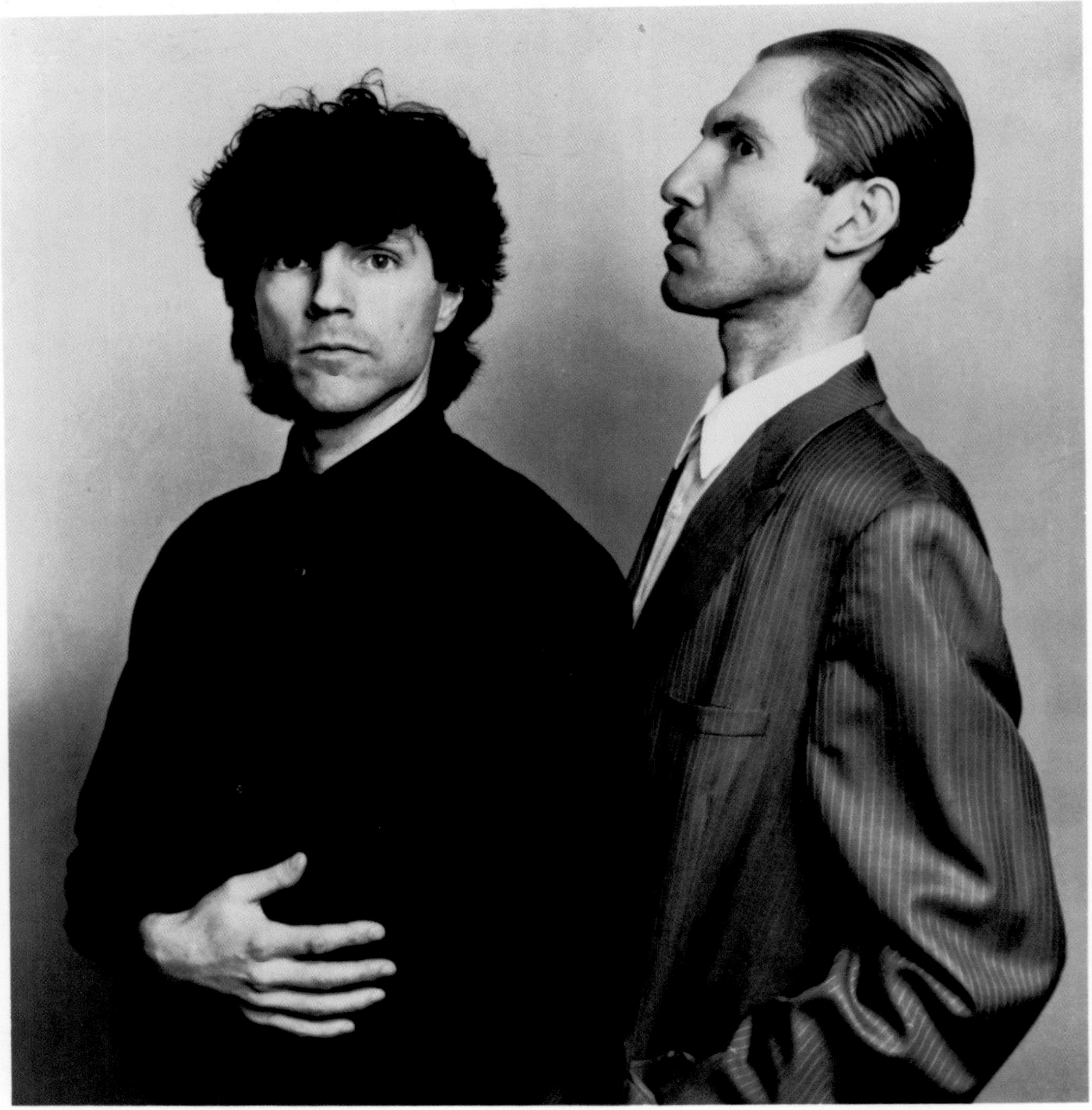

Sparks

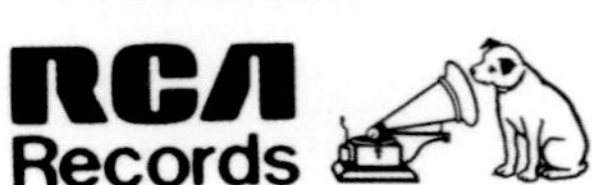

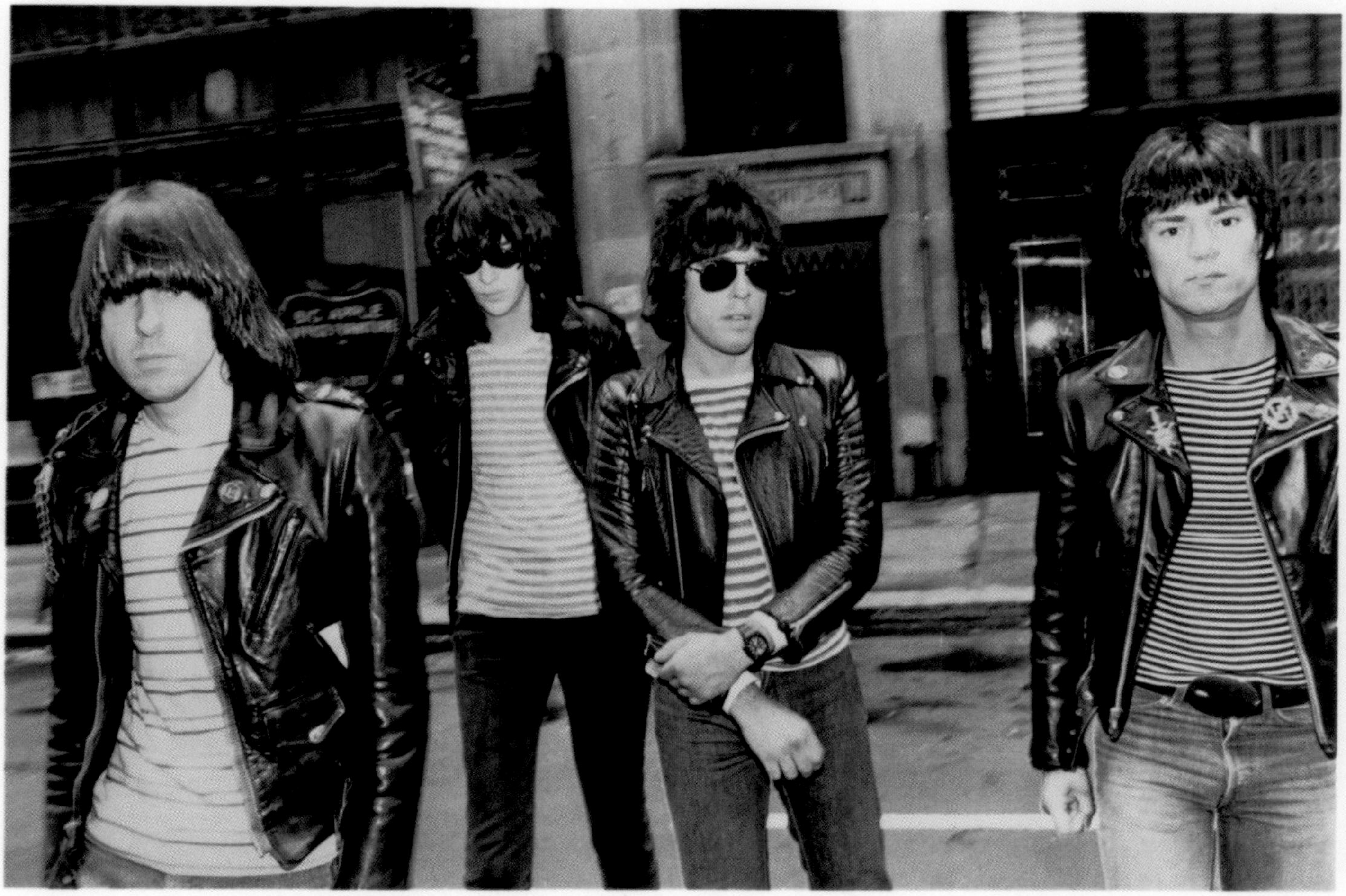

Photo Credit EBET ROBERTS July 1981

JOHNNY JOEY MARKY DEE DEE

RAMONES

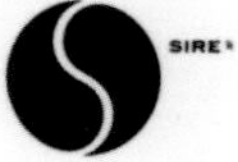

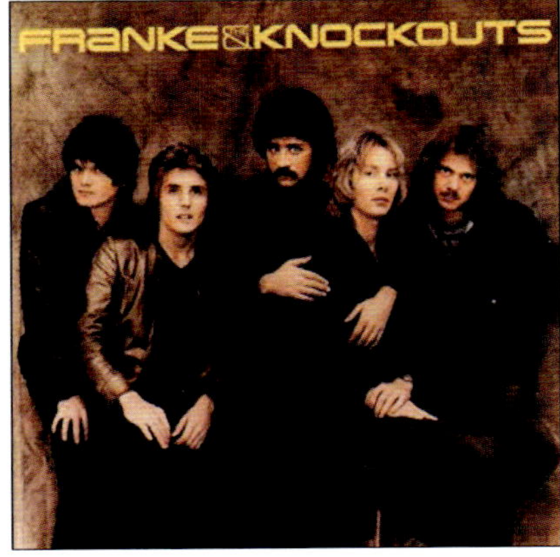

Fronted by singer Franke Previte, the New Jersey quintet **Franke & the Knockouts** scored with a one-two punch of pop-rock hits, "Sweetheart" and "You're My Girl."

Billboard 200: *Franke & the Knockouts* (#31)
Billboard Hot 100: "Sweetheart" (#10);
"You're My Girl" (#27)

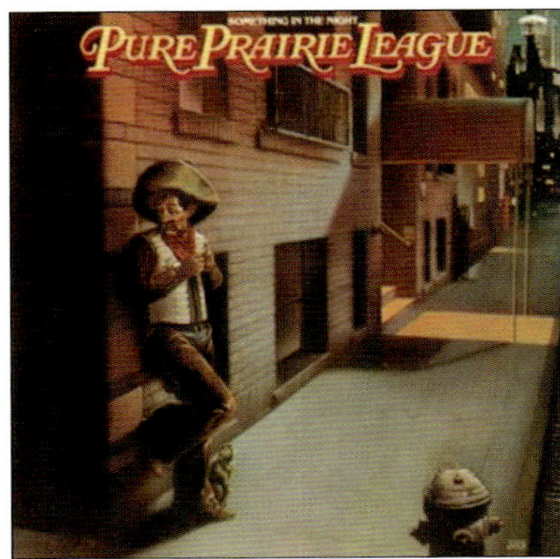

Pure Prairie League's *Something in the Night,* guitarist and vocalist Vince Gill's last album with the country-rock band, charted with the hit, "Still Right Here in My Heart."

Billboard 200: *Something in the Night* (#72)
Billboard Hot 100: "Still Right Here in My Heart" (#28);
"You're Mine Tonight" (#68)

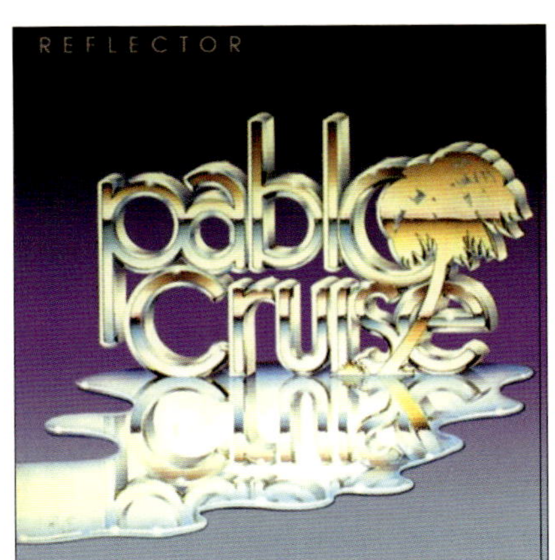

Reflector, the sixth album by **Pablo Cruise**, generated "Cool Love," marking the San Francisco-based soft-rock group's fifth and final single to crack the Top 40.

Billboard 200: *Reflector* (#34)
Billboard Hot 100: "Cool Love" (#13); "Slip Away" (#75)

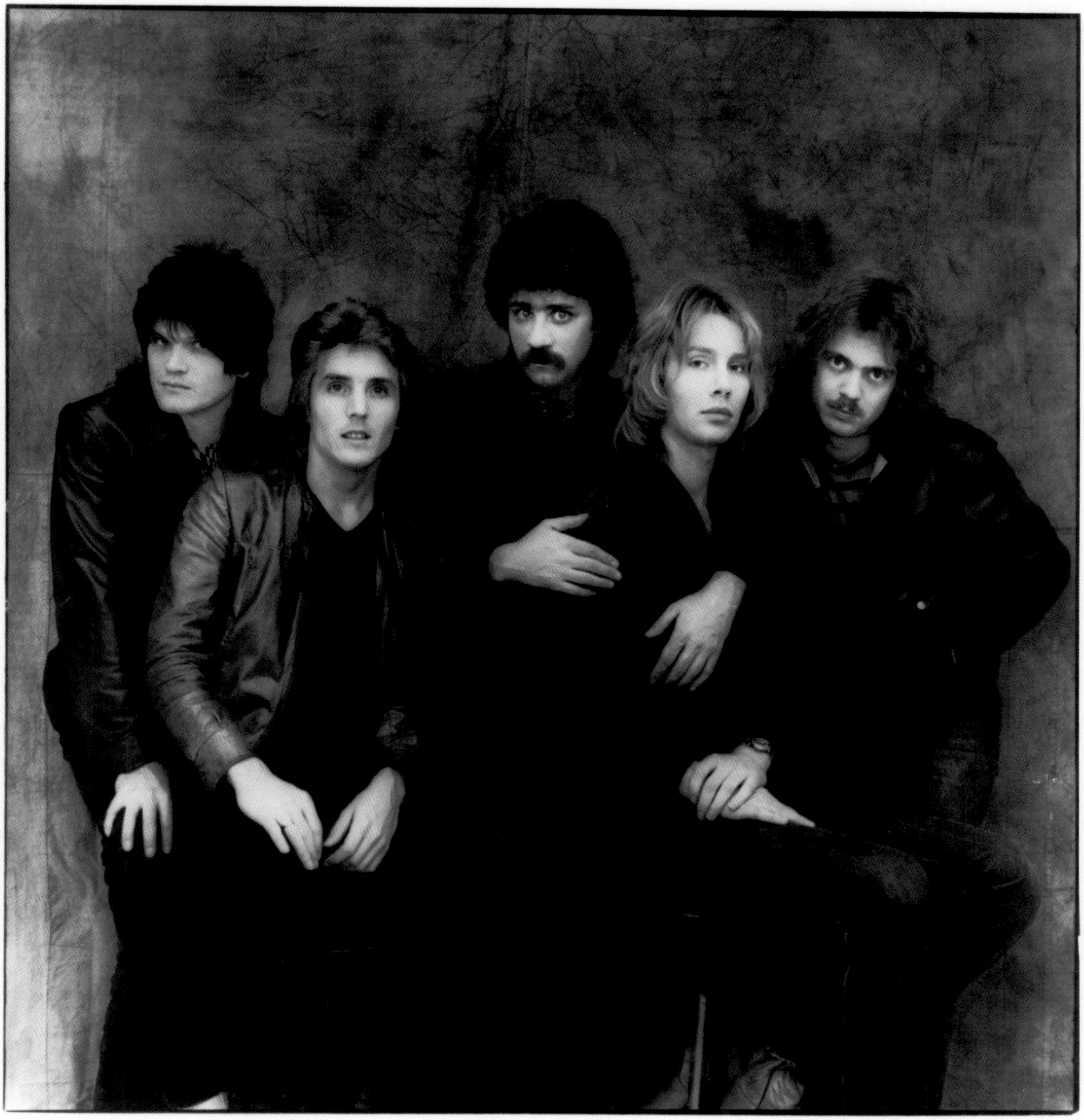

FRANKE & THE KNOCKOUTS

DIRECTION: MICHAEL KLENFNER.

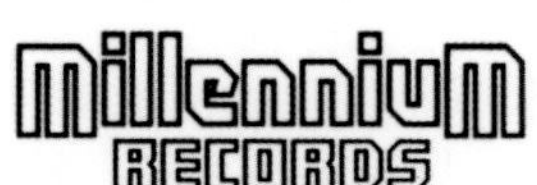

Manufactured and Distributed by RCA Records

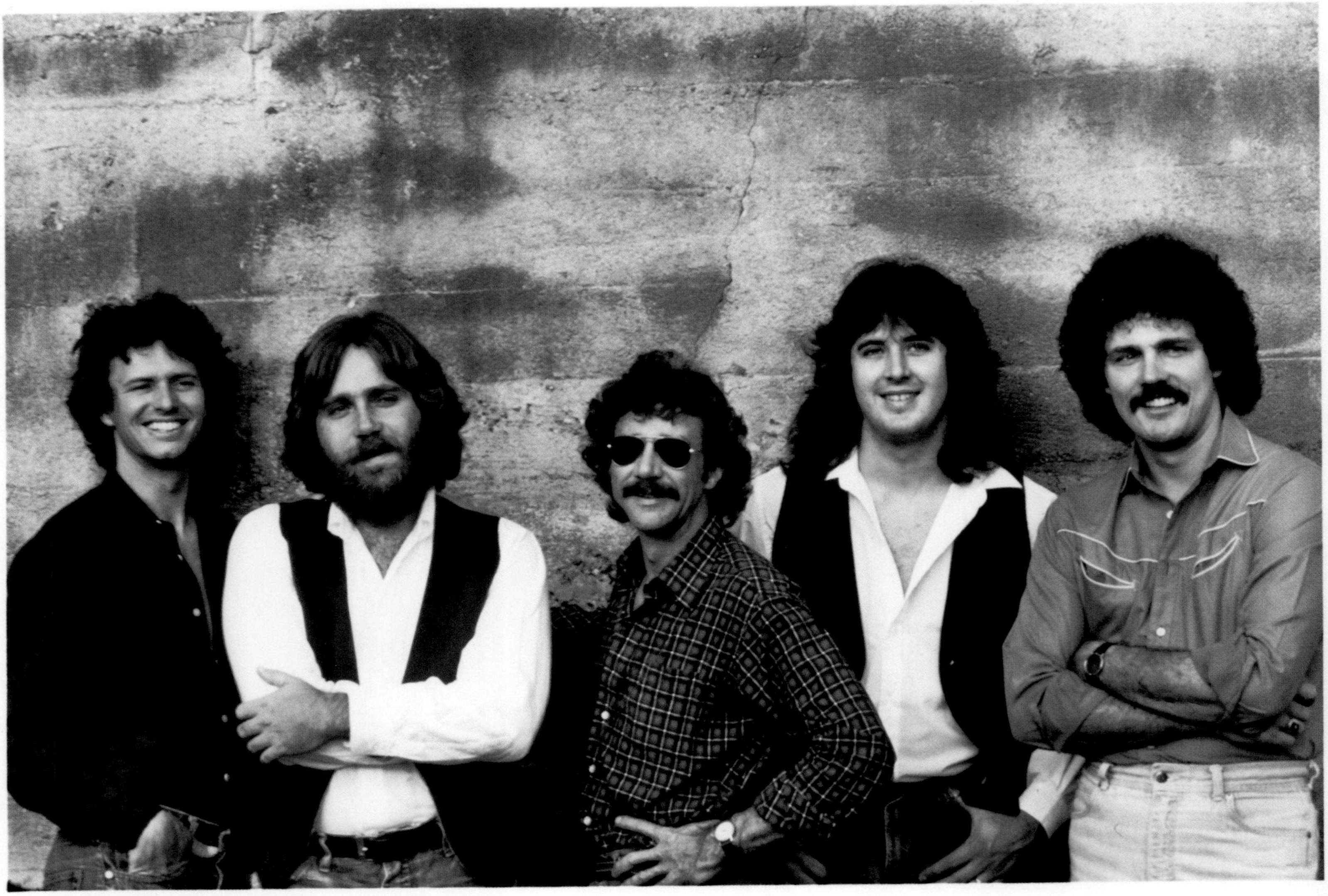

PURE PRAIRIE LEAGUE

PolyGram Records

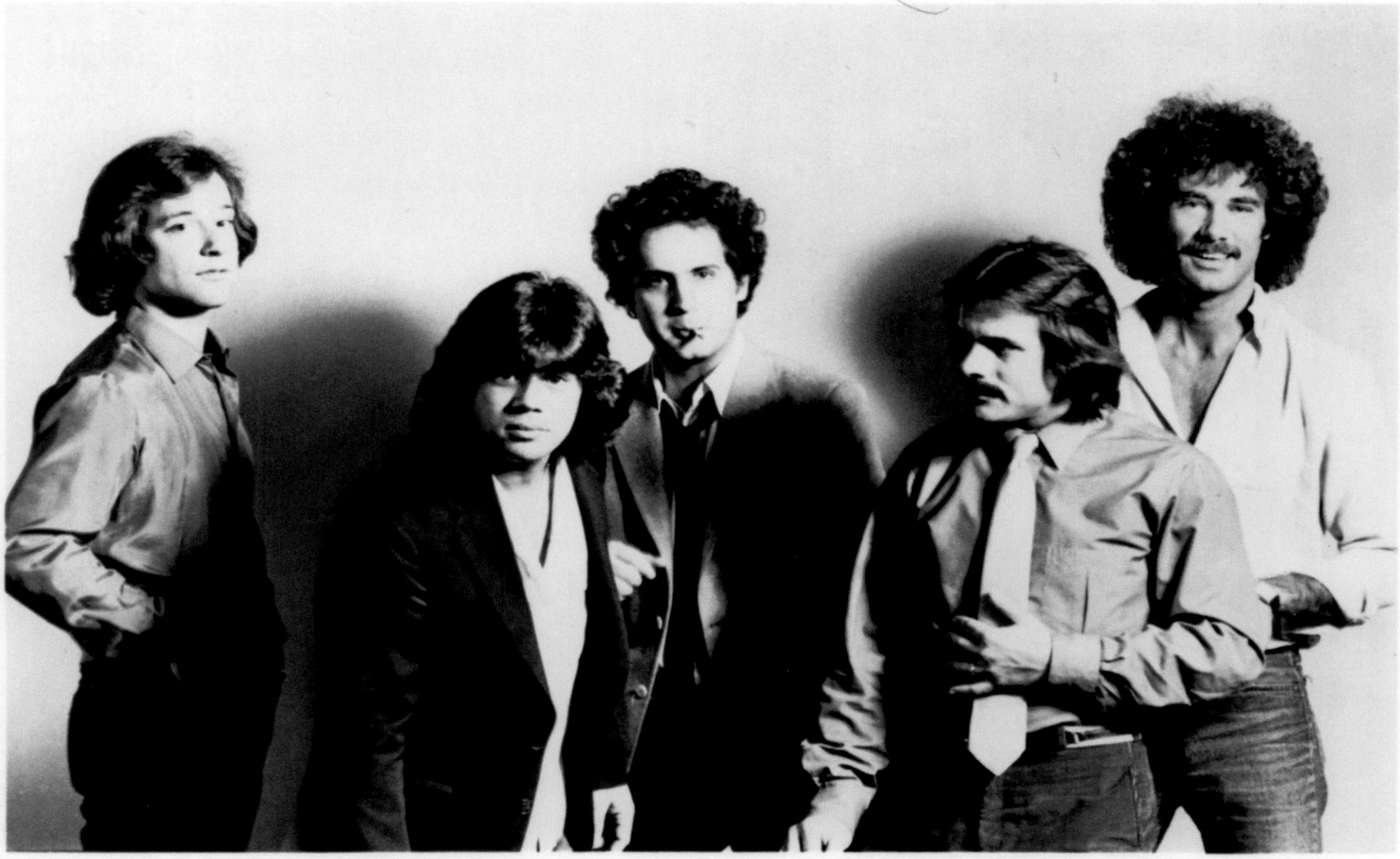

Angelo Rossi | Cory Lerios | John Pierce | Steve Price | David Jenkins

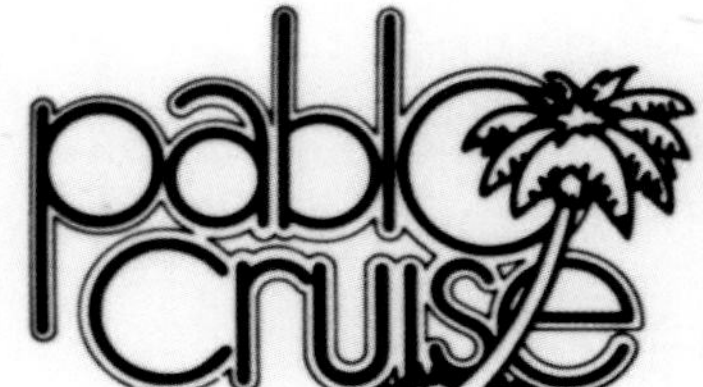

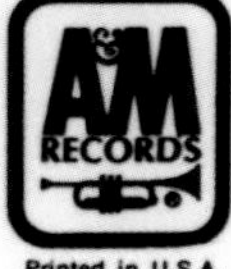

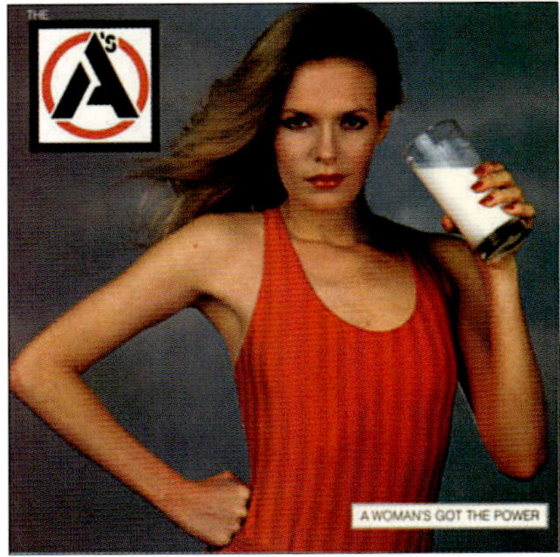

The A's released their second album, *A Woman's Got the Power*, and the R&B-influenced title track garnered the new-wave band a following outside of Philadelphia.

Billboard 200: *A Woman's Got the Power* (#146)

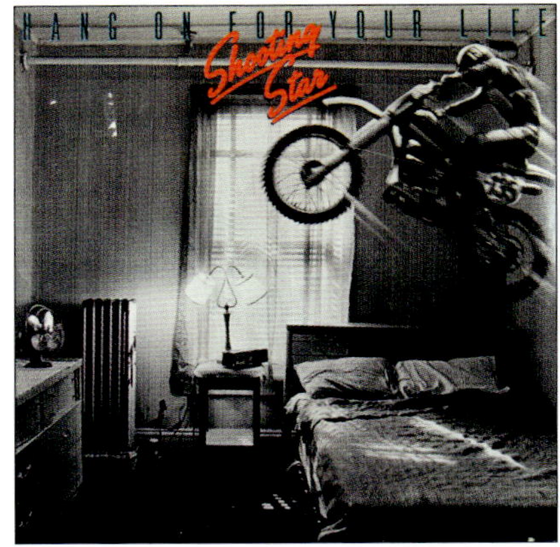

Coming out of Kansas City, the melodic hard-rock quintet **Shooting Star** benefited from a blast of AOR airplay with its sophomore effort, *Hang On for Your Life*.

Billboard 200: *Hang On for Your Life* (#92)
Billboard Hot 100: "Hollywood" (#70)

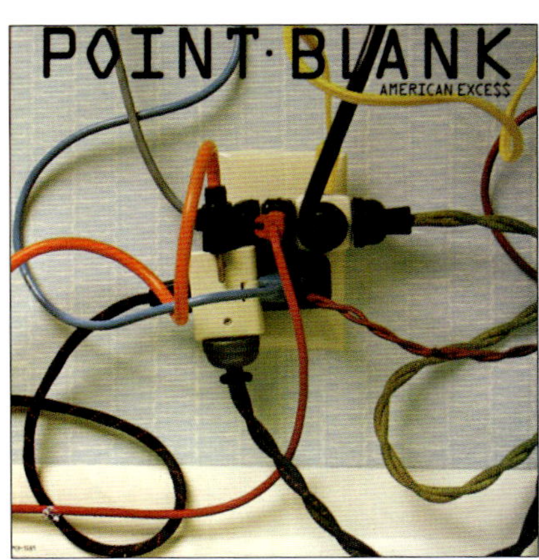

Point Blank caught some chart action with its fifth album, *American Exce$$*, which sported the Southern blues-rock outfit's most renowned hit, "Nicole."

Billboard 200: *American Exce$$* (#80)
Billboard Hot 100: "Nicole" (#39)

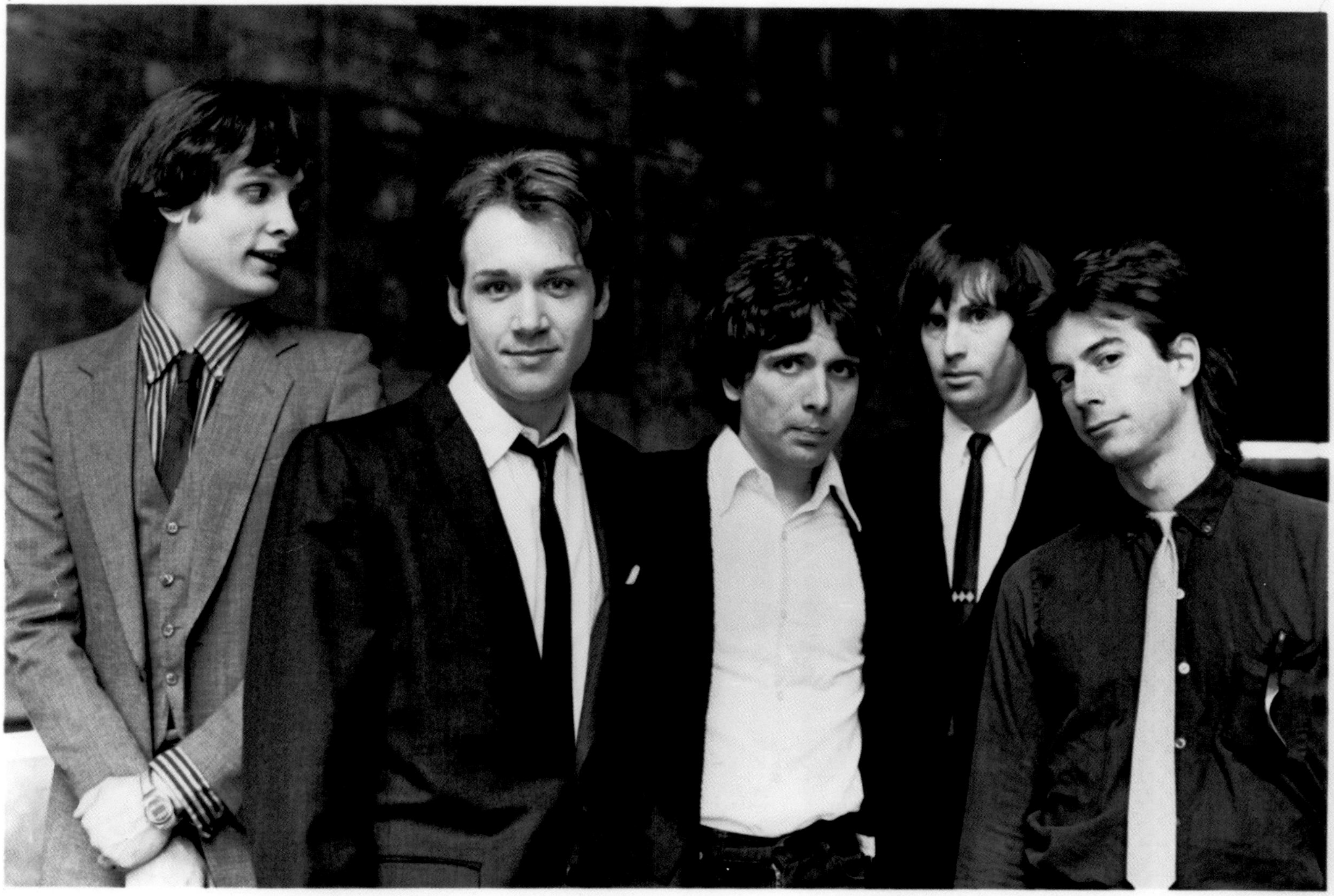

Management:
Apple/Chipetz
1746 Lombard Street
Philadelphia, PA 19146

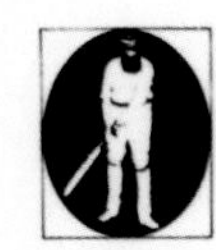

Cricket Talent & Booking Inc.
Suite 1416, 250 West 57th Street,
New York, NY 10019
Telephone: (212) 977 9806

THE A's

ARISTA™

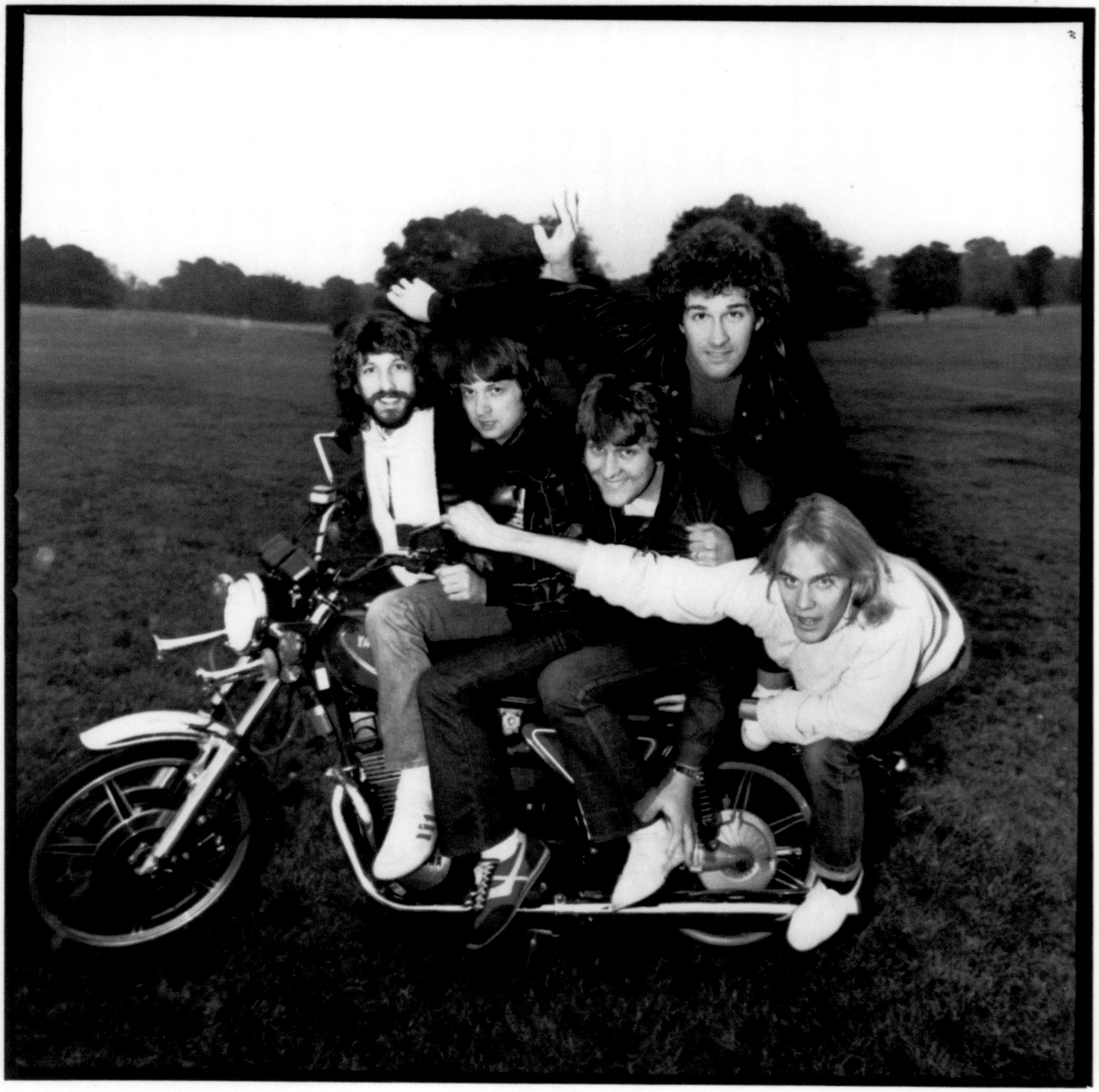

Left to right   Steve Thomas   Gary West   Van McClain   Ron Verlin, Charles Waltz

Virgin RECORDS

SHOOTING STAR

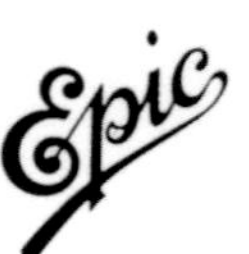

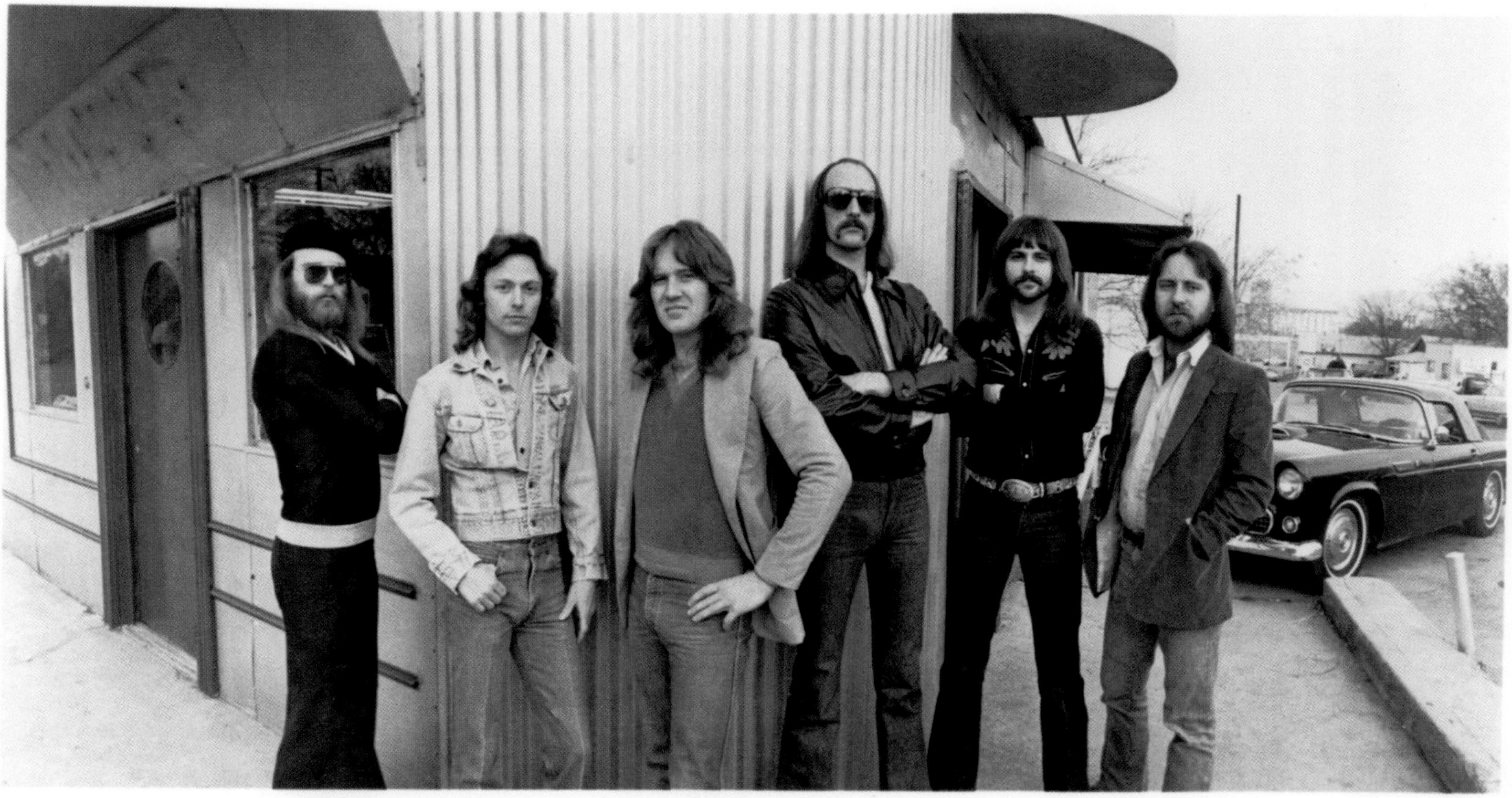

2/81

RUSTY BURNS BUBBA KEITH BILL RANDOLPH BUZZY GRUEN KIM DAVIS MIKE HAMILTON

POINT BLANK

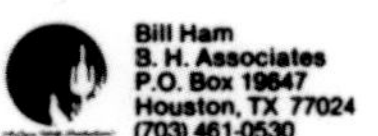

Bill Ham
B. H. Associates
P.O. Box 19647
Houston, TX 77024
(703) 461-0530

Exclusively On
MCA RECORDS

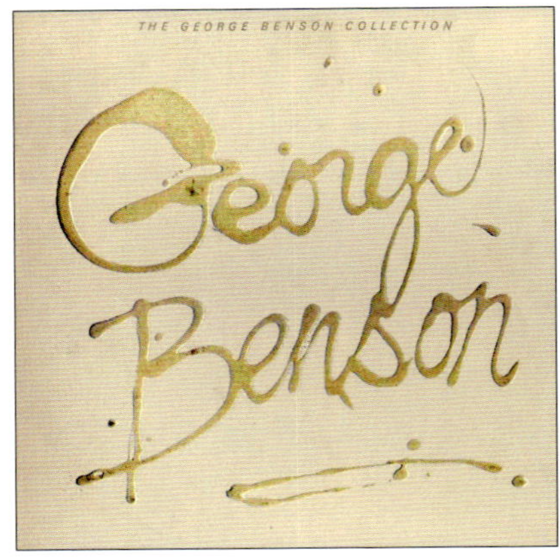

George Benson's No. 1 R&B hit, "Turn Your Love Around," was one of two previously unrecorded tracks compiled for the double-LP, *The George Benson Collection*.

Billboard Hot 100: "Never Give Up on a Good Thing" (#52); "Turn Your Love Around" (#5)

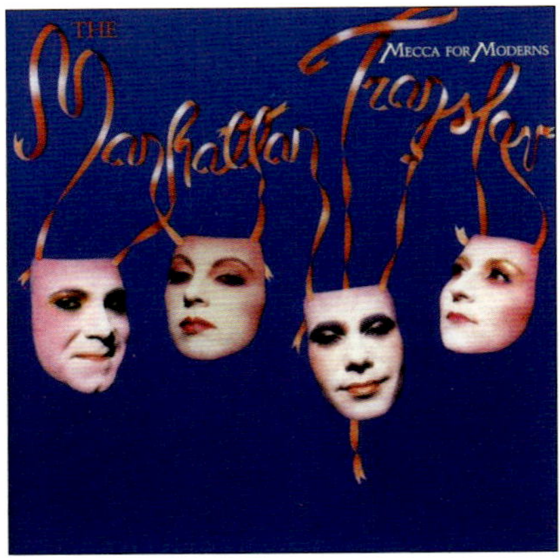

Manhattan Transfer became the first act to win pop and jazz Grammys in the same year with "The Boy from New York City" and "Until I Met You (Corner Pocket)."

Billboard 200: *Mecca for Moderns* (#22)
Billboard Hot 100: "The Boy from New York City" (#7)

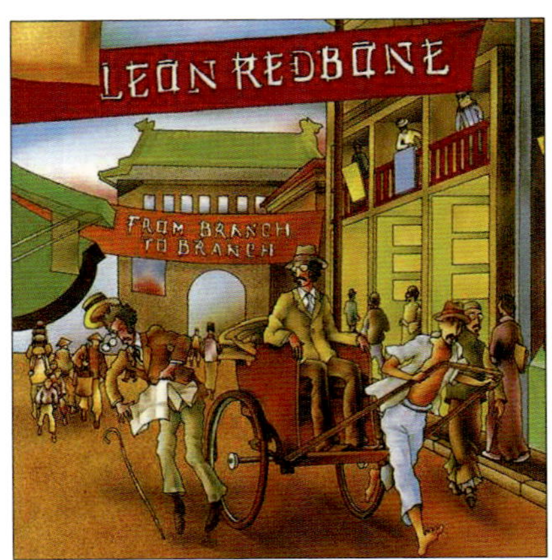

After a three-year break from recording, the enigmatic **Leon Redbone** cut *From Branch to Branch*, reviving a diverse range of vintage jazz, blues and ragtime songs.

Billboard 200: *From Branch to Branch* (#152)

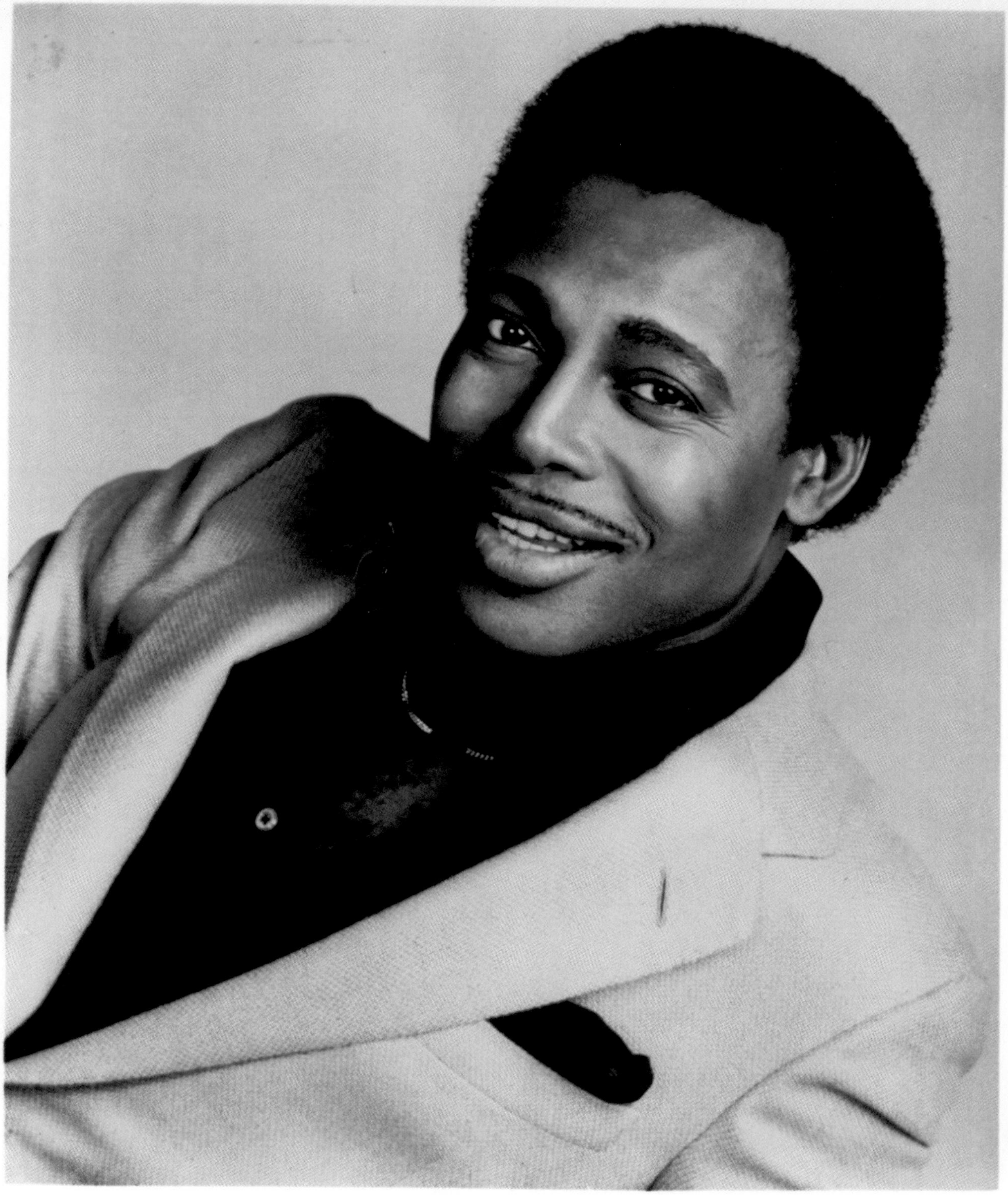

OCTOBER 1981

GEORGE BENSON

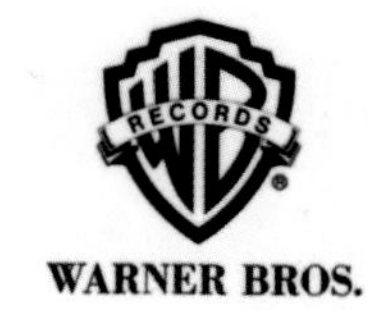

WARNER BROS.

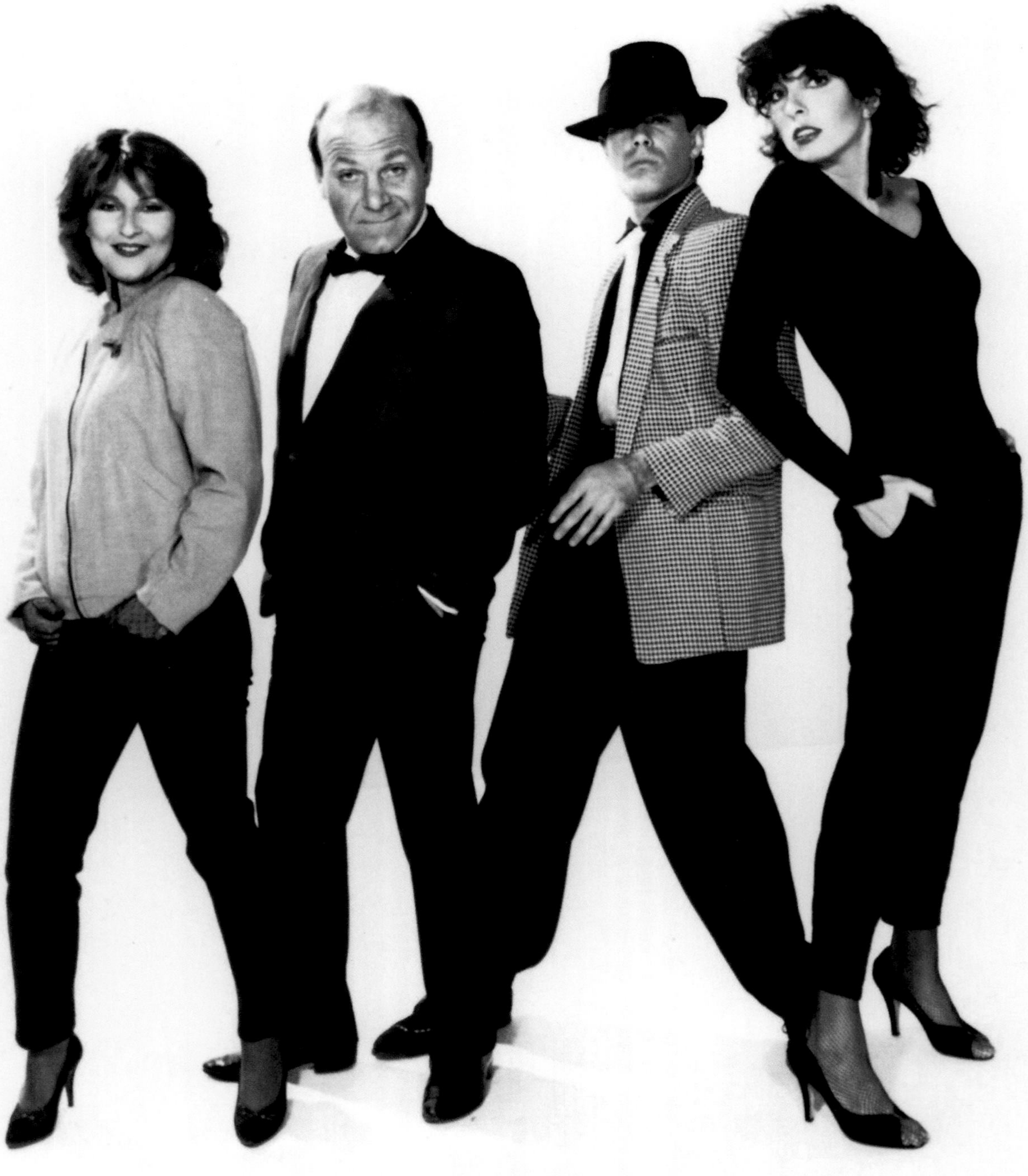

Janis Siegel   Tim Hauser   Alan Paul   Cheryl Bentyne

MANHATTAN TRANSFER

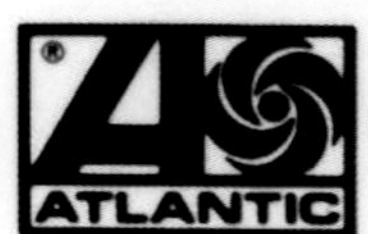

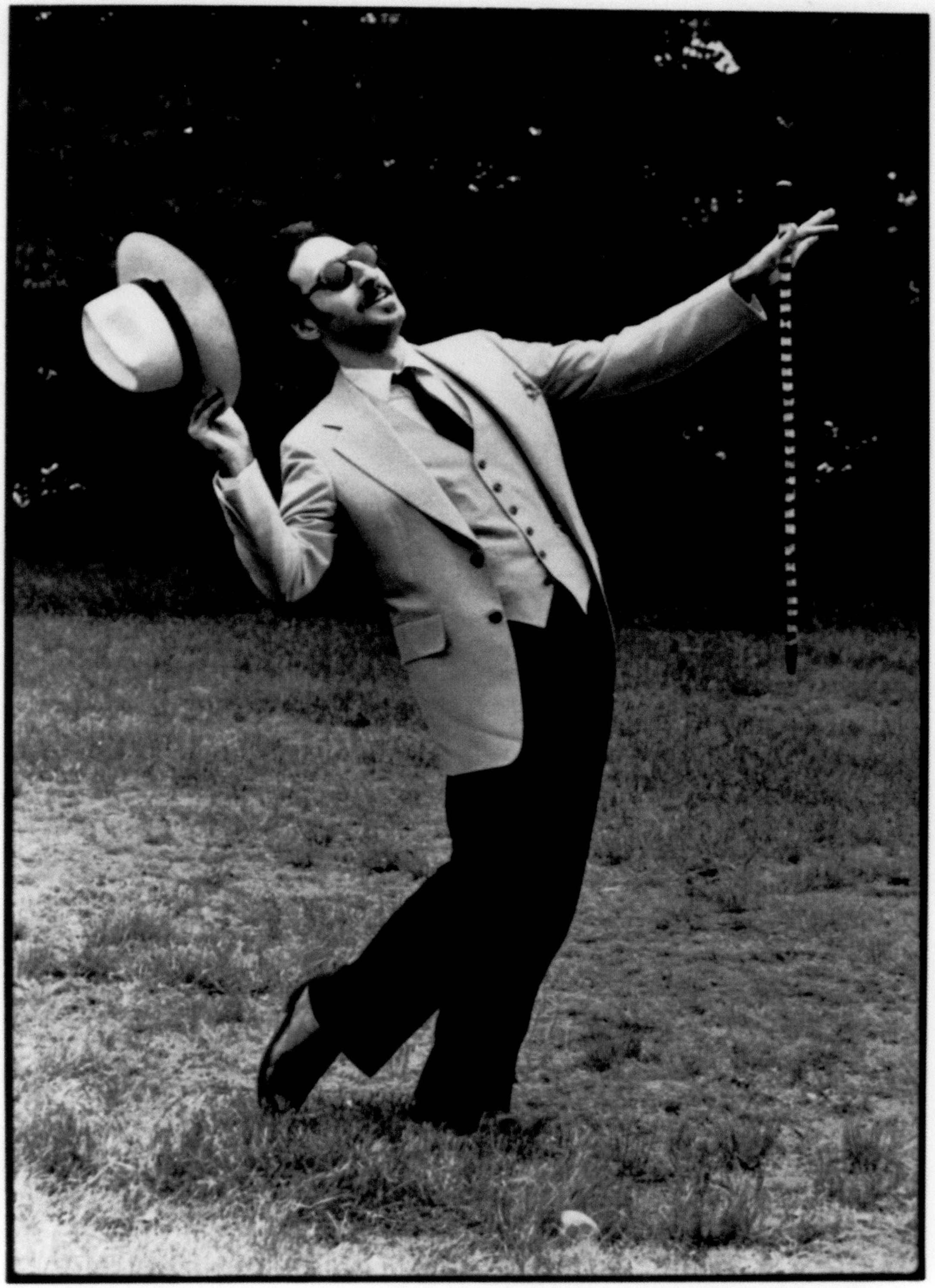

LEON REDBONE

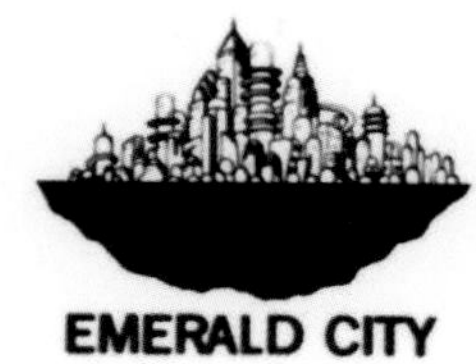

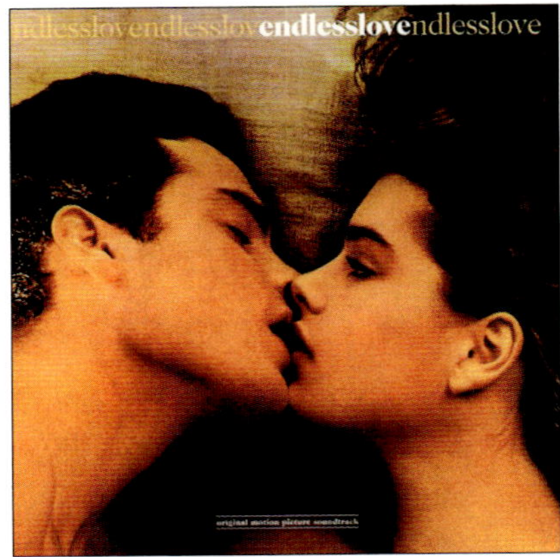

The theme song to *Endless Love*, performed by **Diana Ross & Lionel Richie**, turned out to be the best thing about the movie, becoming a No. 1 hit for nine weeks.

Billboard 200: *Endless Love* (#9)
Billboard Hot 100: "Endless Love" (No. 1)

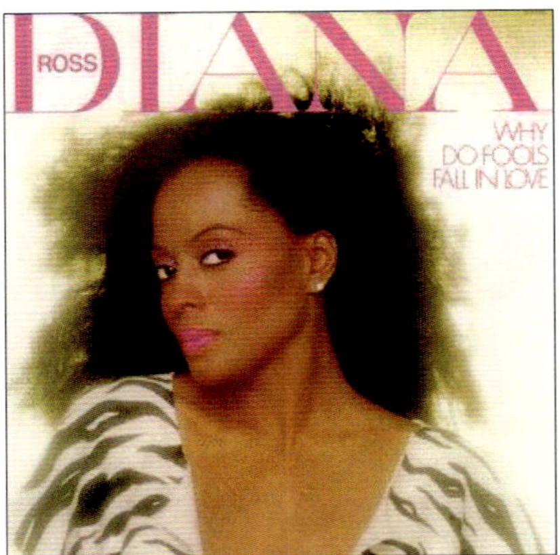

Leaving the Motown label, **Diana Ross** enjoyed a huge hit with *Why Do Fools Fall in Love*, highlighted by "Mirror Mirror" and the pop-soul diva's version of the title song.

Billboard 200: *Why Do Fools Fall in Love* (#15)
Billboard Hot 100: "Why Do Fools Fall in Love" (#7); "Mirror, Mirror" (#8); "Work That Body" (#44)

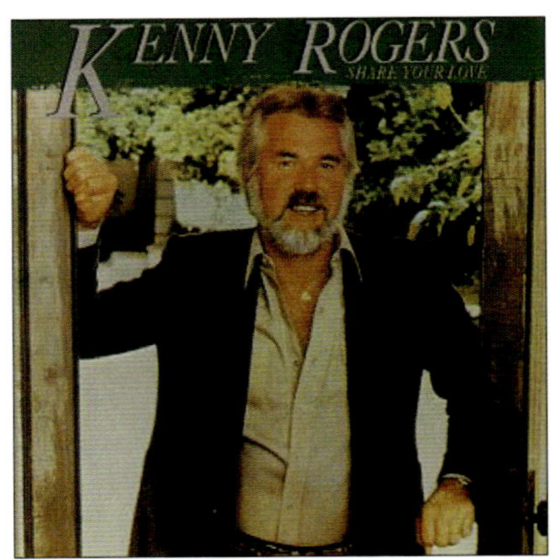

Country-pop icon **Kenny Rogers** asked Lionel Richie to produce *Share Your Love*, netting three hits, "I Don't Need You," "Through the Years" and "Share Your Love with Me."

Billboard 200: *Share Your Love* (#6)
Billboard Hot 100: "I Don't Need You" (#3); "Share Your Love with Me" (#14); "Blaze of Glory" (#66); "Through the Years" (#13)

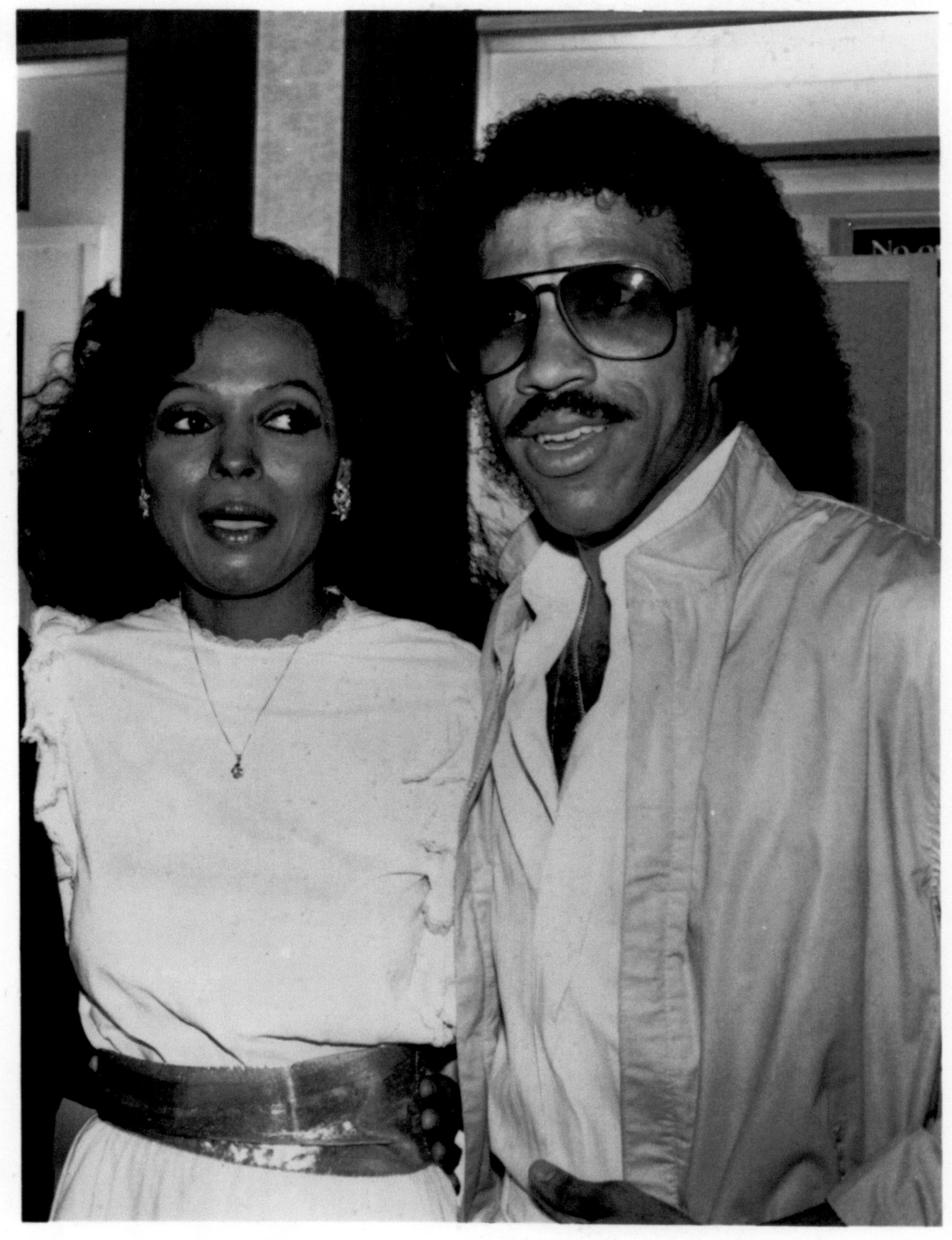

SHOWN IN NEW YORK CITY ON THE OPENING NIGHT OF "ENDLESS LOVE" ARE DIANA ROSS AND LIONEL RICHIE.

Public Relations
Guy Thomas
Vice President/Creative Services
Kragen & Company
1112 N. Sherbourne Dr.
(213) 854-4400

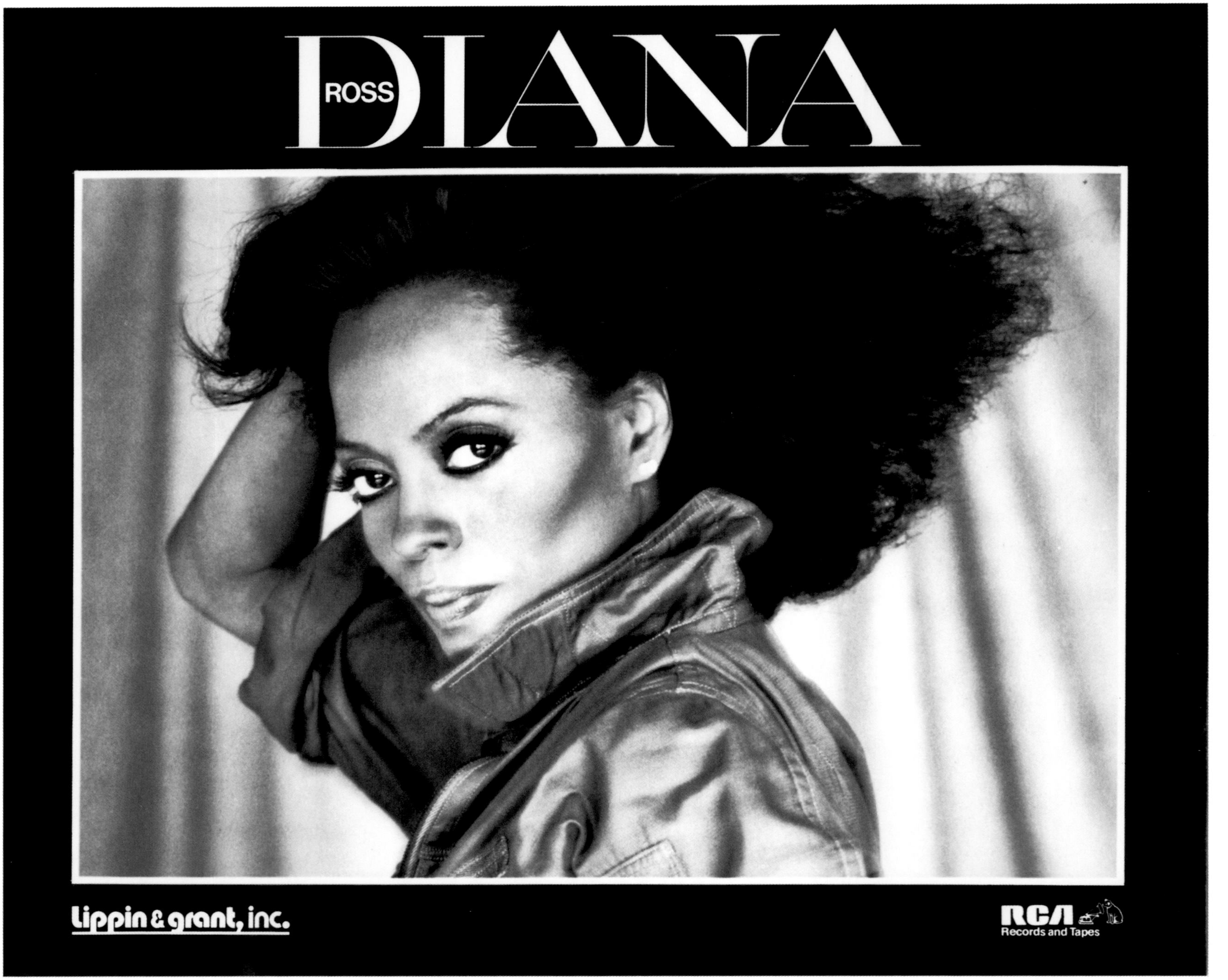

ROSS DIANA

lippin & grant, inc.

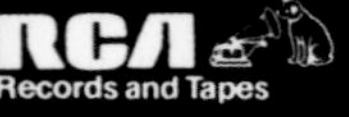

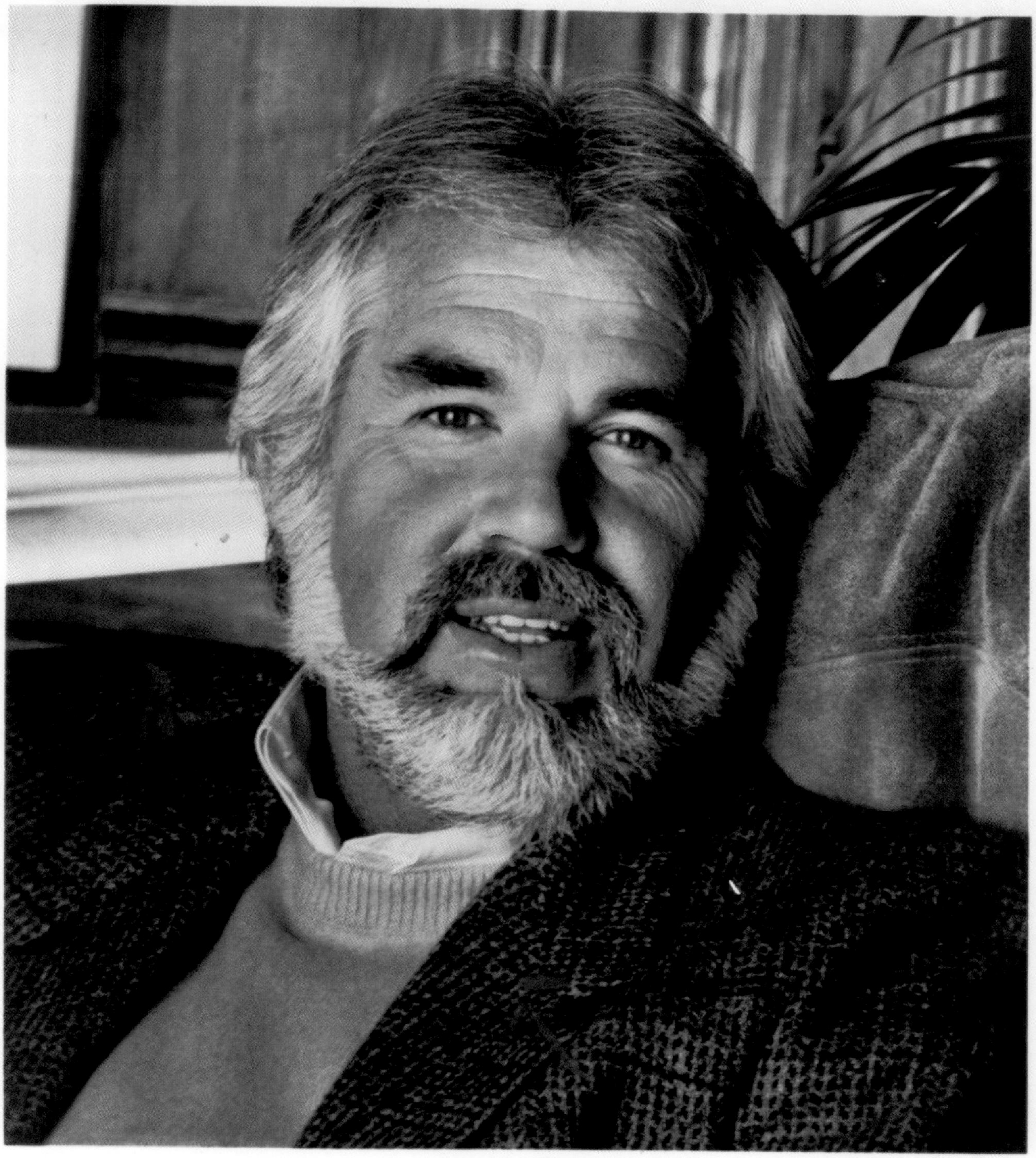

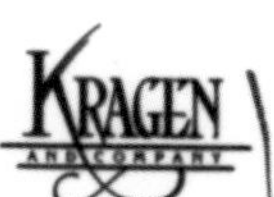

Management/Public Relations:
(213) 854-4400

Photo: Matthew Rolston

KENNY ROGERS

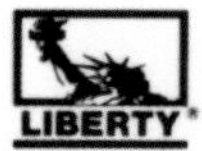

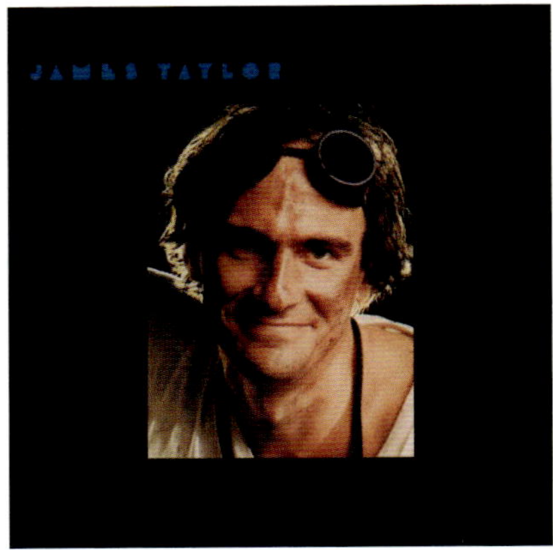

Singer-songwriter **James Taylor**'s tenth album, the platinum-selling *Dad Loves His Work,* provided the hit single, "Her Town Too," a duet with co-writer J.D. Souther.

Billboard 200: *Dad Loves His Work* (#10)
Billboard Hot 100: "Her Town Too" (#11);
"Hard Times" (#72)

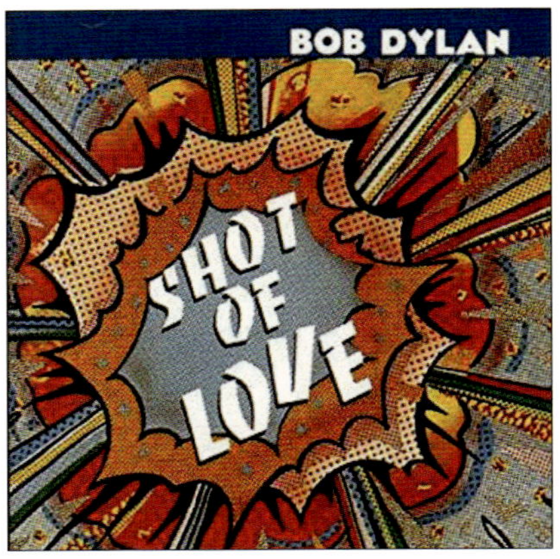

Shot of Love, considered the last and most rock-oriented album of **Bob Dylan**'s "born again" trilogy, included the standout closing track, "Every Grain of Sand."

Billboard 200: *Shot of Love* (#33)

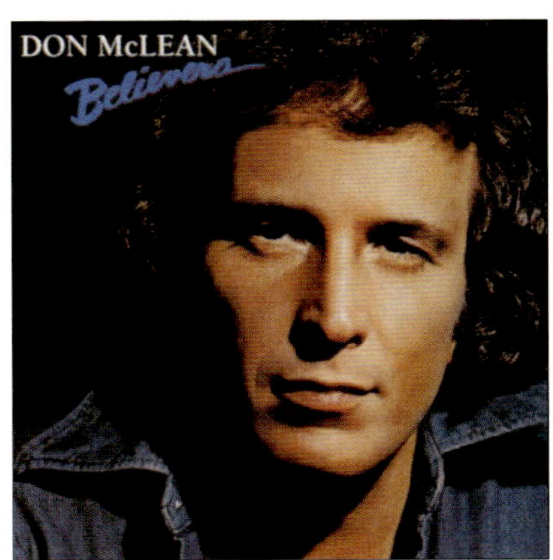

Don McLean's *Believers* led off with a Top 40 hit—a rerecording of "Castles in the Air," which originally appeared on *Tapestry*, the singer-songwriter's 1970 debut album.

Billboard 200: *Believers* (#156)
Billboard Hot 100: "Castles in the Air" (#36)

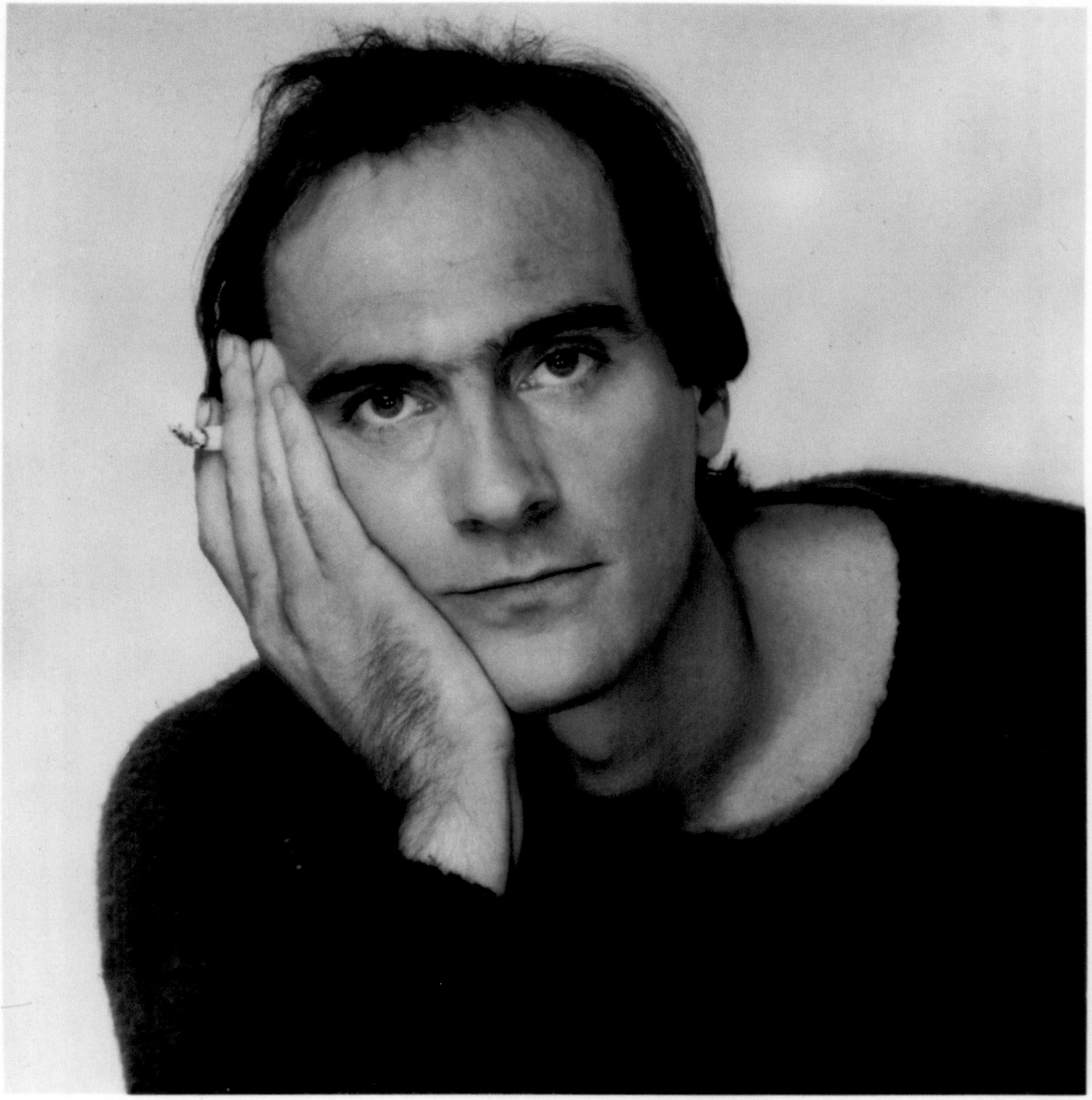

JAMES TAYLOR

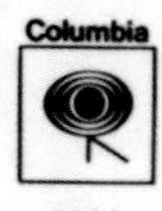

8102

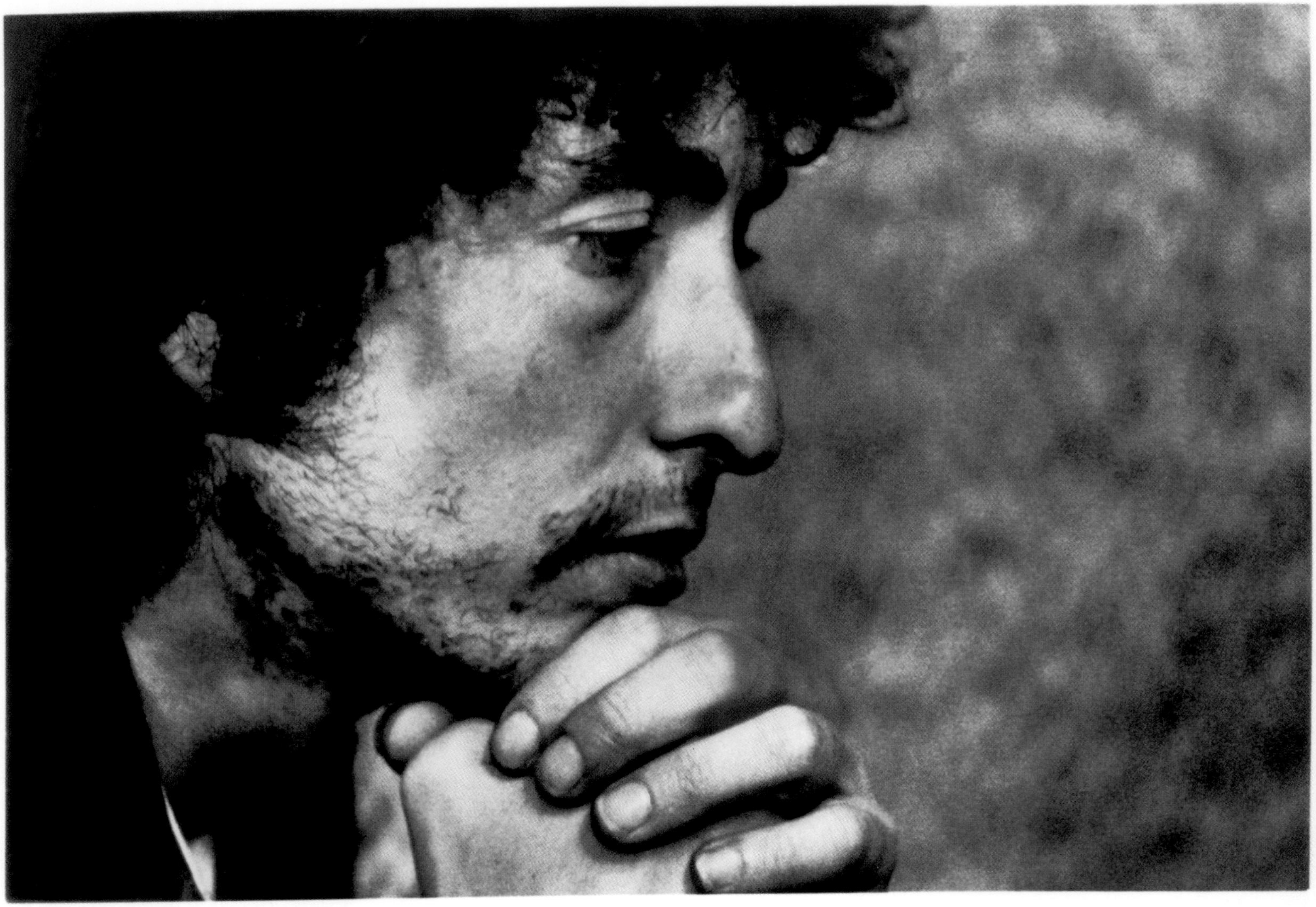

BOB DYLAN

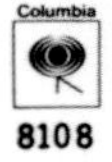

8108

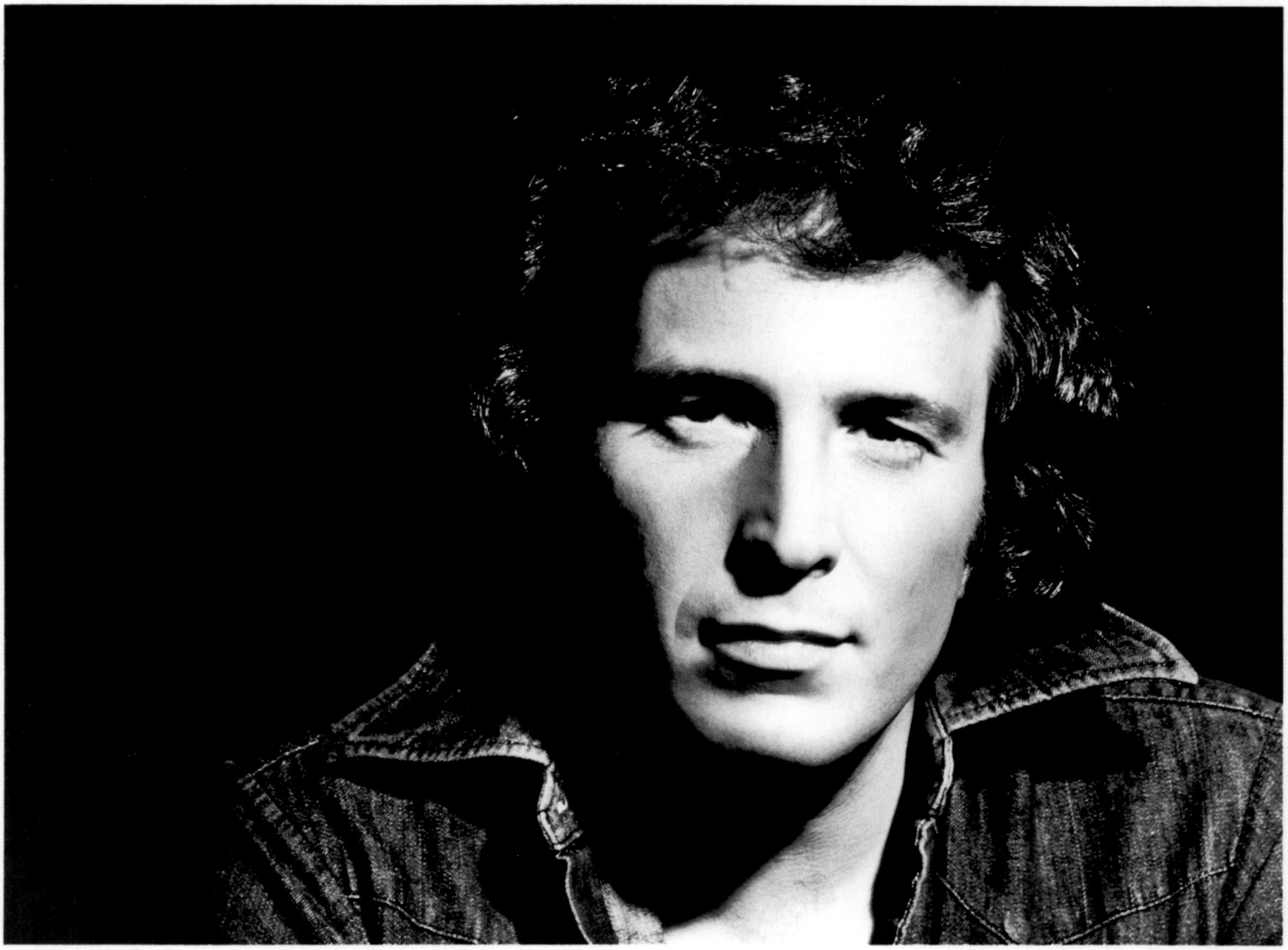

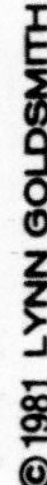

DON McLEAN

HERBERT S. GART MANAGEMENT INC.
101 West 57th Street, Suite 2A
New York, New York 10019
(212) 765-8160

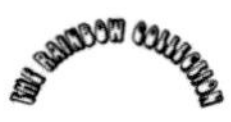

millennium
RECORDS

Manufactured and Distributed by RCA Records and Tapes

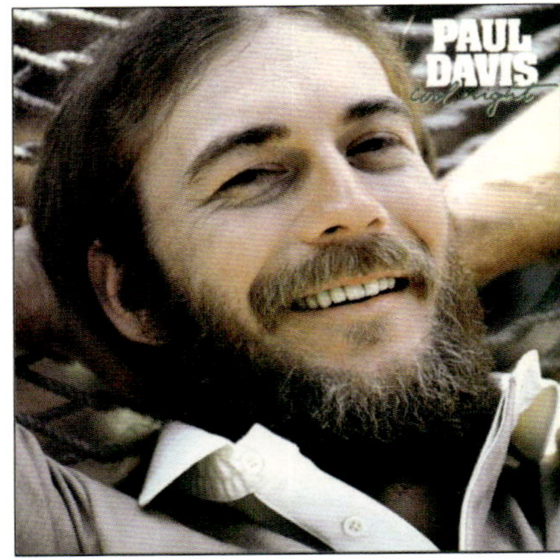

Cool Night, singer-songwriter **Paul Davis**' last studio album, spawned two pop and adult contemporary hits, the title track and his highest-charting single, "'65 Love Affair."

Billboard 200: *Cool Night* (#52)
Billboard Hot 100: "Cool Night" (#11); "'65 Love Affair" (#6); "Love or Let Me Be Lonely" (#40)

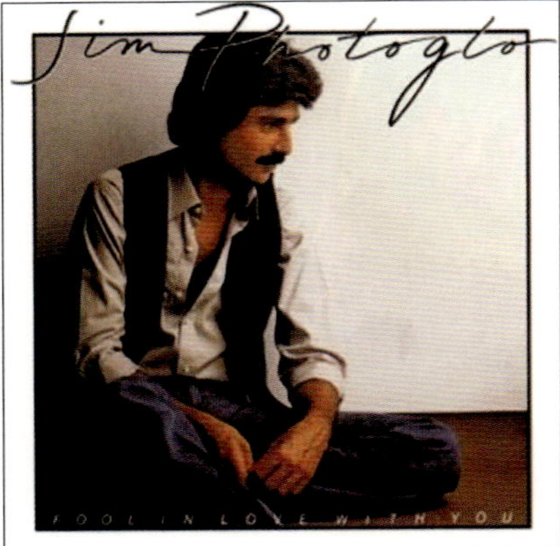

Songwriter and touring musician **Jim Photoglo**'s brief solo career culminated in "Fool in Love with You," his second charting single as a soft-rock performer.

Billboard 200: *Fool in Love with You* (#119)
Billboard Hot 100: "Fool in Love with You" (#25)

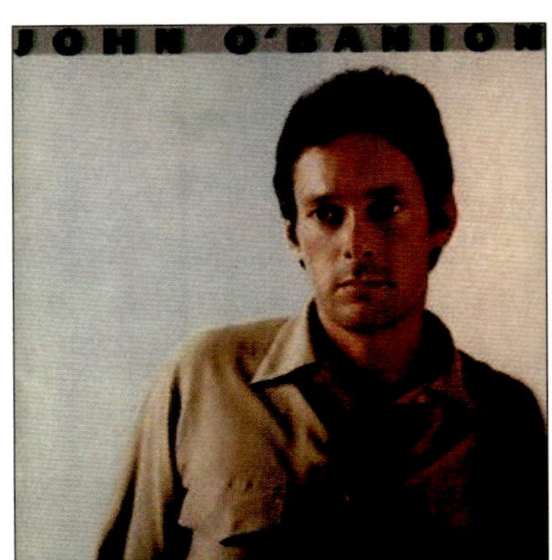

John O'Banion's song, "Love You Like I Never Loved Before," clambered up the Top 40, cementing the singer and actor's ranking as a one-hit wonder.

Billboard 200: *John O'Banion* (#164)
Billboard Hot 100: "Love You Like I Never Loved Before" (#24)

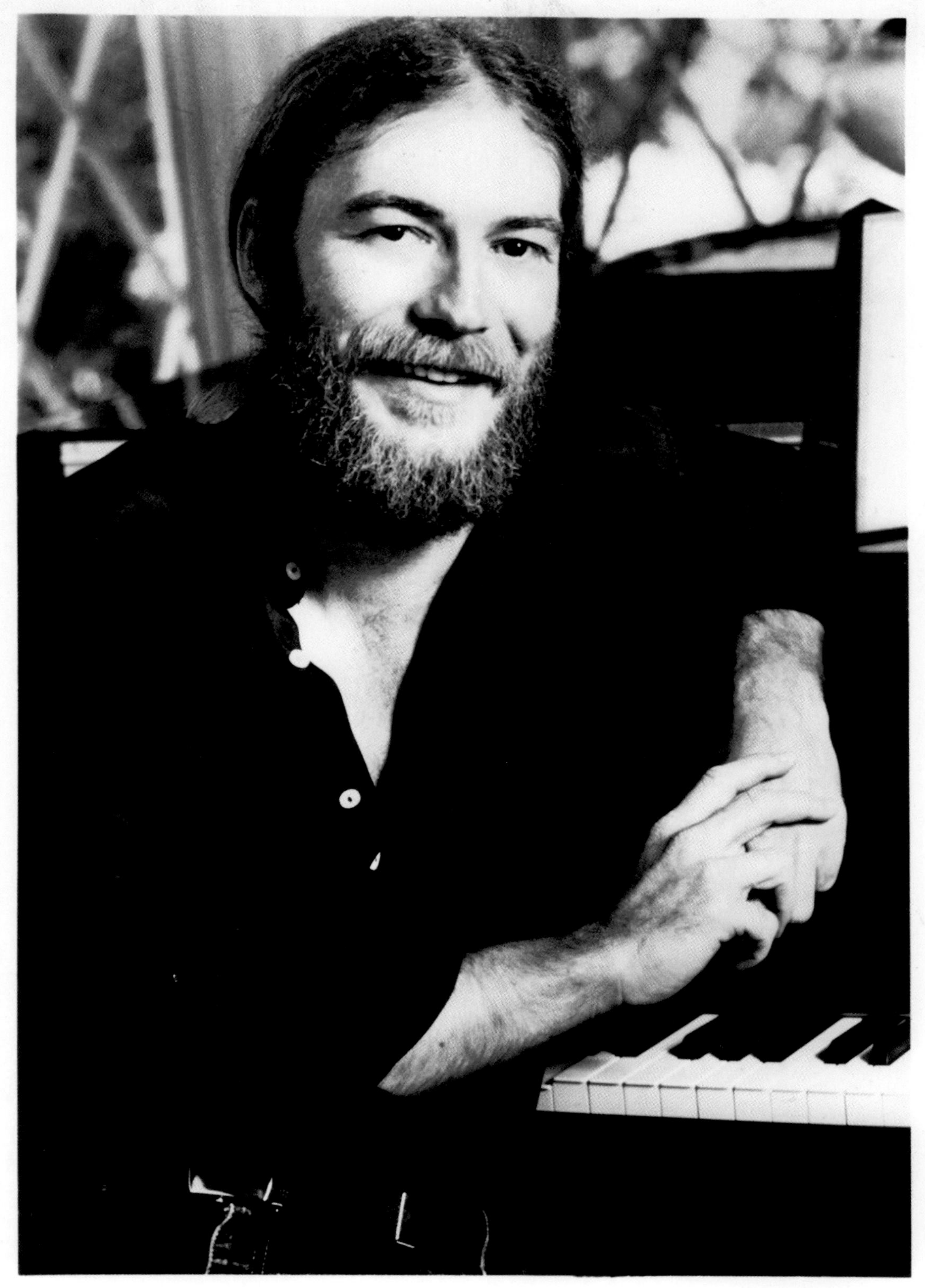

PAUL DAVIS

ARISTA™

PHOTOGLO

20th CENTURY FOX RECORDS
Manufactured and Distributed by RCA Records

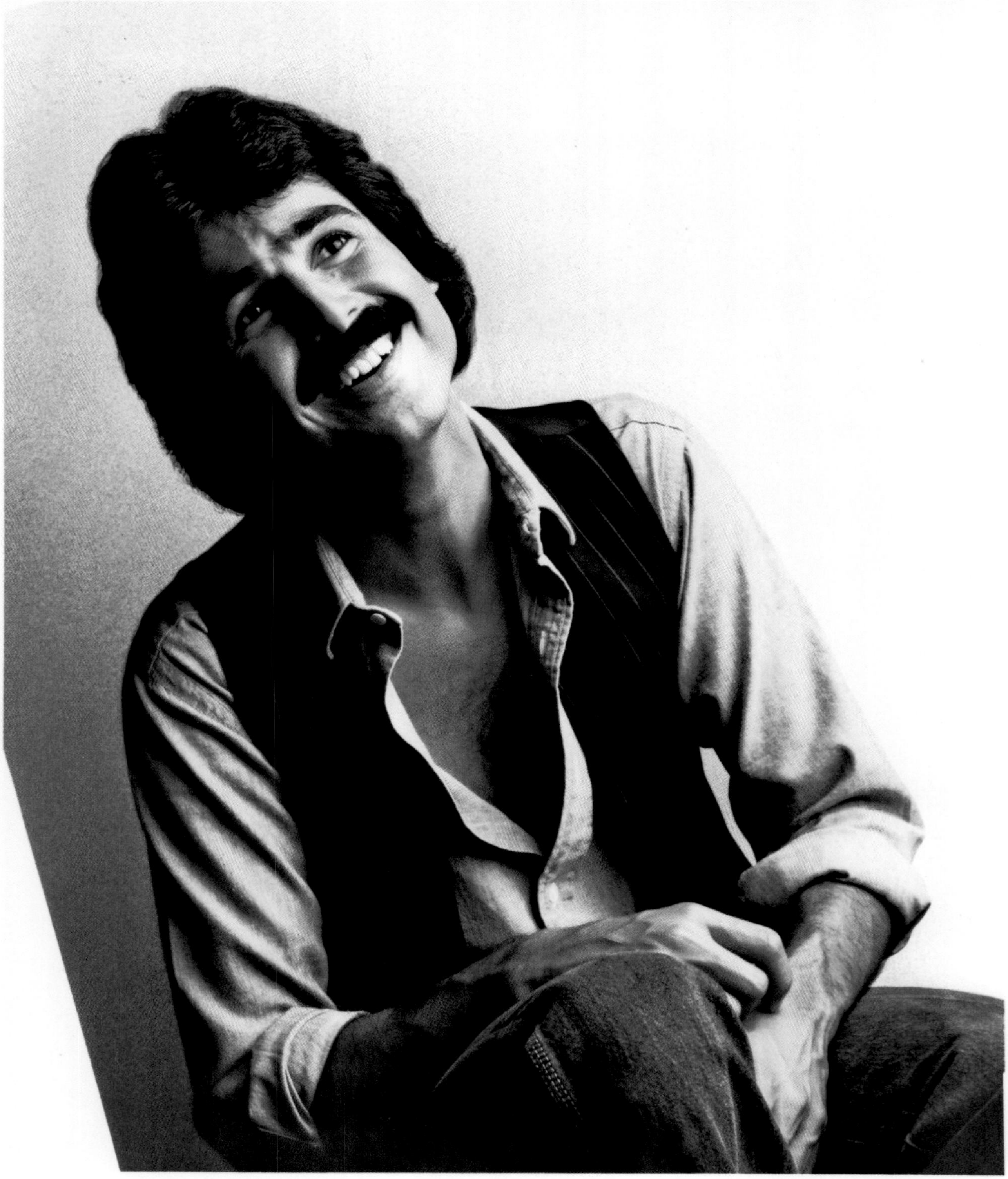

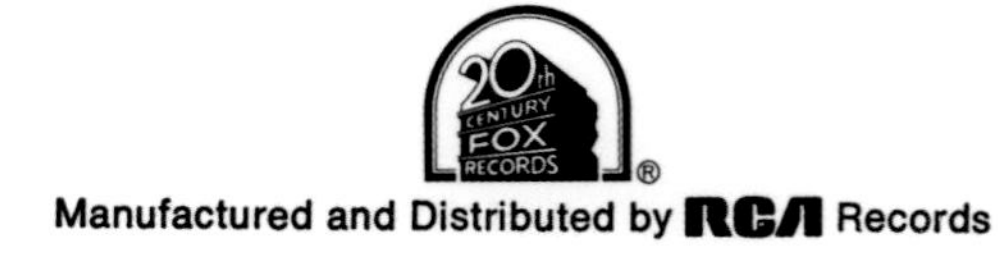

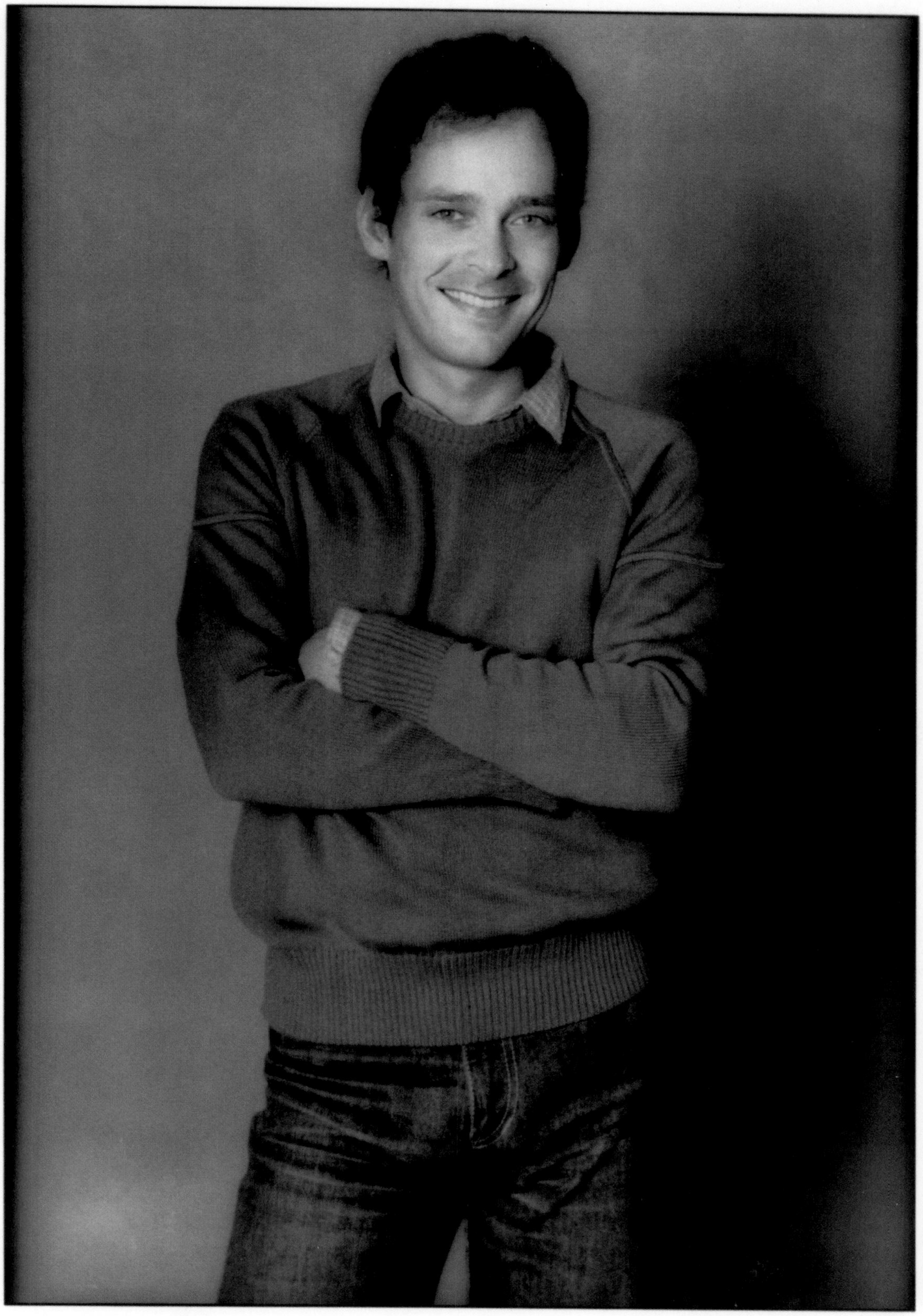

PHOTO CREDIT: JACKI SALLOW/1981

JOHN O'BANION

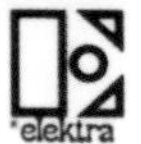

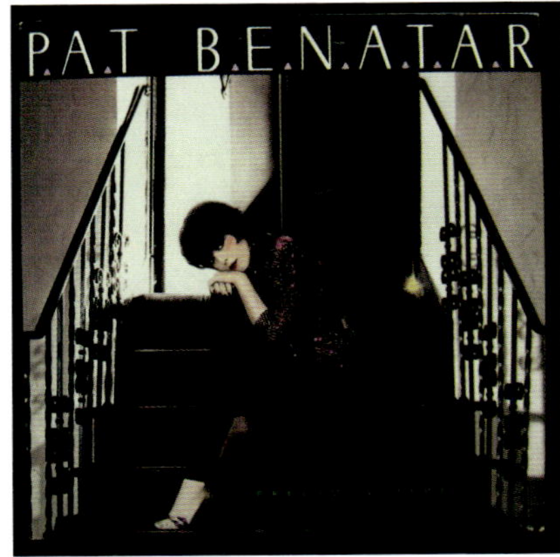

"Fire and Ice," from **Pat Benatar**'s third platinum-selling album, *Precious Time*, earned the artist a second Grammy Award for Best Female Rock Vocal Performance.

Billboard 200: *Precious Time* (No. 1)
Billboard Hot 100: "Fire and Ice" (#17); "Promises in the Dark" (#38)

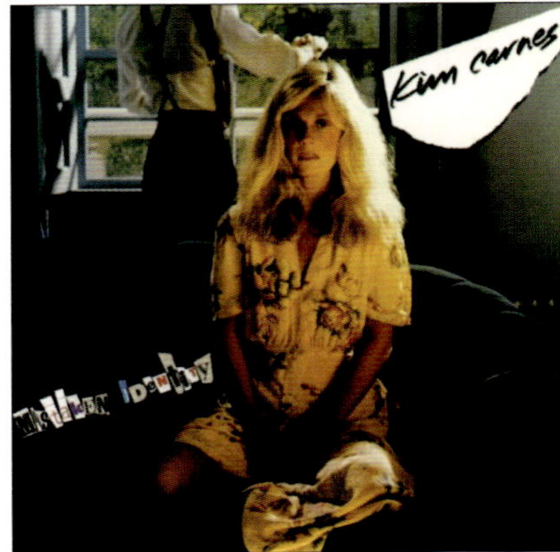

Kim Carnes' raspy voice graced the worldwide smash, "Bette Davis Eyes," which captured Grammys for Song of the Year and Record of the Year.

Billboard 200: *Mistaken Identity* (No. 1)
Billboard Hot 100: "Bette Davis Eyes" (No. 1); "Draw of the Cards" (#28); "Mistaken Identity" (#60)

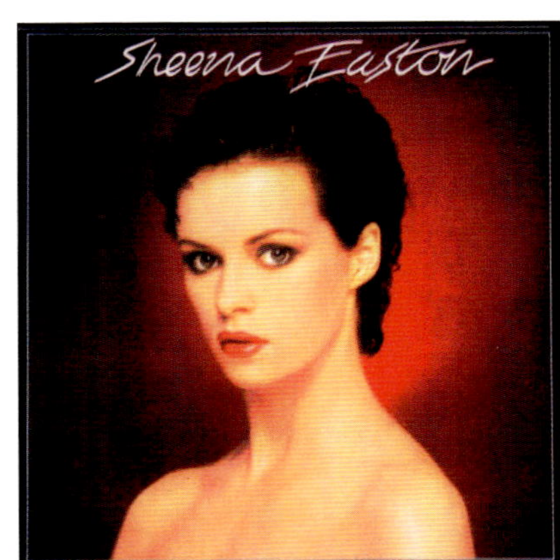

Sheena Easton's first two singles, "Modern Girl" and the No. 1 "Morning Train (Nine to Five)," promptly made her a staple on pop and adult contemporary radio.

Billboard 200: *Sheena Easton* (#24)
Billboard Hot 100: "Morning Train (9 to 5)" (No. 1); "Modern Girl" (#18)

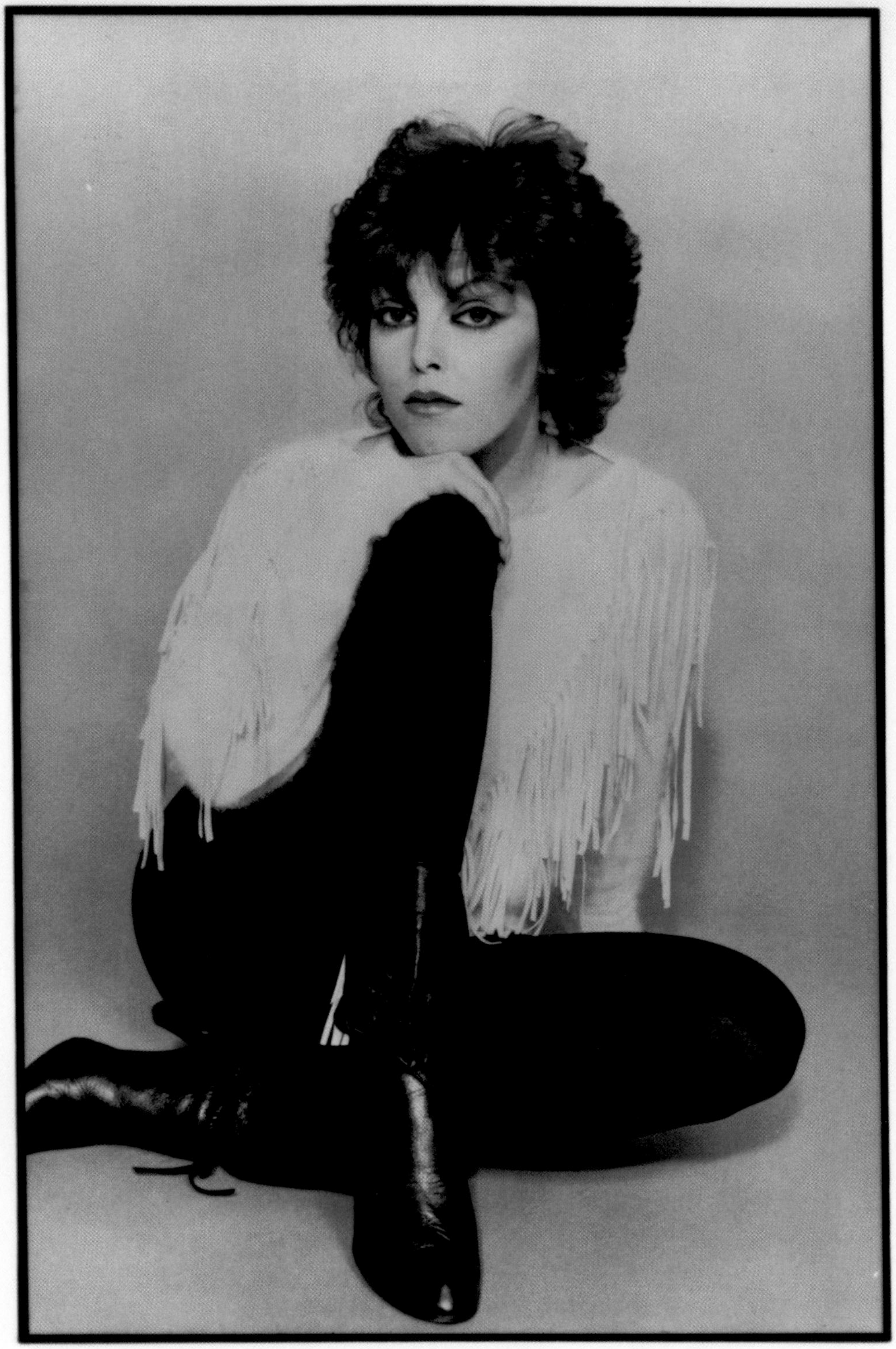

PAT BENATAR

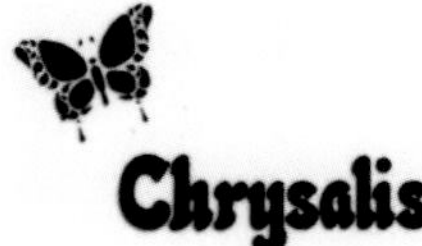

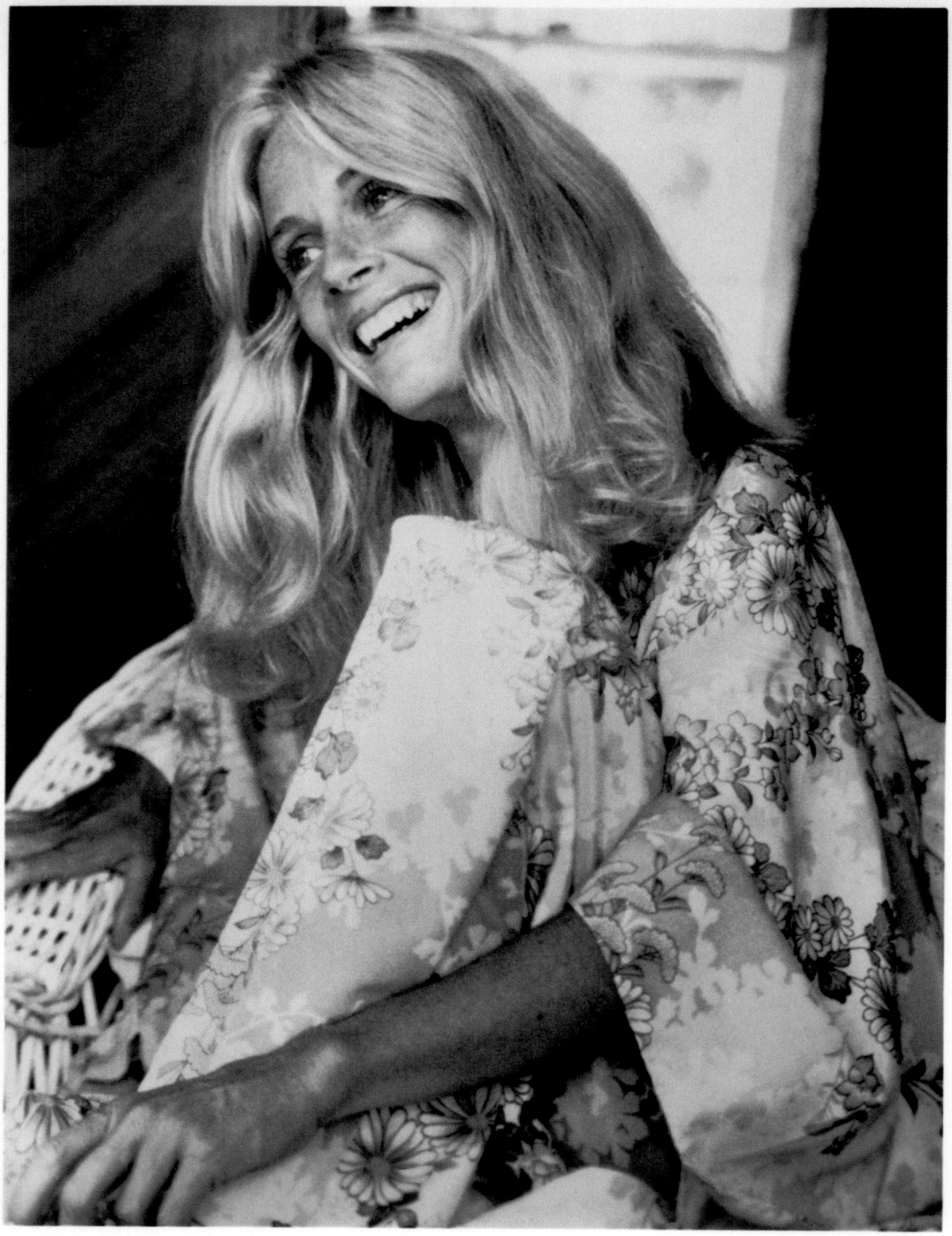

KIM CARNES

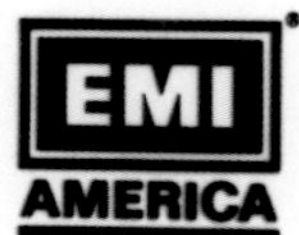

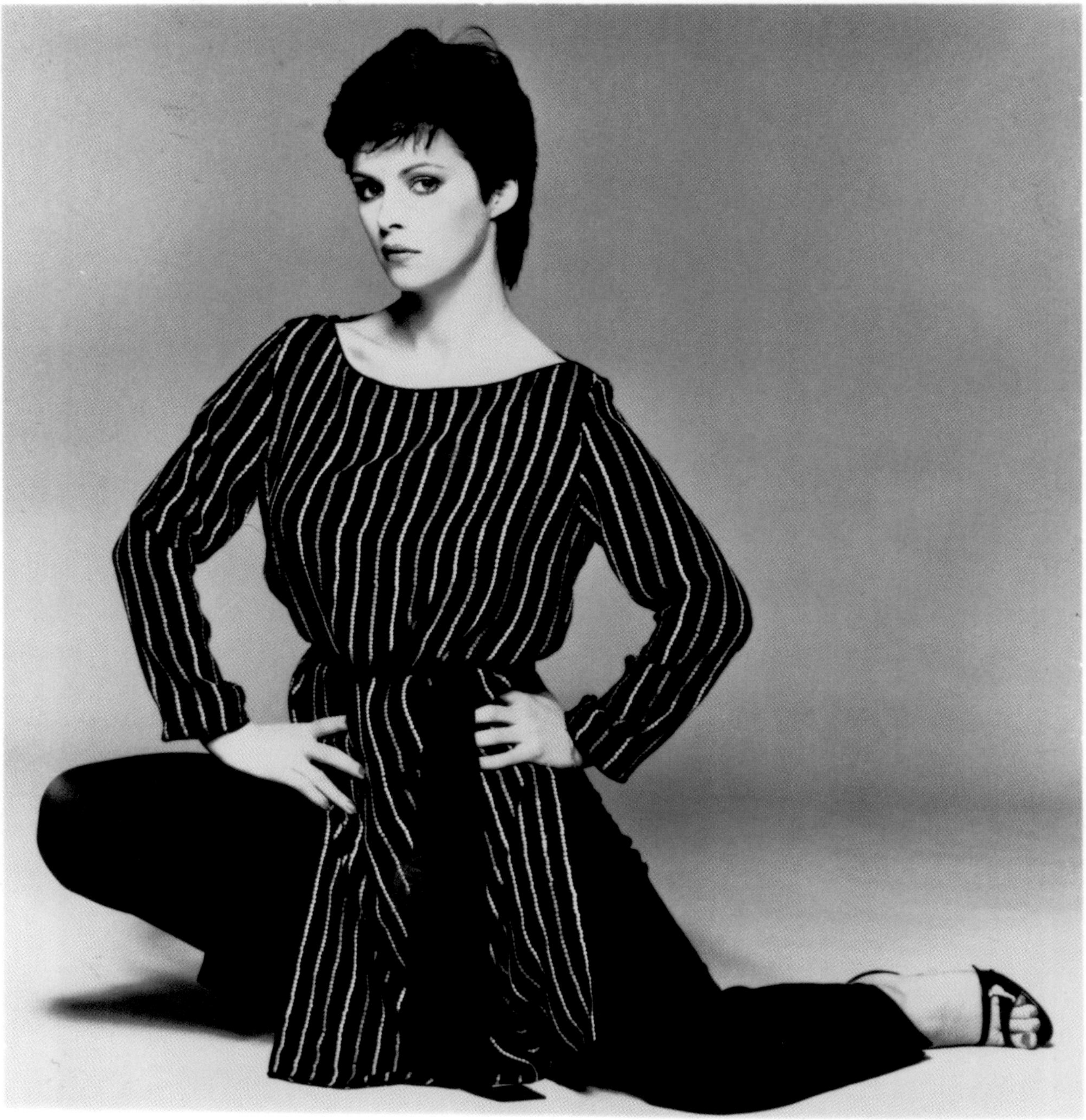

SHEENA EASTON

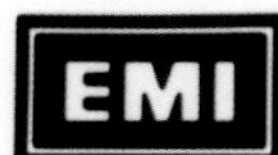

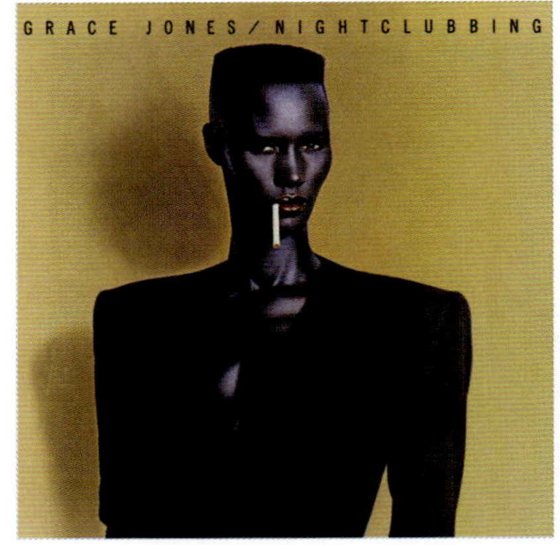

The acclaimed *Nightclubbing* became **Grace Jones**' highest-charting album, and "Pull Up to the Bumper" one of the dance maverick's signature tunes.

Billboard 200: *Nightclubbing* (#32)

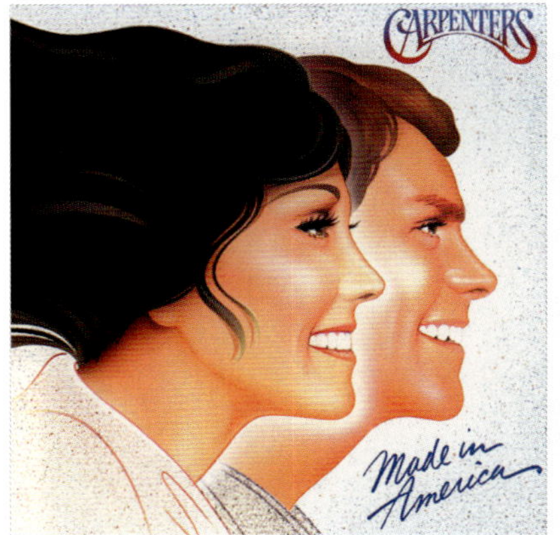

Made in America, the final **Carpenters** album as a duo, produced their 15th No. 1 hit on the adult contemporary charts, "Touch Me When We're Dancing."

Billboard 200: *Made in America* (#52)
Billboard Hot 100: "I Believe You" (#68); "Touch Me When We're Dancing" (#16); "(Want You) Back in My Life Again" (#72); "Those Good Old Dreams" (#63); "Beechwood 4-5789" (#74)

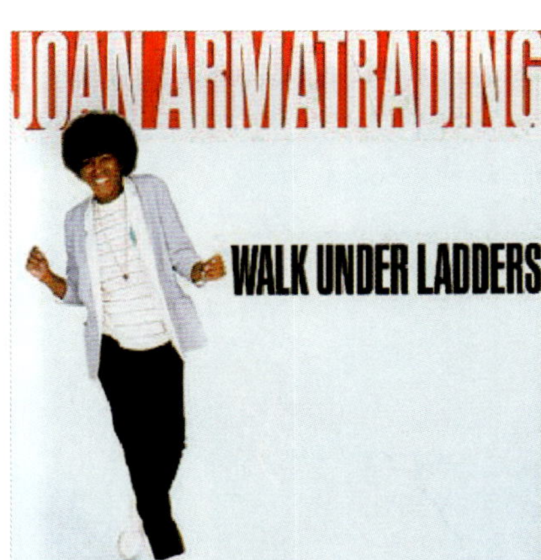

Singer-songwriter **Joan Armatrading**'s devoted fans responded favorably to the new-wave sounds of *Walk Under Ladders*, highlighted by "No Love" and "I'm Lucky."

Billboard 200: *Walk Under Ladders* (#88)

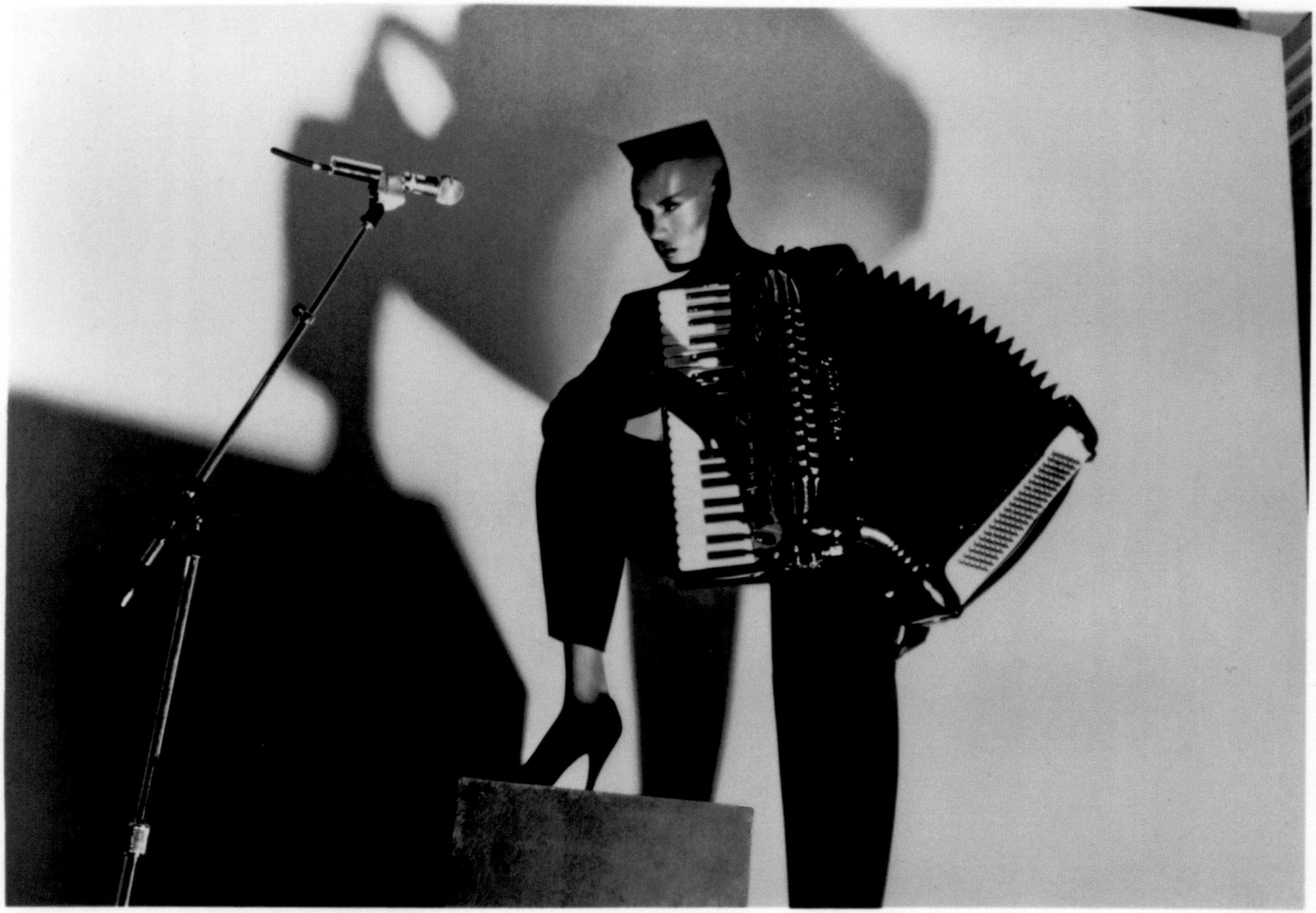

GRACE JONES

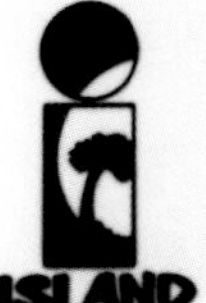

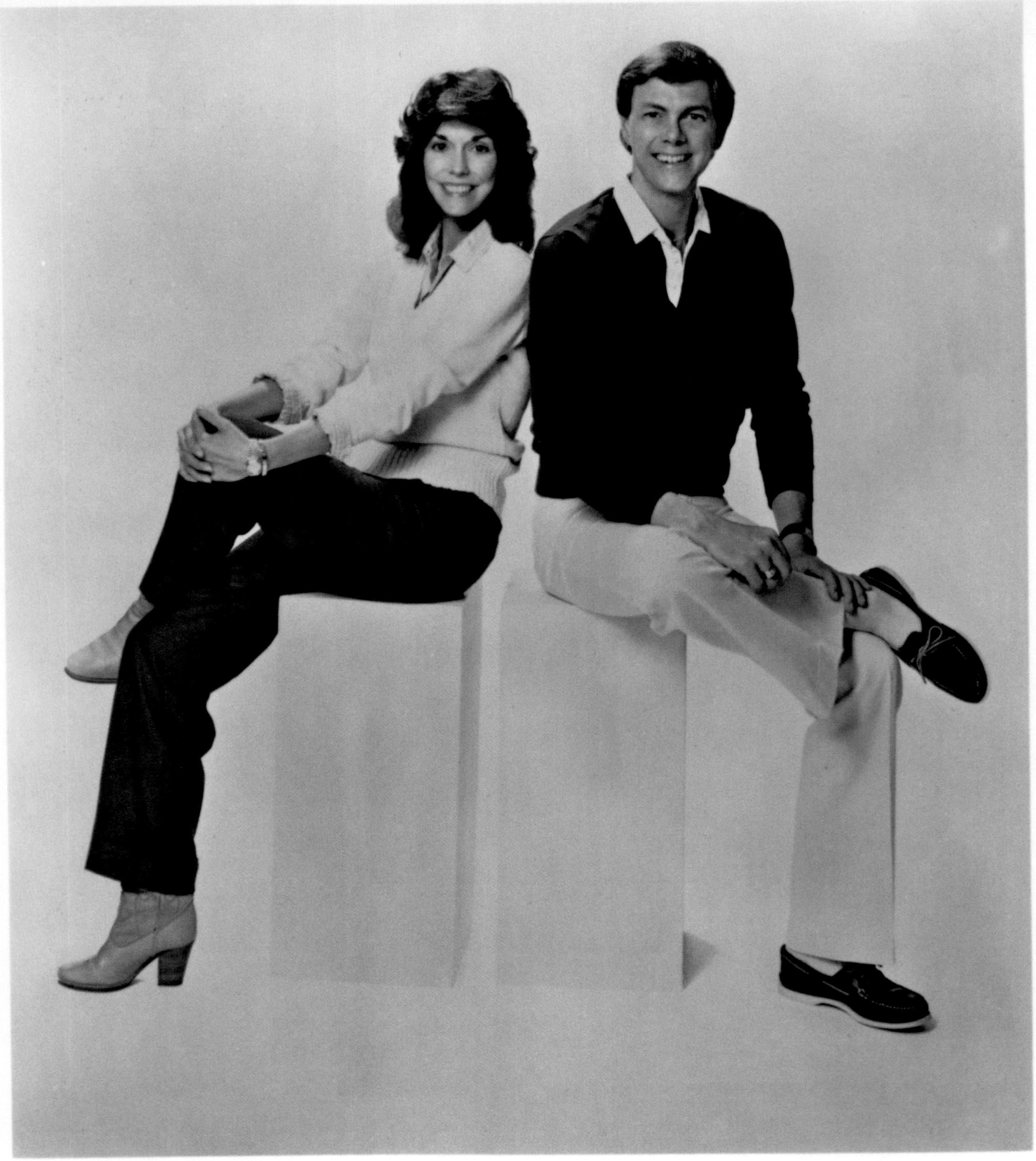

Jerry Weintraub

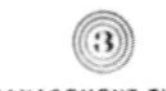

MANAGEMENT THREE
9744 WILSHIRE BOULEVARD
BEVERLY HILLS, CALIF. 90212

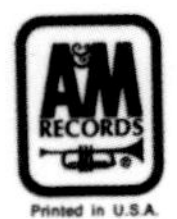

Printed in U.S.A.

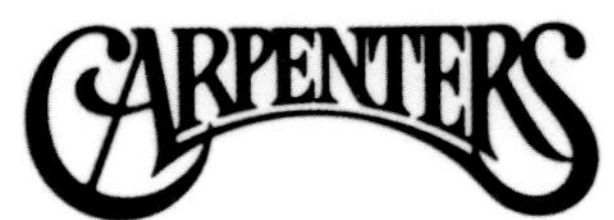

ROGERS & COWAN INC.

Public Relations
9665 Wilshire Blvd.
Beverly Hills, California 90212
(213) 275-4581

NEW YORK
BEVERLY HILLS
CHICAGO
NASHVILLE
LONDON
ROME
MUNICH

WILLIAM MORRIS AGENCY

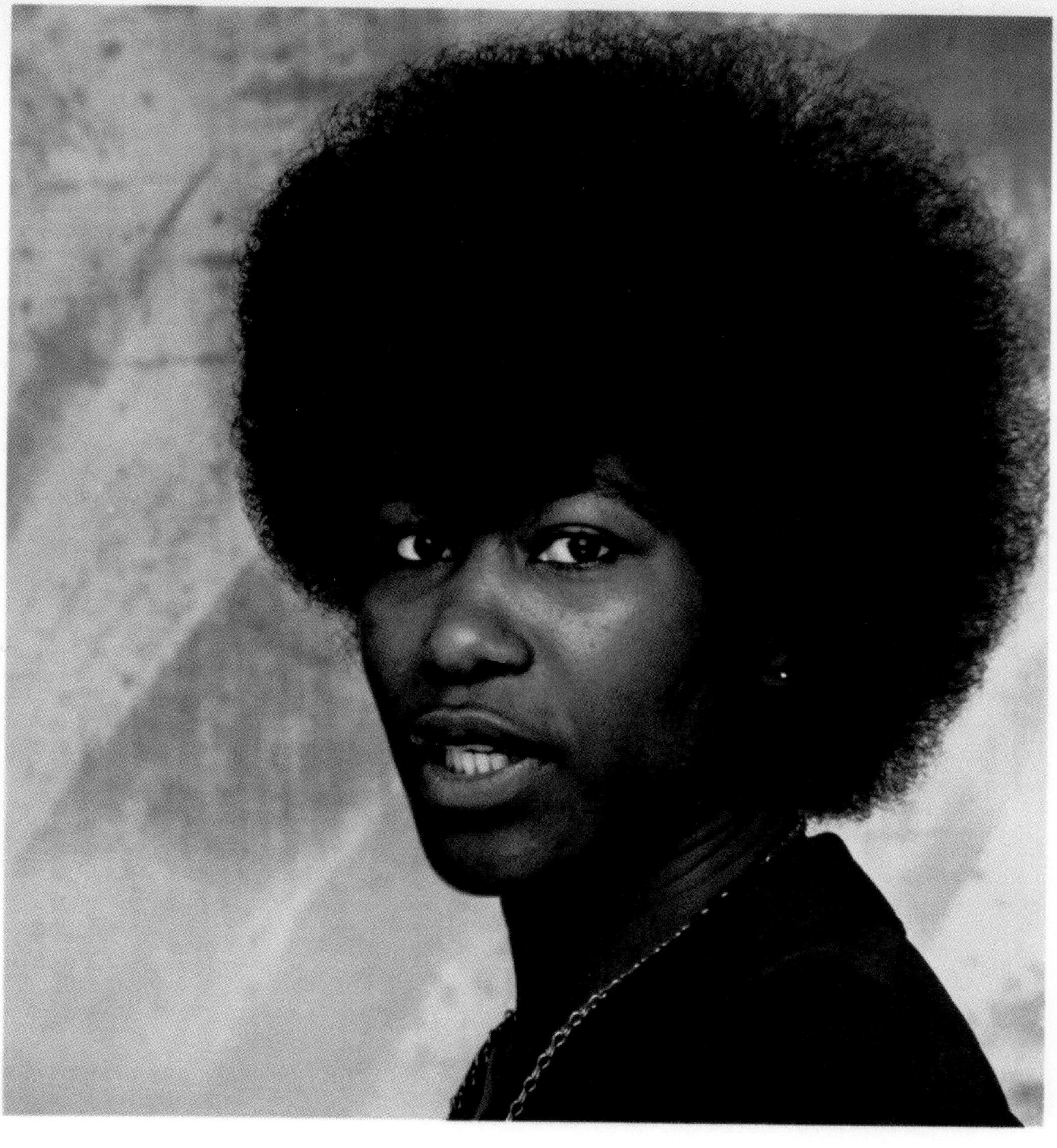

JOAN ARMATRADING

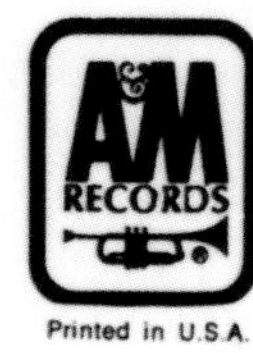

Printed in U.S.A.

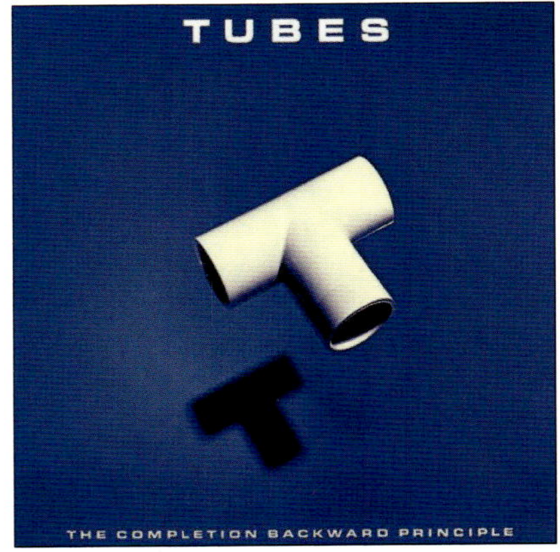

Tubes' *The Completion Backward Principle* featured the rock radio staple, "Talk To Ya Later," and the band's first Top 40 hit in "Don't Want to Wait Anymore."

Billboard 200: The *Completion Backward Principle* (#36)
Billboard Hot 100: "Don't Want to Wait Anymore" (#35)

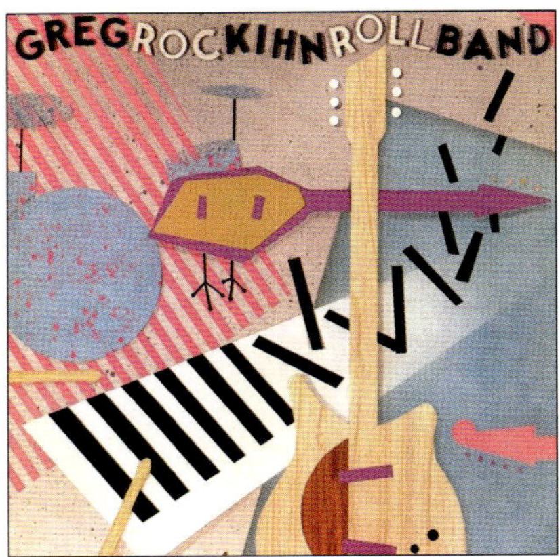

After years of performing, Greg Kihn Band finally broke through with "The Breakup Song (They Don't Write 'Em)," a pop-rock lament from the *Rockihnroll* album.

Billboard 200: *Rockihnroll* (#32)
Billboard Hot 100: "The Breakup Song (They Don't Write 'Em)" (#15)

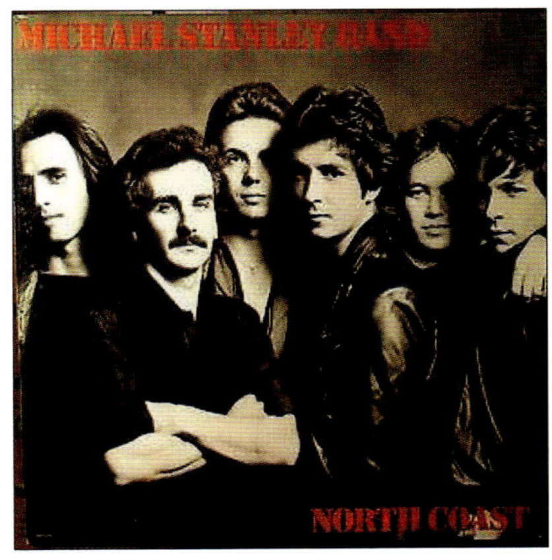

A regional phenomenon, the Cleveland-based Michael Stanley Band reached national popularity with its brand of heartland rock delivered on *North Coast*.

Billboard 200: *North Coast* (#79)
Billboard Hot 100: "Falling in Love Again" (#64)

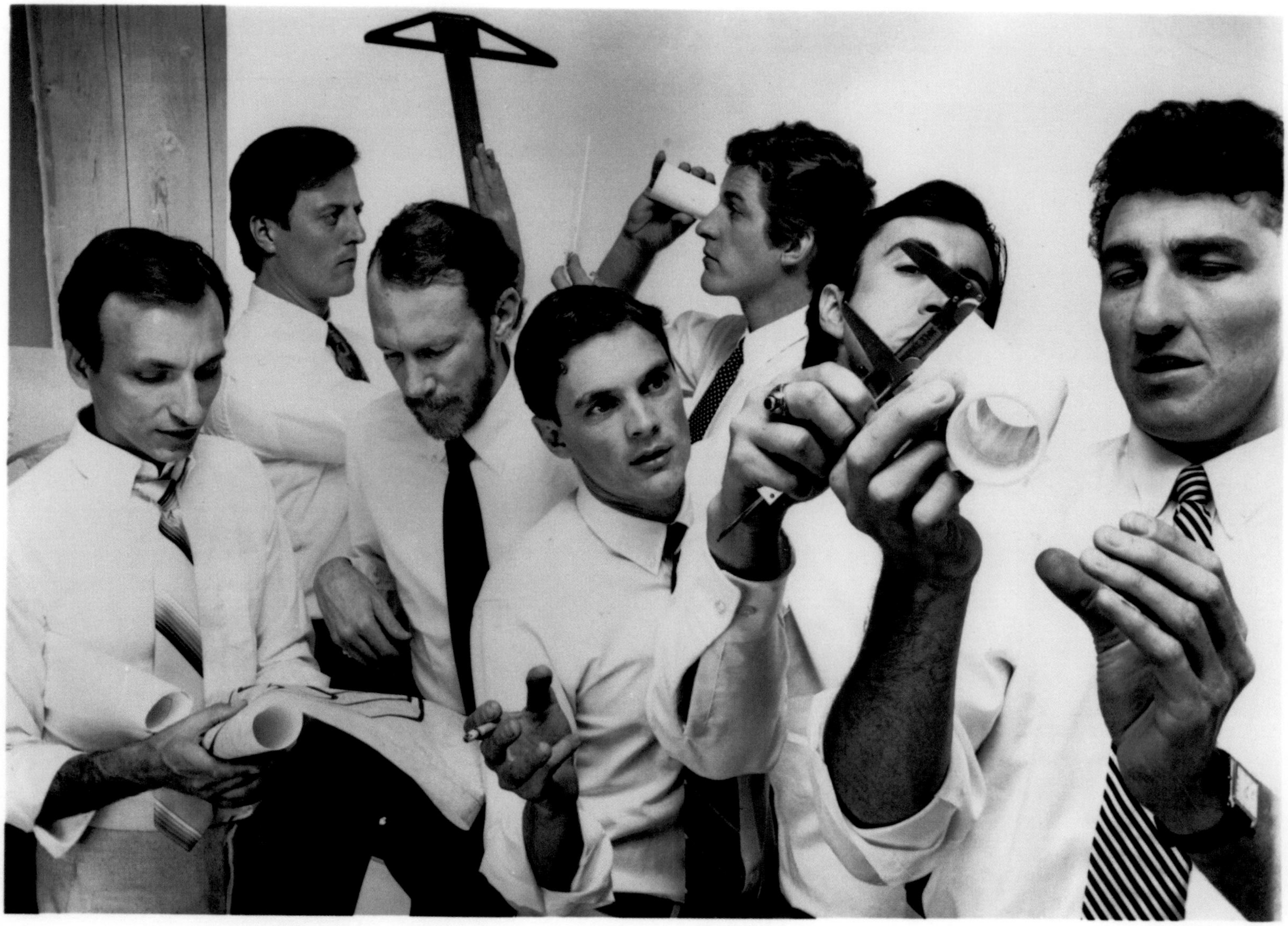

Photo: EXLEY / 1981

TUBES

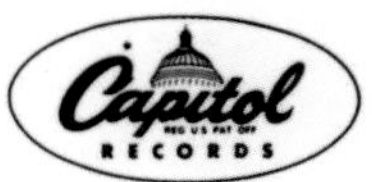

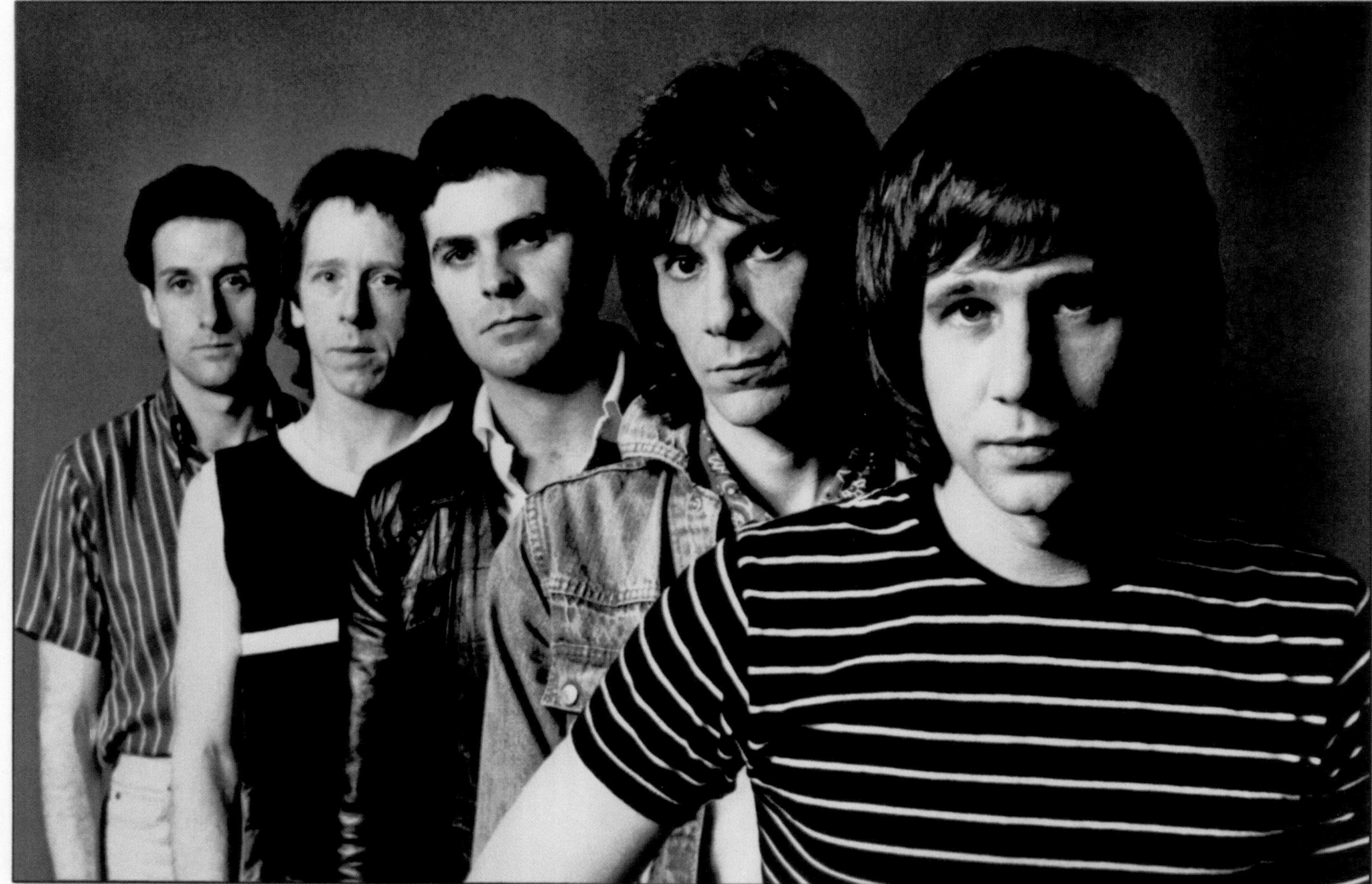
RICHARD MCCAFFREE/1981

LARRY LYNCH DAVE CARPENDER STEVE WRIGHT GARY PHILLIPS GREG KIHN

GREG KIHN BAND

Beserkley "Home of the Hits"

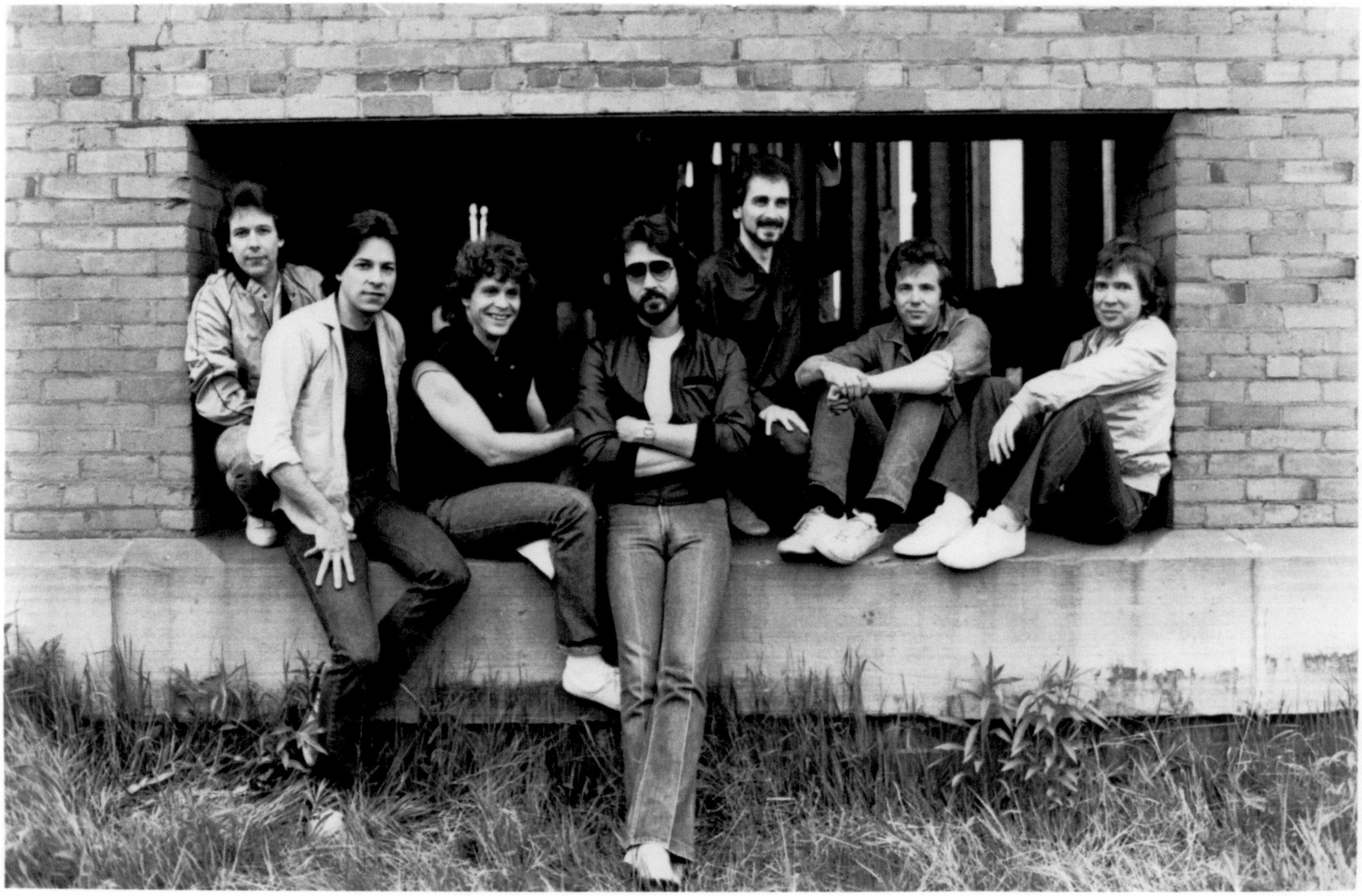

MICHAEL STANLEY BAND

DIRECTION: BELKIN/MADURI MANAGEMENT
28001 CHAGRIN BLVD., CLEVE., OH 44122
(216) 464-5990

MONTEREY PENINSULA ARTISTS
P.O. BOX 7308
CARMEL, CALIFORNIA 93921 (408) 624-4889

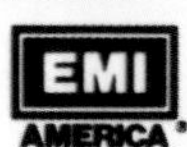

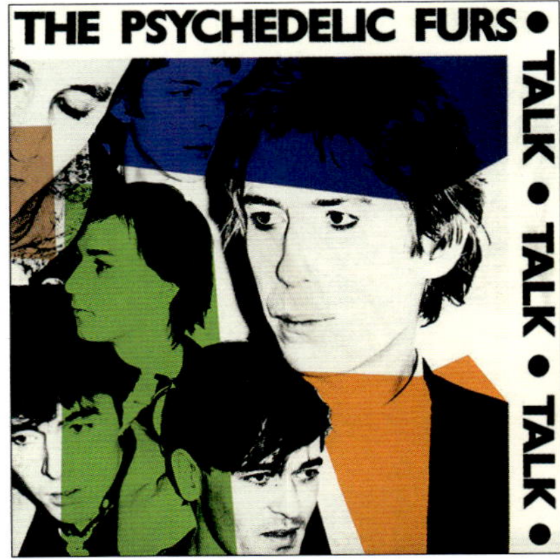

The Psychedelic Furs found success in the US with their second album, *Talk Talk Talk*, with the British alternative rockers producing the original version of "Pretty in Pink."

Billboard 200: *Talk Talk Talk* (#89)

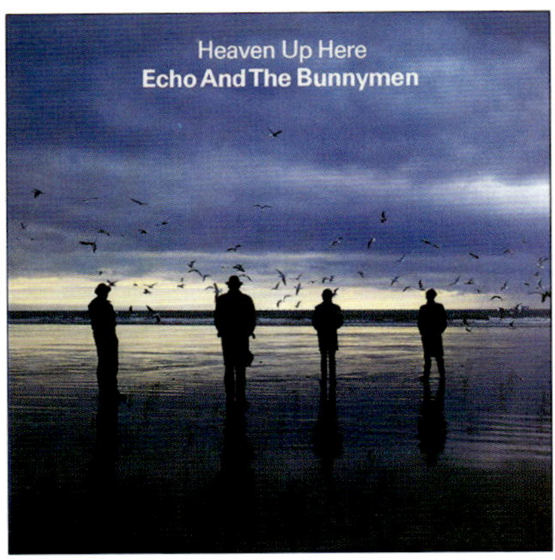

The atmospheric post-punk of *Heaven Up Here*, **Echo & the Bunnymen**'s first album to crack the US charts, elevated the British alternative group to cult status.

Billboard 200: *Heaven Up Here* (#184)

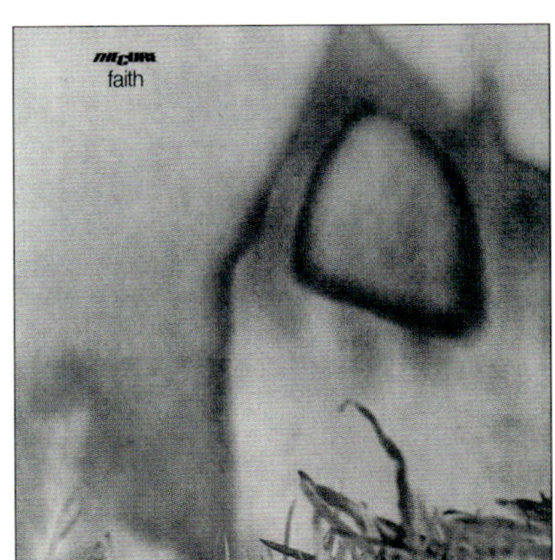

The Cure acquired a reputation as the somber stewards of the nascent gothic rock style for the dark and tormented dirges collected on the *Faith* album.

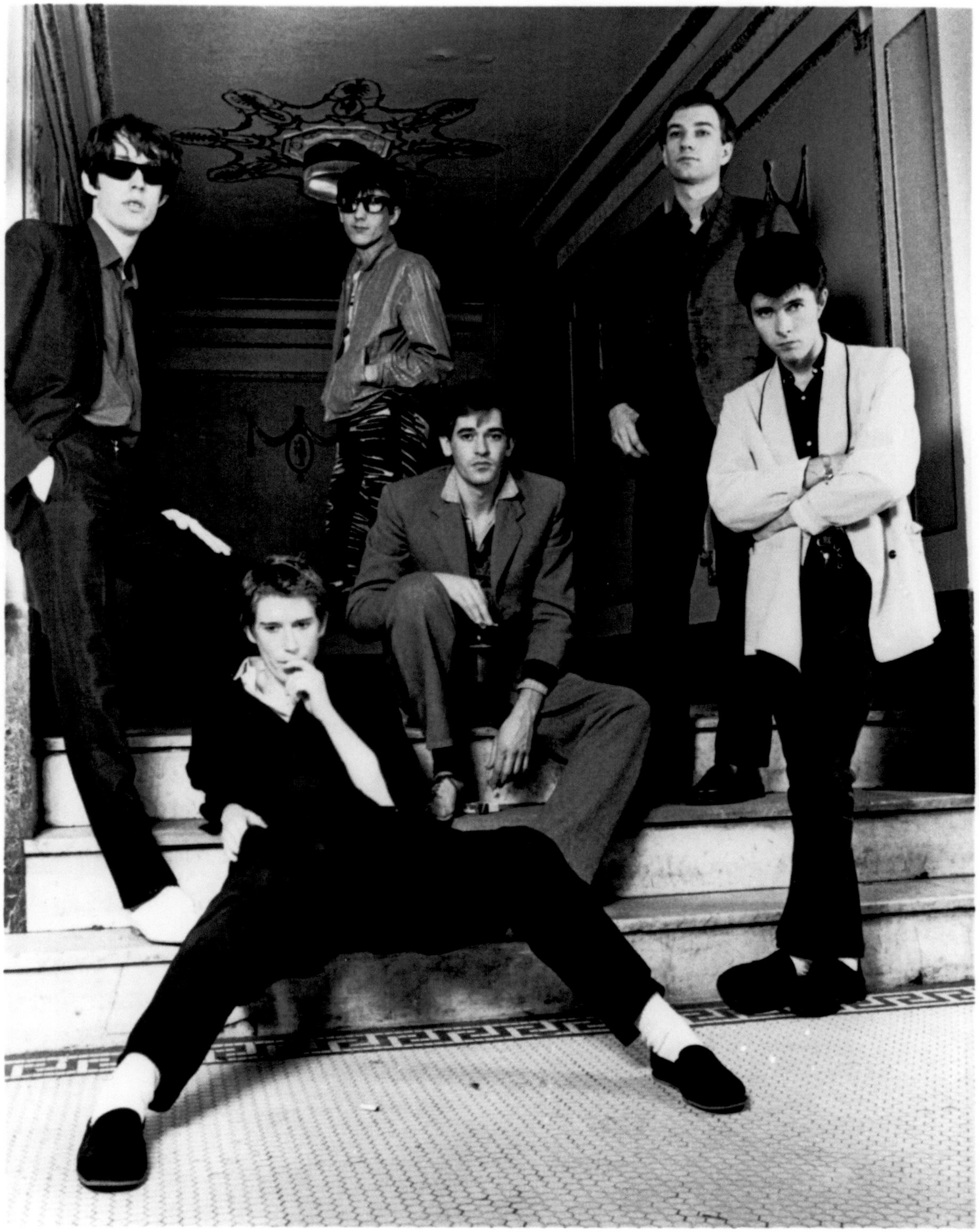

Photograph: Ebet Roberts

PSYCHEDELIC FURS

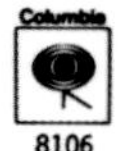

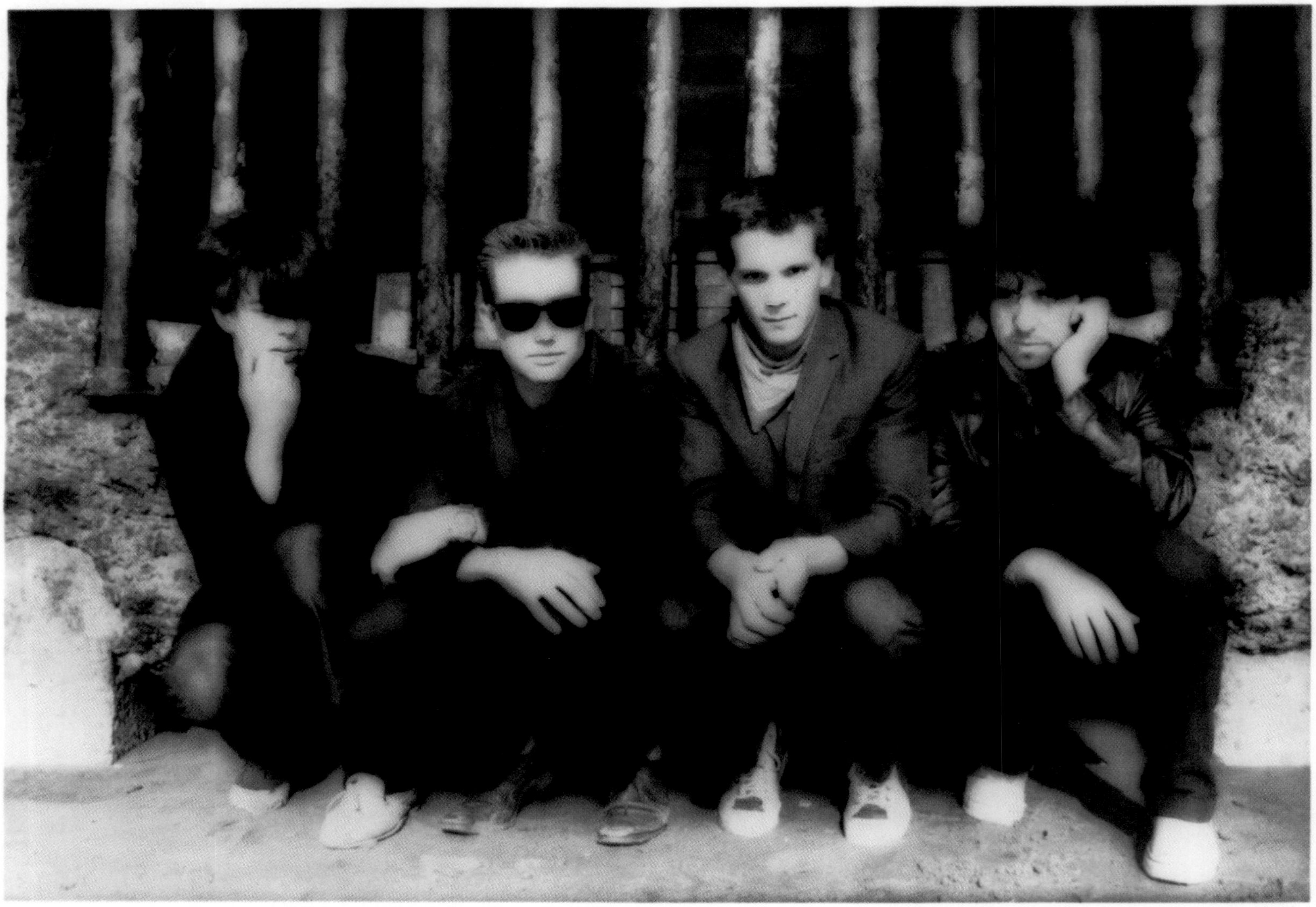

JUNE 1981

ECHO AND THE BUNNYMEN

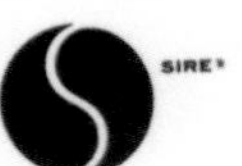

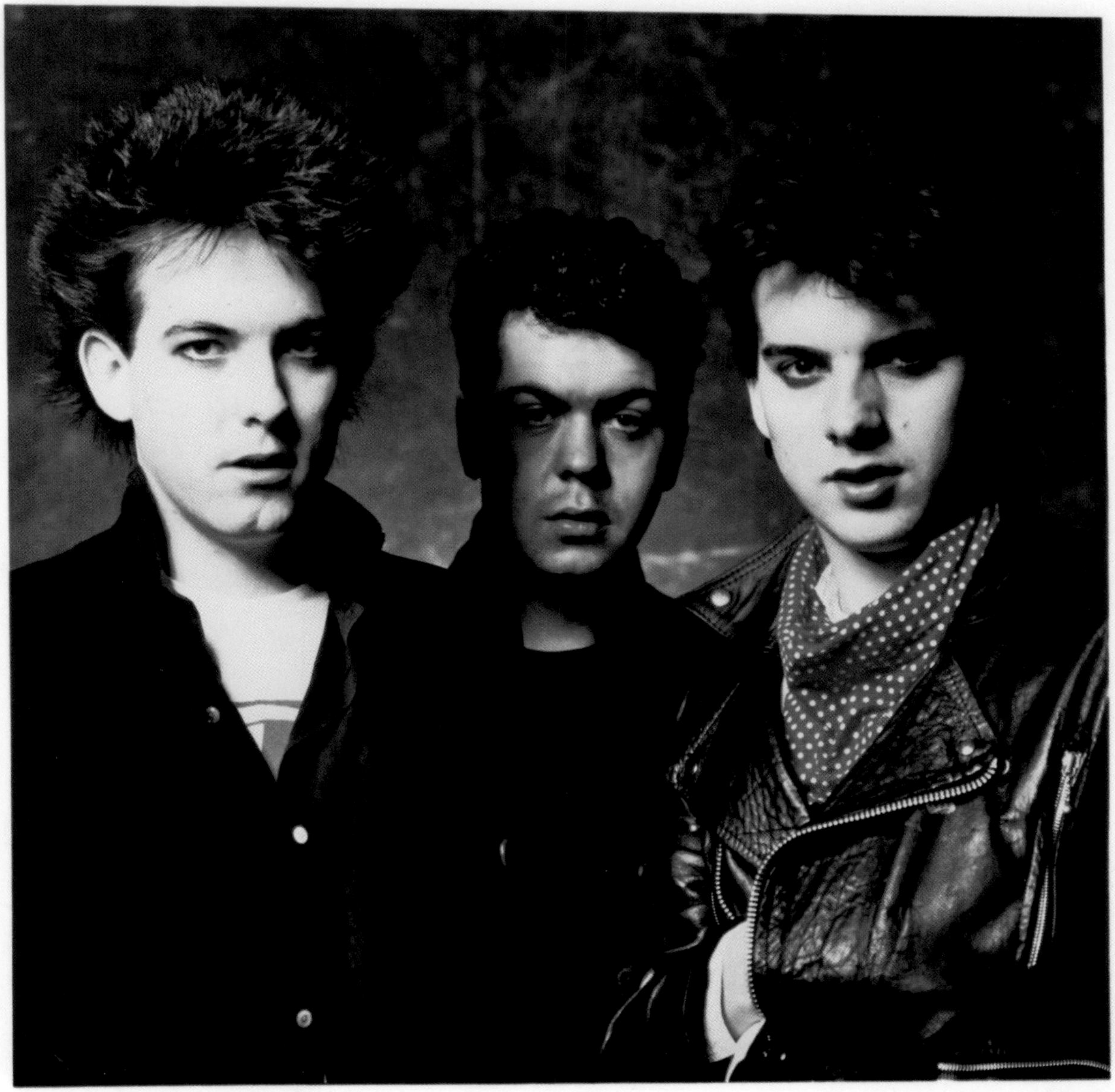

THE CURE

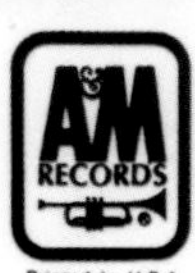

Printed in U.S.A.

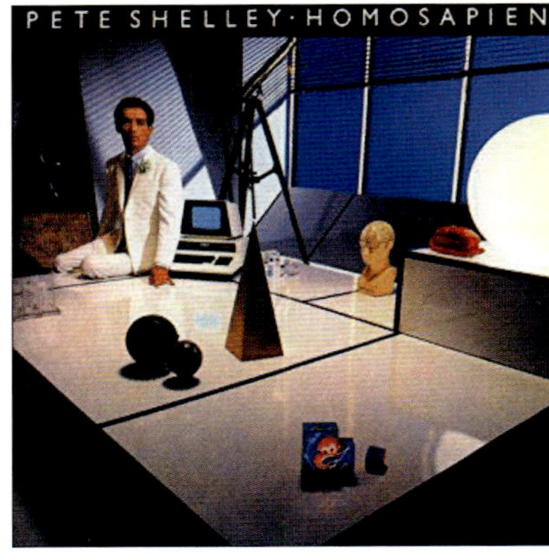

The punk band Buzzcocks broke up, and frontman **Pete Shelley** began a solo career, adopting an electronic sensibility on the new-wave hit, "Homosapien."

Billboard 200: *Homosapien* (#121)

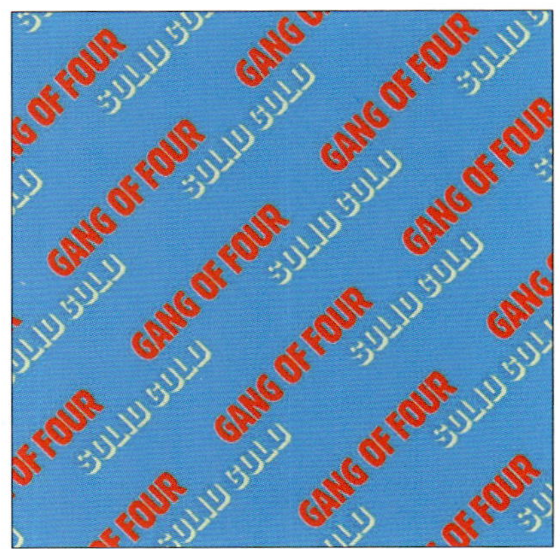

Gang of Four's politically charged *Solid Gold* became the British post-punk band's first US-charting album, and "What We All Want" received heavy dance-club play.

Billboard 200: *Solid Gold* (#190)

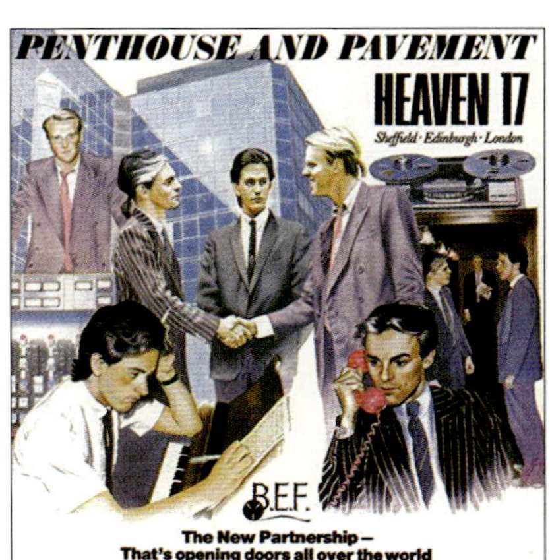

Banned by the BBC for its left-wing extremism, British electro-pop band **Heaven 17**'s "(We Don't Need This) Fascist Groove Thang" became a minor US dance hit.

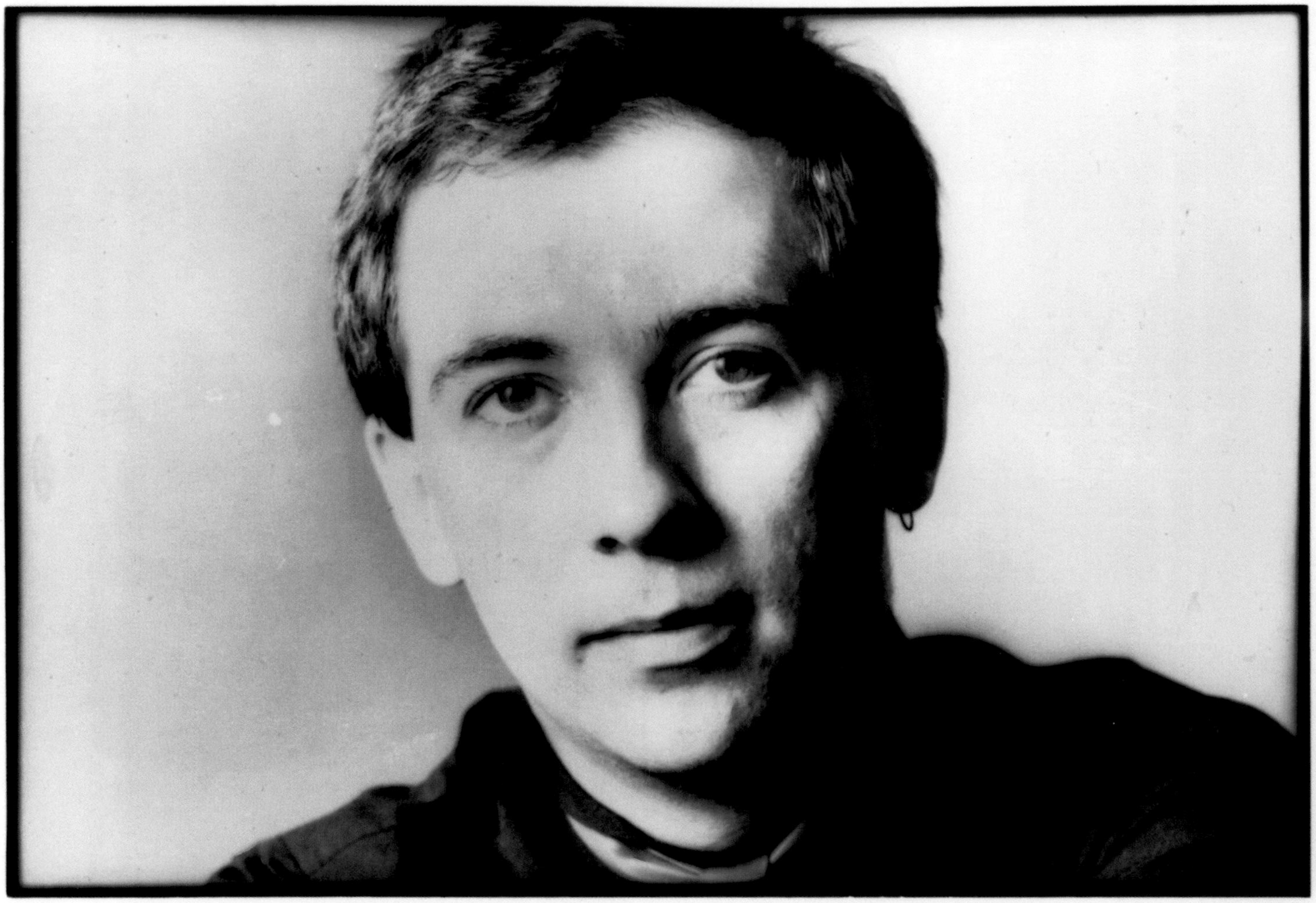

PETE SHELLEY

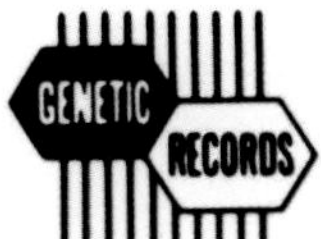

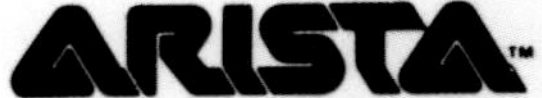

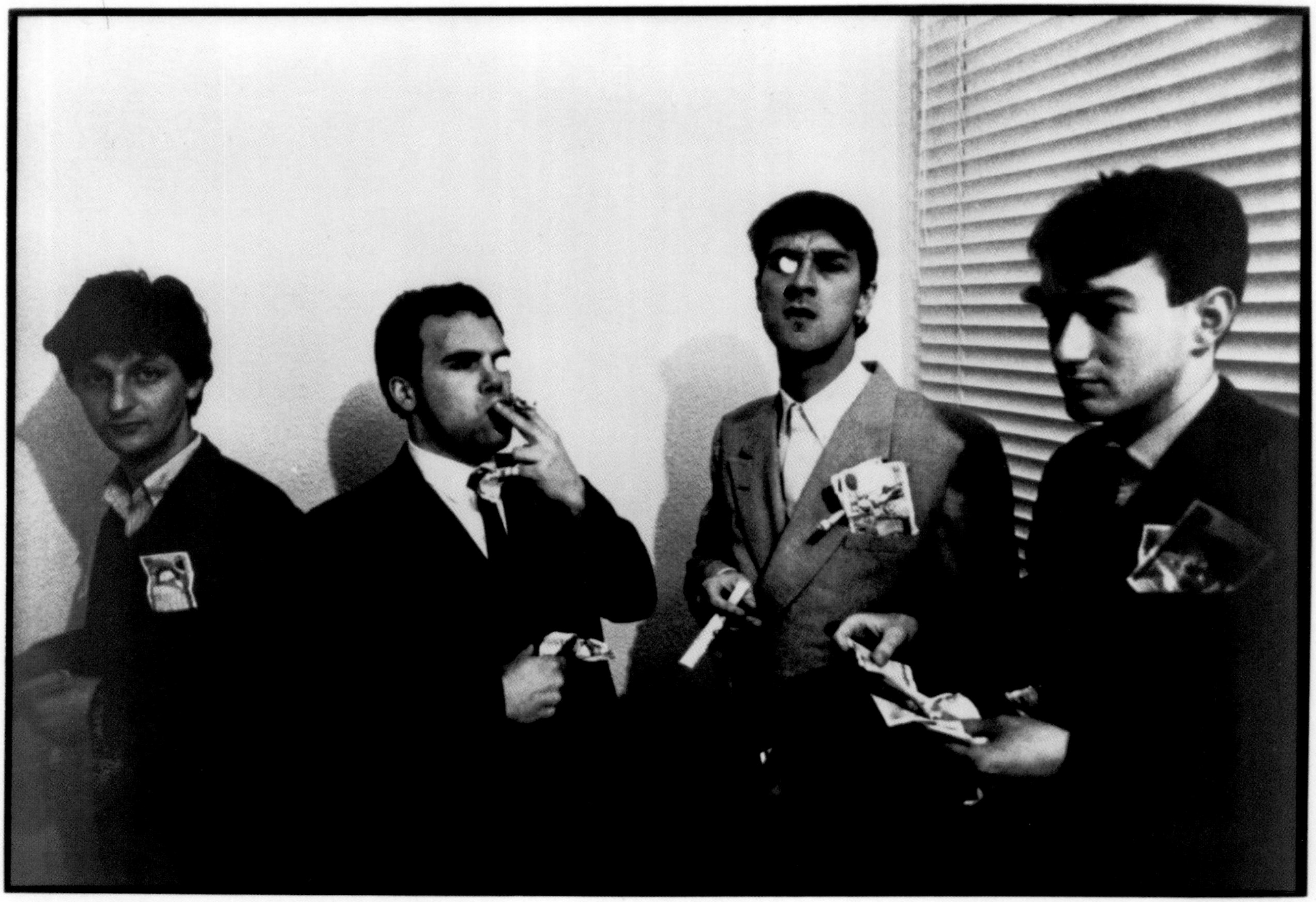

GANG OF FOUR

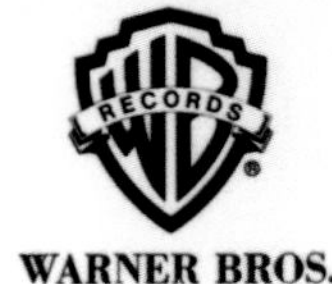

WARNER BROS.

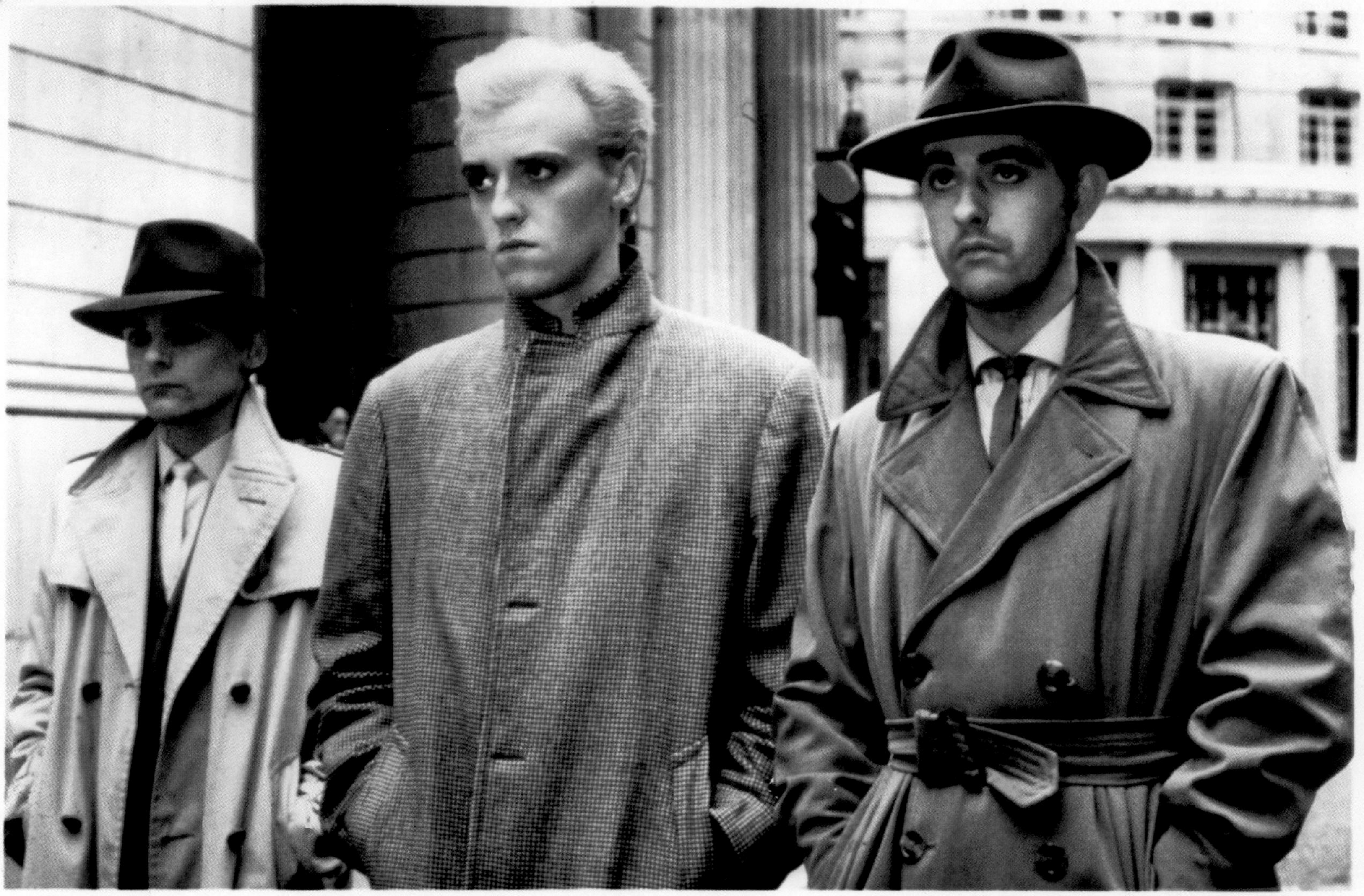

Direction:

Bill Gerber
LOOKOUT MANAGEMENT
9120 Sunset Blvd
Los Angeles CA 90069

(213) 278-0881

HEAVEN 17

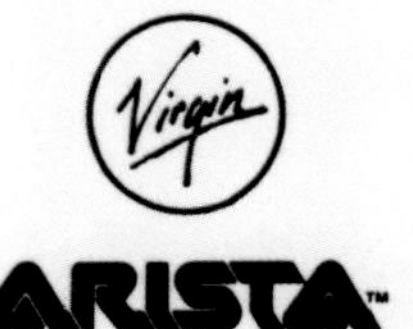

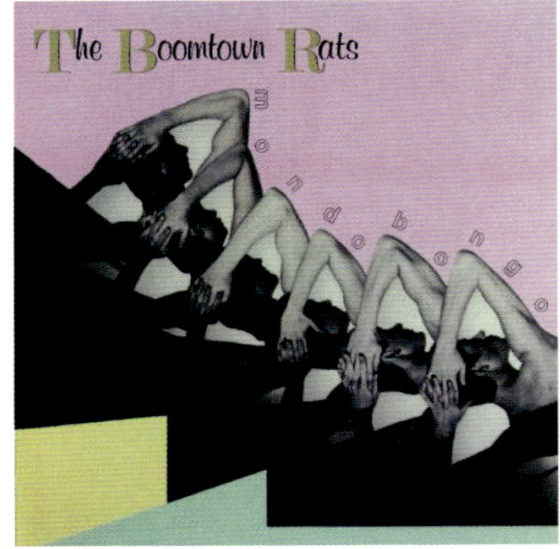

The Boomtown Rats' *Mondo Bongo* included its final UK Top 10 hit, "Banana Republic," a reproach of the band's Irish homeland, which had banned its performances.

Billboard 200: *Mondo Bongo* (#116)

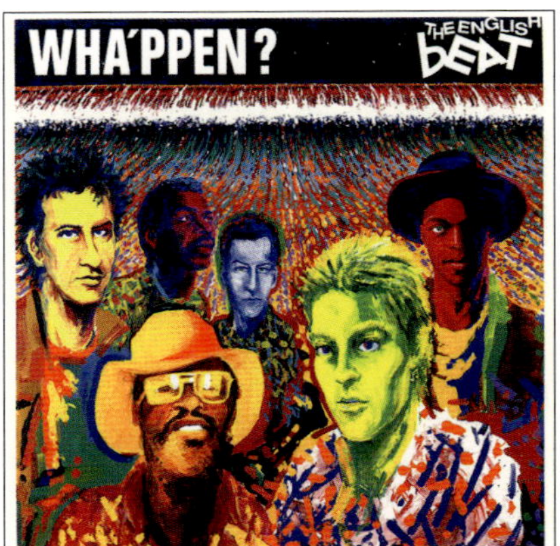

The English Beat won a larger US audience with *Wha'ppen?*, as the racially integrated ska revivalists incorporated more diversified stylings and sophisticated sounds.

Billboard 200: *Wha'ppen?* (#126)

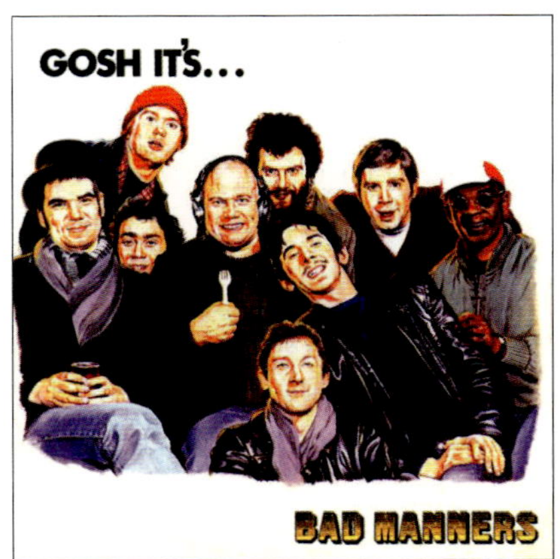

Led by outlandish frontman Buster Bloodvessel, ska revival band Bad Manners scored its biggest UK hit with a rowdy rendition of the Parisian music-hall classic, "Can Can."

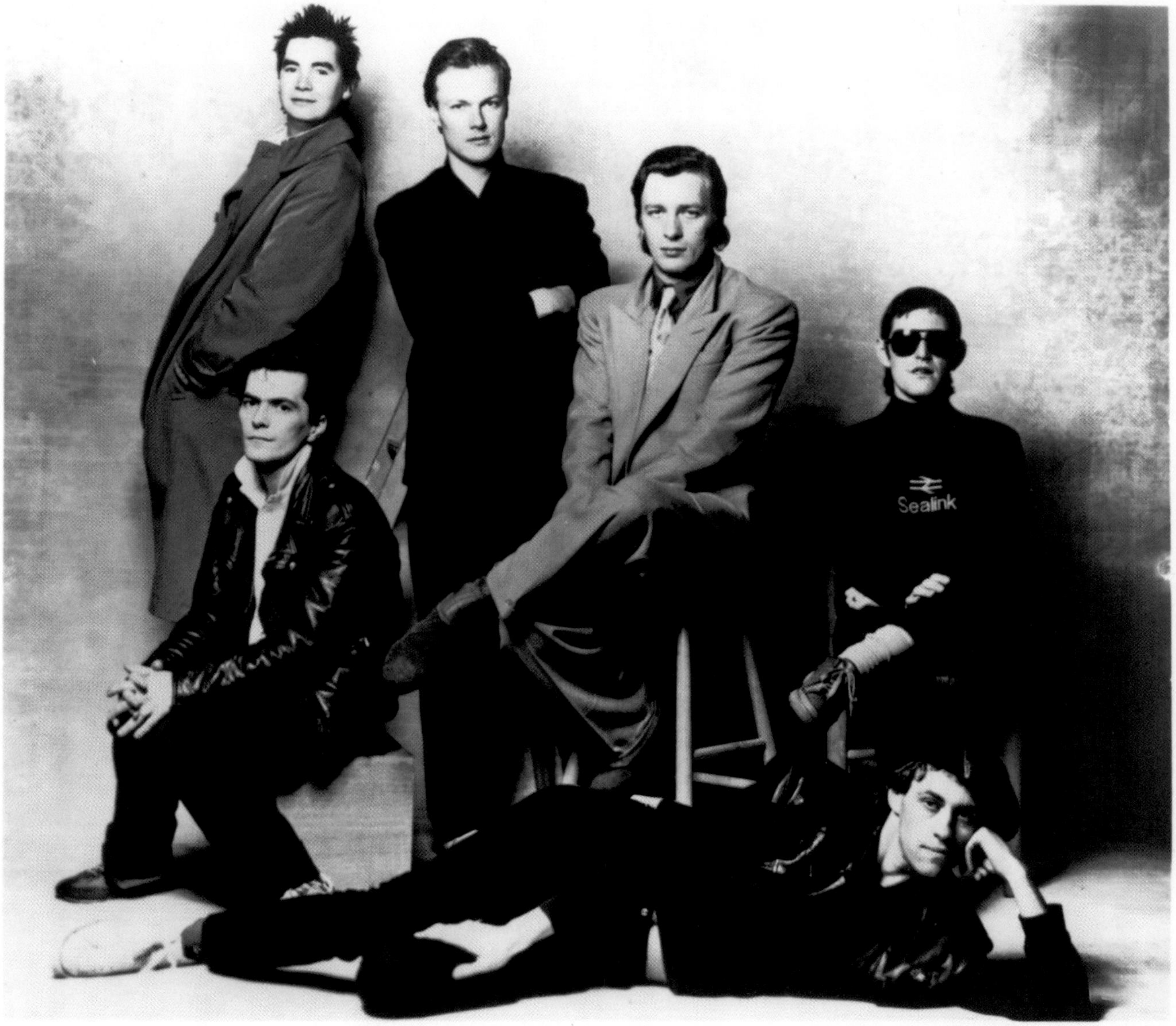

Boomtown Rats

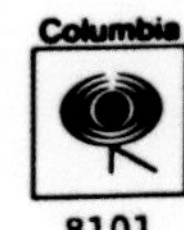

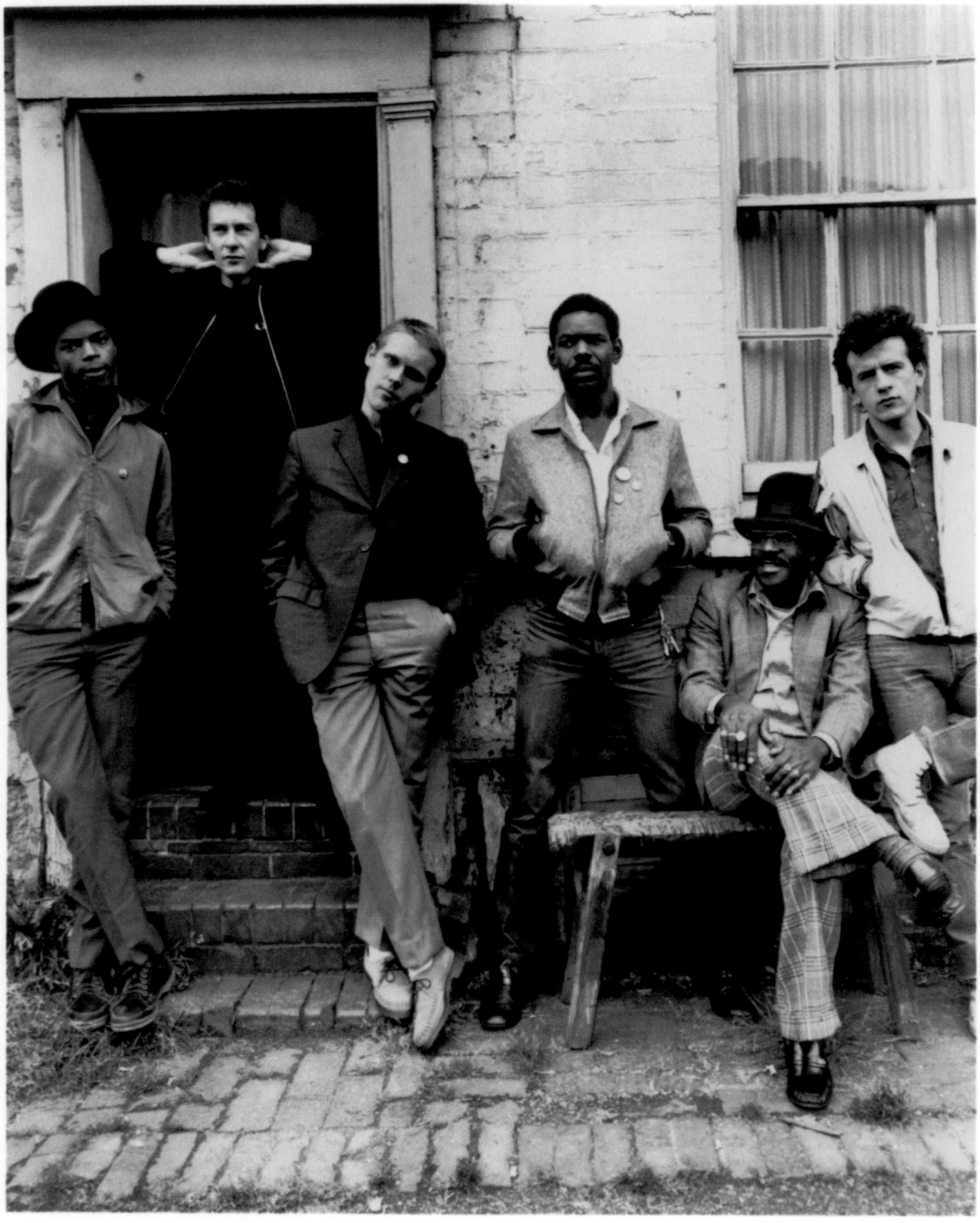

THE ENGLISH BEAT

MAY 1981

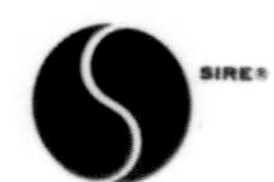

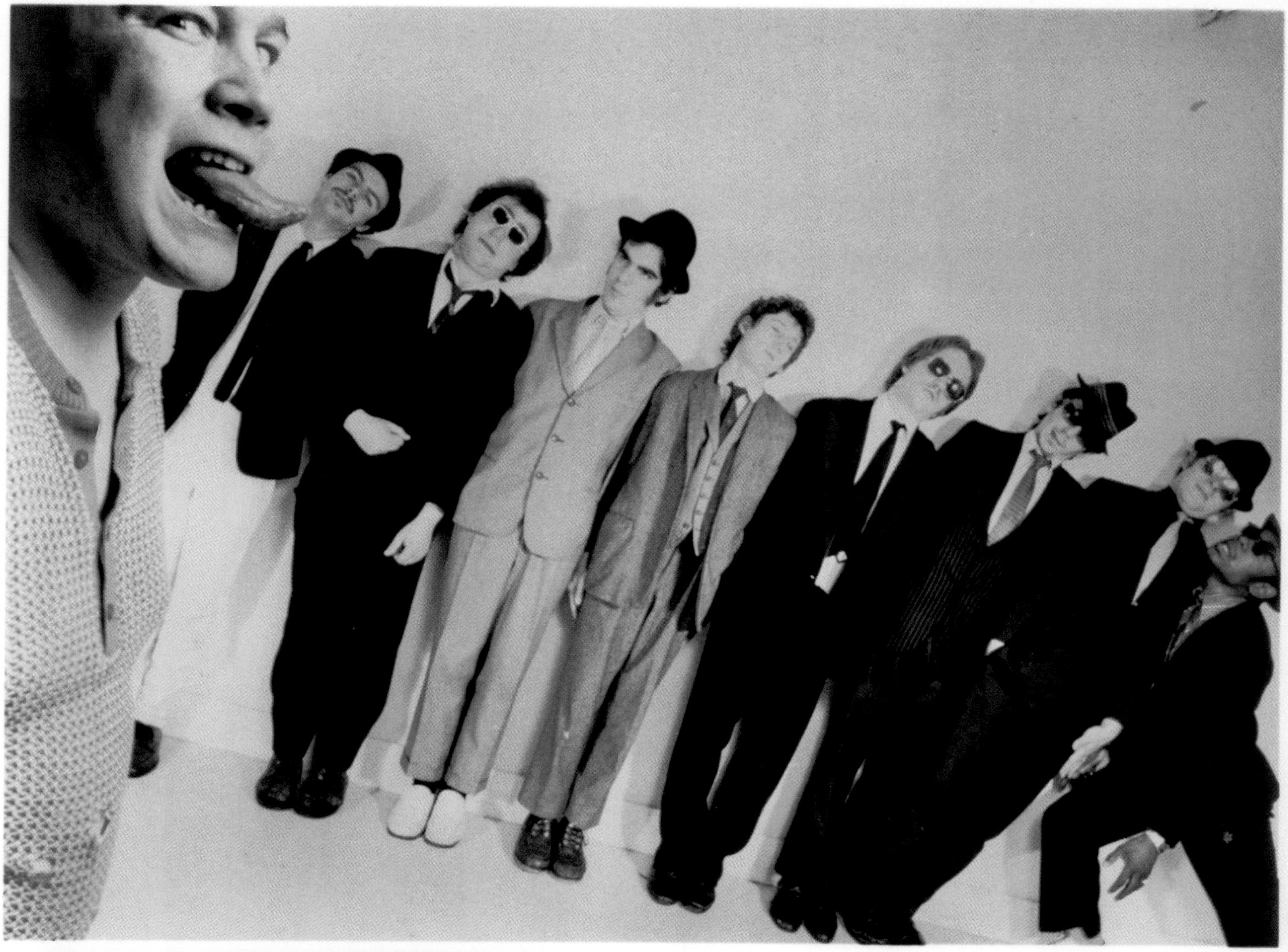

BAD MANNERS

6/81

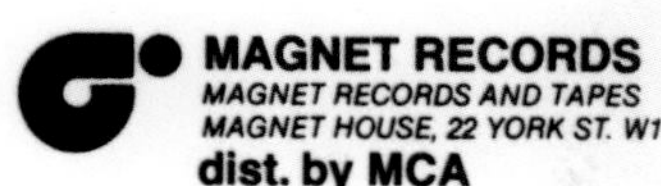

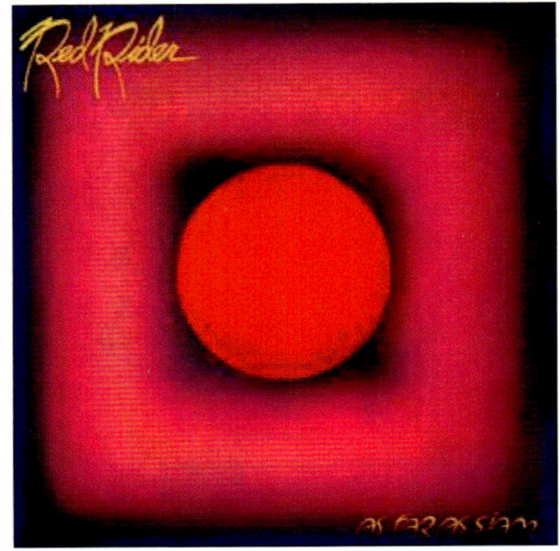

Held dear in Canada, the group **Red Rider** became popular on US rock radio with the haunting, cautionary "Lunatic Fringe," written by bandleader Tom Cochrane.

Billboard 200: *As Far as Siam* (#65)

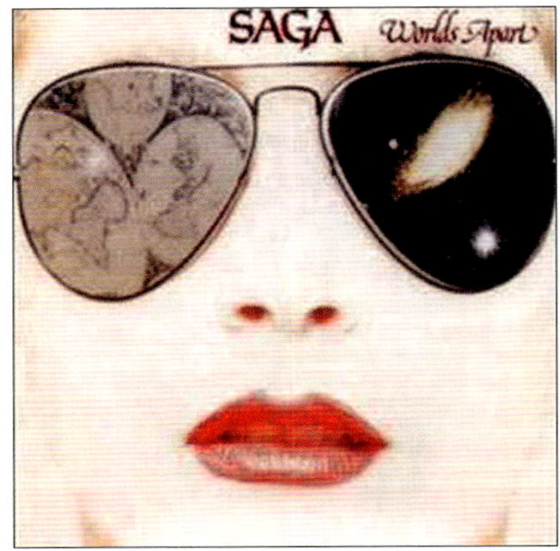

"On the Loose" proved to be the breakthrough hit in the US for Canadian prog-rockers **Saga**, with the help of MTV video play and an expanded tour schedule.

Billboard 200: *Worlds Apart* (#29)
Billboard Hot 100: "Wind Him Up" (#64); "On the Loose"

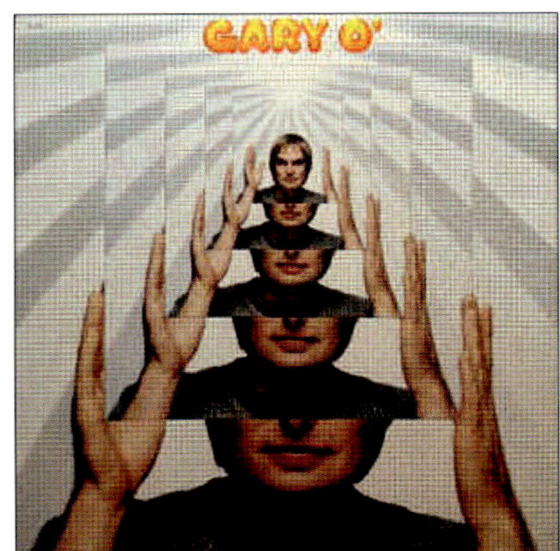

Canadian singer and songwriter **Gary O'** cracked the US charts with a stylish remake of "Pay You Back with Interest," a 1967 song originally recorded by the Hollies.

Billboard Hot 100: "Pay You Back with Interest" (#70)

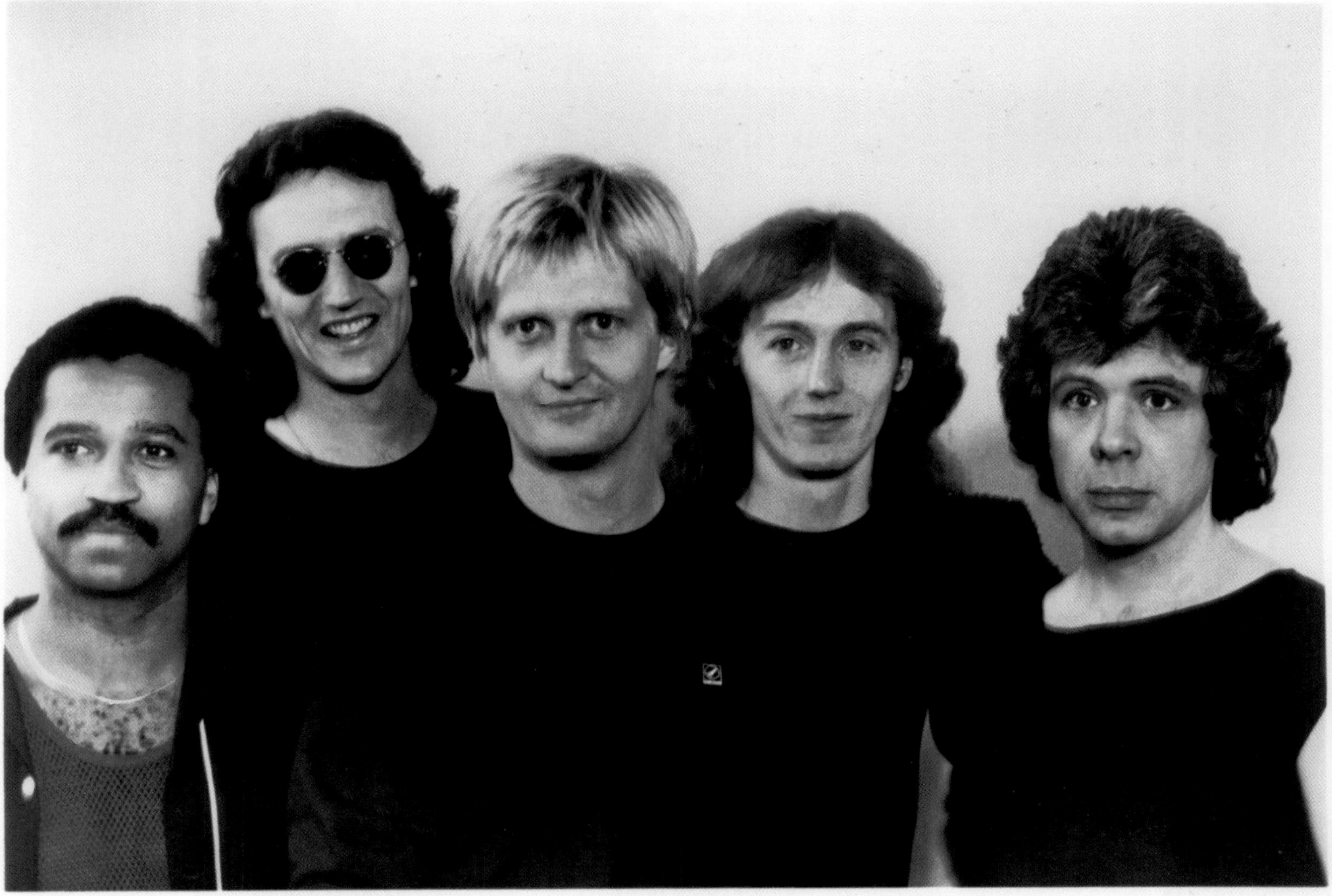

Jeff Jones Peter Boynton Tom Cochrane Ken Greer Rob Baker

Photo: Peter Gravelle / 1981

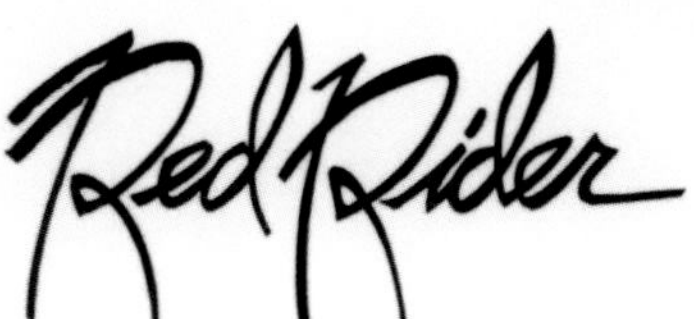

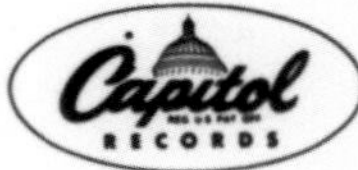

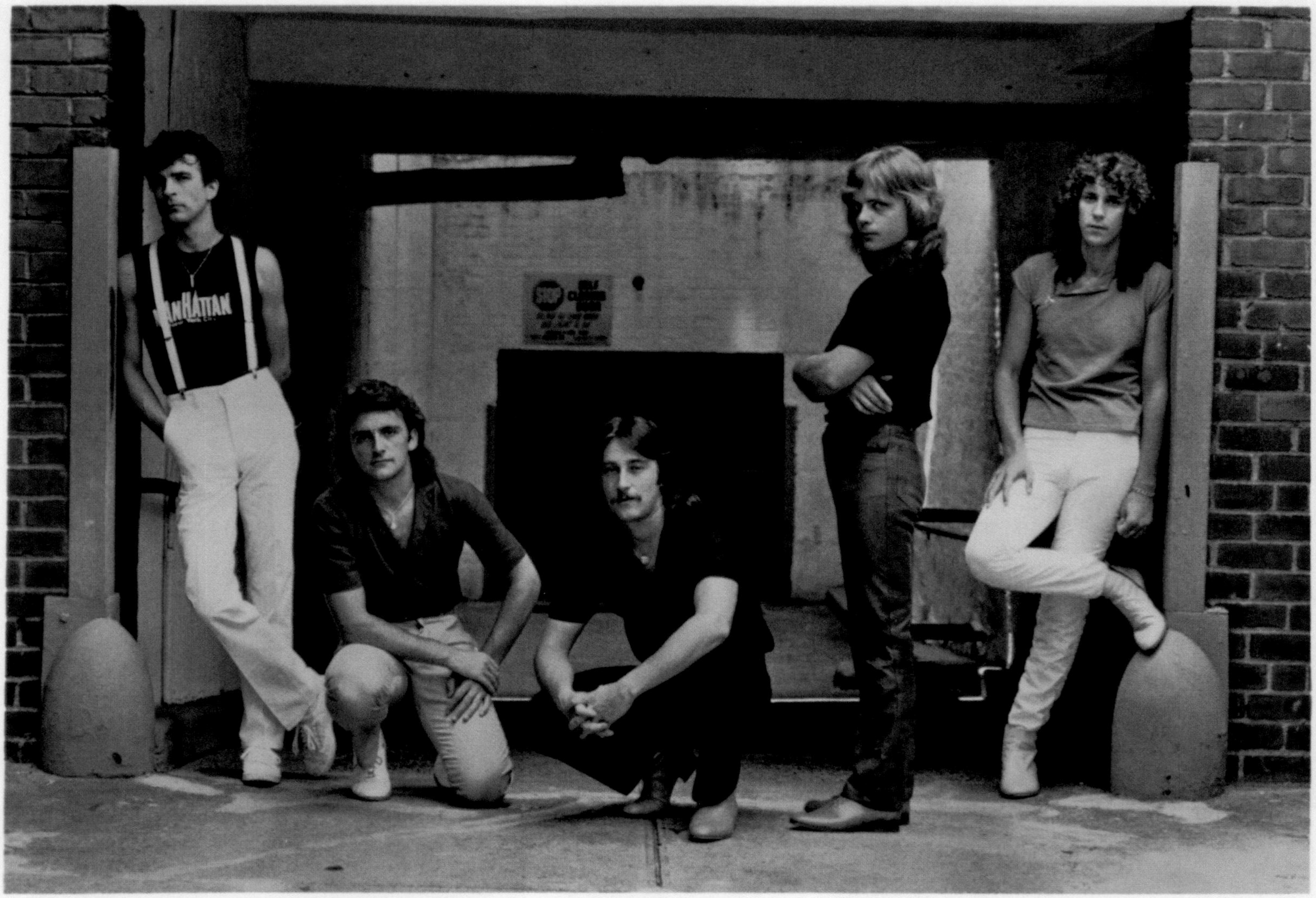

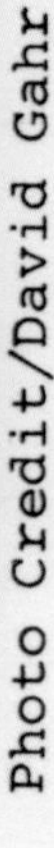

Left to right Michael Sadler, Jim Crichton, Steve Negus, Ian Crichton, Jim Gilmour

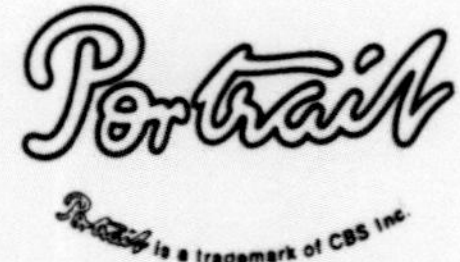

SAGA

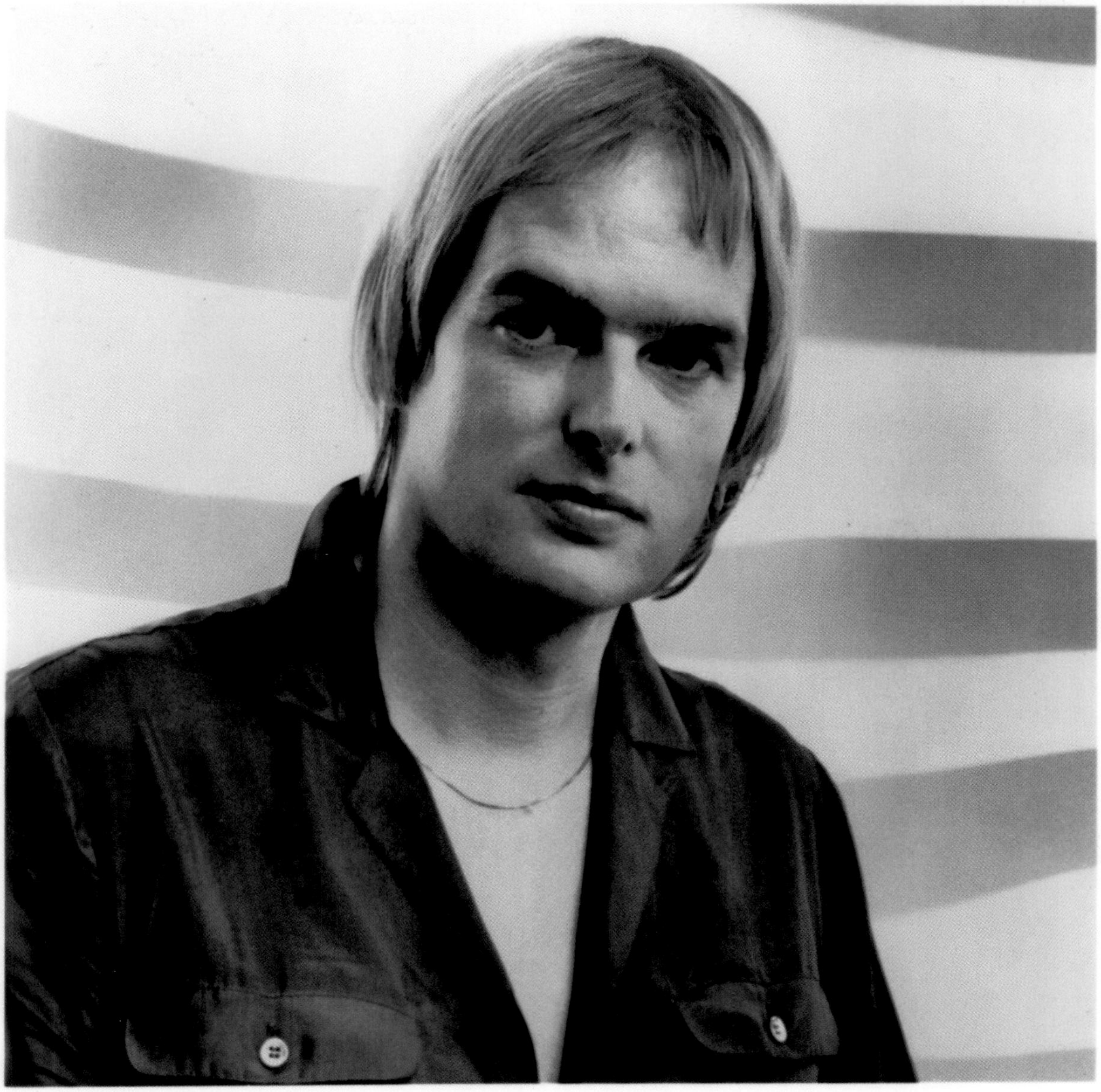

Photo: Sam Scrivano / 1981

GARY O'

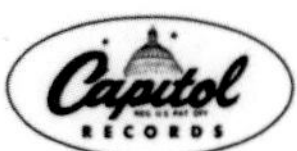

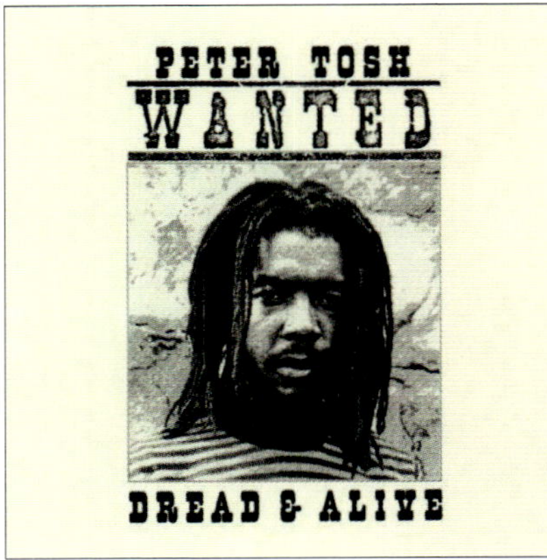

Reggae artist **Peter Tosh** returned with the *Wanted Dread & Alive* album and "Nothing But Love," the Jamaican firebrand's buoyant duet with singer Gwen Guthrie.

Billboard 200: *Wanted Dread & Alive* (#91)

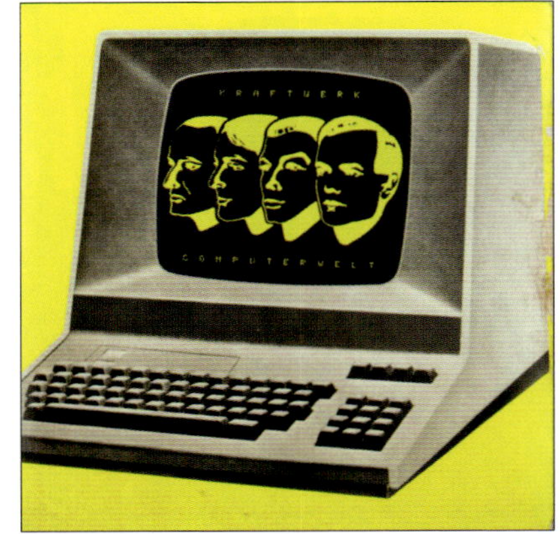

The German electronic band **Kraftwerk** released *Computer World*, ruminating on the global rise of technology with two singles, "Computer Love" and "Pocket Calculator."

Billboard 200: *Computer World* (#72)

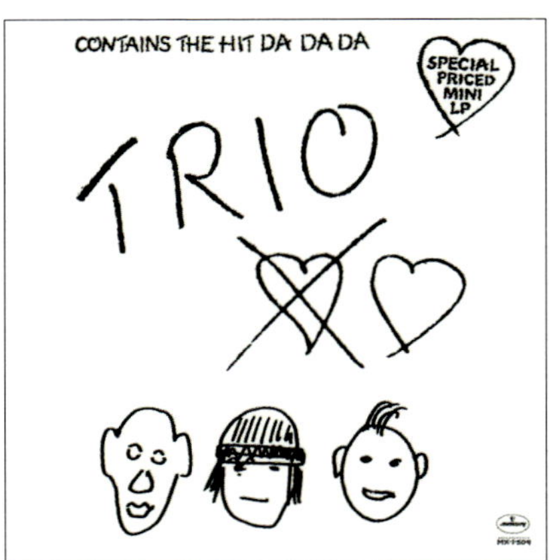

The German outfit **Trio** produced the quirky but oddly captivating "Da Da Da," which eventually became an international synth-pop phenomenon.

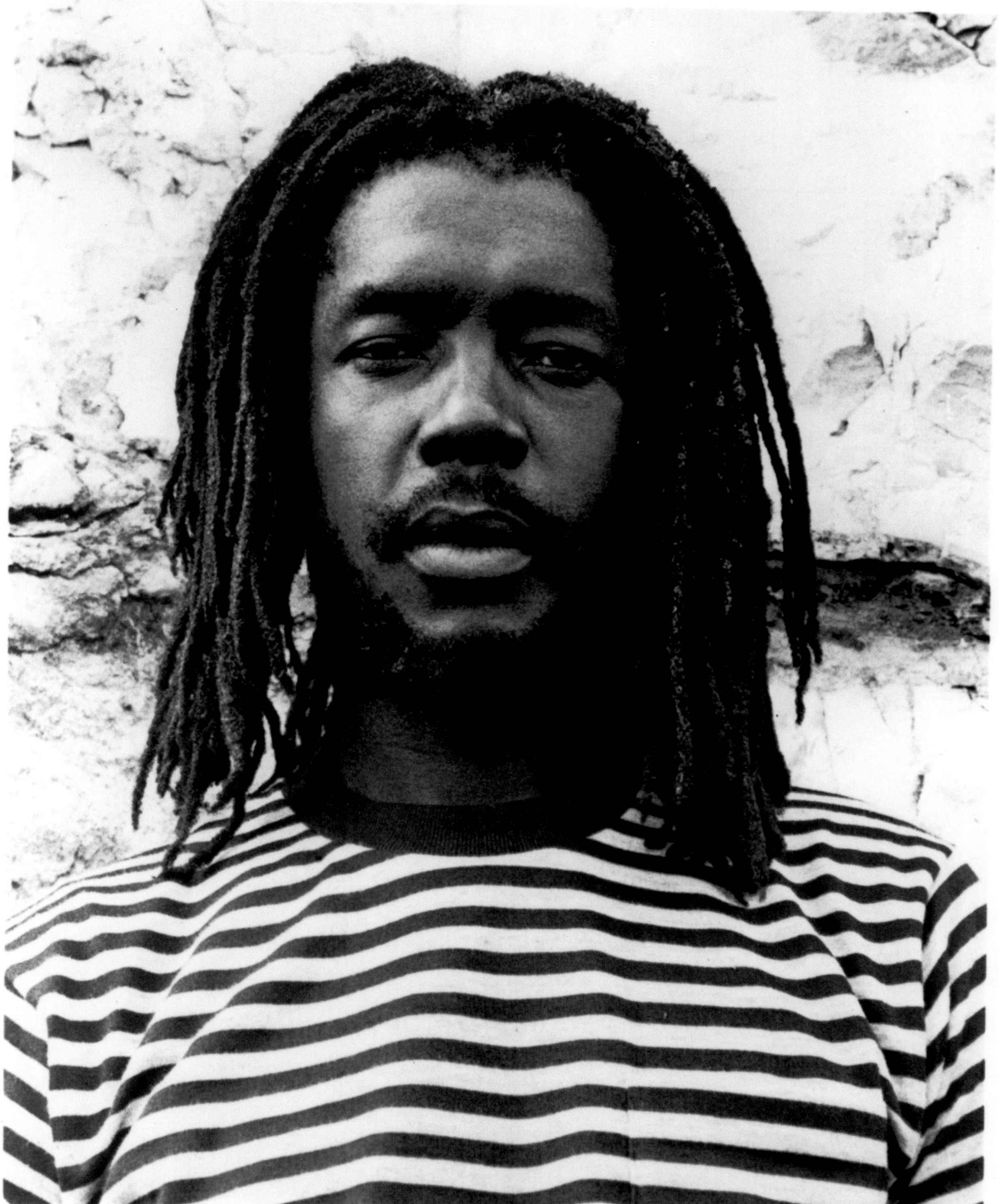

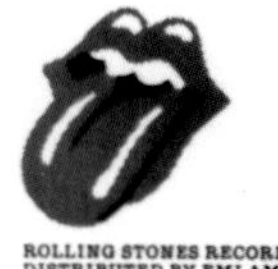

ROLLING STONES RECORDS
DISTRIBUTED BY EMI AMERICA/LIBERTY RECORDS

PETER TOSH

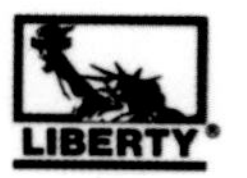

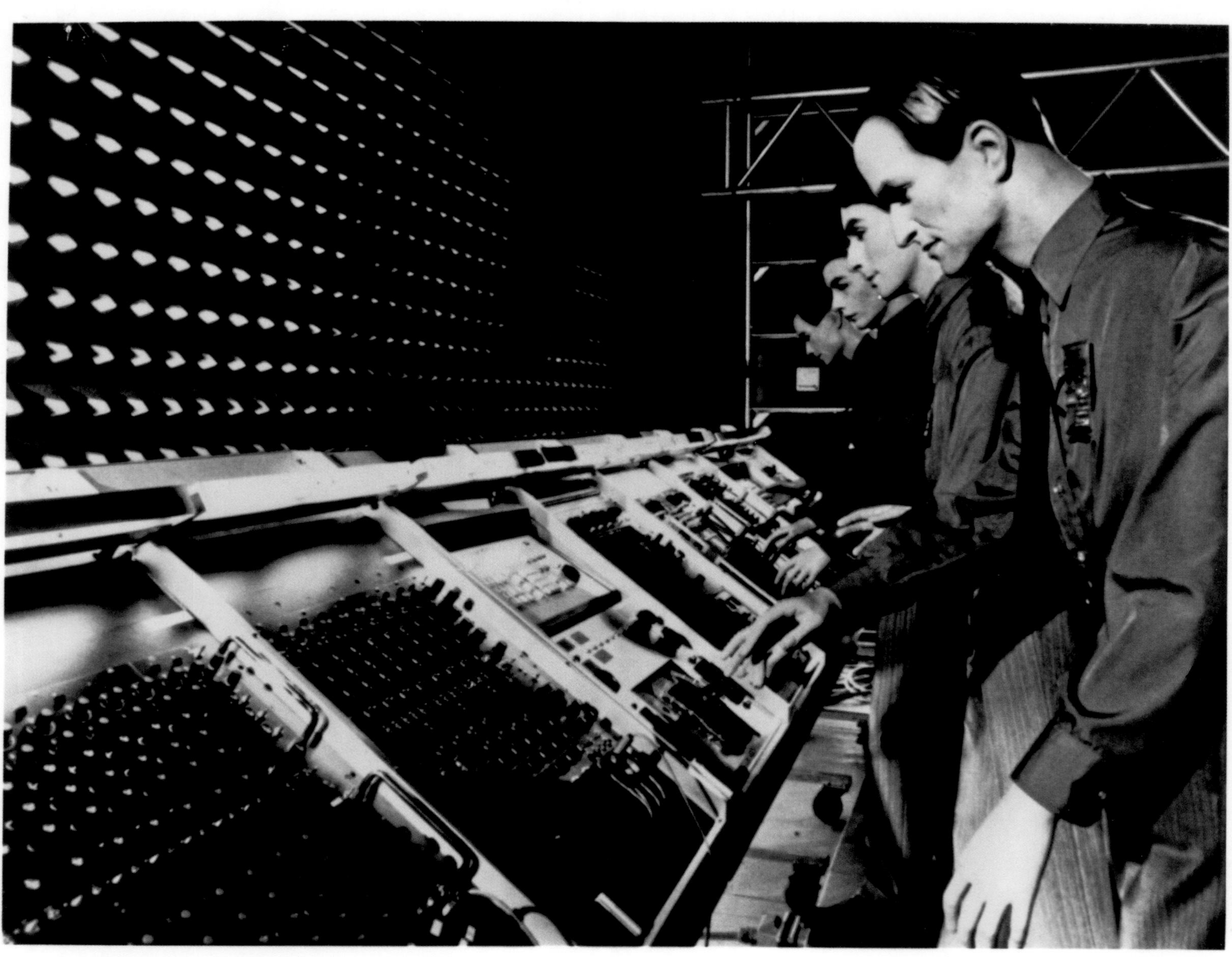

KRAFTWERK

EMI

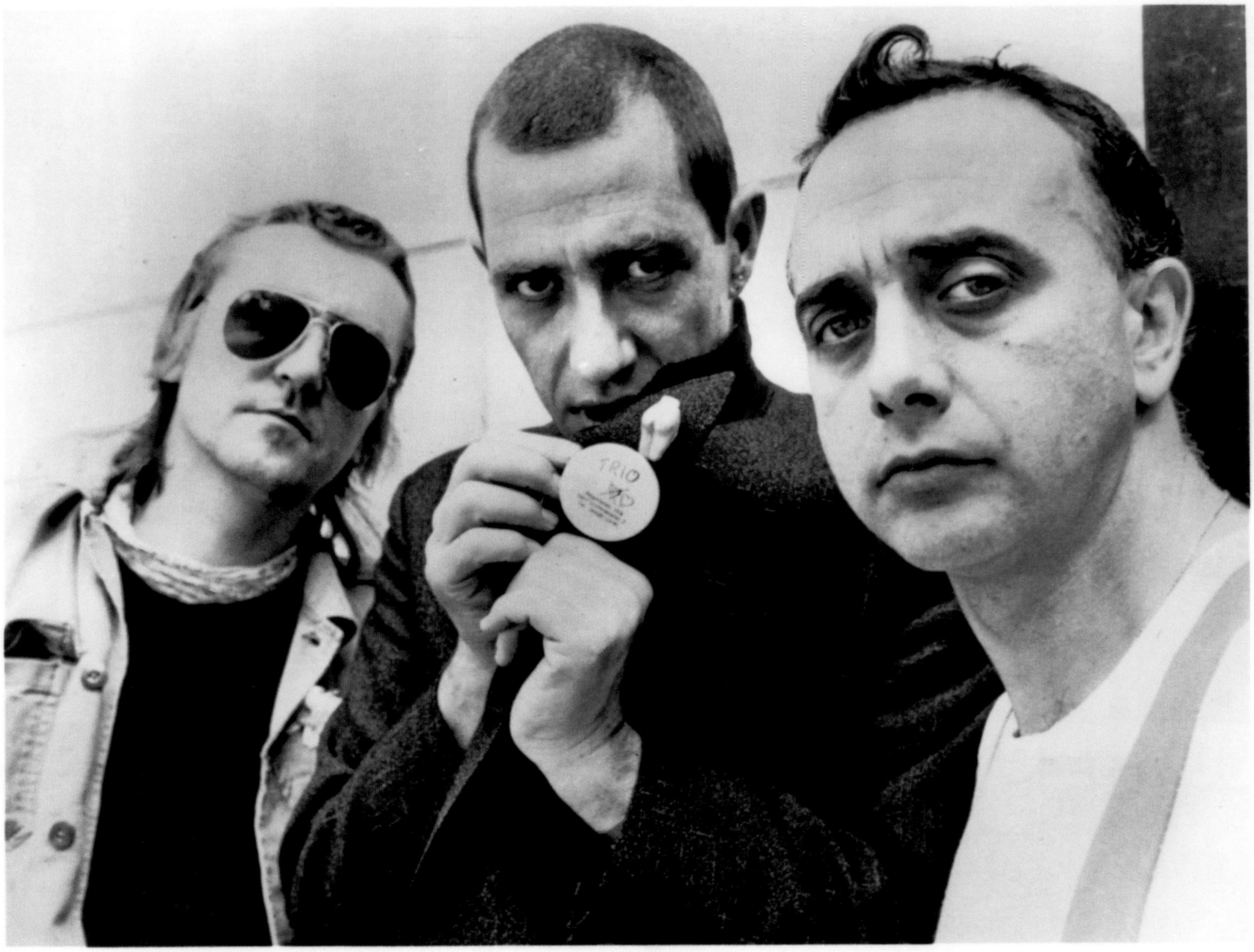

TRIO

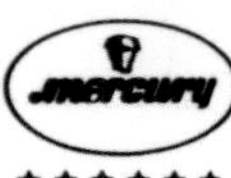

PolyGram Records

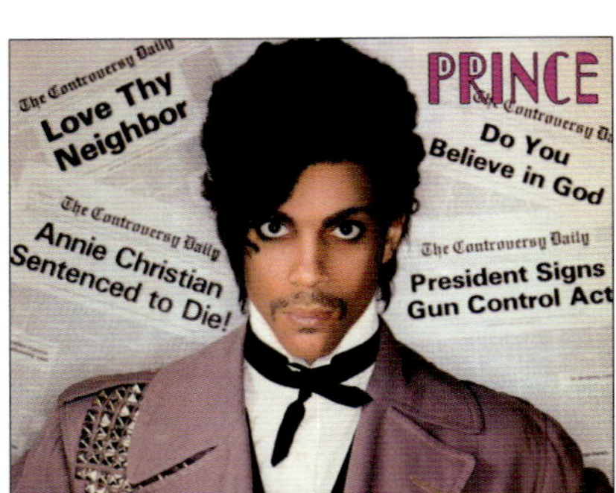

Prince's success continued with *Controversy,* his fourth album, which spotlighted the gifted artist's conspicuously explicit lyrics and synthesis of new wave and funk.

Billboard 200: *Controversy* (#21)
Billboard Hot 100: "Controversy" (#70)

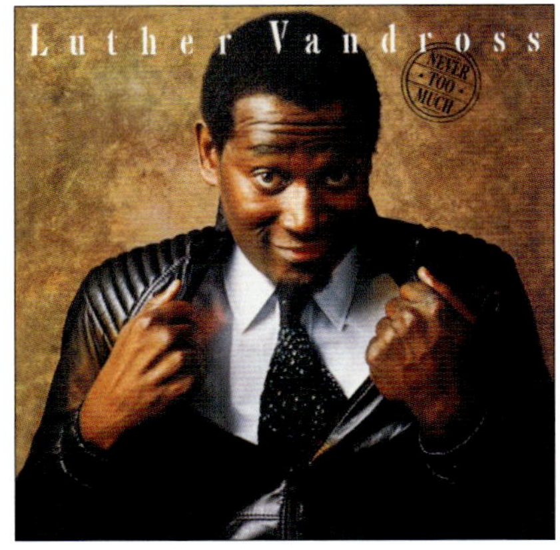

Singer **Luther Vandross**' debut solo album, *Never Too Much,* stormed to No. 1 on the R&B chart, boosted by the hit title track and his epic ownership of "A House Is Not a Home."

Billboard 200: *Never Too Much* (#19)
Billboard Hot 100: "Never Too Much" (#33)

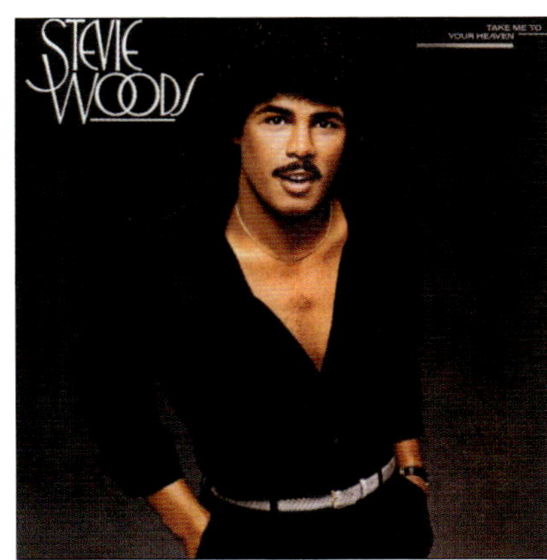

R&B singer **Stevie Woods** enjoyed a brief moment of celebrity when the singles "Steal the Night" and "Just Can't Win 'Em All" climbed into the Top 40.

Billboard 200: *Take Me to Your Heaven* (#153)
Billboard Hot 100: "Steal the Night" (#25); "Just Can't Win 'Em All" (#38); "Fly Away" (#84)

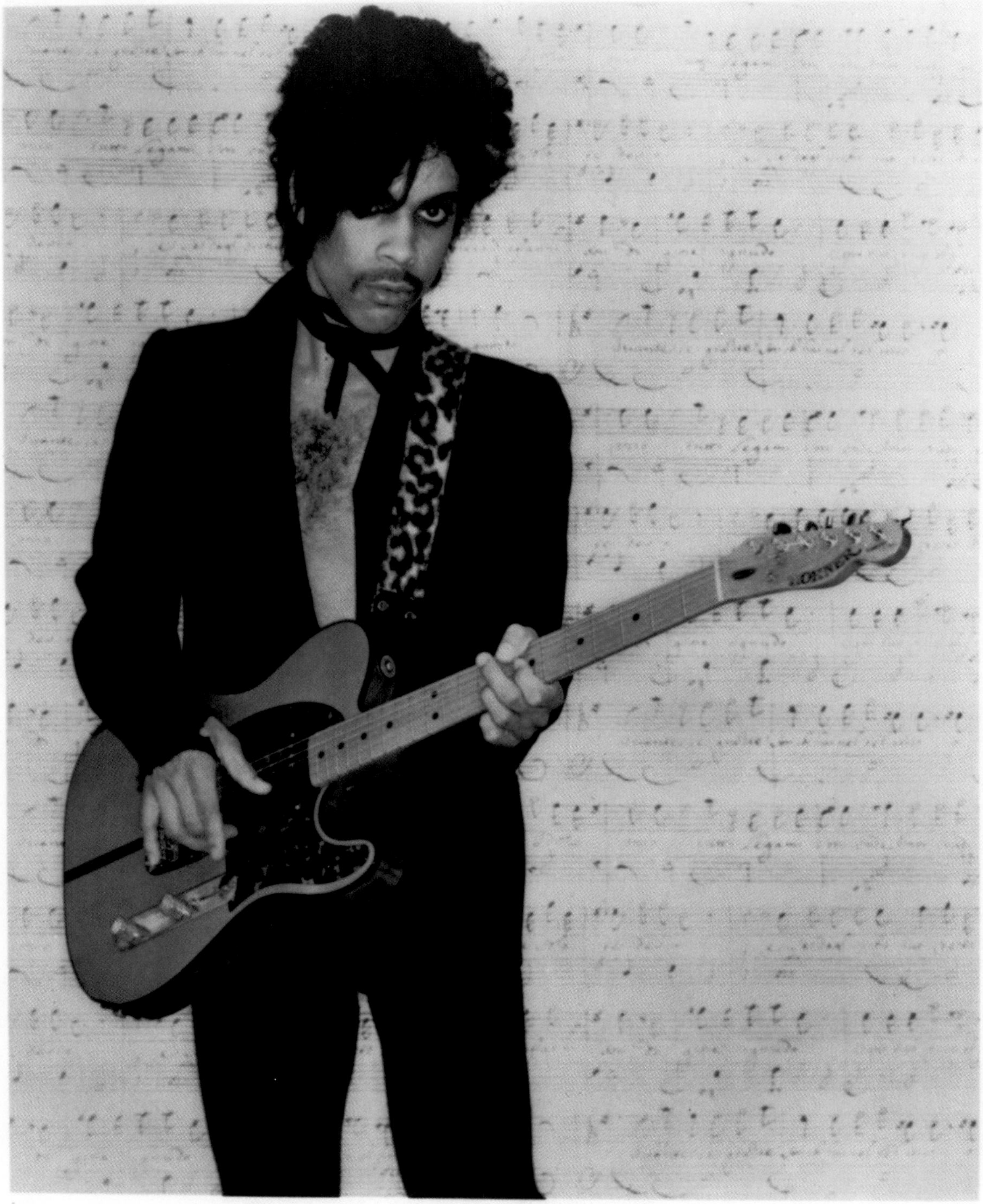

PRINCE

OCTOBER 1981

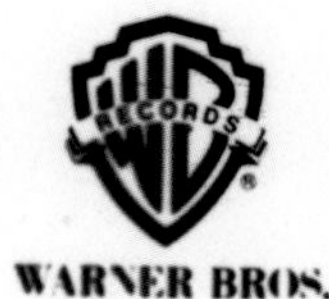

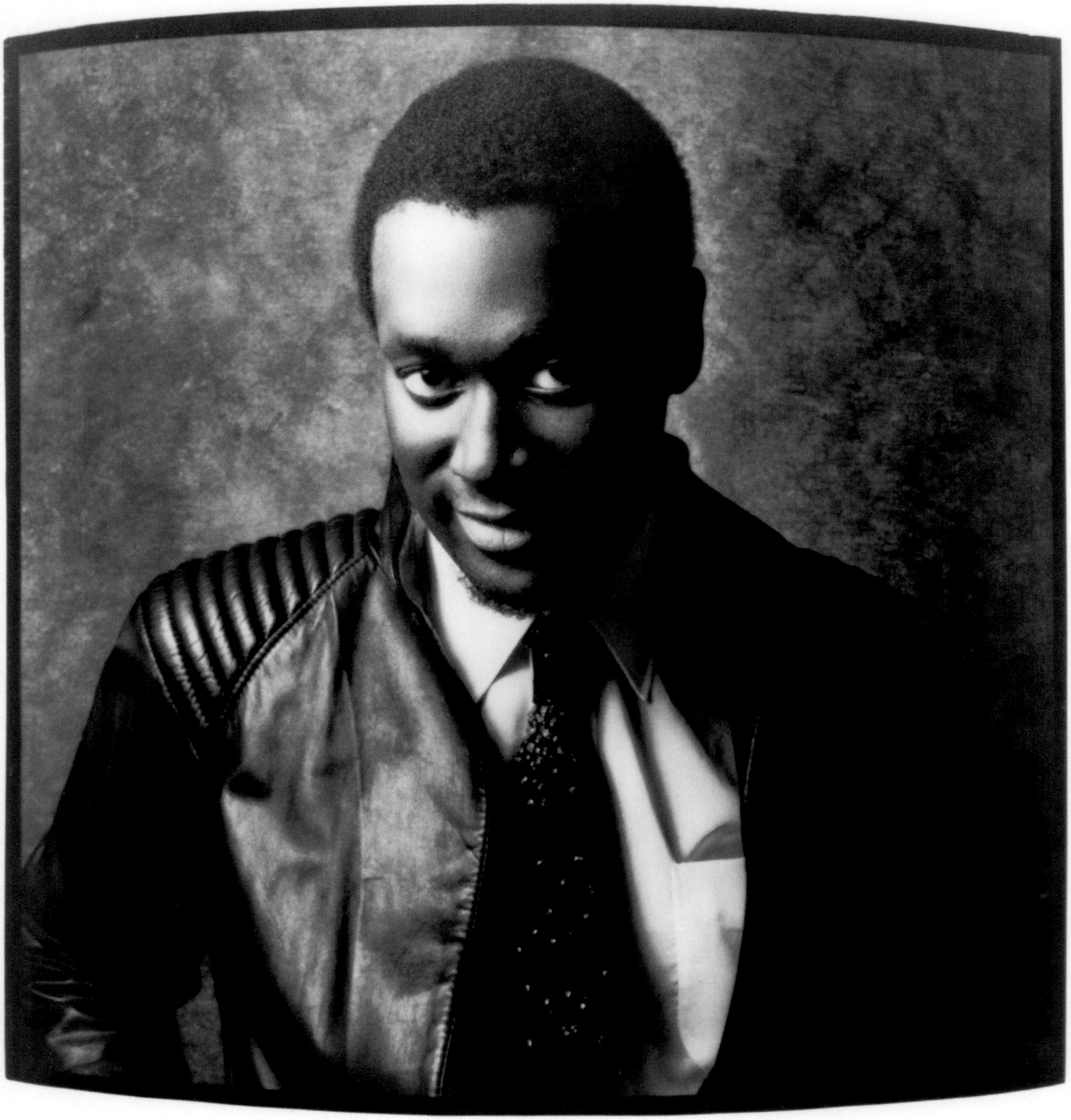

Luther Vandross

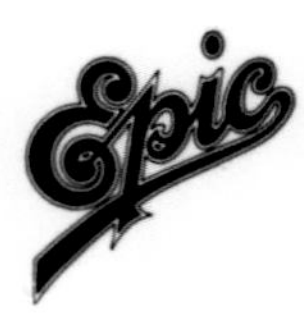

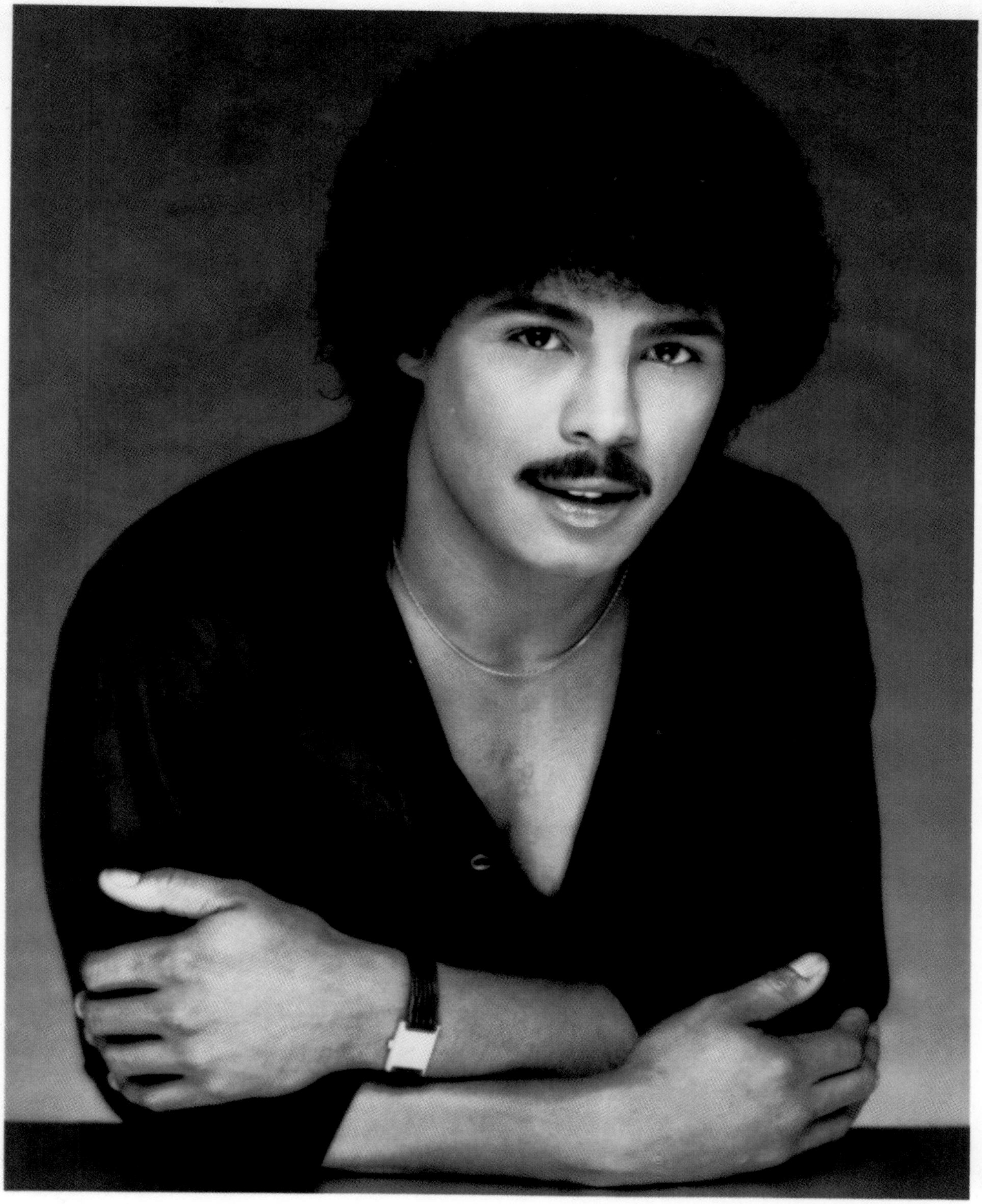

STEVIE WOODS

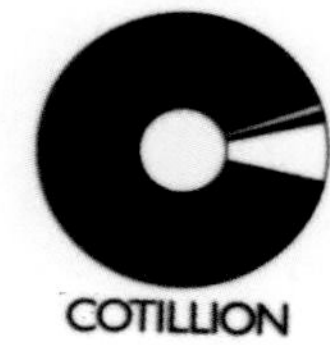

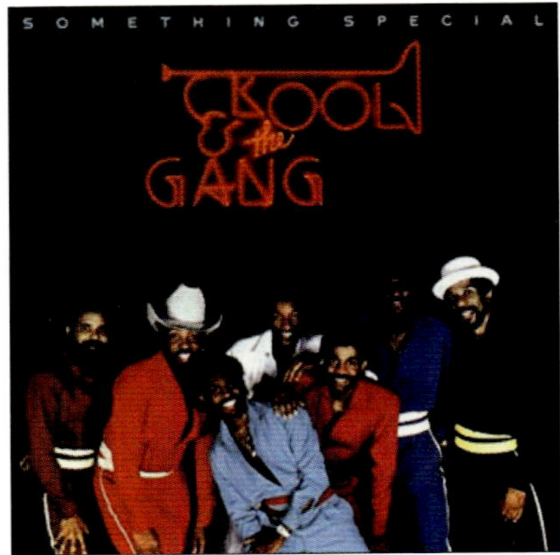

Something Special continued **Kool & the Gang**'s platinum-selling success, due largely to the singles "Get Down on It" and the No. 1 R&B hit, "Take My Heart."

Billboard 200: *Something Special* (#12)
Billboard Hot 100: "Take My Heart (You Can Have It If You Want It)" (#17); "Steppin' Out" (#89); "Get Down on It" (#10)

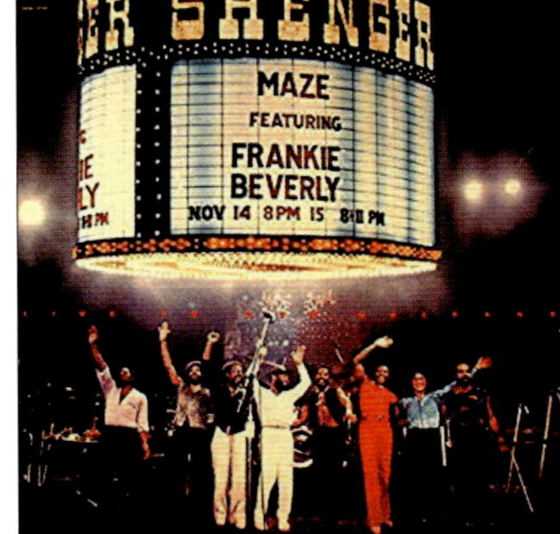

The double-album set *Live in New Orleans* by **Maze featuring Frankie Beverly** captured the expressive spirit and spontaneity of the R&B act's concert dates.

Billboard 200: *Live in New Orleans* (#34)

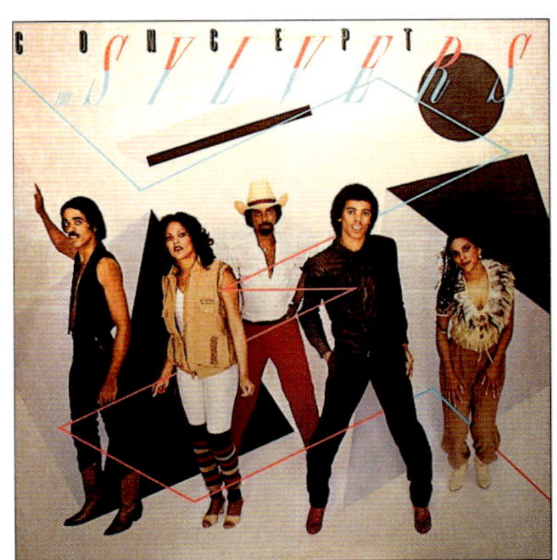

The Sylvers, a popular R&B act of nine performing siblings known predominantly for the 1976 No. 1 hit "Boogie Fever," pared down to a quintet with *Concept*.

Billboard 200: *Concept* (#49)

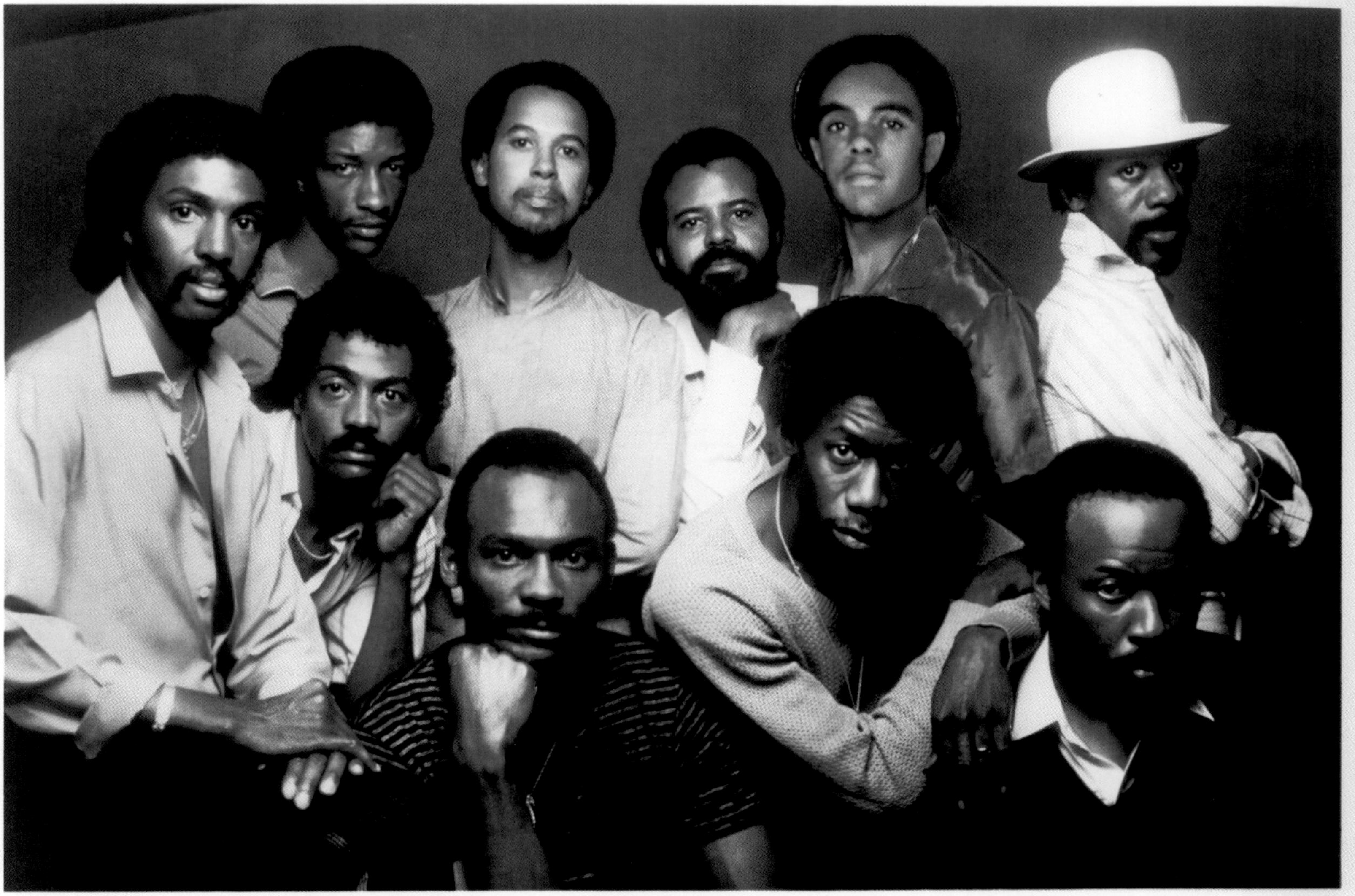

KOOL & THE GANG

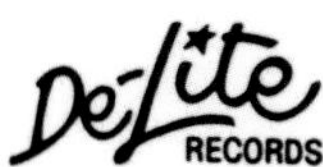

Management & Direction
Quintet Assoc. Ltd.
527 Madison Ave.
New York N.Y 10022
Bookings:
Norby Walters Assoc.

PolyGram Records

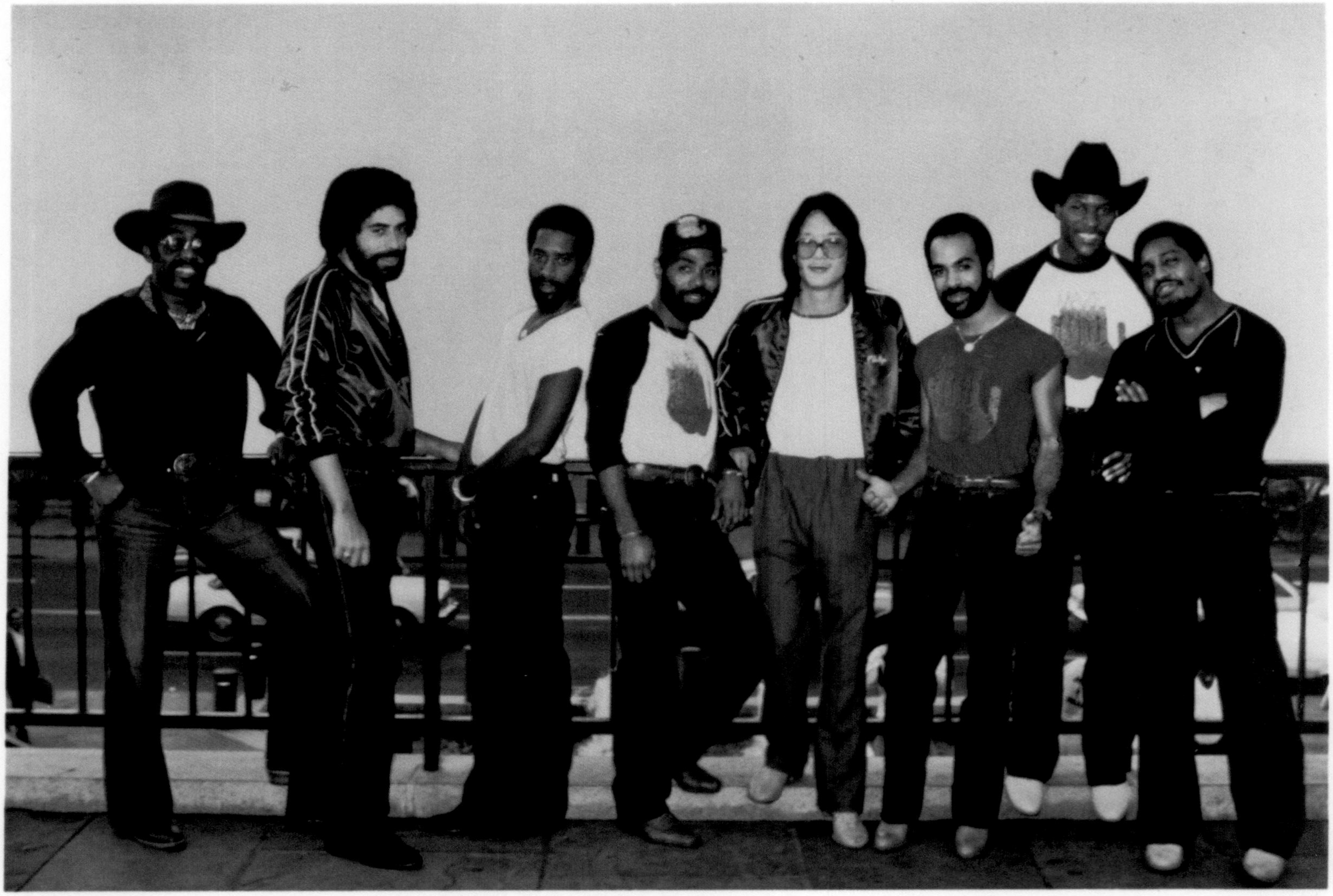

Photo: Todd Gray / 1981

MAZE featuring **Frankie Beverly**

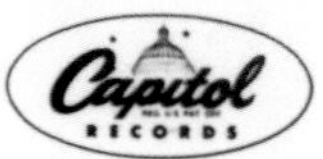

L-R: McKinley Williams, Robin Duhe, Roame Lowry, Frankie Beverly, Phillip Woo, Billy Johnson, Ron Smith, Sam Porter

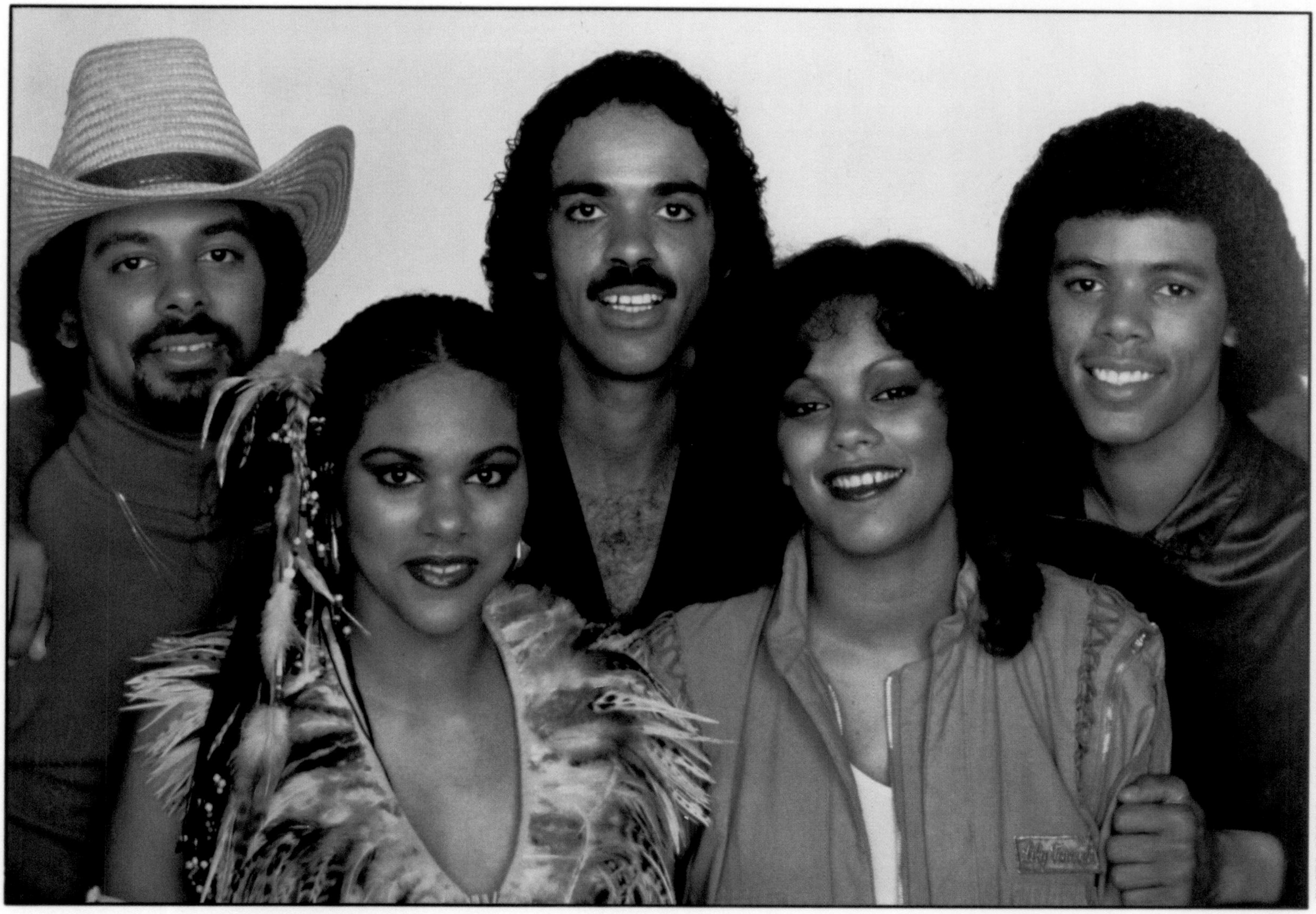

JOHNATHAN PAT RICKY ANGIE FOSTER

PHOTO CREDIT: AARON RAPOPORT/1981

The Sylvers

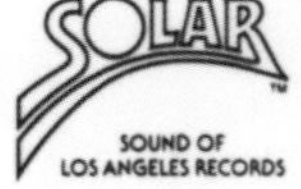

Distributed by Elektra/Asylum Records

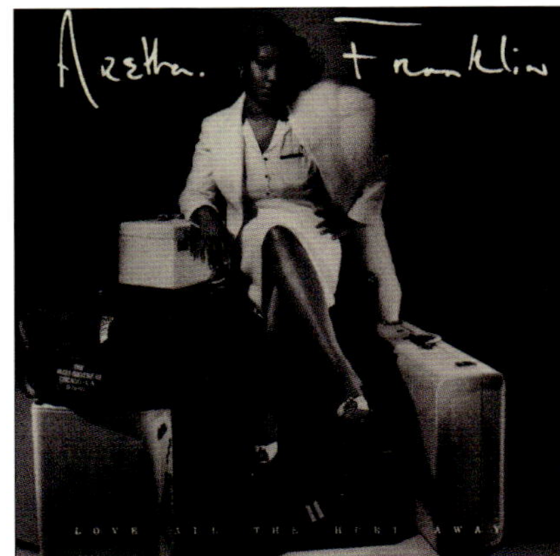

Love All the Hurt Away contained **Aretha Franklin**'s duet with George Benson on the title track and her Grammy-winning cover of Sam & Dave's "Hold On, I'm Comin'."

Billboard 200: *Love All the Hurt Away* (#36)
Billboard Hot 100: "Love All the Hurt Away" (#46)

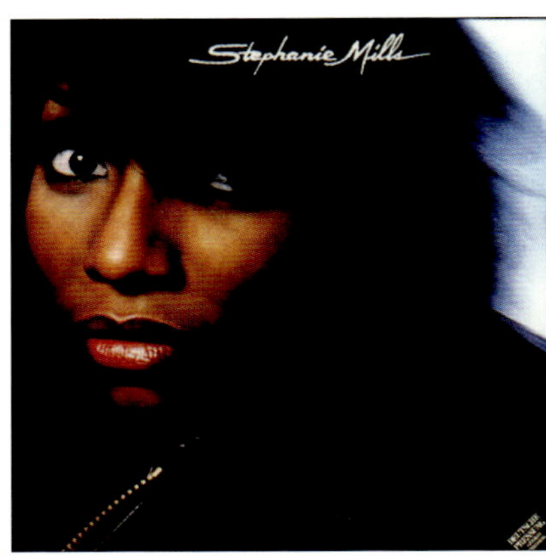

R&B singer **Stephanie Mills** fared well with "Two Hearts," a hit midtempo duet with megastar Teddy Pendergrass from her fifth studio album, *Stephanie*.

Billboard 200: *Stephanie* (#30)
Billboard Hot 100: "Two Hearts" (#40)

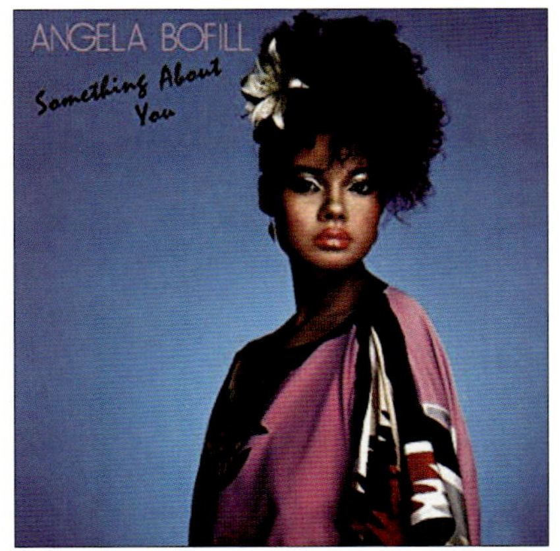

With her third album, *Something About You*, vocalist **Angela Bofill** made a seamless transition from contemporary jazz to a commercial R&B-pop sound.

Billboard 200: *Something About You* (#61)

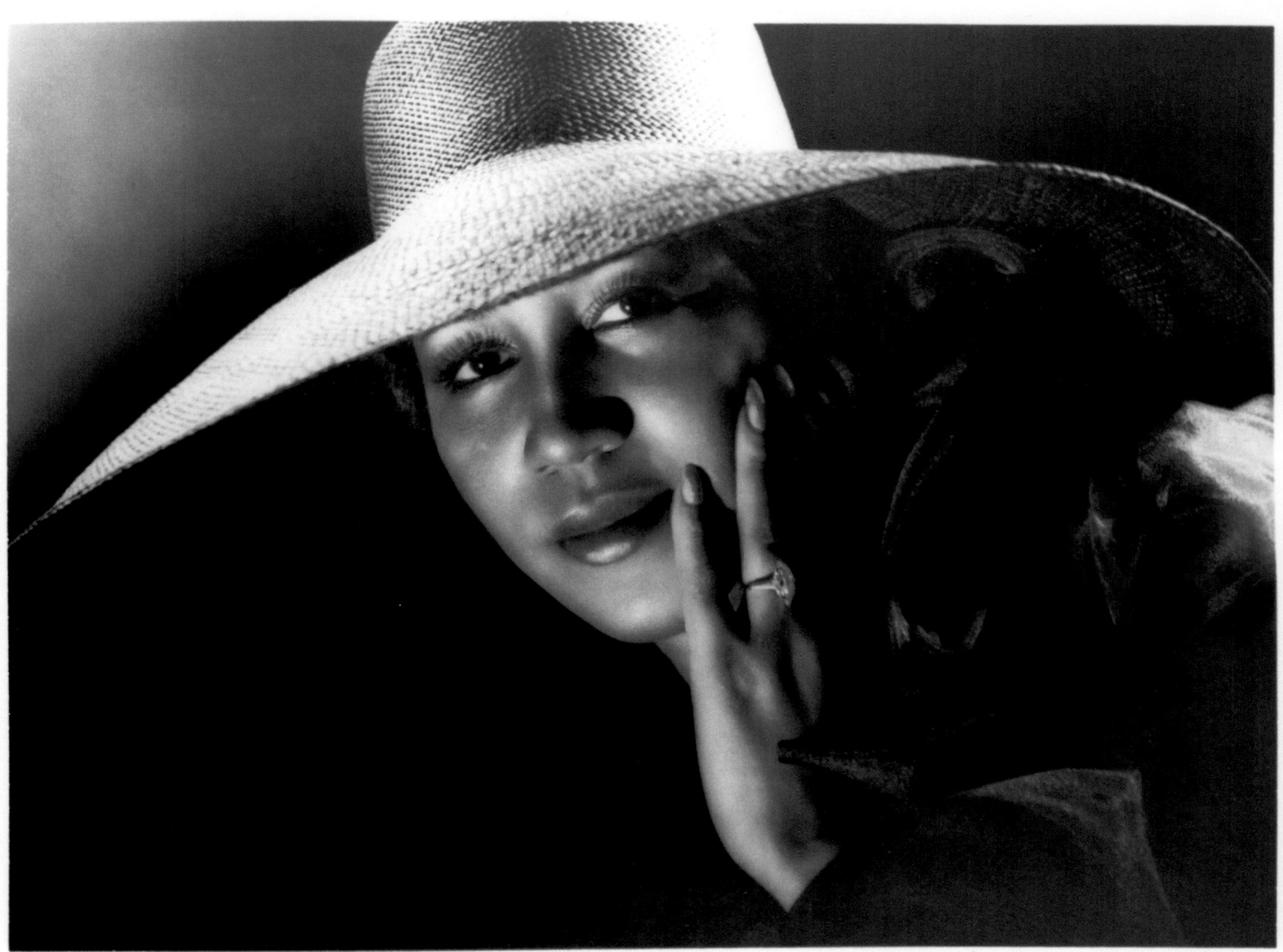

Aretha. Franklin

Management: Reverend Cecil Franklin
(313) 341-3743
Press Agent: Howard Brandy
(213) 657-7940

ARISTA™

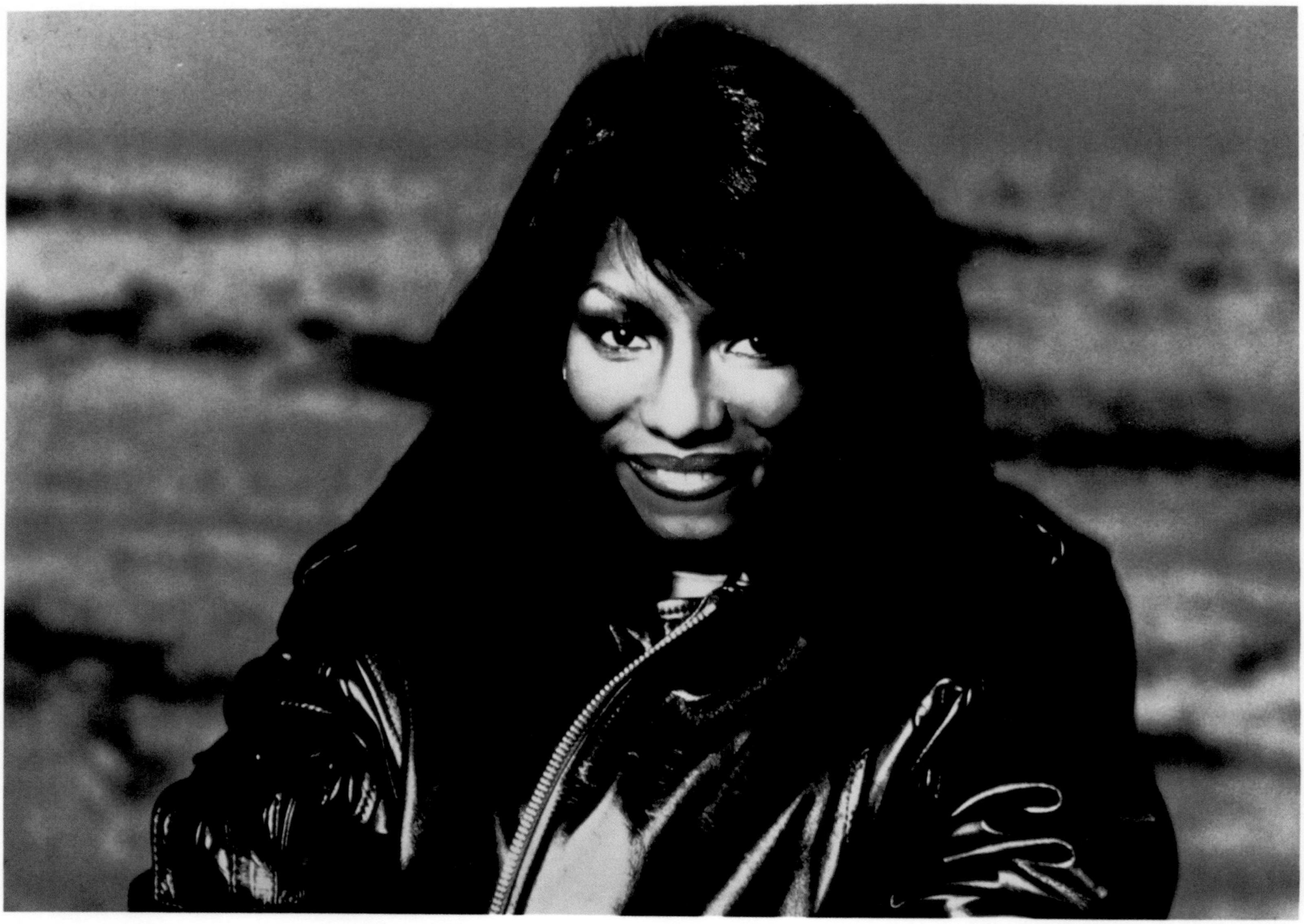

STEPHANIE MILLS

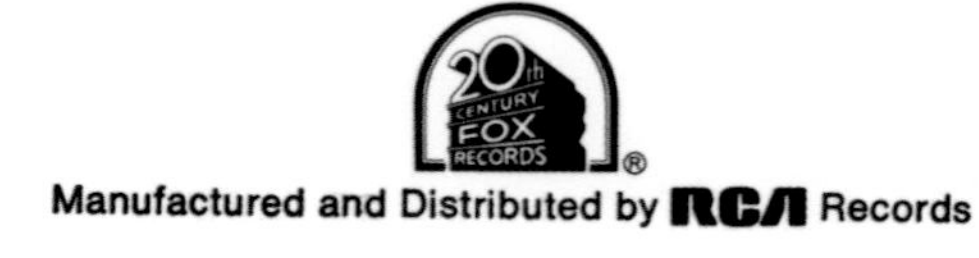

Manufactured and Distributed by RCA Records

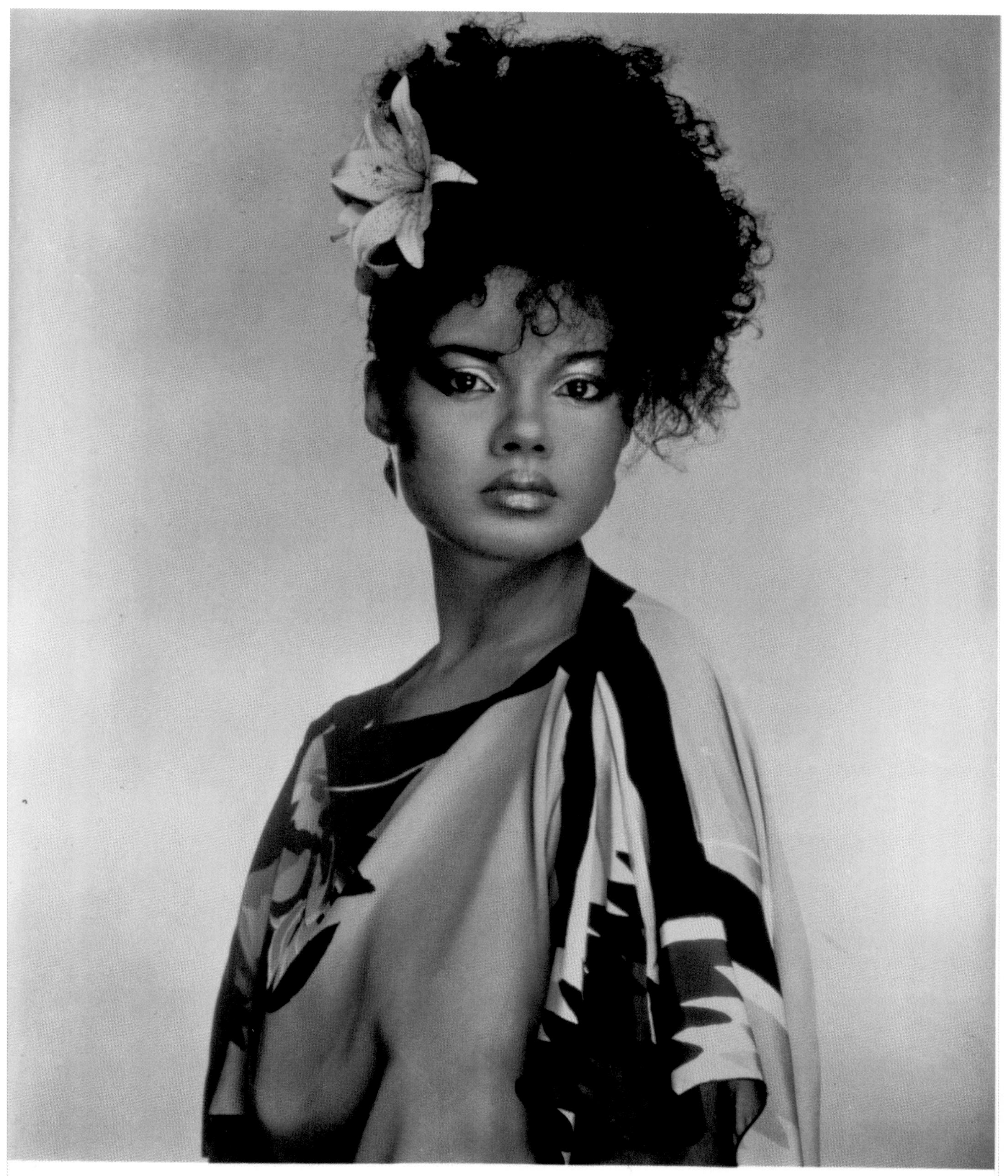

Angela Bofill

ARISTA™

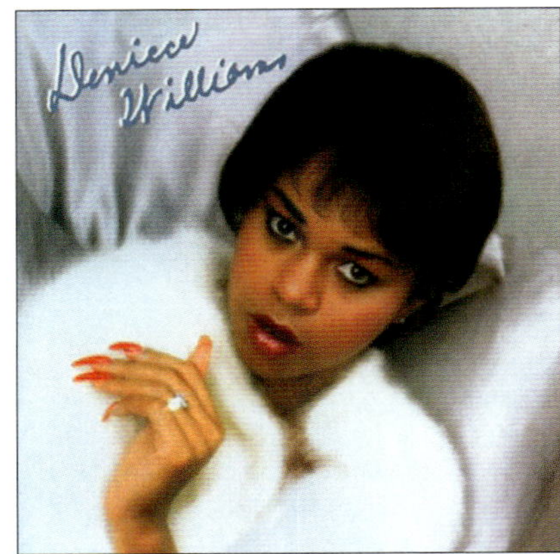

Deniece Williams issued *My Melody*, her fifth album, scoring an R&B hit with "Silly," a ballad she co-produced with famed Philadelphia soul architect Thom Bell.

Billboard 200: *My Melody* (#74)
Billboard Hot 100: "Silly" (#53)

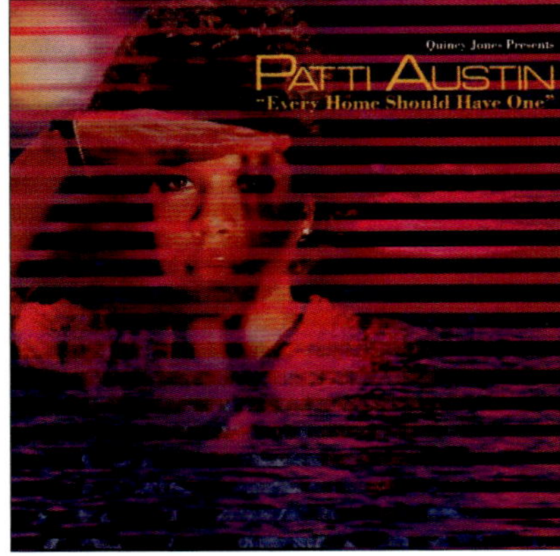

Exposure as a love theme on the TV soap opera *General Hospital* boosted **Patti Austin**'s duet with James Ingram, "Baby, Come to Me," to No. 1 on the charts.

Billboard 200: *Every Home Should Have One* (#36)
Billboard Hot 100: "Every Home Should Have One (#62); "Baby, Come to Me" (No. 1)

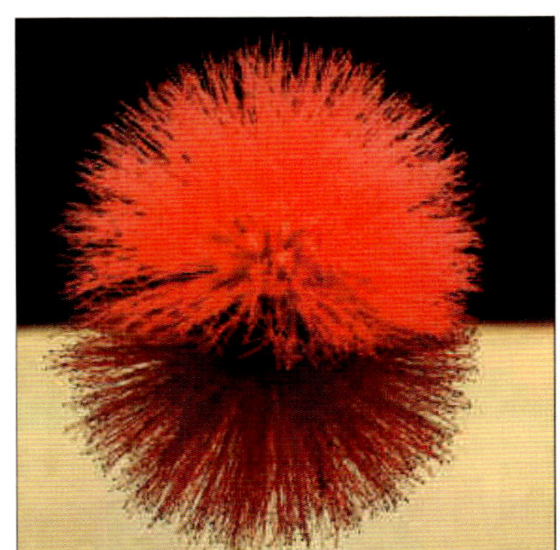

Recorded in 1978 and released in the US in 1981, Japanese keyboardist and kotoist **Yutaka**'s *Love Light* charted with a title track featuring a vocal by Patti Austin.

Billboard 200: *Love Light* (#174)
Billboard Hot 100: "Love Light" (#81)

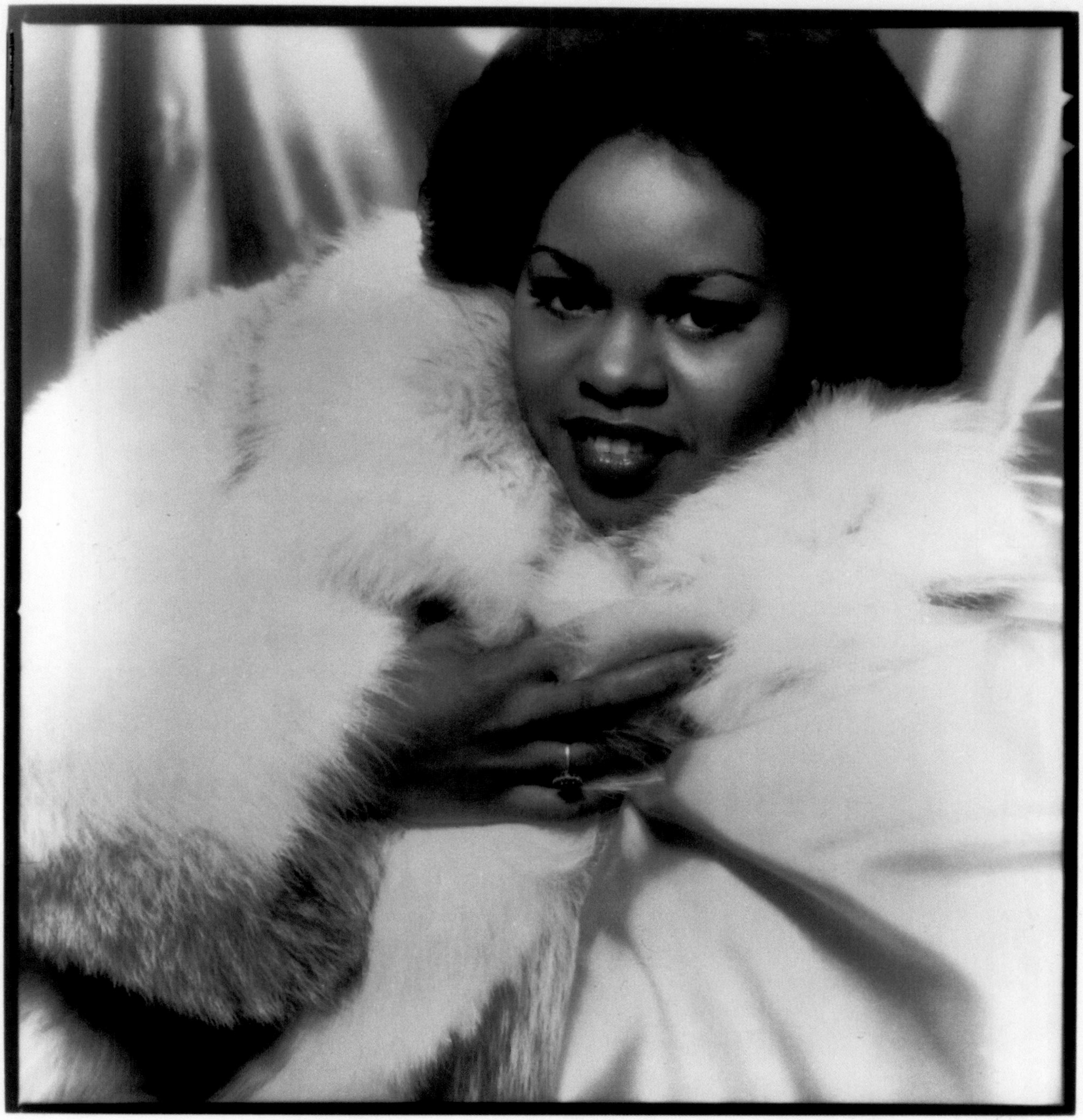

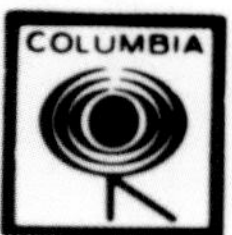

DENIECE WILLIAMS

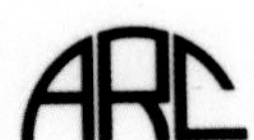

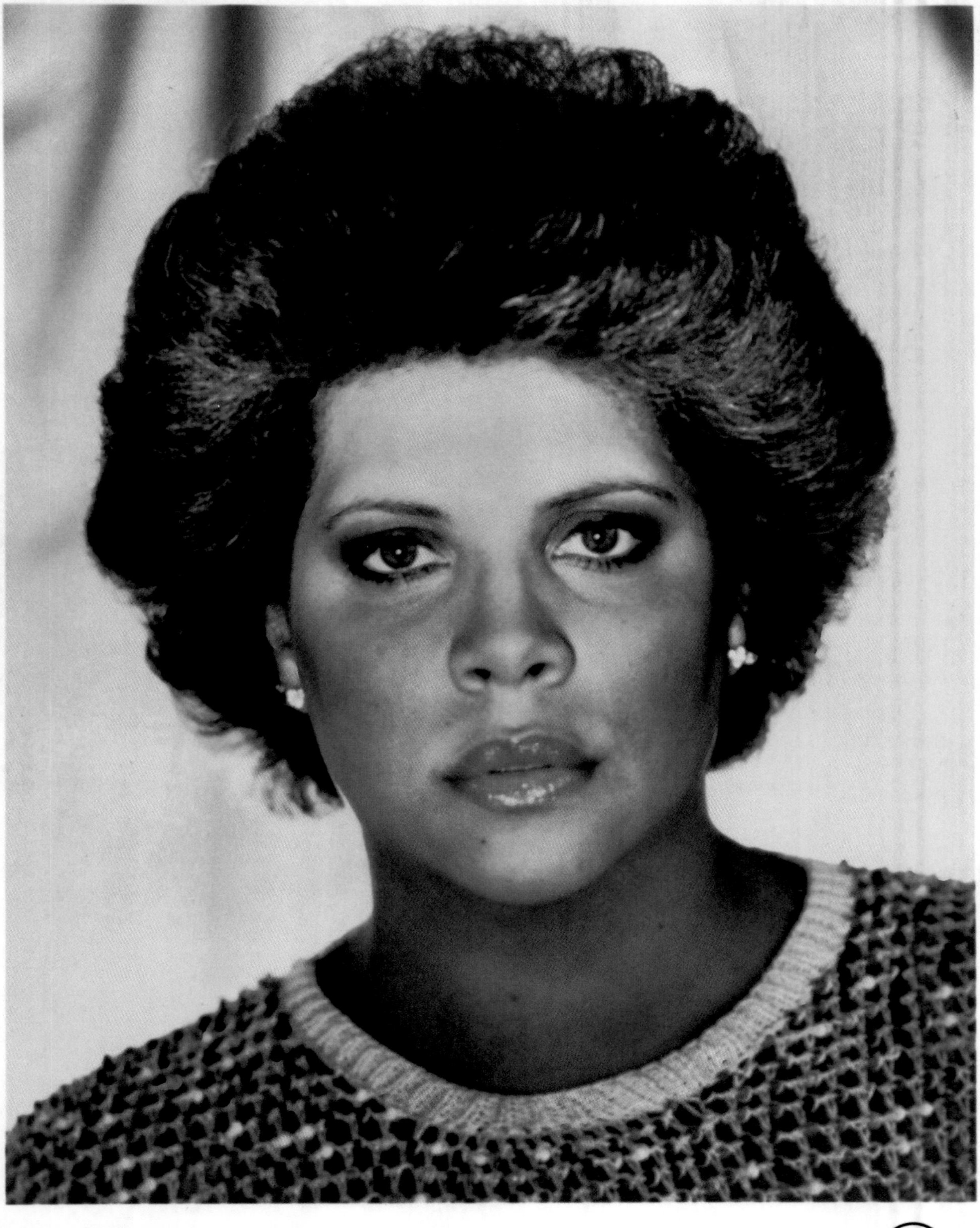

PHOTO: Raul Vega

PATTI AUSTIN

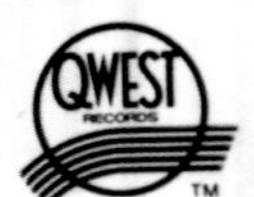

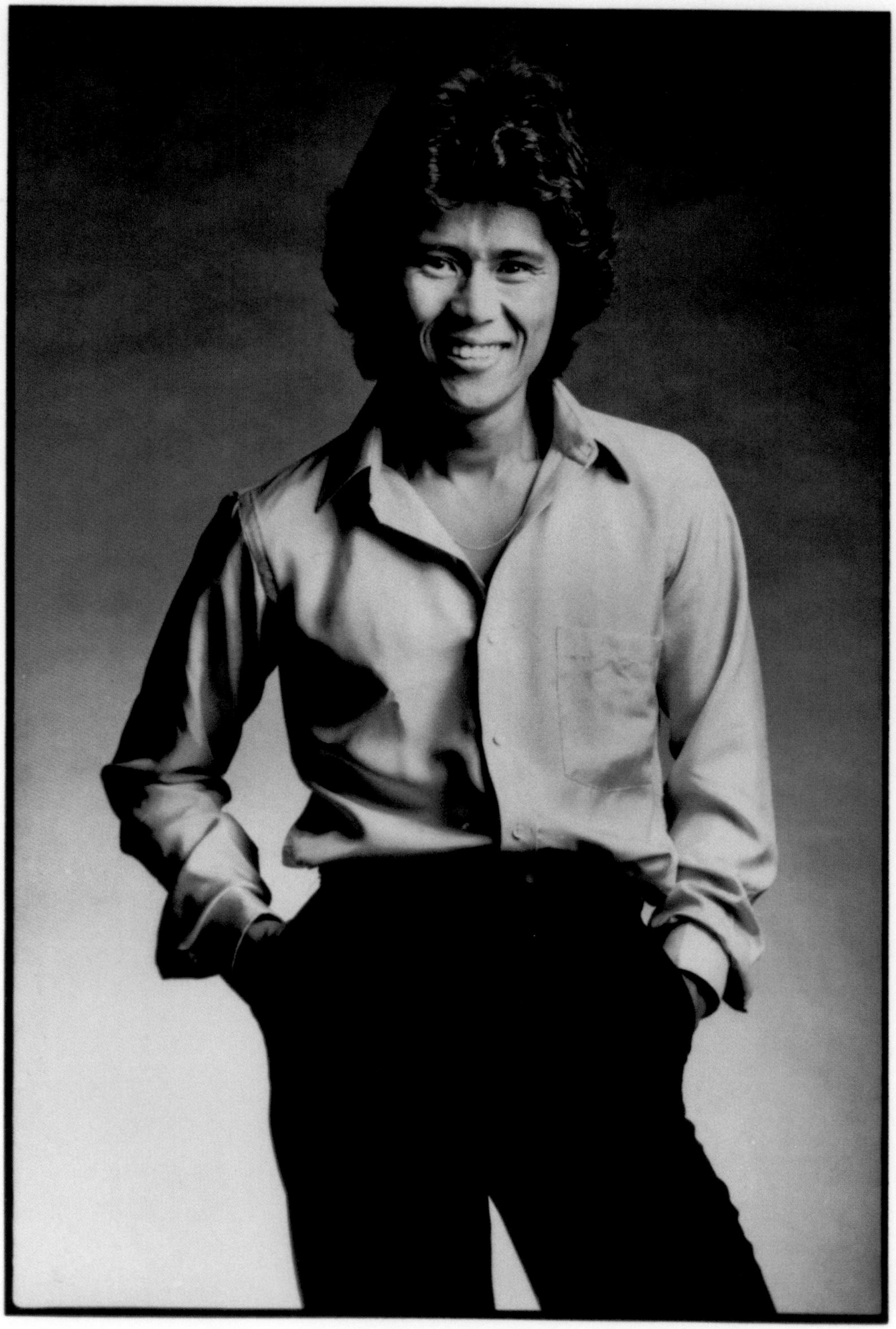

Yutaka Yokokura

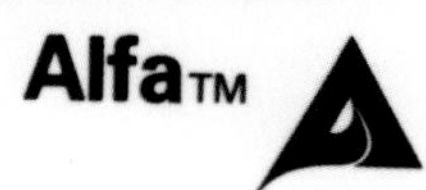

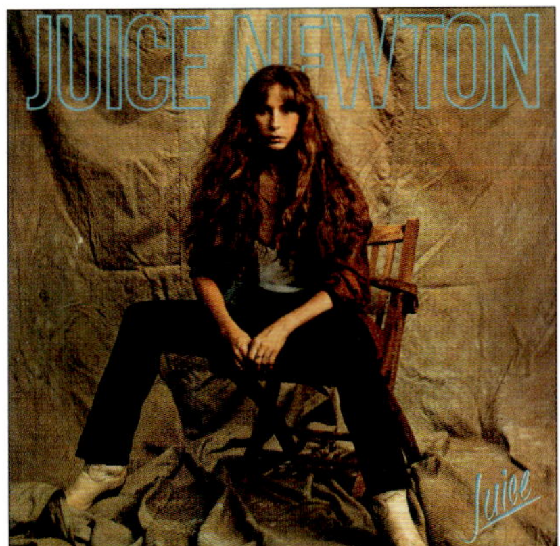

Straddling country and pop, **Juice Newton**'s *Juice* produced a trio of breakthrough hits "Angel of the Morning," "Queen of Hearts" and "The Sweetest Thing (I've Ever Known)."

Billboard 200: *Juice* (#22)
Billboard Hot 100: "Angel of the Morning" (#4); "Queen of Hearts" (#2); "The Sweetest Thing (I've Ever Known)" (#7)

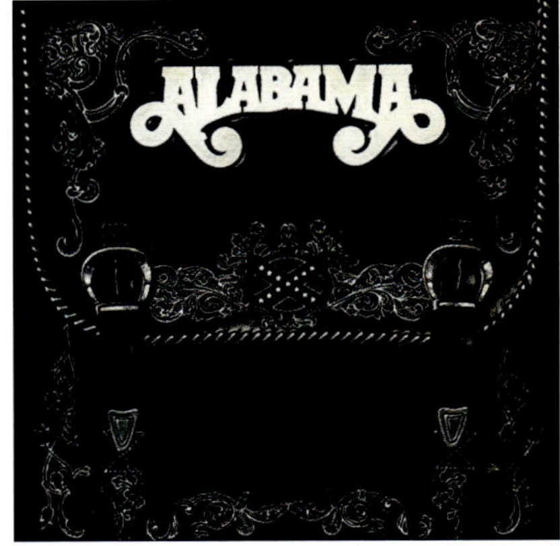

Three No. 1 country singles–"Love in the First Degree," "Old Flame" and the title track–would keep **Alabama**'s *Feels So Right* on the *Billboard* 200 for three years.

Billboard 200: *Feels So Right* (#16)
Billboard Hot 100: "Feels So Right" (#20); "Love in the First Degree" (#15)

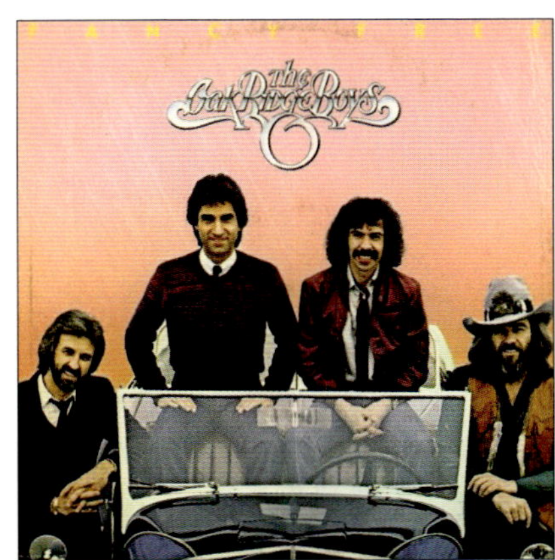

The Oak Ridge Boys recorded their signature country and crossover hit, "Elvira," a doo-wop-style ditty from the Sixties that made them a genuine sensation.

Billboard 200: *Fancy Free* (#14)
Billboard Hot 100: "Elvira" (#5)

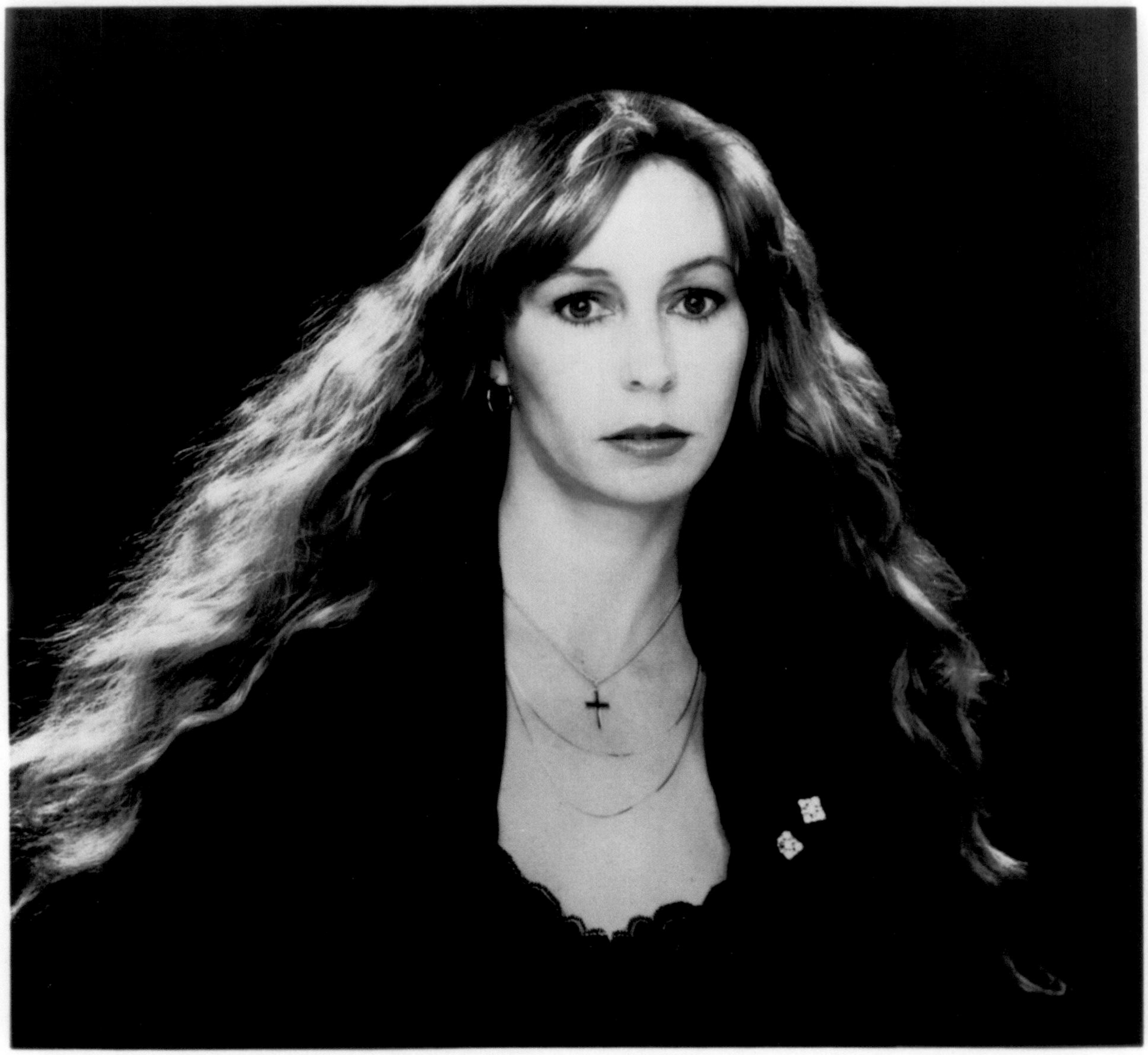

Photo: Charles Bush / 1981

JUICE NEWTON

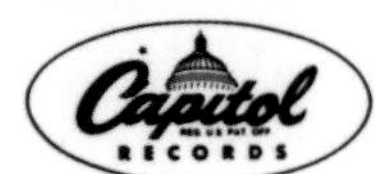

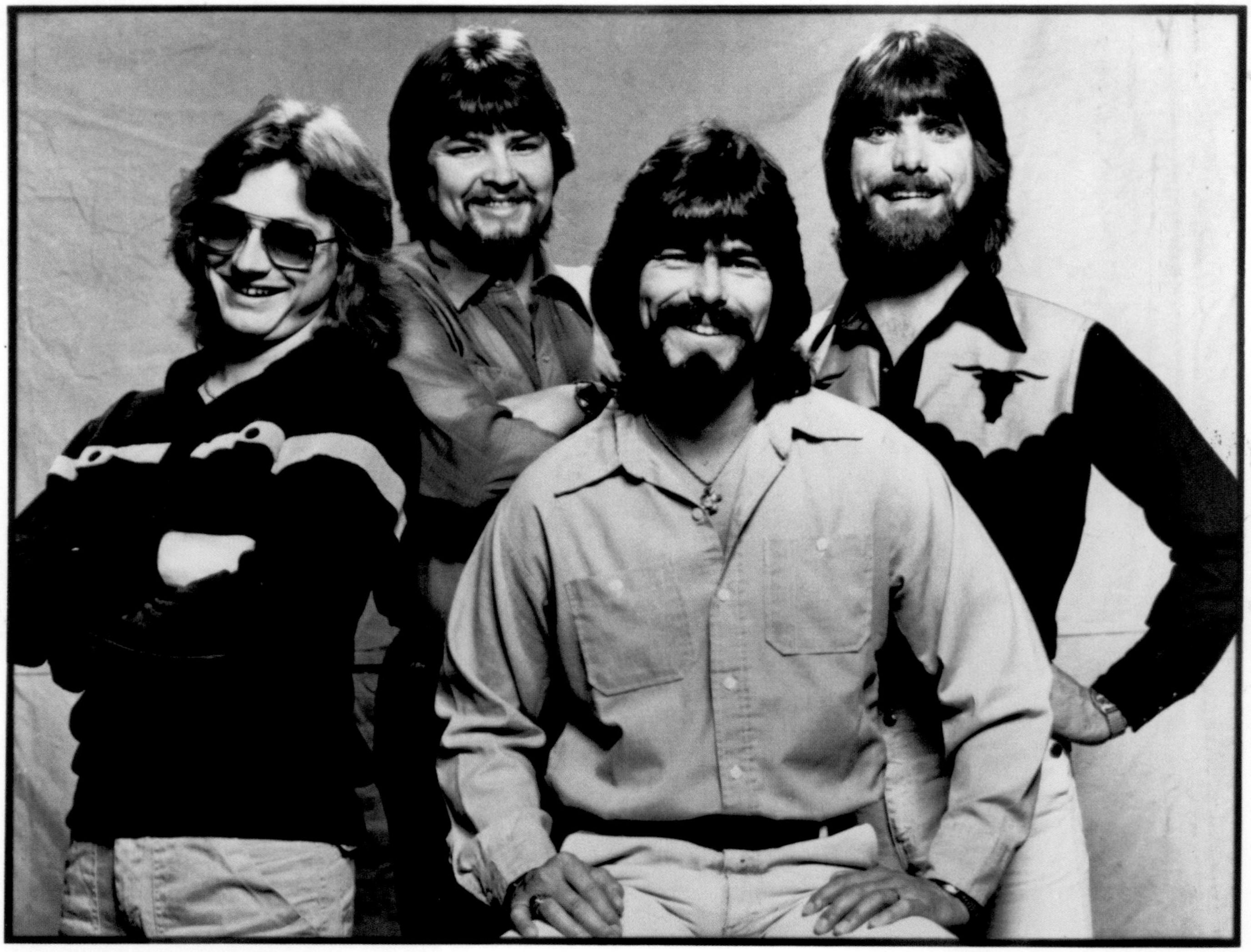

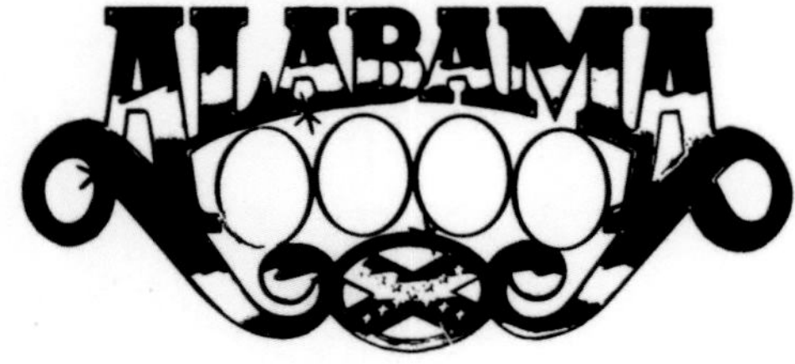
ALABAMA

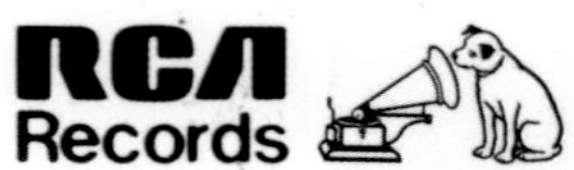
RCA
Records

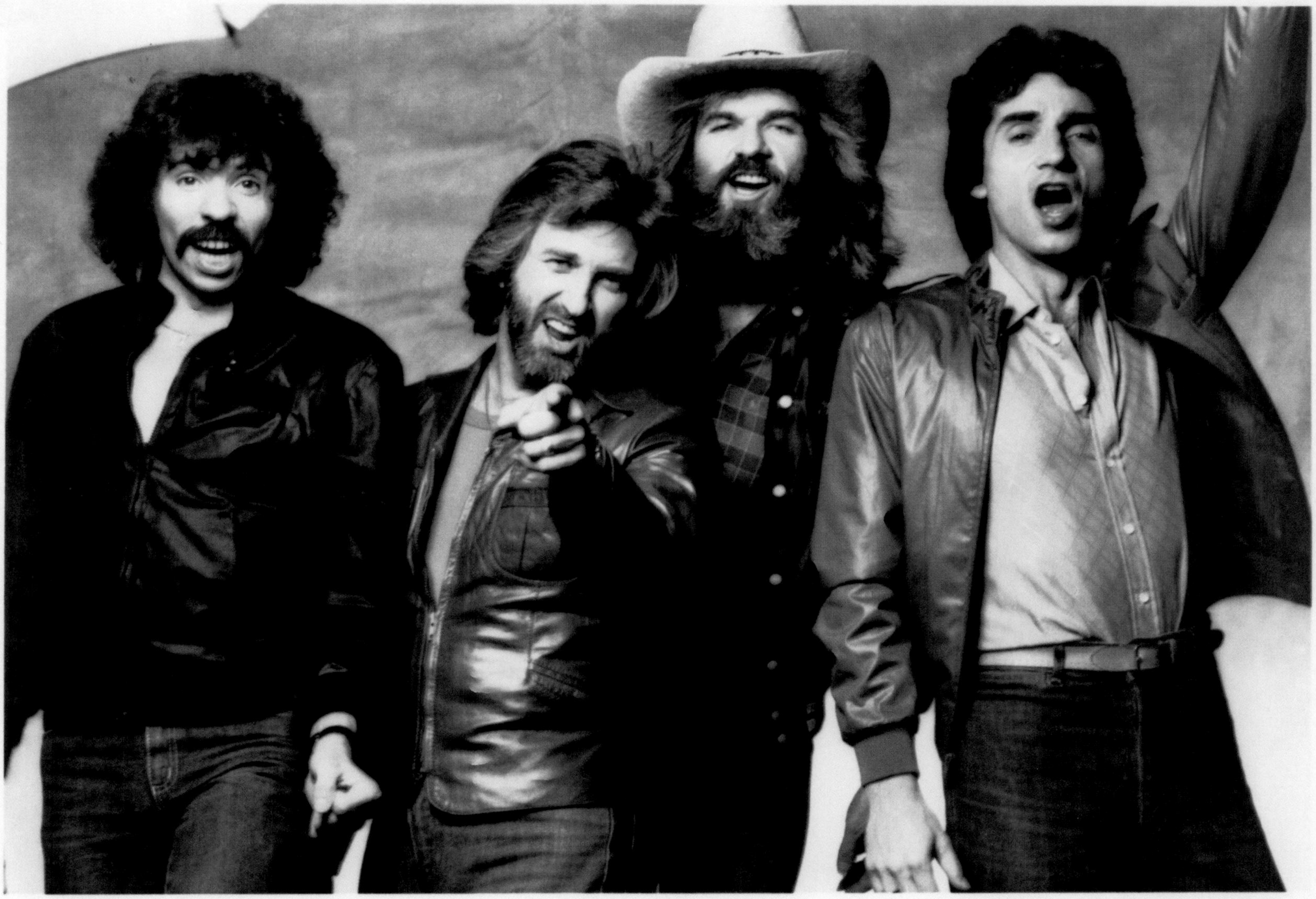

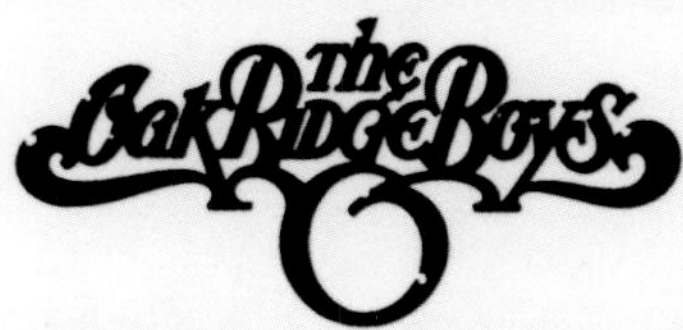

JOE–DUANE–BILL–RICHARD

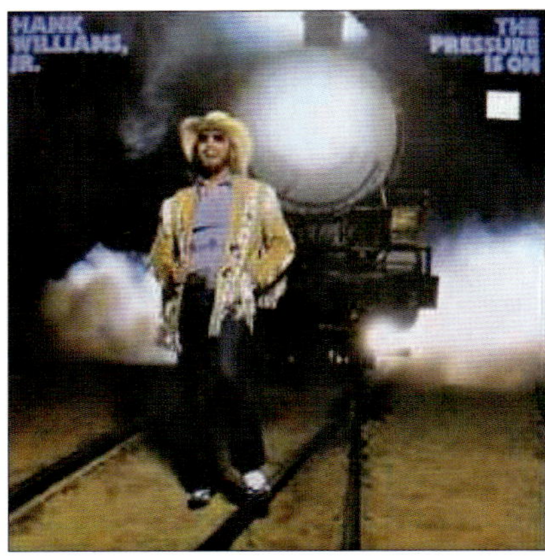

The prolific **Hank Williams, Jr.** recorded two signature redneck rockers, "A Country Boy Can Survive" and the No. 1 country track, "All My Rowdy Friends (Have Settled Down)."

Billboard 200: *The Pressure Is On* (#76)

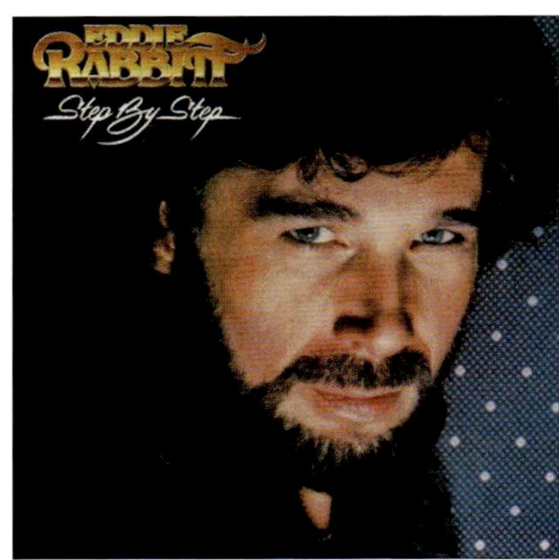

Step by Step continued country artist **Eddie Rabbitt**'s crossover success, as the title track reached the Top 5 on country, adult contemporary and pop charts.

Billboard 200: *Step by Step* (#23)
Billboard Hot 100: "Step by Step" (#5);
"Someone Could Lose a Heart Tonight" (#15);
"I Don't Know Where to Start" (#35)

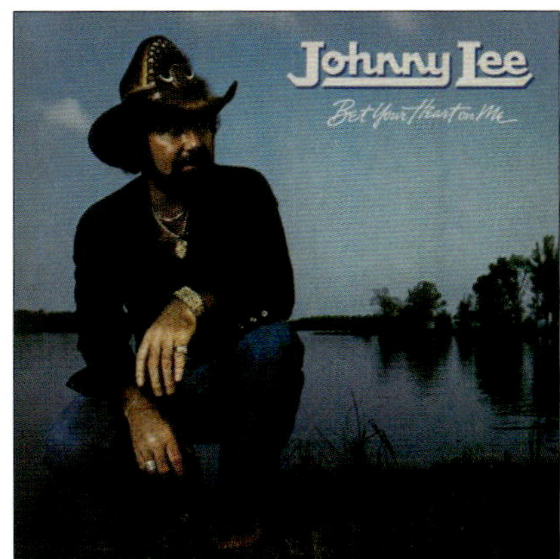

After the *Urban Cowboy* soundtrack had catapulted **Johnny Lee** to fame, "Bet Your Heart on Me" became the singer's third single to top the country chart.

Billboard 200: *Bet Your Heart on Me* (#147)
Billboard Hot 100: "Bet Your Heart on Me" (#54)

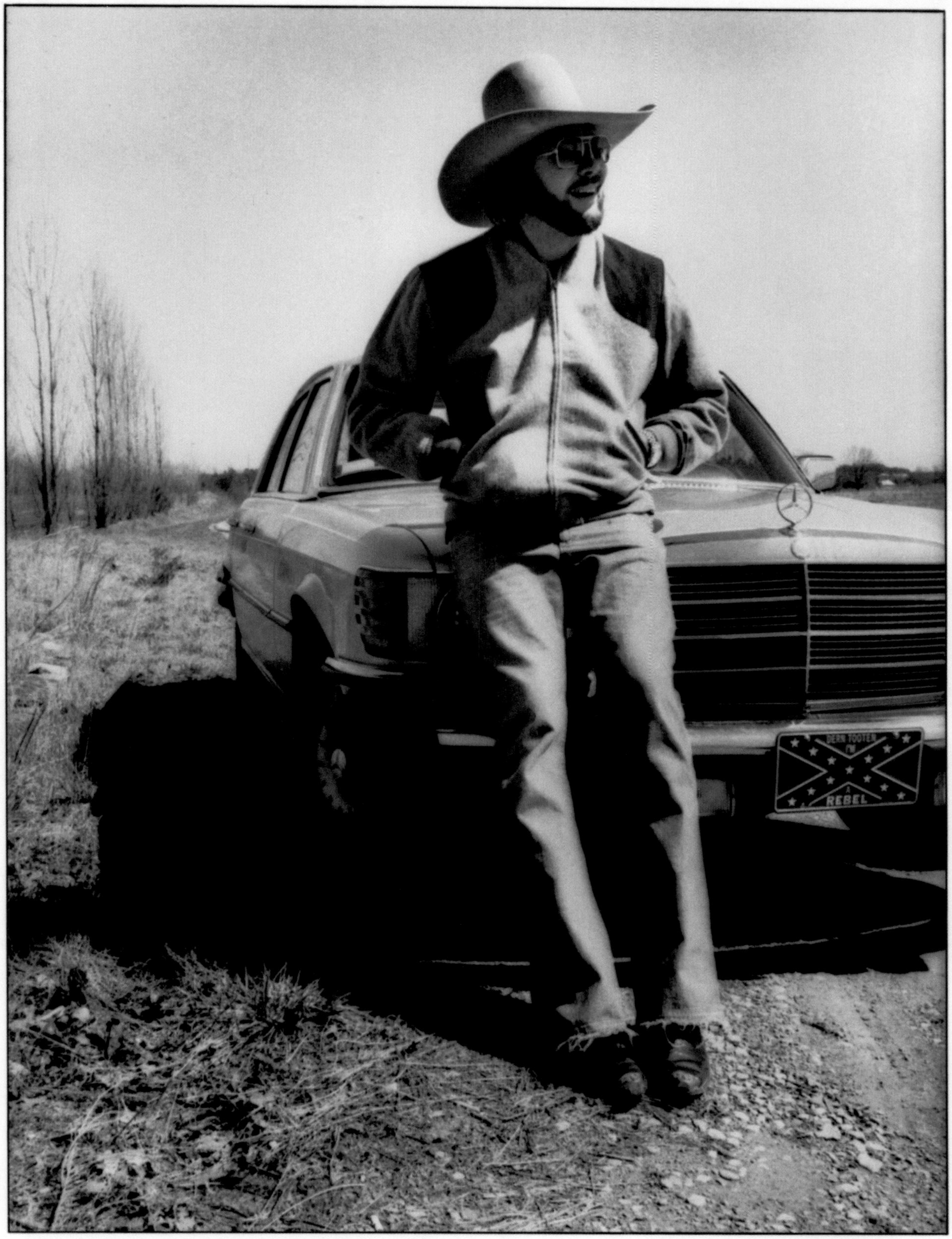

HANK WILLIAMS, Jr.

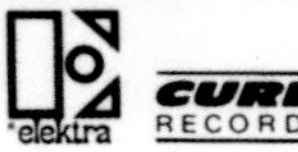

PHOTO CREDIT: JIM SHEA/1981

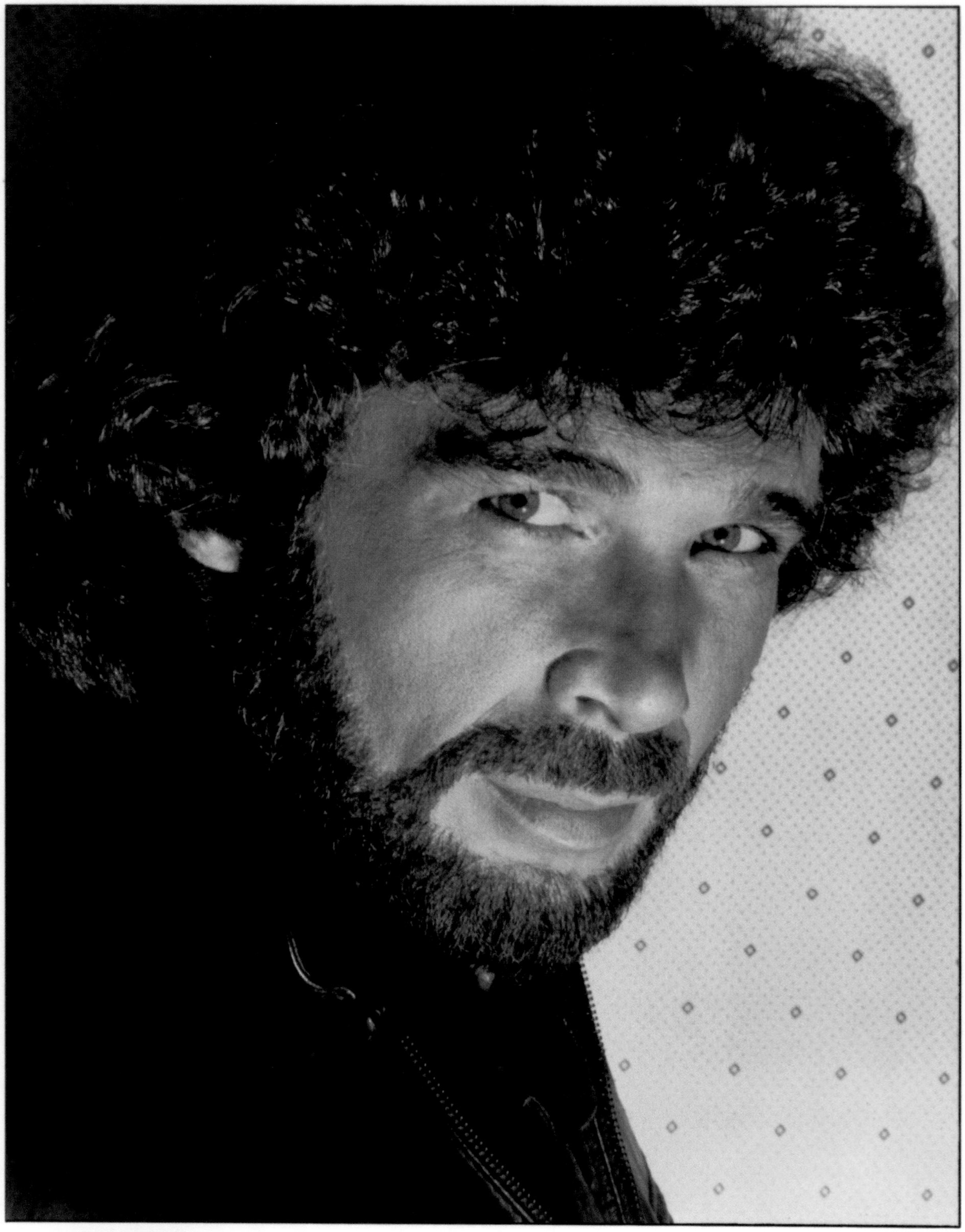

PHOTO CREDIT: LYNN GOLDSMITH, INC./1981

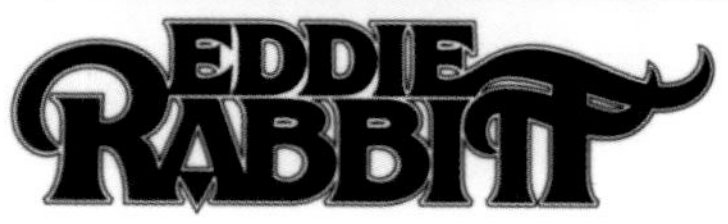

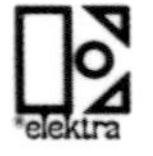

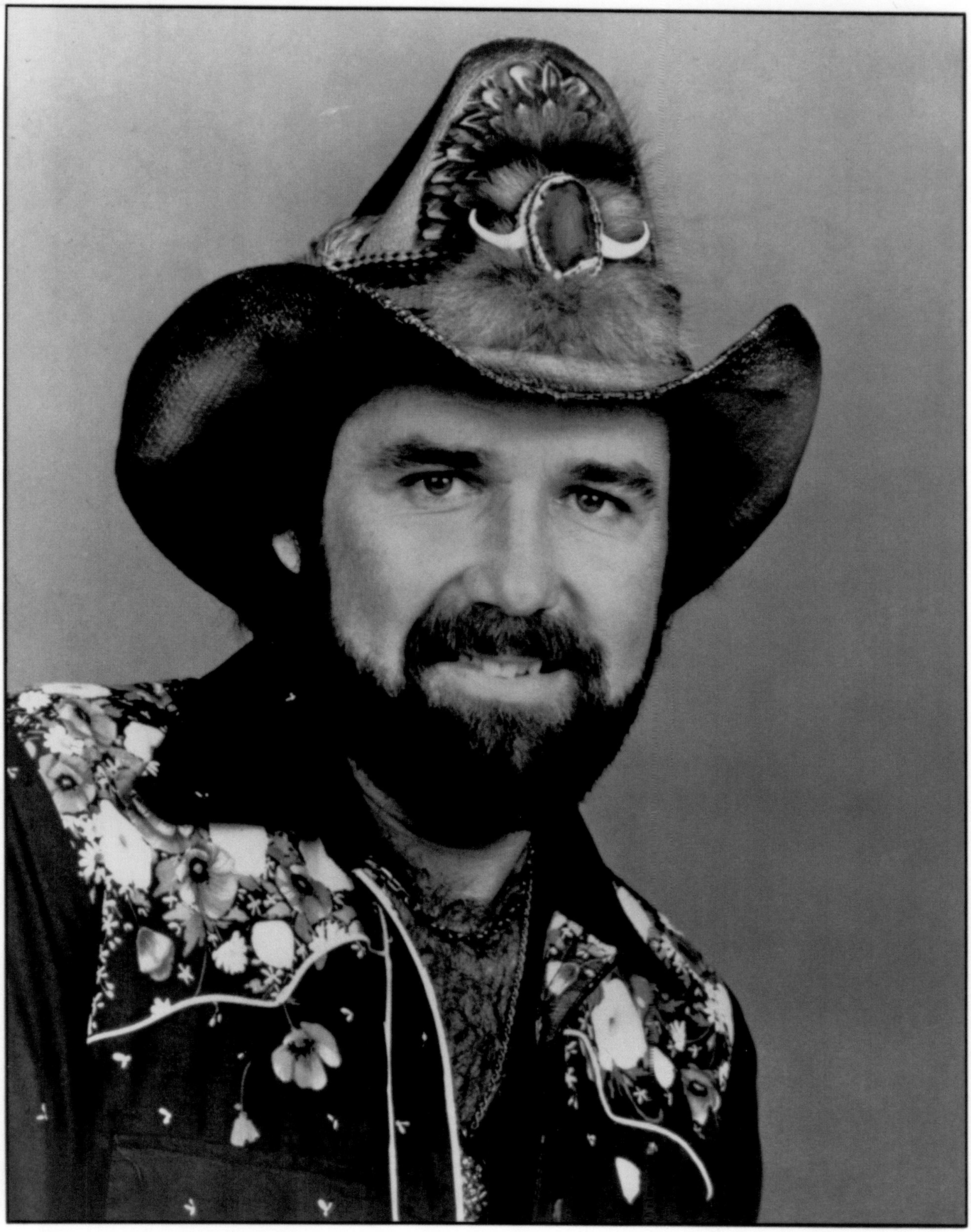

1981

JOHNNY LEE

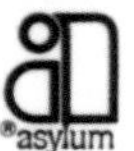

Glen Campbell's *It's the World Gone Crazy* included "Any Which Way You Can," the title song to the Clint Eastwood movie and a Top 10 hit on the country music charts.

Billboard 200: *It's the World Gone Crazy* (#178)
Billboard Hot 100: "I Don't Want to Know Your Name" (#65)

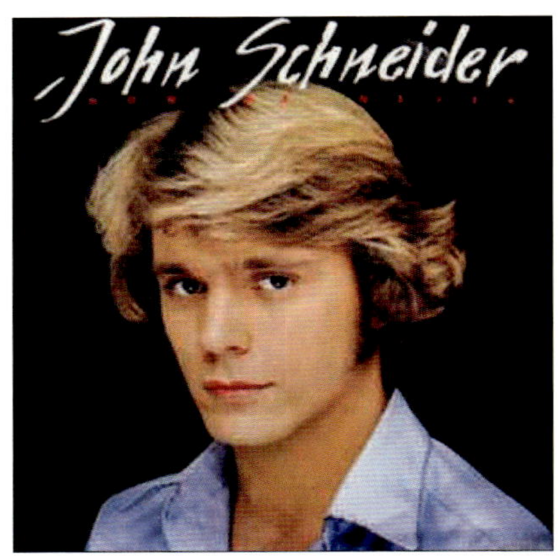

Known as "Bo Duke" on TV's *The Dukes of Hazzard*, **John Schneider** covered Elvis Presley's "It's Now or Never," making the Top 5 on the country and adult contemporary charts.

Billboard 200: *Now or Never* (#37)
Billboard Hot 100: "It's Now or Never" (#14); "Still" (#69)

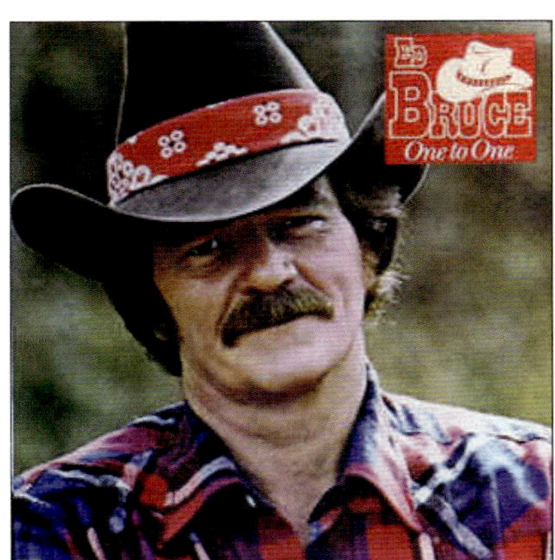

A No. 1 on the country chart, "You're the Best Break This Old Heart Ever Had" gave veteran songwriter, singer and actor **Ed Bruce** his greatest success as a vocalist.

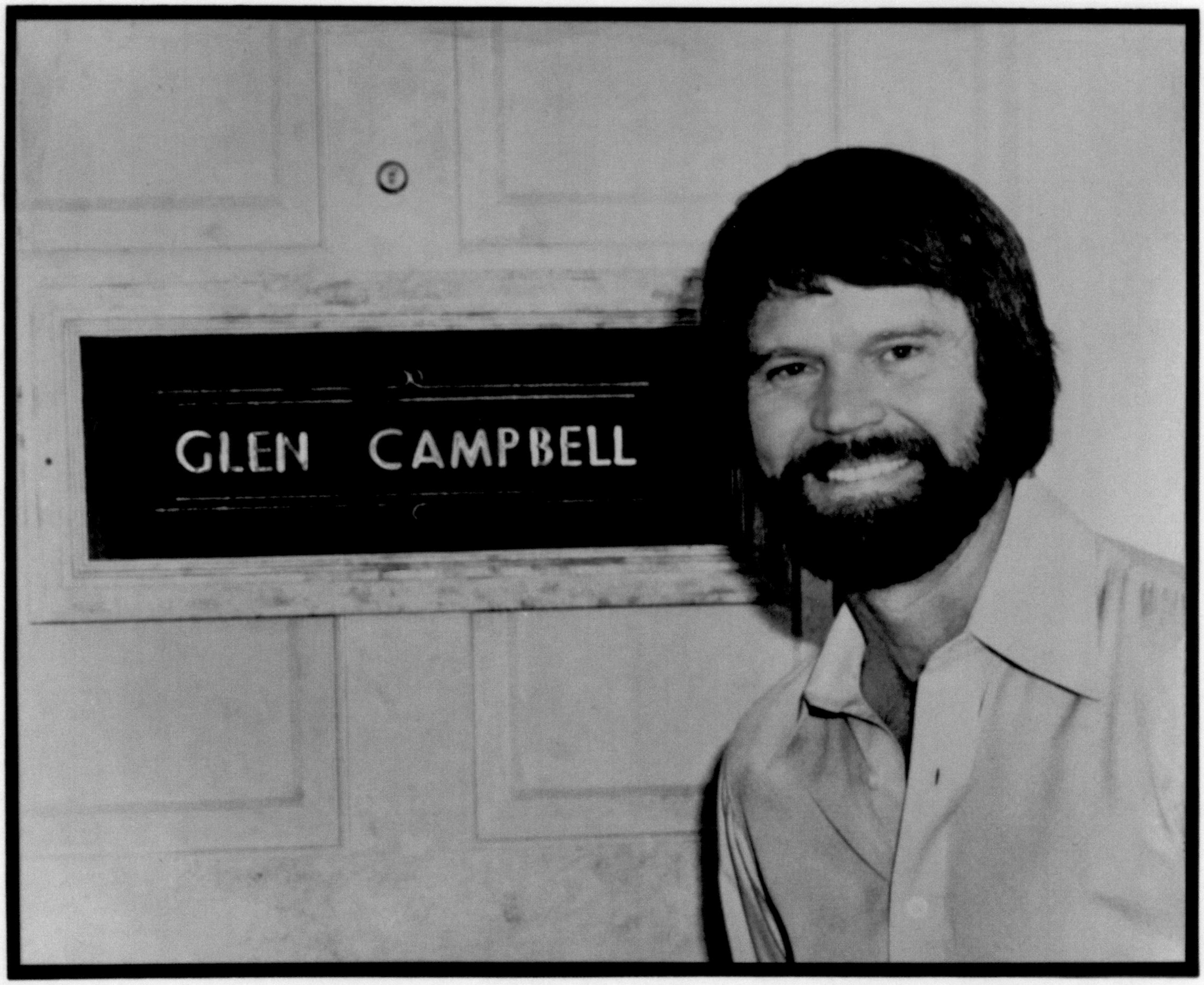

GLEN CAMPBELL

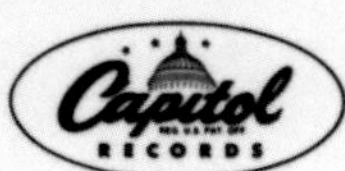

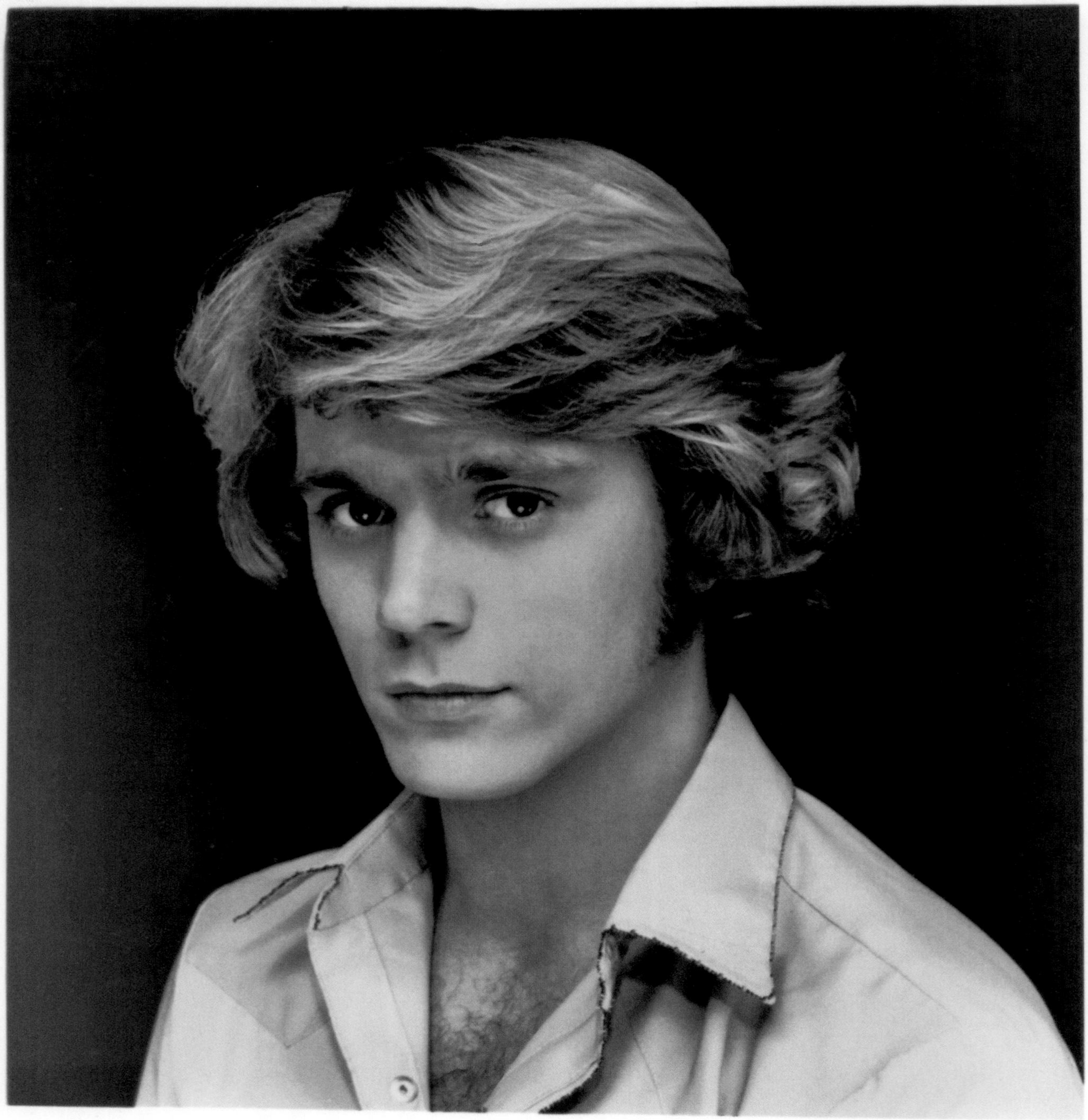

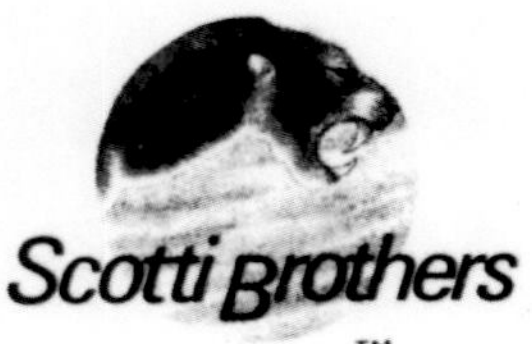

JOHN SCHNEIDER

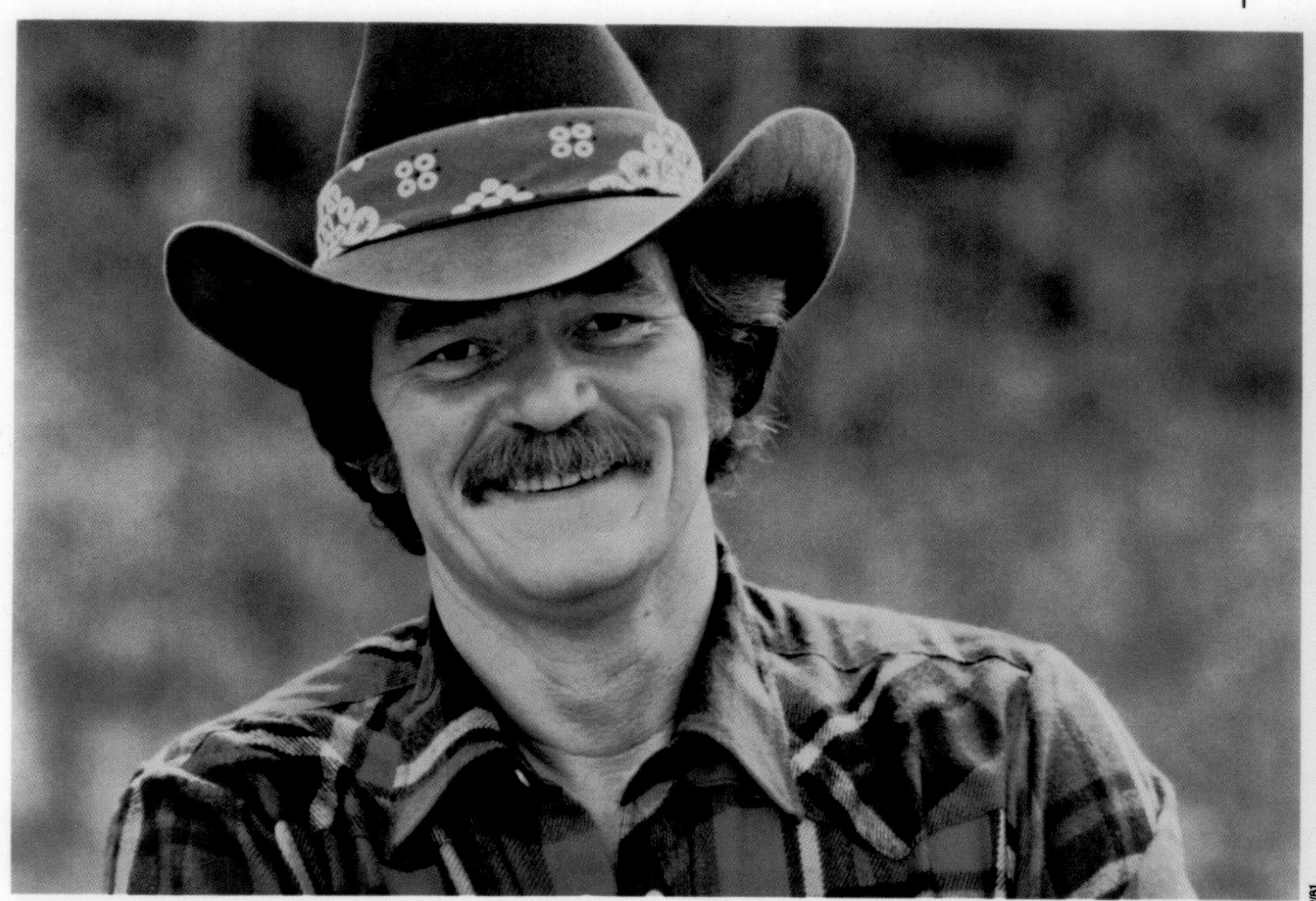

2/81

Ed Bruce

Exclusively On
MCA RECORDS

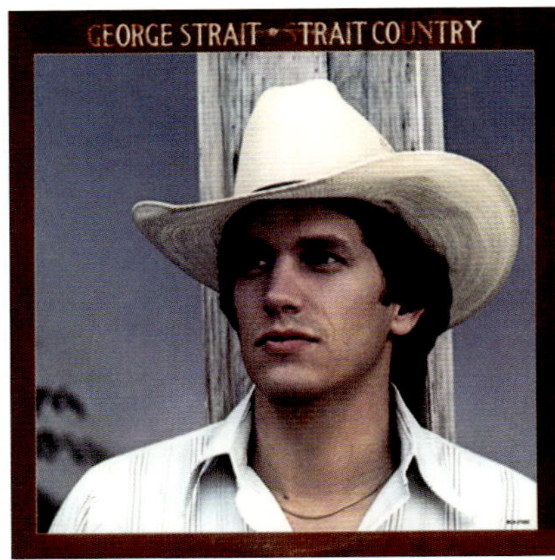

The traditional country music approach of **George Strait**'s "Unwound," the first single from his aptly named debut album, *Strait Country*, sparked a succession of hits.

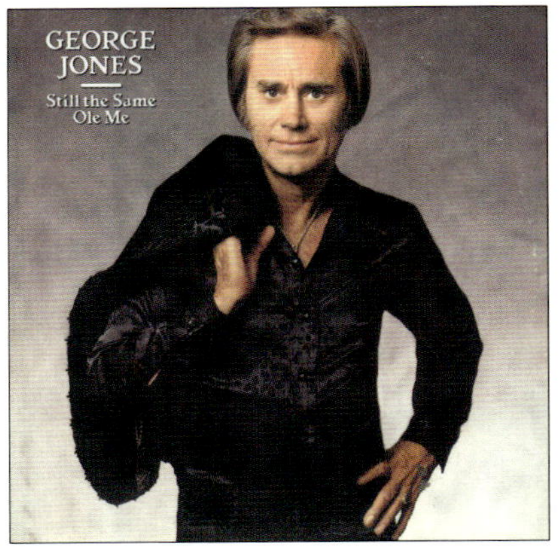

"Still Doin' Time," an autobiographical honkytonk ballad of a man held captive by alcohol, gave **George Jones** another No. 1 smash on the country charts.

Billboard 200: *Still the Same Ole Me* (#115)

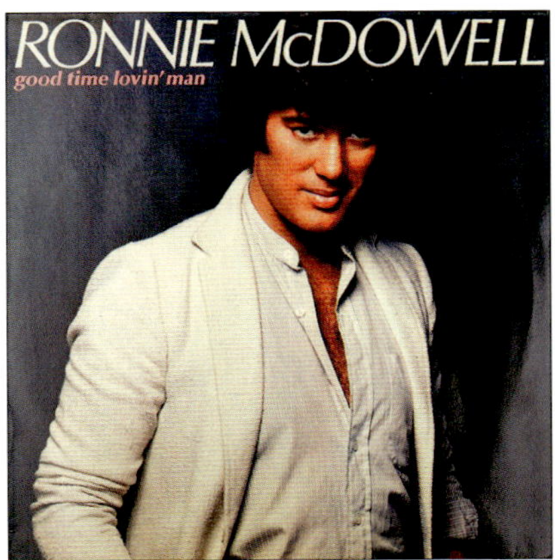

Four years after his elegiac hit, "The King Is Gone," country singer and Elvis soundalike **Ronnie McDowell** enjoyed his first No. 1 on the country chart with "Older Women."

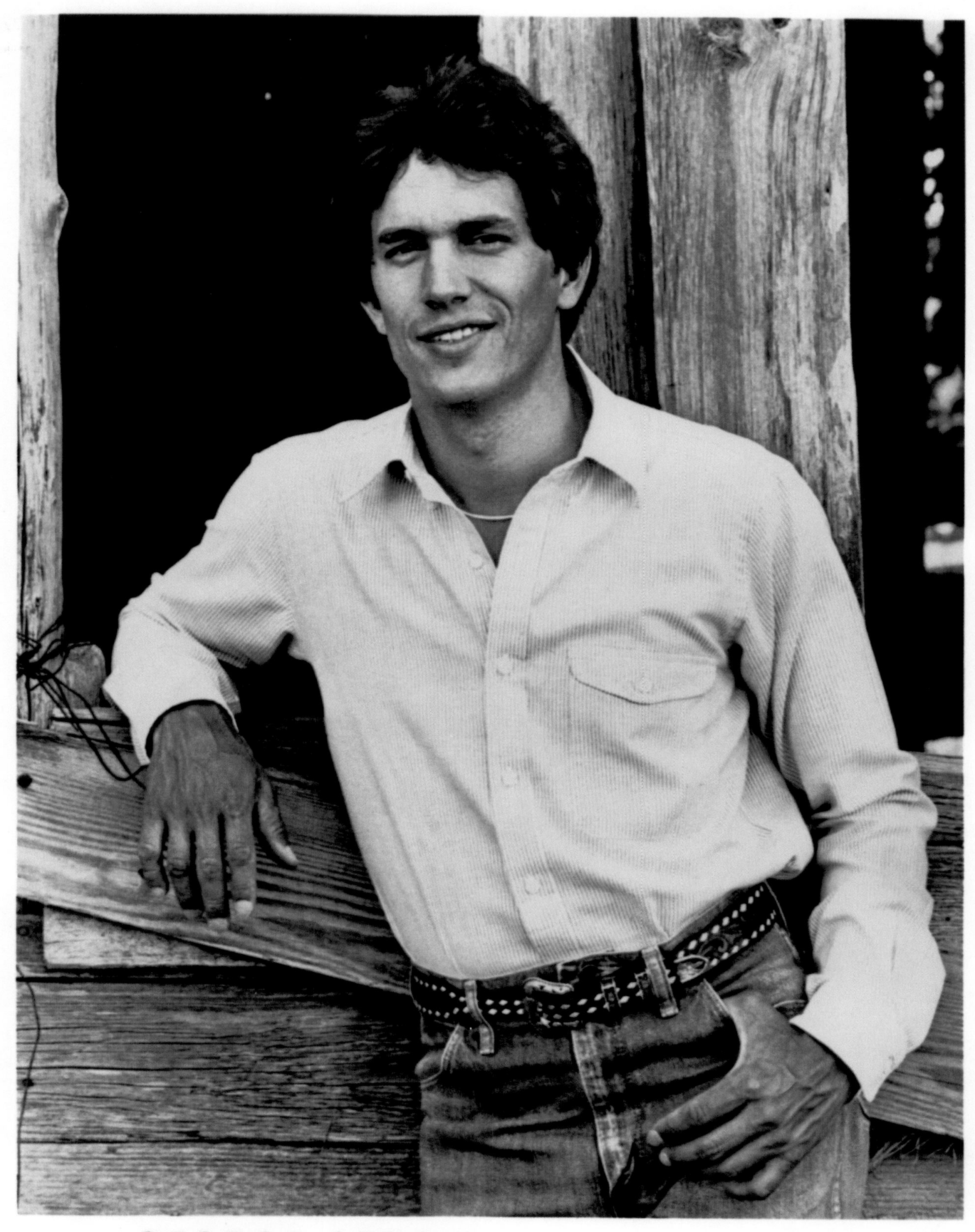

GEORGE STRAIT

MCA RECORDS

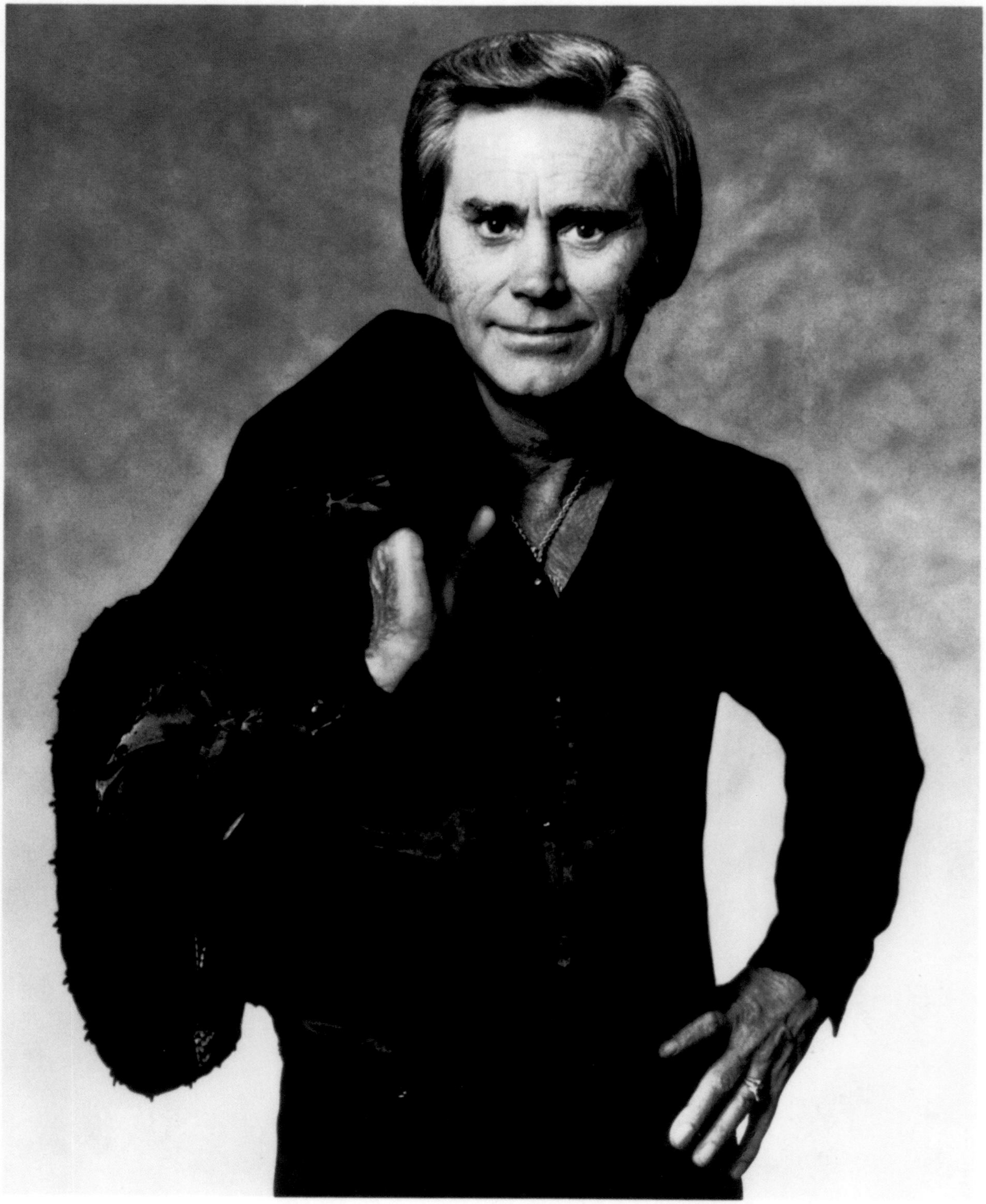

photo credit: Anthony Darius

GEORGE JONES

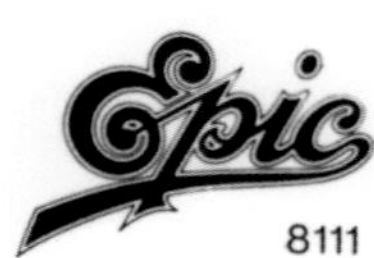

8111

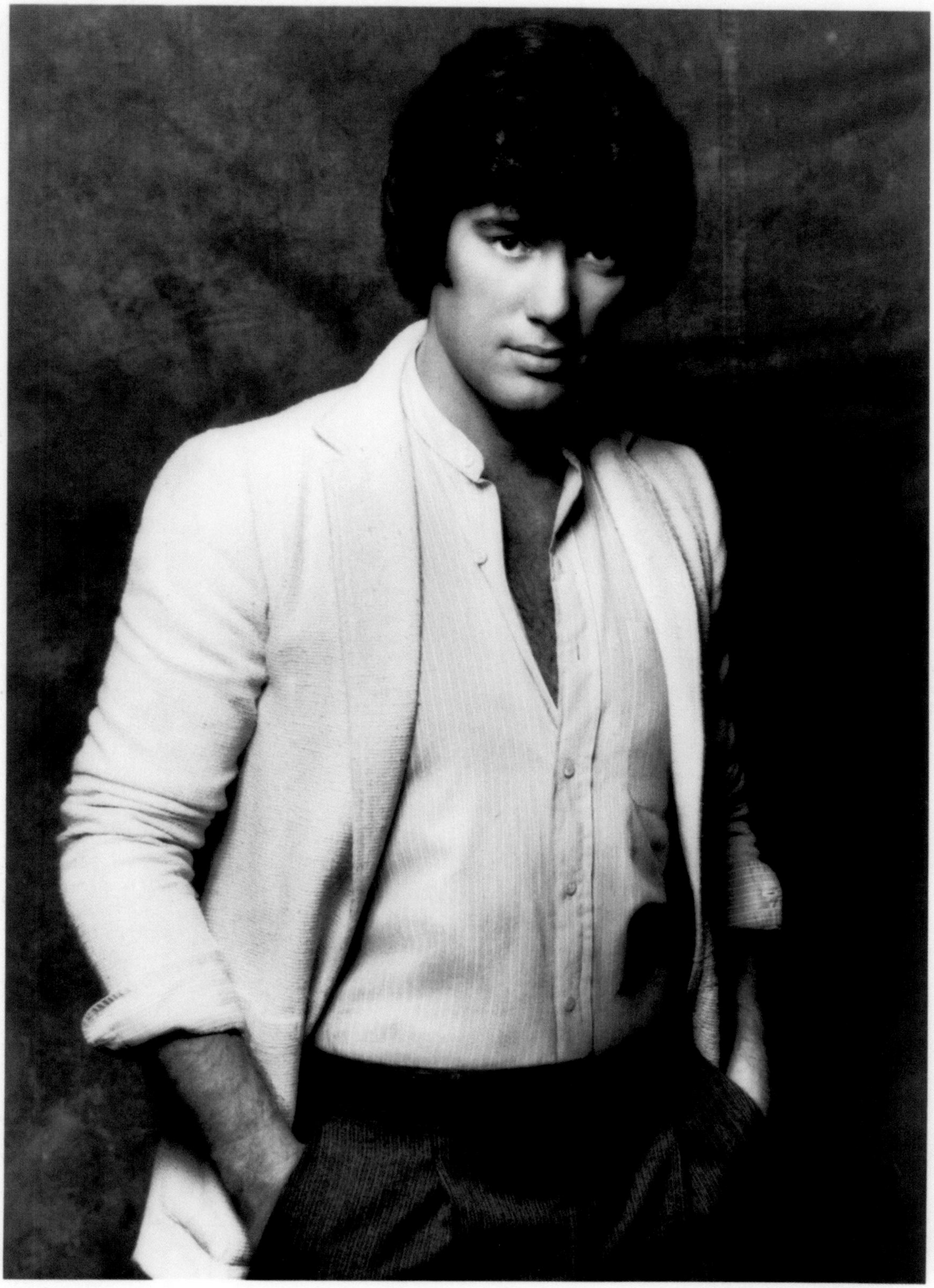

photo credit NORMAN SEEFF

RONNIE McDOWELL

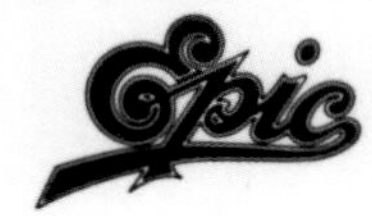

8107

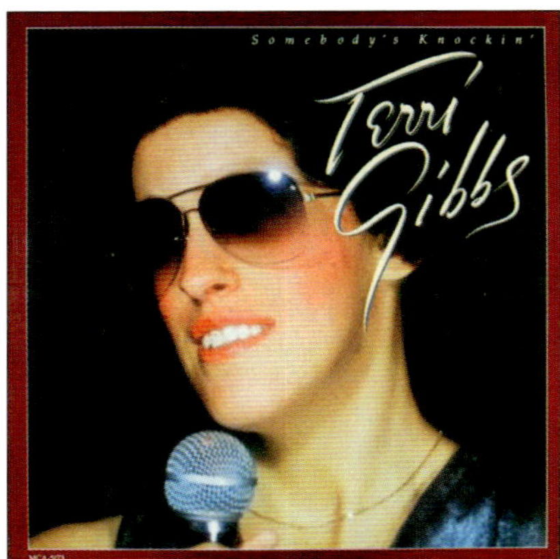

"Somebody's Knockin'," the first single from blind country singer **Terri Gibbs**, became a crossover sensation, ascending into the pop and adult contemporary charts.

Billboard 200: *Somebody's Knockin'* (#53)
Billboard Hot 100: "Somebody's Knockin'" (#13); "Rich Man" (#89)

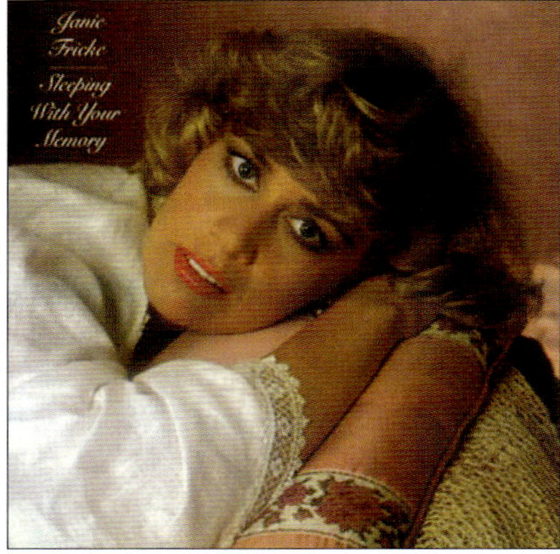

Singer **Janie Fricke** recorded two successful singles, the gently suggestive "Do Me with Love" and "Don't Worry 'Bout Me Baby," her first country chart-topper.

Billboard 200: *En-Tact* (#138)
Billboard Hot 100: "Move Any Mountain" (#38)

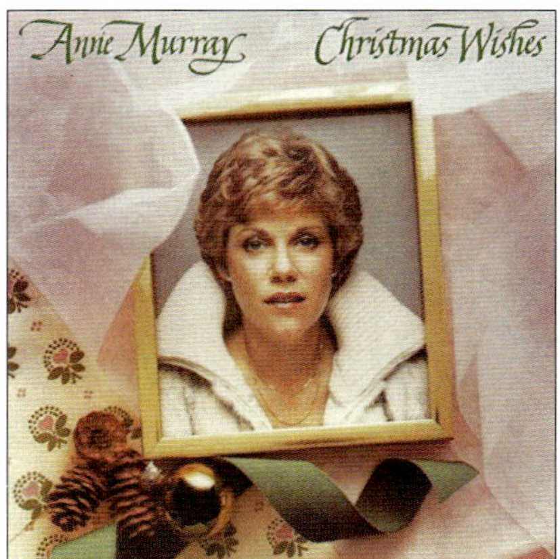

Christmas Wishes, **Anne Murray**'s first holiday album, stood as one of the best-selling recordings of the Canadian country vocalist's distinguished career.

Billboard 200: *Christmas Wishes* (#54)

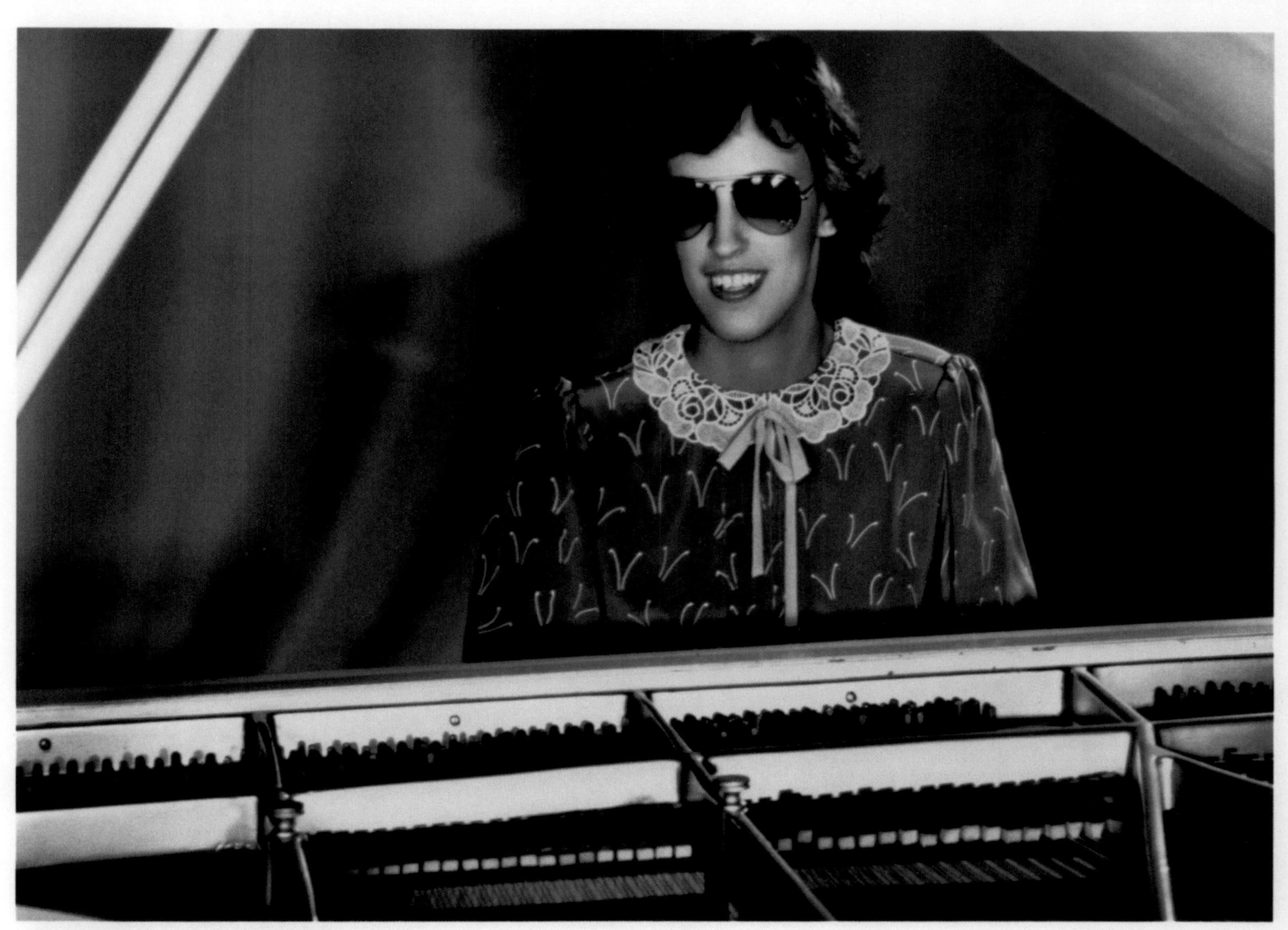

TERRI GIBBS

.MCA RECORDS

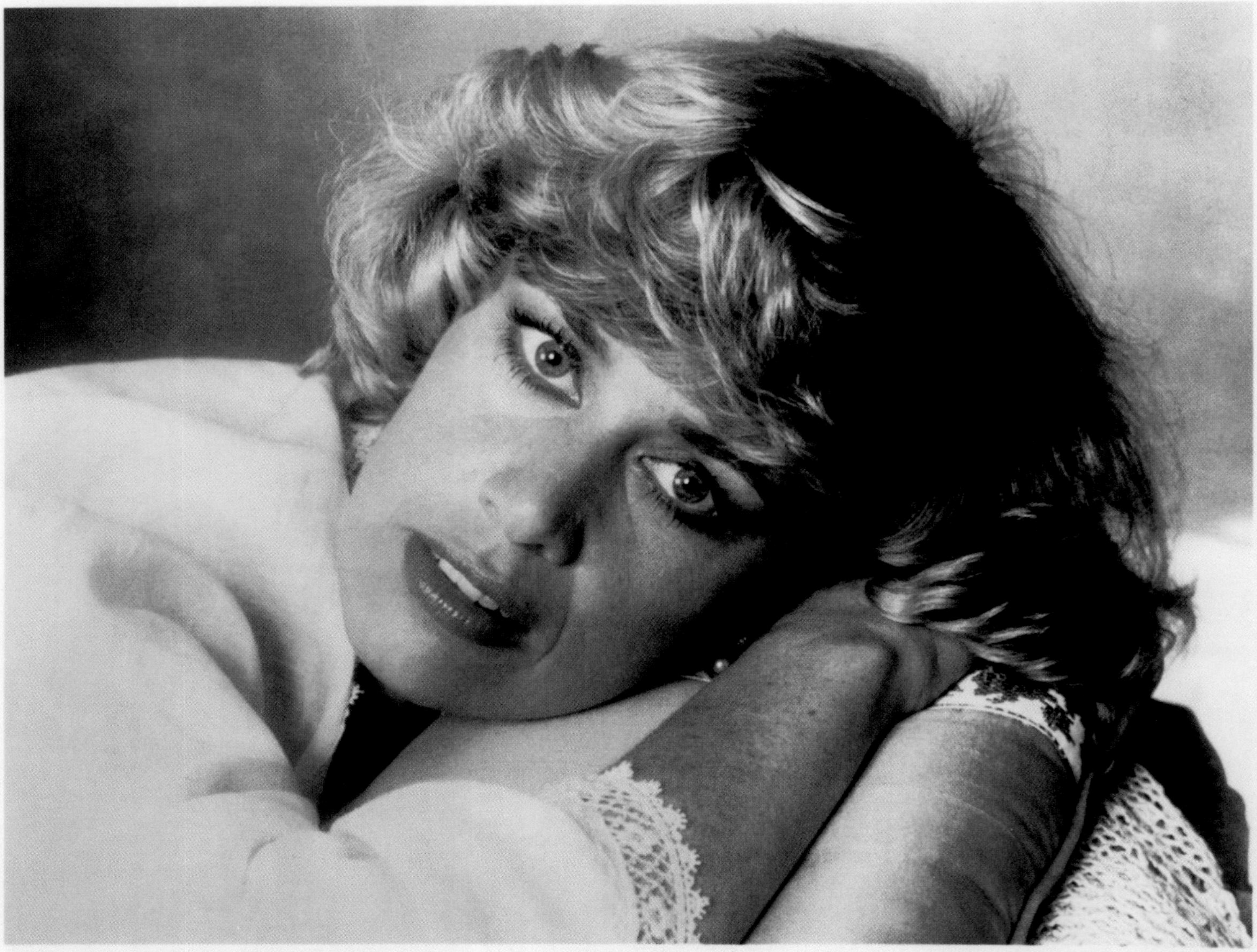

Janie Fricke

photo credit: Alan Messer

Columbia

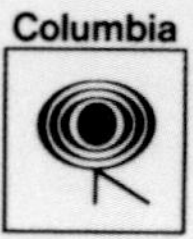

8109

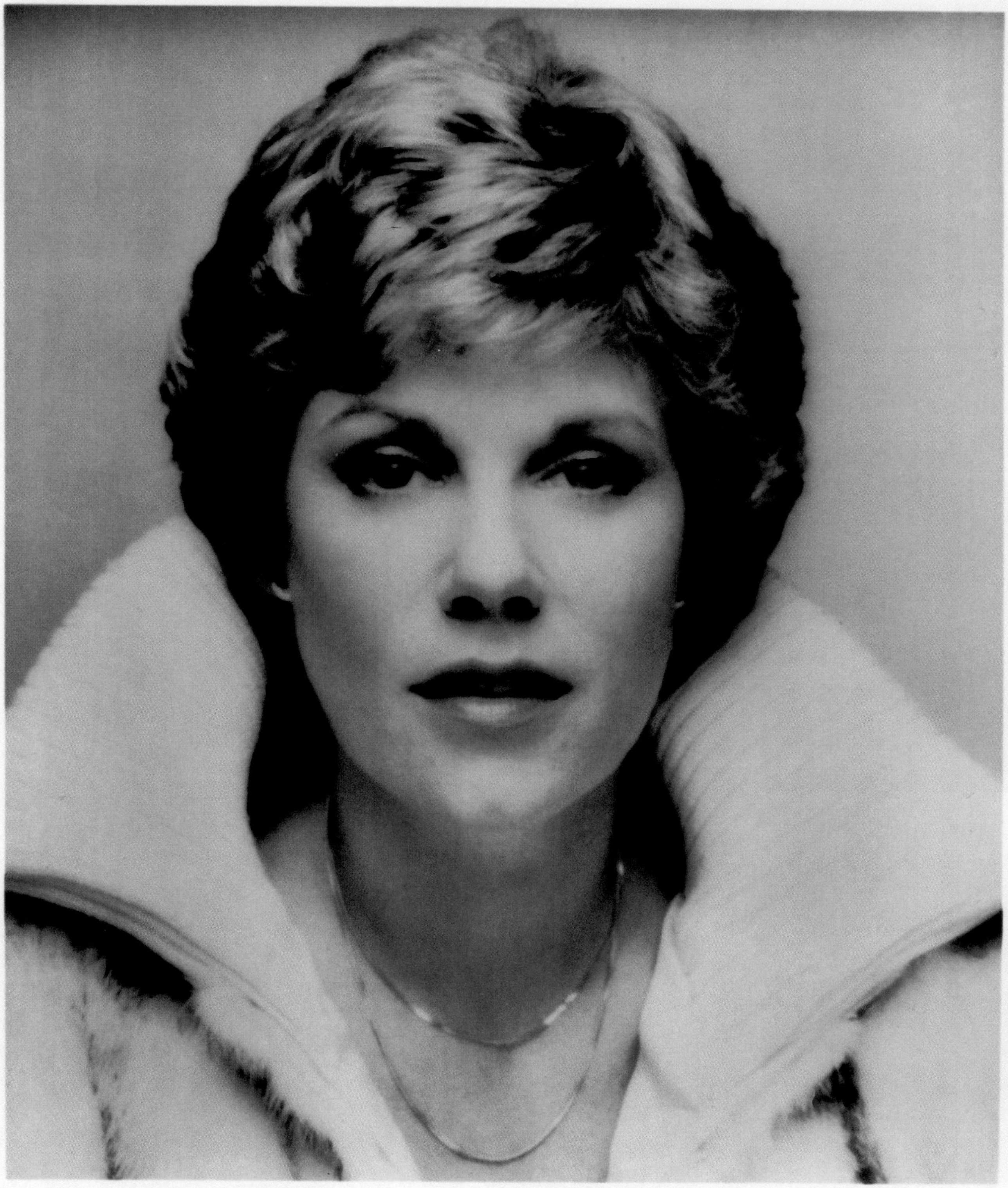

Photo: Tim Saunders / 1981

Anne Murray

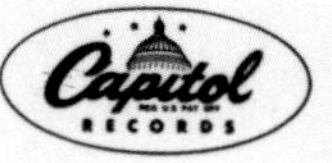

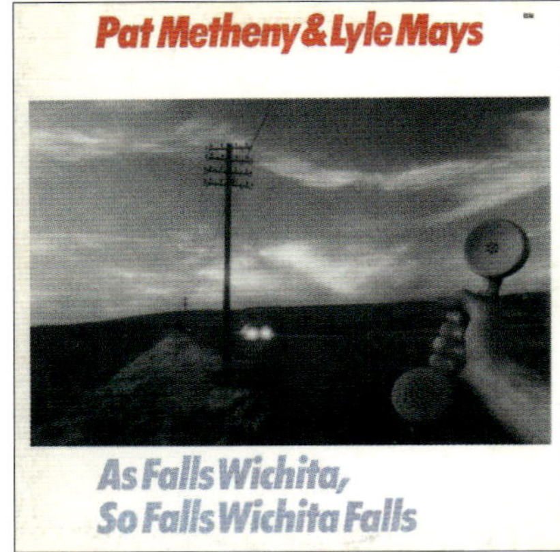

As Falls Wichita, So Falls Wichita Falls by **Pat Metheny & Lyle Mays** found the guitar ace and his keyboardist collaborator stretching out on the 21-minute-long title track.

Billboard 200: *As Falls Wichita, So Falls Wichita Falls*

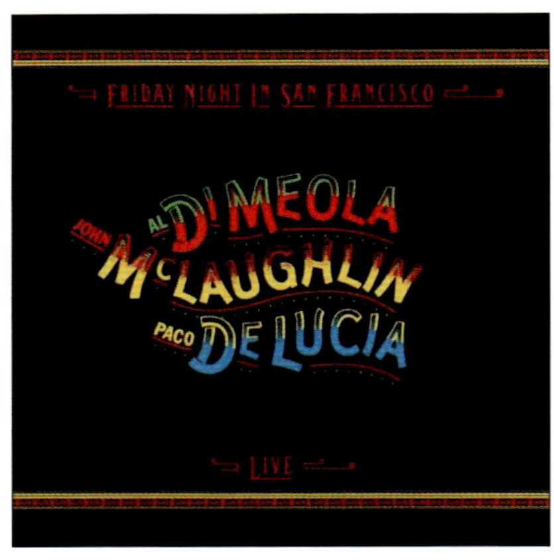

Jazz guitarists **Al Di Meola, John McLaughlin & Paco De Lucia** collaborated on a highly acclaimed and influential acoustic live album, *Friday Night in San Francisco.*

Billboard 200: *Friday Night in San Francisco* (#97)

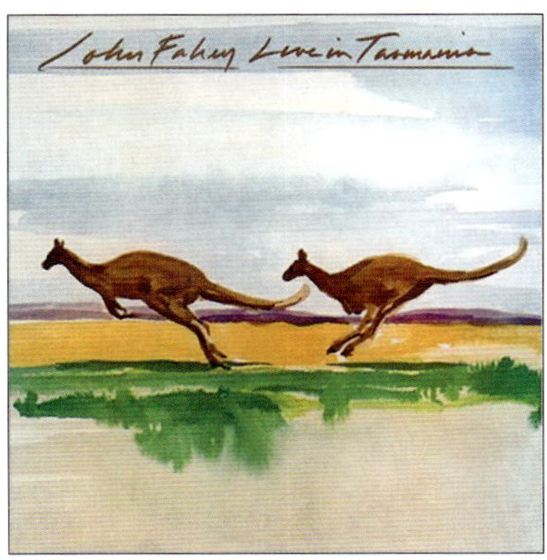

After 18 innovative albums and two decades of concerts, the extraordinary and eccentric fingerstyle guitarist **John Fahey** released his first live recording, *Live in Tasmania.*

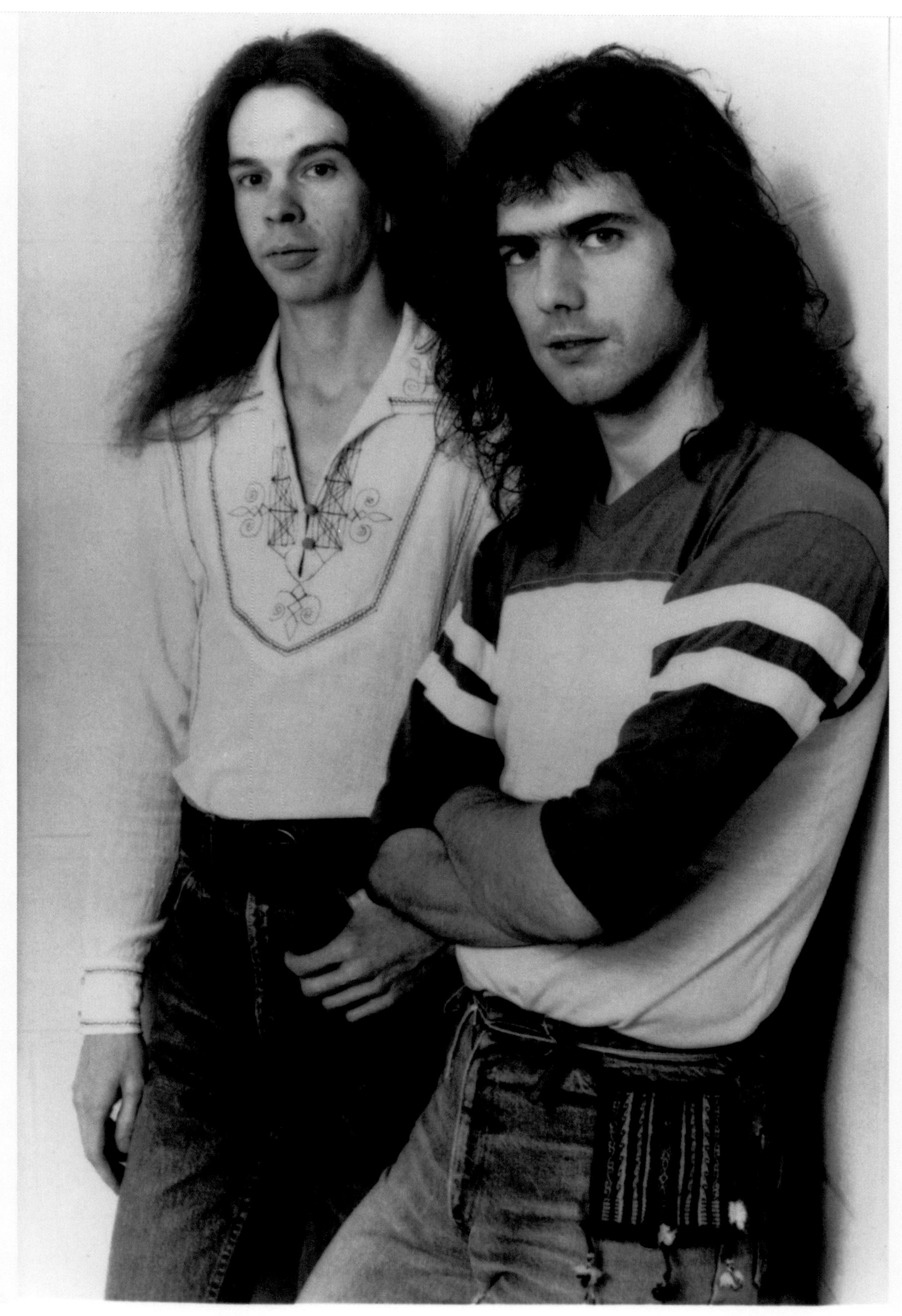

LYLE MAYS, PAT METHENY

ECM RECORDS

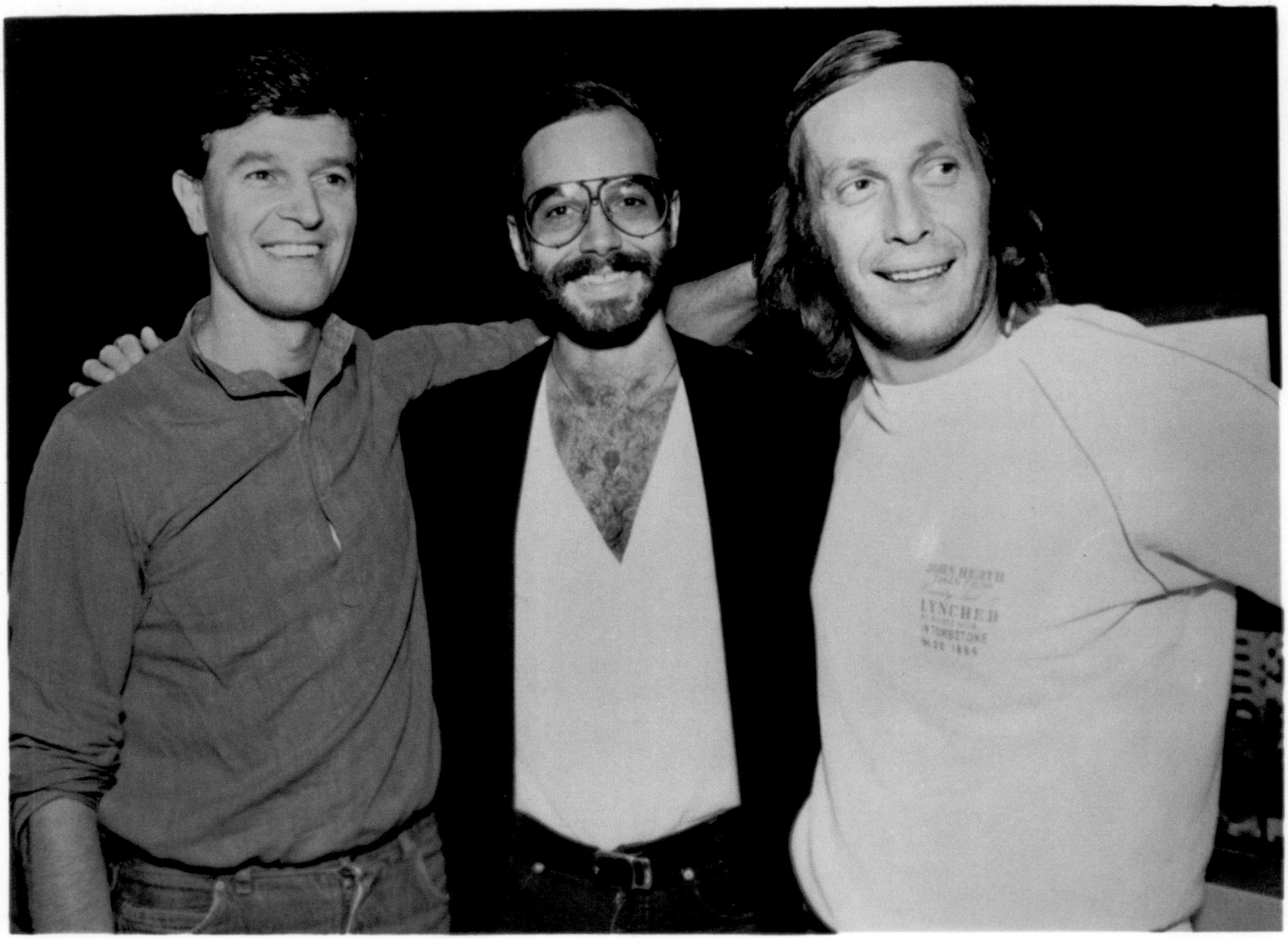

JOHN McLAUGHLIN, AL Di MEOLA, PACO De LUCIA

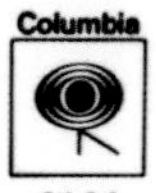

8104

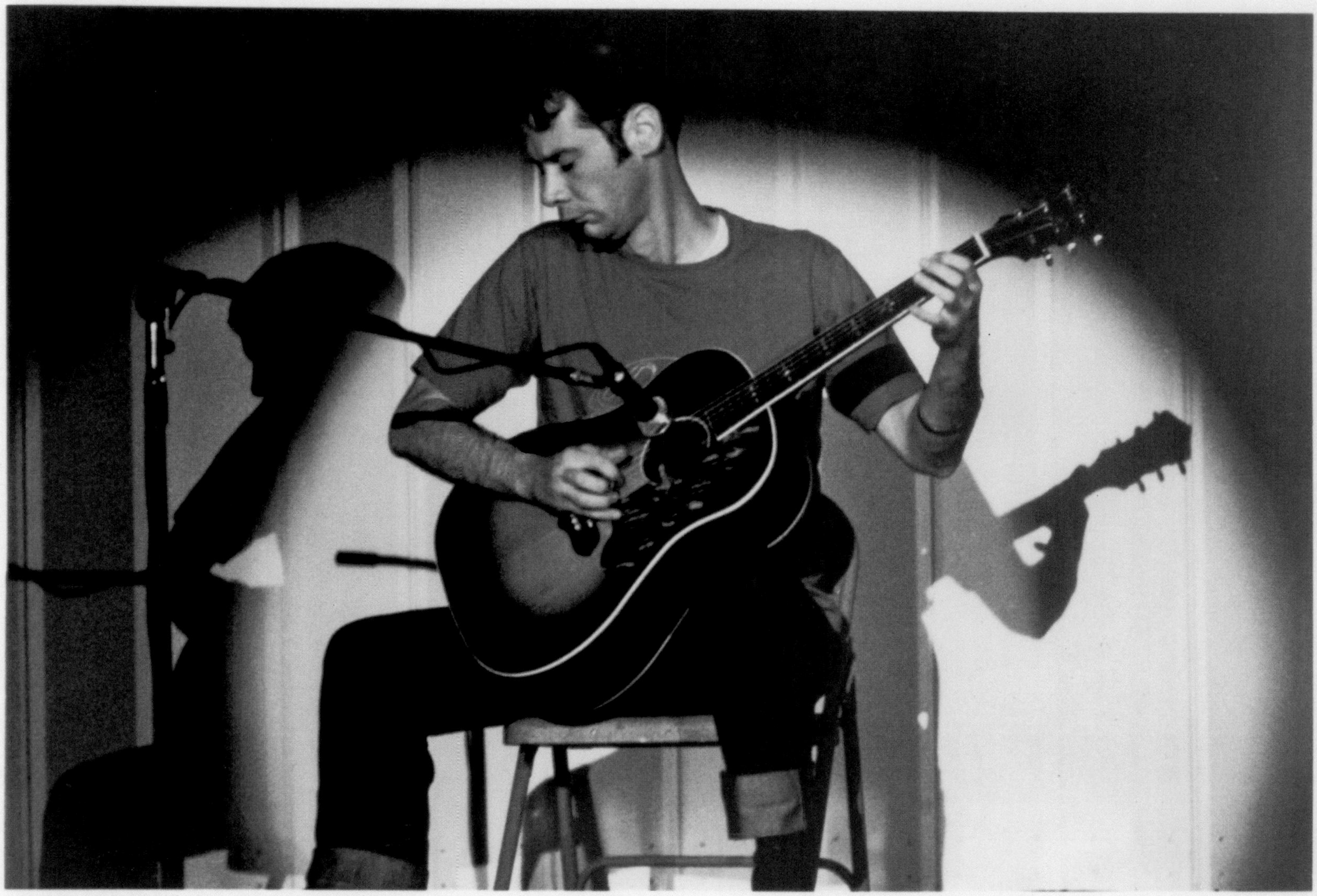

JOHN FAHEY

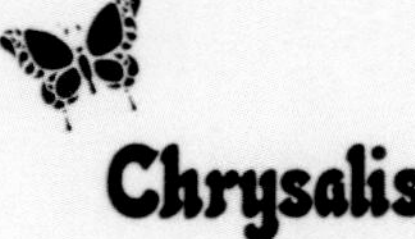

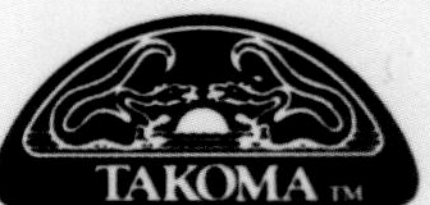

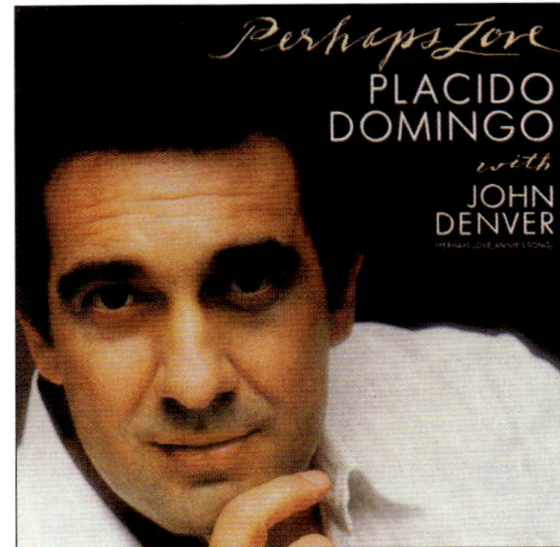

One of the world's leading tenors, **Plácido Domingo** spread his reputation beyond the opera world, recording "Perhaps Love" as a duet with John Denver.

Billboard 200: *Perhaps Love* (#18)
Billboard Hot 100: "Perhaps Love" (#59)

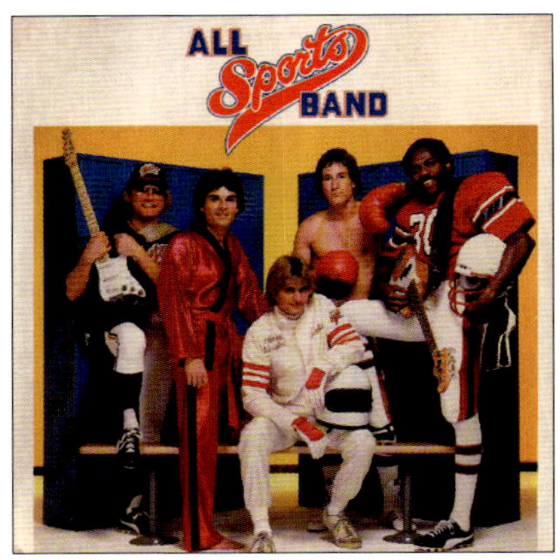

A manufactured group à la Village People, **All Sports Band** comprised "athletes" from auto racing, baseball, boxing, football and martial arts—and saw slight success.

Billboard Hot 100: "I'm Your Superman" (#93);
"Opposites Do Attract" (#78)

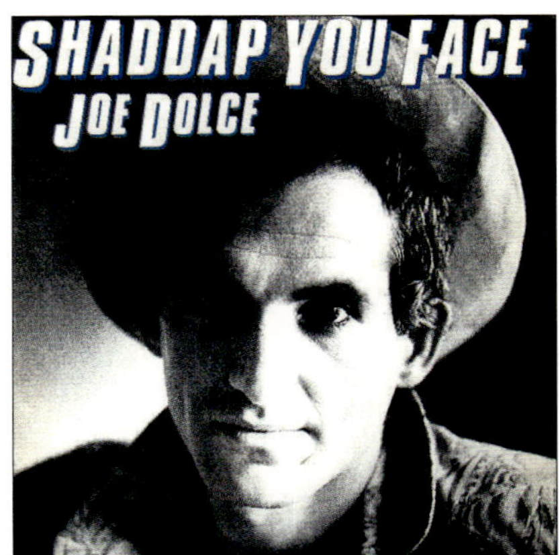

Inspired by his Italian grandparents, Australian **Joe Dolce**'s multimillion-selling novelty song, "Shaddap You Face," became a global hit, reaching No. 1 in 10 countries.

Billboard Hot 100: "Shaddap You Face" (#53)

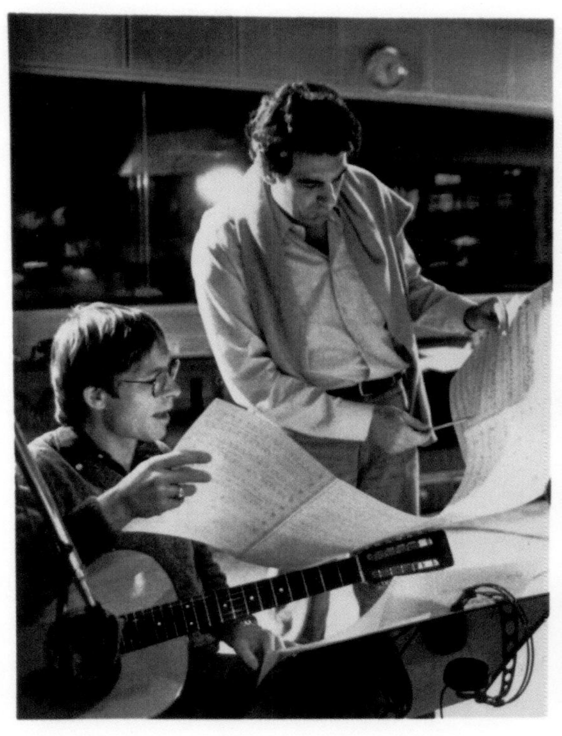

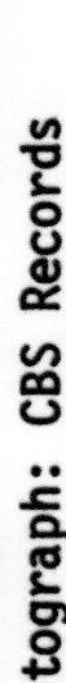

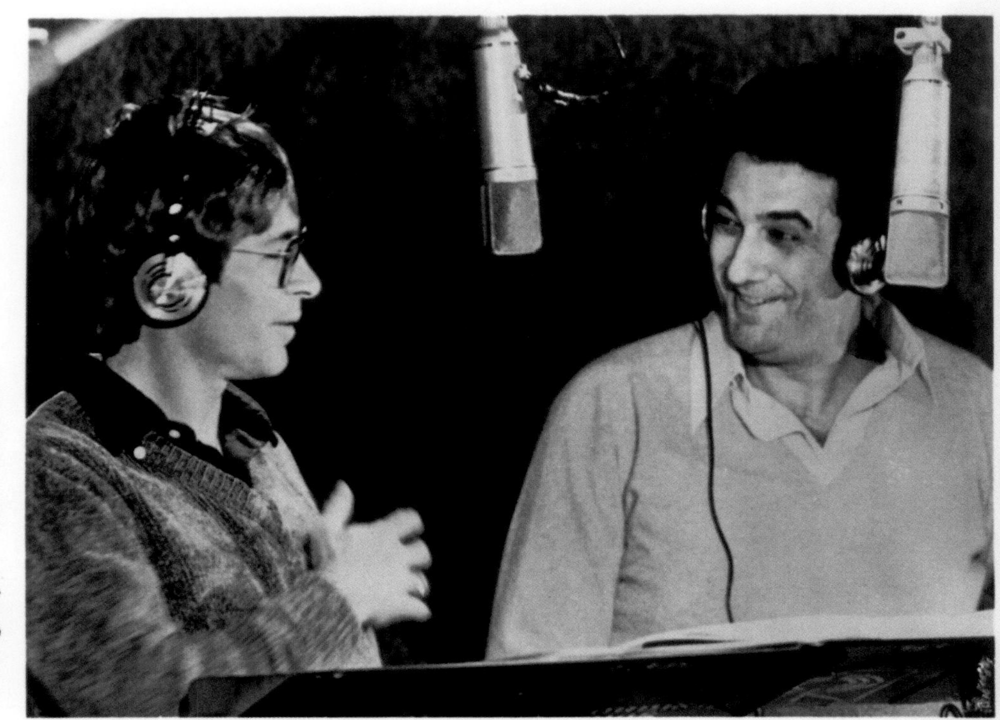

JOHN DENVER AND PLACIDO DOMINGO AT NEW YORK CITY RECORDING OF PERHAPS LOVE.

PLACIDO DOMINGO

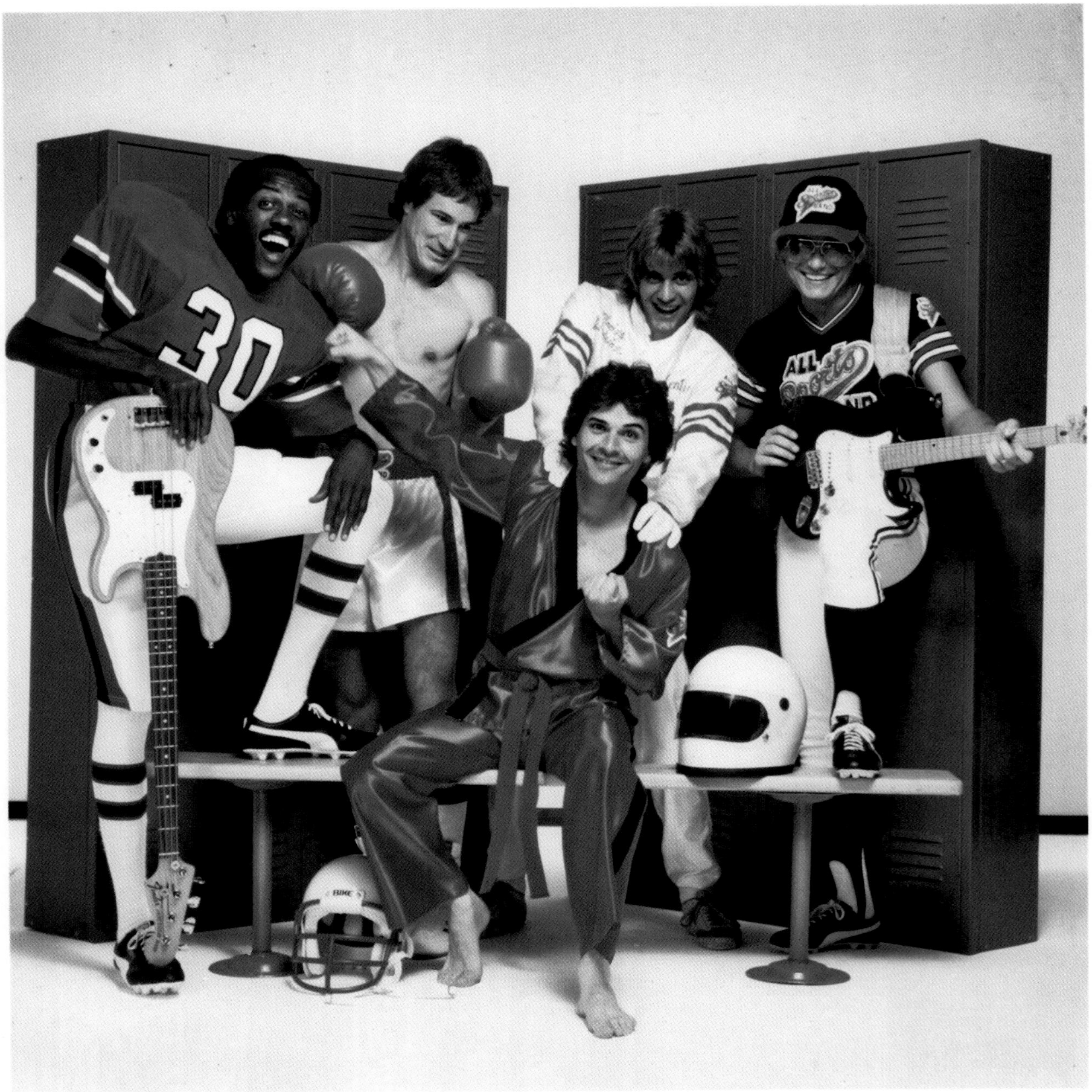

Alfonso Carey The Boxer Chuck Kentis Cy Sulack
Michael Toste

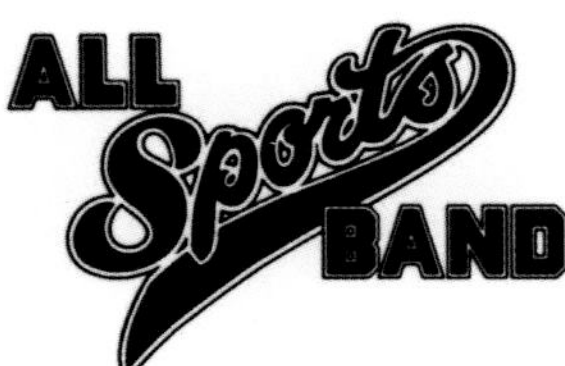

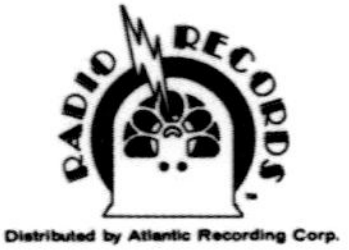

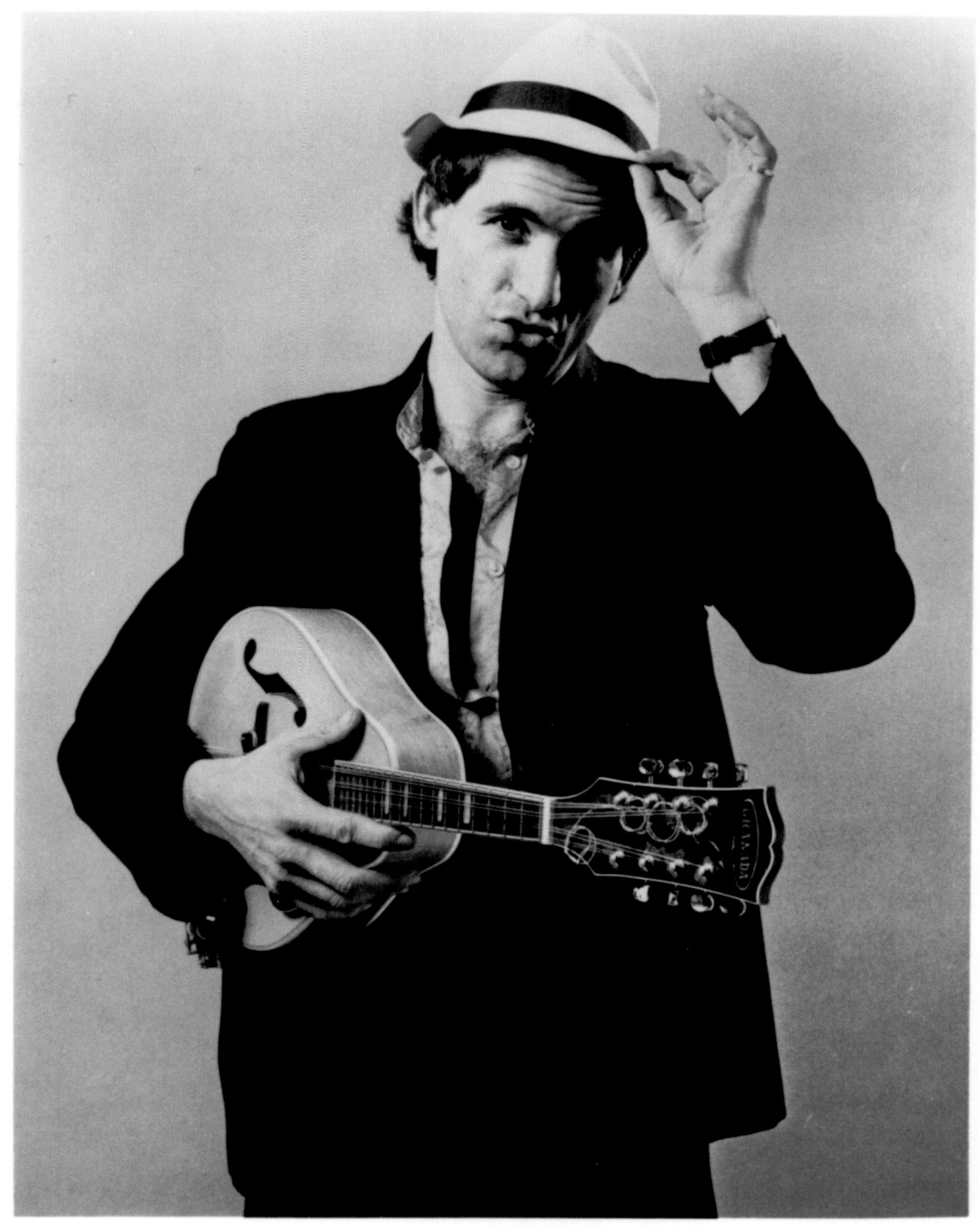

5/81

Joe Dolce

Exclusively On
MCA RECORDS

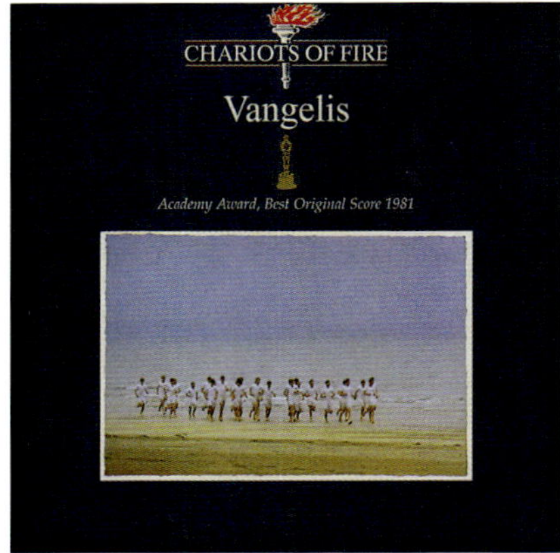

Greek composer Vangelis composed the Oscar-winning score to *Chariots of Fire*, with the triumphant instrumental theme topping the charts.

Billboard 200: *Chariots of Fire* (No. 1)
Billboard Hot 100: "Chariots of Fire - Titles" (No. 1)

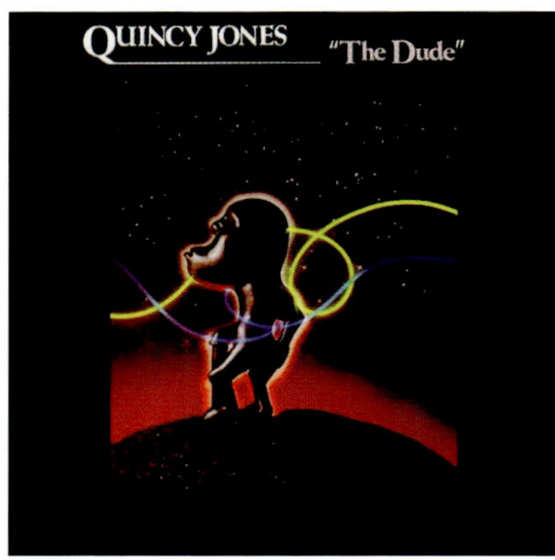

Quincy Jones' *The Dude* bore the hits "Just Once" and "One Hundred Ways," both sung by James Ingram, and "Ai No Corrida," a Chaz Jankel composition.

Billboard 200: *The Dude* (#10)
Billboard Hot 100: "Ai No Corrida" (#28); "Just Once" (#17); "One Hundred Ways" (#14)

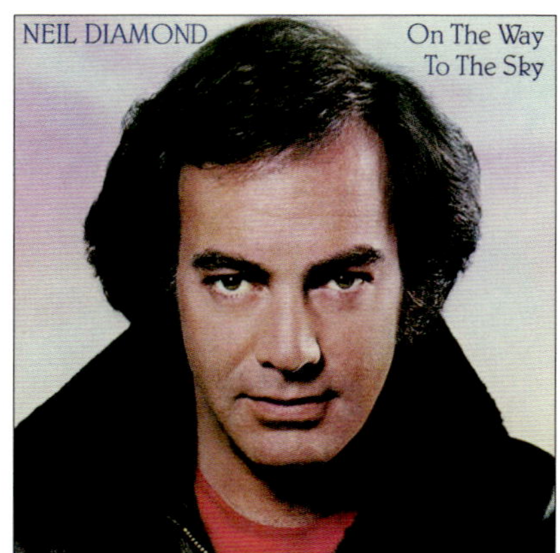

On the Way to the Sky, Neil Diamond's 16th album, delivered another No. 1 adult contemporary smash with the slickly produced "Yesterday's Songs."

Billboard 200: *On the Way to the Sky* (#17)
Billboard Hot 100: "Yesterday's Songs" (#11); "On the Way to the Sky" (#27); "Be Mine Tonight" (#35)

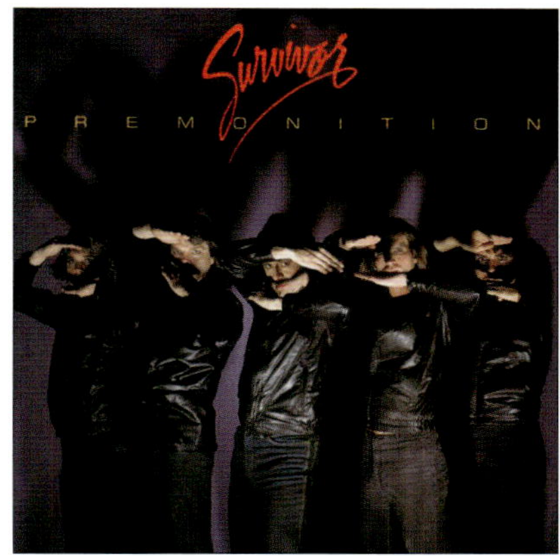

Premonition, the second album from **Survivor**, provided the melodic rockers from Chicago with their first single to crack the Top 40, "Poor Man's Son."

Billboard 200: *Premonition* (#82)
Billboard Hot 100: "Poor Man's Son" (#33); "Summer Nights" (#62)

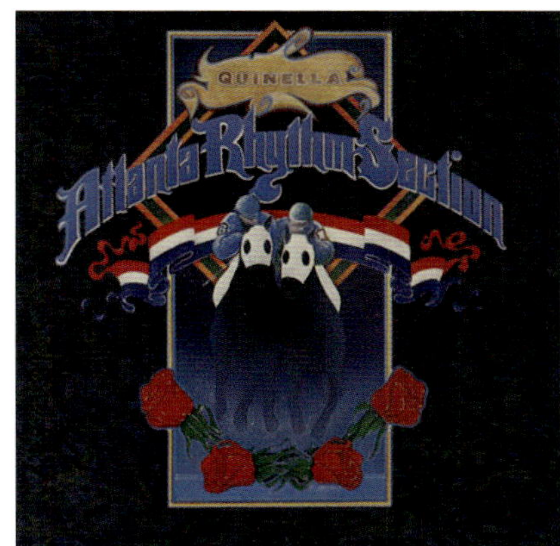

Quinella, **Atlanta Rhythm Section**'s 11th album, marked the Southern rock band's reappearance on the singles chart with the harmony-enriched "Alien."

Billboard 200: *Quinella* (#70)
Billboard Hot 100: "Alien" (#29)

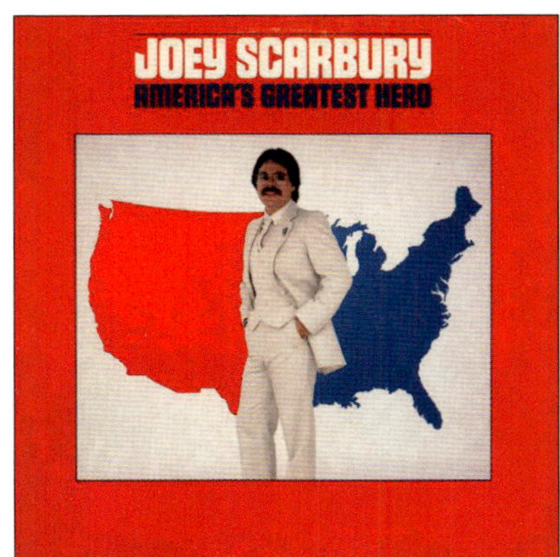

Singer **Joey Scarbury** retreated from the public eye after releasing his only hit, the catchy "Theme from *The Greatest American Hero* (Believe It or Not)."

Billboard 200: *America's Greatest Hero* (#104)
Billboard Hot 100: "Theme from *The Greatest American Hero* (Believe It or Not" (#2); "When She Dances" (#49)

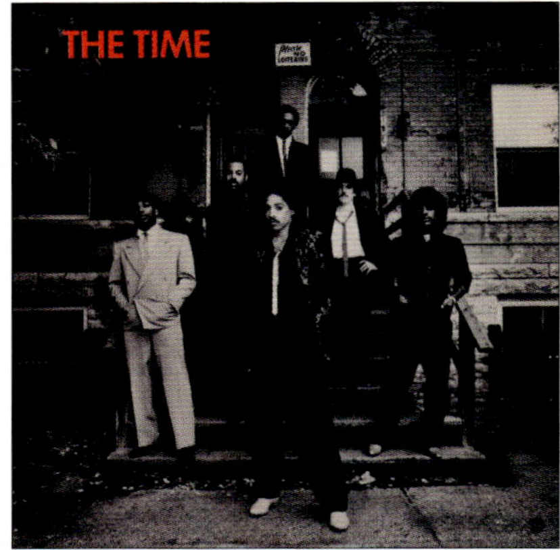

The Time, led by Morris Day and recruited by Prince, fashioned a self-titled debut album produced and arranged by the latter using the alias "Jamie Starr."

Billboard 200: *The Time* (#50)
Billboard Hot 100: "Cool" (#90)

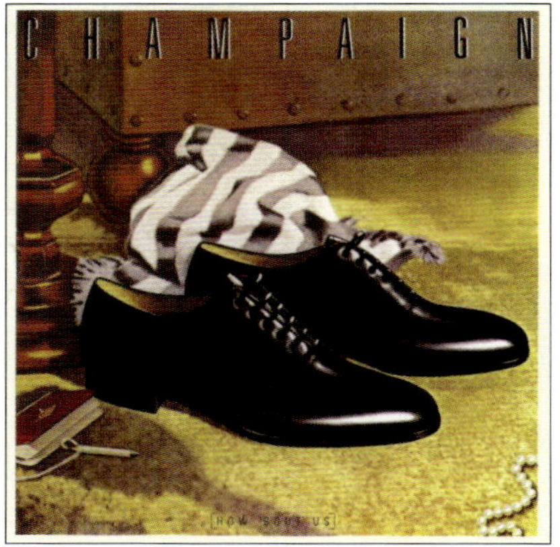

The R&B band Champaign debuted with *How 'Bout Us*, an album whose smooth and sultry title song reached the pop, soul and adult contemporary charts.

Billboard 200: *How 'Bout Us* (#53)
Billboard Hot 100: "How 'Bout Us" (#12)

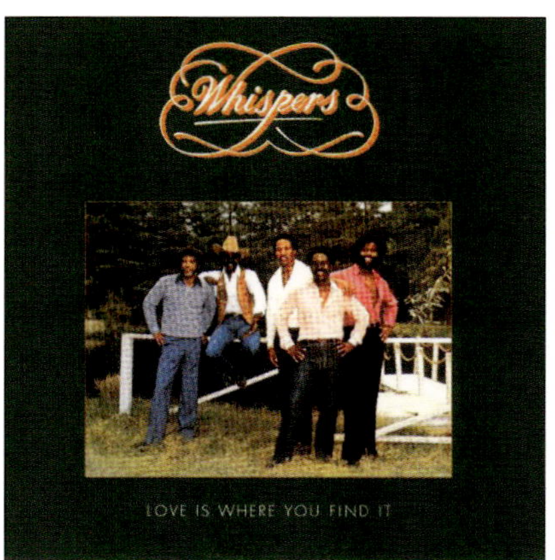

The Whispers, a veteran R&B vocal group, scored a smash when the album *Love Is Where You Find It* climbed to No. 1 on the soul charts.

Billboard 200: *Love Is Where You Find It* (#35)
Billboard Hot 100: "It's a Love Thing" (#28)

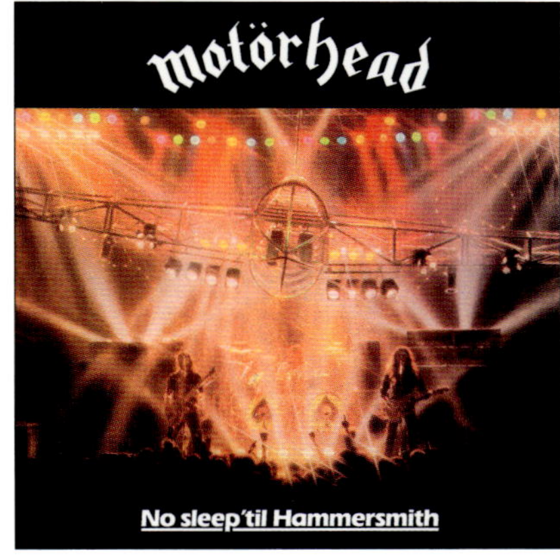

The English heavy metal/punk band Motörhead entered the UK charts at No. 1 with the landmark breakneck live album, *No Sleep 'Til Hammersmith.*

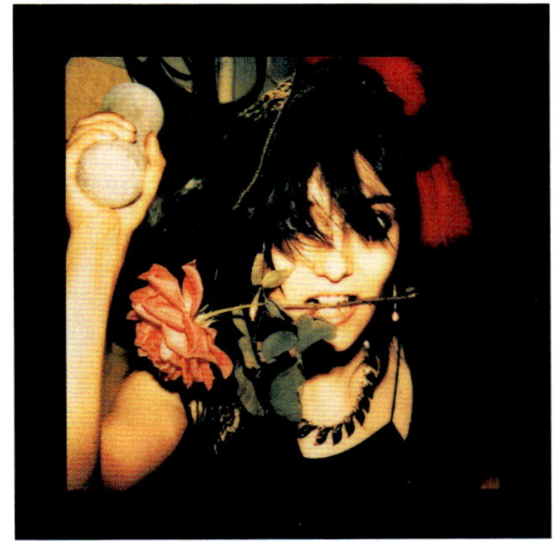

The departure of bassist Jah Wobble prompted Public Image Ltd's John Lydon and guitarist Keith Levene to record the minimalist *The Flowers of Romance*.

Billboard 200: *The Flowers of Romance* (#114)

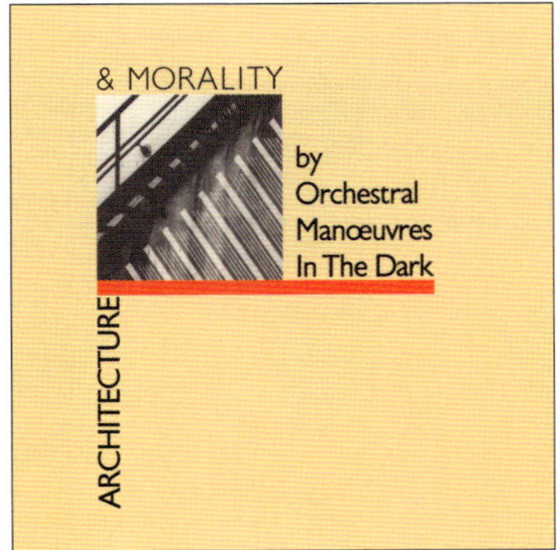

Orchestral Manoeuvres in the Dark's mellotron experiments on *Architecture & Morality* yielded three global hits, "Souvenir," "Joan of Arc" and "Maid of Orleans."

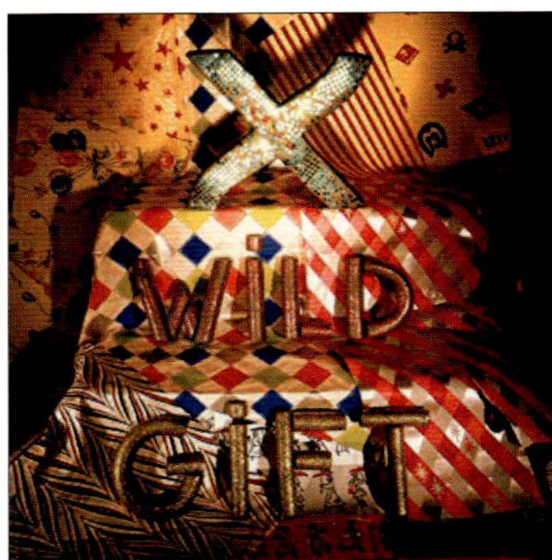

The second independent release by X, one of Los Angeles punk's chief emissaries, *Wild Gift* was produced by former Doors keyboardist Ray Manzarek.

Billboard 200: *Wild Gift* (#165)

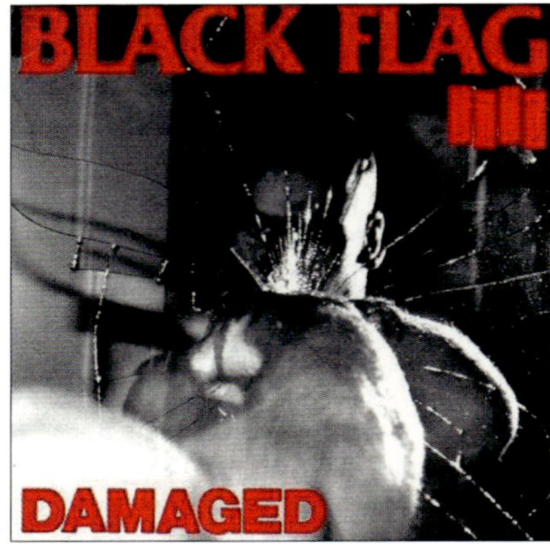

With Henry Rollins joining as lead singer, L.A. hardcore punk band Black Flag released its first full-length album, the controversial and influential *Damaged.*

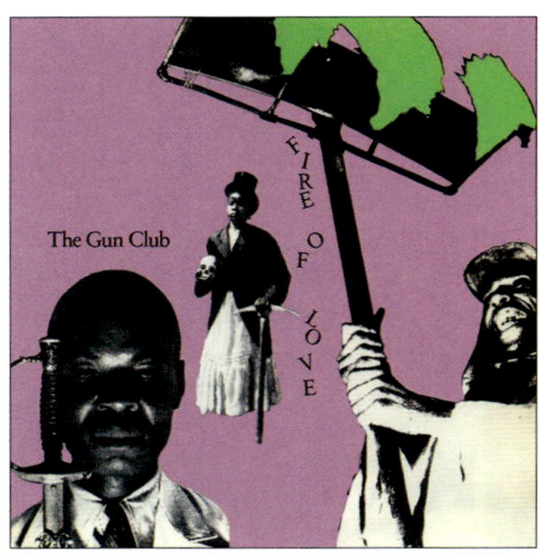

The Gun Club, led by maverick Jeffrey Lee Pierce, confected an uncompromising and inspiring punk-blues hybrid on *Fire of Love*, the L.A. band's debut album.

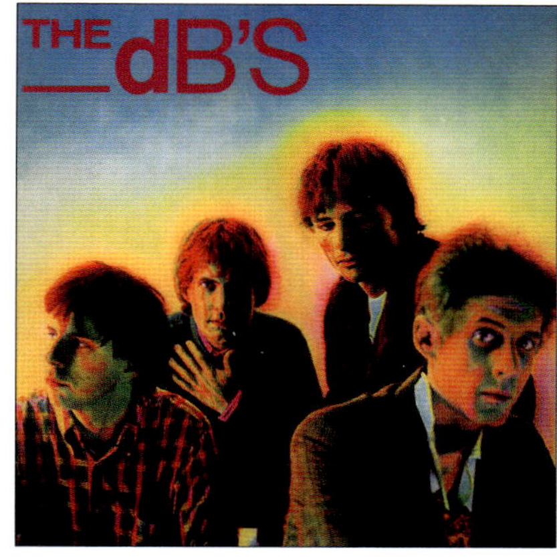

The dB's, a North Carolina-via-New York power-pop foursome, released *Stands for Decibles* on an independent UK label to critical acclaim but paltry sales.

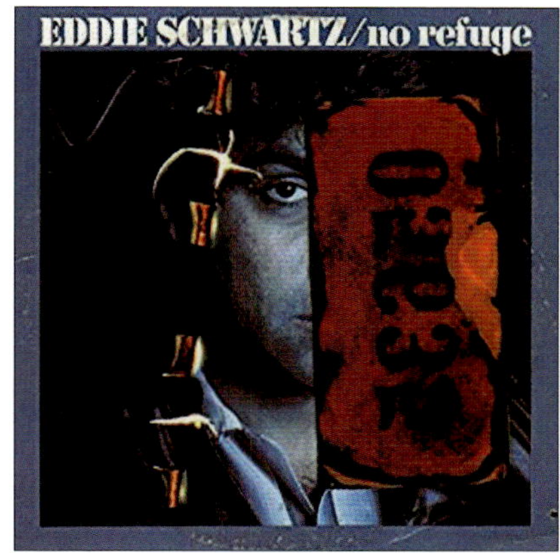

After Pat Benatar recorded his song, "Hit Me with Your Best Shot," Canada's Eddie Schwartz had consequential success with "All Our Tomorrows."

Billboard 200: *No Refuge* (#195)
Billboard Hot 100: "All Our Tomorrows" (#23); "Over the Line" (#91)

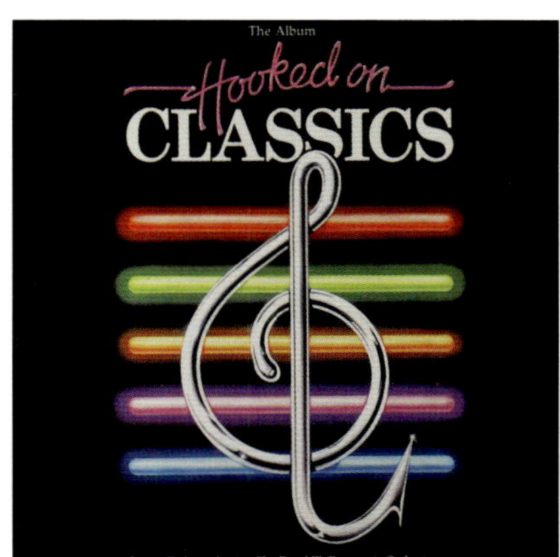

The Royal Philharmonic Orchestra, conducted by Louis Clark, fused synthetic dance beats and iconic classical works on *Hooked on Classics*, selling millions.

Billboard 200: *Hooked on Classics* (#4)
Billboard Hot 100: "Hooked on Classics" (#10)

{ IN MEMORY OF **MARIAN C. RIZZI** }

ACKNOWLEDGMENTS

Many people were essential to the creation of this book. My first thanks go to my amazing publishing team—Jon Rizzi for bringing his special brand of editorial wit and intelligence, and Kate Glassner Brainerd for her design artistry and unflagging pursuit of excellence. Special appreciation goes to Eric Pirritt's The Love We Bring Foundation and the Michael & Patricia Matthews Fund, whose facilitation was indispensable, as well as John Cerullo and Kevin Votel.

Mike Dickson, Chip Garofalo, Jennifer Soulé, Mark Zaremba, Peter Marcus, Matt Rue, Jay Elowsky, Dave Zobl and Mark Lewis contributed expertise and resources. I am especially indebted to my dear friend Michael Jensen, as well as Sue Satriano, Janice Azrak, Bryn Bridenthal, Byron Hontas, Kathy Acquaviva, Shelly Selover, Sue Sawyer, Glen Brunman, Rick Ambrose, Bob Merlis, Bill Bentley, Heidi Ellen Robinson, Les Schwartz, Rick Gershon, Jim Merlis, Judi Kerr and Susan Blond—all of whom supported my efforts.

I specifically treasure the beneficence of Dave Rothstein, Greg Phifer, John Tope, Kevin Knee, Dick Merkle, Jeff Cook, Michael Brannen, Zak Phillips, Rich Garcia, Jason Minkler, Burt Baumgartner, Mitch Kampf, Don Zucker, Carl Walters, Charlie Reardon, Robin Wren, Jimmy Smith, Sharona White, John Ryland, Geina Horton, Michael Linehan, Mike Prince and Jeffrey Naumann, who all graciously furnished information and assistance.

I gratefully acknowledge the editing and reviewing skills of Dick Kreck, Tom Walker, Diane Carman, Mike Rudeen, Ed Smith, Jay Whearley, Mark Sims, Jeff Bradley and Peggy McKay.

I also salute David Gans, Leland Rucker, Steve Knopper, David Menconi, Jon Iverson, Gil Asakawa, Mark Bliesener, Butch Hause, Ricardo Baca, John Moore, Justin Mitchell, Michael Mehle and Harvey Kubernik, whose writings formed a vital index for the music-obsessed.

Finally, I would like to acknowledge with gratitude my beloved wife, Bridget, for her constant devotion and kindness. I cherish her—the love of my life.

BIBLIOGRAPHY

Wall, **Mick**. 1998. *Run to the Hills: Iron Maiden - The Official Biography.* Sanctuary. London.

EDITOR | **JON RIZZI**
ART DIRECTOR | **KATE GLASSNER BRAINERD**

ISBN 978-0-9915668-6-0 PRINTED IN CHINA | Asia Pacific Offset

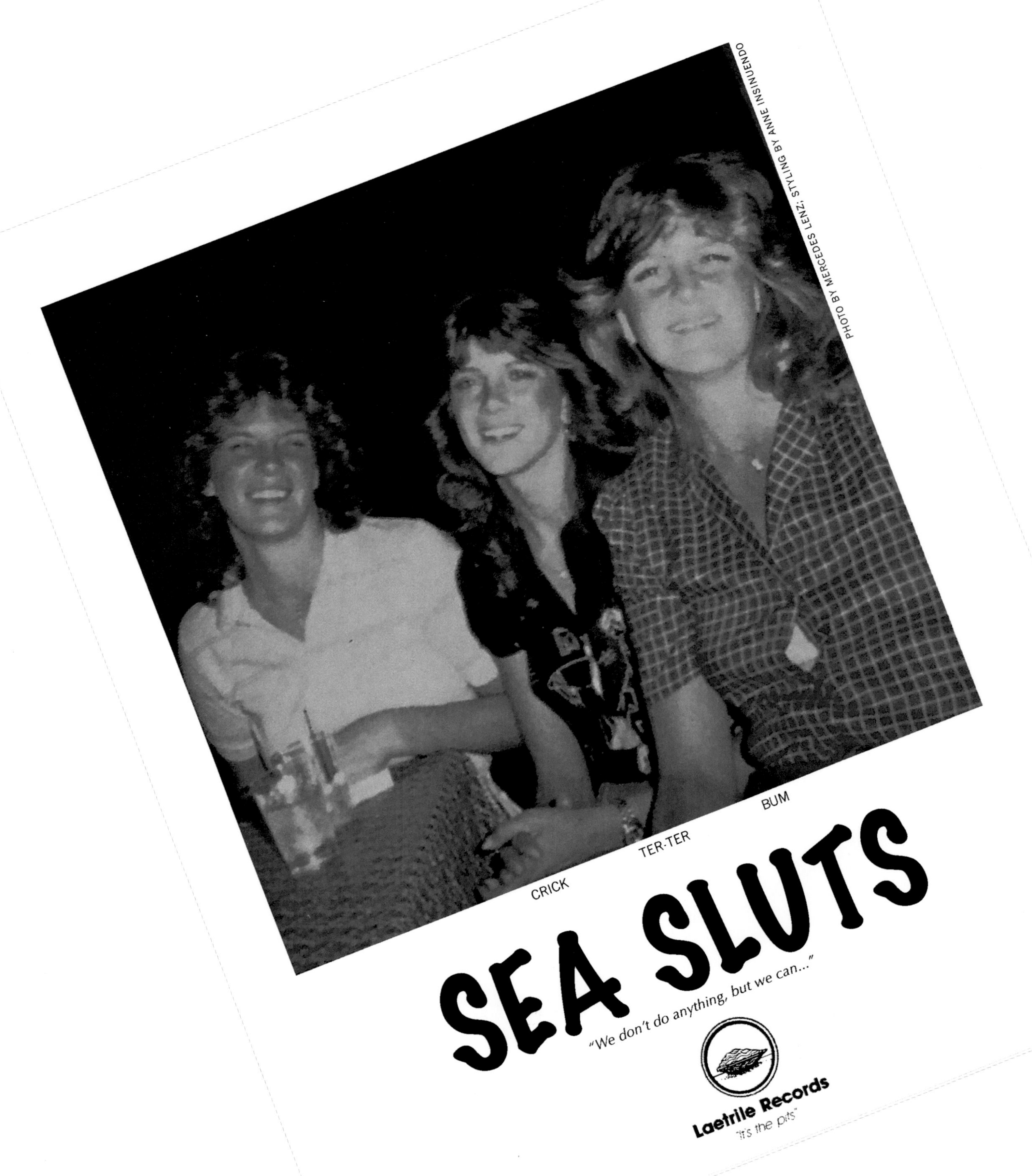
PHOTO BY MERCEDES LENZ; STYLING BY ANNE INSINUENDO
CRICK
TER-TER
BUM
SEA SLUTS
"We don't do anything, but we can..."
Laetrile Records
"It's the pits"

Next in the *ON RECORD* book series

Vol. 5 1988

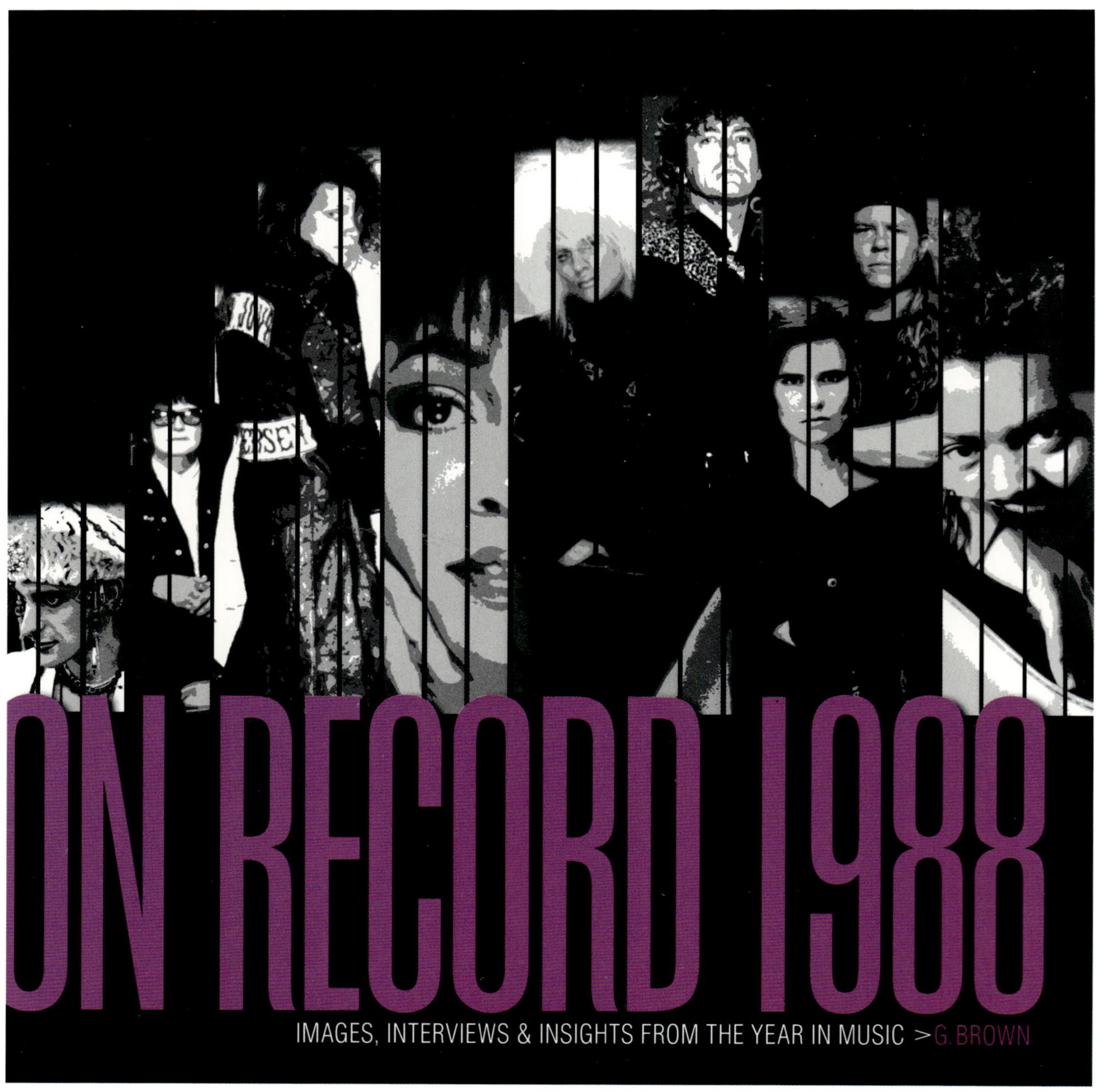